# Oxford Beginner's French Dictionary

**First edition**

P9-CND-004

OXFORD
UNIVERSITY PRESS

# OXFORD
UNIVERSITY PRESS

Great Clarendon Street, Oxford OX2 6DP

Oxford University Press is a department of the University of Oxford.
It furthers the University's objective of excellence in research, scholarship,
and education by publishing worldwide in

Oxford New York

Auckland Cape Town Dar es Salaam Hong Kong Karachi
Kuala Lumpur Madrid Melbourne Mexico City Nairobi
New Delhi Shanghai Taipei Toronto

With offices in

Argentina Austria Brazil Chile Czech Republic France Greece
Guatemala Hungary Italy Japan Poland Portugal Singapore
South Korea Switzerland Thailand Turkey Ukraine Vietnam

Oxford is a registered trade mark of Oxford University Press
in the UK and in certain other countries

Published in the United States
by Oxford University Press Inc., New York

© Oxford University Press 2006

The moral rights of the author have been asserted

Database right Oxford University Press (maker)

First published as Oxford Starter French Dictionary 1997

All rights reserved. No part of this publication may be reproduced,
stored in a retrieval system, or transmitted, in any form or by any means
without the prior permission in writing of Oxford University Press,
or as expressly permitted by law, or under terms agreed with the
appropriate reprographics rights organization. Enquiries concerning
reproduction outside the scope of the above should be sent to the
Rights Department, Oxford University Press, at the address above

You must not circulate this book in any other binding or cover and
you must impose this same condition on any acquirer

British Library Cataloguing in Publication Data
Data available

Library of Congress Cataloging in Publication Data
Data available

ISBN 0-19-929858-0
ISBN 978-0-19-929858-7

10 9 8 7 6 5 4 3 2 1

Typeset in Swift and Arial
Printed in Italy by Legoprint S.p.A.

# Contents

## Contributors

**Chief Editor**
Marie-Hélène Corréard

**Associate Editor**
Mary O'Neill

**Editors**
Gearóid Cronin
Françoise de Peretti
Natalie Pomier

Henri Béjoint
Richard Wakely
Tim Horner
Carol Petersen

**Appendices**
Graham Bishop
Mary O'Neill
Martyn Bird
Lexus Ltd.

# Introduction

## A fresh approach

Created to meet the specific needs of English speakers who are starting to learn French, this dictionary takes a completely fresh approach to helping you make sense of the new language. We have changed the design of the entries to make them different from entries in traditional dictionaries. What exactly is it that makes the entries so different?

- they have a new, clearer layout
- they are designed to provide the information you need in a helpful, readable way with the minimum of clutter
- since you will be using the English–French and the French–English sides of the dictionary for different tasks, each side works differently and it shows in the way the information is presented.

Because of these major changes, you will find that the dictionary is a far more efficient language-learning tool for you as a beginner. Finding the right information quickly and easily will make French more satisfying to learn.

## A clearer layout

Each page of the dictionary presents the information you will need in entries which are well-spaced, easy to read, and which have a consistent layout both in English and French. The main features of the new design are:

- bullet points and numbers to indicate the various uses of each word
- different typefaces as well as the symbol = to indicate the switch from one language to the other
- use of the symbol ! to indicate important grammar points
- use of the symbol ✶ to indicate informal or colloquial words
- use of the symbol ⬦ to indicate words which should be used with care.

## More helpful and easy to use

The entries have been designed so that you can find the information you need quickly. Many of the conventions in traditional dictionaries which you may find confusing or offputting have been avoided, so:

- PARTS OF SPEECH and grammatical terms are written out in full for you. A separate section explains all the terms used if you should need to find out more about them
- explanations of specific grammar points and notes on how a word is actually used are provided in short paragraphs at appropriate places in the dictionary text
- groups of words which behave in a similar way, or which present similar difficulties, are treated in a consistent manner which you will quickly

*Words in capital letters are found in the glossary*

come to recognize. In many entries you are guided to other parts of the dictionary, to VERB tables, for instance, where you will find all the forms of the main French verbs. You will also find handy language notes which deal with such concepts as colours, countries, and dates.

- the language used in the examples and in the signposts to the right translation has been carefully chosen to ensure that it is clear and up to date.

This dictionary, with its precise and lively examples, contains all the words you will need as a beginner and includes plenty of examples of British as well as American English in both the English–French and French–English texts.

## Using the two sides of the dictionary to do different things

Each side of the dictionary has been separately designed to take account of the different ways in which you will use it.

The English–French side is longer. Since you are moving from your own language into French, you will need more detailed guidance. We have provided regular reminders about essential grammar rules. The signposts which pinpoint the precise context in which a word is used are there to help you choose the right translation. These 'sense indicators' are also supported with a wide selection of useful examples.

The French–English side makes the most of what you already know about your own language. The presentation of translations from French is therefore more streamlined. There is detailed treatment of the more irregular and unpredictable features of French which you may come across in newspapers and magazines, for example. A particularly useful feature is that the variations in spelling of IRREGULAR VERBS, ADJECTIVES and PLURAL NOUNS are all listed as separate entries in the WORD LIST. These words then send you to the main dictionary form where you will find the translation you are looking for.

# How to use the dictionary

## Where to look for a word

Bilingual dictionaries are divided into two sections. The first section gives you a list of French words followed by their English equivalents as well as information about the contexts in which they are used.

The second section gives you a list of English words followed by the French words which match their exact meaning according to the contexts in which they are used.

- *Decide first which section you need to look at.*

This dictionary is particularly good at listing as HEADWORDS the various forms that VERBS, NOUNS, and ADJECTIVES may take in French when they are being used to indicate TENSE, GENDER, or NUMBER. From these more unpredictable forms, you will be referred to the main entry of the BASE FORM for the meaning and any further information.

## What information does the dictionary provide you with?

Your dictionary gives you information which falls into three broad categories:

1. information about meaning
2. information about the grammatical characteristics of the words
3. information about the circumstances in which a word may be safely used –
   either from the point of view of CONTEXT (e.g. medical, sport, school contexts) or
   REGISTER (e.g. formal, polite, informal registers)

## How to recognize the information given in the dictionary

Study carefully the diagrams given in **The Structure of French–English and English–French entries**. There you will see how the three categories of information mentioned above are displayed to help you. If you need help finding out what PART OF SPEECH you are dealing with, have a look at the **Definitions of Grammatical Terms**.

## Finding meanings and translating

When you are looking up words for meaning in order to translate them either from your own language or from French, dictionaries can only give you lists of choices. You must look carefully at the information provided to help you choose the right translation in English or in French for the CONTEXT you are in.

If you look up the French word for '**right**', you need to be clear whether you mean '**right**' as opposed to '**left**' or whether you mean '**right** 'as opposed to '**wrong**'.

Scan the whole entry to find the word in French which matches the meaning you need. The context indicators or 'signposts' will help you to pinpoint this meaning. This will be easier to select when you are looking up French words to translate into English since you will know what each of the choices given in English means and how it is used.

If the entry is a long one, first identify the PART OF SPEECH of the word you want to translate. When you have found the right section of the entry, check the range of meanings covered in that section to find the appropriate one. For example:

- '**ring**' could be a verb, in which case the correct French translation may be
  '**sonner**' which is also a verb;

*Words in capital letters are found in the glossary*

- **'ring'** could be a noun, in which case the correct French equivalent might be **'une bague'** ( *a piece of jewellery*) or **'la piste'** ( *in a circus*) or **'un cercle'** (*a circle*).

Your dictionary will give you the context clearly so that you can decide on the appropriate word.

## Using the entries to find information about a word other than the meaning

- Sometimes you will want to use your dictionary simply to check the spelling of the FEMININE or PLURAL form of a NOUN or ADJECTIVE.
- You may wish to check to see if the word has ACCENTS.
- You may wish to check the GENDER of a noun.
- You may wish to find out how a verb is spelled in a particular TENSE.
- The entry will often tell you which pattern of CONJUGATION the VERB follows by referring you to the tables at the back of the book.

### How to use the verb tables

Where you see a French verb followed by a number in a box, look at the back of the dictionary where you will find tables of verbs. The number given against the verb indicates the spelling pattern that the verb follows.

For example: **'arriver'** and **'informer'** are both followed by the number 1. In the verb tables this spelling pattern is represented by the verb **'chanter'**.

Verbs can be split into two parts: the *stem* and the *ending*.

e.g. **arriv + *er*; inform + *er***

The endings of **'chant + *er*'** should be used with the stems of **arriv + *er*** and **inform + *er*** to form the tenses you need.

Where the verb is REGULAR the stem does not change, only the endings.

Where the verb is IRREGULAR the stem may alter as well. Just follow the pattern indicated.

| e.g. 19 **rappeler** | [rappel + *er*] | note the change from **'l'** to double **'ll'** |
| 52 **comprendre** | [comprend + *re*] | note how the **'d'** is not always there |
| 56 **joindre** | [joind + *re*] | note how the **'d'** is not always there and the change to **'gn'** from **'nd'** in certain TENSES |

### Getting to know your dictionary

In the central section of this dictionary (pages 171–184) you will find a short section of games and exercises which will help you get to know your dictionary better and to use it more effectively. Your dictionary is a very important study aid which can greatly help you to find out how the French language works and how to expand your vocabulary.

### Proprietary terms

This dictionary contains some words which are, or are asserted to be, proprietary names or trademarks. Their inclusion does not imply that they have acquired for legal purposes a non-proprietary or general significance, nor is any other judgement implied concerning their legal status. In cases where the editors have some evidence that a word is used as a proprietary name or trademark, this is indicated by the symbol ®, but no judgement concerning the legal status of such words is made or implied thereby.

# The structure of French–English entries

HEADWORD ········ **bête**
**1** *adjective*
numbers indicating ··········· = stupid, silly
grammatical ········· **2** *noun, feminine*
categories   une bête = an animal ·········································· translation clearly
indicated by =

**champion/championne** *noun,*
*masculine/feminine*
un champion/une championne = a ·····→ FEMININE form
champion   of HEADWORD

ABBREVIATION ········· **DOM-TOM** *noun, masculine plural*
(*abbreviation of* **départements et**
**territoires d'outre-mer**)
explanation of a ········· *French overseas departments and*
feature of French   *territories*
culture

**eau** *noun, feminine* ································ PART OF SPEECH plus
(*plural*) **eaux**   GENDER
l'eau = water
compounds ········· **l'eau gazeuse** = fizzy water, sparkling
presented in ···.   water
block at end ···.  **l'eau minérale** = mineral water
of ENTRY   **l'eau potable** = drinking water

········································· number of the
**informer** *verb* [1]   spelling pattern this
**1** (**!** + *avoir*)   verb follows (tables
= to inform ·······································   on pages 380–413)
**2 s'informer** (**!** + *être*)························· information
• s'informer = to keep oneself informed   on correct
• s'informer de = to enquire about   grammatical usage

**pleut ▸ pleuvoir** ································· cross-reference to
HEADWORD

**rattraper** *verb* [1]
bullet points ·········• = to catch up with
indicating a ···.   rattraper un concurrent = to catch up
separate meaning of···.   with a competitor
the HEADWORD   • = to make up for ································· examples
rattraper le temps perdu = to make up
for lost time
• = to recapture, to catch

symbol drawing ···············
attention to   **zut×** *exclamation*
REGISTER   = blast!
= oh dear!

*Words in capital letters are found in the glossary*

# The structure of English–French entries

HEADWORD ········ **circus** *noun*
a circus = un cirque

GENDER of French
NOUNS made clear

**delicious** *adjective*
= délicieux/délicieuse ········ FEMININE form of
ADJECTIVES made
clear

PART OF SPEECH ········
made clear

**fed up** *adjective*
to be fed up = en avoir marre✱ ········ symbol drawing
attention to
REGISTER

**fire**
numbers indicating ········ **1** *noun*
grammatical
categories
fire = le feu
a fire (*for heat*) = un feu
(*causing damage*) = un incendie
to catch fire = prendre feu
to be on fire = être en feu
**2** *verb*
bullet points ········ • (*to shoot*) = tirer
indicating a ········ • (*to dismiss*) = renvoyer
separate meaning
of the HEADWORD

indicators which
spell out the
different meanings
of the HEADWORD

**fireman** *noun* ▶ **315** | ········ page number
where more
information is given

a fireman = un pompier
separate entries for ········ **fire station** *noun*
COMPOUND NOUNS
a fire station = une caserne de pompiers

translation clearly
indicated by =

**kick** *verb*
to kick someone = donner un coup de
pied à quelqu'un
he kicked the ball = il a donné un coup de
pied dans le ballon
PHRASAL VERBS ········ **kick off** = donner le coup d'envoi
presented in ········ **kick out**
separate
blocks
to kick someone out = mettre
quelqu'un à la porte

**need** *verb*
• (*to have to*)
you don't need to ask permission = tu
n'es pas obligé de demander la
permission
they'll need to come early = il va falloir
qu'ils viennent de bonne heure

information on ········
correct grammatical
usage

! *Note that the subjunctive is used after*
*falloir que.*

basic structure to
use as a model

example of a model ········
structure which can
be imitated

• (*to want*) = avoir besoin de
they need [money | help | friends...] = ils ont
besoin [d'argent | d'aide | d'amis...]
we need to see the doctor = nous avons
besoin de voir le médecin
everything you need = tout ce qu'il
vous faut

*Words in capital letters are found in the glossary*

**a** ▶ **avoir** 8

**à** *preposition*
(**!** à + le becomes au; à + les becomes aux)

> **!** You will find translations for phrases with à such as à côté de, à l'étranger, penser à, etc. under the entries côté, étranger, penser, etc.

- (*showing destination*) = to
  **se rendre** [à Nice | à l'école | aux courses …] = to go [to Nice | to school | to the races …]
- (*showing location*) = in
  = at
  = on
  **habiter** [à la campagne | au Portugal | aux États-Unis …] = to live [in the country | in Portugal | in the United States …]
- (*in a description*) = with
  **la maison aux volets verts** = the house with the green shutters
- (*showing ownership*)
  **le livre est** [à moi | à eux | à Isabelle …] = the book is [mine | theirs | Isabelle's …]
- (*indicating a time, a speed, a price*) = at
  **à minuit** = at midnight
  **un timbre à trois euros** = a three-euro stamp
- (*meaning during a period of time*) = in
  **au printemps** = in (the) spring
- (*indicating a distance*)
  **à cinq kilomètres** = five kilometres away
- (*showing how something is done*)
  **écrire au crayon** = to write in pencil
  **à pied** = on foot

**abandonner** *verb* 1
- = to abandon
- = to give up

**abeille** *noun, feminine*
**une abeille** = a bee

**abîmer** *verb* 1
**1** (**!** + *avoir*)
= to damage, to spoil
**2 s'abîmer** (**!** + *être*)
**s'abîmer** = to get damaged

**abonné/abonnée** *noun, masculine/feminine*
**un abonné/une abonnée** = a subscriber

**abonnement** *noun, masculine*
**un abonnement** = a subscription

**abonner**: **s'abonner à** *verb* 1 (**!** + *être*)
**s'abonner à** = to subscribe to

**abord**: **d'abord** *adverb*
**d'abord** = first, at first
**tout d'abord** = first of all

**abri** *noun, masculine*
**un abri** = (a) shelter

**abricot** *noun, masculine*
**un abricot** = an apricot

**abriter** *verb* 1
**1** (**!** + *avoir*)
= to shelter
**2 s'abriter** (**!** + *être*)
**s'abriter** = to shelter, to take shelter

**absent/absente** *adjective*
= absent, missing

**absolument** *adverb*
= absolutely

**accélérer** *verb* 14
= to accelerate

**accepter** *verb* 1
- = to accept
- = to agree to

**accès** *noun, masculine* (**!** *never changes*)
**l'accès** = access
**'accès interdit'** = 'no entrance', 'do not enter'

**accident** *noun, masculine*
**un accident** = an accident

**accompagner** *verb* 1
- = to accompany, to go with
- = to take

**accomplir** *verb* 3
= to carry out, to accomplish

**accord** *noun, masculine*
- **un accord** = an agreement
- **d'accord!** = OK!, all right!
  **je suis d'accord avec toi** = I agree with you

**accorder** *verb* 1
= to give, to grant

**accotement** *noun, masculine*
**un accotement** = a verge, a shoulder
**accotement non stabilisé** = soft verge, soft shoulder

**accroc** *noun, masculine*
**un accroc** (*in material*) = a tear, a rip

**accrocher** *verb* 1
**1** (**!** + *avoir*)
= to hang
**2 s'accrocher** (**!** + *être*)
**s'accrocher** = to hang on, to cling
**accroche-toi à la branche** = hang on to the branch

**accueil** *noun, masculine*
**un accueil** = a welcome, a reception
**ils nous ont fait bon accueil** = they made us welcome, they made us feel at home
**la famille d'accueil** = the host family

**accueillir** verb 27
• (if it's a host) = to welcome
• (if it's a stadium, a hotel) = to accommodate

**achat** noun, masculine
un achat = a purchase
faire des achats = to do some shopping

**acheter** verb 18
= to buy

**acheteur/acheteuse** noun,
masculine/feminine
un acheteur/une acheteuse = a buyer

**acte de propriété** noun, masculine
(of a house)
un acte de propriété = a deed

**acteur/actrice** noun,
masculine/feminine
un acteur/une actrice = an actor/an actress

**actif/active** adjective
= active

**activité** noun, feminine
une activité = an activity

**actrice** ▶ acteur

**actualité**
**1** noun, feminine
l'actualité = current affairs, current events
**2 actualités** noun, feminine plural
les actualités = the news

**actuel/actuelle** adjective
= present, current

**actuellement** adverb
= currently, at the moment

**addition** noun, feminine
• (in a restaurant, a café)
l'addition = the bill, the check
• (in arithmetic)
une addition = an addition

**additionner** verb 1
= to add

**adhérent/adhérente** noun,
masculine/feminine
un adhérent/une adhérente = a member

**adhésion** noun, feminine
l'adhésion = membership

**adieu** noun, masculine
(plural) **adieux**
= goodbye, farewell

**adjectif** noun, masculine
un adjectif = an adjective

**admettre** verb 60
• = to admit
• = to allow
• être admis à un examen = to pass an
exam, to pass a test
• admettons qu'il vienne = (let's) suppose he
comes

**admis/admise** ▶ admettre 60

**admission** noun, feminine
l'admission = admission

**adolescent/adolescente** noun,
masculine/feminine
un adolescent/une adolescente = a
teenager, an adolescent

**adorer** verb 1
= to love, to adore

**adresse** noun, feminine
une adresse = an address
changer d'adresse = to move
une adresse électronique = an email
address

**adresser** verb 1
**1** (! + avoir)
• = to send
• = to address
**2 s'adresser** (! + être)
• s'adresser à un employé = to talk to an
employee
• s'adresser à la banque = to contact the
bank

**adroit/adroite** adjective
• = skil(l)ful
• = clever, smart

**adversaire** noun, masculine/feminine
un adversaire/une adversaire = an
opponent

**aérer** verb 14
= to air

**aérien/aérienne** adjective
= air

**aérobic** noun, masculine
l'aérobic = aerobics

**aérogare** noun, feminine
une aérogare = an air terminal

**aéroglisseur** noun, masculine
un aéroglisseur = a hovercraft

**aéroport** noun, masculine
un aéroport = an airport

**affaire**
**1** noun, feminine
une affaire = a bargain
**2 affaires** noun, feminine plural
• les affaires = business
• mes affaires = my things, my belongings

**affairer: s'affairer** verb 1 (! + être)
s'affairer = to bustle about

**affectueusement** adverb
= affectionately
(ending a letter) = love

**affectueux/affectueuse** adjective
= affectionate

**affiche** noun, feminine
une affiche = a poster
= a notice

**afficher** verb 1
* = to put up, to hang up
* = to display
afficher complet = to be fully booked

**affoler** verb 1
1 (! + avoir)
= to throw into a panic
2 **s'affoler** (! + être)
s'affoler = to get into a panic

**affreux/affreuse** adjective
= awful

**afin**
1 **afin de** preposition
afin de = in order to
2 **afin que** conjunction
afin que = so that

**africain/africaine** adjective
= African

**Afrique** noun, feminine
l'Afrique = Africa

**agacer** verb 12
= to annoy, to irritate

**âge** noun, masculine
l'âge = age
quel âge as-tu? = how old are you?

**âgé/âgée** adjective
* = old, elderly
* être âgé de 18 ans = to be 18 years old

**agence** noun, feminine
une agence = an agency
**une agence immobilière** = an estate
agent's, a real estate agency
**une agence de voyages** = a travel
agency

**agenda** noun, masculine
un agenda = a diary, a date book

**agent** noun, masculine
un agent = an agent
**un agent de la circulation** = a traffic
policeman
**un agent de police** = a policeman, a
police officer

**agglomération** noun, feminine
une agglomération = a town
= a village

**agile** adjective
= agile

**agir** verb 3
1 (! + avoir)
= to act
2 **s'agir de** (! + être)
s'agir de = to be about
de quoi s'agit-il? = what's it about?

**agitation** noun, feminine
* l'agitation = (the) bustle
* l'agitation = (the) excitement

**agité/agitée** adjective
(describing the sea) = rough, choppy

**agiter** verb 1
1 (! | avoir)
* agiter un mouchoir = to wave a
handkerchief
* agiter un flacon = to shake a bottle
2 **s'agiter** (! + être)
* s'agiter = to fidget
* s'agiter = to become restless

**agneau** noun, masculine
(plural) **agneaux**
* (the animal)
un agneau = a lamb
* (the meat)
l'agneau = lamb

**agréable** adjective
= pleasant

**agressif/agressive** adjective
= aggressive

**agression** noun, feminine
* une agression = an attack
* une agression = a mugging

**agricole** adjective
= agricultural

**agriculteur/agricultrice** noun,
masculine/feminine
un agriculteur/une agricultrice = a farmer

**ai ▶ avoir** 8

**aide**
1 noun, feminine
l'aide = help
= assistance
2 noun, masculine/feminine
un aide/une aide = an assistant

**aider** verb 1
1 (! + avoir)
= to help
2 **s'aider de** (! + être)
s'aider de = to use

**aïe** exclamation
= ouch!

**aigle** noun, masculine
un aigle = an eagle

**aigre** adjective
* (tasting unpleasant) = sour
* (sounding unpleasant) = sharp

**aiguille** noun, feminine
* une aiguille = a needle
une aiguille à tricoter = a knitting needle
* les aiguilles d'une montre = the hands on
a watch

**ail** noun, masculine
l'ail = garlic

**aile** noun, feminine
une aile = a wing

**aille ▶ aller 1** 9

A

**ailleurs**
**1** *adverb*
ailleurs = elsewhere, somewhere else
**2 d'ailleurs** = besides

**aimable** *adjective*
= kind, friendly

**aimer** *verb* 1
• = to love
aimer ses enfants = to love one's children
• = to like, to be fond of
j'aime mieux le vin = I prefer wine

**aîné/aînée** *adjective*
= eldest, oldest
= elder, older

**ainsi**
**1** *adverb*
• = in this way
et ainsi de suite = and so on
• = so
ainsi tu t'en vas? = so you're leaving?
**2 ainsi que** = and, as well as

**air** *noun, masculine*
• l'air = (the) air
en plein air = in the open (air), outdoors
allons prendre l'air = let's go and get some fresh air
• de l'air = a wind, a breeze
• (*appearance*)
un air = a look
avoir l'air heureux = to look happy
il n'a pas l'air de comprendre = he doesn't seem to understand
• (*for a song*)
un air = a tune

**aire** *noun, feminine*
une aire = an area
**une aire de jeux** = a playground
**une aire de loisirs** = a recreation area

**aise**: **à l'aise** *adverb*
à l'aise = at ease

**ajouter** *verb* 1
**1** (**!** + *avoir*)
= to add
**2 s'ajouter à** (**!** + *être*)
s'ajouter à = to be added to

**alarme** *noun, feminine*
donner l'alarme = to raise the alarm

**album** *noun, masculine*
un album = an album
**un album à colorier** = a colo(u)ring book

**alcool** *noun, masculine*
l'alcool = alcohol
sans alcool = nonalcoholic, alcohol-free

**alcoolisé/alcoolisée** *adjective*
= alcoholic

**alcootest** *noun, masculine*
un alcootest = a Breathalyzer   test

**algèbre** *noun, feminine*
l'algèbre = algebra

**Alger** *noun*
= Algiers

**Algérie** *noun, feminine*
l'Algérie = Algeria

**algérien/algérienne** *adjective*
= Algerian

**aliment** *noun, masculine*
un aliment = a food

**alimentation** *noun, feminine*
• (*the foods usually eaten*)
une alimentation saine = a healthy diet
• (*food retailing*)
un magasin d'alimentation = a grocery store

**allais** ▶ **aller 1** 9

**allée**
**1** *noun, feminine*
une allée = a path
(*wider*) = an avenue
(*leading to a garage*) = a drive, a driveway
**2 allées** *noun, feminine plural*
leurs allées et venues = their comings and goings

**Allemagne** *noun, feminine*
l'Allemagne = Germany

**allemand/allemande**
**1** *adjective*
= German
**2 allemand** *noun, masculine*
l'allemand = German

**aller**
**1** *verb* 9 (**!** + *être*)
• = to go
où vas-tu? = where are you going?
il faut que j'aille les voir = I must go and see them
allons-y! = let's go!
• (*when talking about the near future*) = to be going to
= to be about to
attention, tu vas tomber! = careful, you're going to fall!
j'allais partir quand il est arrivé = I was about to leave when he arrived
• (*when talking about health, business*)
comment vas-tu?, comment allez-vous? = how are you?
je vais bien = I'm fine
qu'est-ce qui ne va pas? = what's the matter?

**!** *For more examples, see* ça.

• (*to be flattering or convenient*) = to suit, to be good for
le rouge te va bien = red suits you, red is right for you
• (*to be of the right size*) = to fit
son costume ne lui va plus = his suit doesn't fit him any more
• (*when urging or encouraging*)
allons, taisez-vous! = come on, be quiet!
allez-y, tirez! = go on, pull!

**2 s'en aller** verb (**!** + être)
(if it's a person)
s'en aller = to leave, to be off, to go (away)
va-t'en!, allez-vous-en! = go away!
• (If it's a stain)
s'en aller = to come out
**3** noun, masculine
un aller simple = a single (ticket), a one-way ticket
un aller retour = a return ticket, a round trip ticket

**allô** exclamation
allô! = hello!

**allonger** verb [13]
**1** (**!** + avoir)
• = to lengthen
• = to stretch out
**2 s'allonger** (**!** + être)
• s'allonger = to lie down
• s'allonger = to get longer

**allumer** verb [1]
• = to light
• = to turn on

**allumette** noun, feminine
une allumette = a match

**allure** noun, feminine
• l'allure = the speed
= the pace
à toute allure = at top speed
• une allure = an appearance
= a look

**alors**
**1** adverb
• = so
et alors? = so what?
• = then
alors je prendrai le bleu = I'll take the blue one then, OK I'll take the blue one
• ça alors! = my goodness!, oh dear!
**2 alors que** = while
= even though

**alouette** noun, feminine
une alouette = a lark

**alpinisme** noun, masculine
l'alpinisme = climbing, mountaineering

**alpiniste** noun, masculine/feminine
un alpiniste/une alpiniste = a mountain-climber

**altitude** noun, feminine
l'altitude = the altitude
= the height

**amande** noun, feminine
une amande = an almond

**amateur** noun, masculine
• (a keen person)
un amateur = an enthusiast
• (not a professional)
un amateur = an amateur

**ambassade** noun, feminine
une ambassade = an embassy

**ambiance** noun, feminine
l'ambiance = the atmosphere
il y a de l'ambiance = it's pretty lively

**ambition** noun, feminine
l'ambition = ambition

**âme** noun, feminine
une âme = a soul

**amélioration** noun, feminine
une amélioration = an improvement

**améliorer** verb [1]
= to improve

**aménagé/aménagée** adjective
• = fully-equipped
• = converted

**aménager** verb [13]
• = to equip
= to fit out
• = to convert
aménager une grange = to convert a barn

**amende** noun, feminine
une amende = a fine

**amener** verb [16]
= to bring
amenez vos amis = bring your friends

**amer/amère** adjective
= bitter

**américain/américaine**
**1** adjective
= American
**2 américain** noun, masculine
l'américain = American English

**Amérique** noun, feminine
l'Amérique = America
l'Amérique du Nord = North America

**ami/amie** noun, masculine/feminine
un ami/une amie = a (male) friend/a (female) friend
un petit ami/une petite amie = a boyfriend/a girlfriend

**amical/amicale** adjective
(plural) **amicaux/amicales**
= friendly

**amicalement** adverb
• = in a friendly way
• (ending a letter) = best wishes

**amitié** noun, feminine
• l'amitié = friendship
• (ending a letter)
amitiés = kindest regards, fondly

**amour** noun, masculine
l'amour = love

**amoureux/amoureuse** adjective
= in love

**ampoule** *noun, feminine*
* *(for lighting)*
  une ampoule = a light bulb
* *(on the skin)*
  une ampoule = a blister

**amusant/amusante** *adjective*
  = entertaining
  = funny

**amuser** *verb* 1
**1** (! + *avoir*)
  = to amuse
**2 s'amuser** (! + *être*)
  s'amuser = to enjoy oneself
  = to have fun

**an** *noun, masculine*
  un an = one year
  avoir seize ans = to be sixteen years old

**ananas** *noun, masculine* (! *never changes*)
  un ananas = a pineapple

**ancêtre** *noun, masculine/feminine*
  un ancêtre/une ancêtre = an ancestor

**anchois** *noun, masculine* (! *never changes*)
  un anchois = an anchovy

**ancien/ancienne** *adjective*
* *(if placed before the noun)* = former
  l'ancienne mairie = the former town hall
* *(if placed after the noun)* = old
  = antique

**âne** *noun, masculine*
  un âne = a donkey

**ange** *noun, masculine*
  un ange = an angel

**angine** *noun, feminine*
  une angine = a throat infection, tonsillitis

**anglais/anglaise**
**1** *adjective*
  = English
**2 anglais** *noun, masculine*
  l'anglais = English

**Anglais/Anglaise** *noun, masculine/feminine*
  un Anglais/une Anglaise = an Englishman/an Englishwoman
  les Anglais = the English

**angle** *noun, masculine*
* un angle = an angle
* un angle = a corner
  le magasin qui fait l'angle = the shop on the corner

**Angleterre** *noun, feminine*
  l'Angleterre = England

**animal** *noun, masculine*
(*plural*) **animaux**
  un animal = an animal
  **un animal de compagnie** = a pet

**animé/animée** *adjective*
  = lively

**anneau** *noun, masculine*
(*plural*) **anneaux**
  un anneau = a ring

**année** *noun, feminine*
  une année = a year
  Bonne année! = Happy New Year!
  les années 60 = the sixties

**anniversaire** *noun, masculine*
  un anniversaire (*of one's birth*) = a birthday
  (*of an event*) = an anniversary
  Joyeux anniversaire! = Happy birthday!

**annonce** *noun, feminine*
* une annonce = an advertisement
  les petites annonces = classified advertisements
* une annonce = an announcement

**annoncer** *verb* 12
**1** (! + *avoir*)
  = to announce
**2 s'annoncer** (! + *être*)
  ça s'annonce bien = it looks promising

**annuaire** *noun, masculine*
  un annuaire (**téléphonique**) = a telephone directory, a phone book
  l'annuaire électronique = *the electronic telephone directory on Minitel*

**annuler** *verb* 1
  = to cancel

**antigel** *noun, masculine*
  l'antigel = antifreeze

**antillais/antillaise** *adjective*
  = West Indian

**Antilles** *noun, feminine plural*
  les Antilles = the West Indies

**antipathique** *adjective*
  = unpleasant

**antivol** *noun, masculine*
  un antivol = an antitheft device

**anxieux/anxieuse** *adjective*
  = anxious

**août** *noun, masculine*
  août = August

**apercevoir** *verb* 5
**1** (! + *avoir*)
  = to catch sight of
  = to see
**2 s'apercevoir** (! + *être*)
  s'apercevoir que = to realize that
  = to notice that

**aperçu/aperçue**
**1 ▶ apercevoir** 5
**2 aperçu** *noun, masculine*
  un aperçu = a general idea

**aplatir** *verb* 3
  = to flatten

**appareil** noun, masculine
• un appareil = a device, a gadget
= an appliance
• un appareil = a telephone
Victor à l'appareil = (this is) Victor speaking
• un appareil = an aeroplane, an airplane
• un appareil (photo) = a camera

**apparence** noun, feminine
l'apparence = appearance

**appartement** noun, masculine
un appartement = a flat, an apartment

**appartenir** verb 36
appartenir à = to belong to
à qui appartiennent les clés? = whose keys are they?

**appel** noun, masculine
• (in order to attract attention)
un appel = a call
• (at school)
l'appel = registration
faire l'appel = to take the register, to call the roll

**appeler** verb 19
1 (! + avoir)
• = to call
• = to phone
2 s'appeler (! + être)
s'appeler = to be called
comment t'appelles-tu? = what's your name?

**appendicite** noun, feminine
l'appendicite = appendicitis

**appétissant/appétissante** adjective
= appetizing

**appétit** noun, masculine
l'appétit = appetite
bon appétit! = enjoy your meal!

**applaudir** verb 3
= to applaud, to clap

**applaudissements** noun, masculine plural
des applaudissements = applause

**appliquer** verb 1
1 (! + avoir)
• (on the skin, on a surface) = to apply
• (to enforce) = to implement
2 s'appliquer (! + être)
• (to do one's best)
s'appliquer = to apply oneself
• (to be relevant)
s'appliquer = to apply

**apporter** verb 1
= to bring

**apprécier** verb 2
= to like, to appreciate

**apprendre** verb 52
• (to get knowledge) = to learn
ils ont appris à lire = they've learned to read
• (to give lessons) = to teach
elle m'apprenait à conduire = she was teaching me to drive
ça t'apprendra! = that'll teach you!
• (to receive information) = to hear
j'ai appris qu'elle était partie = I heard that she'd left
• (to give information) = to tell

**apprentissage** noun, masculine
• l'apprentissage = training

**appris/apprise ▶ apprendre** 52

**approcher** verb 1
1 (! + avoir)
• = to get nearer, to get closer
• = to bring nearer, to bring closer
2 approcher de (! + avoir)
approcher de = to be getting close to
3 s'approcher de (! + être)
s'approcher de = to go closer to
= to come closer to

**approuver** verb 1
= to approve of

**approximativement** adverb
= approximately

**appuyer** verb 22
1 (! + avoir)
• = to press, to push
• = to rest
• = to lean
2 s'appuyer (! + être)
s'appuyer = to lean

**après**
1 preposition
= after
2 adverb
= afterward(s), after
= later
3 d'après
d'après moi = in my opinion
d'après [lui | eux | le journal ...] = according to [him | them | the newspaper ...]

**après-demain** adverb
= the day after tomorrow

**après-midi** noun, masculine or feminine
(! never changes)
un or une après-midi = an afternoon

**après-shampooing** noun, masculine
un après-shampooing = a conditioner

**après-vente** adjective (! never changes)
le service après-vente = after-sales service

**aquarium** noun, masculine
un aquarium = an aquarium, a fish tank

**arabe**
1 adjective
= Arab
= Arabic

**2** *noun, masculine*
l'arabe = Arabic

**Arabe** *noun, masculine|feminine*
un Arabe/une Arabe = an Arab

**araignée** *noun, feminine*
une araignée = a spider

**arbitre** *noun, masculine*
un arbitre = a referee

**arbre** *noun, masculine*
un arbre = a tree
**un arbre de Noël** = a Christmas tree

**arc-en-ciel** *noun, masculine*
(*plural*) **arcs-en-ciel**
un arc-en-ciel = a rainbow

**arche** *noun, feminine*
une arche = an arch

**ardoise** *noun, feminine*
l'ardoise = slate

**arête** *noun, feminine*
• (*in a fish*)
  une arête = a fishbone
• (*of a mountain*)
  l'arête = the ridge

**argent** *noun, masculine*
• (*metal*)
  l'argent = silver
• (*currency*)
  l'argent = money
**l'argent liquide** = cash
**l'argent de poche** = pocket money,
spending money

**argot** *noun, masculine*
l'argot = slang

**arme** *noun, feminine*
une arme = a weapon
**une arme à feu** = a firearm

**armée** *noun, feminine*
une armée = an army

**armoire** *noun, feminine*
une armoire = a wardrobe, a closet
**une armoire à pharmacie** = a medicine
cupboard, a medicine cabinet

**arobas(e)** *noun, masculine*
(*in an email address*)
un arobas(e) = an at sign

**arracher** *verb* 1
• = to pull out
  = to tear out
• = to snatch

**arranger** *verb* 13
**1** (**!** + *avoir*)
• = to arrange
• = to fix, to repair
• = to tidy, to clean up
• = to suit
  ça m'arrange d'y aller avec eux = it suits
  me to go with them

**2 s'arranger** (**!** + *être*)
• s'arranger = to improve
  le temps s'est arrangé = the weather has
  improved
• s'arranger = to sort itself out, to work out
• s'arranger = to come to an agreement

**arrestation** *noun, feminine*
une arrestation = an arrest

**arrêt** *noun, masculine*
un arrêt = a stop
un arrêt d'autobus = a bus stop

**arrêter** *verb* 1
**1** (**!** + *avoir*)
• = to stop
  arrête de crier = stop shouting
  arrête! = stop it!
• = to arrest
**2 s'arrêter** (**!** + *être*)
s'arrêter = to stop

**arrhes** *noun, feminine plural*
des arrhes = a deposit

**arrière**
**1** *adjective*
  = back
  = rear
**2** *noun, masculine*
• (*the rear part*)
  l'arrière = the back
• (*in sport*)
  un arrière = a fullback
  = a defender
**3 en arrière** *adverb*
• = backward(s)
  se pencher en arrière = to lean back
• = behind
  rester en arrière = to stay behind

**arrivée** *noun, feminine*
• (*of a plane, a passenger*)
  une arrivée = an arrival
  aller chercher un ami à l'arrivée du train
  = to meet a friend off the train, to meet
  a friend from the train
• (*of a race*)
  l'arrivée = the finish

**arriver** *verb* 1 (**!** + *être*)
• = to arrive
• = to come
  j'arrive! = I'm coming!
  ils sont arrivés en courant = they came up
  running, they ran up
• = to reach
• arriver à faire = to manage to do, to
  succeed in doing
  je n'y arrive pas = I can't manage it, I can't
  do it
• = to happen
  c'est arrivé à mon frère = it happened to
  my brother
  que t'est-il arrivé? = what happened to
  you?
  il m'arrive d'oublier = I sometimes forget

**arrondir** verb [3]
arrondir un chiffre = to round off a figure

**arrondissement** noun, masculine
un arrondissement = an arrondissement, a
district

**arroser** verb [1]
= to water
= to spray

**arrosoir** noun, masculine
un arrosoir = a watering can

**art** noun, masculine
l'art = art
**les arts ménagers** = home economics

**artichaut** noun, masculine
un artichaut = an artichoke

**article** noun, masculine
• (in grammar)
un article = an article
• (in a shop)
un article = an item
des articles de sport = sports equipment
des articles de toilette = toiletries

**artificiel/artificielle** adjective
= artificial
= man-made

**artisan** noun, masculine
un artisan = a craftsman

**artisanal/artisanale** adjective
(plural) **artisanaux/artisanales**
une méthode artisanale = a traditional
method
de fabrication artisanale = hand-crafted,
hand-made
= home-made

**artisanat** noun, masculine
l'artisanat = the craft industry
magasin d'artisanat = arts and crafts shop

**artiste** noun, masculine/feminine
un artiste/une artiste = an artist
(in films, plays) = an actor/an actress
un artiste peintre = a painter

**as¹** ▶ avoir [8]

**as²** noun, masculine (**!** never changes)
un as = an ace

**ascenseur** noun, masculine
un ascenseur = a lift, an elevator

**ascension** noun, feminine
une ascension = an ascent

**Ascension** noun, feminine
l'Ascension = Ascension

**asiatique** adjective
= from the Far East, Asian

**Asie** noun, feminine
l'Asie = Asia

**asperge** noun, feminine
des asperges = asparagus

**asphyxier: s'asphyxier** verb [2]
(**!** + être)
s'asphyxier = to suffocate

**aspirateur** noun, masculine
un aspirateur = a vacuum cleaner

**assassin** noun, masculine
un assassin = a murderer

**assassinat** noun, masculine
un assassinat = a murder

**assassiner** verb [1]
= to murder

**asseoir: s'asseoir** verb [34] (**!** + être)
s'asseoir = to sit (down)
(in bed) = to sit up

**assez** adverb
= enough
= quite, pretty

**assiette** noun, feminine
une assiette = a plate
**une assiette anglaise** = assorted cold
meats, cold cuts

**assis/assise**
1 ▶ asseoir [34]
2 adjective
= seated

**assister** verb [1]
• assister à = to attend, to be at
• assister à = to witness

**association** noun, feminine
une association sportive = a sports
association, a (sports) club

**assorti/assortie** adjective
• = matching
• = assorted

**assurance** noun, feminine
• (a feeling)
l'assurance = (self-)confidence
• (against accidents)
une assurance = insurance
**l'assurance maladie** = health insurance
**l'assurance au tiers** = third-party
insurance
**l'assurance tous risques**
= comprehensive insurance

**assuré/assurée**
1 adjective
• = confident
• = certain
2 noun, masculine/feminine
l'assuré/l'assurée = the insured party

**assurer** verb [1]
1 (**!** + avoir)
• (to tell confidently) = to assure
il m'a assuré que c'était vrai = he assured
me that it was true
• (against accidents) = to insure
2 s'assurer (**!** + être)
• s'assurer = to take out insurance
• s'assurer que = to make sure that

**astrologue** noun, masculine|feminine
un astrologue/une astrologue = an
astrologer

**astronaute** noun, masculine|feminine
un astronaute/une astronaute = an
astronaut

**astuce** noun, feminine
• une astuce = a trick
• l'astuce = cleverness
= shrewdness

**astucieux/astucieuse** adjective
= clever, smart
= shrewd

**atelier** noun, masculine
un atelier (for a craftsman) = a workshop
(for a painter) = a studio

**athlétisme** noun, masculine
l'athlétisme = athletics

**Atlantique** noun, masculine
l'(océan) Atlantique = the Atlantic (Ocean)

**atout** noun, masculine
• (at cards)
un atout = a trump
atout trèfle! = clubs are trumps!
• (in life)
un atout = an asset, an advantage

**attacher** verb 1
1 (! + avoir)
= to tie
= to fasten
2 s'attacher à (! + être)
s'attacher à = to become attached to

**attaquer** verb 1
1 (! + avoir)
= to attack
2 s'attaquer à (! + être)
s'attaquer à = to attack

**atteindre** verb 55
• = to reach
• = to hit
• être atteint d'une maladie = to suffer from
a disease

**atteint/atteinte** ▶ atteindre 55

**attendre** verb 6
1 (! + avoir)
• = to wait
= to wait (for)
• = to expect
j'attends une visite = I'm expecting a visit
2 s'attendre à (! + être)
s'attendre à = to expect
il fallait s'y attendre = it was to be expected

**attendu/attendue** ▶ attendre 6

**attentat** noun, masculine
un attentat (on a person) = an
assassination attempt
(on a group, a building) = an attack

**attente** noun, feminine
l'attente = wait(ing)

**attention** noun, feminine
l'attention = attention
faire attention (to take care) = to be careful
(to concentrate) = to pay attention
attention! = careful!, watch out!
attention à la marche! = mind the step!,
watch the step!

**attentivement** adverb
= attentively

**atterrir** verb 3
= to land

**atterrissage** noun, masculine
un atterrissage = a landing

**attirer** verb 1
1 (! + avoir)
= to attract
2 s'attirer (! + être)
s'attirer des ennuis = to get into trouble

**attraction** noun, feminine
• l'attraction = attraction
• des attractions = entertainment
un parc d'attractions = an amusement
park

**attraper** verb 1
= to catch

**au** ▶ à

**auberge** noun, feminine
une auberge = an inn
**une auberge de jeunesse** = a youth
hostel

**aucun/aucune**
1 adjective
= no, not any
en aucun cas = under no circumstances
aucune idée! = I've no idea!
2 pronoun
= none, not any
aucun d'entre nous = none of us
aucune des deux = neither of them

**audace** noun, feminine
l'audace (bravery) = boldness
(guts) = audacity, nerve

**audacieux/audacieuse** adjective
= bold

**au-delà de** preposition
= beyond
= over

**au-dessous de** preposition
= below
= under

**au-dessus de** preposition
= above
= over

**auditeur/auditrice** noun,
masculine|feminine
un auditeur/une auditrice = a listener

**A**

**augmenter** verb [1]
= to increase

**aujourd'hui** adverb
* = today
* = nowadays

**aurai ▶ avoir** [8]

**aussi**
1 adverb
* = also, as well
  = too
  eux aussi ont faim = they are hungry too
* = so
  je ne savais pas que c'était aussi cher = I
  didn't know it was so expensive
  il n'avait jamais vu un aussi gros chien
  = he'd never seen such a large dog
* = as
  aussi [riche | vieux | petit ...] que = as [rich |
  old | small ...] as
2 conjunction
  = so, consequently
  aussi sommes-nous partis = (and) so we
  left

**aussitôt**
1 adverb
= immediately, right away
2 **aussitôt que** = as soon as

**Australie** noun, feminine
l'Australie = Australia

**australien/australienne** adjective
= Australian

**autant** adverb
1 **autant que** = as much as
  il gagne autant que toi = he earns as much
  as you
2 **autant de** = as much
  = as many
  autant de [valeur | patience | temps ...] que
  = as much [value | patience | time ...] as
  autant de [fautes | lettres | soucis ...] que = as
  many [mistakes | letters | worries ...] as

**auteur** noun, masculine
l'auteur (of a book) = the author
(of a song) = the composer

**auto** noun, feminine
une auto = a car

**autobus** noun, masculine (! never
changes)
un autobus = a bus

**autocar** noun, masculine
un autocar = a coach, a bus

**autocollant/autocollante**
1 adjective
= self-adhesive
2 **autocollant** noun, masculine
un autocollant = a sticker

**auto-école** noun, feminine
(plural) **auto-écoles**
une auto-école = a driving school

**automne** noun, masculine
l'automne = autumn, fall

**automobile** noun, feminine
une automobile = a (motor)car, an
automobile

**automobiliste** noun, masculine/feminine
un automobiliste/une automobiliste = a
motorist

**autoritaire** adjective
= authoritarian

**autoroute** noun, feminine
une autoroute = a motorway, a highway

**auto-stop** noun, masculine
l'auto-stop = hitchhiking
faire de l'auto-stop = to hitchhike

**autour de** preposition
= around

**autre**
1 determiner
= other
l'autre jour = the other day
rien d'autre = nothing else
2 **d'autre part** = besides
= on the other hand

**autrefois** adverb
= in the past
= before

**autrement** adverb
* = in a different way, differently
  autrement dit = in other words
* (if not) = otherwise
  autrement il ne viendra pas = otherwise he
  won't come

**Autriche** noun, feminine
l'Autriche = Austria

**autrichien/autrichienne** adjective
= Austrian

**autruche** noun, feminine
une autruche = an ostrich

**aux ▶ à**

**avais ▶ avoir** [8]

**avaler** verb [1]
= to swallow

**avance**
1 noun, feminine
* (of an army)
  l'avance = the advance
* (on a competitor)
  une avance = a lead
* (money)
  une avance = an advance
2 **à l'avance** = in advance
3 **d'avance**
* payer d'avance = to pay in advance
* avoir cinq minutes d'avance = to be five
  minutes early

# avoir  *verb* 8

| present | imperfect | future | past participle |
|---------|-----------|--------|-----------------|
| j'ai | j'avais | j'aurai | eu / eue |
| tu as | tu avais | tu auras | |
| il / elle a | ill / elle avait | il / elle aura | |
| nous avons | nous avions | nous aurons | |
| vous avez | vous aviez | vous aurez | |
| ils / elles ont | ils / elles avaient | ils / elles auront | |

- **1 avoir** functions as an ordinary verb:
  = to have (got)
  > ils **ont** un chien = *they have a dog*
- = to get
  > réussir à **avoir** des billets = *to manage to get tickets*

**2 avoir** is used as an auxiliary verb to conjugate most other verbs, except all reflexive verbs and those verbs labelled (**!** + *être*):
> elle **a** bu son lait = *she drank her milk*
> ils **auraient** aimé te voir = *they would have liked to see you*

**3 avoir** is used in the phrase **il y a**:
> il y **a** = *there is* or *there are*
> il y **aura** = *there will be*

**4 avoir** is used in expressions like **avoir faim, avoir soif, avoir l'air, avoir besoin de** etc. You will find translations at **faim, soif, air, besoin** etc.

---

**4 en avance**
arriver en avance = to arrive early
être en avance sur les autres = to be ahead of the others

## avancer *verb* 12
**1** (**!** + *avoir*)
- = to move forward
  avancer d'un mètre = to move forward one metre
- = to make progress
  avancer lentement = to make slow progress
- = to be fast
  ta montre avance de cinq minutes = your watch is five minutes fast
- = to bring forward
  avancer une réunion = to bring a meeting forward, to push a meeting up
- = to lend
  avancer de l'argent à un ami = to lend money to a friend
**2 s'avancer** (**!** + *être*)
s'avancer = to move forward
il s'est avancé vers la table = he moved toward(s) the table

## avant
**1** *noun, masculine*
- (*the front part*)
  l'avant = the front

- (*in sport*)
  un avant = a forward
**2** *adjective* (**!** *never changes*)
= front
les roues avant = the front wheels
**3** *preposition*
= before
juste avant de partir = just before leaving
**4** *adverb*
= before
= first
que faisait-il avant? = what was he doing before?
la semaine d'avant = the week before
la dame était avant = the lady was first
**5 en avant** = forward(s)
- se pencher en avant = to lean forward(s)
- partir en avant = to go (on) ahead

**avantage** *noun, masculine*
un avantage = an advantage

**avant-hier** *adverb*
= the day before yesterday

**avare** *adjective*
= mean, miserly

**avec** *preposition*
= with

**avenir** *noun, masculine*
l'avenir = the future
à l'avenir = in (the) future

---

**✗** in informal situations

**aventure** *noun, feminine*
une aventure = an adventure
partir à l'aventure = to set off in search of
adventure

**aventurier/aventurière** *noun,*
*masculine/feminine*
un aventurier/une aventurière = an
adventurer

**averse** *noun, feminine*
une averse = a shower, a downpour

**avertir** *verb* 3
• = to warn
• = to inform

**aveugle** *adjective*
= blind

**avez** ▶ **avoir** 8

**avion** *noun, masculine*
un avion = an aeroplane, an airplane
un avion = a jet (plane)

**aviron** *noun, masculine*
• l'aviron = rowing
• un aviron = an oar

**avis** *noun, masculine* (**!** never changes)
• (a belief)
un avis = an opinion
changer d'avis = to change one's mind
• (an announcement)
un avis = a notice, a sign

**avocat¹** *noun, masculine*
un avocat = an avocado

**avocat²/avocate** *noun,*
*masculine/feminine*
un avocat/une avocate = a lawyer
= a barrister, an attorney

**avoir** *verb* 8
▶ See the boxed note.

**avons** ▶ **avoir** 8

**avouer** *verb* 1
= to confess

**avril** *noun, masculine*
avril = April

**ayant** ▶ **avoir** 8

# Bb

**baby-foot** *noun, masculine* (**!** never
changes)
le baby-foot = table football

**bac**, **baccalauréat** *noun, masculine*
le baccalauréat = the baccalaureate (*a*
*school-leaving diploma taken at 17–18*)

**badaud** *noun, masculine*
un badaud = an onlooker

**bagage** *noun, masculine*
un bagage = a piece of luggage

**bagarre** *noun, feminine*
une bagarre = a fight

**bagarrer: se bagarrer** *verb* 1 (**!** + *être*)
se bagarrer = to fight

**bague** *noun, feminine*
une bague = a ring

**baguette** *noun, feminine*
• (bread)
une baguette = a baguette, a French stick,
French bread
• (a thin piece of wood)
une baguette = a stick
**une baguette magique** = a magic wand

**baie** *noun, feminine*
• (on the coast)
une baie = a bay
• (fruit)
une baie = a berry

**baignade** *noun, feminine*
la baignade = swimming

**baigner: se baigner** *verb* 1 (**!** + *être*)
se baigner = to go for a swim

**baignoire** *noun, feminine*
une baignoire = a bathtub

**bâiller** *verb* 1
= to yawn

**bain** *noun, masculine*
• (at home)
un bain = a bath
prendre un bain = to have a bath, to take a
bath
• (at the swimming pool)
le grand bain = the (main) pool
le petit bain = the shallow pool, the
learners' pool

**baiser** *noun, masculine*
un baiser = a kiss

**baisser** *verb* 1
**1** (**!** + *avoir*)
• = to lower
baisser le store = to lower the blinds
• = to drop
la température a baissé = the temperature
has dropped
**2 se baisser** (**!** + *être*)
se baisser = to bend down, to reach down

**bal** *noun, masculine*
un bal = a dance, a ball

**balade** *noun, feminine*
une balade (on foot) = a walk, a stroll
(by car) = a drive
(on a bicycle) = a ride

**balader**: se balader *verb* [1] (**!** + *être*)
se balader (*on foot*) = to go for a walk
(*by car*) = to go for a drive
(*on a bicycle*) = to go for a ride

**baladeur** *noun, masculine*
un baladeur = a walkman

**balai** *noun, masculine*
un balai = a broom

**balance** *noun, feminine*
une balance = scales

**Balance** *noun, feminine*
la Balance = Libra

**balançoire** *noun, feminine*
une balançoire = a swing
= a see-saw

**balayer** *verb* [21]
= to sweep

**balcon** *noun, masculine*
un balcon = a balcony

**baleine** *noun, feminine*
une baleine = a whale

**balle** *noun, feminine*
* (*for playing*)
une balle = a (small) ball
* (*for a gun*)
une balle = a bullet

**ballerine** *noun, feminine*
* (*a person*)
une ballerine = a ballerina
* (*footwear*)
une ballerine (*for dancing*) = a ballet
pump, a ballet slipper
(*for walking*) = a flat pump, a slipper

**ballon** *noun, masculine*
un ballon = a (large) ball

**bambou** *noun, masculine*
le bambou = bamboo

**banal/banale** *adjective*
= commonplace, ordinary

**banane** *noun, feminine*
* une banane = a banana
* une banane = a bum bag, a fanny pack

**banc** *noun, masculine*
un banc = a bench

**bancaire** *adjective*
= bank, banking

**bande** *noun, feminine*
* (*of people*)
une bande = a group, a bunch
* (*with sound*)
une bande = a tape
* (*something long and narrow*)
une bande = a strip
**une bande dessinée** = a comic strip

**bandeau** *noun, masculine*
(*plural*) **bandeaux**
un bandeau (*holding the hair*) = a
hairband, a headband
(*over the eyes*) = a blindfold

**banlieue** *noun, feminine*
la banlieue = the suburbs

**banque** *noun, feminine*
une banque = a bank

**banquette** *noun, feminine*
une banquette = a seat

**banquier** *noun, masculine*
un banquier = a banker

**baptême** *noun, masculine*
un baptême = a christening

**bar** *noun, masculine*
un bar = a bar

**barbant/barbante✗** *adjective*
= boring

**barbare** *noun, masculine|feminine*
un barbare/une barbare = a barbarian

**barbe** *noun, feminine*
* une barbe = a beard
* quelle barbe✗! = what a bore!
**la barbe à papa** = candyfloss, cotton
candy

**barber**: se barber✗ [1] (**!** + *être*)
se barber = to be bored

**barboter** *verb* [1]
= to paddle

**barbu** *noun, masculine*
un barbu = a bearded man

**barque** *noun, feminine*
une barque = a (small) boat

**barrage** *noun, masculine*
* (*on a river*)
un barrage = a dam
* (*on a road*)
un barrage de police = a police roadblock

**barre** *noun, feminine*
* (*of metal, chocolate*)
une barre = a bar
* (*a line*)
une barre = a stroke, a mark
* (*on a ship*)
la barre = the tiller, the helm

**barreau** *noun, masculine*
(*plural*) **barreaux**
un barreau (*on a cage*) = a bar

**barrer** *verb* [1]
* = to cross out
* = to block

**barrière** *noun, feminine*
* (*enclosing an area*)
une barrière = a fence

---

* (an obstacle)
une barrière – a barrier

**bar-tabac** noun, masculine
(plural) **bars-tabac**
  un bar-tabac = a café (also selling stamps and cigarettes)

**bas/basse**
**1** adjective
  = low
**2 bas** adverb
* = low
  voir plus bas = see below
* = quietly
  parler tout bas = to speak in a whisper
**3 bas** noun, masculine (**!** never changes)
* (the lower part)
  le bas = the bottom
  en bas = downstairs
* à bas les patrons! = down with bosses!
* (a garment)
  un bas = a stocking

**basculer** verb [1]
* (to fall over) = to topple over
* (to tilt) = to tip up

**basilic** noun, masculine
  le basilic = basil

**basket**
**1** noun, masculine
  le basket = basketball
**2** noun, feminine
  des baskets = trainers, sneakers

**basse ▸ bas 1**

**bassin** noun, masculine
  un bassin = a pool

**bataille** noun, feminine
  une bataille = a battle
  la bataille navale = battleships

**bateau** noun, masculine
(plural) **bateaux**
  un bateau = a boat
  faire du bateau = to go boating
  = to go sailing

**bateau-mouche** noun, masculine
(plural) **bateaux-mouches**
  un bateau-mouche a large river boat for sightseeing

**bâtiment** noun, masculine
  un bâtiment = a building

**bâtir** verb [3]
  = to build

**bâton** noun, masculine
  un bâton = a stick

**batterie** noun, feminine
* (in a car)
  la batterie = the battery
* (in a band)
  la batterie = the percussion, the drums

**battre** verb [61]
**1** (**!** + avoir)
  = to beat
  battre un record = to break a record
* le cœur battant = with a beating heart
* battre des mains = to clap
**2 se battre** (**!** + être)
  se battre = to fight

**battu/battue ▸ battre** [61]

**baudruche** noun, feminine
  un ballon en baudruche = a balloon

**bavard/bavarde** adjective
  = talkative

**bavarder** verb [1]
  = to chat

**bazar** noun, masculine
  un bazar (a shop) = a general store

**BD** noun, feminine
  une BD = a comic strip

**beau/belle** adjective
(plural) **beaux/belles**

> **!** bel is used instead of beau before masculine nouns beginning with a vowel or a mute h. The plural of bel is beaux.

  = beautiful, handsome
  = fine
  il fait beau = the weather is fine

**beaucoup** adverb
  = a lot
  = much
  c'est beaucoup trop = it's far too much
  beaucoup de [patience | temps | livres ...] = a lot of [patience | time | books ...]
  il ne me reste plus beaucoup d'argent = I haven't got much money left

**beau-frère** noun, masculine
(plural) **beaux-frères**
  un beau-frère = a brother-in-law

**beau-père** noun, masculine
(plural) **beaux-pères**
  un beau-père = a father-in-law
  = a stepfather

**beauté** noun, feminine
  la beauté = beauty

**beaux-arts** noun, masculine plural
  les beaux-arts = fine arts

**bébé** noun, masculine
  un bébé = a baby

**bec** noun, masculine
  un bec = a beak

**bêche** noun, feminine
  une bêche = a spade, a shovel

**beignet** noun, masculine
  un beignet = a fritter
  = a doughnut, a donut

**bel ▶ beau**

**belge** *adjective*
= Belgian

**Belgique** *noun, feminine*
la Belgique = Belgium

**Bélier** *noun, masculine*
le Bélier = Aries

**belle ▶ beau**

**belle-fille** *noun, feminine*
(*plural*) **belles-filles**
une belle-fille = a daughter-in-law

**belle-mère** *noun, feminine*
(*plural*) **belles-mères**
une belle-mère = a mother-in-law
= a stepmother

**belle-sœur** *noun, feminine*
(*plural*) **belles-sœurs**
une belle-sœur = a sister-in-law

**bénéfice** *noun, masculine*
faire un bénéfice = to make a profit

**béquille** *noun, feminine*
une béquille = a crutch

**berceau** *noun, masculine*
(*plural*) **berceaux**
un berceau = a cradle

**bercer** *verb* 12
= to rock

**berge** *noun, feminine*
la berge (de la rivière) = the (river)bank

**berger/bergère** *noun,*
*masculine/feminine*
un berger/une bergère = a shepherd/a
shepherdess
**un berger allemand** = a German
shepherd dog, an Alsatian

**bermuda** *noun, masculine*
un bermuda = bermuda shorts

**besoin** *noun, masculine*
un besoin = a need
avoir besoin d'argent = to need money

**bête**
**1** *adjective*
= stupid, silly
**2** *noun, feminine*
une bête = an animal

**bêtise** *noun, feminine*
• la bêtise = stupidity
• faire une bêtise = to do something silly
dire des bêtises = to talk nonsense

**béton** *noun, masculine*
le béton = concrete

**betterave** *noun, feminine*
une betterave = a beetroot, a beet

---

**\*** in informal situations

**beurre** *noun, masculine*
le beurre = butter

**bibelot** *noun, masculine*
un bibelot = an ornament

**biberon** *noun, masculine*
un biberon = a (baby's) bottle, a (nursing)
bottle

**bibliothèque** *noun, feminine*
une bibliothèque (*a room or a building*) = a
library
(*a piece of furniture*) = a bookcase

**bic** *noun, masculine*
un bic = a biro , a ballpoint pen

**bicyclette** *noun, feminine*
• (*the equipment*)
une bicyclette = a bicycle
• (*the sport*)
faire de la bicyclette = to cycle, to go
cycling

**bidon**
**1** *adjective***\*** (**!** *never changes*)
= bogus, phoney
**2** *noun, masculine*
un bidon = a can
= a drum

**bidonville** *noun, masculine*
un bidonville = a shanty town

**bien**
**1** *adjective* (**!** *never changes*)
• = good
**2** *adverb*
• = well
ils vont bien = they're well
ça s'est bien passé = it went well
c'est bien fait pour lui! = it serves him
right!
• = very
c'est bien triste = it's very sad
je l'espère bien = I very much hope so, I
hope so
• = exactly
• = definitely
c'est bien ce que je pensais = that's
(exactly) what I thought
la voiture rouge est bien à eux = the red
car is definitely theirs
je te l'avais bien dit! = I told you so!
**3** *noun, masculine*
le bien = good
c'est pour ton bien = it's for your own good
**4 bien sûr** = of course
**5 bien entendu** = naturally

**bientôt** *adverb*
= soon

**bienvenu/bienvenue** *adjective*
= welcome

**bière** *noun, feminine*
la bière = beer
la bière (à la) pression = draught beer,
draft beer

**la bière blonde** = lager, light beer
**la bière brune** = stout

**bifteck** noun, masculine
le bifteck = steak

**bifurquer** verb [1]
- (if it's a road) = to fork
- (if it's a driver) = to turn off

**bijou** noun, masculine
(plural) **bijoux**
un bijou = a piece of jewellery, a piece of
  jewelry

**bijouterie** noun, feminine
une bijouterie = a jeweller's, a jewellery
  shop, a jewelry store

**bijoutier/bijoutière** noun,
masculine/feminine
un bijoutier/une bijoutière = a jeweller, a
  jeweler

**bilingue** adjective
= bilingual

**billard** noun, masculine
le billard = billiards
**le billard américain** = pool
**le billard anglais** = snooker

**bille** noun, feminine
une bille = a marble

**billet** noun, masculine
- (on a train, at the theatre)
un billet = a ticket
- (money)
un billet (de banque) = a (bank)note, a bill

**biscotte** noun, feminine
une biscotte = a rusk

**bise\*** noun, feminine
une bise\* = a kiss

**bisou\*** noun, masculine
un bisou\* = a kiss

**bissextile** adjective
une année bissextile = a leap year

**bistro(t)\*** noun, masculine
un bistro(t)\* = a bistro, a café

**bizarre** adjective
= strange, peculiar

**blague\*** noun, feminine
- une blague\* = a funny story
- (a piece of mischief)
une blague\* = a trick
faire une blague\* à un ami = to play a trick
  on a friend

**blanc/blanche**
**1** adjective
- = white
- = blank
**2 blanc** noun, masculine
un blanc (a space) = a blank
**un blanc d'œuf** = an egg white

**du blanc de poulet** = a piece of chicken
breast

**blanchisserie** noun, feminine
une blanchisserie = a laundry, a dry
  cleaner's

**blé** noun, masculine
le blé = wheat, corn

**blessé/blessée**
**1** adjective
= injured
= wounded
**2** noun, masculine/feminine
un blessé/une blessée = an injured
  person
= a casualty

**blesser** verb [1]
**1** (! + avoir)
= to hurt
= to wound
**2 se blesser** (! + être)
se blesser = to hurt oneself
elle s'est blessée à la jambe = she hurt
  her leg

**blessure** noun, feminine
une blessure = an injury
= a wound

**bleu/bleue**
**1** adjective
= blue
bleu marine = navy blue
**2 bleu** noun, masculine
un bleu = a bruise

**bloc**
**1** noun, masculine
(for writing)
un bloc = a notepad
**2 à bloc** = completely
vissé à bloc = tightly screwed
gonflé à bloc = fully inflated

**blond/blonde** adjective
(describing hair) = blonde, blond
(describing tobacco) = light, Virginia

**bloquer** verb [1]
**1** (! + avoir)
- = to block
- = to jam
- bloquer les salaires = to freeze wages
**2 se bloquer** (! + être)
se bloquer = to jam

**blouse** noun, feminine
- (worn for protection)
une blouse = an overall
- (a kind of shirt)
une blouse = a blouse

**blouson** noun, masculine
un blouson = a blouson, a jacket

**bobo\*** noun, masculine
ce n'est qu'un bobo\* = it's only a scratch

**bocal** *noun, masculine*
(*plural*) **bocaux**
  un bocal = a jar

**bœuf** *noun, masculine*
• (*the animal*)
  un bœuf = an ox
• (*the meat*)
  le bœuf = beef

**boire** *verb* 51
  = to drink

**bois**
**1** ▶ **boire** 51
**2** *noun, masculine* (**!** *never changes*)
• (*timber*)
  le bois = wood
• (*a place*)
  un bois = a wood

**boisson** *noun, feminine*
  une boisson = a drink

**boîte** *noun, feminine*
  une boîte = a box
**une boîte de conserve** = a tin, a can
**une boîte aux lettres** = a postbox, a
  mailbox
  = a letter box, a mailbox
**une boîte de nuit** = a nightclub
**une boîte de vitesses** = a gearbox

**boiter** *verb* 1
  = to limp

**boiteux/boiteuse** *adjective*
  = lame

**bol** *noun, masculine*
  un bol = a bowl

**bombe** *noun, feminine*
• (*a weapon*)
  une bombe = a bomb
• (*an aerosol*)
  une bombe = a spray

**bon/bonne¹**
**1** *adjective*
• = good
• = right
  la bonne réponse = the right answer
• = valid
  le billet est encore bon = the ticket is still
  valid
• bon anniversaire! = happy birthday!
  bonne journée! = have a nice day
**2 bon** *adverb*
  il fait bon dehors = it's nice outside
  sentir bon = to smell nice
**3 bon** *noun, masculine*
  un bon = a coupon
  = a voucher
**4 bon** *exclamation*
  bon! = right!
  ah bon? = really?

---

**✕** in informal situations

**bon marché** = cheap
**le bon sens** = common sense

**bonbon** *noun, masculine*
  un bonbon = a sweet, a candy

**bonbonne** *noun, feminine*
  une bonbonne (*for wine*) = a demijohn
  (*for gas*) = a cylinder

**bond** *noun, masculine*
  un bond = a leap

**bondé/bondée** *adjective*
  = packed

**bondir** *verb* 3
  = to leap

**bonhomme✕** *noun, masculine*
(*plural*) **bonshommes**
  un bonhomme✕ = a chap, a guy, a fellow
**un bonhomme de neige** = a snowman

**bonjour** *noun, masculine*
  bonjour! = hello!, good morning!, good
  afternoon!

**bonne²** *noun, feminine*
  une bonne = a maid

**bonnet** *noun, masculine*
  un bonnet = a cap, a hat

**bonsoir** *noun, masculine*
  bonsoir = good evening!, good night!

**bonté** *noun, feminine*
  la bonté = kindness

**bord**
**1** *noun, masculine*
  le bord (*of a bed, a cliff*) = the edge
  (*of a road*) = the side
  (*of a river*) = the bank
  des vacances au bord de la mer = seaside
  holidays, a seaside vacation
**2 à bord** = on board, aboard

**bordeaux**
**1** *adjective* (**!** *never changes*)
  = burgundy
**2** *noun, masculine* (**!** *never changes*)
  le Bordeaux = Bordeaux wine

**bordure** *noun, feminine*
  la bordure (*the limit*) = the edge
  (*ornamental*) = the border

**bosse** *noun, feminine*
  une bosse (*on the head*) = a lump
  (*on the back*) = a hump
  (*on a car*) = a dent

**botte** *noun, feminine*
• (*footwear*)
  une botte = a boot
• (*a bundle*)
  une botte = a bunch

**bouc** *noun, masculine*
• (*an animal*)
  un bouc = a billy goat

- (a beard)
  un bouc = a goatee

**bouche** noun, feminine
la bouche = the mouth
**une bouche de métro** = a tube entrance,
a subway entrance

**bouchée** noun, feminine
une bouchée = a mouthful

**boucher**[1] verb [1]
- = to plug
  = to fill up
- = to block
  = to clog up
- = to cork

**boucher**[2]/**bouchère** noun,
masculine/feminine
le boucher/la bouchère = the butcher

**boucherie** noun, feminine
une boucherie = a butcher's (shop)

**bouchon** noun, masculine
- (on a bottle)
  un bouchon = a cork
  = a top
- (on the road)
  un bouchon = a traffic jam

**boucle** noun, feminine
- (on a belt)
  une boucle = a buckle
- (of hair)
  une boucle = a curl
- (a curved shape)
  une boucle = a loop
**une boucle d'oreille** = an earring

**bouclé/bouclée** adjective
= curly

**boucler** verb [1]
- = to buckle
- = to fasten

**boudin** noun, masculine
le boudin = black pudding, blood pudding

**boue** noun, feminine
la boue = mud

**bouffer**× verb [1]
= to eat

**bouger** verb [13]
= to move

**bougie** noun, feminine
- (for lighting)
  une bougie = a candle
- (in an engine)
  une bougie = a sparking plug, a spark
  plug

**bouillir** verb [31]
= to boil

**bouilloire** noun, feminine
une bouilloire = a kettle

**bouillotte** noun, feminine
une bouillotte = a hot water bottle

**boulanger/boulangère** noun,
masculine/feminine
un boulanger/une boulangère = a baker

**boulangerie** noun, feminine
une boulangerie = a baker's (shop)

**boule** noun, feminine
- (a shape)
  une boule = a ball
  une boule de neige = a snowball
- (in games)
  une boule = a bowl
  = a boule

**boulevard** noun, masculine
un boulevard = an avenue

**boulot**× noun, masculine
- le boulot× = work
- un boulot× = a job

**boum**× noun, feminine
une boum× = a party

**bouquet** noun, masculine
un bouquet = a bunch

**bouquin**× noun, masculine
un bouquin× = a book

**bourgeon** noun, masculine
un bourgeon = a bud

**bousculer** verb [1]
- = to bump into
  = to jostle
- = to rush
  ne me bouscule pas = don't rush me

**boussole** noun, feminine
une boussole = a compass

**bout** noun, masculine
- un bout = a piece
- le bout = the end
  = the tip

**bouteille** noun, feminine
une bouteille = a bottle
une bouteille de gaz = a gas cylinder

**boutique** noun, feminine
une boutique = a shop

**bouton** noun, masculine
- (on a coat, for a doorbell)
  un bouton = a button
- (on the skin)
  un bouton = a spot, a pimple
- (on an appliance)
  un bouton = a switch
- (on a plant)
  un bouton = a bud

**boxe** noun, feminine
la boxe = boxing

**bracelet** noun, masculine
un bracelet = a bracelet
= a bangle

**un bracelet de montre** = a watchstrap, a watchband

**branche** *noun, feminine*
* (*on a tree*)
  **une branche** = a branch
* (*an area of work, study*)
  **une branche** = a field

**branché/branchée✗** *adjective*
= trendy, cool

**brancher** *verb* ☐1
= to plug in
= to connect

**braquer** *verb* ☐1
* **braquer un revolver sur quelqu'un** = to aim a gun at someone
* **braquer le volant à gauche** = to turn the wheel hard (to the) left

**bras** *noun, masculine* (**!** *never changes*)
**un bras** = an arm
**en bras de chemise** = in one's shirtsleeves

**brasserie** *noun, feminine*
* (*for meals*)
  **une brasserie** = a brasserie, a café
* (*a factory*)
  **une brasserie** = a brewery

**bravo** *exclamation*
= bravo!, well done!

**brebis** *noun, feminine* (**!** *never changes*)
**une brebis** = a ewe

**bref/brève**
**1** *adjective*
= brief, short
**2 (en) bref** *adverb*
= in short

**Bretagne** *noun, feminine*
**la Bretagne** = Brittany

**breton/bretonne**
**1** *adjective*
= Breton
**2 breton** *noun, masculine*
**le breton** = Breton

**brève ▶ bref 1**

**brevet** *noun, masculine*
**un brevet** (*a qualification*) = a certificate
**un brevet des collèges** = a certificate of general education
**un brevet de pilote** = a pilot's licence

**bricolage** *noun, masculine*
**le bricolage** = DIY, do-it-yourself

**brillant/brillante** *adjective*
* = shiny
* = brilliant

**briller** *verb* ☐1
= to shine

**brin** *noun, masculine*
**un brin** (*of parsley, mimosa*) = a sprig
(*of grass*) = a blade

**brioche** *noun, feminine*
**une brioche** = a brioche, a (sweet) bun

**briquet** *noun, masculine*
**un briquet** = a cigarette lighter

**britannique** *adjective*
= British

**brocante** *noun, feminine*
**une brocante** = a flea market

**brocanteur/brocanteuse** *noun,*
*masculine/feminine*
**un brocanteur/une brocanteuse** = a bric-à-brac dealer

**broche** *noun, feminine*
* (*an ornament*)
  **une broche** = a brooch, a pin
* (*for cooking*)
  **une broche** = a spit

**brochette** *noun, feminine*
**une brochette** = a kebab, a brochette

**brochure** *noun, feminine*
**une brochure** = a brochure

**broder** *verb* ☐1
= to embroider

**bronzage** *noun, masculine*
**un bronzage** = a (sun)tan

**bronzé/bronzée** *adjective*
= tanned, brown

**bronzer** *verb* ☐1
= to get a tan, to go brown

**brosse** *noun, feminine*
**une brosse** = a brush
**avoir les cheveux (taillés) en brosse** = to have a crew cut
**une brosse à dents** = a toothbrush

**brosser** *verb* ☐1
= to brush

**brouillard** *noun, masculine*
**le brouillard** = fog

**brouillé/brouillée** *adjective*
= jumbled, mixed up

**brouillon** *noun, masculine*
**un brouillon** = a rough draft

**broussailles** *noun, feminine plural*
**les broussailles** = the undergrowth

**brugnon** *noun, masculine*
**un brugnon** = a nectarine

**bruit** *noun, masculine*
**le bruit** = noise

**brûlant/brûlante** *adjective*
= burning hot

---

**✗** in informal situations

**brûlé** noun, masculine
ça sent le brûlé = there's a smell of burning

**brûler** verb ⬚1⬚
**1** (**!** + avoir)
• = to burn
• brûler un feu (rouge) = to jump the lights, to run the lights
**2 se brûler** (**!** + être)
se brûler = to burn oneself

**brume** noun, feminine
la brume = mist

**brumeux/brumeuse** adjective
= misty

**brun/brune** adjective
• = brown, dark
• = dark-haired

**brunir** verb ⬚3⬚
= to tan

**brusque** adjective
• = abrupt
• = sudden

**Bruxelles** noun
= Brussels

**bruyant/bruyante** adjective
= noisy

**bu/bue** ▶ **boire** ⬚51⬚

**bûche** noun, feminine
une bûche = a log

**buffet** noun, masculine
• (a piece of furniture)
un buffet = a sideboard
• (a meal, a place)
un buffet = a buffet

**buisson** noun, masculine
un buisson = a bush
= a shrub

**buissonnière** adjective, feminine
faire l'école buissonnière = to play truant, to play hooky

**bulle** noun, feminine
• (of soap)
une bulle = a bubble
faire des bulles = to blow bubbles
• (in a cartoon)
une bulle = a speech bubble

**bulletin** noun, masculine
un bulletin = a report
= a form
= a certificate
**un bulletin météorologique** = a weather report
**un bulletin scolaire** = a school report, a report card

**bureau** noun, masculine
(plural) **bureaux**

• (a piece of furniture)
un bureau = a desk
• (a room)
un bureau = an office
**le bureau de poste** = the post office
**le bureau des renseignements** = the information office, the information desk

**bus** noun, masculine (**!** never changes)
un bus = a bus

**but** noun, masculine
• (what one has in mind)
un but = a goal
= an aim, a purpose
= an intention
dans le but de = with the intention of
• (in football)
un but = a goal

**buvable** adjective
= drinkable
(on a medicine label) = to be taken orally

**buveur/buveuse** noun, masculine/feminine
un buveur/une buveuse = a drinker

**c'** ▶ **ce**

**ça** pronoun
• = this
= that
donne-moi ça = give me that
ça, c'est bizarre = that's strange
• = it
ça ne fait rien = it doesn't matter
c'est ça! = that's right!, that's it!
c'est pour ça que ... = that's why ...
et avec ça? = anything else?
• où ça? = where?
• comment ça va? = how are you?
ça va mal = things are bad
ça y est, j'ai fini = that's it, I've finished

**cabane** noun, feminine
une cabane = a hut, a shack

**cabillaud** noun, masculine
le cabillaud = cod

**cabine** noun, feminine
une cabine (for sleeping) = a cabin
(for changing) = a cubicle, a changing room
**une cabine d'essayage** = a fitting room
**une cabine téléphonique** = a telephone box, a telephone booth

**cabinet** *noun, masculine*
• (*a place of work*)
un cabinet = an office
(*for a doctor*) = a surgery, an office
• (*a W.C.*)
le cabinet = the toilet

**câble** *noun, masculine*
un câble = a cable

**cacahuète** *noun, feminine*
une cacahuète = a peanut

**cacao** *noun, masculine*
le cacao = cocoa

**cache-cache** *noun, masculine* (**!** *never changes*)
jouer à cache-cache = to play hide and seek

**cacher** *verb* ⃞1
= to hide

**cachet** *noun, masculine*
• (*a medicine*)
un cachet = a tablet, a pill
• (*on a form*)
un cachet = a stamp

**cachette** *noun, feminine*
une cachette = a hiding place
en cachette = secretly

**c-à-d** *conjunction*
(*abbreviation of* **c'est-à-dire**)
c-à-d = i.e.

**cadastre** *noun, masculine*
le cadastre = the land registry

**cadeau** *noun, masculine*
(*plural*) **cadeaux**
un cadeau = a present, a gift

**cadet/cadette** *adjective*
= younger, youngest

**cadre** *noun, masculine*
• (*for a picture*)
un cadre = a frame
• (*an employee*)
un cadre = an executive
• (*the space around a person or a thing*)
le cadre = the surroundings

**cafard** *noun, masculine*
• un cafard = a cockroach
• avoir le cafard = to feel down, to feel blue

**café** *noun, masculine*
• (*a product*)
le café = coffee
• (*a place*)
un café = a café, a diner
**un café crème** = an espresso with milk
**un café au lait** = a coffee with milk

**cafetière** *noun, feminine*
une cafetière = a coffee maker

**cage** *noun, feminine*
une cage = a cage

**cahier** *noun, masculine*
un cahier = an exercise book
**un cahier de brouillon** = a rough book, a notebook
**un cahier de textes** = a homework notebook

**caillou** *noun, masculine*
(*plural*) **cailloux**
un caillou = a stone

**Caire** *noun, masculine*
le Caire = Cairo

**caisse** *noun, feminine*
• (*for goods*)
une caisse = a crate
• (*for money*)
une caisse = a till, a cash register
• (*where you pay in a shop*)
la caisse = the cash desk
= the checkout

**calcul** *noun, masculine*
• (*the study of numbers*)
le calcul = arithmetic
• (*an operation*)
un calcul = a calculation

**calculatrice** *noun, feminine*
une calculatrice = a (pocket) calculator

**calculer** *verb* ⃞1
= to calculate, to work out

**calé/calée✘** *adjective*
= clever

**caleçon** *noun, masculine*
un caleçon (*for men*) = boxer shorts
(*for women*) = leggings
**un caleçon long** = long johns

**calendrier** *noun, masculine*
un calendrier = a calendar

**caler** *verb* ⃞1
• (*in order to fix in a position*) = to wedge
• (*when driving*) = to stall

**calmant** *noun, masculine*
un calmant = a sedative

**calmar** *noun, masculine*
un calmar = a squid

**calme**
**1** *adjective*
= calm, quiet
**2** *noun, masculine*
le calme = peace (and quiet)

**calmer** *verb* ⃞1
**1** (**!** + *avoir*)
= to calm (down)
**2 se calmer** (**!** + *être*)
se calmer = to calm down

**camarade** *noun, masculine/feminine*
un camarade/une camarade = a friend

**cambriolage** *noun, masculine*
un cambriolage = a burglary

**cambrioler** *verb* 1
= to burgle

**caméra** *noun, feminine*
une caméra = a (ciné-)camera, a movie camera

**caméscope** *noun, masculine*
un caméscope = a camcorder

**camion** *noun, masculine*
un camion = a lorry, a truck

**camionnette** *noun, feminine*
une camionnette = a van

**campagne** *noun, feminine*
* (*the area around towns*)
la campagne = the country
= the countryside
* (*for an election, in war*)
une campagne = a campaign

**camper** *verb* 1
= to camp

**campeur/campeuse** *noun, masculine/feminine*
un campeur/une campeuse = a camper

**camping** *noun, masculine*
* (*the activity*)
le camping = camping
* (*the place*)
un camping = a campsite, a campground

**camping-car** *noun, masculine*
(*plural*) **camping-cars**
un camping-car = a camper-van, an RV

**Canada** *noun, masculine*
le Canada = Canada

**canadien/canadienne** *adjective*
= Canadian

**canal** *noun, masculine*
(*plural*) **canaux**
* (*a waterway*)
un canal = a canal
* (*in telecommunications*)
un canal = a channel

**canapé** *noun, masculine*
un canapé = a settee, a sofa

**canard** *noun, masculine*
un canard = a duck

**Cancer** *noun, masculine*
le Cancer = Cancer

**candidat/candidate** *noun, masculine/feminine*
un candidat/une candidate (*in an examination, an election*) = a candidate
(*for a job*) = an applicant

**caniche** *noun, masculine*
un caniche = a poodle

**canif** *noun, masculine*
un canif = a penknife, a pocketknife

**canne** *noun, feminine*
une canne = a (walking) stick, a cane
**une canne à pêche** = a fishing rod

**canoë** *noun, masculine*
* (*the equipment*)
un canoë = a (Canadian) canoe
* (*the sport*)
le canoë = canoeing

**canot** *noun, masculine*
un canot = a (small) boat, a dinghy
**un canot de sauvetage** = a lifeboat

**cantine** *noun, feminine*
une cantine = a canteen

**caoutchouc** *noun, masculine*
le caoutchouc = rubber

**CAP** *noun, masculine* ▶ **certificat**

**capitaine** *noun, masculine*
un capitaine = a captain

**capitale** *noun, feminine*
* (*a town*)
une capitale = a capital (city)
* (*a letter*)
une capitale = a capital

**capot** *noun, masculine*
le capot = the bonnet, the hood

**Capricorne** *noun, masculine*
le Capricorne = Capricorn

**capuchon** *noun, masculine*
* (*for the head*)
un capuchon = a hood
* (*for a pen*)
un capuchon = a cap

**car**
**1** *noun, masculine*
un car = a coach, a bus
**2** *conjunction*
car = because, for

**caractère** *noun, masculine*
* (*a personality*)
un caractère = a character, a nature
* (*in writing*)
un caractère = a letter

**Caraïbes** *noun, feminine plural*
les Caraïbes = the Caribbean islands

**carambolage** *noun, masculine*
un carambolage = a pile-up

**caramel** *noun, masculine*
* (*on ice cream, custard*)
le caramel = caramel
* (*a sweet*)
un caramel = a toffee

**caravane** *noun, feminine*
une caravane = a caravan, a trailer

**carburateur** *noun, masculine*
le carburateur = the carburettor

**caresser** *verb* [1]
= to stroke

**carnet** *noun, masculine*
* (*in which to write*)
un carnet = a notebook
* (*a set of tickets, stamps*)
un carnet = a book
**un carnet d'adresses** = an address book
**un carnet de chèques** = a cheque book,
a checkbook

**carotte** *noun, feminine*
une carotte = a carrot

**carré/carrée** *adjective*
= square

**carreau** *noun, masculine*
(*plural*) **carreaux**
* (*on a window*)
un carreau = a window pane
* (*on the wall, the floor*)
un carreau = a tile
du tissu à carreaux = check(ed) material
* (*at cards*)
carreau = diamonds

**carrefour** *noun, masculine*
le carrefour = the crossroads

**carrière** *noun, feminine*
* (*a profession*)
une carrière = a career
* (*a place*)
une carrière = a quarry

**carrosserie** *noun, feminine*
la carrosserie = bodywork

**cartable** *noun, masculine*
un cartable = a satchel, a schoolbag
= a briefcase

**carte** *noun, feminine*
* (*in games*)
une carte = a card
* (*of a country*)
une carte = a map
* (*in a restaurant*)
la carte = the menu
**une carte bleue** = a credit card
**une carte électronique** = a swipe card
**une carte de fidélité** = a loyalty card
**une carte grise** = a logbook
**une carte d'identité** = an ID card
**une carte mémoire** = a memory card
**une carte orange** = a season ticket (*in the
Paris area*)
**une carte postale** = a postcard
**une carte à puce** = a smart card
**une carte de recharge** = a top-up card
**une carte SIM** = a SIM card
**une carte de visite** = a business card
**une carte de vœux** = a greeting(s) card

**carton** *noun, masculine*
* (*the substance*)
le carton = cardboard
* (*a container*)
un carton = a cardboard box

**cas** *noun, masculine* (**!** *never changes*)
un cas = a case

**case** *noun, feminine*
une case = a box

**casier** *noun, masculine*
un casier (*for messages*) = a pigeonhole
(*for keeping things organized*) = a locker

**casque** *noun, masculine*
* (*for protection*)
un casque = a helmet, a hard hat
* (*for listening to music*)
un casque = headphones

**casquette** *noun, feminine*
une casquette = a cap

**casse-croûte** *noun, masculine* (**!** *never
changes*)
un casse-croûte = a snack

**casser** *verb* [1]
**1** (**!** + *avoir*)
= to break
**2 se casser** (**!** + *être*)
se casser = to break
je me suis cassé le poignet = I broke my
wrist

**casserole** *noun, feminine*
une casserole = a saucepan, a pan

**cassis** *noun, masculine* (**!** *never changes*)
le cassis = blackcurrants

**catastrophe** *noun, feminine*
une catastrophe = a disaster

**catch** *noun, masculine*
le catch = wrestling

**catégorie** *noun, feminine*
une catégorie = a category

**cauchemar** *noun, masculine*
un cauchemar = a nightmare

**cause** *noun, feminine*
la cause = the cause
à cause de = because of

**causer** *verb* [1]
* = to cause
causer un accident = to cause an accident
* **✱** = to chat, to talk

**caution** *noun, feminine*
une caution = a deposit

**cave** *noun, feminine*
une cave = a cellar

---

**✱** in informal situations

**ce¹/cette** *adjective*
(*plural*) **ces**

> ! **cet** *is used instead of* **ce** *before a masculine noun beginning with a vowel or a mute h. The plural of* **cet** *is* **ces**

= this, that
ce livre(-ci) = this book
cet oiseau(-là) = that bird
ces enfants = these children, those children

**ce²** *pronoun* (**c'** *before e*)
• (*when the verb* **être** *is in the singular*)
c'est un cadeau = it's a present
ce serait dommage = it would be a shame
qui est-ce? = who is it?
qu'est-ce que c'est? = what is it?
c'est moi qui l'ai cassé = I was the one who broke it
• (*when the verb* **être** *is in the plural*)
ce sont des insectes = they're insects
ce sont des détails sans importance = these are unimportant details
• voilà ce que j'ai dit = that's what I said
prenez ce dont vous avez besoin = take what you need
c'est ce qui les inquiète = that's what worries them
ce qui m'ennuie le plus, c'est qu'il faudra se lever tôt = what bothers me most is that we'll have to get up early
il est venu, ce qui est étonnant = he came, which is surprising

> ! *Look up the verb* **être** *for translations of* **est-ce que**.

**ceci** *pronoun*
= this

**céder** *verb* 14
• = to give up
• = to give in
céder le passage = to give way, to yield
• = to collapse

**cédille** *noun, feminine*
une cédille = a cedilla

**CEE** *noun, feminine* ▶ **communauté**

**ceinture** *noun, feminine*
une ceinture = a belt
**une ceinture de sécurité** = a seatbelt

**cela** *pronoun*
= it, that

**célèbre** *adjective*
= famous

**célébrer** *verb* 14
= to celebrate

**céleri** *noun, masculine*
le céleri = celery

**célibataire**
**1** *adjective*
= single

**2** *noun, masculine/feminine*
un célibataire/une célibataire = a single man/woman

**celle** ▶ **celui**

**celle-ci** ▶ **celui-ci**

**celle-là** ▶ **celui-là**

**celles-ci** ▶ **celui-ci**

**celles-là** ▶ **celui-là**

**celui/celle** *pronoun*
(*plural*) **ceux/celles**
celui/celle = the one
ceux/celles = the ones
= those
celle de ma sœur = my sister's

**celui-ci/celle-ci** *pronoun*
(*plural*) **ceux-ci/celles-ci**
celui-ci/celle-ci = this one
ceux-ci/celles-ci = these

**celui-là/celle-là** *pronoun*
(*plural*) **ceux-là/celles-là**
celui-là/celle-là = that one
ceux-là/celles-là = those

**cendre** *noun, feminine*
la cendre = ash

**cendrier** *noun, masculine*
un cendrier = an ashtray

**censé/censée** *adjective*
être censé = to be meant to

**cent** *number*
= hundred
pour cent = per cent

**centaine** *noun, feminine*
une centaine = about a hundred

**centième** *number*
= hundredth

**centime** *noun, masculine*
• (*of euro*)
un centime (d'euro) = a cent
• (*of franc*)
un centime = a centime

**centimètre** *noun, masculine*
• (*a unit of length*)
un centimètre = a centimetre, a centimeter
• (*a measuring device*)
un centimètre = a tape measure

**central/centrale¹**
(*plural*) **centraux/centrales**
**1** *adjective*
= central
**2 central** *noun, masculine*
le central (téléphonique) = the (telephone) exchange

**centrale²** *noun, feminine*
une centrale = a power station

**centre** *noun, masculine*
le centre = the centre, the center
**un centre aéré** = a children's outdoor activity centre
**un centre commercial** = a shopping centre, a shopping mall
**un centre d'appels** = a call centre

**centre-ville** *noun, masculine*
(*plural*) **centres-villes**
le centre-ville = the town centre, the town center

**cependant** *conjunction*
= however

**cercle** *noun, masculine*
un cercle = a circle

**cercueil** *noun, masculine*
un cercueil = a coffin

**céréale** *noun, feminine*
une céréale = a cereal, a grain

**cérémonie** *noun, feminine*
une cérémonie = a ceremony

**cerf-volant** *noun, masculine*
(*plural*) **cerfs-volants**
un cerf-volant = a kite

**cerise** *noun, feminine*
une cerise = a cherry

**cerisier** *noun, masculine*
un cerisier = a cherry tree

**certain/certaine**
**1** *adjective*
= certain, sure
**2** *determiner*
= some
**3 certains/certaines** *pronoun, plural*
= some
certains d'entre vous = some of you

**certainement** *adverb*
= most probably
= certainly

**certificat** *noun, masculine*
un certificat = a certificate
**un certificat d'aptitude professionnelle, un CAP** = a vocational training qualification
**un certificat médical** = a doctor's certificate
**un certificat de naissance** = a birth certificate

**cerveau** *noun, masculine*
(*plural*) **cerveaux**
le cerveau = the brain

**cervelle** *noun, feminine*
la cervelle = the brain

**ces** ▶ **ce**[1]

**CES** *noun, masculine* ▶ **collège**

**cesser** *verb* [1]
= to stop

**c'est-à-dire** *adverb*
= that is (to say)

**cet** ▶ **ce**[1]

**CET** *noun, masculine* ▶ **collège**

**cette** ▶ **ce**[1]

**ceux** ▶ **celui**

**chacun/chacune** *pronoun*
• = each (one)
   chacun d'entre vous = each one of you
• = everybody

**chahut** *noun, masculine*
du chahut = a racket

**chaîne** *noun, feminine*
• (*linked metal rings*)
   une chaîne = a chain
• (*on television*)
   une chaîne = a channel
• (*in a factory*)
   la chaîne = the assembly line
**une chaîne hi-fi** = a hi-fi system
**une chaîne laser** = a CD system
**une chaîne de montagnes** = a mountain range

**chair** *noun, feminine*
la chair = flesh
**la chair de poule** = goose pimples, goose bumps

**chaise** *noun, feminine*
une chaise = a chair
**une chaise longue** = a deckchair

**chaleur** *noun, feminine*
la chaleur = heat, warmth

**chambre** *noun, feminine*
une chambre = a room, a bedroom
une chambre pour une personne
   = a single room
une chambre pour deux personnes
   = a double room
**une chambre d'hôte** = a room in a B & B
'**chambres d'hôte**' = 'bed and breakfast'

**chameau** *noun, masculine*
(*plural*) **chameaux**
un chameau = a camel

**champ**
**1** *noun, masculine*
un champ = a field
**2 à tout bout de champ**�ল* = all the time

**champignon** *noun, masculine*
un champignon = a mushroom

**champion/championne** *noun, masculine/feminine*
un champion/une championne
   = a champion

---

✲ in informal situations

**championnat** noun, masculine
un championnat = a championship

**chance** noun, feminine
* (good fortune)
la chance = luck
* (possibility)
avoir des chances de gagner = to stand a chance of winning

**change** noun, masculine
le taux de change = the exchange rate

**changement** noun, masculine
un changement = a change
**le changement climatique** = climate change

**changer** verb 13
= to change
changer d'avis = to change one's mind

**chanson** noun, feminine
une chanson = a song

**chant** noun, masculine
un chant = a song

**chanter** verb 1
= to sing

**chanteur/chanteuse** noun,
masculine/feminine
un chanteur/une chanteuse = a singer

**chantier** noun, masculine
un chantier = a building site

**chantilly** noun, feminine (! never changes)
la chantilly = whipped cream

**chapeau** noun, masculine
(plural) **chapeaux**
* un chapeau = a hat
* (when praising)*
chapeau*! = well done!, good job!
**un chapeau melon** = a bowler hat, a derby hat

**chapitre** noun, masculine
un chapitre = a chapter

**chaque** determiner
= each, every

**char** noun, masculine
* (in a carnival)
un char = a float
* (a military vehicle)
un char = a tank

**charcuterie** noun, feminine
* (a shop)
une charcuterie = a pork butcher's
* (a type of food)
la charcuterie = cooked pork meats

**charcutier/charcutière** noun,
masculine/feminine
un charcutier/une charcutière = a pork butcher

**charger** verb 13
**1** (! + avoir)

* = to load
charger un camion de légumes = to load a truck with vegetables
* = to ask
charger quelqu'un [de poster une lettre | d'arroser les plantes | de transmettre un message …] = to ask someone [to post a letter | to water the plants | to pass on a message …]
* ils sont chargés de surveiller les enfants = they're responsible for looking after the children
**2 se charger** (! + être)
se charger d'une tâche = to take responsibility for a job, to see to a job
je me charge de le leur dire = I'll tell them

**chariot** noun, masculine
un chariot = a trolley, a cart

**charité** noun, feminine
la charité = charity

**charmant/charmante** adjective
= charming

**chasse** noun, feminine
la chasse = hunting
**la chasse d'eau** = the (toilet) flush

**chasse-neige** noun, masculine (! never changes)
un chasse-neige = a snowplough, a snowplow

**chasser** verb 1
* = to hunt
* = to shoot
* = to drive away

**chasseur** noun, masculine
un chasseur = a hunter

**chat** noun, masculine
un chat = a cat

**châtaigne** noun, feminine
une châtaigne = a (sweet) chestnut

**châtain** adjective
= brown

**château** noun, masculine
(plural) **châteaux**
un château = a castle
**un château fort** = a fortified castle

**chaton** noun, masculine
un chaton = a kitten

**chatte** noun, feminine
une chatte = a (female) cat

**chaud/chaude**
**1** adjective
= hot, warm
**2 chaud** adverb
il fait chaud ici = it's hot in here
**3 chaud** noun, masculine
avoir chaud = to be hot

**chaudière** noun, feminine
une chaudière = a boiler

**chauffage** *noun, masculine*
le chauffage = the heating

**chauffard**✶ *noun, masculine*
un chauffard✶ = a reckless driver

**chauffer** *verb* ⓵
* = to heat
* = to overheat
le moteur chauffe = the engine is overheating
* = to give out heat, to give off heat
le poêle chauffe bien = the stove gives out a lot of heat
le soleil chauffe aujourd'hui = the sun is hot today

**chauffeur** *noun, masculine*
un chauffeur = a driver

**chaumière** *noun, feminine*
une chaumière = a thatched cottage

**chaussée** *noun, feminine*
la chaussée = the road, the highway
'chaussée déformée' = 'uneven road surface'

**chausser** *verb* ⓵
chausser du 39 = to take a size 39 (in shoes), to take a size 6

**chaussette** *noun, feminine*
une chaussette = a sock

**chausson** *noun, masculine*
* (*footwear*)
un chausson = a slipper
* (*a cake*)
un chausson = a turnover

**chaussure** *noun, feminine*
une chaussure = a shoe
des chaussures de ski = ski boots

**chauve** *adjective*
= bald

**chauve-souris** *noun, feminine*
(*plural*) **chauves-souris**
une chauve-souris = a bat

**chef**
**1** *noun, masculine*
* (*the person in charge*)
le chef = the leader
* (*in a restaurant*)
un chef (cuisinier) = a chef
**2 en chef**
l'ingénieur en chef = the chief engineer
un chef d'entreprise = a company manager
un chef d'État = a head of state
un chef de gare = a station master
un chef d'orchestre = a conductor

**chef-d'œuvre** *noun, masculine*
(*plural*) **chefs-d'œuvre**
un chef-d'œuvre = a masterpiece

---

✶ in informal situations

**chemin** *noun, masculine*
* un chemin = a country lane, a path
* le chemin = the way
le chemin de fer = the railway, the railroad

**cheminée** *noun, feminine*
une cheminée = a chimney
= a fireplace
= a mantelpiece, a mantel

**chemise** *noun, feminine*
une chemise = a shirt

**chemisier** *noun, masculine*
un chemisier = a blouse

**chêne** *noun, masculine*
un chêne = an oak (tree)

**chenille** *noun, feminine*
une chenille = a caterpillar

**chèque** *noun, masculine*
un chèque = a cheque, a check
un chèque sans provision = a bad cheque, a dud check

**chèque-voyage** *noun, masculine*
(*plural*) **chèques-voyage**
un chèque-voyage = a traveller's cheque, a traveler's check

**chéquier** *noun, masculine*
un chéquier = a cheque book, a checkbook

**cher/chère** *adjective*
* = dear
* = expensive

**chercher** *verb* ⓵
* = to look for
* aller chercher de l'eau = to go and get some water

**chère** ▶ cher

**chéri/chérie** *noun, masculine/feminine*
(mon) chéri/(ma) chérie = (my) darling

**cheval** *noun, masculine*
(*plural*) **chevaux**
* (*an animal*)
un cheval = a horse
monter à cheval = to ride (a horse)
* (*the sport*)
le cheval = horseriding, horseback riding
* (*meat*)
le cheval = horsemeat

**chevalier** *noun, masculine*
un chevalier = a knight

**chevet** *noun, masculine*
une lampe de chevet = a bedside lamp

**cheveu** *noun, masculine*
(*plural*) **cheveux**
les cheveux = hair

**cheville** *noun, feminine*
une cheville = an ankle

**chèvre** noun, feminine
une chèvre = a goat

**chez** préposition
* = at
  je serai chez moi = I'll be at home
  il est chez eux ce matin? = is he at their
   place this morning?
* = to
  aller chez le dentiste = to go to the
   dentist's

**chic** adjective
* (elegant) = chic, smart
* (kind, obliging)✖ = nice

**chien** noun, masculine
* un chien = a dog
  un chien d'aveugle = a guide dog
* il fait un temps de chien✖ = the weather is
  awful

**chienne** noun, feminine
une chienne = a female dog, a bitch

**chiffon** noun, masculine
un chiffon = a rag, a cloth
un chiffon (à poussière) = a duster, a dust
  cloth

**chiffre** noun, masculine
un chiffre = a figure

**chignon** noun, masculine
un chignon = a bun, a chignon

**chimie** noun, feminine
la chimie = chemistry

**chimique** adjective
= chemical

**chinois/chinoise**
1 adjective
= Chinese
2 **chinois** noun, masculine
le chinois = Chinese

**chiot** noun, masculine
un chiot = a puppy

**chips** noun, feminine (**!** never changes)
une chips = a crisp, a (potato) chip

**chirurgien** noun, masculine
un chirurgien = a surgeon

**choc** noun, masculine
un choc = a shock

**chocolat** noun, masculine
le chocolat = chocolate

**choisir** verb [3]
= to choose

**choix** noun, masculine (**!** never changes)
un choix = a choice
des produits de choix = choice products
de premier choix = top quality

**chômage** noun, masculine
le chômage = unemployment
être au chômage = to be unemployed

**chômeur/chômeuse** noun,
masculine/feminine
un chômeur/une chômeuse = an
  unemployed man/woman

**choquer** verb [1]
= to shock

**chorale** noun, feminine
une chorale = a choir

**chose** noun, feminine
une chose = a thing
quelque chose = something
= anything
pas grand chose = not much

**chou** noun, masculine
(plural) **choux**
* (a vegetable)
  un chou = a cabbage
* (a cake)
  un chou = a choux bun, a pastry shell
* (a person)
  mon chou = my darling
**un chou de Bruxelles** = a Brussels sprout
**un chou à la crème** = a cream puff

**choucroute** noun, feminine
la choucroute = sauerkraut

**chouette**
1 adjective✖
= nice, great
2 noun, feminine
une chouette = an owl

**chou-fleur** noun, masculine
(plural) **choux-fleurs**
un chou-fleur = a cauliflower

**chronométrer** verb [14]
= to time

**chrysanthème** noun, masculine
un chrysanthème = a chrysanthemum

**chuchoter** verb [1]
= to whisper

**chut** exclamation
chut! = shh!, hush!

**chute** noun, feminine
une chute = a fall

**cicatrice** noun, feminine
une cicatrice = a scar

**ci-contre** adverb
= opposite

**ci-dessous** adverb
= below

**ci-dessus** adverb
= above

**cidre** noun, masculine
le cidre = cider, hard cider

**ciel** noun, masculine
* le ciel = the sky
* le ciel = heaven

**cieux** *noun, masculine plural*
les cieux = heaven

**cigale** *noun, feminine*
une cigale = a cicada

**ci-joint/ci-jointe** *adjective*
= enclosed

**cil** *noun, masculine*
un cil = an eyelash

**cime** *noun, feminine*
la cime = the top

**cimetière** *noun, masculine*
un cimetière = a graveyard, a cemetery

**ciné✶** *noun, masculine*
le ciné✶ = the pictures, the movies

**cinéma** *noun, masculine*
• un cinéma = a cinema, a movie theater
• le cinéma = the cinema, the movies

**cinglé/cinglée✶** *adjective*
= mad, crazy

**cinq** *number*
= five

**cinquantaine** *noun, feminine*
une cinquantaine = about fifty

**cinquante** *number*
= fifty

**cinquième**
1 *number*
= fifth
2 *noun, feminine*
la cinquième = *the class for secondary
school students aged 12 to 13*

**cirage** *noun, masculine*
le cirage = shoe polish

**circuit** *noun, masculine*
• (*visiting several places*)
un circuit = a tour
• (*in a race*)
un circuit = a circuit

**circulation** *noun, feminine*
la circulation = the traffic

**circuler** *verb* [1]
• = to move
• = to run
ce train ne circule pas le dimanche = this
train doesn't run on Sundays
• = to circulate

**cirque** *noun, masculine*
le cirque = the circus

**ciseaux** *noun, masculine plural*
des ciseaux = scissors

**citadelle** *noun, feminine*
une citadelle = a fortress

**cité** *noun, feminine*
• une cité = a city, a town
• une cité = a housing estate, a housing
development
**une cité universitaire** = student halls of
residence, dormitories

**citoyen/citoyenne** *noun,
masculine/feminine*
un citoyen/une citoyenne = a citizen

**citron** *noun, masculine*
un citron = a lemon
**un citron pressé** = a freshly squeezed
lemonade

**citronnade** *noun, feminine*
la citronnade = lemon squash, (still)
lemonade

**clair/claire**
1 *adjective*
• = clear
• = light
2 **clair** *noun, masculine*
le clair de lune = moonlight

**claqué/claquée✶** *adjective*
= exhausted

**claquer** *verb* [1]
• = to slam
claquer la porte = to slam the door
• = to bang
une porte claquait = a door was banging
• faire claquer ses doigts = to snap one's
fingers
il claque des dents = his teeth are
chattering

**claquettes** *noun, feminine plural*
les claquettes = tap dancing

**clarinette** *noun, feminine*
une clarinette = a clarinet

**classe** *noun, feminine*
• (*a room*)
une (salle de) classe = a classroom
aller en classe = to go to school
• (*a category*)
une classe = a class
un billet de première classe = a first-class
ticket
**une classe de mer** = a seaside trip (*with a
school*)
**une classe de neige** = a skiing trip (*with
a school*)
**une classe verte** = a field trip (*with a
school*)

**classeur** *noun, masculine*
un classeur = a folder

**clavier** *noun, masculine*
un clavier = a keyboard

**clé** *noun, feminine*
• (*for a lock*)
une clé = a key
fermer à clé = to lock

• (a tool)
une clé = a spanner, a wrench

**clef ▶ clé**

**client/cliente** noun, masculine/feminine
un client/une cliente = a customer, a client

**clignotant** noun, masculine
un clignotant = an indicator, a turn signal

**climat** noun, masculine
le climat = the climate

**climatisation** noun, feminine
la climatisation = air-conditioning

**clinique** noun, feminine
une clinique = a (private) clinic

**cliquer** verb
= to click
cliquer à gauche = to left-click
cliquer à droite = to right-click

**clochard/clocharde** noun,
masculine/feminine
un clochard/une clocharde = a tramp, a
bum

**cloche** noun, feminine
• une cloche = a bell
• une cloche✱ = an idiot

**cloche-pied, à cloche-pied** adverb
sauter à cloche-pied = to hop

**clocher** noun, masculine
un clocher = a church tower

**clochette** noun, feminine
une clochette = a small bell

**cloison** noun, feminine
une cloison = a partition

**cloque** noun, feminine
une cloque = a blister

**clos/close** adjective
• = (en)closed

**clôture** noun, feminine
une clôture = a fence

**clou**
1 noun, masculine
un clou = a nail
2 clous noun, masculine plural
les clous = the pedestrian crossing, the
crosswalk

**clouer** verb 1
= to nail (down)

**clouté** adjective, masculine
un passage clouté = a pedestrian crossing,
a crosswalk

**clown** noun, masculine
un clown = a clown

**club** noun, masculine
un club = a club

**cobaye** noun, masculine
un cobaye = a guinea pig

**coca** noun, masculine
un coca = a Coke , a Coca-Cola

**cocher** verb 1
= to tick, to check (off)

**cochon** noun, masculine
un cochon = a pig
**un cochon d'Inde** = a guinea pig

**coco** noun, masculine
une noix de coco = a coconut

**cocotier** noun, masculine
un cocotier = a coconut tree

**code**
1 noun, masculine
un code = a code
2 codes noun, masculine plural
les codes = dipped headlights, dimmed
headlights
se mettre en codes = to dip one's
headlights, to dim one's headlights
**un code confidentiel (d'identification)**
= a personal identification number
**un code postal** = a postcode, a zip code
**le code de la route** = the highway code,
the rules of the road

**cœur**
1 noun, masculine
• le cœur = the heart
avoir mal au cœur = to feel sick, to feel
nauseous
avoir bon cœur = to be kind-hearted
• (at cards)
cœur = hearts
2 **par cœur** = by heart

**coffre** noun, masculine
• un coffre (for storage) = a chest, a trunk
(for valuables) = a safe
• (in a car)
le coffre = the boot, the trunk

**coffre-fort** noun, masculine
(plural) **coffres-forts**
un coffre-fort = a safe

**cognac** noun, masculine
le cognac = brandy

**coiffer; se coiffer** verb 1 (! + être)
se coiffer = to do one's hair

**coiffeur/coiffeuse** noun,
masculine/feminine
un coiffeur/une coiffeuse = a hairdresser, a
hairstylist

**coin** noun, masculine
• (an angle)
un coin = a corner
au coin de la rue = on the corner of the
street
au coin du feu = by the fire
• (a place)
un coin = a spot
un petit coin tranquille = a nice quiet spot

- (*the surrounding area*)
  **le coin** = the neighbo(u)rhood
  **le café du coin** = the local café
  **dans le coin** = in the area

**coincer** *verb* 12
= to jam, to wedge

**col** *noun, masculine*
- (*on a garment*)
  **un col** = a collar
  **un col roulé** = a polo neck, a turtleneck
- (*in the mountain*)
  **un col** = a pass

**colère** *noun, feminine*
  **la colère** = anger

**coléreux/coléreuse** *adjective*
= quick-tempered, short-tempered

**colique** *noun, feminine*
  **la colique** = diarrh(o)ea

**colis** *noun, masculine* (**!** *never changes*)
  **un colis** = a parcel, a package

**collant/collante**
**1** *adjective*
= sticky
**2 collant** *noun, masculine*
  **un collant** = (a pair of) tights, pantyhose

**colle** *noun, feminine*
  **la colle** = glue

**collectionner** *verb* 1
= to collect

**collège** *noun, masculine*
  **un collège** (*d'enseignement secondaire*),
  **un CES** = a secondary school, ≈ a junior
  high school (*for students aged 11 to 14*)
  **un collège d'enseignement technique, un
  CET** = a technical secondary school (*for
  students aged 11 to 14*)

**collègue** *noun, masculine/feminine*
  **un collègue/une collègue** = a colleague

**coller** *verb* 1
- = to stick, to glue
- (*in an examination*)✱
  **se faire coller✱ à un examen** = to fail an
  examination

**collier** *noun, masculine*
  **un collier** (*on a person*) = a necklace
  (*on an animal*) = a collar

**colline** *noun, feminine*
  **une colline** = a hill

**colonie** *noun, feminine*
  **une colonie** = a colony
  **une colonie de vacances** = a holiday
  camp, a summer camp (*for children*)

**colonne** *noun, feminine*
  **une colonne** = a column

**colorier** *verb* 2
= to colo(u)r

**coloris** *noun, masculine* (**!** *never changes*)
  **un coloris** = a colo(u)r

**combien**
**1** *adverb*
  **combien (de)** = how much, how many
**2** *noun* (**!** *never changes*)
  **le combien sommes-nous?** = what's the
  date today?
  **du combien chaussez-vous?** = what size
  shoe do you take?

**combinaison** *noun, feminine*
  **une combinaison** (*a fashion garment*) = a
  jumpsuit
  (*protective clothing*) = overalls, coveralls
**une combinaison de plongée** = a
  wetsuit
**une combinaison de ski** = a ski-suit

**combiné** *noun, masculine*
  **le combiné** = the handset, the receiver

**comédie** *noun, feminine*
- (*a play*)
  **une comédie** = a comedy
- (*pretence*)
  **de la comédie** = an act

**comédien/comédienne** *noun,
masculine/feminine*
  **un comédien/une comédienne** = an
  actor/an actress

**comestible** *adjective*
= edible

**comique** *adjective*
- = comic
- = funny

**commandant** *noun, masculine*
  **le commandant** = the major
**le commandant de bord** = the captain

**commande** *noun, feminine*
- (*for goods*)
  **une commande** = an order
- (*a device*)
  **une commande** = a control
  **être aux commandes** = to be at the
  controls

**commander** *verb* 1
- (*in a restaurant*) = to order
- (*in a group*) = to be in command

**comme**
**1** *adverb*
  **comme c'est beau!** = it's so beautiful!
**2** *conjunction*
- = like
  **il conduit comme un fou** = he drives like a
  maniac
- = as
  **comme toujours** = as always
  **gros comme mon poing** = as big as my fist

---

✱ in informal situations

- = as, since
  comme il pleuvait, je ne suis pas sorti = as
  it was raining I didn't go out
- = as a
  travailler comme serveuse = to work as a
  waitress
  comme ci comme ça* = so so
- **3 comme il faut** = properly, correctly

**commencer** verb 12
= to start, to begin

**comment** adverb
- = how
  comment allez-vous? = how are you?
- = what
  comment s'appelle-t-il? = what's his
  name?
  comment trouves-tu leur jardin? = what do
  you think of their garden?
  c'est comment? = what's it like?
- (when asking someone to repeat)
  comment? = sorry?, pardon?, excuse me?

**commentaire** noun, masculine
- (on a text, on a match)
  un commentaire = a commentary
- (a remark)
  un commentaire = a comment

**commerçant/commerçante** noun,
masculine/feminine
un commerçant/une commerçante = a
shopkeeper

**commerce** noun, masculine
- (a place)
  un commerce = a shop, a store
- (an activity)
  le commerce = trade

**commettre** verb 60
commettre un meurtre = to commit a
murder
commettre une erreur = to make a mistake

**commis/commise** ▶ commettre 60

**commissariat** noun, masculine
le commissariat (de police) = the police
station

**commode**
**1** adjective
= convenient, handy
**2** noun, feminine
une commode = a chest of drawers, a
dresser

**commun/commune** adjective
= common

**communauté** noun, feminine
une communauté = a community
**la Communauté Européenne, la CE**
= the European Community, the EC

**communication** noun, féminine
une communication (téléphonique) = a
(phone) call

**communiquer** verb 1
= to communicate

**compagne** noun, feminine
une compagne = a (female) companion

**compagnie** noun, feminine
- (a firm, a group of actors)
  une compagnie = a company
- (the presence of other people)
  la compagnie = company
**une compagnie aérienne** = an airline

**compagnon** noun, masculine
un compagnon = a (male) companion

**comparaison** noun, feminine
une comparaison = a comparison

**comparer** verb 1
= to compare

**compartiment** noun, masculine
un compartiment = a compartment

**compétition** noun, feminine
- la compétition = competition, rivalry
- une compétition (sportive) = a sporting
  event

**complet/complète** adjective
- = complete
- = full

**compliment** noun, masculine
un compliment = a compliment
tous mes compliments! = congratulations!

**compliqué/compliquée** adjective
= complicated

**comporter** verb 1
**1** (! + avoir)
= to consist of
**2 se comporter** (! + être)
se comporter = to behave

**composer** verb 1
**1** (! + avoir)
- = to dial
  composer un numéro = to dial a number
- = to put together
  composer un menu = to put a menu
  together
- = to make up
  les joueurs qui composent l'équipe = the
  players who make up the team
  composé de = made up of
- = to compose
  qui a composé la musique du film? = who
  composed the score for the film?
**2 se composer de** (! + être)
se composer de = to be made up of

**compositeur/compositrice** noun,
masculine/feminine
un compositeur/une compositrice = a
composer

**composter** verb 1
= to punch

C

**compote** noun, feminine
la compote de pommes = stewed apple

**comprendre** verb 52
**1** (**!** + avoir)
- = to understand
- = to include
**2 se comprendre** (**!** + être)
- se comprendre = to understand each other
- se comprendre = to be understandable

**comprimé** noun, masculine
un comprimé = a tablet, a pill

**compris/comprise**
**1 ▶ comprendre** 52
**2** adjective
= included
**3 y compris** = including

**compte** noun, masculine
- (in a bank, a post office)
un compte = an account
- se rendre compte = to realize
- tenir compte de = to take into account
- travailler à son compte = to be self-employed

**compter** verb 1
- = to count
- = to intend
- compter sur = to count on

**comptoir** noun, masculine
le comptoir (in a shop) = the counter
(in a café) = the bar, the counter

**con✱** noun, masculine
un con✱° = a stupid jerk

**concerner** verb 1
- = to concern
- = to affect

**concessionnaire** noun, masculine/feminine
un concessionnaire/une concessionnaire = a distributor, an agent

**concierge** noun, masculine/feminine
un concierge/une concierge = a caretaker, a superintendent

**concombre** noun, masculine
un concombre = a cucumber

**concours** noun, masculine (**!** never changes)
- (a game, an event)
un concours = a competition, a contest
- (an examination)
un concours = a competitive examination

**concurrence** noun, feminine
la concurrence = competition

**concurrent/concurrente** noun, masculine/feminine
un concurrent/une concurrente = a competitor

**condamner** verb 1
- (to declare someone guilty) = to convict
- (to punish) = to sentence
être condamné à une amende = to be fined

**condition** noun, feminine
une condition = a condition
à condition de, à condition que = provided (that), on condition that

**condoléances** noun, feminine plural
des condoléances = condolences

**conducteur/conductrice** noun, masculine/feminine
un conducteur/une conductrice = a driver

**conduire** verb 62
**1** (**!** + avoir)
- = to drive
- = to lead
le sentier conduit au village = the path leads to the village
**2 se conduire** (**!** + être)
se conduire = to behave

**conduite** noun, feminine
ta conduite = your behavio(u)r
= your conduct

**confection** noun, feminine
la confection = ready-to-wear clothes

**confiance** noun, feminine
- (in someone's honesty)
la confiance = trust
faire confiance = to trust
- (in someone's ability)
la confiance = confidence
la confiance en soi = (self-)confidence

**confier** verb 2
**1** (**!** + avoir)
= to entrust
**2 se confier** (**!** + être)
se confier à quelqu'un = to confide in someone

**confiserie** noun, feminine
une confiserie = a sweet shop, a candy store

**confisquer** verb 1
= to confiscate

**confiture** noun, feminine
la confiture = jam, jelly
la confiture d'orange = marmalade

**confort** noun, masculine
le confort = comfort

**confortable** adjective
= comfortable

**congé** noun, masculine
un congé = a holiday, a vacation
être en congé = to be on holiday, to be on vacation
**un congé de maladie** = sick leave

---

**congélateur** noun, masculine
　un congélateur = a freezer

**conjuguer** verb [1]
　= to conjugate

**connaissance** noun, feminine
• la connaissance = knowledge
• une connaissance = an acquaintance
　j'ai fait la connaissance de leur fils = I met
　　their son
• perdre connaissance = to lose
　consciousness
　sans connaissance = unconscious

**connaître** verb [63]
**1** (! + avoir)
　= to know
**2 se connaître** (! + être)
• se connaître = to know each other
• se connaître = to know oneself
**3 s'y connaître en** (! + être)
　s'y connaître en = to know about
　tu t'y connais en voitures? = do you know
　　about cars?

**connu/connue**
**1** ▶ **connaître** [63]
**2** adjective
　= well-known

**consciencieux/consciencieuse**
adjective
　= conscientious

**conseil** noun, masculine
• (an opinion)
　un conseil = a piece of advice
　des conseils = advice
• (a group of people)
　un conseil = a council
**un conseil de classe** = a staff meeting
　(for those teaching a given class)
**le conseil municipal** = the town council

**conseiller¹** verb [1]
• = to advise
• = to recommend

**conseiller²/conseillère** noun,
masculine/feminine
• (an expert)
　un conseiller/une conseillère = an adviser,
　　a consultant
• (an elected member)
　un conseiller/une conseillère = a
　　councillor
**un conseiller d'éducation** = a
　supervisor
**un conseiller municipal** = a town
　councillor
**un conseiller d'orientation** = a careers
　adviser

**conservatoire** noun, masculine
　un conservatoire = an academy, a
　　conservatory

**conserve** noun, feminine
　les conserves (in tins) = canned food

　(in jars) = preserves
　une boîte de conserve = a can (of food)

**conserver** verb [1]
• = to keep
• = to preserve

**consigne** noun, feminine
• la consigne = the left luggage office
• la consigne = orders, instructions
**la consigne automatique** = the left
　luggage lockers, the baggage lockers

**consoler** verb [1]
　= to comfort
　= to console

**consommateur/consommatrice**
noun, masculine/feminine
　un consommateur/une consommatrice (of
　　goods, services) = a consumer
　(in a café) = a customer

**consommation** noun, feminine
• (in a café)
　une consommation = a drink
• (of gas, food)
　la consommation = consumption

**consommer** verb [1]
　= to consume

**constater** verb [1]
　= to notice

**construire** verb [62]
　= to build

**construit** ▶ **construire** [62]

**consulat** noun, masculine
　un consulat = a consulate

**consulter** verb [1]
　= to consult

**contacter** verb [1]
　= to contact, to get in touch with

**contagieux/contagieuse** adjective
　= contagious

**conte** noun, masculine
　un conte = a story, a tale
　un conte de fées = a fairy tale

**contenir** verb [36]
• = to contain
• = to hold

**content/contente** adjective
　= happy, pleased, glad
　il est content de te voir = he's happy to see
　　you

**contenu/contenue**
**1** ▶ **contenir** [36]
**2 contenu** noun, masculine
　le contenu = the contents

**continuellement** adverb
　= continuously

**continuer** verb [1]
　= to continue

**contourner** verb [1]
= to go (a)round
= to bypass

**contraire** adjective
= opposite

**contrarier** verb [2]
= to upset

**contravention** noun, feminine
une contravention = a fine

**contre**
1 preposition
= against
2 noun, masculine
le pour et le contre = the pros and cons
3 **par contre** = on the other hand

**contrebande** noun, feminine
la contrebande = smuggling
des produits de contrebande = smuggled
goods

**contrebasse** noun, feminine
une contrebasse = a double bass, an
upright bass

**contribuer** verb [1]
contribuer à = to contribute to

**contrôle** noun, masculine
* (a way of checking)
un contrôle = a check
= an inspection
(in class) = a test
un contrôle de qualité = a quality check
un contrôle des billets = a ticket
inspection
* (over a vehicle)
le contrôle = control
**le contrôle (continu) des
connaissances** = (continuous)
assessment

**contrôler** verb [1]
= to check
= to inspect

**contrôleur/contrôleuse** noun,
masculine/feminine
un contrôleur/une contrôleuse = an
inspector

**convaincre** verb [57]
= to convince
= to persuade

**convaincu/convaincue** ▶
convaincre [57]

**convenable** adjective
* = suitable
* = proper

**convenir** verb [36]
convenir à = to suit
= to be suitable for

**convenu/convenue** ▶ convenir [36]

**convoi** noun, masculine
un convoi = a convoy

**convoquer** verb [1]
= to summon
= to send for

**copain** noun, masculine
mon copain = my friend
= my boyfriend

**copie** noun, feminine
* (of a letter, a painting)
une copie = a copy
* (a piece of schoolwork)
une copie = a paper

**copier** verb [2]
= to copy

**copine** noun, feminine
ma copine = my friend
= my girlfriend

**coq** noun, masculine
un coq = a cock, a rooster

**coquillage** noun, masculine
* un coquillage = a shell
* les coquillages = shellfish

**coquille** noun, feminine
une coquille = a shell
**une coquille Saint-Jacques** = a scallop

**cor** noun, masculine
un cor = a horn

**corbeau** noun, masculine
(plural) **corbeaux**
un corbeau = a crow

**corbeille** noun, feminine
une corbeille = a basket
**une corbeille à papier** = a wastepaper
basket

**corde** noun, feminine
* une corde = a rope
* (on a violin, a bow, a racket)
une corde = a string
**une corde à sauter** = a skipping rope, a
jumprope

**corne** noun, feminine
une corne = a horn

**cornet** noun, masculine
* (for ice cream)
un cornet = a cornet
* (for fries, sweets)
un cornet = a bag

**Cornouailles** noun, feminine
la Cornouailles = Cornwall

**corps** noun, masculine (! never changes)
le corps = the body

**correct/correcte** adjective
* = correct

---

**✗** in informal situations

* = proper
* = polite

**correspondance** noun, feminine
* (when travelling)
  une correspondance = a connection
* (when writing letters)
  la correspondance = correspondence

**correspondant/correspondante**
noun, masculine/feminine
  un correspondant/une correspondante = a
  penfriend, a penpal

**correspondre** verb 6
* = to write
* correspondre à = to correspond to, to
  match

**corrigé** noun, masculine
  le corrigé = the correct version

**corriger** verb 13
* = to correct
* = to mark, to grade

**Corse** noun, feminine
  la Corse = Corsica

**cortège** noun, masculine
  un cortège = a procession

**corvée** noun, feminine
  une corvée = a chore

**costaud✲** adjective
  = strong, sturdy

**costume** noun, masculine
* (a man's outfit)
  un costume = a suit
* (worn by actors)
  un costume = a costume

**côte**
1 noun, feminine
* (by the sea)
  la côte = the coast
* (an incline)
  une côte = a hill
  = a slope
* (in the body)
  une côte = a rib
2 **côte à côte** = side by side

**côté**
1 noun, masculine
  un côté = a side
2 **à côté** = nearby
  j'habite à côté = I live nearby
  la maison d'à côté = the house next door
3 **à côté de** = next to

**Côte-d'Ivoire** noun, feminine
  la Côte-d'Ivoire = the Ivory Coast

**côtelette** noun, feminine
  une côtelette = a chop, a cutlet

**cotisation** noun, feminine
  une cotisation = a subscription

**coton** noun, masculine
* (a natural fibre)
  le coton = cotton
* (fluffy wadding)
  le coton (hydrophile) = cotton wool,
  (absorbent) cotton

**cou** noun, masculine
  le cou = the neck

**couche** noun, feminine
* (a thickness)
  une couche = a layer
* (on a baby)
  une couche = a nappy, a diaper

**coucher**
1 verb 1 (! + avoir)
* = to put to bed
* = to sleep
2 **se coucher** verb 1 (! + être)
* se coucher = to go to bed
  ils sont couchés = they're in bed
* se coucher = to lie (down)
* se coucher = to set, to go down
  le soleil se couche vers 8 heures = the sun
  sets at about 8 o'clock
3 noun, masculine
  le coucher du soleil = sunset

**couchette** noun, feminine
  une couchette = a couchette, a berth

**coucou** exclamation
  coucou! = peekaboo!

**coude** noun, masculine
  un coude = an elbow

**coudre** verb 66
  = to sew

**couette** noun, feminine
* (on a bed)
  une couette = a duvet, a comforter
* (a hairstyle)
  des couettes = bunches, pigtails

**couler** verb 1
  = to flow

**couleur** noun, feminine
  une couleur = a colo(u)r

**couloir** noun, masculine
  un couloir = a corridor, a hallway
  = a passage

**coup** noun, masculine
  ! For translations of phrases such as coup
  de foudre, coup de fil, coup de soleil etc
  look up the entries at foudre, fil, soleil etc.
* (a hard hit)
  un coup = a blow
  donner un coup de [pied | poing | couteau …]
  à quelqu'un = [to kick | to punch | to stab …]
  someone
  à coups de marteau = with a hammer

C

- (a loud noise)
  un coup = a knock
  frapper trois coups à la porte = to knock
      three times on the door
- (the firing of a gun)
  un coup de [feu | fusil | revolver …] = a shot
  tué d'un coup de fusil = shot dead
- (an attempt, an occasion)
  du premier coup = first time
  à chaque coup = every time
  ce coup-ci = this time
  sur le coup = at the time
  = instantly
  tout d'un coup, tout à coup = suddenly, all
      of a sudden

**coupable**
1 adjective
  = guilty
2 noun, masculine|feminine
  un coupable/une coupable = a culprit

**coupe** noun, feminine
- (a trophy)
  une coupe = a cup
- (at the hairdresser's)
  une coupe = a haircut
- (a container)
  une coupe = a bowl

**couper** verb 1
1 (! + avoir)
  = to cut off
2 se couper (! + être)
  se couper = to cut oneself
  se couper le doigt = to cut one's finger

**cour** noun, feminine
- (an enclosed area)
  une cour = a yard
  = a courtyard
  = a farmyard
- (a play area at school)
  une cour (de récréation) = a playground, a
      schoolyard
- (for royalty, trials)
  la cour = the court

**courageux/courageuse** adjective
  = courageous, brave

**couramment** adverb
- = fluently
- = widely

**courant**
1 ▶ courir 26
2 noun, masculine
  un courant = a current
3 au courant
  être au courant de ce qui se passe = to
      know what's going on
  je vous tiendrai au courant = I'll keep you
      informed
**un courant d'air** = a draught, a draft

---

**coureur/coureuse** noun, masculine|
feminine
  un coureur/une coureuse = a runner
**un coureur cycliste** = a racing cyclist

**courir** verb 26
- = to run
- = to race
- = to rush

**couronne** noun, feminine
- (on a king's head)
  une couronne = a crown
- (on a grave)
  une couronne = a wreath

**courriel** noun, masculine
  le courriel = email

**courrier** noun, masculine
  le courrier = the post, the mail
  par retour du courrier = by return (post),
      by return mail
**le courrier du cœur** = the advice column
**le courrier électronique** = email
**le courrier rebut** = junk mail

**cours** noun, masculine (! never changes)
- (a teaching session)
  un cours = a lesson, a class
  faire cours = to teach
- (a series of lessons)
  un cours = a course
- (on the foreign exchange)
  le cours du dollar = the (exchange) rate for
      the dollar
- au cours de la journée = during the course
      of the day
  en cours de route = along the way
**un cours du soir** = an evening class

**course**
1 noun, feminine
- (a competition)
  une course = a race
- (some business to attend to)
  une course = an errand
2 courses noun, feminine plural
  des courses = shopping

**coursier/coursière** noun, masculine|
feminine
  un coursier/une coursière = a messenger

**court/courte** adjective
  = short
  de courte durée = short-lived

**couru/courue** ▶ courir 26

**cousin/cousine** noun,
masculine|feminine
  un cousin/une cousine = a cousin

**coussin** noun, masculine
  un coussin = a cushion

**cousu/cousue** ▶ coudre 66

**coût** noun, masculine
  le coût = the cost

**couteau** noun, masculine
(plural) **couteaux**
  un couteau = a knife

**coûter** verb ①
= to cost

**coûteux/coûteuse** adjective
= costly

**coutume** noun, feminine
une coutume = a custom

**couture** noun, feminine
• (an activity)
la couture = sewing
• (in a garment)
une couture = a seam

**couvercle** noun, masculine
un couvercle = a lid

**couvert¹** noun, masculine
un couvert = a place setting
mettre le couvert = to set the table

**couvert²/couverte** ▶ couvrir ③②

**couverture** noun, feminine
• (on a bed)
une couverture = a blanket
• (on a book)
une couverture = a cover
• (of mobile phone reception)
la couverture = coverage

**couvrir** verb ③②
= to cover

**crabe** noun, masculine
un crabe = a crab

**cracher** verb ①
• = to spit
• = to spit out

**craie** noun, feminine
la craie = chalk

**craindre** verb ⑤④
• = to fear, to be afraid
ne craignez rien = don't be afraid
• = to be sensitive to

**craint/crainte¹** ▶ craindre ⑤④

**crainte¹** noun, feminine
la crainte = fear

**cramoisi/cramoisie** adjective
= crimson

**crampe** noun, feminine
une crampe = a cramp

**crâne** noun, masculine
le crâne = the skull

**crapaud** noun, masculine
un crapaud = a toad

**craquer** verb ①
• = to break
• = to creak
• (emotionally)✶ = to crack up

**cravate** noun, feminine
une cravate = a tie

**crayon** noun, masculine
un crayon = a pencil

**un crayon à bille** = a ballpoint pen
**un crayon de couleur** = a colo(u)red pencil
**un crayon feutre** = a felt-tip pen

**crèche** noun, feminine
• (for babies)
une crèche = a day-nursery, a nursery
• (a Christmas scene)
une crèche = a crib, a crèche

**crédit** noun, masculine
le crédit = credit
acheter à crédit = to buy on credit
'la maison ne fait pas de crédit' = 'no credit'

**créer** verb ⑪
• = to create
• = to set up, to found

**crème**
**1** noun, feminine
la crème = cream
**2** noun, masculine
un crème = an espresso with milk

**crémerie** noun, feminine
une crémerie = a cheese shop, a cheese store

**crêpe** noun, feminine
une crêpe = a pancake

**crêperie** noun, feminine
une crêperie = a pancake restaurant

**cresson** noun, masculine
le cresson = watercress

**crête** noun, feminine
• (of a hill, a wave)
la crête = the crest
• (of a roof)
la crête = the ridge
• (on a bird)
la crête = the comb

**creuser** verb ①
• = to dig
• l'exercice, ça creuse✶! = exercise gives you an appetite!

**creux/creuse** adjective
= hollow

**crevaison** noun, feminine
une crevaison = a puncture

**crevant/crevante✶** adjective
• = exhausting
• = hilarious

**crevé/crevée✶** adjective
• = exhausted
• = flat, punctured

**crever** verb ⑯
• = to have a puncture
• = to burst
= to puncture
• = to die
un chat crevé = a dead cat

- (to exhaust)✗ = to wear out
  la course m'a crevé✗ = the race wore me
  out

**crevette** noun, feminine
  une crevette grise = a shrimp
  une crevette rose = a prawn

**cri** noun, masculine
- (by a person)
  un cri = a cry, a shout
  = a scream
  pousser un cri = to scream
- (by an animal)
  un cri = a cry
  = a call

**crier** verb 2
  = to shout
  = to scream

**crime** noun, masculine
  un crime (a criminal action) = a crime
  (an unlawful killing) = a murder

**criminel/criminelle**
**1** adjective
  = criminal
**2** noun, masculine/feminine
  un criminel/une criminelle = a criminal
  = a murderer

**crise** noun, feminine
- (a difficult situation)
  une crise = a crisis
- (an outburst)
  une crise = a fit
- (a sudden illness)
  une crise = an attack
  **une crise cardiaque** = a heart attack

**critiquer** verb 1
  = to criticize

**crochet** noun, masculine
- (a piece of bent metal)
  un crochet = a hook
- (on a journey)
  un crochet = a detour

**croire** verb 53
**1** (! + avoir)
- = to believe
  je te crois = I believe you
- = to think
  je ne crois pas = I don't think so
**2 se croire** (! + être)
  il se croit malin = he thinks he's smart

**croisement** noun, masculine
  un croisement = a junction, an
  intersection

**croiser** verb 1
**1** (! + avoir)

- = to cross
  les jambes croisées = legs crossed
  les bras croisés = arms folded
- = to pass
  croiser une voiture = to pass a car (coming
  the other way)
**2 se croiser** (! + être)
- se croiser = to cross
- se croiser = to pass each other

**croisière** noun, feminine
  une croisière = a cruise

**croissance** noun, feminine
  la croissance = growth

**croissant** noun, masculine
- (a pastry)
  un croissant = a croissant
- (a shape)
  un croissant = a crescent

**croix** noun, feminine (! never changes)
  une croix = a cross

**croque-monsieur** noun, masculine
(! never changes)
  un croque-monsieur = a grilled ham and
  cheese sandwich

**crotte** noun, feminine
  de la crotte de chien = dog mess, dog poop

**croûte** noun, feminine
- (on bread)
  la croûte = the crust
- (on cheese)
  la croûte = the rind
- (on the skin)
  une croûte = a scab

**croûton** noun, masculine
  un croûton = a crouton

**CRS** noun, masculine (! never changes)
  un CRS a member of the French riot police

**cru/crue**
**1 ▶ croire** 53
**2** adjective
  = raw

**crudités** noun, feminine plural
  des crudités = raw vegetables

**cruel/cruelle** adjective
  = cruel

**cueillir** verb 27
  = to pick

**cuiller, cuillère** noun, feminine
  une cuiller, une cuillère = a spoon
  **une cuillère à café, une petite**
  **cuillère** = a teaspoon
  **une cuillère à soupe** = a soup spoon

---

✗ in informal situations   ✦ may be considered offensive

**cuillerée** *noun, feminine*
  une cuillerée = a spoonful

**cuir** *noun, masculine*
  le cuir = leather

**cuire** *verb* 62
  = to cook
  = to bake

**cuisine** *noun, feminine*
• (*a room*)
  une cuisine = a kitchen
• (*the preparation of food*)
  la cuisine = cooking

**cuisinier/cuisinière¹** *noun,*
*masculine/feminine*
  un cuisinier/une cuisinière = a cook

**cuisinière²** *noun, feminine*
  une cuisinière = a cooker, a stove, a range

**cuisse** *noun, feminine*
  une cuisse = a thigh
  des cuisses de grenouille = frog's legs

**cuit/cuite ▶ cuire** 62

**cul✳** *noun, masculine*
  le cul✳ = the arse, the ass

**culot✗** *noun, masculine*
  le culot✗ = cheek, nerve

**culotte** *noun, feminine*
  une culotte = pants, panties, knickers

**cultiver** *verb* 1
• = to cultivate
• = to grow

**cure** *noun, feminine*
  une cure = a course of treatment (*in a*
  *spa*)

**curé** *noun, masculine*
  un curé = a (parish) priest

**curieux/curieuse**
**1** *adjective*
• = inquisitive
• = odd, strange
**2 curieux** *noun, masculine plural*
  les curieux = onlookers

**curiosité** *noun, feminine*
  la curiosité = curiosity

**cuvette** *noun, feminine*
  une cuvette = a bowl

**CV** *noun, masculine*
• (*personal details*)
  un CV = a CV, a résumé
• (*a unit of power*)
  un CV = one HP

**cyclable** *adjective*
  une piste cyclable = a cycle lane

**cycliste** *noun, masculine/feminine*
  un cycliste/une cycliste = a cyclist

**cygne** *noun, masculine*
  un cygne = a swan

**cyprès** *noun, masculine* (**!** *never changes*)
  un cyprès = a cypress

# Dd

**d' ▶ de**

**dactylo** *noun, masculine/feminine*
  un dactylo/une dactylo = a typist

**daim** *noun, masculine*
• (*an animal*)
  un daim = a deer
• (*a type of leather*)
  le daim = suede

**dame**
**1** *noun, feminine*
  une dame = a lady
**2 dames** *noun, feminine plural*
  les dames = draughts, checkers

**Danemark** *noun, masculine*
  le Danemark = Denmark

**danger** *noun, masculine*
  le danger = danger
  'danger de noyade' = 'unsafe for
  swimming'

**dangereux/dangereuse** *adjective*
  = dangerous

**danois/danoise**
**1** *adjective*
  = Danish
**2 danois** *noun, masculine*
  le danois = Danish

**dans** *preposition*
• = in
  vivre dans une ville = to live in a town
  être dans les affaires = to be in business
  aller dans la bonne direction = to go in the
    right direction
  dans une semaine = in a week's time
• = into
  entrer dans une maison = to go into a
    house
  sortir dans le jardin = to go out into the
    garden
• = on
  être dans un train = to be on a train
  monter dans un avion = to get on a plane
  dans l'ensemble = on the whole
• = through
  fouiller dans un sac = to rummage
    through a bag
• = out of
  prendre un verre dans un placard = to take
    a glass out of a cupboard

**danse** *noun, feminine*
• la danse = dancing
• une danse = a dance
**la danse classique** = ballet dancing

**danser** *verb* ⎡1⎤
= to dance

**danseur/danseuse** *noun,*
*masculine/feminine*
un danseur/une danseuse = a dancer

**date** *noun, feminine*
la date = the date
'date limite de consommation' = 'use-by
  date'

**dater** *verb* ⎡1⎤
= to date
dater de = to date from

**datte** *noun, feminine*
une datte = a date

**daube** *noun, feminine*
la daube  beef stew cooked in wine

**dauphin** *noun, masculine*
un dauphin = a dolphin

**davantage** *adverb*
• = more
• = longer

**de** (**d'** *before vowel or mute h;* de + le
*becomes* du; de + les *becomes* des)

> ❗ *You will find translations for phrases with*
> de *such as* d'abord, pomme de terre,
> chemin de fer *etc. under the words* abord,
> pomme, chemin, *etc.*

**1** *preposition*
• = of
  un verre d'eau = a glass of water
  la voiture de mon père = my father's car
• = from
  le paquet vient de Paris = the package
    comes from Paris
  du matin au soir = from morning till night
• = by
  un tableau de Picasso = a painting by
    Picasso
  il était suivi de son chien = he was
    followed by his dog
• = about
  elle parle des voisins = she's talking about
    the neighbo(u)rs
  de quoi s'agit-il? = what's it about?
• = than
  plus de trois heures après mon arrivée
    = more than three hours after I'd
    arrived
  moins de dix pour cent = less than ten per
    cent
**2** *determiner*
  = some
  = any
  voulez-vous de la bière? = would you like
    some beer?
  il n'a pas de monnaie = he hasn't got any
    change
  as-tu des courses à faire? = have you got
    any shopping to do?

**dé** *noun, masculine*
• (*in games*)
  un dé = a dice
• (*in sewing*)
  un dé = a thimble

**déballer** *verb* ⎡1⎤
• = to unpack
• = to display

**débarquer** *verb* ⎡1⎤
• = to disembark, to get off
• = to unload

**débarras** *noun, masculine* (❗ *never*
*changes*)
• (*a room*)
  un débarras = a junk room
• bon débarras! = good riddance!

**débarrasser** *verb* ⎡1⎤
**1** (❗ + *avoir*)
• = to clear (out)
  débarrasser (la table) = to clear the table
• = to rid
  je vous débarrasse de votre manteau?
    = shall I take your coat?
**2 se débarrasser de** (❗ + *être*)
  se débarrasser de = to get rid of

**débattre**: **se débattre** *verb* ⎡61⎤ (❗ + *être*)
  se débattre = to struggle

**débit** *noun, masculine*
haut débit = broadband

**déborder** *verb* ⎡1⎤
= to overflow

**débouché** *noun, masculine*
un débouché = an opening

**déboucher** *verb* ⎡1⎤
• = to open
  déboucher une bouteille = to open a bottle
• = to unblock, to unclog
  déboucher un évier = to unblock a sink
• = to lead to
  le sentier débouche sur une route = the
    path leads to a road
• = to come out
  la voiture a débouché d'une petite rue
    = the car came out of a side street

**debout** *adverb*
• = standing
  se mettre debout = to stand up
  rester debout = to stand
• = upright
  mets la caisse debout = stand the crate in
    an upright position
• = up
  être debout à six heures du matin = to be
    up at six in the morning
  debout! = get up!

**déboutonner** *verb* ⎡1⎤
= to unbutton

**débraillé/débraillée** *adjective*
= dishevelled

**D**

**débrancher** verb [1]
= to unplug

**débrayer** verb [21]
= to put the clutch in

**débris** noun, masculine (**!** never changes)
* (of glass, china)
un débris = a fragment
* (of car, plane)
un débris = a piece of wreckage

**débrouiller** verb [1]
**1** (**!** + avoir)
* = to unscramble
* = to disentangle
**2 se débrouiller** (**!** + être)
* se débrouiller = to manage
se débrouiller pour avoir des billets = to manage to get tickets
* se débrouiller = to get by
se débrouiller en anglais = to get by in English

**début** noun, masculine
le début = the beginning
au début = at the beginning
début avril = at the beginning of April, in early April

**débutant/débutante** noun, masculine/feminine
un débutant/une débutante = a beginner

**décacheter** verb [20]
= to unseal

**décaféiné/décaféinée** adjective
= decaffeinated

**décalage** noun, masculine
le décalage horaire = the time difference
= jet lag

**décapsuleur** noun, masculine
un décapsuleur = a bottle-opener

**décéder** verb [14]
= to die
être décédé = to be dead

**décembre** noun, masculine
décembre = December

**déception** noun, feminine
une déception = a disappointment

**décès** noun, masculine (**!** never changes)
un décès = a death

**décevant/décevante** adjective
= disappointing

**décevoir** verb [5]
= to disappoint

**déchaîner: se déchaîner** verb [1]
(**!** + être)
se déchaîner = to go wild

**décharger** verb [13]
= to unload

**déchets** noun, masculine plural
les déchets = waste

**déchiffrer** verb [1]
= to decipher
= to decode

**déchirer** verb [1]
**1** (**!** + avoir)
= to tear (up)
**2 se déchirer** (**!** + être)
se déchirer = to tear

**décidément** adverb
= really

**décider** verb [1]
**1** (**!** + avoir)
* = to decide
elle a décidé de les inviter = she's decided to invite them
c'est décidé = it's settled
* = to persuade
j'ai décidé mes amis à venir = I persuaded my friends to come
**2 se décider** (**!** + être)
se décider = to make up one's mind

**déclarer** verb [1]
**1** (**!** + avoir)
* = to declare
rien à déclarer = nothing to declare
* = to report
déclarer un vol = to report a theft
**2 se déclarer** (**!** + être)
se déclarer = to break out
un incendie s'est déclaré = a fire broke out

**déclencher** verb [1]
= to set off
= to trigger

**décollage** noun, masculine
le décollage = take-off

**décoller** verb [1]
**1** (**!** + avoir)
* = to peel off
décoller une étiquette = to peel off a label
* = to take off
l'avion va décoller = the plane is about to take off
**2 se décoller** (**!** + être)
se décoller = to come off

**décolleté/décolletée** adjective
= low-cut

**décolorer** verb [1]
* = to bleach
* = to cause to fade

**décombres** noun, masculine plural
les décombres = the rubble

**décongeler** verb [17]
= to defrost

**décontracté/décontractée**
adjective
* = relaxed, laid-back
* = casual

**décorer** verb 1
= to decorate

**découper** verb 1
= to cut out
= to cut up
= to carve

**décourager** verb 13
= to discourage

**découvert/découverte¹**
▶ **découvrir** 32

**découverte²** noun, feminine
une découverte = a discovery

**découvrir** verb 32
• = to discover
• = to uncover

**décrire** verb 42
= to describe

**décrocher** verb 1
• (to remove from its hook) = to take down
  décrocher le téléphone = to pick up the
  receiver
  = to take the phone off the hook
• (in a competition, an exam)✷ = to pass
  = to get
  décrocher✷ son permis = to pass one's
  driving test

**déçu/déçue** ▶ **décevoir** 5

**dedans** adverb
= inside

**défaire** verb 10
1 (! + avoir)
= to undo
défaire sa valise = to unpack one's
  suitcase
2 se défaire (! + être)
se défaire = to come undone

**défaut** noun, masculine
un défaut = a fault

**défavorisé/défavorisée** adjective
• = underprivileged
• = disadvantaged

**défectueux/défectueuse** adjective
= faulty

**défendre** verb 6
1 (! + avoir)
• = to forbid
  je vous défends de sortir = I forbid you to
  go out
  c'est défendu = it's forbidden, it's not
  allowed
• = to defend
2 se défendre (! + être)
se défendre = to defend oneself

**défendu/défendue** ▶ **défendre** 6

**défense** noun, feminine
• (an order)
  'défense de fumer' = 'no smoking'
• (against an attack, an accusation)
  la défense = the defence, the defense
  prendre la défense d'un ami = to stand up
  for a friend
  sans défense = helpless, defenceless,
  defenseless
• (of an elephant, a walrus)
  une défense = a tusk

**défilé** noun, masculine
• (a military display)
  un défilé = a parade
• (people filing past)
  un défilé = a procession
  = a march
• (a constant flow of people)
  un défilé de visiteurs = a stream of visitors

**défiler** verb 1
• = to march past
• (on a computer)
  défiler vers le haut/le bas = to scroll up/down

**défoncer** verb 12
défoncer une porte = to break down a
  door

**déformé/déformée** adjective
= distorted
= misshapen
'chaussée déformée' = 'uneven road
  surface'

**dégager** verb 13
1 (! + avoir)
• = to clear
  ciel dégagé = clear sky
• = to free
• = to give off
  dégager de la chaleur = to give off heat
2 se dégager (! + être)
• se dégager = to clear
  le temps s'est dégagé = the weather has
  cleared
• se dégager (de) = to free oneself (from)

**dégâts** noun, masculine plural
les dégâts = the damage

**dégonfler** verb 1
1 (! + avoir)
• = to deflate, to let down
2 se dégonfler (! + être)
• se dégonfler = to deflate, to go down
• (when faced with a challenge)✷
  se dégonfler✷ = to lose one's nerve, to
  chicken out

**dégoûtant/dégoûtante** adjective
• = filthy
• = disgusting

**degré** noun, masculine
• (a unit of measurement)
  un degré = one degree

---

✷ in informal situations

- (a level)
  l'enseignement du second degré
  = secondary education, high school
  education (for students aged 11 to 18)

**dégringoler** verb [1]
= to take a tumble
= to tumble down

**déguiser** verb [1]
1 (! + avoir)
= to disguise
2 se déguiser (! + être)
* se déguiser = to disguise oneself
* se déguiser = to dress up

**dégustation** noun, feminine
une dégustation de vin = a wine tasting

**déguster** verb [1]
* = to taste, to sample
* = to enjoy

**dehors** adverb
= outside

**déjà** adverb
= already

**déjeuner**
1 noun, masculine
* (in the middle of the day)
  le déjeuner = lunch
* (in the morning)
  le (petit) déjeuner = breakfast
2 verb
* = to have lunch
* = to have breakfast

**delà : au delà de** preposition
au delà de = beyond

**délabré/délabrée** adjective
= dilapidated

**délai** noun, masculine
* (time allowed)
  dans un délai de 24 heures = within 24
  hours
  sans délai = immediately
  mardi, dernier délai = Tuesday at the latest
* (additional time)
  un délai = an extension

**délasser** verb [1]
= to refresh
= to relax

**délicieux/délicieuse** adjective
= delicious

**délit** noun, masculine
un délit = an offence, an offense

**délivrer** verb [1]
* = to free
  délivrer un prisonnier = to free a prisoner
* = to issue
  délivrer un passeport = to issue a passport

**deltaplane** noun, masculine
* (the equipment)
  un deltaplane = a hang-glider

* (the sport)
  le deltaplane = hang-gliding

**demain** adverb
= tomorrow
à demain = see you tomorrow

**demande** noun, feminine
* une demande = a request
  faire une demande de prêt = to apply for a
  loan
  'demandes d'emploi' = 'jobs wanted'
* (in business)
  l'offre et la demande = supply and
  demand

**demander** verb [1]
1 (! + avoir)
* = to ask (for)
  elle a demandé de l'argent à ses parents
  = she's asked her parents for money
* = to require
  ça demande trop d'efforts = it requires too
  much effort
2 se demander (! + être)
se demander = to wonder

**demandeur/demandeuse d'asile** noun,
masculine/feminine
un demandeur/une demandeuse d'asile
= an asylum-seeker

**démarrer** verb [1]
* (if it's a vehicle) = to pull away
* (if it's a driver) = to drive off

**démarreur** noun, masculine
le démarreur = the starter

**déménagement** noun, masculine
* (going to live elsewhere)
  un déménagement = a move
* (transporting furniture)
  un déménagement = a removal

**déménager** verb [10]
= to move (house)

**demeurer** verb [1]
* = to live
* = to remain

**demi/demie**[1]
1 adjective
* demi- (! comes before the noun, never
  changes)
  = half
  = semi
  une demi-heure = half an hour
  un demi-tarif = a half-price ticket
  une demi-finale = a semi-final
* et demi/et demie (! comes after the noun,
  never plural)
  = and a half
  deux et demi = two and a half
  à cinq heures et demie = at half past five
2 demi noun, masculine
* (a drink)
  un demi = a glass of beer
* (in rugby)
  un demi de mêlée = a scrum half
3 à demi = half
  à demi éveillé = half awake

**demie²** *noun, feminine*
la demie = half past
il est déjà la demie = it's already half past

**demi-frère** *noun, masculine*
(*plural*) **demi-frères**
un demi-frère = a stepbrother, a half-brother

**demi-pension** *noun, feminine*
la demi-pension = half board, accommodation with one meal only

**demi-sœur** *noun, feminine*
(*plural*) **demi-sœurs**
une demi-sœur = a stepsister, a half-sister

**démissionner** *verb* 1
= to resign

**demi-tour** *noun, masculine*
(*plural*) **demi-tours**
un demi-tour = a half-turn
faire demi-tour = to turn back

**démodé/démodée** *adjective*
= old-fashioned

**demoiselle** *noun, feminine*
une demoiselle = a young lady
**une demoiselle d'honneur** = a bridesmaid

**démolir** *verb* 3
= to demolish

**démonter** *verb* 1
• = to take apart, to dismantle
• = to remove, to take off

**démontrer** *verb* 1
= to demonstrate

**denrée** *noun, feminine*
une denrée = a product

**dent** *noun, feminine*
une dent = a tooth
avoir mal aux dents = to have (a) toothache

**dentelle** *noun, feminine*
la dentelle = lace

**dentifrice** *noun, masculine*
le dentifrice = toothpaste

**dentiste** *noun, masculine/feminine*
un dentiste/une dentiste = a dentist

**dépannage** *noun, masculine*
'service de dépannage' = 'breakdown service', 'emergency service'

**dépanner** *verb* 1
• = to fix, to repair
• (*if someone's in difficulty*)✖ = to help out

**dépanneur/dépanneuse¹** *noun,*
*masculine/feminine*
un dépanneur/une dépanneuse = an engineer

**dépanneuse²** *noun, feminine*
une dépanneuse = a breakdown truck, a tow truck

**dépareillé/dépareillée** *adjective*
= odd

**départ** *noun, masculine*
• (*the act of leaving*)
le départ = the departure
• (*the beginning*)
le départ = the start
au départ = at first

**département** *noun, masculine*
un département = a department (*an administrative district*)

**dépasser** *verb* 1
• = to overtake, to pass
• = to exceed
elle le dépasse de 5 centimètres = she's 5 centimetres taller than him
• = to be ahead of, to outstrip
• = to pass, to go past
nous avons dépassé l'école = we've gone past the school

**dépêcher: se dépêcher** *verb* 1
(**!** + *être*)
se dépêcher = to hurry up
dépêchez-vous! = hurry up!

**dépendre** *verb* 6
dépendre de = to depend on
ça dépendra du temps = it'll depend on the weather
ça dépend! = it depends!

**dépense** *noun, feminine*
la dépense du ménage = the household expenditure
faire une dépense = to spend some money

**dépenser** *verb* 1
= to spend (money)

**déplacer** *verb* 12
**1** (**!** + *avoir*)
= to move
**2 se déplacer** (**!** + *être*)
• se déplacer = to move
• se déplacer = to travel

**dépliant** *noun, masculine*
un dépliant = a leaflet

**déplier** *verb* 2
= to unfold

**déposer** *verb* 1
**1** (**!** + *avoir*)
• déposer des ordures = to dump rubbish, to dump garbage
• déposer une gerbe = to lay a wreath
• déposer de l'argent sur un compte = to deposit money in an account
• déposer une valise à la consigne automatique = to leave a suitcase in a left-luggage locker

---

✖ in informal situations

- déposer un passager = to drop a passenger off
- déposer une plainte = to lodge a complaint, to make a complaint
- une marque déposée = a registered trademark

**2 se déposer** (! + *être*)
se déposer = to settle
= to collect

**dépositaire** *noun, masculine/feminine*
un dépositaire/une dépositaire = an agent, a representative
un dépositaire de journaux = a newsagent, a newsdealer

**dépôt** *noun, masculine*
- (*for goods*)
un dépôt = a warehouse
- (*in a shop*)
faire dépôt de gaz = to sell bottled gas
- (*in a bottle*)
un dépôt = a deposit, a residue

**déprime**✳ *noun, feminine*
la déprime✳ = depression

**déprimer** *verb* ⬛1
- (*to cause sadness*) = to depress
- (*to feel sadness*)✳ = to be depressed

**déprogrammer** *verb* ⬛1
= to cancel

**depuis**
**1** *preposition*
- = since
depuis lundi = since Monday
depuis quand est-il à Paris? = how long has he been in Paris?
- = for
depuis un an = for a year
je le connais depuis longtemps = I've known him for a long time
il pleuvait depuis trois jours = it had been raining for three days
depuis combien de temps le sais-tu? = how long have you known?
**2** *adverb*
= since
je n'ai pas de nouvelles depuis = since then I haven't heard any news
**3 depuis que** = since, ever since

**député** *noun, masculine*
un député = a Member of the National Assembly
un député européen = a member of the European Parliament, a Euro-MP

**dérailler** *verb* ⬛1
= to be derailed

**déranger** *verb* ⬛13
**1** (! + *avoir*)
- = to bother, to disturb
excusez-moi de vous déranger = I'm sorry to bother you
ça vous dérange si je mets la radio? = do you mind if I turn the radio on?
- = to disturb, to upset, to mess up

**2 se déranger** (! + *être*)
- se déranger = to get up
= to move
- se déranger = to put oneself out

**déraper** *verb* ⬛1
= to skid

**dériveur** *noun, masculine*
un dériveur = a dinghy

**dernier/dernière**
**1** *adjective*
= last
= latest
au dernier étage = on the top floor
**2** *noun, masculine/feminine*
- le dernier/la dernière = the last one
c'est le dernier qui me reste = it's my last one
arriver le dernier = to arrive last
- ce dernier/cette dernière = the latter
**3 en dernier** = lastly
= last

**dernièrement** *adverb*
= recently, lately

**déroulant** *adjective*
un menu déroulant = a pop-up menu

**derrière**
**1** *preposition*
= behind
**2** *adverb*
= behind
= at the back, in the back
**3** *noun, masculine*
- (*the rear*)
le derrière = the back
la porte de derrière = the back door
- (*part of the body*)✳
le derrière✳ = the behind, the backside

**des** ▶ **de**

**dès**
**1** *preposition*
= from
dès ce soir = from tonight
dès mon arrivée = as soon as I arrive(d)
**2 dès que** = as soon as

**désagréable** *adjective*
= unpleasant

**désastre** *noun, masculine*
un désastre = a disaster

**descendre** *verb* ⬛6
**1** (! + *être*)
- = to go down, to come down
il est descendu au village = he's gone down to the village
tu es descendu à pied? = did you walk down?
nous sommes descendus en courant = we ran down
- = to go downstairs, to come downstairs
- = to get off
je descendrai à la prochaine gare = I'll get off at the next station

- (*other uses*)
  **descendre dans un hôtel** = to stop (off) at a hotel
**2** (**!** + *avoir*)
- = to go down
  **descendre la rue** = to go down the street
  **il a descendu l'escalier en courant** = he ran down the stairs
- = to take down, to bring down
  **je dois descendre mes bagages** = I must take my luggage down
  **peux-tu me descendre mes lunettes?** = can you bring my glasses down to me?

**descente** *noun, feminine*
- (*a steep surface*)
  **une descente** = a slope
- (*in a plane*)
  **la descente** = the descent
- (*in a skiing competition*)
  **la descente** = the downhill event

**désert/déserte**
**1** *adjective*
= deserted
**2 désert** *noun, masculine*
  **le désert** = the desert

**désespéré/désespérée** *adjective*
  (*describing a person*) = in despair
  (*describing a situation*) = hopeless

**désespoir** *noun, masculine*
  **le désespoir** = despair
  **être au désespoir** = to be in despair

**déshabiller** *verb* 1
**1** (**!** + *avoir*)
= to undress
**2 se déshabiller** (**!** + *être*)
  **se déshabiller** = to get undressed

**désigner** *verb* 1
- = to point out
- = to choose, to designate

**désirer** *verb* 1
= to want
  **que désirez-vous?** = what would you like?

**désobéir** *verb* 3
- = to be disobedient
- = to disobey
  **désobéir à son père** = to disobey one's father

**désobéissant/désobéissante**
*adjective*
= disobedient

**désolé/désolée** *adjective*
  **je suis désolé** = I'm sorry

**désordre** *noun, masculine*
- (*in a room*)
  **le désordre** = untidiness, messiness
  **quel désordre!** = what a mess!
  **être en désordre** = to be untidy
  **mettre du désordre dans une pièce** = to make a room untidy, to make a room messy

- (*unrest*)
  **le désordre** = disorder

**désormais** *adverb*
= from now on
= from then on

**dessert** *noun, masculine*
  **un dessert** = a dessert

**dessin** *noun, masculine*
- (*a picture*)
  **un dessin** = a drawing
- (*a subject*)
  **le dessin** = art, drawing
= design
**un dessin animé** = a cartoon (film)

**dessinateur/dessinatrice** *noun,*
*masculine/feminine*
  **un dessinateur/une dessinatrice** = a draughtsman, a draftsman
= an illustrator
= a designer

**dessiner** *verb* 1
= to draw

**dessous**
**1** *adverb*
= underneath
**2** *noun, masculine* (**!** *never changes*)
  **le dessous** = the underside
= the bottom
  **le drap de dessous** = the bottom sheet
  **les voisins du dessous** = the people who live (on the floor) below
**3 en dessous** = underneath
  **la taille en dessous** = the next size down, the smaller size
**4 en dessous de** = below
  **en dessous de la moyenne** = below average

**dessus**
**1** *adverb*
= on top
  **écris ton nom dessus** = write your name on it
**2** *noun, masculine* (**!** *never changes*)
  **le dessus** = the top
  **le drap de dessus** = the top sheet
  **les voisins du dessus** = the people who live (on the floor) above

**destinataire** *noun, masculine/feminine*
  **le destinataire/la destinataire** = the addressee

**destination**
**1** *noun, feminine*
  **une destination** = a destination
**2 à destination de** = bound for
  **vol 802 à destination de Nice** = flight 802 to Nice

**détacher** *verb* 1
**1** (**!** + *avoir*)
- = to undo
- = to untie
- = to unfasten
- = to tear off, to detach

**2 se détacher** (! + être)
* se détacher = to come undone
* se détacher = to come off

**détail** noun, masculine
* (a minor point)
un détail = a detail
des détails supplémentaires = extra
information
* (selling direct to the public)
le détail = retail

**détendre** verb [6]
**1** (! + avoir)
* = to relax
* = to be relaxing
**2 se détendre** (! + être)
se détendre = to relax

**détenu/détenue** noun,
masculine/feminine
un détenu/une détenue = a prisoner

**détester** verb [1]
= to detest, to hate

**détraquer** verb [1]
= to damage

**détresse** noun, feminine
la détresse = distress

**détroit** noun, masculine
un détroit = a strait

**détruire** verb [62]
= to destroy

**dette** noun, feminine
une dette = a debt

**deuil** noun, masculine
* un deuil = a bereavement
* le deuil = mourning

**deux** number
= two
ils iront tous les deux = both of them will
go

**deuxième** number
= second

**deux-roues** noun, masculine (! never
changes)
un deux-roues = a two-wheeler

**devant**
**1** preposition
* = in front of
le livre est devant toi = the book is in front
of you
* = ahead of
Paul était loin devant nous = Paul was (a
long) way ahead of us
* = outside
attends-moi devant la bibliothèque = wait
for me outside the library
* = past
passer devant un magasin = to walk past
a shop

**2** adverb
= in front
= at the front
**3** noun, masculine
le devant = the front
la fenêtre de devant = the front window

**devenir** verb [36] (! + être)
= to become

**déviation** noun, feminine
une déviation = a diversion, a detour

**deviner** verb [1]
= to guess

**devinette** noun, feminine
une devinette = a riddle

**devis** noun, masculine (! never changes)
un devis = an estimate

**devise** noun, feminine
* (money)
une devise = a currency
* (a short saying)
une devise = a motto

**devoir**
**1** noun, masculine
* (work set by a teacher)
un devoir = a piece of homework, an
assignment
faire ses devoirs = to do one's homework
* (responsibility)
le devoir = duty
faire son devoir = to do one's duty
**2** verb [44]
* = to owe
devoir de l'argent à un ami = to owe a
friend money
je leur dois des excuses = I owe them an
apology
* (to be obliged to) = to have to
je dois aller travailler = I have to go to
work, I must go to work
tu aurais dû téléphoner = you should have
phoned
vous devriez les remercier = you ought to
thank them
* (meaning that something is likely) = must
il doit être arrivé = he must have arrived
elle devait avoir 11 ans = she must have
been 11
ils ont dû oublier = they must have
forgotten
* (meaning that something is certain or
expected)
cela devait arriver = it was bound to
happen
le train doit partir vers neuf heures = the
train is due to leave at about nine
o'clock

**devrai ▶ devoir 2** [44]

**diabétique** adjective
= diabetic

**diabolo menthe** *noun, masculine*
(*plural*) **diabolos menthe**
  un diabolo menthe = a mint cordial and
    lemonade, a mint cordial and soda

**diamètre** *noun, masculine*
  le diamètre = the diameter

**diapositive** *noun, feminine*
  une diapositive = a slide

**diarrhée** *noun, feminine*
  la diarrhée = diarrh(o)ea

**dictée** *noun, feminine*
  une dictée = a dictation

**dicter** *verb* 1
  = to dictate

**dictionnaire** *noun, masculine*
  un dictionnaire = a dictionary

**diète** *noun, feminine*
  être à la diète = to be on a restricted diet

**diététicien/diététicienne** *noun,*
*masculine/feminine*
  un diététicien/une diététicienne = a
    dietician

**dieu** *noun, masculine*
(*plural*) **dieux**
  un dieu = a god
  mon Dieu! = my God!

**différence** *noun, feminine*
  une différence = a difference
  à la différence des animaux = unlike
    animals

**difficile** *adjective*
• = difficult
• = fussy

**difficulté** *noun, feminine*
  une difficulté = a difficulty

**difforme** *adjective*
  = deformed

**diffuser** *verb* 1
  (*on radio*) = to broadcast

**dimanche** *noun, masculine*
  dimanche = Sunday

**dinde** *noun, feminine*
  une dinde = a turkey

**dîner**
**1** *noun, masculine*
  le dîner = dinner
  à l'heure du dîner = at dinner time
**2** *verb* 1
  = to have dinner

**dingue✘** *adjective*
  = crazy

---

✘ in informal situations

**diplôme** *noun, masculine*
  un diplôme = a diploma
  = a qualification

**dire** *verb* 40
**1** (**!** + *avoir*)
• = to say
  on dit que l'usine va fermer = they say the
    factory is going to close down
• = to tell
  dire des mensonges = to tell lies
  dites-leur de venir = tell them to come
• = to think
  qu'est-ce que tu en dis? = what do you
    think?
  on ne dirait pas qu'elle a 20 ans = you
    wouldn't think she was 20, she doesn't
    look 20
  on dirait qu'il va pleuvoir = it looks like
    rain
• vouloir dire = to mean
  qu'est-ce que ça veut dire? = what does it
    mean?
• ça ne me dit rien = it doesn't appeal to me,
    I don't feel like it
  = it doesn't mean anything to me, it
    doesn't ring a bell
**2 se dire** (**!** + *être*)
• se dire = to tell oneself
• se dire = to claim to be
  il se dit médecin = he claims to be a doctor
• ça ne se dit pas = you can't say that

**direct/directe**
**1** *adjective*
  = direct
**2 direct** *noun, masculine*
• (*a train*)
  un direct = an express (train)
• (*on radio, TV*)
  le direct = live broadcasting
  en direct de Rome = live from Rome

**directement** *adverb*
• = straight
• = directly

**directeur/directrice** *noun,*
*masculine/feminine*
• (*in a school*)
  le directeur/la directrice = the headteacher,
    the principal
• (*in an organization, a business*)
  un directeur/une directrice = a director
  = a manager

**direction** *noun, feminine*
• (*when moving*)
  une direction = a direction
  dans quelle direction? = which way?
  en direction de Calais = toward(s) Calais
• (*in an organization*)
  la direction = (the) management
• (*on a car*)
  la direction = the steering

**directrice ▶ directeur**

**diriger** verb 13
**1** (! + avoir)
• diriger une affaire = to run a business
• diriger une opération = to direct an operation
• diriger un orchestre = to conduct an orchestra
**2 se diriger** (! + être)
• se diriger vers Paris = to make for Paris, to head toward(s) Paris
• se diriger dans le noir = to find one's way in the dark

**disco** noun, masculine
le disco – disco music

**discothèque** noun, feminine
• (a library)
une discothèque = a record library
• (a nightclub)
une discothèque = a disco(theque)

**discours** noun, masculine (! never changes)
un discours = a speech

**discuter** verb 1
• = to chat, to talk
• = to argue
• discuter de = to discuss

**disparaître** verb 63
• = to disappear
• = to die

**disparition** noun, feminine
la disparition = the disappearance

**disparu/disparue** ▶ disparaître 63

**disponible** adjective
= available

**disposer** verb 1
**1** (! + avoir)
• = to arrange, to position
• disposer de = to have (at one's disposal)
**2 se disposer** (! + être)
se disposer à partir = to be about to leave

**dispute** noun, feminine
une dispute = an argument, a quarrel

**disputer; se disputer** verb 1 (! + être)
se disputer = to argue, to quarrel

**disque** noun, masculine
• (in music)
un disque = a record, an LP
un disque compact = a compact disc
• (in sport)
le disque = the discus
• (in computers)
le disque dur = the hard disk

**disquette** noun, feminine
une disquette = a diskette, a floppy disk

**dissimuler** verb 1
= to conceal, to hide

**distance** noun, feminine
la distance = distance
à une distance de 25 kilomètres = 25 kilometres away
la ville est à quelle distance? = how far is the town?
commande à distance = remote control

**distingué/distinguée** adjective
= distinguished

**distraction** noun, feminine
• (leisure activity)
une distraction = entertainment
• (lack of concentration)
la distraction = absent-mindedness

**distraire** verb 58
**1** (! + avoir)
• = to entertain, to amuse
• = to distract
**2 se distraire** (! + être)
se distraire = to amuse oneself

**distrait/distraite**
**1** ▶ distraire 58
**2** adjective
= absent-minded

**distribuer** verb 1
= to give out, to distribute
distribuer le courrier = to deliver the mail
distribuer les cartes = to deal

**distributeur** noun, masculine
un distributeur automatique de billets = a cash dispenser

**divan** noun, masculine
un divan = a sofa

**divers/diverse** adjective
• = various
• = miscellaneous

**diviser** verb 1
= to divide

**divorcé/divorcée** noun, masculine/feminine
un divorcé/une divorcée = a divorcee

**divorcer** verb 12
= to get divorced

**dix** number
= ten

**dix-huit** number
= eighteen

**dix-huitième** number
= eighteenth

**dixième** number
= tenth

**dix-neuf** number
= nineteen

**dix-neuvième** number
= nineteenth

D

**dix-sept** *number*
= seventeen

**dix-septième** *number*
= seventeenth

**dizaine** *noun, feminine*
une dizaine = about ten
= ten

**docteur** *noun, masculine*
un docteur = a doctor

**documentaire** *noun, masculine*
un documentaire = a documentary

**documentation** *noun, feminine*
de la documentation = brochures,
literature

**dodo\*** *noun, masculine*
au dodo\*! = beddy-byes!, bed time!

**doigt** *noun, masculine*
• (*on the hand*)
un doigt = a finger
montrer du doigt = to point at
un doigt de pied = a toe
• (*small amount*)
un doigt de vin = a drop of wine

**dois** ▶ **devoir 2** 44

**doive** ▶ **devoir 2** 44

**domestique**
1 *adjective*
= domestic
2 *noun, masculine/feminine*
un domestique/une domestique = a
servant

**domicile**
1 *noun, masculine*
un domicile = a (place of) residence
2 à domicile
travailler à domicile = to work from home
livrer à domicile = to deliver, to do home
deliveries

**domicilié/domiciliée** *adjective*
être domicilié à Londres = to live in
London

**dominer** *verb* 1
1 (**!** + *avoir*)
• = to dominate
• = to tower over
le monument dominait le village = the
monument towered over the village
• = to control
dominer sa peur = to overcome one's fear
• = to be predominant
2 se dominer (**!** + *être*)
se dominer = to control oneself

**domino** *noun, masculine*
un domino = a domino

---

\* in informal situations

**dommage** *noun, masculine*
• (*in expressions of regret*)
(quel) dommage! = what a pity!, what a
shame!
• (*harm*)
un dommage = damage
des dommages et intérêts = damages

**DOM-TOM** *noun, masculine plural*
(*abbreviation of* **départements et
territoires d'outre-mer**)
*French overseas departments and territories*

**don** *noun, masculine*
• (*talent*)
un don = a gift
• (*something given*)
un don = a donation

**donc** *conjunction*
= so, therefore
il est malade, donc il restera au lit = he's
unwell, so he'll stay in bed
taisez-vous donc! = be quiet, will you?
sers-toi donc! = do help yourself!

**donjon** *noun, masculine*
un donjon = a keep

**donner** *verb* 1
• = to give
donner un jouet à un enfant = to give a
child a toy
donner des coups à un animal = to hit an
animal
• donner une veste à nettoyer = to take a
jacket to be dry-cleaned
• donner sur = to overlook
la chambre donne sur la baie = the
bedroom overlooks the bay

**dont** *pronoun*
• = whose
voici le chauffeur dont la voiture a pris feu
= this is the driver whose car caught
fire
• = of which
= of whom
c'est le dessin dont il est si fier = it's the
drawing of which he's so proud
ils ont cinq fils, dont deux sont étudiants
= they've got five sons, two of whom are
students
j'ai lu le livre dont tu m'avais parlé = I read
the book that you'd told me about
il a pris les outils dont il avait besoin = he's
taken the tools that he needed
le pays dont elle vient = the country she
comes from
la façon dont il parle = the way he talks
c'est tout ce dont je me souviens = that's
all I can remember

**doré/dorée** *adjective*
= gilt
= golden
= gold

**dormir** *verb* 30
= to sleep

**dortoir** noun, masculine
un dortoir = a dormitory

**dos** noun, masculine (! never changes)
le dos = the back
avoir mal au dos = to have (a) backache
je l'ai vu de dos = I saw him from behind

**dose** noun, feminine
une dose = a dose

**dossier** noun, masculine
• (part of a seat)
le dossier = the back(rest)
• (documents)
un dossier = a file

**douane** noun, feminine
la douane = the customs

**douanier/douanière** noun,
masculine/feminine
un douanier/une douanière = a customs
officer

**double**
**1** adjective
= double
**2** noun, masculine
• (a quantity)
payer le double = to pay twice as much
le double de la taille normale = twice the
normal size
• (a duplicate)
un double = a copy
le double des clés = a spare set of keys

**doubler** verb 1
• (to increase twofold) = to double
• (in a car) = to overtake, to pass
• (for a film) = to dub
• (in dressmaking) = to line

**douce ▶ doux**

**doucement** adverb
• = gently
• = softly
• = slowly

**douche** noun, feminine
une douche = a shower

**doucher: se doucher** verb 1 (! + être)
se doucher = to take a shower

**doué/douée** adjective
= gifted, talented

**douleur** noun, feminine
• une douleur = a pain
• la douleur = grief

**douloureux/douloureuse** adjective
= painful

**doute**
**1** noun, masculine
le doute = doubt
ça ne fait aucun doute = there's no doubt
about it
**2 sans doute** = probably

**Douvres** noun
= Dover

**doux/douce**
**1** adjective
• = soft
une voix douce = a soft voice
• = mild
un temps doux = mild weather
• = gentle
une pente douce = a gentle slope
**2 doux** adverb
doux = mild
il fait doux aujourd'hui = it's mild today

**douzaine** noun, feminine
une douzaine = a dozen
= about twelve

**douze** number
= twelve

**douzième** number
= twelfth

**dragée** noun, feminine
une dragée = a sugared almond

**draguer\*** verb 1
= to chat up, to come on to

**drap** noun, masculine
un drap = a sheet

**drapeau** noun, masculine
(plural) **drapeaux**
un drapeau = a flag

**dresser** verb 1
**1** (! + avoir)
• = to train
dresser un animal = to train an animal
• = to put up
dresser une tente = to put up a tent
• = to raise
dresser la tête = to raise one's head
dresser l'oreille = to prick up one's ears
**2 se dresser** (! + être)
se dresser = to stand (up)

**drogue** noun, feminine
la drogue = drugs

**drogué/droguée** noun,
masculine/feminine
un drogué/une droguée = a drug addict

**droguer: se droguer** verb 1 (! + être)
se droguer = to take drugs

**droguerie** noun, feminine
une droguerie = a hardware shop, a
hardware store

**droguiste** noun, masculine/feminine
un droguiste/une droguiste = a hardware
dealer, an ironmonger

## droit/droite[1]
**1** adjective
* = straight
  = upright
* = right
  **du côté droit** = on the right-hand side
**2 droit** adverb
  = straight
  **continuez tout droit** = carry straight on
**3 droit** noun, masculine
* (something one is entitled to)
  **un droit** = a right
  **avoir le droit d'aller où l'on veut** = to have the right to go wherever one wants
* (money that has to be paid)
  **un droit** = a fee
  = a tax
* (a course of study)
  **le droit** = law
  **les droits de douane** = customs duties
  **les droits de succession** = inheritance tax

## droite[2] noun, feminine
  **la droite** = the right

## droitier/droitière noun,
masculine/feminine
  **un droitier/une droitière** = a right-handed person

## drôle adjective
  = funny

## du ▶ de

## dû/due ▶ devoir 2 [44]

## duc noun, masculine
  **un duc** = a duke

## dur/dure
**1** adjective
  = hard, tough
  = harsh
**2 dur** adverb
  **travailler dur** = to work hard

## durée noun, feminine
* (of a reign, of a course)
  **la durée** = the length
  = the duration
  **un séjour de courte durée** = a short stay
* (of a cassette)
  **la durée** = the playing time
* (of a battery)
  **la durée** = the life
  **pile longue durée** = long-life battery

## durer verb [1]
  = to last

## duvet noun, masculine
* (for sleeping in)
  **un duvet** = a sleeping bag
* (feathers)
  **le duvet** = down

## dynamique adjective
  = dynamic

# Ee

## eau noun, feminine
(plural) **eaux**
  **l'eau** = water
  **l'eau gazeuse** = fizzy water, sparkling water
  **l'eau minérale** = mineral water
  **l'eau potable** = drinking water

## eau-de-vie noun, feminine
(plural) **eaux-de-vie**
  **l'eau-de-vie** = brandy

## éboueur noun, masculine
  **un éboueur** = a dustman, a garbage collector

## éboulement noun, masculine
  **un éboulement (de rochers)** = a rockfall

## écarlate adjective
  = scarlet

## écarter verb [1]
**1** (**!** + avoir)
* (to open) = to spread
  = to part
* (to remove) = to push aside
  = to move away
**2 s'écarter** (**!** + être)
  **s'écarter** = to move out of the way
  = to move away

## échafaudage noun, masculine
  **un échafaudage** = scaffolding

## échalote noun, feminine
  **une échalote** = a shallot

## échange
**1** noun, masculine
  **un échange** = an exchange
  **faire un échange** = to swap
**2 en échange (de)** = in exchange (for), in return (for)

## échanger verb [13]
  = to exchange

## échangeur noun, masculine
  **un échangeur** = an interchange, a clover junction

## échapper: s'échapper verb [1]
(**!** + être)
  **s'échapper** = to escape

## écharpe noun, feminine
  **une écharpe** = a scarf

## échasse noun, feminine
  **une échasse** = a stilt

## échauffer: s'échauffer verb [1]
(**!** + être)
  **s'échauffer** = to warm up

**échec**
1 *noun, masculine*
un óohoc = a failure
2 **échecs** *noun, masculine plural*
les échecs = chess

**échelle** *noun, feminine*
* (*a piece of equipment*)
une échelle = a ladder
faire la courte échelle à Roger = to give
Roger a leg-up
* (*on a map*)
l'échelle = the scale

**échiquier** *noun, masculine*
un échiquier = a chessboard

**échouer** *verb* 1
1 (**!** + *avoir*)
= to fail
échouer à un examen = to fail an
examination
2 **s'échouer** (**!** + *être*)
s'échouer = to run aground

**éclair** *noun, masculine*
* (*in the sky*)
un éclair = a flash of lightning
* (*a cake*)
un éclair = an éclair

**éclairage** *noun, masculine*
l'éclairage = the lighting

**éclaircie** *noun, feminine*
une éclaircie = a sunny spell

**éclairer** *verb* 1
1 (**!** + *avoir*)
* = to light
* = to give light
2 **s'éclairer** (**!** + *être*)
s'éclairer (*if it's a face, a screen*) = to light
up

**éclater** *verb* 1
(*if it's a tyre, a pipe*) = to burst
(*if it's a bomb*) = to explode
(*if it's a storm*) = to break
(*if it's war*) = to break out
éclater de rire = to burst out laughing

**école** *noun, feminine*
une école = a school
**une école libre** = an independent school
**une école maternelle** = a nursery school
(*for children aged 2 to 6*)
**une école primaire** = a primary school
(*for children aged 6 to 11*)
**une école secondaire** = a secondary
school (*for students aged 11 to 18*)
**une école publique** = a state school
(*in the US*) = a public school

**écolier/écolière** *noun,*
*masculine/feminine*
un écolier/une écolière = a schoolboy/a
schoolgirl

**écologie** *noun, feminine*
l'écologie = ecology

**écologiste** *noun, masculine/feminine*
* (*a scientist*)
un écologiste/une écologiste = an
ecologist
* (*a person who is against pollution*)
un écologiste/une écologiste = an
environmentalist

**économe** *adjective*
= thrifty

**économie** *noun, feminine*
une économie = a saving
faire des économies = to save up, to save
money

**écorce** *noun, feminine*
l'écorce (*on a tree*) = the bark
(*on an orange*) = the peel

**écossais/écossaise** *adjective*
* = Scottish
* une veste écossaise = a tartan jacket, a
plaid jacket

**Écosse** *noun, feminine*
l'Écosse = Scotland

**écouter** *verb* 1
= to listen to
écouter un disque = to listen to a record

**écran** *noun, masculine*
* (*on a television set*)
un écran = a screen
* (*protection from the sun*)
une crème écran total = a sun block

**écraser** *verb* 1
1 (**!** + *avoir*)
* = to crush
* = to run over
se faire écraser = to get run over
2 **s'écraser** (**!** + *être*)
s'écraser = to crash

**écrevisse** *noun, feminine*
une écrevisse = a crayfish, a crawfish

**écrire** *verb* 42
1 (**!** + *avoir*)
= to write
2 **s'écrire** (**!** + *être*)
* s'écrire = to write (to each other)
* s'écrire = to be spelled

**écriture** *noun, feminine*
* (*the activity*)
l'écriture = writing
* (*the way one writes*)
ton écriture = your handwriting

**écrivain** *noun, masculine*
un écrivain = a writer

**écrou** *noun, masculine*
un écrou = a nut

**écrouler: s'écrouler** *verb* 1 (**!** + *être*)
s'écrouler = to collapse

**écurie** *noun, feminine*
une écurie = a stable

**écusson** noun, masculine
un écusson (*on a garment*) = a (cloth) badge

**éducation** noun, feminine
• (*teaching*)
l'éducation = education
• (*politeness*)
l'éducation = manners
**l'éducation physique** = PE, physical education

**effacer** verb 12
= to erase
= to delete
effacer le tableau = to wipe the board, to erase the board

**effet**
1 noun, masculine
• (*result*)
un effet = an effect
n'avoir aucun effet = to have no effect
faire de l'effet = to be effective
• (*impact*)
un effet = an impression
faire bon effet = to make a good impression
ça m'a fait un drôle d'effet = it made me feel strange
2 **en effet** = indeed

**efficace** adjective
• = effective
• = efficient

**effondrer**: **s'effondrer** verb 1 (**!** + *être*)
s'effondrer = to collapse

**effort** noun, masculine
un effort = an effort

**effrayant/effrayante** adjective
= frightening

**effrayer** verb 21
= to frighten, to scare

**effronté/effrontée** adjective
= cheeky

**égal/égale** adjective
(*plural*) **égaux/égales**
= equal
ça m'est égal = I don't mind either way
= I don't care

**égaler** verb 1
= to be equal to

**égalité** noun, feminine
l'égalité = equality

**égarer** verb 1
1 (**!** + *avoir*)
= to lose
2 **s'égarer** (**!** + *être*)
s'égarer = to get lost

**église** noun, feminine
une église = a church

**égoïste** adjective
= selfish

**eh bien** exclamation
eh bien! = well!

**électricien/électricienne** noun,
masculine/feminine
un électricien/une électricienne = an electrician

**électroménager**
1 adjective, masculine
un appareil électroménager = an electrical household appliance
2 noun, masculine
l'électroménager = electrical household appliances

**électrophone** noun, masculine
un électrophone = a record player

**élégant/élégante** adjective
= elegant

**éléphant** noun, masculine
un éléphant = an elephant

**élève** noun, masculine/feminine
un élève/une élève = a pupil, a student

**élevé/élevée** adjective
• = high
• bien élevé = well brought-up, well-mannered
mal élevé = ill-mannered

**élever** verb 16
1 (**!** + *avoir*)
• (*if it's children*) = to bring up, to raise
• (*if it's animals*) = to breed
• (*if it's a wall, a statue*) = to erect, to raise
2 **s'élever** (**!** + *être*)
• s'élever = to rise
• s'élever à 500 euros = to add up to 500 euros

**éliminer** verb 1
• = to eliminate
= to knock out, to eliminate
être éliminé en quart de finale = to be knocked out in the quarter final
• = to rule out

**elle** pronoun, feminine
(*plural*) **elles**
• = she
= it
elles n'ont rien dit = they said nothing
elle est cassée = it's broken
• = her
à cause d'elle = because of her
la valise bleue est à elle = the blue suitcase is hers
c'est à elle de jouer = it's her turn to play
les livres sont pour elles = the books are for them

---

**✗** in informal situations

**elle-même** *pronoun, feminine*
(*plural*) **elles-mêmes**
= herself
= itself
**elles-mêmes** = themselves

**elles ▶ elle**

**éloigné/éloignée** *adjective*
= distant
éloigné de = far from

**éloigner: s'éloigner** *verb* 1 (**!** + *être*)
s'éloigner = to move away

**Élysée** *noun, masculine*
(le palais de) l'Élysée = the Élysée palace
(*the official residence of the French
President*)

**email** *noun, masculine*
un email = an email

**emballage** *noun, masculine*
l'emballage = the packaging
= the wrapping

**embarquer** *verb* 1
**1** (**!** + *avoir*)
• = to load
• = to board
**2 s'embarquer** (**!** + *être*)
s'embarquer = to board

**embêtant/embêtante** *adjective*
= annoying

**embêter** *verb* 1
**1** (**!** + *avoir*)
• = to annoy
= to pester
• ça m'embête d'y aller = I don't really want
to go
**2 s'embêter** (**!** + *être*)
s'embêter = to be bored

**emblée: d'emblée** *adverb*
d'emblée = right away, straightaway

**embouteillage** *noun, masculine*
un embouteillage = a traffic jam

**embrasser** *verb* 1
**1** (**!** + *avoir*)
= to kiss
**2 s'embrasser** (**!** + *être*)
s'embrasser = to kiss (each other)

**embrayage** *noun, masculine*
l'embrayage = the clutch

**émeute** *noun, feminine*
une émeute = a riot

**émigrer** *verb* 1
= to emigrate

**émission** *noun, feminine*
une émission = a broadcast, a
program(me)

**emménager** *verb* 13
= to move in

**emmener** *verb* 16
= to take
= to take away

**empêcher** *verb* 1
**1** (**!** + *avoir*)
• = to prevent
empêcher un enfant de sortir = to prevent
a child from going out
• (il) n'empêche que = nevertheless
**2 s'empêcher** (**!** + *être*)
je n'ai pas pu m'empêcher de rire
= I couldn't help laughing

**empiffrer: s'empiffrer\*** *verb* 1
(**!** + *être*)
s'empiffrer = to stuff oneself

**emplacement** *noun, masculine*
un emplacement (*for a building*) = a site
(*for a tent*) = a pitch
(*for a vehicle*) = a parking space

**emploi** *noun, masculine*
• (*a post*)
un emploi = a job
• (*the job market*)
l'emploi = employment
• (*of a word, a product*)
l'emploi = the use
**un emploi du temps** = a timetable

**employé/employée** *noun,
masculine/feminine*
un employé/une employée = an employee
**un employé de banque** = a bank clerk
**un employé de bureau** = an office
worker

**employer** *verb* 23
• = to employ
• = to use

**empoisonné/empoisonnée**
*adjective*
= poisoned

**emporter** *verb* 1
**1** (**!** + *avoir*)
• = to take
emporte un parapluie = take an umbrella
• = to take away
'plats à emporter' = 'take away food',
'food to go'
• = to sweep away
le pont a été emporté = the bridge has
been swept away
• l'emporter = to win
l'emporter sur = to get the better of, to
beat
**2 s'emporter** (**!** + *être*)
s'emporter = to lose one's temper

**empreinte** *noun, feminine*
une empreinte (*left by a foot*) = a footprint
les empreintes digitales = fingerprints

**emprunter** *verb* 1
= to borrow
emprunter de l'argent à la banque = to
borrow money from the bank

## en

! *You will find translations for phrases with* en *such as* en train de, s'en aller *etc at the entries* train, aller, *etc.*

**1** *preposition*
- = in
  vivre en France = to live in France
  en mai = in May
  faire le trajet en deux heures = to do the journey in two hours
- = to
  = into
  aller en Espagne = to go to Spain
  aller en ville = to go into town
  monter en voiture = to get into the car
- = by
  voyager en [train | bateau | voiture ...] = to travel by [train | boat | car ...]
- = made of
  c'est en bois = it's (made of) wood
  une chaîne en or = a gold chain
- (*showing that two things are done at the same time*) = while
  chanter en travaillant = to sing while working
  j'ai lu le journal en attendant = I read the paper while I was waiting
- (*showing the manner in which something is done*)
  sortir en courant = to run out
  se réveiller en pleurant = to wake up crying
  j'ai fini le travail en me levant tous les jours à six heures = I finished the work by getting up at six every day
- (*showing the circumstances in which something occurs*)
  il est tombé en traversant la rue = he fell as he was crossing the street
  tu t'es trompé en mesurant la pièce = you made a mistake when you measured the room

**2** *pronoun*
- = of it
  = of them
  il en boit beaucoup = he drinks a lot of it
  il y en a quatre = there are four (of them)
  combien en voulez-vous? (*if it's cheese*) = how much (of it) would you like?
  (*if it's cakes*) = how many (of them) would you like?
  je m'en souviens = I remember
- = some/any
  encore un peu de thé? il en reste = a little more tea? there's some left
  des roses? il n'y en a plus = roses? there aren't any left
- (*representing a place*)
  j'en arrive à l'instant = I've just got back from there

**enchanter** *verb* [1]
= to delight
  enchanté (de faire votre connaissance) = pleased to meet you

**enchères** *noun, feminine plural*
une vente aux enchères = an auction

**encombré/encombrée** *adjective*
  (*describing a street*) = congested
  (*describing a room, a cupboard*) = cluttered

**encombrement** *noun, masculine*
  l'encombrement (*on the road*) = traffic congestion

**encore** *adverb*
- = still
  tu es encore jeune = you're still young
- = again
  il a encore écrit = he's written again
- = more
  = another
  tu veux encore un peu de thé? = would you like some more tea?
  essaie encore une fois = try again
  encore un gâteau? = another cake?
- pas encore = not yet
  elle n'est pas encore arrivée = she hasn't arrived yet
- encore plus = even more
  c'est encore plus cher = it's even more expensive
  il fait encore plus chaud ici = it's even hotter here

**encourager** *verb* [13]
= to encourage

**encre** *noun, feminine*
  l'encre = ink

**endormi/endormie** *adjective*
= asleep

**endormir** *verb* [30]
**1** (! + *avoir*)
= to put to sleep
  la télévision m'endort = television puts me to sleep
**2 s'endormir** (! + *être*)
  s'endormir = to fall asleep
  = to get to sleep

**endroit** *noun, masculine*
- (*a spot*)
  un endroit = a place
  au bon endroit = in the right place
  par endroits = in places
  à quel endroit? = where?
- (*a side*)
  l'endroit = the right side
  à l'endroit = the right way round, the right way around

**énergie** *noun, feminine*
  l'énergie = energy

**énergique** *adjective*
= energetic

**énervé/énervée** *adjective*
= irritable
= on edge

**énerver** verb 1
**1** (! + avoir)
= to irritate
ça m'énerve = it irritates me, it gets on
my nerves
**2 s'énerver** (! + être)
s'énerver = to get irritable, to get annoyed

**enfance** noun, feminine
l'enfance = childhood

**enfant** noun, masculine/feminine
un enfant/une enfant = a child

**enfer** noun, masculine
l'enfer = Hell
un bruit d'enfer = a hell of a noise

**enfermer** verb 1
**1** (! + avoir)
= to lock up
**2 s'enfermer** (! + être)
s'enfermer = to lock oneself in

**enfin** adverb
• = finally
• = at last
• mais enfin, cesse de crier! = for heaven's
sake, stop shouting!

**enflammer**: **s'enflammer** verb 1
(! + être)
s'enflammer = to go up in flames
= to catch fire

**enfler** verb 1
= to swell (up)

**enfoncer** verb 12
**1** (! + avoir)
• = to push in
enfoncer un clou = to drive a nail in
enfoncer une épingle = to stick a pin in
enfoncer ses mains dans ses poches = to
dig one's hands into one's pockets
• enfoncer une porte = to break down a
door
**2 s'enfoncer** (! + être)
• s'enfoncer = to sink
s'enfoncer dans la boue = to sink in the
mud
s'enfoncer dans un fauteuil = to sink back
into an armchair
• s'enfoncer une épine dans le doigt = to get
a thorn in one's finger

**enfreindre** verb 55
enfreindre le règlement = to break the
rules

**enfuir**: **s'enfuir** verb 29 (! + être)
s'enfuir = to run away
= to escape

**engin** noun, masculine
• un engin = a device
• un engin = a vehicle

**engorger** verb 13
= to block
= to clog up

**enlever** verb 18
**1** (! + avoir)
• = to remove
• = to kidnap
**2 s'enlever** (! + être)
s'enlever = to come off

**enneigé/enneigée** adjective
= covered in snow

**ennui** noun, masculine
• un ennui = a problem
• l'ennui = boredom

**ennuyer** verb 22
**1** (! + avoir)
• = to bore
• = to bother
= to annoy
ça t'ennuie qu'il vienne? = do you mind if
he comes?
**2 s'ennuyer** (! + être)
s'ennuyer = to be bored

**ennuyeux/ennuyeuse** adjective
• = boring
• = tedious
• = annoying

**énorme** adjective
= huge, enormous

**énormément** adverb
= tremendously, immensely

**enquête** noun, feminine
• (into a crime)
une enquête = an inquiry, an
investigation
• (on opinions, lifestyles)
une enquête = a survey

**enquêteur/enquêtrice** noun,
masculine/feminine
un enquêteur/une enquêtrice = an
investigator

**enregistrement** noun, masculine
• (for sound)
un enregistrement = a recording
• (for air passengers)
l'enregistrement = checking-in

**enregistrer** verb 1
• (if it's sound, statistics) = to record
• (if it's luggage) = to register
(at an airport) = to check in

**enrhumer**: **s'enrhumer** verb 1
(! + être)
s'enrhumer = to catch a cold
être enrhumé = to have a cold

**enseignant/enseignante** noun,
masculine/feminine
un enseignant/une enseignante = a
teacher

**enseigne** noun, feminine
une enseigne = a sign

**enseignement** noun, masculine
• (as a career)
  l'enseignement = teaching
• (a system)
  l'enseignement = education
  l'enseignement par correspondance
  = correspondence courses

**ensemble**
1 adverb
  = together
2 noun, masculine
• (clothes)
  un ensemble = an outfit
  = a lady's suit
• (the entirety)
  l'ensemble = the whole
  = all
  une vue d'ensemble = an overall view
• (a collection)
  un ensemble = a set
  = a group
  un grand ensemble = a high-density
  housing complex, a high-rise housing
  complex
3 dans l'ensemble = on the whole

**ensoleillé/ensoleillée** adjective
  = sunny

**ensuite** adverb
  = then
  = later
  = next

**entendre** verb 6
1 (! + avoir)
  = to hear
  j'ai entendu dire qu'il était de retour = I've
  heard that he's back
  as-tu entendu parler de ce film? = have
  you heard about this film?
2 s'entendre (! + être)
  s'entendre = to get on, to get along
  elles s'entendent bien = they get on well,
  they get along well

**entendu/entendue**
1 ▶ entendre 6
2 adjective
  = agreed
  entendu! = OK then!
3 bien entendu = of course

**enterrement** noun, masculine
  un enterrement = a funeral

**enterrer** verb 1
  = to bury

**enthousiasmer** verb 1
1 (! + avoir)
  = to fill with enthusiasm
2 s'enthousiasmer (! + être)
  s'enthousiasmer = to get enthusiastic

**enthousiaste** adjective
  = enthusiastic

**entier/entière** adjective
  = whole, entire

**entourer** verb 1
• = to surround
  des collines entourent la ville = the town
  is surrounded by hills
  un jardin entouré d'une haie = a garden
  surrounded by a hedge
• = to circle
  entourer une date en rouge = to circle a
  date in red
• entourer son doigt d'un mouchoir = to put
  a handkerchief round one's finger

**entracte** noun, masculine
  un entracte = an interval, an intermission

**entraînement** noun, masculine
  l'entraînement (for an athlete) = training
  (for a musician) = practice

**entraîner** verb 1
1 (! + avoir)
• = to lead to
  entraîner des problèmes = to lead to
  problems, to cause problems
• = to drag along
  entraîner un ami à la plage = to drag a
  friend along to the beach
• = to coach, to train
  entraîner une équipe = to coach a team
2 s'entraîner (! + être)
  s'entraîner = to train
  = to practise, to practice

**entraîneur** noun, masculine
  un entraîneur = a coach

**entre** preposition
  = between
  l'un d'entre eux = one of them

**entrée** noun, feminine
• (way in)
  l'entrée = the entrance
  = the (entrance) hall
• (access)
  l'entrée = entry
  = admission
  'entrée interdite' = 'no entry', 'do not
  enter'
  'entrée gratuite' = 'free admission'
• (on a menu)
  une entrée = a starter, an appetizer

**entreprise** noun, feminine
  une entreprise = a firm
  = a company

**entrer** verb 1 (! + être)
  = to enter, to go in
  = to enter, to come in
  entrez! = come in!
  entrer dans la cuisine = to go into the
  kitchen
  = to come into the kitchen

**entretien** noun, masculine
• un entretien (a conversation) = a
  discussion
  (for a job) = an interview

- l'entretien (of a house, a garden) = the upkeep, the maintenance
  (of clothes, furniture) = the care

**enveloppe** noun, feminine
une enveloppe = an envelope

**envelopper** verb [1]
= to wrap

**envers**
**1** preposition
= toward, towards, to
**2** noun, masculine (! never changes)
l'envers = the back
= the wrong side
= the reverse
**3 à l'envers** = the wrong way

**envie** noun, feminine
une envie = a desire
avoir envie de pleurer = to want to cry, to feel like crying

**environ** adverb
= about

**environs** noun, masculine plural
les environs = the surrounding area

**envoler: s'envoler** verb [1] (! + être)
s'envoler (if it's a bird) = to fly away
(if it's a plane) = to take off

**envoyer** verb [24]
- = to send
- = to throw

**épais/épaisse** adjective
= thick

**épaule** noun, feminine
une épaule = a shoulder

**épeler** verb [19]
= to spell

**épice** noun, feminine
une épice = a spice

**épicerie** noun, feminine
une épicerie = a grocer's, a grocery store

**épicier/épicière** noun,
masculine/feminine
un épicier/une épicière = a grocer

**épinards** noun, masculine plural
des épinards = spinach

**épine** noun, feminine
une épine = a thorn

**épingle** noun, feminine
une épingle = a pin
une épingle à nourrice, une épingle
de sûreté = a safety pin

**épisode** noun, masculine
un épisode = an episode
un roman à épisodes = a serialized novel

**éplucher** verb [1]
= to peel

**épluchure** noun, feminine
des épluchures = peelings

**éponge** noun, feminine
- (a type of material)
  l'éponge = (terry-)towelling, terrycloth
- (a sea creature)
  une éponge = a sponge

**époque** noun, feminine
une époque = a period, an era
à notre époque = nowadays, in our times
à l'époque = at the time

**épouse** noun, feminine
une épouse = a wife

**épouser** verb [1]
= to marry

**épouvantable** adjective
= dreadful

**épouvante** noun, feminine
l'épouvante = terror
= horror
un film d'épouvante = a horror film, a horror movie

**époux** (! never changes)
**1** noun, masculine singular
un époux = a husband
**2** noun, masculine plural
les époux = the (married) couple
les jeunes époux = the newly weds

**épreuve** noun, feminine
une épreuve (at school) = an examination
(in sport) = an event

**éprouver** verb [1]
= to feel

**EPS** noun, feminine (! never changes)
l'EPS = PE

**épuisé/épuisée** adjective
= exhausted

**équateur** noun, masculine
l'équateur = the equator

**équilibre** noun, masculine
l'équilibre = balance
perdre l'équilibre = to lose one's balance
en équilibre = balanced

**équilibrer** verb [1]
= to balance

**équipage** noun, masculine
un équipage = a crew

**équipe** noun, feminine
- (of players, workers)
  une équipe = a team
- (in a factory)
  l'équipe de nuit = the night shift

**équipement** noun, masculine
l'équipement = the equipment

**équitation** noun, feminine
l'équitation = (horse-)riding

E

**erreur** noun, feminine
une erreur = a mistake

**es** ▶ **être** 7

**escalade** noun, feminine
l'escalade = rock climbing

**escalader** verb 1
= to climb

**escalier** noun, masculine
• un escalier = a staircase
= (a flight of) stairs
• les escaliers = the stairs
un **escalier roulant** = an escalator

**escargot** noun, masculine
un escargot = a snail

**esclave** noun, masculine/feminine
un esclave/une esclave = a slave

**escrime** noun, feminine
l'escrime = fencing

**escroc** noun, masculine
un escroc = a crook

**espace** noun, masculine
• l'espace = space
• un espace = a space, a gap
un **espace vert** = an open space, a green
area, a park

**Espagne** noun, feminine
l'Espagne = Spain

**espagnol/espagnole**
**1** adjective
= Spanish
**2 espagnol** noun, masculine
l'espagnol = Spanish

**espèce** noun, feminine
• (a sort)
une espèce de roue = a kind of wheel
• (a group of animals or plants)
une espèce = a species

**espérer** verb 14
= to hope (for)

**espionnage** noun, masculine
l'espionnage = espionage, spying

**esquimau/esquimaude**
(plural) **esquimaux/esquimaudes**
**1** adjective
= Eskimo
**2 esquimau** noun, masculine
un esquimau = a choc-ice, an ice cream
bar

**essayer** verb 21
• = to try
essayer d'ouvrir la porte = to try to open
the door
• = to try on
essayer un chapeau = to try on a hat

**essence** noun, feminine
l'essence = petrol, gas(oline)

l'**essence sans plomb** = unleaded petrol,
unleaded gas

**essorage** noun, masculine
l'essorage = spinning

**essuie-glace** noun, masculine
(plural) **essuie-glaces**
un essuie-glace = a windscreen wiper, a
windshield wiper

**essuyer** verb 22
**1** (! + avoir)
• = to dry
• = to wipe (up)
**2 s'essuyer** (! + être)
s'essuyer = to wipe oneself
= to dry oneself
s'essuyer les mains = to wipe one's hands

**est¹** ▶ **être** 7

**est²**
**1** noun, masculine
l'est = the east
**2** adjective (! never changes)
= east
= eastern

**est-ce que** ▶ **être** 7

**estivant/estivante** noun,
masculine/feminine
un estivant/une estivante = a summer
visitor

**estomac** noun, masculine
l'estomac = the stomach

**et** conjunction
= and
et avec ceci? = anything else?

**étage** noun, masculine
un étage = a floor, a story
habiter au premier étage (in Britain) = to
live on the first floor
(in the US) = to live on the second floor
à l'étage = upstairs

**étagère** noun, feminine
une étagère (a flat piece of wood, glass)
= a shelf
(a piece of furniture) = a bookshelf

**étais** ▶ **être** 7

**étaler** verb 1
= to spread (out)

**étang** noun, masculine
un étang = a pond

**étant** ▶ **être** 7

**étape** noun, feminine
• (a place)
une étape = a stop
faire étape à Nice = to stop in Nice
• (part of a journey)
une étape = a stage
(in a race) = a leg

**état** noun, masculine
un état = a state

**États-Unis** noun, masculine plural
les États-Unis = the United States

**été**
1 ▶ être [7]
2 noun, masculine
l'été = summer

**éteindre** verb [55]
1 (! + avoir)
* = to put out
* = to switch off, to turn off
2 s'éteindre (! + être)
* s'éteindre = to go out
* s'éteindre = to go off

**éteint/éteinte** ▶ éteindre [55]

**étendre** verb [6]
1 (! + avoir)
* (to put down flat)
étendre une nappe = to spread out a
tablecloth
* (to put out to dry)
étendre le linge = to hang out the
washing, to hang out the laundry
2 s'étendre (! + être)
* (if it's a person)
s'étendre = to lie down
* (if it's land)
s'étendre = to stretch
* (if it's a conflict)
s'étendre = to spread

**étendu/étendue¹**
1 ▶ étendre [6]
2 adjective
= extensive

**étendue²** noun, feminine
* (of land, water)
une étendue = an expanse
= a stretch
* (of a disaster)
l'étendue = the scale, the size

**éternuer** verb [1]
= to sneeze

**êtes** ▶ être [7]

**étiquette** noun, feminine
une étiquette = a label
= a tag

**étirer**; **s'étirer** verb [1] (! + être)
s'étirer = to stretch

**étoile** noun, feminine
une étoile = a star

**étonnant/étonnante** adjective
= surprising
= amazing

**étonner** verb [1]
1 (! + avoir)
= to surprise
2 s'étonner (! + être)
s'étonner = to be surprised

**étouffant/étouffante** adjective
= stifling

**étouffer** verb [1]
1 (! + avoir)
* = to smother
* = to suffocate
on étouffe ici! = it's stifling in here!
2 s'étouffer (! + être)
s'étouffer = to choke

**étourdi/étourdie** adjective
= scatterbrained

**étrange** adjective
= strange

**étranger/étrangère**
1 adjective
= foreign
2 noun, masculine|feminine
un étranger/une étrangère (from another
country) = a foreigner
(an unknown person) = a stranger
3 à l'étranger = abroad

**être** verb [7] (! + avoir)
▶ 64 | See the boxed note.

**étroit/étroite** adjective
= narrow

**étude**
1 noun, feminine
* (an activity)
l'étude = study
* (a room in a school)
l'étude = the study room, the study hall
* (on the school timetable)
'étude' = 'private study', 'study hall'
2 études noun, feminine plural
les études = studies, higher education
faire des études = to study, to be a student

**étudiant/étudiante** noun,
masculine|feminine
un étudiant/une étudiante = a student

**étudier** verb [2]
* = to study
* = to examine

**étui** noun, masculine
un étui = a case
un étui à lunettes = a glasses case

**eu/eue** ▶ avoir [8]

**euro** noun, masculine
un euro = a euro

**Europe** noun, feminine
l'Europe = Europe

**européen/européenne** adjective
= European

**eux** pronoun
* = them
à cause d'eux = because of them

E

# être verb 7

| present | imperfect | future | past participle |
|---------|-----------|--------|-----------------|
| je suis | j'étais | je serai | été |
| tu es | tu étais | tu seras | |
| il / elle est | il / elle était | il / elle sera | |
| nous sommes | nous étions | nous serons | |
| vous êtes | vous étiez | vous serez | |
| ils / elles sont | ils / elles étaient | ils / elles seront | |

**1 être** functions as an ordinary verb:
* (*showing a quality or state*) = to be
  - je **suis** fatigué = *I'm tired*
  - le ciel **est** bleu = *the sky is blue*
  - elle **est** fatiguée = *she is tired*
  - **sois** sage! = *be good!*
  - ils **ont été** malades = *they've been ill*
* (*showing ownership*)
  - la maison **est** à Pierre = *the house belongs to Pierre, the house is Pierre's*
  - à qui **sont** ces gants? = *who do these gloves belong to, whose gloves are they?*
  - ils **sont** à moi = *they belong to me, they're mine*

**2 être** is used as an auxiliary verb to conjugate some verbs, notably reflexive verbs and a few others, all of which are labelled (**!** + *être*):
  - je **suis** né en Italie = *I was born in Italy*
  - elle n'**est** pas encore rentrée = *she hasn't come home yet*
  - ils **sont** partis = *they've left*
  - tu t'**es** lavé les mains? = *did you wash your hands?*

**3 être** is used to form questions in the phrase **est-ce que**:
  - **est-ce que** tu aimes le jazz? = *do you like jazz?*
  - **est-ce qu'**il fait froid? = *is it cold?*
  - **est-ce que** tu viendras? = *will you come?*
  - **est-ce qu'**ils ont fini? = *have they finished?*
  - **est-ce que** tu as de l'argent? = *have you got any money?*

---

* (*indicating possession, turn*)
  **le chien est à eux** = the dog is theirs
  **c'est à eux de jouer** = it's their turn to play
* (*when used for emphasis*) = they
  **je suis resté, mais eux sont partis** = I stayed but they left

**eux-mêmes** *pronoun*
  = themselves

**évaluer** *verb* 1
* = to assess
* = to estimate
* = to value

**évanouir**: **s'évanouir** *verb* 3 (**!** + *être*)
  s'évanouir = to faint

**évasion** *noun, feminine*
  une évasion = an escape

**événement** *noun, masculine*
  un événement = an event

**éventail** *noun, masculine*
  un éventail = a fan

**éventuellement** *adverb*
* = possibly
* = if necessary

**évidemment** *adverb*
  = obviously
  = of course

**évident/évidente** *adjective*
  = obvious

**évier** *noun, masculine*
  un évier = a (kitchen) sink

**éviter** *verb* 1
  = to avoid

**exact/exacte** *adjective*
* = correct
* = exact

---

**✘** in informal situations

**exactement** adverb
= exactly

**exagérer** verb 14
= to exaggerate

**examen** noun, masculine
* (for pupils, students)
un examen = an examination, an exam, a test
passer un examen = to take an exam
réussir à un examen = to pass an exam
* (by a doctor)
un examen = an examination

**examiner** verb 1
= to examine

**excursion** noun, feminine
une excursion = an excursion, a trip
faire une excursion = to go on an excursion

**excuse** noun, feminine
* (a reason)
une excuse = an excuse
* (when saying that one is sorry)
des excuses = an apology
présenter des excuses = to apologize

**excuser** verb 1
1 (! + avoir)
= to excuse
excusez-moi (when apologizing) = I'm sorry
(when interrupting) = excuse me
2 s'excuser (! + être)
s'excuser = to apologize

**exemple** noun, masculine
un exemple = an example
par exemple = for example, for instance

**exercer; s'exercer** verb 12 (! + être)
s'exercer = to practise, to practice
s'exercer à sauter à la corde = to practise skipping

**exercice** noun, masculine
un exercice = an exercise

**exiger** verb 13
= to demand
= to require

**expédier** verb 2
= to send

**expéditeur/expéditrice** noun, masculine/feminine
un expéditeur/une expéditrice = a sender

**expérience** noun, feminine
* (skill, knowledge)
l'expérience = experience
* (a test)
une expérience = an experiment

**expliquer** verb 1
= to explain

**explorateur/exploratrice** noun, masculine/feminine
un explorateur/une exploratrice = an explorer

**exploser** verb 1
= to explode

**exposer** verb 1
* (in a shop window) = to display
* (in a gallery) = to exhibit
* (to the sun, to a danger) = to expose

**exposition** noun, feminine
une exposition = an exhibition

**exprès** adverb
= on purpose

**express** noun, masculine (! never changes)
un express = an express, a fast train

**exprimer** verb 1
= to express

**extérieur/extérieure**
1 adjective
= outside
2 extérieur noun, masculine
l'extérieur = the outside
à l'extérieur de la boîte = outside the box

**externe**
1 adjective
= external
2 noun, masculine/feminine
un externe/une externe = a day pupil, a day student

**extra** adjective
= first-class, great

**extrait** noun, masculine
un extrait = an extract

# Ff

**fabrication** noun, feminine
la fabrication = manufacture

**fabriquer** verb 1
* = to make, to manufacture
* qu'est-ce que tu fabriques*? = what are you up to?

**façade** noun, feminine
la façade = the front

**face**
1 noun, feminine
la face (on a box) = the side
(of a coin) = the heads side
pile ou face = heads or tails

**2 de face** = from the front
**3 en face (de)** = opposite

**fâcher: se fâcher** *verb* [1]
  se fâcher = to get angry

**facile** *adjective*
  = easy

**facilement** *adverb*
  = easily

**façon** *noun, feminine*
  une façon = a way
  la façon dont il parle = the way he talks
  de toute façon = anyway

**façonner** *verb* [1]
  = to shape, to mould

**facteur/factrice** *noun,*
*masculine/feminine*
  un facteur/une factrice = a postman/a
  postwoman, a mail carrier

**facture** *noun, feminine*
  une facture = a bill, an invoice

**faible** *adjective*
  = weak

**faillir** *verb* [28]
  j'ai failli y aller = I (very) nearly went, I
  almost went

**faim** *noun, feminine*
  la faim = hunger
  avoir faim = to be hungry

**fainéant/fainéante** *adjective*
  = lazy

**faire** *verb* [10]

  **!** *You will find translations for phrases with*
  faire *such as* faire attention, faire le clown,
  faire pousser *etc under the words*
  attention, clown, pousser *etc.*

**1** (**!** + *avoir*)
• = to make
  faire [un gâteau | un effort | une faute …] = to
  make [a cake | an effort | a mistake …]
• = to do
  faire [la vaisselle | ses devoirs | un travail …]
  = to do [the dishes | one's homework | a job …]
  que fait-il? (*for a living*) = what does he do?
  (*at this very moment*) = what's he doing?
• = to go
  faire [de l'escalade | du vélo | des courses …]
  = to go [climbing | cycling | shopping …]
• (*when talking about the weather*)
  il fait [chaud | gris | du vent …] = it's [hot |
  overcast | windy …]
  il faisait 30° à l'ombre = it was 30° in the
  shade
  il fera beau demain = the weather will be
  fine tomorrow

• (*when talking about a particular length of
  time*)
  ça fait deux heures que j'attends = I've
  been waiting for two hours
  ça fait longtemps qu'il est parti = he left a
  long time ago
• (*when talking about measurements*)
  faire 1,75 m = to be 1.75 m tall
  faire du 42 = to take a size 42
• (*to cause something to happen*)
  il m'a fait [tomber | manquer le train |
  travailler …] = he made me [fall | miss the
  train | work …]
• (*to get something done*)
  faire nettoyer une veste = to have a jacket
  cleaned
• (*some other uses*)
  ça ne fait rien = it doesn't matter
  qu'est-ce que ça peut bien te faire?
  = what's it to you?
  fais comme tu veux = do as you like
  faites comme chez vous = make yourself
  at home
**2 se faire** (**!** + *être*)
• (*to do something for oneself*)
  se faire = to make
  elle s'est fait du café = she made herself
  some coffee
  se faire des amis = to make friends
  se faire comprendre = to make oneself
  understood
• (*to get someone to do something for you*)
  se faire couper les cheveux = to have one's
  hair cut
  elle s'est fait faire une robe = she's had a
  dress made
• (*when something is done to you*)
  se faire [attraper | menacer | écraser …] = to be
  [caught | threatened | run over …]
• (*other uses*)
  ça ne se fait pas = it isn't the done thing,
  it isn't the thing to do
**3 s'en faire** (**!** + *être*)
  s'en faire = to worry
  ne t'en fais pas = don't worry

**faire-part** *noun, masculine* (**!** *never
changes*)
  un faire-part = an announcement card

**fais ▶ faire** [10]

**faisable** *adjective*
  = feasible
  c'est faisable = it can be done

**faisais ▶ faire** [10]

**faisan** *noun, masculine*
  un faisan = a pheasant

**faisons ▶ faire** [10]

**fait/faite**
**1 ▶ faire** [10]
**2** *adjective*
• = done
  un travail bien fait = a job well done
  c'est bien fait pour lui! = it serves him
  right!

- tout fait = ready-made
  des rideaux tout faits = ready-made
  curtains, store-bought drapes
- c'est fait pour nettoyer les vitres = it's
  meant for cleaning windows
**3 fait** noun, masculine
  un fait = a fact
**4 au fait** = by the way
**5 en fait** = in fact
**un fait divers** = a (short) news item

**faites ▶ faire** ⑩

**falaise** noun, feminine
  une falaise = a cliff

**falloir** verb ⑩
  il faut une clé pour ouvrir la porte = you
  need a key to open the door
  il me fallait de l'argent = I needed some
  money
  allons, il faut partir = come on, we've got to
  go
  il ne faut jamais arriver en retard = one
  must never be late
  achète ce qu'il faut pour le jardin = buy
  whatever is necessary for the garden
  il le fallait = it was necessary
  il faudra que tu ailles au garage = you will
  have to go to the garage
  il va falloir que vous le fassiez = you will
  have to do it

**fallu ▶ falloir** ⑩

**familial/familiale** adjective
(plural) **familiaux/familiales**
  = family

**familier/familière** adjective
  = familiar

**famille** noun, feminine
  une famille = a family
  en famille = with the family
  = as a family

**fana*** noun, masculine/feminine
  un fana*/une fana* = a fanatic

**fantastique** adjective
  = fantastic

**fantôme** noun, masculine
  un fantôme = a ghost

**farce** noun, feminine
- (a trick)
  une farce = a practical joke
- (in cooking)
  la farce = the stuffing

**farci/farcie** adjective
  = stuffed

**fard** noun, masculine
  le fard = make-up

**farfelu/farfelue*** adjective
- = scatterbrained
- = eccentric

**farine** noun, feminine
  la farine = flour

**fasse ▶ faire** ⑩

**fatigant/fatigante** adjective
  = tiring

**fatigue** noun, feminine
  la fatigue = tiredness

**fatigué/fatiguée**
  = tired

**fauché/fauchée*** adjective
  = broke

**faudra ▶ falloir** ⑤

**faune** noun, feminine
  la faune = wildlife

**fausse ▶ faux**

**faut ▶ falloir** ⑤

**faute** noun, feminine
- (an error)
  une faute = a mistake
- (responsibility)
  c'est (de) ta faute = it's your fault

**fauteuil** noun, masculine
  un fauteuil = an armchair
**un fauteuil roulant** = a wheelchair

**faux/fausse**
**1** adjective
- (not right) = wrong
- (not genuine) = false
  = fake
**2 faux** adverb
  chanter faux = to sing out of tune

**favori/favorite** adjective
  = favo(u)rite

**féculent** noun, masculine
  un féculent = a starchy food

**fêlé/fêlée** adjective
  = cracked

**félicitations** noun, feminine plural
  des félicitations = congratulations

**femme** noun, feminine
  une femme = a woman
  = a wife
**une femme d'affaires** = a businesswoman
**une femme de ménage** = a cleaning lady

**fenêtre** noun, feminine
  une fenêtre = a window

**fente** noun, feminine
  une fente (for a coin) = a slot
  (in a wall) = a crack
  (in a mask) = a slit

**fer** noun, masculine
  le fer = iron
  un fer à repasser = an iron

F

**ferai** ▶ **faire** 50

**férié/fériée** *adjective*
un jour férié = a public holiday, a holiday

**ferme** *noun, feminine*
une ferme = a farm

**fermer** *verb* 1
= to close, to shut

**fermeture** *noun, feminine*
• (*of a shop*)
la fermeture = closing (down)
'fermeture annuelle' = 'annual closing'
• (*a device*)
une fermeture = a fastener
**une fermeture éclair** = a zip(per)

**fermier/fermière** *noun,
masculine/feminine*
un fermier/une fermière = a farmer

**féroce** *adjective*
= fierce

**ferroviaire** *adjective*
= rail, railroad

**fesse** *noun, feminine*
une fesse = a buttock

**fête** *noun, feminine*
• (*a special day in a country*)
une fête = a public holiday, a holiday
• (*a special day for a person*)
ma fête = my (saint's) name-day
bonne fête! = happy saint's day!
• (*an organized event*)
une fête = a festival
• (*at home*) = a celebration
= a party
faire une fête = to have a party
**une fête foraine** = a funfair, a carnival
**la fête des Mères** = Mother's day
(*celebrated in France on the last Sunday in
May*)
**la fête du travail** = May Day

**fêter** *verb* 1
= to celebrate

**feu** *noun, masculine*
(*plural* **feux**)
• (*flames*)
un feu = a fire
mettre le feu à une maison = to set fire to
a house
au feu! = fire!
en feu = on fire
• (*the flame from a match or a lighter*)
du feu = a light
demander du feu = to ask for a light
• (*on a car, in the street*)
un feu = a light
les feux = the traffic lights
**un feu d'artifice** = a fireworks display
**les feux de détresse** = hazard lights

**les feux de signalisation, les feux
tricolores** = the traffic lights

**feuille** *noun, feminine*
• (*on a tree*)
une feuille = a leaf
• (*paper*)
une feuille = a sheet

**feuilleter** *verb* 20
= to flick through

**feuilleton** *noun, masculine*
un feuilleton = a serial
= a soap opera

**feutre** *noun, masculine*
un feutre = a felt-tip pen

**fève** *noun, feminine*
• une fève = a broad bean, a fava bean
• une fève = a lucky charm (*hidden in the
galette des rois*)

**février** *noun, masculine*
février = February

**fiançailles** *noun, feminine plural*
des fiançailles = an engagement

**fiancer: se fiancer** *verb* 12 (**!** + *être*)
se fiancer = to get engaged

**ficelle** *noun, feminine*
• (*around a parcel*)
de la ficelle = string
• (*bread*)
une ficelle = a thin baguette

**fiche** *noun, feminine*
une fiche = a form
= card

**ficher\*** *verb* 1
**1** (**!** + *avoir*)
• = to do
il n'a rien fiché\* *or* fichu\* de la journée
= he's done nothing all day
• ficher\* à la poubelle = to bin, to throw out
• fiche-moi la paix\*! = leave me alone!
**2 se ficher\*** (**!** + *être*)
• se ficher de quelqu'un\*
(*to mock*) = to make fun of someone
(*to lack consideration*) = to mess someone
around
• je m'en fiche\* = I couldn't care less
je me fiche\* de ce qu'on dit = I couldn't
care less what people say

**fichu/fichue\***
**1** ▶ **ficher** 1
**2** *adjective*
• = rotten, nasty
avoir un fichu\* caractère = to have a nasty
temper
• = done for
ma voiture est fichue\* = my car's had it
s'il pleut c'est fichu\* = if it rains that's the
end of that
• être fichu\* de faire = to be capable of
doing

---

**\*** in informal situations

**fidèle** *adjective*
– faithful

**fier/fière** *adjective*
= proud

**fièvre** *noun, feminine*
une fièvre = a fever
avoir de la fièvre = to have a temperature

**fiévreux/fiévreuse** *adjective*
= feverish

**figue** *noun, feminine*
une figue = a fig

**figure** *noun, feminine*
• la figure = the face
• une figure = a figure
= a diagram

**figurer** *verb* 1
**1** (! + *avoir*)
= to appear, to feature
figurer sur une liste = to appear on a list
**2 se figurer** (! + *être*)
se figurer = to think, to imagine

**fil** *noun, masculine*
• (*for sewing*)
le fil = thread
• (*connecting a telephone*)
un fil = a wire
un coup de fil = a phone call
passe-moi un coup de fil = give me a call
**le fil de fer** = wire
**sans fil** = wireless

**file** *noun, feminine*
• (*a row of people or cars*)
une file = a line
(*at a cinema, a bus stop, a store*)
une file d'attente = a queue, a line
• (*part of a road*)
une file = a lane

**filer*** *verb* 1
• (*to leave*)✖ = to go off
• (*to escape*)✖ = to get away

**filet** *noun, masculine*
un filet = a net
**un filet à provisions** = a string bag

**fille** *noun, feminine*
une fille = a girl
= a daughter

**fillette** *noun, feminine*
une fillette = a little girl

**filleul/filleule** *noun, masculine/feminine*
un filleul/une filleule = a godson/a
goddaughter

**film** *noun, masculine*
un film = a film, a movie
**un film d'animation** = a cartoon (film)
**un film policier** = a detective film

**fils** *noun, masculine* (! *never changes*)
un fils = a son

**fin¹** *noun, feminine*
la fin = the end
en fin de matinée = late in the morning
en fin de compte = in the end, finally

**fin²/fine** *adjective*
= thin
= slender
= fine

**finalement** *adverb*
= finally, in the end

**finir** *verb* 3
• = to finish
j'ai fini d'écrire = I've finished writing
• = to end
Il a fini par avoir un accident = he ended
up having an accident
l'histoire finit bien = the story has a happy
ending

**fioul** *noun, masculine*
le fioul = fuel oil

**firme** *noun, feminine*
une firme = a firm

**fixe** *adjective*
un prix fixe = a fixed price
une résidence fixe = a permanent address
manger à heure fixe = to eat at a set time

**flamme** *noun, feminine*
une flamme = a flame

**flan** *noun, masculine*
un flan ≈ custard
= a custard tart, a custard flan

**flâner** *verb* 1
= to stroll

**flaque** *noun, feminine*
une flaque = a puddle

**flèche** *noun, feminine*
une flèche = an arrow

**fléchette** *noun, feminine*
une fléchette = a dart

**fleur** *noun, feminine*
une fleur = a flower

**fleuriste** *noun, masculine/feminine*
un fleuriste/une fleuriste = a florist

**fleuve** *noun, masculine*
un fleuve = a (large) river

**flic*** *noun, masculine*
un flic✖ = a cop, a policeman

**flipper** *noun, masculine*
le flipper (*the machine*) = the pinball
machine
(*the device in the machine*) = the flipper
(*the game*) = pinball

**flocon** *noun, masculine*
un flocon de neige = a snowflake

**flotter** *verb* 1
= to float

**F**

**flotteur** *noun, masculine*
un flotteur = a float

**fluo** *adjective* (**!** *never changes*)
= fluorescent

**fluorescent/fluorescente** *adjective*
= fluorescent

**flûte** *noun, feminine*
• (*an instrument*)
une flûte = a flute
une flûte à bec = a recorder
• (*bread*)
une flûte = a French stick, French bread

**foie** *noun, masculine*
le foie = (the) liver

**foire** *noun, feminine*
une foire = a fair
= a trade fair

**fois**
**1** *noun, feminine* (**!** *never changes*)
encore une fois = one more time
une fois = once
deux fois = twice
trois fois = three times
une fois qu'il aura fini = once he's finished
une fois pour toutes = once and for all
**2 à la fois** = at the same time
= at once
**3 des fois*** = sometimes

**folklorique** *adjective*
= folk

**folle ▶ fou**

**foncé/foncée** *adjective*
= dark

**foncer** *verb* 12
foncer sur quelqu'un = to charge at
someone

**fonctionnaire** *noun, masculine/feminine*
un fonctionnaire/une fonctionnaire = a
civil servant

**fonctionner** *verb* 1
= to work

**fond**
**1** *noun, masculine*
• (*the deepest part*)
le fond = the bottom
au fond du verre = at the bottom of the
glass
• (*the furthest part*)
le fond (*of a cupboard, a shop*) = the back
(*of a room, a yard*) = the far end
(*on a picture*) = the background
**2 à fond**
respirer à fond = to breathe deeply
appuyer à fond = to press hard

**3 au fond, dans le fond**
au fond, ce n'est pas bête = it's a rather
good idea
dans le fond, il a raison = he's right, really
**un fond de teint** = a foundation, a make-
up base

**fonder** *verb* 1
= to found

**fondre** *verb* 6
= to melt
faire fondre = to melt

**fondu/fondue** *adjective*
= melted

**font ▶ faire** 10

**fontaine** *noun, feminine*
une fontaine = a fountain

**foot*** *noun, masculine*
le foot* = football, soccer

**football** *noun, masculine*
le football = football, soccer

**footing** *noun, masculine*
le footing = jogging

**force**
**1** *noun, feminine*
• (*energy*)
la force = strength
avoir de la force = to be strong
• (*violence*)
la force = force
de force = by force
**2 à force de**
réussir à force de travailler = to succeed by
dint of hard work
j'ai mal au bras à force d'écrire = I've done
so much writing that my arm hurts

**forcer** *verb* 12
**1** (**!** + *avoir*)
= to force
forcer un enfant à manger = to force a
child to eat
**2 se forcer** (**!** + *être*)
se forcer = to force oneself

**forêt** *noun, feminine*
une forêt = a forest

**forfaitaire** *adjective*
= inclusive

**forgeron** *noun, masculine*
un forgeron = a blacksmith

**formation** *noun, feminine*
• (*the learning of skills*)
la formation = training
• (*the process of creating or developing*)
la formation = the formation

---

**forme** *noun, feminine*
* (*an outline*)
  une forme = a shape
  = a form
  en forme de I = I-shaped
* (*a person's energy*)
  avoir la forme = to be in good form
  être en (pleine) forme = to be in (very)
    good form

**former** *verb* $\boxed{1}$
* = to form
* = to train

**formidable** *adjective*
* = tremendous
* = great

**formulaire** *noun, masculine*
  un formulaire = a form

**fort/forte**
**1** *adjective*
* (*not weak*) = strong
* (*not slim*) = stout
  = broad
* (*not soft*) = loud
* (*not slight*)
  de fortes pluies = heavy rain
  une forte chaleur = intense heat
  une forte pente = a steep slope
* (*gifted*)
  fort en = good at
  être fort en chimie = to be good at
    chemistry
**2 fort** *adverb*
* = hard
  taper fort = to hit hard
* = loudly
  parler fort = to speak loudly

**fortement** *adverb*
  = strongly
  = deeply

**fortune** *noun, feminine*
  une fortune = a fortune
  faire fortune = to make one's fortune

**fossé** *noun, masculine*
  un fossé = a ditch

**fou/folle**
**1** *adjective*
  = mad, crazy
  être fou✱/folle✱ de quelqu'un = to be mad
    about someone
**2** *noun, masculine|feminine*
  un fou/une folle = a madman/a
    madwoman

**foudre** *noun, feminine*
* la foudre = lightning
* le coup de foudre = love at first sight

**fouiller** *verb* $\boxed{1}$
* = to search
* fouiller dans un tiroir = to rummage
    around in a drawer

**foulard** *noun, masculine*
  un foulard = a scarf

**foule** *noun, feminine*
  la foule = the crowd

**fouler: se fouler** *verb* $\boxed{1}$ (**!** + *être*)
  se fouler la cheville = to sprain one's ankle

**four** *noun, masculine*
  un four = an oven
  faire cuire au four = to roast
  = to bake
**un four à micro-ondes** = a microwave
  (oven)

**fourche** *noun, feminine*
  une fourche = a garden fork
  = a pitchfork

**fourchette** *noun, feminine*
  une fourchette = a fork

**fourgonnette** *noun, feminine*
  une fourgonnette = a (small) van

**fourmi** *noun, feminine*
  une fourmi = an ant

**fournir** *verb* $\boxed{3}$
  = to provide, to supply

**fourrer✱** *verb* $\boxed{1}$
**1** (**!** + *avoir*)
  = to shove, to put
  fourrer✱ des lettres dans un sac = to shove
    letters into a bag
**2 se fourrer✱** (**!** + *être*)
  se fourrer = to put oneself

**fourrure** *noun, feminine*
  la fourrure = fur

**foutre: se foutre de✱✱** *verb* $\boxed{6}$ (**!** + *être*)
  se foutre de✱✱ = not to give a damn about
  je m'en fous✱✱ = I couldn't care less, I don't
    give a damn

**foyer** *noun, masculine*
* (*for a large group*)
  un foyer = a hostel
* (*where a family lives*)
  un foyer = a home
* (*in a fireplace*)
  le foyer = the hearth

**fracture** *noun, feminine*
  une fracture = a fracture

**fragile** *adjective*
  = fragile
  = delicate

**fraîche ▶ frais 1**

**frais/fraîche**
**1** *adjective*
* = cool
  = chilled
  des boissons fraîches = cool drinks, cold
    drinks
  'servir frais' = 'serve chilled'

F

• = fresh
des légumes frais = fresh vegetables
des nouvelles fraîches = fresh news
**2 frais** *adverb*
• = cool
= chilly
il fait frais ce matin = it's cool this morning
= it's chilly this morning
**3 frais** *noun, masculine* (**!** *never changes*)
'garder au frais' = 'keep in a cool place'
prendre le frais = to take a breath of fresh air
**4 frais** *noun, masculine plural*
des frais = expenses

**fraise** *noun, feminine*
une fraise = a strawberry

**framboise** *noun, feminine*
une framboise = a raspberry

**franc/franche**
**1** *adjective*
= frank
**2 franc** *noun, masculine*
un franc = one franc

**français/française**
**1** *adjective*
= French
**2 français** *noun, masculine*
le français = French

**Français/Française** *noun, masculine/feminine*
un Français/une Française = a Frenchman/a Frenchwoman
les Français = the French

**France** *noun, feminine*
la France = France

**franchement** *adverb*
= frankly

**franchir** *verb* 3
• = to cross
franchir une frontière = to cross a border
• = to get over
franchir une clôture = to get over a fence
• = to cover
franchir dix kilomètres = to cover ten kilometres

**francophone** *adjective*
= French-speaking

**frange** *noun, feminine*
une frange = a fringe, bangs

**frapper** *verb* 1
• = to hit
• = to knock

**fraternité** *noun, feminine*
la fraternité = fraternity

**frein** *noun, masculine*
un frein = a brake
le frein à main = the handbrake
donner un coup de frein = to brake

**freiner** *verb* 1
= to brake

**fréquenter** *verb* 1
• = to mix with, to associate with
fréquenter des voyous = to mix with hooligans
• = to go to
= to visit
= to attend

**frère** *noun, masculine*
un frère = a brother

**frigidaire** *noun, masculine*
un frigidaire = a refrigerator

**frigo✕** *noun, masculine*
un frigo✕ = a fridge

**frimeur/frimeuse✕** *noun, masculine/feminine*
un frimeur✕/une frimeuse✕ = a show-off

**fringues✕** *noun, feminine plural*
des fringues✕ = clothes

**frire** *verb* 39
= to fry

**frisé/frisée** *adjective*
= curly

**frisson** *noun, masculine*
un frisson = a shiver
= a shudder

**frit/frite** *adjective*
= fried

**frites** *noun, feminine plural*
les frites = chips, French fries

**froid/froide**
**1** *adjective*
= cold
**2 froid** *adverb*
il fait froid = it's cold
**3 froid** *noun, masculine*
le froid = the cold
avoir froid = to feel cold, to be cold
prendre froid = to catch (a) cold

**fromage** *noun, masculine*
le fromage = cheese
le fromage blanc ≈ fromage frais

**front** *noun, masculine*
le front = the forehead

**frontière** *noun, feminine*
une frontière = a border, a frontier

**frotter** *verb* 1
= to rub

**fruit** *noun, masculine*
un fruit = a piece of fruit
des fruits = fruit
**des fruits de mer** = seafood

**fuir** *verb* 29
• (*if it's a person*) = to flee
• (*if it's a tap, a hose*) = to leak

**fuite** noun, feminine
• (of a person)
  la fuite = the flight
  = the escape
• (in a pipe, a hose)
  une fuite = a leak

**fumée** noun, feminine
  la fumée = smoke

**fumer** verb [1]
  = to smoke

**fumeur/fumeuse** noun,
masculine/feminine
  un fumeur/une fumeuse = a smoker

**funiculaire** noun, masculine
  un funiculaire = a funicular (railway)

**fur: au fur et à mesure** adverb
  au fur et à mesure = as one goes along
  au fur et à mesure que = as
  au fur et à mesure qu'on fait des progrès
   = as one improves

**furieux/furieuse** adjective
  = furious, angry

**fuseau** noun, masculine
(plural) **fuseaux**
  un fuseau = ski pants
**un fuseau horaire** = a time zone

**fusée** noun, feminine
  une fusée = a rocket

**fusil** noun, masculine
  un fusil = a (shot)gun
  = a rifle
  un coup de fusil = a shot

# Gg

**gâcher** verb [1]
  = to waste
  = to spoil

**gaffe\*** noun, feminine
• une gaffe = a blunder
• faire gaffe\* = to watch out

**gagnant/gagnante**
**1** adjective
  = winning
**2** noun, masculine/feminine
  un gagnant/une gagnante = a winner

**gagner** verb [1]
• = to win
• = to earn
  il gagne bien sa vie = he makes a good
   living

  • = to save
  gagner du temps = to save time
  gagner de la place = to make more room

**gai/gaie** adjective
  = happy
  = cheerful

**gain** noun, masculine
  c'est un gain de temps = it saves time

**gala** noun, masculine
  un gala = a gala, a gala event

**galerie** noun, feminine
• (a passage)
  une galerie = a gallery
• (on a car)
  la galerie = the roof rack
• une galerie d'art = an art gallery
**une galerie marchande** = a shopping
  centre, a shopping mall

**galet** noun, masculine
  un galet = a pebble

**galette** noun, feminine
  une galette = a biscuit, a cookie
  = a pancake
**la galette des rois** = the Twelfth Night
  cake (eaten on the Epiphany)

**Galles** noun, plural
  le pays de Galles = Wales

**gallois/galloise**
**1** adjective
  = Welsh
**2 gallois** noun, masculine
  le gallois = Welsh

**galop** noun, masculine
  un galop = a gallop
  au galop = at a gallop

**galoper** verb [1]
  = to gallop

**gamin/gamine\*** noun,
masculine/feminine
  un gamin\*/une gamine\* = a kid, a child

**gamme** noun, feminine
• (of products)
  une gamme = a range
• (in music)
  une gamme = a scale

**gant** noun, masculine
  un gant = a glove
**un gant de toilette** ≈ a face flannel, a
  wash cloth

**garage** noun, masculine
  un garage = a garage
  un garage à vélos = a bicycle shed

**garagiste** noun, masculine/feminine
  un garagiste/une garagiste = a garage
   owner
  = a car mechanic

**G**

**garantie** *noun, feminine*
une garantie = a guarantee
= a warranty
un bon de garantie = a guarantee

**garçon** *noun, masculine*
• un garçon = a boy
= a young man
• un garçon (de café) = a waiter
**un garçon d'honneur** = a best man
**un garçon manqué** = a tomboy

**garde**
**1** *noun, feminine*
• la garde (*of a child*) = the care
(*of a building*) = guarding
• être de garde (*if it's a doctor*) = to be on call
(*if it's a pharmacist*) = to be on duty
**2** *noun, masculine*
un garde = a guard
**un garde du corps** = a bodyguard

**garde-chasse** *noun, masculine*
(*plural*) **gardes-chasses**
un garde-chasse = a game warden
= a gamekeeper

**garde-fou** *noun, masculine*
(*plural*) **garde-fous**
un garde-fou = a parapet
= a safeguard

**garder** *verb* 1
• = to keep (on)
• = to look after
• = to guard

**gardien/gardienne** *noun,*
*masculine/feminine*
un gardien/une gardienne (*in a prison*) = a
warder, a guard
(*in a museum*) = an attendant, a museum
security guard
(*on work premises*) = a security guard
(*in an apartment block*) = a caretaker, a
janitor
**un gardien de but** = a goalkeeper
**une gardienne d'enfant** = a childminder,
a day-care lady

**gare**
**1** *noun, feminine*
une gare = a railway station
**2** *exclamation*
gare à toi! = watch it!
**une gare maritime** = a harbo(u)r station
**une gare routière** = a coach station, a bus
station

**garer** *verb* 1
**1** (**!** + *avoir*)
= to park
**2 se garer** (**!** + *être*)
se garer = to park
= to pull over

**garni/garnie** *adjective*
= served with vegetables

**gars✗** *noun, masculine* (**!** *never changes*)
• un (petit) gars✗ = a (young) lad, a (young)
guy
• un gars✗ = a chap, a guy

**gas-oil** *noun, masculine*
le gas-oil = diesel oil, fuel oil

**gaspiller** *verb* 1
= to waste

**gâteau** *noun, masculine*
(*plural*) **gâteaux**
un gâteau = a cake
**le gâteau de riz** = rice pudding
**un gâteau sec** = a biscuit, a cookie

**gâter** *verb* 1
**1** (**!** + *avoir*)
= to spoil
un enfant gâté = a spoiled child
**2 se gâter** (**!** + *être*)
• (*if it's fruit*)
se gâter = to go bad
• (*if it's the weather*)
se gâter = to take a turn for the worse

**gauche**
**1** *adjective*
• = left
• = awkward
= clumsy
**2** *noun, feminine*
la gauche = the left
tournez à gauche = turn left
conduire à gauche = to drive on the left-
hand side

**gaucher/gauchère** *adjective*
= left-handed

**gaufre** *noun, feminine*
une gaufre = a waffle

**Gaulois/Gauloise** *noun,*
*masculine/feminine*
un Gaulois/une Gauloise = a Gaul

**gaz** *noun, masculine* (**!** *never changes*)
le gaz = gas
se chauffer au gaz = to have gas heating
**le gaz carbonique** = carbon dioxide
**le gaz de ville** = mains gas

**gazeux/gazeuse** *adjective*
= fizzy, sparkling
une boisson gazeuse = a fizzy drink

**gazon** *noun, masculine*
le gazon = grass, lawn

**géant/géante**
**1** *adjective*
= huge
**2** *noun, masculine/feminine*
un géant/une géante = a giant/a giantess

**gel** *noun, masculine*
• (*in winter*)
le gel = frost

- (for hair)
  **un gel coiffant** = a styling gel

**gelé/gelée¹** adjective
= frozen

**gelée²** noun, feminine
- (on the ground)
  **la gelée** = frost
- (in cooking)
  **la gelée de groseilles** = redcurrant jelly

**geler** verb 17
**1** (! + avoir)
= to freeze
**il gèle** = it's freezing
**2 se geler*** (! + être)
**se geler*** = to be freezing

**gélule** noun, feminine
**une gélule** = a capsule

**Gémeaux** noun, masculine plural
**les Gémeaux** = Gemini

**gémir** verb 3
= to moan
= to whimper

**gênant/gênante** adjective
= embarrassing

**gendarme** noun, masculine
**un gendarme** = a gendarme, a French
  policeman

**gendarmerie** noun, feminine
- **la gendarmerie (nationale)** = the
  gendarmerie
- **une gendarmerie** ≈ a police station

**gendre** noun, masculine
**un gendre** = a son-in-law

**généalogique** adjective
**un arbre généalogique** = a family tree

**gêner** verb 1
**1** (! + avoir)
- = to disturb
  = to bother
  **ça te gêne si j'allume?** = do you mind if
  I switch the light on?
- = to be in the way
- = to embarrass
**2 se gêner** (! + être)
- **se gêner** = to get in each other's way
- **ne te gêne pas pour moi** = don't mind me

**général/générale**
(plural) **généraux/générales**
**1** adjective
- = general
  **de l'avis général** = in most people's
  opinion
  **dans l'intérêt général** = in the public
  interest
- **en général** = generally
  = usually
**2 général** noun, masculine
**un général** = a general

**généralement** adverb
= generally
= normally

**généraliste** adjective
- = non-specialized
- **un médecin généraliste** = a general
  practitioner, a GP, a family doctor

**généreux/généreuse** adjective
= generous

**génétique** adjective
= genetic

**Genève** noun
= Geneva

**génial/géniale*** adjective
(plural) **géniaux/géniales**
= brilliant

**génie** noun, masculine
**le génie** = genius
**une idée de génie** = a brainwave

**genou** noun, masculine
(plural) **genoux**
**un genou** = a knee
**être sur les genoux de sa mère** = to be on
  one's mother's lap
**à genoux** = on one's knees
**se mettre à genoux** = to kneel down

**genre** noun, masculine
- (a type)
  **un genre** = a kind
  **ce genre de travail** = this kind of work
  **un peu dans le genre de ta robe** = a little
  bit like your dress
- (a look)
  **avoir un drôle de genre** = to look a bit
  shady
  **pour se donner un genre** = to make
  oneself look different
- (in grammar)
  **le genre** = gender
- (in literature, cinema)
  **un genre** = a genre

**gens** noun, masculine plural
**les gens** = people

**gentil/gentille** adjective
= kind, nice

**gentillesse** noun, feminine
**la gentillesse** = kindness

**gentiment** adverb
= nicely, kindly

**géographie** noun, feminine
**la géographie** = geography

**gérant/gérante** noun,
masculine/feminine
- (in a shop)
  **un gérant/une gérante** = a manager
- (for a property)
  **un gérant/une gérante** = a managing
  agent

**G**

**gerboise** *noun, feminine*
une gerboise = a gerbil

**germain/germaine** *adjective*
un cousin germain = a first cousin

**geste** *noun, masculine*
un geste = a movement
= a gesture

**gibier** *noun, masculine*
le gibier = game

**gifle** *noun, feminine*
une gifle = a slap in the face

**gigantesque** *adjective*
= huge, gigantic

**gigot** *noun, masculine*
un gigot d'agneau = a leg of lamb

**gilet** *noun, masculine*
• un gilet = a cardigan
• un gilet = a waistcoat, a vest
**un gilet de sauvetage** = a lifejacket

**girafe** *noun, feminine*
une girafe = a giraffe

**gîte** *noun, masculine*
un gîte rural = a self-catering cottage

**givrant** *adjective, masculine*
du brouillard givrant = freezing fog

**givre** *noun, masculine*
le givre = frost

**glace** *noun, feminine*
• (*frozen water*)
la glace = ice
• (*a confection*)
la glace = ice cream
une glace à la vanille = a vanilla ice cream
• (*a looking glass*)
une glace = a mirror

**glacé/glacée** *adjective*
• = ice-cold
= frozen
• = glossy

**glaçon** *noun, masculine*
un glaçon = an ice cube

**glisser** *verb* $\boxed{1}$
**1** (**!** + *avoir*)
• = to slip
= to slide
• = to be slippery
**2 se glisser** (**!** + *être*)
se glisser dans = to slip into
= to sneak into
= to creep into

**globe** *noun, masculine*
le globe (terrestre) = the globe, the Earth

**gloire** *noun, feminine*
la gloire = glory, fame

**goal** *noun, masculine*
un goal = a goalkeeper

**gogo**: **à gogo**✻ *adverb*
à gogo✻ = galore

**golfe** *noun, masculine*
un golfe = a gulf

**gomme** *noun, feminine*
• une gomme = a rubber, an eraser
• la gomme = gum

**gonflé/gonflée** *adjective*
• = inflated
• = swollen
• être gonflé✻ = to have a nerve
= to have guts

**gonfler** *verb* $\boxed{1}$
• = to inflate
• = to swell (up)

**gorge** *noun, feminine*
la gorge = the throat
avoir mal à la gorge = to have a sore throat
avoir la gorge serrée = to have a lump in
one's throat

**gorgée** *noun, feminine*
une gorgée = a sip
= a gulp

**gorille** *noun, masculine*
• un gorille = a gorilla
• un gorille✻ = a bodyguard

**gosse**✻ *noun, masculine/feminine*
un gosse✻/une gosse✻ = a kid, a child

**goudron** *noun, masculine*
le goudron = tar

**goudronner** *verb* $\boxed{1}$
= to tarmac, to blacktop

**gourde** *noun, feminine*
une gourde = a gourd
= a flask

**gourmand/gourmande** *adjective*
être gourmand = to be fond of good food
(*to like sweet things*) = to have a sweet
tooth

**goût** *noun, masculine*
le goût = taste

**goûter**
**1** *verb* $\boxed{1}$
= to taste
**2** *noun, masculine*
• le goûter = an afternoon snack
• un goûter = a children's party

**goutte** *noun, feminine*
une goutte = a drop
goutte à goutte = drop by drop

**grâce**
**1** *noun, feminine*
la grâce = grace
**2 grâce à** = thanks to

---

✻ in informal situations

**gradins** noun, masculine plural
les gradins = the terraces, the bleachers

**graine** noun, feminine
une graine = a seed

**graisse** noun, feminine
la graisse (in food) = fat
(for machinery) = grease

**graisser** verb 1
= to grease
= to lubricate

**grammaire** noun, feminine
la grammaire = grammar

**gramme** noun, masculine
un gramme = a gram

**grand/grande**
1 adjective
• = tall
= big, large
= long
Théo est grand = Théo is tall
un grand jardin = a large garden
un grand voyage = a long journey
il n'y avait pas grand monde = there
  weren't many people
faire de grands gestes = to wave one's
  arms around
• = great
un grand homme = a great man
un train à grande vitesse = a high-speed
  train
2 grand adverb
= wide
grand ouvert = wide open
voir grand = to think big
le grand bassin = the main pool
un grand magasin = a department store
le grand public = the general public
une grande personne = a grown-up
une grande surface = a supermarket
les grandes lignes = main train routes
les grandes vacances = the summer
  holidays, the summer vacation

**grand-chose** pronoun
pas grand-chose = not much, not a lot
ça ne sert pas à grand-chose = it's not
  much use

**Grande-Bretagne** noun, feminine
la Grande-Bretagne = Great Britain

**grandir** verb 3
= to grow

**grand-mère** noun, feminine
(plural) **grands-mères**
une grand-mère = a grandmother

**grand-père** noun, masculine
(plural) **grands-pères**
un grand-père = a grandfather

**grands-parents** noun, masculine plural
des grands-parents = grandparents

**grange** noun, feminine
une grange = a barn

**granulé** noun, masculine
un granulé = a granule

**graphique**
1 adjective
= graphic
2 noun, masculine
un graphique = a graph

**grappe** noun, feminine
une grappe = a bunch
= a cluster

**gras/grasse**
1 adjective
• = greasy
= fatty
• = fat
• (if it's a letter) = bold
2 gras noun, masculine (! never changes)
le gras (on meat) = fat

**gratin** noun, masculine
un gratin = a gratin (a dish topped with
  browned cheese and breadcrumbs)
un gratin de pommes de terre = potatoes
  au gratin

**gratis**
1 adjective (! never changes)
= free
2 adverb
= free, for free

**gratter** verb 1
1 (! + avoir)
• = to scratch
= to scrape (off)
• ça me gratte partout = I'm itching all over
2 se gratter (! + être)
se gratter = to scratch

**gratuit/gratuite** adjective
= free

**gratuitement** adverb
= free, for free

**grave** adjective
• = serious
• = grave, solemn
• une voix grave = a deep voice

**graveur** noun, masculine
(for CDs, DVDs)
un graveur = a burner

**gravement** adverb
• = seriously
• = gravely, solemnly

**gravier** noun, masculine
du gravier = gravel

**gravillon** noun, masculine
un gravillon = a bit of grit, some grit

**grec/grecque**
1 adjective
= Greek
2 grec noun, masculine
le grec = Greek

**G**

**Grèce** noun, feminine
la Grèce = Greece

**grecque** ▶ **grec 1**

**grêle** noun, feminine
la grêle = hail
il tombe de la grêle = it's hailing

**grêlon** noun, masculine
un grêlon = a hailstone

**grelotter** verb [1]
= to shiver

**grenier** noun, masculine
un grenier = an attic, a loft

**grenouille** noun, feminine
une grenouille = a frog

**grève** noun, feminine
• (at work)
une grève = a strike
faire grève = to go on strike
• (by the sea)
la grève = the shore
**une grève de la faim** = a hunger strike

**griffe** noun, feminine
une griffe = a claw

**griffer** verb [1]
= to scratch

**grignoter** verb [1]
= to nibble

**grillade** noun, feminine
une grillade = grilled meat

**grillage** noun, masculine
le grillage = wire netting

**grille** noun, feminine
• (in a garden)
une grille = a gate
• (for a crossword)
une grille = a grid

**grille-pain** noun, masculine (**!** never changes)
un grille-pain = a toaster

**griller** verb [1]
• (in cooking)
(faire) griller = to grill
= to toast
• griller* un feu = to go through a red light

**grimace** noun, feminine
une grimace = a (funny) face
faire des grimaces = to make faces
faire la grimace devant un plat = to turn one's nose up at a dish

**grimper** verb [1]
= to climb

**grippe** noun, feminine
la grippe = flu

---

**gris/grise** adjective
• = grey, gray
• = dull, dreary
un temps gris = dull weather

**grive** noun, feminine
une grive = a thrush

**grognon** adjective
= grumpy, grouchy

**gros/grosse**
**1** adjective
• = big
• = heavy
un gros fumeur = a heavy smoker
**2 gros** adverb
• écrire gros = to write in big letters
• perdre gros = to lose a lot
**3 gros** noun, masculine (**!** never changes)
• le gros du travail = the bulk of the work
• le prix de gros = the wholesale price
**4 en gros**
• en gros = roughly
• en gros = wholesale
• en gros = in big letters
**le gros lot** = the first prize
**un gros mot** = a swearword
**les gros titres** = the headlines

**groseille** noun, feminine
une groseille = a redcurrant
une groseille à maquereau = a gooseberry

**grosse** ▶ **gros 1**

**grossier/grossière** adjective
• = rude
• = coarse

**grotte** noun, feminine
une grotte = a cave
= a grotto

**groupe** noun, masculine
un groupe = a group
**un groupe scolaire** = a school

**guépard** noun, masculine
un guépard = a cheetah

**guêpe** noun, feminine
une guêpe = a wasp

**guère** adverb
= hardly
il n'avait guère le choix = he didn't really have a choice

**guérir** verb [3]
= to cure
= to heal
= to recover

**guerre** noun, feminine
une guerre = a war

**guetter** verb [1]
= to watch
= to watch out for

---

**✖** in informal situations

**gueule** noun, feminine
une gueule = a mouth
avoir une grande gueule✱ = to have a big
    mouth

**gui** noun, masculine
le gui = mistletoe

**guichet** noun, masculine
un guichet (in a bank, a post office) = a
    counter
= a window
(in a museum, a station) = a ticket office
(in a theatre, a cinema) = a box office
**un guichet automatique** = an automatic
cash dispenser

**guide** noun, masculine
un guide = a guide

**guidon** noun, masculine
le guidon = the handlebars

**guignol** noun, masculine
un guignol = a puppet show

**guillemets** noun, masculine plural
des guillemets = inverted commas
= quotation marks

**guitare** noun, feminine
une guitare = a guitar

**gym✱** noun, feminine
• (at school)
la gym✱ = physical education
• (as a sport)
la gym✱ = gymnastics

**gymnase** noun, masculine
un gymnase = a gymnasium

**gymnastique** noun, feminine
la gymnastique (the sport) = gymnastics
(to keep fit) = exercise

# Hh

**habile** adjective
= clever
= skil(l)ful

**habiller** verb |1|
**1** (! + avoir)
= to dress
**2 s'habiller** (! + être)
s'habiller = to get dressed
= to dress up

**habitant/habitante** noun,
masculine/feminine
un habitant/une habitante = an inhabitant

**habiter** verb |1|
= to live (in)
habiter la campagne = to live in the
    country
habiter à Paris = to live in Paris

**habitude**
**1** noun, feminine
une habitude = a habit
avoir l'habitude de se lever tôt = to be in
    the habit of getting up early
= to be used to getting up early
avoir l'habitude des enfants = to be used
    to children
**2 d'habitude** = usually
comme d'habitude = as usual

**habituel/habituelle** adjective
= usual

**haché/hachée** adjective
= minced
= chopped

**hachis** noun, masculine (! never changes)
le hachis = mince, ground meat
**le hachis Parmentier** = shepherd's pie

**haie** noun, feminine
une haie = a hedge

**haleine** noun, feminine
l'haleine = the breath
hors d'haleine = out of breath

**halte** noun, feminine
une halte (a pause) = a stop
(a place) = a stopping place
faire halte = to stop

**haltérophilie** noun, feminine
l'haltérophilie = weightlifting

**hameau** noun, masculine
(plural) **hameaux**
un hameau = a hamlet

**hameçon** noun, masculine
un hameçon = a fish-hook

**hanche** noun, feminine
une hanche = a hip

**handicapé/handicapée**
**1** adjective
= handicapped
**2** noun, masculine/feminine
un handicapé/une handicapée = a
    handicapped person

**hanté/hantée** adjective
= haunted

**hareng** noun, masculine
un hareng = a herring

**haricot** noun, masculine
un haricot = a bean
**les haricots verts** = French beans

**hasard** noun, masculine
le hasard = chance
un hasard = a coincidence

**H**

**hâte** noun, feminine
* la hâte = haste
  à la hâte = hastily
* j'ai hâte de partir = I can't wait to leave

**hausse** noun, feminine
une hausse = a rise, an increase

**hausser** verb [1]
= to raise
hausser les épaules = to shrug one's
  shoulders

**haut/haute**
**1** adjective
* = high
  = tall
* à haute voix = aloud
  = loudly
**2 haut** adverb
* = high
  haut les mains! = hands up!
* = loud(ly)
  tout haut = aloud
**3 haut** noun, masculine
* le haut = the top
  les pièces du haut = the upstairs rooms
* faire 15 mètres de haut = to be 15 metres
  high
**4 en haut** = at the top
  = upstairs

**hauteur** noun, masculine
la hauteur = the height

**Haye** noun, feminine
la Haye = the Hague

**hebdomadaire** adjective
= weekly

**hébergement** noun, masculine
l'hébergement = accommodation, lodging

**héberger** verb [13]
= to put up

**hein✕** exclamation
* hein✕? = what?
* tu n'iras pas, hein✕? = you won't go, will
  you?

**hélas** exclamation
hélas! = unfortunately!

**hélice** noun, feminine
une hélice = a propeller

**hélicoptère** noun, masculine
un hélicoptère = a helicopter

**herbe** noun, feminine
* de l'herbe = grass
* une herbe = a(n) herb
* une mauvaise herbe = a weed

**hérisson** noun, masculine
un hérisson = a hedgehog

**héritage** noun, masculine
un héritage = an inheritance

**hériter** verb [1]
= to inherit

**héritier/héritière** noun,
masculine/feminine
un héritier/une héritière = an heir/an
  heiress

**héros** noun, masculine (❗ never changes)
un héros = a hero

**hésiter** verb [1]
= to hesitate

**heure** noun, feminine
* l'heure = the time
  quelle heure est-il? = what time is it?
  il est huit heures = it's eight o'clock
  il est huit heures dix = it's ten past eight
  il est huit heures moins dix = it's ten to
    eight
  l'heure du déjeuner = lunchtime
  être à l'heure = to be on time
  de bonne heure = early
  mettre sa montre à l'heure = to set one's
    watch
* une heure = an hour
  toutes les trois heures = every three hours
  faire du 100 à l'heure✕ = to do 100 km per
    hour
  les heures d'affluence = peak times
  les heures de pointe = the rush hour
  les heures supplémentaires = overtime

**heureuse ▶ heureux**

**heureusement** adverb
= fortunately
= luckily

**heureux/heureuse** adjective
= happy

**heurter** verb [1]
= to bump into
= to hit, to crash into

**hibou** noun, masculine
(plural) **hiboux**
un hibou = an owl

**hier** adverb
= yesterday
hier soir = yesterday evening

**hippodrome** noun, masculine
un hippodrome = a racecourse

**hippopotame** noun, masculine
un hippopotame = a hippopotamus

**hirondelle** noun, feminine
une hirondelle = a swallow

**histoire** noun, feminine
* l'histoire = history
* une histoire = a story
* faire des histoires✕ = to make trouble

---

✕ in informal situations

**historique** adjective
* = historic
* = historical

**hit-parade** noun, masculine
(plural) **hit-parades**
 le hit-parade = the charts

**hiver** noun, masculine
 l'hiver = winter

**HLM** noun, masculine or feminine
 un(e) HLM ≈ a council flat, a low-rent
  apartment
 = a block of council flats, a low-rent
  apartment building

**hocher** verb [1]
 hocher la tête (in agreement) = to nod
 (to say no) = to shake one's head

**hollandais/hollandaise**
**1** adjective
 = Dutch
**2 hollandais** noun, masculine
 le hollandais = Dutch

**Hollande** noun, feminine
 la Hollande = Holland

**homard** noun, masculine
 un homard = a lobster

**homme** noun, masculine
 un homme = a man
**un homme d'affaires** = a businessman

**Hongrie** noun, feminine
 la Hongrie = Hungary

**hongrois/hongroise**
**1** adjective
 = Hungarian
**2 hongrois** noun, masculine
 le hongrois = Hungarian

**honnête** adjective
 = honest

**honoraire**
**1** adjective
 = honorary
**2 honoraires** noun, masculine plural
 les honoraires = the fee(s)

**honte** noun, feminine
 la honte = shame
 avoir honte = to be ashamed

**hôpital** noun, masculine
(plural) **hôpitaux**
 un hôpital = a hospital

**hoquet** noun, masculine
 le hoquet = hiccoughs, hiccups

**horaire** noun, masculine
 un horaire = a timetable
**les horaires à la carte, les horaires
libres** = flexitime, flextime

**horizon** noun, masculine
 l'horizon = the horizon
 à l'horizon = on the horizon

**horizontal/horizontale** adjective
(plural) **horizontaux/horizontales**
 = horizontal, flat

**horizontalement** adverb
* = horizontally
* (in a crossword) = across

**horloge** noun, feminine
 une horloge = a clock

**horloger/horlogère** noun,
masculine/feminine
 un horloger/une horlogère = a
  watchmaker

**horreur** noun, feminine
* l'horreur = horror
 quelle horreur! = how horrible!
 = it's hideous!
* l'horreur = loathing
 avoir horreur de laver la voiture = to loathe
  washing the car

**horrible** adjective
 = awful, horrible

**hors** preposition
 hors (de) = outside, out of
 hors d'haleine = out of breath
 hors jeu = offside
 hors de prix = ridiculously expensive
 hors (de) saison = out of season
 'hors service' = 'out of order'
 hors taxes, HT (describing a shop) = duty-
  free
 (describing a price) = excluding tax
 hors d'usage = worn out

**hors-d'œuvre** noun, masculine (**!** never
changes)
 un hors-d'œuvre = a starter

**hospitalité** noun, feminine
 l'hospitalité = hospitality

**hôte**
**1** noun, masculine
 un hôte = a host
**2** noun, masculine/feminine
 un hôte/une hôte = a guest

**hôtel** noun, masculine
 un hôtel = a hotel
**l'hôtel de ville** = the town hall

**hôtelier/hôtelière** noun,
masculine/feminine
 un hôtelier/une hôtelière = a hotel-keeper,
  a hotel manager

**hôtesse** noun, feminine
* (a person who has guests)
 une hôtesse = a hostess
* (a person who deals with customers)
 une hôtesse (in a firm) = a receptionist
 (on a train, a boat) = a stewardess
**une hôtesse d'accueil** = a receptionist
**une hôtesse de l'air** = a flight attendant,
 an air hostess

**H**

**houx** *noun, masculine* (**!** *never changes*)
le houx = holly

**HT ▶ hors**

**hublot** *noun, masculine*
un hublot = a porthole

**huile** *noun, feminine*
l'huile = oil

**huissier** *noun, masculine*
un huissier (de justice) = a bailiff

**huit** *number*
= eight
huit jours = a week
= eight days
lundi en huit = a week on Monday

**huitaine** *noun, feminine*
une huitaine = about a week
= about eight

**huitante** *number*
= eighty

**huitième** *number*
= eighth

**huître** *noun, feminine*
une huître = an oyster

**humain/humaine** *adjective*
• = human
• = humane

**humeur** *noun, feminine*
une humeur = a mood
être de bonne humeur = to be in a good mood
être de mauvaise humeur = to be in a bad mood

**humide** *adjective*
= damp
= humid

**hurlement** *noun, masculine*
un hurlement = a howl

**hurler** *verb* 1
= to howl

**hydroglisseur** *noun, masculine*
un hydroglisseur = a hydrofoil

**hydrophile** *adjective*
= absorbent

**hygiénique** *adjective*
le papier hygiénique = toilet paper

**hyper\*** *adverb*
= extremely

**hypermarché** *noun, masculine*
un hypermarché = a hypermarket, a large supermarket

# I i

**ici** *adverb*
= here
venez par ici = come this way

**idéal/idéale** *adjective*
(*plural*) **idéaux/idéales**
= ideal

**idée** *noun, feminine*
une idée = an idea

**identifier** *verb* 2
= to identify

**identité** *noun, feminine*
l'identité = identity

**idiot/idiote**
**1** *adjective*
= stupid
**2** *noun, masculine/feminine*
un idiot/une idiote = an idiot

**ignorer** *verb* 1
• = not to know
j'ignore où il habite = I don't know where he lives
• = to ignore

**il** *pronoun, masculine*
**1** (*referring to a person, an animal or a thing*)
= he
= it
ils = they
**2** (*impersonal use*)
• = it
il fait froid = it's cold
il est facile d'obtenir des billets = it's easy to get tickets
• il y a = there is
= there are
il y a une fuite = there is a leak
• (*when talking about time*)
il y a une heure que j'attends = I've been waiting for an hour
il y a un an qu'il est parti = he left a year ago

**île** *noun, feminine*
une île = an island
les îles Anglo-Normandes = the Channel Islands

**illégal/illégale** *adjective*
(*plural*) **illégaux/illégales**
= illegal

**illettré/illettrée** *adjective*
= illiterate

**illimité/illimitée** *adjective*
= unlimited

---

**illisible** adjective
• = illegible
• = unreadable

**illuminé/illuminée** adjective
= lit up
= illuminated

**illustre** adjective
= illustrious

**illustré** noun, masculine
un illustré = an illustrated magazine
= a comic, a comic book

**illustrer** verb [1]
= to illustrate

**ils** pronoun, masculine plural
= they

**image** noun, feminine
une image = a picture
= an image

**imaginaire** adjective
= imaginary

**imaginer** verb [1]
= to imagine

**imbattable** adjective
= unbeatable

**imbécile** noun, masculine/feminine
un imbécile/une imbécile = an idiot
faire l'imbécile = to be silly

**imiter** verb [1]
= to imitate

**immatriculation** noun, feminine
l'immatriculation = registration
= the registration number

**immédiatement** adverb
= immediately

**immense** adjective
= huge
= great

**immeuble** noun, masculine
un immeuble = a building
= a block of flats, an apartment block

**immigré/immigrée** adjective
= immigrant

**immobile** adjective
= still

**immobilier** noun, masculine
l'immobilier = property, real estate

**impair/impaire** adjective
les nombres impairs = odd numbers

**imparfait/imparfaite**
1 adjective
= imperfect
2 imparfait noun, masculine
l'imparfait = the imperfect (tense)

**impasse** noun, feminine
une impasse = a cul-de-sac, a dead end

**impatienter: s'impatienter** [1]
(**1** + être)
s'impatienter = to get impatient

**imper\*** noun, masculine
un imper\* = a mac, a raincoat

**imperméable**
1 noun, masculine
un imperméable = a raincoat
2 adjective
= waterproof

**impoli/impolie** adjective
= impolite, rude

**important/importante** adjective
= important
= considerable
= sizeable

**importer** verb [1]
• = to import
• = to be important
il importe de [faire | dire | savoir ...] = it's
important to [do | say | know ...]
**n'importe**
n'importe lequel = any
n'importe où = anywhere
n'importe quel = any
n'importe qui = anybody
n'importe quoi = anything

**impôt** noun, masculine
un impôt = a tax

**impressionnant/impressionnante**
adjective
= impressive

**impressionner** verb [1]
= to impress

**imprévu/imprévue** adjective
= unexpected

**imprimé/imprimée**
1 adjective
= printed
2 imprimé noun, masculine
• (paper)
un imprimé = a leaflet
• (on material)
un imprimé = a print

**imprimer** verb [1]
= to print

**imprimeur** noun, masculine
un imprimeur = a printer

**improviser** verb [1]
= to improvise

**improviste: à l'improviste** adverb
à l'improviste = unexpectedly

**imprudence** noun, feminine
• l'imprudence = recklessness
• faire une imprudence = to do something
reckless

**imprudent/imprudente** adjective
= reckless

**inabordable** *adjective*
* (*describing a price*) = prohibitive, unaffordable
* (*describing a person*) = unapproachable

**inadmissible** *adjective*
= unacceptable

**inattendu/inattendue** *adjective*
= unexpected

**incapable** *adjective*
= incompetent
être incapable de conduire = to be incapable of driving
= to be unable to drive

**incendie** *noun, masculine*
un incendie = a fire

**incident** *noun, masculine*
un incident = an incident

**inclus/incluse** *adjective*
* = including
* = enclosed

**inconnu/inconnue**
**1** *adjective*
= unknown
**2** *noun, masculine|feminine*
un inconnu/une inconnue = a stranger
= an unknown man/woman

**inconvénient** *noun, masculine*
un inconvénient = a drawback, a disadvantage
si vous n'y voyez pas d'inconvénient = if you have no objection

**incroyable** *adjective*
= unbelievable

**incroyablement** *adverb*
= incredibly

**inculpé/inculpée** *noun, masculine|feminine*
l'inculpé/l'inculpée = the accused

**inculper** *verb* [1]
= to charge
on l'a inculpé de meurtre = he's been charged with murder

**Inde** *noun, feminine*
l'Inde = India

**indemne** *adjective*
= unharmed

**indépendant/indépendante** *adjective*
= independent

**index** *noun, masculine* (**!** *never changes*)
l'index = the index finger, the forefinger

**indicateur** *noun, masculine*
* (*a book giving information*)
un indicateur (*for trains*) = a timetable
(*for streets*) = a directory
* (*an instrument*)
un indicateur = a gauge

**indicatif** *noun, masculine*
* (*when making a phone call*)
l'indicatif = the dialling code, the area code
* (*of a radio or TV programme*)
l'indicatif = the signature tune, the theme music
* (*in grammar*)
l'indicatif = the indicative

**indice** *noun, masculine*
un indice = a sign, an indication
(*in a police inquiry*) = a clue

**indien/indienne** *adjective*
= Indian

**indigestion** *noun, feminine*
une indigestion = a stomach upset

**indigner**: **s'indigner** *verb* [1] (**!** + *être*)
s'indigner = to be indignant

**indiquer** *verb* [1]
* (*with one's hand*) = to indicate, to point to
* (*to give information*) = to tell
pouvez-vous m'indiquer la banque la plus proche? = could you tell me where the nearest bank is?
je leur ai indiqué le moyen d'entrer sans payer = I told them how to get in for free
il m'a indiqué un bon restaurant = he recommended a good restaurant
indiquez votre nom et votre adresse = give your name and address
* (*to display information*) = to show
le village n'est pas indiqué sur la carte = the village isn't shown on the map
* (*to be a sign or a clue*) = to suggest
rien n'indique qu'il changera d'avis = there's nothing to suggest that he'll change his mind

**individu** *noun, masculine*
un individu = an individual
= a person

**individuel/individuelle** *adjective*
= individual

**industrie** *noun, feminine*
l'industrie = industry

**industriel/industrielle** *adjective*
= industrial

**inédit/inédite** *adjective*
* = (previously) unpublished
* = new

**infect/infecte** *adjective*
= horrible, revolting

**infecter**: **s'infecter** *verb* [1] (**!** + *être*)
s'infecter = to become infected, to go septic

**inférieur/inférieure** *adjective*
* = lower
* = inferior

**infirme**
1 *adjective*
= disabled
2 *noun, masculine/feminine*
un infirme/une infirme = a disabled person

**infirmerie** *noun, feminine*
l'infirmerie = the sick bay

**infirmier/infirmière** *noun,*
*masculine/feminine*
un infirmier/une infirmière = a nurse

**inflammable** *adjective*
= flammable

**infliger** *verb* 13
= to inflict

**informaticien/informaticienne**
*noun, masculine/feminine*
un informaticien/une informaticienne = a
computer scientist

**informations** *noun, feminine plural*
les informations = the news

**informatique** *noun, feminine*
l'informatique = computer science,
computing

**informer** *verb* 1
1 (**!** + *avoir*)
= to inform
2 s'informer (**!** + *être*)
• s'informer = to keep oneself informed
• s'informer de = to enquire about

**ingénieur** *noun, masculine*
un ingénieur = an engineer

**ingrat/ingrate** *adjective*
• (*not thankful*) = ungrateful
• (*not pretty*) = unattractive

**inhabité/inhabitée** *adjective*
= uninhabited

**inhabituel/inhabituelle** *adjective*
= unusual

**inhumer** *verb* 1
= to bury

**initiale** *noun, feminine*
une initiale = an initial

**injure** *noun, feminine*
une injure = an insult

**injuste** *adjective*
= unfair

**inquiet/inquiète** *adjective*
= worried, anxious

**inquiéter** *verb* 14
1 (**!** + *avoir*)
= to worry
2 s'inquiéter (**!** + *être*)
s'inquiéter = to worry

**inquiétude** *noun, feminine*
l'inquiétude = worry

**inscrire** *verb* 42
1 (**!** + *avoir*)
• = to enrol(l), to register
• = to write down
2 s'inscrire (**!** + *être*)
s'inscrire = to register
= to enrol

**inscrit/inscrite** ▶ **inscrire** 42

**insecte** *noun, masculine*
un insecte = an insect

**insolation** *noun, feminine*
une insolation = sunstroke

**insolent/insolente** *adjective*
= insolent, cheeky

**insomniaque** *adjective*
= insomniac, unable to sleep

**inspecter** *verb* 1
= to inspect

**inspecteur/inspectrice** *noun,*
*masculine/feminine*
un inspecteur/une inspectrice = an
inspector
**un inspecteur de police** = a detective
constable, a police detective

**inspirer** *verb* 1
1 (**!** + *avoir*)
• = to inspire
• = to breathe in
2 s'inspirer de (**!** + *être*)
s'inspirer de = to be inspired by, to draw
one's inspiration from

**Installation**
1 *noun, feminine*
• (*the fact of fitting*)
l'installation = installing, putting in
• (*going to new premises*)
une installation = a move
2 **installations** *noun, feminine plural*
des installations = facilities
**des installations sanitaires** = toilets

**installer** *verb* 1
1 (**!** + *avoir*)
• (*to fit*) = to install, to put in
(*if it's gas, water, electricity*) = to connect
faire installer le téléphone = to have the
telephone connected
• (*to position*)
installer une tente sous un arbre = to put
up a tent under a tree
installer un invité dans un fauteuil = to sit
a guest in an armchair
2 s'installer (**!** + *être*)
s'installer dans une ville = to settle in a
town
s'installer près du feu = to sit by the fire

**instant** *noun, masculine*
un instant = a moment
à chaque instant = constantly

**instinctivement** *adverb*
= instinctively

I

**instituteur/institutrice** *noun,*
*masculine/feminine*
  un instituteur/une institutrice = a (primary
  school) teacher

**instruction** *noun, feminine*
• **des instructions** = instructions
• **l'instruction** = education
**l'instruction civique** = social studies
**l'instruction religieuse** = religious
  education

**instrument** *noun, masculine*
  un instrument = an instrument
**un instrument de musique** = a musical
  instrument

**insuffisant/insuffisante** *adjective*
  = insufficient

**insulter** *verb* 1
  = to insult

**insupportable** *adjective*
  = unbearable

**intelligent/intelligente** *adjective*
  = intelligent, clever

**intention** *noun, feminine*
  une intention = an intention
  **avoir l'intention de voyager** = to intend to
  travel

**interdire** *verb* 40
  = to forbid
  **elle nous a interdit de sortir** = she forbade
  us to go out

**interdit/interdite** *adjective*
  = forbidden, not allowed
  'baignade interdite' = 'no swimming'

**intéressant/intéressante** *adjective*
  = interesting

**intéresser** *verb* 1
**1** (**!** + *avoir*)
  = to interest
  **ça ne m'intéresse pas** = I'm not interested
**2 s'intéresser** (**!** + *être*)
  **s'intéresser à** = to be interested in

**intérêt** *noun, masculine*
  un intérêt = an interest

**intérieur/intérieure**
**1** *adjective*
  = inside
  = inner
**2 extérieur** *noun, masculine*
  **l'intérieur** = the inside
  **à l'intérieur de la boîte** = inside the box

**internat** *noun, masculine*
  un internat = a boarding school

**interne**
**1** *adjective*
  = internal

**2** *noun, masculine/feminine*
  **un interne/une interne** (*a pupil*) = a
  boarder, a boarding student

**Internet** *noun, masculine*
  **l'Internet** = the Internet

**interprète** *noun, masculine/feminine*
  **un interprète/une interprète** = an
  interpreter

**interro**✶ *noun, feminine*
(*abbreviation of* **interrogation**)
  **une interro**✶ = a test

**interrogation** *noun, feminine*
• (*in class*)
  **une interrogation** = a test
• (*in grammar*)
  **une interrogation** = a question

**interroger** *verb* 13
• = to question
• = to test

**interviewer** *verb* 1
  = to interview

**intituler** *verb* 1
**1** (**!** + *avoir*)
  = to call, to entitle
**2 s'intituler** (**!** + *être*)
  **s'intituler** = to be called

**intoxication** *noun, feminine*
  **une intoxication alimentaire** = food
  poisoning

**introduire** *verb* 62
**1** (**!** + *avoir*)
  = to insert
**2 s'introduire dans** (**!** + *être*)
  **s'introduire dans** (*to go in*) = to enter

**intrus/intruse** *noun, masculine/feminine*
(*a person*)
  **un intrus/une intruse** = an intruder

**inutile** *adjective*
  = useless
  = pointless

**inutilisable** *adjective*
  = unusable

**inventer** *verb* 1
  = to invent

**inverse** *noun, masculine*
  **l'inverse** = the opposite

**investissement** *noun, masculine*
  un investissement = an investment

**invité/invitée** *noun, masculine/feminine*
  un invité/une invitée = a guest

**inviter** *verb* 1
  = to invite

**irai** ▶ **aller 1** 9

**irlandais/irlandaise**
**1** *adjective*
  = Irish

---

✶ in informal situations

**2 irlandais** *noun, masculine*
l'irlandais = Irish

**Irlande** *noun, feminine*
l'Irlande = Ireland
la République d'Irlande = the Republic of Ireland
l'Irlande du Nord = Northern Ireland

**irriter** *verb* 1
= to irritate

**islamique** *adjective*
= Islamic

**isolé/isolée** *adjective*
= isolated
= lonely

**issue** *noun, feminine*
une issue = an exit, a way out
une issue de secours = an emergency exit
'voie sans issue' = 'no through road'

**Italie** *noun, feminine*
l'Italie = Italy

**italien/italienne**
**1** *adjective*
= Italian
**2 italien** *noun, masculine*
l'italien = Italian

**italique** *noun, masculine*
en italique(s) = in italics

**itinéraire** *noun, masculine*
un itinéraire = a route, an itinerary
'itinéraire bis' = 'alternative route'

**ivoire** *noun, masculine*
l'ivoire = ivory

**ivre** *adjective*
= drunk

**ivresse** *noun, feminine*
l'ivresse = drunkenness, intoxication

**ivrogne** *noun, masculine/feminine*
un ivrogne/une ivrogne = a drunkard

# Jj

**j'** ▶ **je**

**jadis** *adverb*
= in the past, a long time ago

**jaloux/jalouse** *adjective*
= jealous

**jamaïcain/jamaïcaine** *adjective*
= Jamaican

**Jamaïque** *noun, feminine*
la Jamaïque = Jamaica

**jamais** *adverb*
• (*at no time*) = never
= ever
il n'écrit jamais = he never writes
plus jamais = never again
rien n'est jamais certain = nothing is ever certain
• (*at any other time*) = ever
il fait plus froid que jamais = it's colder than ever

**jambe** *noun, feminine*
une jambe = a leg

**jambon** *noun, masculine*
le jambon = ham

**janvier** *noun, masculine*
janvier = January

**Japon** *noun, masculine*
le Japon = Japan

**japonais/japonaise**
**1** *adjective*
= Japanese
**2 japonais** *noun, masculine*
le japonais = Japanese

**jardin** *noun, masculine*
un jardin = a garden, a yard
faire son jardin = to work in one's garden
**un jardin potager** = a vegetable garden
**un jardin public** = a park
**un jardin zoologique** = a zoo

**jardinage** *noun, masculine*
le jardinage = gardening

**jardinier/jardinière** *noun, masculine/feminine*
un jardinier/une jardinière = a gardener

**jaune** *adjective*
= yellow

**javelot** *noun, masculine*
un javelot = a javelin

**J.-C.** (*abbreviation of* **Jésus-Christ**)
avant J.-C. = BC
après J.-C. = AD

**je** (**j'** *before vowel or mute h*) *pronoun*
= I

**jean** *noun, masculine*
un jean = (a pair of) jeans

**jetable** *adjective*
= disposable

**jeter** *verb* 20
= to throw (away)

**jeton** *noun, masculine*
un jeton = a counter

**jeu** *noun, masculine*
(*plural* **jeux**)
• (*the activity*)
un jeu = a game
faire un jeu = to play a game

J

- (*the equipment*)
  un jeu = a set
  un jeu d'échecs = a chess set
  **un jeu de mots** = a pun
  **le jeu de l'oie** ≈ snakes and ladders,
  chutes and ladders
  **un jeu de société** = a board game
  = a party game
  **un jeu télévisé** = a game show
  **les jeux Olympiques** = the Olympic
  Games

**jeudi** *noun, masculine*
  jeudi = Thursday

**jeun**: **à jeun** *adverb*
  être à jeun = to have had nothing to eat

**jeune**
**1** *adjective*
  = young
**2** *noun, masculine*
  un jeune = a youth, a lad
  les jeunes = young people
  **une jeune fille** = a girl
  **un jeune homme** = a young man

**jeunesse** *noun, feminine*
- (*the young years*)
  la jeunesse = youth
- (*young boys and girls*)
  la jeunesse = young people

**jf** (*abbreviation of* **jeune fille**)
  = young woman

**jh** (*abbreviation of* **jeune homme**)
  = young man

**Joconde** *noun, feminine*
  la Joconde = the Mona Lisa

**joie** *noun, feminine*
  la joie = joy

**joindre** *verb* 56
**1** (**!** + *avoir*)
- (*to add*) = to attach
  = to enclose
- (*to link, to fasten*) = to join
  = to put together
- (*to make contact*) = to get hold of
  = to get in touch with
**2 se joindre à** (**!** + *être*)
  se joindre à = to join

**joli/jolie** *adjective*
  = pretty, attractive
  = nice

**jongler** *verb* 1
  = to juggle

**jongleur/jongleuse** *noun,*
*masculine/feminine*
  un jongleur/une jongleuse = a juggler

**jonquille** *noun, feminine*
  une jonquille = a daffodil

**joue** *noun, feminine*
  une joue = a cheek

**jouer** *verb* 1
- = to play
  jouer à [cache-cache | la marelle | colin-
  maillard …] = to play [hide-and-seek |
  hopscotch | blind man's buff …]
  jouer aux cartes = to play cards
  à quoi jouez-vous? = what are you
  playing?
  jouer de [la guitare | la flûte | la harpe …] = to
  play [the guitar | the flute | the harp …]
  jouer du piano = to play the piano
  de quoi joue-t-il? = what does he play?
- = to gamble
- qu'est-ce qu'on joue au théâtre? = what's
  on at the theatre?, what's showing at the
  theater?

**jouet** *noun, masculine*
  un jouet = a toy

**joueur/joueuse** *noun,*
*masculine/feminine*
  un joueur/une joueuse (*in a game, in sport*)
  = a player
  (*at the casino*) = a gambler
  être mauvais joueur = to be a bad loser

**jour** *noun, masculine*
- (*24 hours*)
  un jour = a day
  tous les jours = every day
  par jour = per day
  un jour de congé = a day off
  il y a quinze jours = a fortnight ago, two
  weeks ago
  de nos jours = nowadays
- (*the light*)
  le jour = daylight
  il fait jour = it's daylight
  en plein jour = in broad daylight
  voyager de jour = to travel by day, to
  travel in the daytime
  **le jour de l'An** = New Year's (Day)
  **un jour férié** = a bank holiday, a legal
  holiday
  **le jour J** = D-day
  **un jour ouvrable** = a working day

**journal** *noun, masculine*
(*plural*) **journaux**
- (*a publication*)
  un journal = a newspaper
- (*a private record*)
  un journal (intime) = a diary
  **le journal télévisé** = the TV news

**journaliste** *noun, masculine/feminine*
  un journaliste/une journaliste = a
  journalist

**journée** *noun, feminine*
  une journée = a day
  dans la journée = during the day

**joyeux/joyeuse** *adjective*
  = happy

**juger** verb [17]
= to judge

**juif/juive**
1 *adjective*
= Jewish
2 *noun, masculine/feminine*
un juif/une juive = a Jew

**juillet** *noun, masculine*
juillet = July
le 14 juillet = Bastille Day

**juin** *noun, masculine*
juin = June

**juive** ▶ juif

**jumeau/jumelle**
(*plural*) **jumeaux/jumelles**
1 *adjective*
= twin
2 *noun, masculine/feminine*
un jumeau/une jumelle = a (male) twin/a (female) twin
des jumeaux/des jumelles = twins

**jumelage** *noun, masculine*
un jumelage = a (town) twinning

**jumelé/jumelée** *adjective*
= twinned
Oxford est jumelé avec Grenoble = the city of Oxford is twinned with Grenoble

**jumelles** *noun, feminine plural*
des jumelles = binoculars

**jupe** *noun, feminine*
une jupe = a skirt

**jurer** verb [1]
= to swear

**jus** *noun, masculine* (**!** *never changes*)
• (*from fruit*)
du jus = juice
un jus de fruit = a fruit juice
• (*from a roast*)
le jus = the gravy

**jusque** (**jusqu'** *before vowel*)
1 *preposition*
• = as far as
aller jusqu'à Rome = to go as far as Rome
• = up to
= down to
de l'eau jusqu'à la taille = water up to the waist
se pencher jusqu'à terre = to bend down to the ground
• = until, till
jusqu'à lundi = until Monday
jusqu'à l'an 2000 = until the year 2000
jusqu'ici, jusqu'à présent = till now, up to now
2 **jusqu'à ce que** = until

**juste**
1 *adjective*
• = right, correct
une réponse juste = a correct answer
• = fair
ce n'est pas juste = it's not fair, it's unfair
• = tight
2 *adverb*
• chanter juste = to sing in tune
• il est huit heures juste = it's exactly eight o'clock
• tout juste = only just
il arrive juste = he's (only) just arrived
juste à temps = just in time
3 **au juste** = exactly

**justement** *adverb*
= exactly

**kaki**
1 *adjective* (**!** *never changes*)
= khaki
2 *noun, masculine*
un kaki = a persimmon

**kangourou** *noun, masculine*
un kangourou = a kangaroo

**karting** *noun, masculine*
le karting = go-karting

**kayak** *noun, masculine*
• (*the equipment*)
un kayak = a kayak
• (*the sport*)
le kayak = canoeing

**kermesse** *noun, feminine*
une kermesse = a fête, a festival

**kilo, kilogramme** *noun, masculine*
un kilo, un kilogramme = a kilo, a kilogram

**kilomètre** *noun, masculine*
un kilomètre = a kilometre, a kilometer

**kiosque** *noun, masculine*
un kiosque = a kiosk
**un kiosque à journaux** = a newspaper kiosk, a newsstand
**un kiosque à musique** = a bandstand

**klaxon** *noun, masculine*
un klaxon = a (car) horn

**klaxonner** verb [1]
= to sound one's horn, to honk the horn

**KO** adjective (**!** never changes)
(abbreviation of **knocked out**)
- = KO'ed
  **mettre son adversaire KO** = to KO one's
  opponent
- **je suis KO�֊** = I'm exhausted

**K-way**    noun, masculine
  **un K-way** = a windcheater, a windbreaker

# L1

**l'** ▶ **le**

**la** ▶ **le**

**là** adverb
- (indicating a place) = there
  **j'habitais là** = I used to live there
  **passez par là** = go that way
  **c'est là qu'il est né** = that's where he was
    born
  **là où elle travaille** = where she works
- (indicating a time) = then
  **d'ici là j'aurai fini** = by then, I'll have
    finished
  **ce jour-là** = that day
  **en ce temps-là** = in those days

**là-bas** adverb
  = over there

**laboratoire** noun, masculine
  **un laboratoire** = a laboratory

**lac** noun, masculine
  **un lac** = a lake

**lacet** noun, masculine
- (for shoes)
  **un lacet** = a lace
- (in a road)
  **un lacet** = a hairpin bend, a hairpin turn
  **une route en lacets** = a twisting road

**lâcher** verb 1
- (to stop holding) = to drop
  = to let go of
- (to collapse) = to give way
- (to stop working) = to fail

**là-dedans** adverb
  = in there

**là-dessous** adverb
  = under there, under it

**là-dessus** adverb
- (on a surface) = there, on it
- (on a subject) = about it

---

**✖** in informal situations

**là-haut** adverb
  = up there
  = upstairs

**laid/laide** adjective
  = ugly

**laine** noun, feminine
  **la laine** = wool
  **de laine, en laine** = wool(l)en, wool

**laisse** noun, feminine
  **une laisse** = a leash

**laisser** verb 1
**1** (**!** + avoir)
- = to leave
  **laisser sa voiture à l'ombre** = to leave one's
    car in the shade
  **laissez-moi tranquille!** = leave me alone!
- = to let
  **laisser couler l'eau** = to let the water run
  **laisser tomber un verre** = to drop a glass
**2 se laisser** (**!** + être)
- **se laisser influencer** = to allow oneself to
  be influenced
- **se laisser tomber sur le sable** = to flop
  down on the sand

**lait** noun, masculine
  **le lait** = milk
  **le lait en poudre** = powdered milk
  **le lait solaire** = suntan lotion

**laitier/laitière**
**1** adjective
  **les produits laitiers** = dairy products
  **une vache laitière** = a dairy cow
**2** noun, masculine|feminine
  **un laitier/une laitière** = a milkman/a
    milkwoman

**laitue** noun, feminine
  **une laitue** = a (head of) lettuce

**lame** noun, feminine
  **une lame** = a blade
  **une lame de rasoir** = a razor blade

**lamentable** adjective
  = pitiful
  = awful

**lampadaire** noun, masculine
  **un lampadaire** (in a house) = a standard
    lamp, a floor lamp
  (in the street) = a streetlamp, a streetlight

**lampe** noun, feminine
  **une lampe** = a lamp
  **une lampe de chevet** = a bedside lamp
  **une lampe électrique** = a torch, a
    flashlight
  **une lampe de poche** = a pocket torch, a
    flashlight

**lancer** verb 12
**1** (**!** + avoir)
- = to throw
- = to launch
**2 se lancer** (**!** + être)

- (to jump)
  se lancer = to throw oneself
- (to dare)
  se lancer = to take the plunge
- (to start)
  se lancer dans les affaires = to go into business

**langage** noun, masculine
un langage = a language

**langouste** noun, feminine
une langouste = a rock lobster

**langue** noun, feminine
- la langue = the tongue
- une langue = a language
- **la langue maternelle** = the mother tongue
- **les langues vivantes** = modern languages

**languir** verb ③
**1** (! + avoir)
  languir de revoir un ami = to be longing to see a friend
**2 se languir de** (! + être)
  se languir de = to be pining for

**lapin** noun, masculine
- un lapin = a rabbit
- poser un lapin* à quelqu'un = to stand someone up

**laquelle ▶ lequel**

**large**
**1** adjective
  = wide
**2** noun, masculine
- faire trois mètres de large = to be three metres wide
- le large = the open sea
  au large de la Bretagne = off the coast of Brittany

**largement** adverb
  avoir largement le temps = to have plenty of time
  c'est largement suffisant = it's more than enough

**largeur** noun, feminine
  la largeur = the width

**larme** noun, feminine
  une larme = a tear

**las/lasse** adjective
  = tired, weary

**lassant/lassante** adjective
  = tedious
  = tiresome

**lasser, se lasser de** verb ① (! + être)
  se lasser de = to grow tired of

**latin** noun, masculine
  le latin = Latin

**laurier** noun, masculine
  le laurier = laurel
  = bay
  une feuille de laurier = a bay leaf

**lavable** adjective
  = washable

**lavabo** noun, masculine
  un lavabo = a washbasin, a wash-hand basin

**lavage** noun, masculine
  le lavage = washing

**lavande** noun, feminine
  la lavande = lavender

**lave-linge** noun, masculine (! never changes)
  un lave-linge = a washing machine

**laver** verb ①
**1** (! + avoir)
  = to wash
**2 se laver** (! + être)
  se laver = to wash oneself
  se laver les mains = to wash one's hands

**laverie** noun, feminine
  une laverie (automatique) = a launderette, a laundromat

**lave-vaisselle** noun, masculine (! never changes)
  un lave-vaisselle = a dishwasher

**le/la** (l' before vowel or mute h)
(plural) **les**
**1** determiner
- = the
  la fenêtre de la cuisine = the kitchen window
  les Martin = the Martins
- (not translated in some cases)
  apprendre le russe = to learn Russian
  aimer le café = to like coffee
  les enfants aiment les animaux = children like animals
- = a
  8 euros le kilo = 8 euros a kilo
  cent kilomètres à l'heure = one hundred kilometres an hour
- (used with nouns relating to a part of the body)
  avoir les yeux bleus = to have blue eyes
  se casser la jambe = to break one's leg
  il m'a serré la main = he shook my hand
- (used with a day of the week)
  travailler le lundi = to work on Mondays
  tous les mardis = every Tuesday
**2** pronoun
- (referring to a person, an animal or a thing)
  = him/her
  = it
  (plural) = them
  il l'a invitée = he invited her
  où les as-tu achetés? = where did you buy them?

L

* (other cases)
  comme vous le savez = as you know
  je te l'avais dit = I told you
  il ne peut pas te le dire = he can't tell you
  espérons-le! = let's hope so!

**lécher** verb 1
　= to lick

**leçon** noun, feminine
　une leçon = a lesson

**lecteur/lectrice**
**1** noun, masculine/feminine
　un lecteur/une lectrice = a reader
**2 lecteur** noun, masculine
　un lecteur de cassettes = a cassette player
　un lecteur laser = a CD player
　un lecteur DVD = a DVD player

**lecture** noun, feminine
　la lecture = reading

**légendaire** adjective
　= legendary

**légende** noun, feminine
* (a story)
  une légende = a legend
* (on a picture, a cartoon)
  la légende = the caption
* (on a map)
  la légende = the key

**léger/légère** adjective
* (not heavy) = light
* (not serious) = slight
* (not strong)
  un café léger = a weak coffee
  une cigarette légère = a mild cigarette
  un vent léger = a light wind

**légèrement** adverb
　= slightly

**légume** noun, masculine
　un légume = a vegetable

**lendemain** noun, masculine
　le lendemain = the next day
　le lendemain matin = the next morning
　le lendemain de mon arrivée = the day
　　after I arrived

**lent/lente** adjective
　= slow

**lentement** adverb
　= slowly

**lentille** noun, feminine
* (food)
  des lentilles = lentils
* (optical device)
  une lentille = a lens
  les lentilles de contact = contact lenses

**lequel/laquelle** pronoun
(plural) **lesquels/lesquelles**
* = which one

lequel d'entre eux a payé? = which one of
　them paid?
lesquelles veux-tu? = which ones do you
　want?
* = which
  la situation dans laquelle je me trouve
  = the situation in which I find myself

**les ▶ le**

**lesquels/lesquelles ▶ lequel**

**lessive** noun, feminine
　la lessive = the washing, the laundry

**lettre** noun, feminine
　une lettre = a letter
　en toutes lettres = in full

**leur**
**1** determiner
　= their
　leur jardin = their garden
　leurs sacs = their bags
**2** pronoun (! never changes)
　= them
　il leur a prêté sa voiture = he lent them his
　　car
　je la leur ai envoyée = I sent it to them
**3** pronoun
　le leur/la leur/les leurs = theirs

**levée** noun, feminine
　une levée (from a post-box) = a collection

**lever**
**1** verb 16 (! + avoir)
　= to raise
　levez les bras = raise your arms
　lever le doigt (in class) ≈ to put up one's
　　hand
**2 se lever** verb 16 (! + être)
* (if it's a person)
  se lever = to get up
  = to stand up
* (if it's the sun, the wind)
  se lever = to rise
**3** noun, masculine
　au lever = when one gets up
　= on getting up
　le lever du soleil = sunrise

**lèvre** noun, feminine
　une lèvre = a lip

**levure** noun, feminine
　la levure = yeast
　**la levure chimique** = baking powder

**lexique** noun, masculine
　un lexique = a vocabulary list

**libérer** verb 14
　= to release, to free

**liberté** noun, feminine
　la liberté = freedom

**libraire** noun, masculine/feminine
　un libraire/une libraire = a bookseller

**librairie** noun, feminine
une librairie = a bookshop, a bookstore

**libre** adjective
- = free
ils sont libres d'y aller = they're free to go
'entrée libre' = 'admission free'
- = clear
la route est libre = the road is clear
- = vacant
une place libre = a vacant seat
- la ligne n'est pas libre = the line is engaged, the line is busy

**librement** adverb
= freely

**libre-service** noun, masculine
(plural) **libres-services**
un libre-service = a self-service

**licence** noun, feminine
une licence (a diploma) = a degree

**licencier** verb [2]
= to dismiss, to lay off
= to make redundant, to let go

**lien** noun, masculine
un lien = a tie
= a bond
= a link

**lieu** noun, masculine
(plural) **lieux**
**1** un lieu = a place
un lieu de rencontre = a meeting place
votre lieu de naissance = your place of birth
**2 avoir lieu** = to take place
**3 au lieu de** = instead of

**lièvre** noun, masculine
un lièvre = a hare

**ligne** noun, feminine
une ligne = a line
**en ligne** = online

**lilas** noun, masculine (! never changes)
le lilas = lilac

**limonade** noun, feminine
la limonade = lemonade

**linge** noun, masculine
- (sheets, towels)
le linge (de maison) = (household) linen
le linge sale = dirty linen
- (when being laundered)
le linge = the washing, the laundry
avoir du linge à laver = to have some washing to do

**lion** noun, masculine
un lion = a lion

**Lion** noun, masculine
le Lion = Leo

**liquide** noun, masculine
- un liquide = a liquid
- payer en liquide = to pay cash

**lire¹** verb [41]
= to read

**lire²** noun, feminine
la lire = the lira

**lisse** adjective
= smooth

**liste** noun, feminine
une liste = a list
une liste d'attente = a waiting list
être sur liste rouge = to be ex-directory, to have an unlisted number

**lit** noun, masculine
un lit = a bed
un lit de camp = a camp bed
un grand lit = a double bed
des lits superposés = bunk beds

**litre** noun, masculine
un litre = a litre, a liter

**littérature** noun, feminine
la littérature = literature

**littoral** noun, masculine
(plural) **littoraux**
le littoral = the coast

**livraison** noun, feminine
une livraison = a delivery

**livre**
**1** noun, masculine
un livre = a book
**2** noun, feminine
une livre = a pound

**livrer** verb [1]
= to deliver

**livret** noun, masculine
un livret = a booklet
**un livret de famille** = a family record book (of births, marriages and deaths)
**un livret scolaire** = a school report book

**local/locale**
(plural) **locaux/locales**
**1** adjective
= local
**2 local** noun, masculine
un local = a place

**locataire** noun, masculine/feminine
un locataire/une locataire = a tenant

**location** noun, feminine
la location (of accommodation) = renting
(of equipment) = hiring
(of seats) = booking, reservation
'location de voitures' = 'car hire', 'car rental'

**loge** noun, feminine
- (for a caretaker)
une loge = a lodge

**L**

- (for an actor)
  **une loge** = a dressing room

**logé/logée** adjective
= housed
**être logé et nourri** = to have room and
  board

**logement** noun, masculine
- **un logement** = accommodation
  = a flat, an apartment
- **le logement** = housing

**loger** verb 13
**1** (**!** + avoir)
- (to provide accommodation) = to house
  (for a short time) = to put up
- (to have accommodation) = to live
  (for a short time) = to stay
**2 se loger** (**!** + être)
**trouver à se loger** = to find somewhere to
  live

**logique** adjective
= logical

**loi** noun, feminine
**une loi** = a law

**loin** adverb
- = a long way, far (away)
  **c'est trop loin** = it's too far
  **c'est encore loin?** = is it much further?
- **de loin** = from a distance
- **au loin** = in the distance

**lointain/lointaine** adjective
= distant

**loisir** noun, masculine plural
- (spare time)
  **le loisir** = leisure
- (activity)
  **un loisir** = a leisure activity, a pastime

**Londres** noun
= London

**long/longue**
**1** adjective
= long
**2 long** noun, masculine
**faire deux mètres de long** = to be two
  metres long
**marcher de long en large** = to pace up and
  down
**3 le long de** = along

**longer** verb 13
= to follow

**longtemps** adverb
= (for) a long time
**il y a longtemps qu'il est parti** = he left a
  long time ago
**ça fait longtemps que tu attends?** = have
  you been waiting long?

**longue** ▶ **long**

**longuement** adverb
= for a long time

**longueur** noun, feminine
**la longueur** = the length
**à longueur de journée** = all day long

**lorsque** (**lorsqu'** before vowel or mute h)
conjunction
= (at the time) when

**loterie** noun, feminine
**une loterie** = a lottery

**lotissement** noun, masculine
**un lotissement** = a housing estate, a
  housing development

**loto** noun, masculine
**le loto** = lotto
= bingo

**louche**
**1** adjective
= shady
**2** noun, feminine
**une louche** = a ladle

**louer** verb 1
- (as the owner) = to rent out
  **'à louer'** = 'to let', 'for rent'
- (as the tenant) = to rent
  (as the hirer) = to hire, to rent

**loufoque✗** adjective
= crazy

**loup** noun, masculine
**un loup** = a wolf

**loupe** noun, feminine
**une loupe** = a magnifying glass

**lourd/lourde** adjective
- (weighty) = heavy
- (describing the weather) = muggy, sultry
  **il fait lourd** = it's muggy

**loyer** noun, masculine
**le loyer** = the rent

**lu/lue** ▶ **lire**[1] 41

**lucarne** noun, feminine
**une lucarne** = a skylight

**lueur** noun, feminine
**une lueur** = a (faint) light
= a glow
= a gleam, a flash

**luge** noun, feminine
- (the equipment)
  **une luge** = a toboggan, a sled
- (the sport)
  **la luge** = tobogganing

---

**✗** in informal situations

**lui**
1 *pronoun, masculine*
- = him
  à cause de lui = because of him
  la voiture est à lui = the car belongs to
  him, the car is his
  c'est à lui de jouer = it's his turn to play
- = he
  elle est restée, mais lui est parti = she
  stayed, but he left
2 *pronoun, feminine*
  = her
  je lui ai prêté ma robe = I lent her my dress

**lui-même** *pronoun, masculine*
= himself
= itself

**luire** *verb* 62
= to shine, to glow

**luisant/luisante** *adjective*
= shining, glowing

**lumière** *noun, feminine*
la lumière = light

**lunch** *noun, masculine*
un lunch = a buffet lunch

**lundi** *noun, masculine*
lundi = Monday

**lune** *noun, feminine*
la lune = the moon

**lunette**
1 *noun, feminine*
  une lunette = a telescope
2 **lunettes** *noun, feminine plural*
  des lunettes = glasses, spectacles
  des lunettes de soleil = sunglasses

**lustrer** *verb* 1
= to polish

**lutin** *noun, masculine*
un lutin = an imp

**lutte** *noun, feminine*
- (*a fight*)
  une lutte = a struggle
- (*the sport*)
  la lutte = wrestling

**lutter** *verb* 1
= to fight
= to struggle

**luxe** *noun, masculine*
le luxe = luxury

**Luxembourg** *noun, masculine*
le Luxembourg = Luxembourg

**lycée** *noun, masculine*
un lycée = a secondary school, ≈ a senior
high school (*for students aged 15 to 18*)

**lycéen/lycéenne** *noun,*
*masculine/feminine*
un lycéen/une lycéenne = a secondary
school student, a high school student
(*aged 15 to 18*)

# Mm

**m** *noun, masculine* (**!** *never changes*)
(*abbreviation of* **mètre**)
m = m

**m'** ▶ **me**

**M.** (*abbreviation of* **Monsieur**)
M. = Mr

**ma** ▶ **mon**

**macaron** *noun, masculine*
un macaron = a macaroon

**macédoine** *noun, feminine*
- une macédoine de légumes = mixed diced
  vegetables
- une macédoine de fruits = a fruit salad

**machin**<sup>×</sup> *noun, masculine*
un machin<sup>×</sup> = a thing, a what's it

**machine** *noun, feminine*
une machine = a machine
**une machine à coudre** = a sewing
machine
**une machine à écrire** = a typewriter
**une machine à laver** = a washing
machine
**une machine à sous** = a one-armed
bandit

**maçon** *noun, masculine*
un maçon = a bricklayer
= a mason
= a builder

**madame** *noun, feminine*
(*plural*) **mesdames**
Madame Martin = Mrs Martin
bonjour madame = good morning
mesdames et messieurs = ladies and
gentlemen

**mademoiselle** *noun, feminine*
(*plural*) **mesdemoiselles**
Mademoiselle Martin = Miss Martin
bonjour mademoiselle = good morning
mesdames, mesdemoiselles et messieurs
= ladies and gentlemen

**magasin** *noun, masculine*
un magasin = a shop, a store
**un grand magasin** = a department store

**magazine** *noun, masculine*
un magazine = a magazine

**magique** *adjective*
= magic

**magnétophone** *noun, masculine*
un magnétophone = a tape recorder

**magnétoscope** *noun, masculine*
un magnétoscope = a video recorder

M

**magnifique** *adjective*
= magnificent
= wonderful

**mai** *noun, masculine*
mai = May
le 1er Mai = May Day

**maigre** *adjective*
• = thin
• = lean

**maigrir** *verb* ③
= to lose weight

**maillot** *noun, masculine*
un maillot (*for a dancer*) = a leotard
(*in football*) = a shirt, a jersey
(*for cyclists*) = a jersey
**un maillot de corps** = a vest, an undershirt
**un maillot de bain** = a swimsuit

**main** *noun, feminine*
une main = a hand
fait (à la) main = handmade
se donner la main = to hold hands
se serrer la main = to shake hands
je vais te donner un coup de main = I'll give you a hand
haut les mains! = hands up!

**maintenant** *adverb*
= now
= nowadays

**maire** *noun, masculine*
le maire = the mayor

**mairie** *noun, feminine*
la mairie = the town hall

**mais** *conjunction*
= but

**maïs** *noun, masculine* (**!** *never changes*)
le maïs = maize, corn
= sweetcorn

**maison**
**1** *adjective* (**!** *never changes*)
= homemade
**2** *noun, feminine*
la maison = the house
= home
rester à la maison = to stay at home
**une maison de campagne** = a house in the country
**une maison de la culture** = a community arts centre
**une maison des jeunes (et de la culture)** = a youth club
**une maison de retraite** = a retirement home

**maître/maîtresse** *noun, masculine/feminine*

---

**×** in informal situations

• (*in a school*)
le maître/la maîtresse = the teacher
• (*of a pet*)
le maître/la maîtresse = the master/the mistress

**majeur/majeure** *adjective*
• = major, main
en majeure partie = for the most part
• être majeur = to be over 18 years of age

**mal**
**1** *adjective* (**!** *never changes*)
= bad
c'est mal de mentir = it's bad to lie
les photos ne sont pas mal× = the photos aren't bad
**2** *adverb*
mal = badly
= not well
ils ont mal dormi = they slept badly
elle va mal = she isn't well at all
être mal élevé = to be bad mannered
**3 faire mal** = to hurt
ça me fait mal = it hurts
tu me fais mal = you're hurting me
je me suis fait mal = I hurt myself
**4 avoir mal**
avoir mal à la tête = to have a headache
avoir mal aux dents = to have (a) toothache
avoir mal à la gorge = to have a sore throat
avoir mal au cœur = to feel sick
il a mal au genou = his knee hurts
avoir le mal de mer = to be seasick

**malade**
**1** *adjective*
= ill, sick
tomber malade = to fall ill
**2** *noun, masculine/feminine*
un malade/une malade = a patient
= a sick person

**maladie** *noun, feminine*
une maladie = an illness, a disease

**maladroit/maladroite** *adjective*
= clumsy

**malaise** *noun, masculine*
• (*faintness*)
un malaise = a dizzy turn
avoir un malaise = to feel faint
• (*nervousness*)
un malaise = unease

**malfaiteur** *noun, masculine*
un malfaiteur = a criminal

**malgré** *preposition*
= despite, in spite of

**malheur** *noun, masculine*
un malheur = a misfortune

**malheureusement** *adverb*
= unfortunately

**malheureux/malheureuse** adjective
= unhappy
= unfortunate

**malhonnête** adjective
= dishonest

**malin/maligne** adjective
= clever
= crafty

**malsain/malsaine** adjective
– unhealthy

**maltraiter** verb [1]
= to ill treat

**maman** noun, feminine
une maman = a mum, a mom

**mamie×** noun, feminine
ma mamie× = my gran, my granny

**manche**
**1** noun, feminine
une manche = a sleeve
sans manches = sleeveless
**2** noun, masculine
un manche = a handle
**un manche à balai** – a broomstick
= a joystick

**Manche** noun, feminine
la Manche = the (English) Channel

**mandat** noun, masculine
un mandat = a money order

**manège** noun, masculine
un manège = a fairground ride

**manger** verb [13]
= to eat
inviter des amis à manger = to invite
friends for a meal
manger au restaurant = to eat out

**mangue** noun, feminine
une mangue = a mango

**manière** noun, feminine
• (a method)
la manière = the way
c'est leur manière de remercier = it's their
way of saying thank you
• (conduct)
des manières = manners

**manif×** noun, feminine
une manif× = a demo

**manifestation** noun, feminine
une manifestation = a demonstration
**une manifestation sportive** = a
sporting event

**mannequin** noun, masculine
un mannequin (in a shop window) = a
dummy, a mannequin
(a person) = a (fashion) model

**manquer** verb [1]
• (to fail to catch, hit, reach, see, hear) = to
miss
manquer le train = to miss the train
• mes amis me manquent = I miss my
friends
ça t'a manqué? = did you miss it?
• (impersonal use) = to be missing
il manque un bouton = there's a button
missing
je ne peux pas l'acheter, il me manque dix
euros = I can't buy it, I'm ten euros short
il te manque cinq euros pour payer la note
= you need five euros more to pay the
bill
• manquer de = to be short of
= to lack
• manquer à sa promesse = to break one's
promise

**mansarde** noun, feminine
une mansarde = an attic room

**manteau** noun, masculine
(plural) **manteaux**
un manteau = a coat

**maquereau** noun, masculine
(plural) **maquereaux**
un maquereau = a mackerel

**maquette** noun, feminine
une maquette = a scale model

**maquillage** noun, masculine
le maquillage = make-up

**maquiller: se maquiller** verb [1]
(! + être)
se maquiller = to put on make-up
= to wear make-up

**marbre** noun, masculine
le marbre = marble

**marchand/marchande** noun,
masculine/feminine
un marchand/une marchande = a
shopkeeper
= a stallholder

**marchandise** noun, feminine
de la marchandise = goods

**marche** noun, feminine
• (stair)
une marche = a step
les marches = the stairs
• (the sport)
la marche = walking
• (when talking about a machine, a
mechanism)
être en marche = to be running
mettre le moteur en marche = to start the
engine up
• (when talking about a vehicle)
un train en marche = a moving train
faire marche arrière = to reverse
**la marche à suivre** = the procedure

**M**

**marché** *noun, masculine*
* (*a place*)
  un marché = a market
  faire son marché = to go shopping
* (*in business*)
  un marché = a deal
* être bon marché = to be cheap
**le Marché Commun** = the Common Market
**un marché aux puces** = a flea market

**marcher** *verb* 1
* = to walk
* = to work
  comment marche la tondeuse? = how does the mower work?
* (*if it's an event, a fest*)✶ = to go well
  les affaires marchent✶ bien = business is going well
  l'examen a marché✶? = how did the exam go?

**mardi** *noun, masculine*
  mardi = Tuesday
**Mardi gras** = Shrove Tuesday

**mare** *noun, feminine*
  une mare = a pond

**marée** *noun, feminine*
  la marée = the tide
  la marée monte = the tide is coming in
  la marée descend = the tide is going out
**une marée noire** = an oil slick

**marelle** *noun, feminine*
  la marelle = hopscotch

**marge** *noun, feminine*
  la marge = the margin

**mari** *noun, masculine*
  un mari = a husband

**mariage** *noun, masculine*
  un mariage = a wedding
  = a marriage

**marié/mariée**
**1** *adjective*
  = married
**2** *noun, masculine/feminine*
  le marié/la mariée = the bridegroom/the bride

**marier** *verb* 2
**1** (**!** + *avoir*)
  = to marry
  ils ont marié leur fille = they married their daughter
**2 se marier** (**!** + *être*)
  se marier = to get married, to marry
  elle s'est mariée avec son cousin = she got married to her cousin, she married her cousin

**marin/marine**[1]
**1** *adjective*

* le sel marin = sea salt
* un pull marin = a seaman's jersey
**2 marin** *noun, masculine*
  un marin = a sailor

**marine**[2] *noun, feminine*
  la marine = the navy

**marionnette** *noun, feminine*
  une marionnette = a puppet

**Maroc** *noun, masculine*
  le Maroc = Morocco

**marocain/marocaine** *adjective*
  = Moroccan

**maroquinerie** *noun, feminine*
  une maroquinerie = a leather shop, a leather store

**marque** *noun, feminine*
* (*in commerce*)
  une marque = a brand, a make
  de marque française = French
* (*a trace*)
  une marque = a mark

**marquer** *verb* 1
* = to note (down), to write
* = to score
* = to mark, to make an impression

**marraine** *noun, feminine*
  une marraine = a godmother

**marrant/marrante**✶ *adjective*
  = funny

**marre**✶ *adverb*
  en avoir marre✶ = to be fed up

**marrer: se marrer**✶ *verb* 1 (**!** + *être*)
* se marrer✶ = to laugh
* se marrer✶ = to have a good laugh

**marron**
**1** *adjective* (**!** *never changes*)
  = brown
**2** *noun, masculine*
  un marron = a chestnut
  un marron (d'Inde) = a horse chestnut
**des marrons chauds** = roast chestnuts

**mars** *noun, masculine*
  mars = March

**Marseillaise** *noun, feminine*
  la Marseillaise = the Marseillaise (*the French national anthem*)

**marteau** *noun, masculine*
  (*plural*) **marteaux**
  un marteau = a hammer
**un marteau piqueur** = a pneumatic drill, a jackhammer

**mas** *noun, masculine* (**!** *never changes*)
  un mas = a farmhouse (*in Provence*)

**masque** *noun, masculine*
  un masque = a mask

---
✶ in informal situations

**mât** noun, masculine
un mât = a mast

**match** noun, masculine
un match de football = a football match, a
football game

**matelas** noun, masculine (**!** never
changes)
un matelas = a mattress
**un matelas pneumatique** = an air bed,
an air mattress

**matériel** noun, masculine
le matériel = the equipment

**mathématiques** noun, feminine plural
les mathématiques = mathematics

**maths\*** noun, feminine plural
les maths\* = math(s)

**matière** noun, feminine
• (something studied)
une matière = a subject
• (a substance)
une matière = a material
**les matières grasses** = fats
**les matières premières** = raw materials

**matin** noun, masculine
un matin = a morning
demain matin = tomorrow morning
de bon matin = early in the morning

**matinal/matinale** adjective
(plural) **matinaux/matinales**
= early
être matinal = to be an early riser

**matinée** noun, feminine
la matinée = the morning
faire la grasse matinée = to have a lie-in,
to sleep in

**mauvais/mauvaise**
**1** adjective
• = bad
le mauvais temps = bad weather
être mauvais en algèbre = to be bad at
algebra
• = wrong
la mauvaise adresse = the wrong address
**2 mauvais** adverb
• il fait mauvais = the weather is bad
• ça sent mauvais = it smells
**une mauvaise herbe** = a weed

**maximum** noun, masculine
un maximum = a maximum
100 euros au maximum = 100 euros at
(the) most

**mayonnaise** noun, feminine
la mayonnaise = mayonnaise

**me** (**m'** before vowel or mute h) pronoun
• = me
Il m'a vu = he saw me
elle ne me parle pas = she won't speak to
me

• = myself
je me suis coupé = I cut myself

**mec\*** noun, masculine
un mec\* = a bloke, a guy

**mécanicien/mécanicienne**
un mécanicien/une mécanicienne (in a
garage) = a mechanic
(on a train) = an engine driver, a
locomotive engineer

**mécanique**
**1** adjective
= mechanical
(describing a toy) = clockwork
**2** noun, feminine
la mécanique = mechanics

**méchant/méchante** adjective
= nasty, mean

**méchoui** noun, masculine
un méchoui = a North African style
barbecue

**mécontent/mécontente** adjective
= dissatisfied, displeased

**médaille** noun, feminine
une médaille = a medal

**médecin** noun, masculine
un médecin = a doctor

**médical/médicale** adjective
(plural) **médicaux/médicales**
= medical

**médicament** noun, masculine
un médicament = a medicine, a drug

**médiéval/médiévale** adjective
(plural) **médiévaux/médiévales**
= medieval

**Méditerranée** noun, feminine
la (mer) Méditerranée = the
Mediterranean (Sea)

**méfiant/méfiante** adjective
= suspicious, mistrustful

**méfier: se méfier** verb [2] (**!** + être)
• se méfier = to distrust
je me méfie de ce garçon = I don't trust
that boy
• se méfier = to be careful
méfie-toi! = be careful

**meilleur/meilleure**
**1** adjective
• = better
le film est meilleur que le roman = the film
is better than the novel
• = best
le meilleur vin de la région = the best wine
in the area
**2** noun, masculine/feminine
le meilleur/la meilleure = the best one

M

**3 meilleur** *adverb*
= better
**il fait meilleur qu'hier** = the weather is
better than yesterday

**mélanger** *verb* 13
• (*to combine*) = to mix
• (*to muddle up*) = to mix up

**melon** *noun, masculine*
**un melon** = a melon

**membre** *noun, masculine*
• (*a person*)
**un membre** = a member
• (*an arm, a leg*)
**un membre** = a limb

**même**
**1** *adjective*
= same
**les mêmes bottes que les miennes** = the
same boots as mine
**2** *pronoun*
**le même/la même** = the same one
**3** *adverb*
• (*used for emphasis*) = even
**il n'a même pas répondu** = he didn't even
reply
**j'irai, même s'il pleut** = I'll go, even if it
rains
• (*exactly*) = very
**aujourd'hui même** = this very day
**ici même** = in this very place, right here

**mémé×** *noun, feminine*
**ma mémé×** = my gran, my granny

**mémoire** *noun, feminine*
**la mémoire** = memory

**mémoriser** *verb* 1
= to memorize

**menacer** *verb* 12
= to threaten

**ménage** *noun, masculine*
• (*cleaning*)
**le ménage** = the housework
• (*the people*)
**un ménage** = a couple
= a household

**ménager/ménagère¹** *adjective*
= domestic
= household

**ménagère²** *noun, feminine*
**une ménagère** = a housewife

**mendiant/mendiante** *noun,*
*masculine/feminine*
**un mendiant/une mendiante** = a beggar

**mener** *verb* 16
• = to lead
• = to take

**mensonge** *noun, masculine*
**un mensonge** = a lie

**mensuel/mensuelle** *adjective*
= monthly

**menteur/menteuse** *noun, masculine/*
*feminine*
**un menteur/une menteuse** = a liar

**menthe** *noun, feminine*
**la menthe** = mint
**une menthe à l'eau** = a mint cordial

**mentionner** *verb* 1
= to mention

**mentir** *verb* 30
= to lie

**menton** *noun, masculine*
**le menton** = the chin

**menu/menue**
**1** *adjective*
= small
**2 menu** *adverb*
**hacher menu** = to chop finely
**3 menu** *noun, masculine*
**le menu** = the menu
**le menu à prix fixe** = the set menu

**mer** *noun, feminine*
**la mer** = the sea

**merci** *noun, masculine* (*also exclamation*)
**merci!** = thank you!

**mercredi** *noun, masculine*
**mercredi** = Wednesday

**merde⬥** *exclamation*
= shit!

**mère** *noun, feminine*
**une mère** = a mother

**méridional/méridionale** *adjective*
(*plural*) **méridionaux/méridionales**
= southern

**mériter** *verb* 1
= to deserve

**merveille** *noun, feminine*
**une merveille** = a marvel, a wonder
**faire des merveilles** = to work wonders

**merveilleux/merveilleuse** *adjective*
= marvellous, wonderful

**mes ▶ mon**

**mesdames ▶ madame**

**mesdemoiselles ▶ mademoiselle**

**messe** *noun, feminine*
**une messe** = a mass

**messieurs ▶ monsieur**

**mesure** *noun, feminine*
• (*when determining size*)
**une mesure** = a measurement
**sur mesure** = made to measure

---

- (a decision, a step)
une mesure = a measure

**mesurer** verb [1]
= to measure
combien mesures-tu? = how tall are you?
Paul mesure 1,80 m = Paul is six foot tall

**météo** noun, feminine
la météo = the weather forecast
la météo marine = the shipping forecast
la météo annonce de la pluie = the forecast is for rain

**méthode** noun, feminine
- (a way of doing things)
une méthode = a method
- (a book)
une méthode = a handbook
= a textbook

**métier** noun, masculine
un métier = a job
= a trade

**mètre** noun, masculine
- (a unit of measurement)
un mètre = a metre, a meter
- (an instrument)
un mètre = a tape measure

**métro** noun, masculine
le métro = the underground, the subway

**mets ▶ mettre** [60]

**mettre** verb [60]
**1** (! + avoir)
- = to put
j'ai mis la lettre sur la table = I put the letter on the table
- = to put on
il a mis son chapeau = he put on his hat
- (other uses)
mettre le couvert = to set the table
elle met une heure pour aller au bureau = it takes her one hour to get to the office
**2 se mettre** (! + être)
- (to place oneself)
se mettre debout = to stand up
il s'est mis à table = he sat down at the table
- (to apply, to wear)
se mettre = to put on
se mettre du rouge à lèvres = to put lipstick on
- (to begin)
se mettre à [chanter | pleurer | écrire …] = to start [singing | crying | writing …]
se mettre en colère = to lose one's temper, to get angry
se mettre en route = to set off

**meuble** noun, masculine
un meuble = a piece of furniture
des meubles = furniture

**meubler** verb [1]
= to furnish

**meurtre** noun, masculine
un meurtre = a murder

**micro** noun, masculine
un micro = a microphone

**microbe** noun, masculine
un microbe = a germ, a microbe

**midi** noun, masculine
- = twelve o'clock, midday, noon
il est midi et demi = it's half past twelve, it's twelve thirty
- = lunchtime

**Midi** noun, masculine
le Midi = the South of France

**miel** noun, masculine
le miel = honey

**mien/mienne** pronoun
le mien/la mienne = mine
les miens/les miennes = mine

**miette** noun, feminine
une miette = a crumb

**mieux** adverb, adjective (! never changes)
= better

**mignon/mignonne** adjective
= sweet, cute

**mijoter** verb [1]
- = to simmer
- = to prepare

**milieu**
(plural) **milieux**
**1** noun, masculine
- (the centre)
le milieu = the middle
- (the world around)
le milieu (nature) = the environment
(family) = the background
**2 au milieu de** = in the middle of
= among

**militaire**
**1** adjective
= military
**2** noun, masculine
un militaire = a soldier

**mille**
**1** number (! never changes)
= a thousand, one thousand
**2** noun, masculine
un mille (marin) = a (nautical) mile

**milliard** noun, masculine
un milliard = a billion

**millier** noun, masculine
un millier = a thousand
= about a thousand

**million** noun, masculine
un million = a million, one million

M

**minable*** *adjective*
= pathetic
= shabby

**mince**
**1** *adjective*
= slim, thin, slender
**2** *exclamation***
mince***! (*expressing annoyance*) = damn!
(*expressing amazement*) = wow!

**minéral/minérale** *adjective*
(*plural*) **minéraux/minérales**
= mineral

**mineur/mineure**
**1** *adjective*
• (*under 18*) = underage
• (*not important*) = minor
**2** *noun, masculine/feminine*
un mineur/une mineure = a minor
**3** **mineur** *noun, masculine*
un mineur = a miner

**Minitel**    *noun, masculine*
le Minitel = Minitel (*a terminal linking
    phone users to interactive databases*)

**minuit** *noun, masculine*
minuit = twelve o'clock, midnight

**minuscule** *adjective*
= tiny, minute

**minute** *noun, feminine*
une minute = a minute, one minute

**miroir** *noun, masculine*
un miroir = a mirror

**mis/mise ▶ mettre** 60

**misérable** *adjective*
= poor
= wretched

**misère** *noun, feminine*
la misère = poverty

**mistral** *noun, masculine*
le mistral = the mistral (*a cold north wind*)

**mite** *noun, feminine*
une mite = a (clothes) moth

**mixte** *adjective*
= mixed
(*describing a school*) = coeducational

**Mlle** (*abbreviation of* **Mademoiselle**)
Mlle = Miss, Ms

**Mme** (*abbreviation of* **Madame**)
Mme = Mrs, Ms

**mobilier** *noun, masculine*
le mobilier = the furniture

**mobylette**    *noun, feminine*
une mobylette = a moped

---

**moche*** *adjective*
• = ugly
• = awful

**mode**
**1** *noun, feminine*
une mode = a fashion
être à la mode (*if it's clothes*) = to be
    fashionable
(*if it's a singer, an actor*) = to be popular
**2** *noun, masculine*
un mode de vie = a lifestyle

**modèle** *noun, masculine*
un modèle = a model
= a pattern

**modéré/modérée** *adjective*
= moderate

**moi** *pronoun*
= me
moi non plus = nor me, me neither
donne-la-moi = give it to me
ce sac est à moi = this bag belongs to me,
    this bag is mine
c'est à moi de jouer = it's my turn to play
viens chez moi = come to my house
moi, je reste ici = I'm staying here

**moi-même** *pronoun*
= myself

**moineau** *noun, masculine*
(*plural*) **moineaux**
un moineau = a sparrow

**moins**
**1** *preposition*
• = minus
= less
il fait moins cinq (degrés) = it's minus five
    (degrees)
550 euros, moins la caution = 550 euros,
    minus the deposit
• (*when talking about time*) = to
il est une heure moins le quart = it's a
    quarter to one
**2** *adverb*
• = less
moins intéressant = less interesting
moins cher que d'habitude = cheaper than
    usual
de moins en moins = less and less
deux fois moins cher = twice as cheap
• moins de = less
= fewer
= less than
= under
un peu moins de sucre = a little less sugar
il a moins d'amis maintenant = he has
    fewer friends now
moins de la moitié = less than half
• moins... moins... = the less... the less...
moins... plus... = the less... the more...
moins je travaille, moins j'ai envie de
    travailler = the less I work, the less I feel
    like working

---

**✕** in informal situations

* le moins/la moins = the least
  = the less
  le coin le moins ensoleillé du jardin = the least sunny spot in the garden
  le moins cher des deux = the cheaper of the two
**3 au moins** = at least
**4 du moins** = at least
**4 à moins que, à moins de** = unless

**mois** *noun, masculine* (**!** *never changes*)
  un mois = a month
  au mois de mai = in May

**moisson** *noun, feminine*
  la moisson = the harvest

**moitié** *noun, feminine*
  une moitié = a half
  à moitié prix = half-price

**molle ▶ mou**

**moment** *noun, masculine*
  un moment = a moment, one moment
  en ce moment = at the moment
  par moments = at times
  juste au moment où il allait partir = just as he was about to leave

**mon/ma** *determiner*
(*plural*) **mes**
  = my

**monde** *noun, masculine*
* le monde = the world
  faire le tour du monde en bateau = to sail around the world
  le monde des affaires = the business world
* Il y a du monde, il y a beaucoup de monde = there are a lot of people
  tout le monde = everybody

**moniteur/monitrice**
**1** *noun, masculine/feminine*
  un moniteur/une monitrice (*for skiers, drivers*) = an instructor
  (*in a holiday camp*) = a group leader, a counselor
**2 moniteur** *noun, masculine*
  un moniteur (*a screen*) = a monitor

**monnaie** *noun, feminine*
* la monnaie = change
* une monnaie = a currency

**monsieur** *noun, masculine*
(*plural*) **messieurs**
  un monsieur = a gentleman
  bonjour messieurs = good morning (gentlemen)
  Monsieur Martin = Mr Martin

**monstre**
**1** *adjective*
  monstre✖ = huge
**2** *noun, masculine*
  un monstre = a monster

**montagne** *noun, feminine*
  une montagne = a mountain

**montagneux/montagneuse**
*adjective*
  = mountainous

**montant/montante**
**1** *adjective*
* un col montant = a high collar
* la marée montante = the rising tide
**2 montant** *noun, masculine*
  le montant (*on a bill*) = the total

**monter** *verb* 1
**1** (**!** + *être*)
* = to go up
  elle est montée au village = she's gone up to the village
  tu es monté à pied? = did you walk up?
  nous sommes montés en courant = we ran up
* = to go upstairs
  montez, le bureau est à l'étage au-dessus = go upstairs, the office is on the next floor
* = to come up
  = to come upstairs
  je suis dans le grenier, monte = I'm in the attic, come up
* = to get in(to)
  = to get on
  elle est montée dans la voiture = she got into the car
  monter dans un avion = to get on a plane
* = to climb
  ne monte pas sur la table = don't climb onto the table
* = to rise, to go up
  les prix montent = prices are rising, prices are going up
* (*other uses*)
  monter à bicyclette = to ride a bicycle
  monter à cheval = to ride
**2** (**!** + *avoir*)
* = to go up
  il a monté la colline en vélo = he cycled up the hill
* = to take up(stairs)
  je vais monter les bagages = I'm going to take the luggage up(stairs)
* = to bring up
  peux-tu me monter mes lunettes? = can you bring my glasses up to me?
* = to put up
  monter une tente = to put up a tent

**montgolfière** *noun, feminine*
  une montgolfière = a hot air balloon

**montre** *noun, feminine*
  une montre = a watch

**montrer** *verb* 1
  = to show

**monument** *noun, masculine*
  un monument = a monument
  **un monument historique** = a historical building
  **un monument aux morts** = a war memorial

**moquer**: **se moquer de** *verb* [1]
(**!** + *être*)
• (*to mock*)
  se moquer de = to make fun of
• (*to dismiss*)
  se moquer de = not to care about
  je m'en moque = I don't care

**moquette** *noun, feminine*
  une moquette = a fitted carpet, wall-to-
  wall carpeting

**moral** *noun, masculine*
  le moral = morale
  avoir le moral, avoir bon moral = to be in
  good spirits
  avoir le moral à zéro✱ = to feel very down

**morceau** *noun, masculine*
(*plural*) **morceaux**
  un morceau = a piece
**un morceau de sucre** = a lump of sugar

**mordre** *verb* [6]
  = to bite

**morpion** *noun, masculine*
  le morpion = noughts and crosses

**mort¹** *noun, feminine*
  la mort = death

**mort²/morte**
**1 ▶ mourir** [25]
**2** *adjective*
  = dead
  être mort de peur = to be scared stiff
**3** *noun, masculine/feminine*
  un mort/une morte = a dead man/a dead
  woman

**mosquée** *noun, feminine*
  une mosquée = a mosque

**mot** *noun, masculine*
• un mot = a word
• (*a message*)
  un mot = a note
**des mots croisés** = a crossword puzzle

**motard** *noun, masculine*
  un motard = a motorcyclist, a biker
  = a police motorcyclist

**mot-clé** *noun, masculine*
(*plural*) **mots-clés**
  un mot-clé = a key word

**moteur** *noun, masculine*
  un moteur = an engine
  = a motor

**moto** *noun, feminine*
  une moto = a motorbike, a motorcycle

**mou/molle** *adjective*
• (*describing things*) = soft
  = limp

✱ in informal situations

• (*describing a person*) = spineless
  = lethargic

**mouche** *noun, feminine*
  une mouche = a fly

**mouchoir** *noun, masculine*
  un mouchoir = a handkerchief

**mouette** *noun, feminine*
  une mouette = a seagull

**mouiller** *verb* [1]
**1** (**!** + *avoir*)
  = to wet
**2 se mouiller** (**!** + *être*)
  se mouiller = to get wet

**moule**
**1** *noun, feminine*
  une moule = a mussel
**2** *noun, masculine*
  un moule = a mould
  = a (baking) tin, a pan

**mourir** *verb* [25] (**!** + *être*)
  = to die
  il est mort en avril = he died in April
  je meurs [de faim | de soif | de froid …]! = I'm
  [starving | parched | freezing …]!
  il meurt d'envie de te le dire = he's dying to
  tell you

**mousse** *noun, feminine*
• (*a plant*)
  la mousse = moss
• (*bubbles*)
  la mousse = foam
  = lather
  = froth
• (*in cooking*)
  une mousse au chocolat = a chocolate
  mousse
• (*a material*)
  la mousse = foam rubber

**moustache** *noun, feminine*
• (*on a man*)
  une moustache = a moustache
• (*on an animal*)
  des moustaches = whiskers

**moustique** *noun, masculine*
  un moustique = a mosquito

**moutarde** *noun, feminine*
  la moutarde = mustard

**mouton** *noun, masculine*
  un mouton = a sheep

**moyen/moyenne¹**
**1** *adjective*
  = average
  = medium
**2 moyen** *noun, masculine*
  un moyen = a means
  = a way
  un moyen de transport = a means of
  transport
  c'est le seul moyen = it's the only way

**3 moyens** *noun, masculine plural*
des moyens *(money)* = means
je n'ai pas les moyens de voyager = I can't
    afford to travel
**le Moyen Âge** = the Middle Ages

**moyenne²** *noun, feminine*
• *(in statistics)*
    la moyenne = the average
    en moyenne = on average
• *(in an exam)*
    la moyenne = half marks, 50%

**moyennement** *adverb*
= moderately
= fairly

**Moyen-Orient** *noun, masculine*
le Moyen-Orient = the Middle East

**muet/muette** *adjective*
• = dumb
• = silent

**muguet** *noun, masculine*
le muguet = lily of the valley

**multiplier** *verb* ☐2
= to multiply

**municipal/municipale** *adjective*
*(plural)* **municipaux/municipales**
= municipal

**municipalité** *noun, feminine*
la municipalité = the (local) council

**munir: se munir de** *verb* ☐3 (**!** + être)
se munir de = to equip oneself with

**mur** *noun, masculine*
un mur = a wall
**le mur du son** = the sound barrier

**mûr/mûre¹** *adjective*
• *(describing fruit)* = ripe
• *(describing people)* = mature

**muraille** *noun, feminine*
une muraille = a great wall

**mûre²** *noun, feminine*
une mûre = a blackberry

**murmurer** *verb* ☐1
• = to murmur
• = to whisper

**musclé/musclée** *adjective*
= muscular

**musculation** *noun, feminine*
la musculation = body-building

**musée** *noun, masculine*
un musée = a museum, a gallery

**musicien/musicienne** *noun,*
*masculine/feminine*
un musicien/une musicienne = a musician

**musique** *noun, feminine*
la musique = music

**mutinerie** *noun, feminine*
une mutinerie = a mutiny

**mystère** *noun, masculine*
un mystère = a mystery

**mystérieux/mystérieuse** *adjective*
= mysterious

# Nn

**n'** ▶ **ne**

**nage** *noun, feminine*
la nage = swimming
traverser le fleuve à la nage = to swim
    across the river

**nager** *verb* ☐13
= to swim

**nain/naine**
**1** *adjective*
= dwarf
= miniature
**2** *noun, masculine/feminine*
un nain/une naine = a dwarf

**naissance** *noun, feminine*
la naissance = birth
à ma naissance = when I was born

**naître** *verb* ☐64 (**!** + être)
= to be born
il est né le 10 janvier = he was born on 10
    January

**nappe** *noun, feminine*
une nappe = a tablecloth
une nappe de brouillard = a blanket of fog

**narine** *noun, feminine*
une narine = a nostril

**natal/natale** *adjective*
*(plural)* **natals/natales**
= native

**natation** *noun, feminine*
la natation = swimming

**national/nationale¹** *adjective*
*(plural)* **nationaux/nationales**
= national

**nationale²** *noun, feminine*
une nationale = a trunk road, a highway

**nature**
**1** *adjective* (**!** *never changes*)
= plain
un yaourt nature = a plain yogurt
un thé nature = a black tea

N

**2** *noun, feminine*
la nature = nature
la protection de la nature = the protection of the environment
**une nature morte** = a still life

**naturel/naturelle**
**1** *adjective*
= natural
**2 naturel** *noun, masculine*
• être d'un naturel timide = to be shy by nature
• il manque de naturel = he's not very natural
• du thon au naturel = tuna in brine

**naufrage** *noun, masculine*
un naufrage = a shipwreck
faire naufrage (*if it's a ship*) = to be wrecked
(*if it's a crew*) = to be shipwrecked

**nausée** *noun, feminine*
la nausée = nausea
avoir la nausée = to feel sick, to feel nauseous

**nautique** *adjective*
les sports nautiques = water sports

**navet** *noun, masculine*
un navet = a turnip

**navette** *noun, feminine*
une navette = a shuttle
= a shuttle service
faire la navette = to travel back and forth
= to commute

**navire** *noun, masculine*
un navire = a ship

**navré/navrée** *adjective*
je suis vraiment navré = I'm terribly sorry
avoir l'air navré = to look upset

**ne** (**n'** *before vowel or mute h*) *adverb*
> **!** *In cases where* ne *is used with* aucun, guère, jamais, pas, personne, plus, rien *etc, one should consult the corresponding entry.* ne + verb + que *is treated in the entry below.*

je ne sais pas = I don't know
je n'ai que 10 euros = I've only got 10 euros
tu n'avais qu'à le dire = you only had to say so

**né/née** ▶ **naître** 64

**néanmoins** *adverb*
= nevertheless

**nécessaire**
**1** *adjective*
= necessary

**2** *noun, masculine*
• faire le nécessaire pour les billets = to see about the tickets
• le strict nécessaire = the bare essentials

**néerlandais/néerlandaise**
**1** *adjective*
= Dutch
**2 néerlandais** *noun, masculine*
le néerlandais = Dutch

**néfaste** *adjective*
= harmful

**négatif/négative** *adjective*
= negative

**négliger** *verb* 13
= to neglect

**neige** *noun, feminine*
la neige = snow
des blancs d'œufs battus en neige = stiffly beaten eggwhites

**neiger** *verb* 13
= to snow
il neige = it's snowing

**nénuphar** *noun, masculine*
un nénuphar = a waterlily

**nerf** *noun, masculine*
un nerf = a nerve
il me tape sur les nerfs✗ = he gets on my nerves

**nerveux/nerveuse** *adjective*
= nervous, tense

**n'est-ce pas** *adverb*
c'est grand, n'est-ce pas? = it's big, isn't it?
tu viendras, n'est-ce pas? = you will come, won't you?

**net/nette**
**1** *adjective*
• (*describing prices or weights*) = net
• (*free from stains or clutter*) = clean
• (*easy to see or understand*) = clear
**2 net** *adverb*
s'arrêter net = to stop dead
refuser net = to refuse flatly

**nettoyer** *verb* 23
= to clean

**neuf¹** *number*
= nine

**neuf²/neuve** *adjective*
= new
une voiture toute neuve = a brand new car

**neuvième** *number*
= ninth

**neveu** *noun, masculine*
(*plural*) **neveux**
un neveu = a nephew

**nez** *noun, masculine* (**!** *never changes*)
le nez = the nose

**ni** *conjunction*
ni anglais ni espagnol = neither English nor Spanish
elle ne veut pas le voir ni lui parler = she doesn't wish to see him or talk to him
ni l'un ni l'autre = neither of them

**niche** *noun, feminine*
• (*for a dog*)
une niche = a kennel, a doghouse
• (*in a wall*)
une niche = a recess

**nid** *noun, masculine*
un nid = a nest

**nièce** *noun, feminine*
une nièce = a niece

**nier** *verb* 2
= to deny

**n'importe** ▸ **importer** 1

**niveau** *noun, masculine*
(*plural*) **niveaux**
un niveau = a level
= a standard
**le niveau de vie** = the standard of living

**noce** *noun, feminine*
une noce = a wedding
**des noces d'argent** = a silver wedding anniversary

**nocturne** *adjective*
= nocturnal
= night

**Noël** *noun, masculine*
Noël = Christmas

**nœud** *noun, masculine*
un nœud = a knot
**un nœud papillon** = a bow tie

**noir/noire** *adjective*
• = black
• = dark

**noisette** *noun, feminine*
une noisette = a hazelnut

**noix** *noun, feminine* (**!** *never changes*)
une noix = a walnut, an English walnut

**nom**
**1** *noun, masculine*
• un nom = a name
• un nom = a noun
**2 au nom de** = in the name of
= on behalf of
**un nom de famille** = a surname, a last name
**un nom de jeune fille** = a maiden name

**nombre** *noun, masculine*
un nombre = a number
un certain nombre de personnes = some people

**nombreux/nombreuse** *adjective*
= large
= many
une foule nombreuse = a large crowd
de nombreuses personnes = many people
ils sont peu nombreux = there are few of them

**nommer** *verb* 1
**1** (**!** + *avoir*)
• = to name
= to call
nommer un enfant Olivier = to name a child Olivier
une plage nommée 'La Salie' = a beach called 'La Salie'
• = to appoint
être nommé à Paris = to be posted to Paris
**2 se nommer** (**!** + *être*)
se nommer = to be called

**non**
**1** *adverb*
• = no
ah, ça non! = definitely not
je pense que non = I don't think so
• = non
non alcoolisé = nonalcoholic
**2 non plus**
je ne suis pas d'accord non plus = I don't agree either
il n'a pas aimé le film, moi non plus = he didn't like the film, neither did I

**nonante** *number*
= ninety

**nord**
**1** *noun, masculine*
le nord = the north
**2** *adjective* (**!** *never changes*)
= north
= northern

**normal/normale** *adjective*
(*plural*) **normaux/normales**
= normal
il est normal qu'il soit triste = it's natural that he should be sad

**normalement** *adverb*
= normally

**normand/normande** *adjective*
= Norman
= from Normandy
la côte normande = the Normandy coast

**Normandie** *noun, feminine*
la Normandie = Normandy

**Norvège** *noun, feminine*
la Norvège = Norway

**norvégien/norvégienne**
**1** *adjective*
= Norwegian
**2 norvégien** *noun, masculine*
le norvégien = Norwegian

**N**

**nos** ▶ **notre**

**note** noun, feminine
* (in a hotel)
  la note = the bill, the check
* (in music)
  une note = a note
* (at school)
  une note = a mark, a grade
* (words taken down)
  des notes = notes

**noter** verb [1]
* = to write down
* = to notice
* = to mark, to grade

**notre** determiner
(plural) **nos**
  = our

**nôtre** pronoun
  le nôtre/la nôtre/les nôtres = ours

**nouille** noun, feminine
  les nouilles = noodles, pasta

**nourrir** verb [3]
**1** (! + avoir)
  = to feed
  = to nourish
**2 se nourrir** (! + être)
  se nourrir = to feed
  = to eat

**nourriture** noun, feminine
  la nourriture = food

**nous** pronoun
* = we
  = us
  nous avons froid = we're cold
  donne-nous le livre = give us the book
  la voiture est à nous = the car is ours
  c'est à nous de jouer = it's our turn to play
  il nous l'a prêté = he lent it to us
* = ourselves
  nous nous soignons = we look after
    ourselves
  nous nous levons tôt = we get up early
* = each other
  nous nous aimons = we love each other

**nouveau/nouvelle¹**
(plural) **nouveaux/nouvelles**
**1** adjective

> ! nouvel is used instead of nouveau
> before masculine nouns that begin with a
> vowel or a mute h. The plural of nouvel is
> nouveaux.

  = new
  le Nouvel An = the New Year
  c'est tout nouveau = it's brand new
**2** noun, masculine/feminine
  le nouveau/la nouvelle (a pupil) = the new
    boy/the new girl

---

**×** in informal situations

**3 de nouveau** = (once) again

**nouveau-né** noun, masculine
(plural) **nouveau-nés**
  un nouveau-né = a newborn baby

**nouvel** ▶ **nouveau 1**

**nouvelle²** noun, feminine
  une nouvelle = a piece of news
  la nouvelle = the news
  les nouvelles = the news
  tu connais la nouvelle? = have you heard
    the news?

**Nouvelle-Zélande** noun, feminine
  la Nouvelle-Zélande = New Zealand

**novembre** noun, masculine
  novembre = November

**noyau** noun, masculine
(plural) **noyaux**
  un noyau = a stone, a pit

**noyé/noyée** noun, masculine/feminine
  un noyé/une noyée = a drowned person

**noyer**
**1** noun, masculine
  un noyer = a walnut tree
**2** verb [23] (! + avoir)
  = to drown
**3 se noyer** (! + être)
  se noyer = to drown

**nu/nue** adjective
  = naked, bare

**nuage** noun, masculine
  un nuage = a cloud

**nuageux/nuageuse** adjective
  = cloudy

**nuance** noun, feminine
* (a colour)
  une nuance = a shade
* (between two things)
  une nuance = a slight difference

**nuée** noun, feminine
  une nuée = a swarm

**nuire** verb [62]
  nuire à = to harm
  = to be harmful to

**nuisible** adjective
  = harmful

**nuit** noun, feminine
  une nuit = a night
  cette nuit = last night
  = tonight
  il fait nuit = it's dark
  **une nuit blanche** = a sleepless night

**nul/nulle**
**1** adjective
* (describing a person)× = hopeless
  (describing a piece of work)× = worthless
  (describing a film, a book)× = trashy

- (*in sports*)
un match nul = a draw, a tie
**2** *determiner*
nul [homme | pays | besoin …] = no [man |
country | need …]
nul autre que vous = no-one else but you
**3** *pronoun*
= no-one
**4 nulle part** = nowhere

**numérique** *adjective*
= digital

**numéro** *noun, masculine*
- (*for a house, a telephone, a ticket*)
un numéro = a number
un numéro de téléphone = a telephone
number
- (*a magazine*)
un numéro = a copy, an issue

**nuque** *noun, feminine*
la nuque = the nape (of the neck)

# Oo

**obéir** *verb* ③
= to obey

**obéissant/obéissante** *adjective*
= obedient

**objet** *noun, masculine*
un objet = an object
des objets de valeur = valuables
**objets trouvés** = lost property, lost and
found

**obligatoire** *adjective*
= compulsory

**obliger** *verb* ⑬
obliger un enfant à manger = to make a
child eat, to force a child to eat
je suis obligé de partir = I have to go

**obscur/obscure** *adjective*
- = dark
- = obscure

**obscurité** *noun, feminine*
l'obscurité = darkness

**obsèques** *noun, feminine plural*
les obsèques = the funeral

**observateur/observatrice** *noun,*
*masculine/feminine*
un observateur/une observatrice = an
observer

**observer** *verb* ①
- = to watch
- = to notice
- = to observe

**obtenir** *verb* ㊱
= to get, to obtain

**occasion** *noun, feminine*
- (*a chance*)
une occasion = an opportunity
- une voiture d'occasion = a second-hand
car
- (*a circumstance*)
une occasion = an occasion

**occident** *noun, masculine*
l'occident = the west

**occidental/occidentale** *adjective*
(*plural*) **occidentaux/occidentales**
= western

**occupé/occupée** *adjective*
- (*having a lot to do*) = busy
- (*not vacant*) = engaged

**occuper** *verb* ①
**1** (**!** + *avoir*)
- = to occupy
- = to keep busy
ça m'occupe = it keeps me busy
**2 s'occuper** (**!** + *être*)
- s'occuper = to keep oneself busy, to
occupy oneself
- s'occuper de = to take care of, to look
after

**océan** *noun, masculine*
un océan = an ocean

**octante** *number*
= eighty

**octobre** *noun, masculine*
octobre = October

**odeur** *noun, feminine*
une odeur = a smell

**odieux/odieuse** *adjective*
= horrible, hateful

**œil** *noun, masculine*
(*plural*) **yeux**
un œil = an eye

**œillet** *noun, masculine*
un œillet = a carnation

**œuf** *noun, masculine*
un œuf = an egg
**un œuf à la coque** = a boiled egg
**un œuf dur** = a hard-boiled egg
**un œuf sur le plat** = a fried egg

**œuvre** *noun, feminine*
une œuvre = a work

**offense** *noun, feminine*
une offense = an insult

**offenser** *verb* ①
= to offend

**office** *noun, masculine*
- (*in church*)
un office = a service

**O**

• (*an organization*)
  un office = an office
  l'office du tourisme = the tourist office

**offre** *noun, feminine*
  une offre = an offer
  'offres d'emploi' = 'situations vacant'

**offrir** *verb* 4
**1** (**!** + *avoir*)
• = to offer
• = to give
**2 s'offrir** (**!** + *être*)
  s'offrir une croisière = to treat oneself to a
  cruise

**oie** *noun, feminine*
  une oie = a goose

**oignon** *noun, masculine*
  un oignon = an onion

**oiseau** *noun, masculine*
(*plural*) **oiseaux**
  un oiseau = a bird

**olivier** *noun, masculine*
  un olivier = an olive tree

**ombre** *noun, feminine*
• (*darkness*)
  l'ombre = shade
• (*a shape*)
  une ombre = a shadow

**ombrelle** *noun, feminine*
  une ombrelle = a sunshade, a parasol

**omnibus** *noun, masculine* (**!** *never
changes*)
  un (train) omnibus = a slow train, a local
  train

**omoplate** *noun, feminine*
  l'omoplate = the shoulder blade

**on** *pronoun*
• = someone
  on t'appelle = someone's calling you
• = we
  on a eu un accident = we had an accident
• = one
  = you
  = they
  on est obligé de payer à l'avance = one
  has to pay in advance
  = you have to pay in advance
  on vend des fleurs au supermarché = they
  sell flowers at the supermarket
• = people
  je me moque de ce qu'on dit = I don't care
  what people say
• (*other possible translations*)
  on m'a demandé ma carte = I was asked
  for my card
  on a réparé la route = the road has been
  repaired

**oncle** *noun, masculine*
  un oncle = an uncle

**ondulé/ondulée** *adjective*
  = wavy

**ongle** *noun, masculine*
  un ongle = a nail

**ont ▶ avoir** 8

**onze** *number*
  = eleven

**onzième** *number*
  = eleventh

**opération** *noun, feminine*
• (*in mathematics*)
  une opération = a calculation
• (*on a patient*)
  une opération = an operation

**opérer** *verb* 14
  = to operate
  se faire opérer = to have an operation

**opinion** *noun, feminine*
  une opinion = an opinion

**opposé/opposée** *adjective*
  = opposite

**optimiste** *adjective*
  = optimistic

**or** *noun, masculine*
  l'or = gold
  une montre en or = a gold watch

**orage** *noun, masculine*
  un orage = a storm

**orageux/orageuse** *adjective*
  = stormy

**orchestre** *noun, masculine*
  un orchestre = an orchestra
  = a band

**ordinaire** *adjective*
  = ordinary

**ordinateur** *noun, masculine*
  un ordinateur = a computer

**ordonnance** *noun, feminine*
  une ordonnance = a prescription

**ordre** *noun, masculine*
• (*a command*)
  un ordre = an order
• (*a way of arranging things*)
  dans l'ordre = in order
• (*neatness*)
  l'ordre = tidiness
  mettre de l'ordre = to tidy up, to clean up

**ordures** *noun, feminine plural*
  les ordures = rubbish, garbage, trash

**oreille** *noun, feminine*
  une oreille = an ear

**oreiller** *noun, masculine*
  un oreiller = a pillow

**organisateur/organisatrice** noun,
masculine/feminine
  un organisateur/une organisatrice = an
  organizer

**organiser** verb 1
**1** (! + avoir)
  = to organize
**2 s'organiser** (! + être)
  s'organiser = to get organized

**organisme** noun, masculine
  un organisme = an organization, a body

**orge** noun, feminine
  l'orge = barley

**orgueil** noun, masculine
  l'orgueil = pride

**orgueilleux/orgueilleuse** adjective
  = proud

**orient** noun, masculine
  l'orient = the east

**oriental/orientale** adjective
(plural) **orientaux/orientales**
  = eastern

**originaire** adjective
  être originaire d'un pays = to come from a
  country, to be a native of a country

**original/originale** adjective
(plural) **originaux/originales**
• = original
• = eccentric, unusual

**origine** noun, feminine
  l'origine = the origin

**orner** verb 1
  = to decorate

**orphelin/orpheline** noun,
masculine/feminine
  un orphelin/une orpheline = an orphan

**orteil** noun, masculine
  un orteil = a toe

**orthographe** noun, feminine
  l'orthographe = spelling

**ortie** noun, feminine
  une ortie = a (stinging) nettle

**os** noun, masculine (! never changes)
  un os = a bone

**oser** verb 1
  = to dare

**osier** noun, masculine
  l'osier = wicker

**otage** noun, masculine
  un otage = a hostage

**ôter** verb 1
  = to take off, to remove

**ou** conjunction
• = or
  ou bien = or else
• ou (bien)... ou (bien)... = either... or...

**où**
**1** adverb
  = where
  d'où vient le bus? = where does the bus
    come from?
**2** pronoun
• = where
  restez où vous êtes = stay where you are
• = when
  juste au moment où il partait = just as he
    was leaving

**oublier** verb 2
  = to forget

**ouest**
**1** noun, masculine
  l'ouest = the west
**2** adjective (! never changes)
  = west, western

**ouf** exclamation
  ouf! = phew!

**oui** adverb
  = yes
  je crois que oui = I think so

**ouragan** noun, masculine
  un ouragan = a hurricane

**ourlet** noun, masculine
  un ourlet = a hem

**ours** noun, masculine (! never changes)
  un ours = a bear
  **un ours en peluche** = a teddy bear

**oursin** noun, masculine
  un oursin = a sea urchin

**outil** noun, masculine
  un outil = a tool

**outre-mer** adverb
  = overseas

**ouvert/ouverte**
**1** ▶ **ouvrir** 32
**2** adjective
  = open

**ouverture** noun, feminine
  une ouverture = an opening

**ouvrable** adjective
  un jour ouvrable = a working day

**ouvrage** noun, masculine
  un ouvrage = a (piece of) work, a project
  = a book, a work

**ouvre-boîtes** noun, masculine (! never
changes)
  un ouvre-boîtes = a can-opener

**ouvreur/ouvreuse** noun,
masculine/feminine
  un ouvreur/une ouvreuse = an usher/an
    usherette

**O**

**ouvrier/ouvrière**
1 *noun, masculine/feminine*
  un ouvrier/une ouvrière = a worker
2 *adjective*
  = working-class

**ouvrir** *verb* 32
1 (**!** + *avoir*)
  = to open
2 **s'ouvrir** (**!** + *être*)
  s'ouvrir = to open

**P**p

**pagaille**✻
1 *noun, feminine*
  une pagaille✻ = a mess
  mettre la pagaille✻ = to cause chaos
2 **en pagaille**✻
  il y a du vin en pagaille✻ = there's loads of
  wine, there's lots of wine

**page** *noun, feminine*
  une page = a page

**paille** *noun, feminine*
  la paille = straw

**pain** *noun, masculine*
• le pain = bread
• un pain = a loaf
**le pain grillé** = toast
**un petit pain** = a bread roll

**pair/paire¹**
1 *adjective*
  les nombres pairs = even numbers
2 **au pair**
  une jeune fille au pair = an au pair

**paire²** *noun, feminine*
  une paire = a pair

**paisible** *adjective*
  = peaceful

**paix** *noun, feminine* (**!** *never changes*)
  la paix = peace
  = peace and quiet

**palais** *noun, masculine* (**!** *never changes*)
• un palais = a palace
• le palais = the palate

**pâle** *adjective*
  = pale

**palier** *noun, masculine*
  le palier = the landing

**palmier** *noun, masculine*
  un palmier = a palm tree

**pamplemousse** *noun, masculine*
  un pamplemousse = a grapefruit

**panaché** *noun, masculine*
  un (demi-)panaché = a shandy, a beer with
  lemonade

**pancarte** *noun, feminine*
  une pancarte = a notice, a sign
  = a placard

**panier** *noun, masculine*
  un panier = a basket

**paniquer**✻ *verb* 1
  = to panic

**panne** *noun, feminine*
  une panne = a breakdown
  tomber en panne = to break down
  tomber en panne d'essence = to run out
  of petrol, to run out of gas
  **une panne de courant** = a power failure

**panneau** *noun, masculine*
  (*plural*) **panneaux**
• un panneau = a panel
• un panneau = a sign
  **un panneau d'affichage** = a noticeboard
  **un panneau de signalisation routière**
  = a road sign

**pansement** *noun, masculine*
  un pansement = a dressing, a bandage
  **un pansement adhésif** = a plaster, a
  Band-Aid

**pantalon** *noun, masculine*
  un pantalon = (a pair of) trousers, (a pair
  of) pants

**pantoufle** *noun, feminine*
  une pantoufle = a slipper

**paon** *noun, masculine*
  un paon = a peacock

**papa** *noun, masculine*
  un papa = a dad

**pape** *noun, masculine*
  le pape = the pope

**papeterie** *noun, feminine*
  une papeterie = a stationer's

**papier** *noun, masculine*
  le papier = paper
  **le papier alu(minium)** = aluminium foil,
  aluminum foil
  **le papier d'emballage** = wrapping paper
  **le papier hygiénique** = toilet paper
  **le papier peint** = wallpaper
  **les papiers (d'identité)** = (identity)
  papers

**papillon** *noun, masculine*
  un papillon = a butterfly

**pâquerette** *noun, feminine*
  une pâquerette = a daisy

**Pâques** *noun, masculine*
  Pâques = Easter

**paquet** noun, masculine
- un paquet = a packet
- un paquet = a parcel, a package

**par**
**1** preposition
- = by
  il a été piqué par une abeille = he was stung by a bee
  payer par carte de crédit = to pay by credit card
- = through
  le chemin passe par la forêt = the path goes through the forest
  par ici = this way, through here
- = per
  = a
  par personne = per person
  trois par [jour | mois | an ...] = three a [day | month | year ...]
- = in
  mettez-vous deux par deux = stand in twos
  sortir par mauvais temps = to go out in bad weather
- = on
  par une froide journée d'hiver = on a cold winter's day
- = out of
  regarder par la fenêtre = to look out (of) the window
  par bêtise = out of stupidity
**2 par contre** = on the other hand

**parachute** noun, masculine
- (the equipment)
  un parachute = a parachute
- (the sport)
  le parachute = parachuting

**parages** noun, masculine plural
dans les parages = in the area

**paraître** verb 63
**1** (! + avoir)
- (to create an impression) = to seem, to look
- (to be seen) = to appear
  paraître en public = to appear in public
**2** (! + être)
  (if it's a book, a record) = to come out
**3 il paraît que** = apparently
  il paraît que non = apparently not

**parapente** noun, masculine
- (the equipment)
  un parapente = a paraglider
- (the sport)
  le parapente = paragliding

**parapluie** noun, masculine
un parapluie = an umbrella

**parasol** noun, masculine
un parasol = a sunshade, a beach umbrella

**parc** noun, masculine
un parc = a park
**un parc d'attractions** = an amusement park

**parce que (parce qu'** before vowel or mute h) conjunction
= because

**par-ci** adverb
par-ci par-là = here and there

**parcmètre** noun, masculine
un parcmètre = a parking meter

**parcourir** verb 26
- = to cover
  parcourir une distance = to cover a distance
- = to go all over
  parcourir toute la ville = to go all over the town
- = to glance through
  parcourir un article = to glance through an article

**parcours** noun, masculine (! never changes)
un parcours = a journey
= a route

**parcouru/parcourue ▶ parcourir** 26

**pardessus** noun, masculine (! never changes)
un pardessus = an overcoat

**pardon** noun, masculine
- le pardon = forgiveness
  demander pardon = to apologize
  = to ask for forgiveness
- pardon! = sorry!
  pardon monsieur, je cherche la mairie = excuse me, I'm looking for the town hall

**pardonner** verb 1
= to forgive

**pare-brise** noun, masculine (! never changes)
un pare-brise = a windscreen, a windshield

**pareil/pareille**
**1** adjective
- = the same
  = similar
  = identical
- = such
  je n'ai jamais vu un luxe pareil = I've never seen such luxury
**2 pareil*** adverb
= the same
faisons pareil* = let's do the same

**parent/parente**
**1** noun, masculine|feminine
un parent/une parente = a relative, a relation
**2 parents** noun, masculine plural
les parents = parents

**parenthèse** noun, feminine
entre parenthèses = between brackets

P

**paresse** *noun, feminine*
la paresse = laziness

**paresseux/paresseuse** *adjective*
= lazy

**parfait/parfaite** *adjective*
= perfect

**parfois** *adverb*
= sometimes

**parfum** *noun, masculine*
un parfum = a perfume
= a flavo(u)r

**parfumé/parfumée** *adjective*
= scented
= flavo(u)red

**parier** *verb* 2
= to bet

**parisien/parisienne** *adjective*
= Parisian

**parking** *noun, masculine*
un parking = a car park, a parking lot
**un parking de délestage** = an overflow car park

**parler** *verb* 1
= to talk
= to speak

**parmi** *preposition*
= among

**paroisse** *noun, feminine*
une paroisse = a parish

**parole** *noun, feminine*
une parole = a word
prendre la parole = to speak
à vous la parole! = your turn to speak!

**parrain** *noun, masculine*
un parrain = a godfather

**part**
**1** *noun, feminine*
• (*when dividing*)
une part (*of food*) = a portion
(*of a legacy*) = a share
• (*meaning direction, place*)
de toutes parts = from all sides, from everywhere
nulle part = nowhere
quelque part = somewhere
d'une part… d'autre part = on the one hand… on the other hand
**2 de la part de** = from
= on behalf of
elle m'a fait part de sa décision = she informed me of her decision
**3 à part** = apart (from)

**partager** *verb* 13
= to share

**partenaire** *noun, masculine/feminine*
un partenaire/une partenaire = a partner

**parterre** *noun, masculine*
• (*in a garden*)
un parterre = a bed
• (*in a theatre*)
le parterre = the stalls, the orchestra

**participer** *verb* 1
• participer (à) = to take part (in)
• participer à = to share in

**particulier/particulière** *adjective*
= particular
= special

**partie**
**1** *noun, feminine*
• (*not the whole*)
une partie = (a) part
• (*at cards, in sport*)
une partie = a game
**2 en partie** = partly, in part
**3 faire partie de** = to be part of
ça fait partie de mon travail = it's part of my job
faire partie d'un club = to be a member of a club

**partir**
**1** *verb* 30 (**!** + *être*)
• = to leave
partir en courant = to run off
• = to go
partir à Paris = to go to Paris
• = to start
le sentier part du bois = the path starts in the wood
**2 à partir de** = from
à partir de maintenant = from now on

**partout** *adverb*
= everywhere

**paru** ▶ **paraître** 63

**parvenir** *verb* 36 (**!** + *être*)
• parvenir à = to achieve
parvenir à son but = to achieve one's goal
parvenir à faire = to manage to do
• parvenir à = to reach
parvenir à New York = to reach New York

**parvenu/parvenue** ▶ **parvenir** 36

**pas**
**1** *adverb*
= not
pas du tout = not at all
le film n'est pas mal✶ = the film isn't bad
**2** *noun, masculine* (**!** *never changes*)
• (*a movement*)
un pas = a step
c'est à deux pas d'ici = it's very near here
• (*speed*)
le pas = the pace
d'un pas lent = slowly

**passage** *noun, masculine*
• (*a section of a text, a film*)
un passage = a passage

- (a means of access)
  un passage = a way
  céder le passage = to give way, to yield
  'passage interdit' = 'no entry'
- être de passage = to be passing through
- **un passage à niveau** = a level crossing, a grade crossing
- **un passage pour piétons** = a pedestrian crossing, a crosswalk
- **un passage souterrain** = a subway, a pedestrian underpass

**passager/passagère** noun,
masculine|feminine
  un passager/une passagère = a passenger
  **un passager clandestin** = a stowaway

**passant/passante** noun,
masculine|feminine
  un passant/une passante = a passer-by

**passé/passée**
**1 ▶ passer** 1
**2** adjective
- l'an passé = last year
- il est cinq heures passées = it's past five o'clock
**3 passé** noun, masculine
  le passé = the past

**passer** verb 1
**1** (! + avoir)
- = to spend
  passer son temps à lire = to spend one's time reading
- = to take, to sit
  passer un examen = to take an examination

  ! Note that réussir à un examen means to pass an exam.

- = to show
  = to play
  passer un film = to show a film
  passer un disque = to play a record
- = to pass
  = to give
  peux-tu passer le sel? = can you pass the salt?
  il m'a passé son rhume = he gave me his cold
  je vous la passe (on the telephone) = I'll put her on
- (to miss)
  passer son tour = to pass
**2** (! + être)
- (to walk, to drive, to fly past) = to go past, to go by
  un bus vient de passer = a bus has just gone past
  passer devant l'église = to go past the church, to pass the church
- (to go a certain way)
  passer par = to go through, to go by
  passer par la porte de derrière = to go through the back door

- (to make one's way) = to get past
  je ne peux pas passer = I can't get past
  laisser passer les enfants = to let the children past
- (to call, to arrive) = to come
  le facteur passe vers dix heures = the postman comes at about ten o'clock
- (to pay a visit) = to drop in
  passer voir un ami = to drop in on a friend
- (to move to a different level)
  passer dans la classe supérieure = to move up to the next class
- = to pass
  le temps passe trop vite = time passes too quickly
**3 se passer** (! + être)
- se passer = to happen
  qu'est-ce qui se passe? = what's happening?, what's going on?
- se passer = to go
  ça s'est bien passé = it went well
- se passer de = to do without

**passerelle** noun, feminine
  une passerelle = a footbridge
  = a gangway

**passe-temps** noun, masculine (! never changes)
  un passe-temps = a hobby

**passion** noun, feminine
  une passion = a passion

**passionnant/passionnante**
adjective
  = fascinating
  = exciting

**passionné/passionnée**
**1 ▶ passionner** 1
**2** adjective
  = passionate
**3** noun, masculine|feminine
  un passionné/une passionnée de football = a football enthusiast, a football fan

**passionner** verb 1
**1** (! + avoir)
  = to fascinate
**2 se passionner pour** (! + être)
  se passionner pour = to have a passion for

**passoire** noun, feminine
  une passoire = a colander
  = a strainer

**pastèque** noun, feminine
  une pastèque = a watermelon

**pasteur** noun, masculine
  un pasteur = a parson, a minister

**pastille** noun, feminine
  une pastille = a lozenge, a cough drop

**patate\*** noun, feminine
  une patate\* = a spud, a potato

**patauger** verb 13
  = to splash about

**pâte**
**1** *noun, feminine*
• la pâte = pastry
  = dough
  = batter
• une pâte = a paste
**2 pâtes** *noun, feminine plural*
  des pâtes (alimentaires) = pasta

**pâté** *noun, masculine*
• le pâté = pâté
  un pâté (en croûte) = a pie
• un pâté de maisons = a block (of houses)

**patience** *noun, feminine*
• (*a virtue*)
  la patience = patience
• (*a game of cards*)
  faire une patience = to play patience, to play solitaire

**patient/patiente**
**1** *adjective*
  = patient
**2** *noun, masculine|feminine*
  un patient/une patiente = a patient

**patienter** *verb* ☐1
  = to wait

**patin** *noun, masculine*
  un patin = a skate
**des patins de frein** = brake blocks
**des patins à glace** = ice-skates
**des patins à roulettes** = roller-skates

**patinage** *noun, masculine*
  le patinage = skating

**patinoire** *noun, feminine*
  une patinoire = an ice rink

**pâtisserie** *noun, feminine*
• (*a place*)
  une pâtisserie = a cake shop
• (*a sweet*)
  une pâtisserie = a pastry, a cake

**pâtissier/pâtissière** *noun, masculine|feminine*
  un pâtissier/une pâtissière = a confectioner

**patron/patronne**
**1** *noun, masculine|feminine*
  le patron/la patronne = the boss
  = the manager
**2 patron** *noun, masculine*
  un patron = a pattern

**patronne ▶ patron 1**

**patte** *noun, feminine*
  une patte = a leg
  = a paw
  = a foot
  à quatre pattes = on all fours

**paupière** *noun, feminine*
  une paupière = an eyelid

**pause** *noun, feminine*
  une pause = a break
  faire une pause = to take a break

**pauvre** *adjective*
  = poor

**pauvreté** *noun, feminine*
  la pauvreté = poverty

**pavé/pavée**
**1** *adjective*
  = cobbled
**2 pavé** *noun, masculine*
  un pavé = a cobblestone

**payant/payante** *adjective*
  (*describing a person*) = paying
  (*describing a show*) = not free

**payer** *verb* 21
**1** (! + *avoir*)
  = to pay
**2 se payer**✶ (! + *être*)
  se payer✶ un repas = to treat oneself to a meal

**pays** *noun, masculine* (! *never changes*)
  un pays = a country

**paysage** *noun, masculine*
  un paysage = a landscape

**Pays-Bas** *noun, masculine plural*
  les Pays-Bas = the Netherlands, Holland

**Pays de Galles** *noun, masculine*
  le Pays de Galles = Wales

**PCV** *noun, masculine*
  appeler en PCV = to make a reverse-charge call, to call collect

**péage** *noun, masculine*
  le péage = the toll
  = the tollbooth

**peau** *noun, feminine*
(*plural*) **peaux**
  la peau = skin

**pêche** *noun, feminine*
• une pêche = a peach
• la pêche = fishing

**péché** *noun, masculine*
  un péché = a sin

**pêcher**
**1** *verb* ☐1
• = to catch
• = to go fishing
**2** *noun, masculine*
  un pêcher = a peach tree

**pêcheur** *noun, masculine*
  un pêcheur = a fisherman

**pédale** *noun, feminine*
  une pédale = a pedal

**pédaler** verb 1
= to pedal

**pédestre** adjective
une randonnée pédestre = a ramble, a walk

**peigne** noun, masculine
un peigne = a comb

**peignoir** noun, masculine
un peignoir = a dressing gown, a robe

**peindre** verb 55
= to paint

**peine**
1 noun, feminine
• avoir de la peine à finir un travail = to have difficulty finishing a job
• ce n'est pas la peine d'essayer = it's not worth trying
ça vaut la peine d'y aller = it's worth going
• (sorrow)
la peine = grief
faire de la peine à ses amis = to upset one's friends
avoir de la peine = to be sad
• (punishment)
une peine de prison = a prison sentence
la peine de mort = capital punishment
2 à peine = hardly

**peint/peinte** ▶ **peindre** 55

**peintre** noun, masculine
un peintre = a painter

**peinture** noun, feminine
• la peinture (substance) = paint
(the activity) = painting
• une peinture = a painting

**pêle-mêle** adverb
= higgledy-piggledy, pell-mell

**peler** verb 17
= to peel

**pèlerinage** noun, masculine
un pèlerinage = a pilgrimage

**pelle** noun, feminine
une pelle = a shovel

**pellicule**
1 noun, feminine
une pellicule = a film
2 **pellicules** noun, feminine plural
des pellicules = dandruff

**pelouse** noun, feminine
la pelouse = the lawn

**peluche** noun, feminine
une peluche = a soft toy
un animal en peluche = a soft toy, a stuffed animal

**pencher** verb 1
1 (! + avoir)
= to tilt
pencher la tête = to bend one's head

2 **se pencher** (! + être)
se pencher = to lean
= to bend down

**pendant**
1 preposition
• = for
pendant des heures = for hours
pendant tout le voyage = for the whole journey, throughout the journey
• = during
pendant la nuit = during the night
pendant ce temps = meanwhile
2 **pendant que** = while

**penderie** noun, feminine
une penderie = a wardrobe, a closet

**pendre** verb 6
• = to hang
• = to dangle

**pendu/pendue**
1 ▶ **pendre** 6
2 **pendu** noun, masculine
jouer au pendu = to play hangman

**pendule** noun, feminine
une pendule = a clock

**pénétrer** verb 14
pénétrer dans un bâtiment = to enter a building, to get into a building

**pénible** adjective
= hard, difficult

**péniblement** adverb
= with difficulty

**péniche** noun, feminine
une péniche = a barge

**pensée** noun, feminine
• (an idea)
une pensée = a thought
• (a flower)
une pensée = a pansy

**penser** verb 1
• = to think
qu'en pensez-vous? = what do you think (about it)?
• penser à = to think of
= to remember
je pense à toi = I'm thinking of you
j'y ai pensé = I thought about it

**pension** noun, feminine
• (money)
une pension = a pension
• (a school)
une pension = a boarding school
• (a hotel)
une pension = a boarding house
la pension complète = full board
une pension de famille = a family hotel

**pensionnaire** noun, masculine/feminine
un pensionnaire/une pensionnaire (in a school) = a boarder
(in a hotel) = a resident

P

**pensionnat** *noun, masculine*
un pensionnat = a boarding school

**pente** *noun, feminine*
une pente = a slope
en pente = sloping

**Pentecôte** *noun, feminine*
la Pentecôte = Whitsun, Pentecost

**pépé*** *noun, masculine*
un pépé* = a grandad

**pépin** *noun, masculine*
• un pépin = a pip, a seed
• un pépin* = a slight problem

**perche** *noun, feminine*
une perche = a pole
la saut à la perche = pole vaulting

**perdant/perdante**
**1** *adjective*
= losing
**2** *noun, masculine/feminine*
un perdant/une perdante = a loser

**perdre** *verb* 6
**1** (**!** + *avoir*)
= to lose
perdre son temps = to waste one's time
**2 se perdre** (**!** + *être*)
se perdre = to get lost

**perdu/perdue**
**1 ▶ perdre** 6
**2** *adjective*
• = lost
= stray
• = wasted
c'est du temps perdu = it's a waste of time
• = remote, isolated

**père** *noun, masculine*
un père = a father
**le père Noël** = Father Christmas, Santa Claus

**perfectionner** *verb* 1
**1** (**!** + *avoir*)
= to perfect
= to improve
= to refine
**2 se perfectionner** (**!** + *être*)
se perfectionner = to improve

**périmé/périmée** *adjective*
= out-of-date

**périphérique** *noun, masculine*
le périphérique = the ring road, the beltway

**permanence**
**1** *noun, feminine*
une permanence = a permanently manned office
(*in school*) = a (supervised) study room, a study hall

**2 en permanence** = permanently

**permettre** *verb* 60
**1** (**!** + *avoir*)
= to allow
permettre à un enfant de sortir = to allow a child to go out
**2 se permettre** (**!** + *être*)
• (*to act without asking*)
se permettre de se servir = to take the liberty of helping oneself
• (*to have money*)
pouvoir se permettre d'aller au restaurant = to be able to afford to eat out

**permis/permise**
**1 ▶ permettre** 60
**2** *adjective*
= permitted, allowed
**3 permis** *noun, masculine* (**!** *never changes*)
un permis = a permit
= a licence, a license
**un permis de conduire** = a driving licence, a driver's license

**perroquet** *noun, masculine*
un perroquet = a parrot

**perruche** *noun, feminine*
une perruche = a budgerigar, a budgie

**perruque** *noun, feminine*
une perruque = a wig

**persienne** *noun, feminine*
une persienne = a shutter

**persil** *noun, masculine*
le persil = parsley

**personnage** *noun, masculine*
un personnage = a character

**personne**
**1** *pronoun*
= nobody
= anybody
**2** *noun, feminine*
une personne = a person
quelques personnes = a few people

**personnel/personnelle**
**1** *adjective*
= personal
**2 personnel** *noun, masculine*
le personnel = the staff

**perte** *noun, feminine*
une perte = a loss
une perte de temps = a waste of time

**peser** *verb* 16
= to weigh

**pétanque** *noun, feminine*
la pétanque = pétanque, *French bowls*

**pétard** *noun, masculine*
un pétard = a banger, a firecracker

**pétillant/pétillante** *adjective*
= sparkling

---

* in informal situations

**petit/petite**
1 *adjective*
(*in size or importance*) = small, little
(*in duration, length*) = short
2 *noun, masculine/feminine*
un petit/une petite – a child
(*in school*) = a junior
3 **petit** *noun, masculine*
un petit = a little one
les petits = the young
4 **petit à petit** = little by little, gradually
**les petits chevaux** ≈ ludo, Parcheesi

**petite-fille** *noun, feminine*
(*plural*) **petites-filles**
une petite-fille = a granddaughter

**petit-fils** *noun, masculine*
(*plural*) **petits-fils**
un petit-fils = a grandson

**petits-enfants** *noun, masculine plural*
des petits-enfants = grandchildren

**pétrole** *noun, masculine*
le pétrole = oil, petroleum

**peu**
1 *noun, masculine*
un peu = a little
un tout petit peu = just a little
2 *adverb*
• = not much
il mange peu = he doesn't eat very much
• = not very
peu intelligent = not very intelligent
peu après = soon afterwards
3 **peu de** *determiner*
= few, not many
= little, not much
peu de livres = few books
peu de nourriture = little food
c'est peu de chose = it's not much
4 **peu à peu** = gradually
5 **à peu près** = more or less
= approximately

**peuple** *noun, masculine*
un peuple = a people

**peur** *noun, feminine*
la peur = fear
avoir peur = to be afraid
faire peur à quelqu'un = to frighten
someone

**peut-être** *adverb*
= perhaps, maybe

**peux ▶ pouvoir 2** 49

**phare** *noun, masculine*
un phare (*on a car*) = a headlight
(*on the coast*) = a lighthouse

**pharmacie** *noun, feminine*
une pharmacie = a chemist's (shop), a
drugstore

**pharmacien/pharmacienne** *noun,
masculine/feminine*
un pharmacien/une pharmacienne = a
chemist, a pharmacist

**philatélie** *noun, feminine*
la philatélie = stamp collecting

**phoque** *noun, masculine*
un phoque = a seal

**photo** *noun, feminine*
• (*a picture*)
une photo = a photograph
• (*the activity*)
la photo = photography

**photocopie** *noun, feminine*
une photocopie = a photocopy

**photocopieuse** *noun, feminine*
une photocopieuse = a photocopier

**photographe** *noun, masculine/feminine*
un photographe/une photographe = a
photographer

**photographie** *noun, feminine*
• (*a picture*)
une photographie – a photograph
• (*the activity*)
la photographie = photography

**phrase** *noun, feminine*
une phrase = a sentence

**physicien/physicienne** *noun,
masculine/feminine*
un physicien/une physicienne = a
physicist

**physique**
1 *adjective*
= physical
2 *noun, feminine*
la physique = physics
3 *noun, masculine*
le physique = physical appearance

**picorer** *verb* 1
= to peck

**pièce** *noun, feminine*
• (*in a house, an apartment*)
une pièce = a room
un trois-pièces cuisine = a three-roomed
apartment with kitchen
• (*money*)
une pièce (de monnaie) = a coin
• (*at the theatre*)
une pièce (de théâtre) = a play
• (*a component*)
une pièce = a part
une pièce de rechange = a spare part
• (*an item*)
une pièce = a piece
ils coûtent dix euros pièce = they cost ten
euros each
un (maillot) deux-pièces = a two-piece
swimsuit
• (*in a file*)
une pièce = a document

P

**une pièce détachée** = a spare part
**une pièce d'identité** = identification
**une pièce jointe** = an attachment

**pied** *noun, masculine*
* (*part of the body*)
  un pied = a foot
  à pied = on foot
  pieds nus = barefoot
  un coup de pied = a kick
* (*the lower end*)
  le pied = the foot, the bottom
  au pied de l'escalier = at the bottom of the
  stairs
* (*an upright part*)
  un pied (*on a table*) = a leg
  (*on a lamp*) = a base
  (*on a glass*) = a stem
* (*a measurement*)
  un pied = a foot

**piège** *noun, masculine*
  un piège = a trap

**pierre** *noun, feminine*
  une pierre = a stone

**piéton/piétonne** *noun,*
*masculine/feminine*
  un piéton/une piétonne = a pedestrian

**pieuvre** *noun, feminine*
  une pieuvre = an octopus

**pigeon** *noun, masculine*
  un pigeon = a pigeon
**pigeon vole** = Simon says

**pile**
**1** *noun, feminine*
* (*in a flashlight, a toy*)
  une pile = a battery
  à piles = battery-operated
* (*on a coin*)
  pile = tails
  jouer à pile ou face = to play heads or tails
* (*things on top of one another*)
  une pile = a pile, a stack
**2** *adverb*�910
  à trois heures pile�910 = at three o'clock on
  the dot
  s'arrêter pile�910 = to stop dead
  tu tombes pile�910 = you've come at just the
  right moment

**pilier** *noun, masculine*
  un pilier = a pillar

**pilote** *noun, masculine*
  un pilote = a pilot
**pilote automobile** = racing driver
**pilote de rallye** = rally driver

**pilule** *noun, feminine*
  une pilule = a pill

**pin** *noun, masculine*
  un pin = a pine (tree)

———————
�910 in informal situations

**pinceau** *noun, masculine*
(*plural*) **pinceaux**
  un pinceau = a (paint)brush

**pincée** *noun, feminine*
  une pincée = a pinch

**pincer** *verb* 12
  = to pinch

**pinède** *noun, feminine*
  une pinède = a pine forest

**pingouin** *noun, masculine*
  un pingouin = a penguin

**ping-pong**   *noun, masculine*
(*plural*) **ping-pongs**
  le ping-pong = table tennis, ping-pong

**pin's** *noun, masculine* (**!** *never changes*)
  un pin's = a (lapel) badge, a pin

**pioche** *noun, feminine*
  une pioche = a pickaxe

**pipe** *noun, feminine*
  une pipe = a pipe

**pipi**�910 *noun, masculine*
  faire pipi�910 = to have a pee, to take a pee

**pique** *noun, masculine*
  pique = spades

**pique-nique** *noun, masculine*
(*plural*) **pique-niques**
  un pique-nique = a picnic

**piquer** *verb* 1
**1** (**!** + *avoir*)
* (*if it's a bee, a nettle, smoke*) = to sting
  (*if it's a snake, a mosquito*) = to bite
  (*if it's a thorn*) = to prick
* (*to take*)�910 = to pinch, to steal
  = to borrow
**2 se piquer** (**!** + *être*)
  se piquer = to prick oneself

**piqûre** *noun, feminine*
  une piqûre (*with a syringe*) = an injection
  (*from an insect*) = a sting
  = a bite

**pire**
**1** *adjective*
  = worse
  = worst
**2** *noun, masculine*
  le pire = the worst (about it)

**piscine** *noun, feminine*
  une piscine = a swimming pool
  une piscine couverte = an indoor
  swimming pool

**pistache** *noun, feminine*
  une pistache = a pistachio nut

**piste** *noun, feminine*
* (*a clearly marked path*)
  une piste (*in a forest*) = a trail, a track
  (*when skiing*) = a piste, a run

(*in racing events*)
= a (race)track
= a racecourse
• (*in a circus*)
la piste = the ring
• (*in a police investigation*)
une piste = a lead
**une piste d'atterrissage** = a runway
**une piste cyclable** = a cycle lane
**une piste de danse** = a dance floor

**pistolet** *noun, masculine*
un pistolet = a gun

**pitre** *noun, masculine*
un pitre = a clown, a buffoon

**pittoresque** *adjective*
= picturesque

**placard** *noun, masculine*
un placard = a cupboard

**place** *noun, feminine*
• (*in a town*)
une place = a square
• (*for a passenger, a spectator*)
une place = a seat
une place assise = a seat
une place debout = a standing ticket
• (*a position*)
une place = a place
remettre un livre à sa place = to put a
book back in its place
obtenir la première place = to take first
place
à la place de = instead of
• (*a vacant spot*)
une place (*at a table*) = a place
(*for a car*) = a parking space
• (*enough empty space*)
de la place = room, space

**plafond** *noun, masculine*
le plafond = the ceiling

**plage** *noun, feminine*
la plage = the beach

**plaie** *noun, feminine*
une plaie = a wound

**plaindre** *verb* 54
**1** (**!** + *avoir*)
= to feel sorry for
**2 se plaindre** (**!** + *être*)
se plaindre = to complain

**plaint/plainte¹** ▶ **plaindre** 54

**plainte²** *noun, feminine*
• (*expressing dissatisfaction*)
une plainte = a complaint
• (*a sound of pain*)
une plainte = a moan, a groan

**plaire** *verb* 59
• s'il te plaît, s'il vous plaît = please
• Marc plaît aux filles = girls find Marc
attractive
le film leur a plu = they liked the film

**plaisanterie** *noun, feminine*
une plaisanterie = a joke

**plaisir** *noun, masculine*
le plaisir = pleasure
ma visite leur a fait plaisir = they were
pleased to see me

**plaît** ▶ **plaire** 59

**plan** *noun, masculine*
• (*of an area*)
un plan = a map
• (*for an essay*)
un plan = an outline
• (*for a line of action*)
un plan = a plan
• (*in films, photography*)
au premier plan = in the foreground
un gros plan = a close-up

**planche** *noun, feminine*
une planche = a plank
= a board
**une planche à repasser** = an ironing
board
**une planche à roulettes** = a skateboard
**une planche à voile** = a windsurfing
board

**plancher** *noun, masculine*
le plancher = the floor

**planète** *noun, feminine*
une planète = a planet

**planeur** *noun, masculine*
• (*the equipment*)
un planeur = a glider
• (*the sport*)
le planeur = gliding

**planifier** *verb* 2
= to plan

**plante** *noun, feminine*
une plante = a plant
**une plante grasse** = a succulent
**une plante verte** = a houseplant

**planter** *verb* 1
• = to plant
• planter une tente = to pitch a tent

**plaque** *noun, feminine*
une plaque (*of metal, glass*) = a plate
**une plaque d'immatriculation** = a
number plate, a license plate

**plastique** *noun, masculine*
le plastique = plastic

**plat/plate**
**1** *adjective*
= flat
**2 plat** *noun, masculine*
un plat = a dish
= a course
le plat du jour = today's special

**P**

**3 à plat**
* (the way something lies)
  à plat = flat
  poser une carte à plat = to lay a map down
    flat
  à plat ventre = flat on one's stomach
* (describing a tyre)
  à plat = flat
* (describing a person)
  à plat✶ = run down

**plateau** noun, masculine
(plural) **plateaux**
  un plateau (for serving) = a tray
  un plateau de fromages = a cheeseboard

**platine** noun, feminine
  une platine = a turntable
  une platine CD = a CD player

**plâtre** noun, masculine
  le plâtre = plaster

**plein/pleine**
**1** adjective
* = full
* en pleine forêt = (right) in the middle of
  the forest
  en plein jour = in broad daylight
  en plein air = in the open air
  en pleine forme = in great shape, really fit
**2 plein** noun, masculine
  faire le plein (d'essence) = to fill up (with
    petrol)

**pleurer** verb [1]
  = to cry, to weep

**pleut ▶ pleuvoir** [33]

**pleuvoir** verb [33]
  = to rain
  il pleut = it's raining

**plier** verb [2]
  = to fold
  = to bend

**plombier** noun, masculine
  un plombier = a plumber

**plongée** noun, feminine
  la plongée = diving
  la plongée sous-marine = deep-sea diving

**plongeoir** noun, masculine
  un plongeoir = a diving-board

**plongeon** noun, masculine
  un plongeon = a dive

**plonger** verb [13]
* = to dive
* = to plunge

**plongeur/plongeuse** noun,
masculine/feminine
  un plongeur/une plongeuse = a diver

---
✶ in informal situations

**plu**
* ▶ **plaire** [59]
* ▶ **pleuvoir** [33]

**pluie** noun, feminine
  la pluie = rain

**plume** noun, feminine
* (on a bird)
  une plume = a feather
* (on a pen)
  une plume = a nib

**plupart** noun, feminine
  la plupart de = most of

**pluriel** noun, masculine
  le pluriel = the plural

**plus**
**1** conjunction
  = plus
**2** adverb
* = more
  c'est plus intéressant = it's more
    interesting
  arriver plus tôt que d'habitude = to arrive
    earlier than usual
  de plus en plus prudent = more and more
    careful
  deux fois plus cher = twice as expensive
* plus de = more
  = more than, over
  plus de la moitié = more than half
  elle a plus de seize ans = she's over sixteen
  il est plus de minuit = it's past midnight
* plus... plus = the more... the more
  plus... moins = the more... the less
  plus... mieux = the more... the better
  plus on lit, plus on apprend = the more
    you read, the more you learn
* le plus/la plus = the most
  = the more
  les plus belles fleurs du jardin = the most
    beautiful flowers in the garden
  le plus cher des deux = the more
    expensive of the two
* en plus = on top (of that)
  il fait froid et en plus il pleut = it's cold and
    on top of that it's raining
  en plus de mon travail = on top of my
    work
**3 ne... plus** = no more, not any more
  = no longer
  il n'y a plus de pain = there's no more
    bread, there's no bread left
  elle ne travaille plus = she doesn't work
    any more, she no longer works
  je n'ai plus que dix euros = I've only got
    ten euros left
  il ne te reste plus rien = you've nothing
    left
  plus jamais = never again
  il n'y va pas, et moi non plus = he's not
    going and neither am I

**plusieurs** adjective
  = several

**plutôt** *adverb*
= rather
= instead

**pluvieux/pluvieuse** *adjective*
= rainy

**pneu** *noun, masculine*
un pneu = a tyre, a tire

**pneumatique** *adjective*
= inflatable

**poche** *noun, feminine*
une poche = a pocket

**poêle**
**1** *noun, feminine*
une poêle (à frire) = a frying pan
**2** *noun, masculine*
un poêle = a stove

**poésie** *noun, feminine*
• la poésie = poetry
• une poésie = a poem

**poids** *noun, masculine* (**!** *never changes*)
le poids = the weight
prendre du poids = to put on weight
**un poids lourd** = a heavy goods vehicle

**poignée** *noun, feminine*
• (*on a door*)
une poignée = a handle
• (*an amount*)
une poignée = a handful
**une poignée de main** = a handshake

**poignet** *noun, masculine*
un poignet = a wrist
= a cuff

**poil** *noun, masculine*
un poil (*on the body, on an animal*) = a hair
(*on a brush*) = a bristle

**poing** *noun, masculine*
le poing = the fist
un coup de poing = a punch

**point**
**1** *noun, masculine*
• (*a punctuation mark*)
un point = a full stop, a period
deux points = a colon
• (*when scoring*)
un point = a point
• (*in sewing, in knitting*)
un point = a stitch
• (*a small round mark*)
un point = a dot, a speck
• (*a particular place or position*)
un point de rencontre = a meeting point
**2** à point
un bifteck (cuit) à point = a medium rare
  steak
**un point de départ** = a starting point
**un point d'exclamation** = an
exclamation mark
**un point d'interrogation** = a question
mark

**un point de repère** = a landmark
**des points de suspension** = suspension
points

**pointe** *noun, feminine*
la pointe = the point, the tip
sur la pointe des pieds = on tiptoe

**pointer: se pointer\*** *verb* |1| (**!** + *être*)
se pointer\* = to show up

**pointu/pointue** *adjective*
= pointed
= with a sharp point

**pointure** *noun, feminine*
une pointure = a shoe size

**point-virgule** *noun, masculine*
(*plural*) **points-virgules**
un point-virgule = a semicolon

**poire** *noun, feminine*
une poire = a pear

**poireau** *noun, masculine*
(*plural*) **poireaux**
un poireau = a leek

**pois** *noun, masculine* (**!** *never changes*)
• (*on material*)
un pois = a dot
à pois = polka dot, dotted
• (*in a pod*)
un pois = a pea
des petits pois = garden peas, petits pois

**poisson** *noun, masculine*
un poisson = a fish
**un poisson d'avril** = an April fool's joke
**un poisson rouge** = a goldfish

**poissonnerie** *noun, feminine*
une poissonnerie = a fishmonger's, a fish
shop

**poissonnier/poissonnière** *noun,*
*masculine/feminine*
un poissonnier/une poissonnière = a
fishmonger, a fish dealer

**Poissons** *noun, masculine plural*
Poissons = Pisces

**poitrine** *noun, feminine*
la poitrine = the chest
= the bust

**poivre** *noun, masculine*
le poivre = pepper

**poivron** *noun, masculine*
un poivron = a sweet pepper, a capsicum

**poli/polie** *adjective*
• (*well-mannered*) = polite
• (*shiny*) = polished

**police** *noun, feminine*
la police = the police
**police secours** ≈ emergency services

**policier** *noun, masculine*
un policier = a policeman

**P**

**polluer** *verb* 1
= to pollute

**Pologne** *noun, feminine*
la Pologne = Poland

**polonais/polonaise**
**1** *adjective*
= Polish
**2 polonais** *noun, masculine*
le polonais = Polish

**pommade** *noun, feminine*
une pommade = an ointment

**pomme** *noun, feminine*
une pomme = an apple
**une pomme de terre** = a potato

**pommier** *noun, masculine*
un pommier = an apple tree

**pompe** *noun, feminine*
une pompe = a pump

**pompier** *noun, masculine*
un pompier = a fireman, a firefighter
les pompiers = the fire brigade, the fire
　department

**pompiste** *noun, masculine/feminine*
un pompiste/une pompiste = a petrol
　pump attendant, a gas station
　attendant

**pont** *noun, masculine*
• (*over a river*)
　un pont = a bridge
• (*on a ship*)
　un pont = a deck
• (*extra time off*)
　**faire le pont** *to have the day(s) off between
　a public holiday and a weekend*

**populaire** *adjective*
• (*describing an area*) = working-class
• (*meaning well-liked*) = popular

**porc** *noun, masculine*
• (*the animal*)
　un porc = a pig
• (*the meat*)
　le porc = pork

**porc-épic** *noun, masculine*
(*plural*) **porc-épics**
　un porc-épic = a porcupine

**porcherie** *noun, feminine*
une porcherie = a pigsty

**portable** *noun, masculine*
un portable = a mobile phone, a cell phone
un portable = a laptop

**port** *noun, masculine*
un port = a harbo(u)r, a port
**un port de plaisance** = a marina

**portail** *noun, masculine*
un portail = a gate

**porte** *noun, feminine*
une porte = a door
= a gate
mettre à la porte = to throw out
**une porte d'embarquement** = a
　departure gate
**la porte d'entrée** = the front door

**porte-clés, porte-clefs** *noun,
masculine* (**!** *never changes*)
un porte-clés = a key ring

**porte-fenêtre** *noun, feminine*
(*plural*) **portes-fenêtres**
une porte-fenêtre = a French window

**portefeuille** *noun, masculine*
un portefeuille = a wallet

**portemanteau** *noun, masculine*
(*plural*) **portemanteaux**
un portemanteau = a coat rack
= a coat stand

**porte-monnaie** *noun, masculine*
(**!** *never changes*)
un porte-monnaie = a purse, a coin purse

**porter** *verb* 1
**1** (**!** + *avoir*)
• = to carry
• = to wear
• **porter bonheur** = to bring good luck
　**porter malheur** = to bring bad luck
**2 se porter** (**!** + *être*)
se porter bien = to be well

**porteur** *noun, masculine*
un porteur = a porter

**portier** *noun, masculine*
un portier = a doorman

**portière** *noun, feminine*
une portière = a door

**portillon** *noun, masculine*
un portillon = a gate, a barrier

**portrait** *noun, masculine*
• (*a likeness*)
　un portrait = a portrait
• (*in words*)
　un portrait = a description

**portrait-robot** *noun, masculine*
(*plural*) **portraits-robots**
　un portrait-robot = a photofit　, an
　identikit

**portugais/portugaise**
**1** *adjective*
= Portuguese
**2 portugais** *noun, masculine*
le portugais = Portuguese

**Portugal** *noun, masculine*
le Portugal = Portugal

---

**✗** *in informal situations*

**poser** verb ①
**1** (! + *avoir*)
- = to put down
  poser un sac sur une table = to put a bag down on a table
- = to ask
  poser une question = to ask a question
**2 se poser** (! + *être*)
  se poser (*if it's a bird*) = to settle, to alight
  (*if it's a plane*) = to land, to touch down

**posséder** verb ⑭
= to own
= to possess

**possible**
**1** *adjective*
= possible
  le plus de temps possible = as much time as possible
  le plus tôt possible = as soon as possible
**2** *noun, masculine*
  faire tout son possible = to do one's utmost

**poste**
**1** *noun, feminine*
  la poste = the post office
**2** *noun, masculine*
- (*employment*)
  un poste = a job, a position
- (*a receiver*)
  un poste de télévision = a television set
- (*a place*)
  le poste (de police) = the police station
- (*for telephoning*)
  un poste = an extension

**poster** verb ①
= to post, to mail

**pot** *noun, masculine*
- un pot = a pot
  = a jar
- un pot✶ = a drink

**potable** *adjective*
  l'eau potable = drinking water

**potage** *noun, masculine*
  le potage = soup

**potager** *noun, masculine*
  un (jardin) potager = a vegetable garden

**poteau** *noun, masculine*
(*plural*) **poteaux**
  un poteau = a post
**un poteau indicateur** = a signpost

**potier/potière** *noun, masculine/feminine*
  un potier/une potière = a potter

**poubelle** *noun, feminine*
  une poubelle = a dustbin, a trash can

**pouce** *noun, masculine*
- un pouce = a thumb
- un pouce = an inch

**poudre** *noun, feminine*
  la poudre = powder

**poule** *noun, feminine*
  une poule = a hen

**poulet** *noun, masculine*
  un poulet = a chicken

**poulpe** *noun, masculine*
  un poulpe = an octopus

**pouls** *noun, masculine* (**l** *never changes*)
  le pouls = the pulse

**poumon** *noun, masculine*
  un poumon = a lung

**poupée** *noun, feminine*
  une poupée = a doll

**pour**
**1** *preposition*
- = for
  c'est pour toi = it's for you
  un produit pour nettoyer les vitres = a product for cleaning windows
- = to, in order to, so as to
  j'ai écrit pour les remercier = I've written to thank them
  pour ne pas manquer le train = so as not to miss the train
- = per
  dix pour cent = ten per cent
**2** *noun, masculine*
  le pour et le contre = the pros and the cons

**pourboire** *noun, masculine*
  un pourboire = a tip

**pourpre** *adjective*
= crimson

**pourquoi** *adverb, conjunction*
= why

**pourrai** ▶ **pouvoir 2** ㊾

**pourri/pourrie** *adjective*
= rotten

**pourtant** *adverb*
= yet

**pousser** verb ①
**1** (! + *avoir*)
- = to push
- = to move
- = to let out
  pousser un cri = to let out a cry
- (*if it's a plant, hair*) = to grow
  faire pousser des fleurs = to grow flowers
**2 se pousser** (! + *être*)
  se pousser = to move over

**poussette** *noun, feminine*
  une poussette = a pushchair, a stroller

**poussière** *noun, feminine*
  la poussière = dust

**poussin** *noun, masculine*
  un poussin = a chick

**pouvoir**
**1** *noun, masculine*
  le pouvoir = power

**P**

**2** verb 49
- = to be able to
  - il ne pourra pas venir = he won't be able to come
  - elle n'a pas pu partir = she wasn't able to leave, she couldn't leave
  - je ne peux pas payer ce prix = I can't pay that sort of price
  - pourriez-vous me dire où se trouve la gare? = could you tell me where the station is?
  - je n'en peux plus! (after an effort) = I've had it!
  - (after a meal) = I'm full!
- = to be allowed to
  - puis-je téléphoner? = may I use the phone?
  - tu ne peux pas te garer là = you can't park there
- (expressing a possibility)
  - attention, tu pourrais glisser = careful, you might slip
  - vous auriez pu m'avertir! = you might have warned me!
  - il pouvait avoir dix ans = he would have been about ten
  - il pouvait être dix heures = it was probably about ten o'clock

**3 il se peut** (! + être)
- il se peut que j'y aille = I might go
- il se pourrait bien que l'avion ait du retard = the plane might well be delayed
- ça se peut = it's possible

**prairie** noun, feminine
- une prairie = a meadow

**pratique** adjective
- = practical
- = handy, convenient

**pratiquer** verb 1
- pratiquer le tennis = to play tennis
- pratiquer le yoga = to do yoga

**pré** noun, masculine
- un pré = a meadow

**précieux/précieuse** adjective
- = precious

**précipiter: se précipiter** verb 1
(! + être)
- se précipiter = to rush
- se précipiter sur le journal = to pounce on the newspaper

**précis/précise** adjective
- = precise
- = accurate
- à trois heures précises = at exactly three o'clock, at three o'clock sharp

**préféré/préférée**
**1 ▶ préférer** 14
**2** adjective
- = favo(u)rite

**préférence** noun, feminine
- une préférence = a preference
- de préférence = preferably

**préférer** verb 14
- = to prefer

**premier/première¹**
**1** adjective
- = first
**2 premier** noun, masculine
- habiter au premier (in Britain) = to live on the first floor
- (in the US) = to live on the second floor
**le premier de l'an** = New Year's Day

**première²** noun, feminine
- (in school)
  - la première the class for secondary school students aged 16 to 17
- (when travelling)
  - voyager en première = to travel first class

**prendre** verb 52
**1** (! + avoir)
- = to take
- = to have
  - allons prendre un verre = let's go and have a drink
  - qu'est-ce que tu prends? = what'll you have?
- = to go
  - prenez à gauche = go left, turn left
- = to catch
  - prendre froid = to catch a chill
  - prendre feu = to catch fire
- qu'est-ce qui te prend✱? = what's up with you?
**2 se prendre** (! + être)
- pour qui se prend-il? = who does he think he is?
- elle s'y prend mal = she's going about it the wrong way

**prénom** noun, masculine
- un prénom = a first name

**préparer** verb 1
**1** (! + avoir)
- préparer un repas = to prepare a meal
- préparer un examen = to prepare for an examination
- préparer ses affaires = to get one's things ready
**2 se préparer** (! + être)
- se préparer = to get ready

**près**
**1** adverb
- = close, near(by)
- tout près du magasin = near the shop
- près de trois mètres = nearly three metres
**2 de près** = closely
**3 à peu près** = about
- = practically

**présenter** verb 1
**1** (! + avoir)
- = to present
- = to show

---

✱ in informal situations

• = to introduce
**présenter son passeport** = to show one's passport
**il m'a présenté à ses amis** = he introduced me to his friends
**2 se présenter** (**!** + *être*)
• (*to give one's name*)
**se présenter** = to introduce oneself
• (*to show up*)
**se présenter** = to present oneself
• (*if it's an opportunity*)
**se présenter** = to arise

**président/présidente** *noun, masculine/feminine*
**un président/une présidente** = a president = a chairman/a chairwoman, a chairperson

**presque** *adverb*
= nearly, almost

**pressé/pressée** *adjective*
**être pressé** = to be in a hurry

**pressing** *noun, masculine*
**un pressing** = a dry cleaner's

**pression** *noun, feminine*
**la pression** = pressure

**prêt/prête**
**1** *adjective*
= ready
**2 prêt** *noun, masculine*
**un prêt** = a loan

**prêt-à-porter** *noun, masculine*
**le prêt-à-porter** = ready-to-wear (clothes)

**prêter** *verb* 1
= to lend

**prêtre** *noun, masculine*
**un prêtre** = a priest

**preuve** *noun, feminine*
• **une preuve** = a piece of evidence
**des preuves** = evidence
• **la preuve** = the proof
**c'est la preuve qu'il est innocent** = it's proof that he's innocent
• **faire preuve de** = to show

**prévenir** *verb* 36
• = to warn
• = to prevent

**prévenu/prévenue** ▶ **prévenir** 36

**prévision** *noun, feminine*
**une prévision** = a forecast
**les prévisions météorologiques** = the weather forecast

**prévoir** *verb* 35
• = to predict
• = to anticipate, to expect
• = to plan
**comme prévu** = as planned

**prévu/prévue** ▶ **prévoir** 35

**prier** *verb* 2
• = to request, to ask
**je vous en prie** = don't mention it

**primaire** *adjective*
= primary

**primeurs** *noun, feminine plural*
**les primeurs** = early produce

**principal/principale** *adjective*
(*plural*) **principaux/principales**
= main

**principauté** *noun, feminine*
**une principauté** = a principality

**printemps** *noun, masculine* (**!** *never changes*)
**le printemps** = spring

**priorité** *noun, feminine*
**la priorité** = priority
(*on the road*) = the right of way

**pris/prise¹** ▶ **prendre** 52

**prise²** *noun, feminine*
• (*electrical*)
**une prise** = a plug
= a socket
• (*when fishing*)
**une prise** = a catch

**prisonnier/prisonnière** *adjective*
**être prisonnier** = to be a prisoner

**privé/privée** *adjective*
= private

**prix** *noun, masculine* (**!** *never changes*)
• (*the cost*)
**le prix** = the price
**à tout prix** = at all costs
• (*a reward*)
**un prix** = a prize

**problème** *noun, masculine*
**un problème** = a problem
= an issue

**procès** *noun, masculine* (**!** *never changes*)
**un procès** = a trial

**prochain/prochaine** *adjective*
= next
**à l'année prochaine!** = see you next year!

**proche** *adjective*
= nearby
**le garage le plus proche** = the nearest garage

**producteur/productrice** *noun, masculine/feminine*
**un producteur/une productrice** = a producer

**produire** *verb* 62
**1** (**!** + *avoir*)
• = to produce
• = to cause

P

**2 se produire** (**!** + *être*)
se produire = to happen

**produit/produite**
**1 ▶ produire** 62
**2 produit** *noun, masculine*
un produit = a product
**un produit de beauté** = a beauty product
**un produit chimique** = a chemical

**prof✗** *noun, masculine/feminine*
un prof✗/une prof✗ = a teacher, a lecturer

**professeur** *noun, masculine*
un professeur = a teacher, a lecturer

**profiter** *verb* 1
profiter de = to take advantage of
= to make the most of

**profond/profonde** *adjective*
= deep
peu profond = shallow

**profondeur** *noun, feminine*
la profondeur = the depth
avoir dix mètres de profondeur = to be ten
metres deep

**programmateur** *noun, masculine*
un programmateur = a timer

**programme** *noun, masculine*
un programme = a program(me)
(*for an examination*) = a syllabus
(*for a computer*) = a program

**programmer** *verb* 1
= to program

**progrès** *noun, masculine* (**!** *never
changes*)
le progrès = progress

**projecteur** *noun, masculine*
• (*a light*)
un projecteur = a floodlight
= a searchlight
• (*for slides*)
un projecteur = a projector

**projet** *noun, masculine*
un projet = a plan
des projets de vacances = holiday plans,
vacation plans

**projeter** *verb* 20
= to plan

**promenade** *noun, feminine*
une promenade (*on foot*) = a walk
(*by car*) = a drive
(*on a bike*) = a ride

**promener** *verb* 16
**1** (**!** + *avoir*)
promener le chien = to take the dog for a
walk
**2 se promener** (**!** + *être*)
se promener (*on foot*) = to go for a walk

(*by car*) = to go for a drive
(*on a bike*) = to go for a ride

**promesse** *noun, feminine*
une promesse = a promise

**promettre** *verb* 60
= to promise

**promis/promise ▶ promettre** 60

**promotion** *noun, feminine*
• (*in a shop*)
une promotion = a special offer
• (*in one's career*)
une promotion = promotion

**pronom** *noun, masculine*
un pronom = a pronoun

**prononcer** *verb* 12
• = to pronounce
• = to deliver

**propos** *noun, masculine plural*
des propos = words
**à propos** = by the way
à propos, je n'y vais pas = by the way, I'm
not going
**à propos de** = about

**proposer** *verb* 1
• = to suggest
• = to offer
elle m'a proposé sa voiture = she offered
me her car

**proposition** *noun, feminine*
une proposition = a suggestion
= a proposal

**propre** *adjective*
• = clean
une serviette propre = a clean towel
• = own
avec mon propre argent = with my own
money

**propriétaire** *noun, masculine/feminine*
le propriétaire/la propriétaire = the owner
(*with tenants*) = the landlord/the landlady

**propriété** *noun, feminine*
la propriété = property
'propriété privée' = 'private property'

**prospère** *adjective*
= prosperous

**protéger** *verb* 15
= to protect

**protester** *verb* 1
= to protest

**prouver** *verb* 1
= to prove

**provenance** *noun, feminine*
la provenance = the origin
le train en provenance de Paris = the train
from Paris

---

**✗** in informal situations

**provençal/provençale**
(*plural*) **provençaux/provençales**
**1** *adjective*
= of Provence
= from Provence
**2 provençal** *noun, masculine*
le provençal – Provençal

**proviseur** *noun, masculine*
le proviseur = the headteacher, the
principal

**provision**
**1** *noun, feminine*
une provision de = a stock of, a supply of
faire une provision de papier = to stock up
on paper
**2 provisions** *noun, feminine plural*
faire des provisions = to go shopping for
food

**provisoire** *adjective*
= provisional, temporary

**provoquer** *verb* ①
• = to cause
• = to provoke

**proximité**: **à proximité** *adverb*
= near(by)

**prudence** *noun, feminine*
la prudence = caution

**prudent/prudente** *adjective*
= careful, cautious

**prune** *noun, feminine*
une prune = a plum

**pruneau** *noun, masculine*
(*plural*) **pruneaux**
un pruneau = a prune

**PTT** *noun, feminine plural*
les PTT *formerly the French postal and
telecommunications service*

**pu** ▶ **pouvoir 2** 49

**pub**✻ *noun, feminine* ▶ **publicité**

**public/publique**
**1** *adjective*
= public
(*describing a school, education*) = state
(*in the US*) = public
**2 public** *noun, masculine*
le public (*all the people*) = the public
(*at a meeting, a show*) = the audience

**publicitaire**
**1** *adjective*
= advertising
**2** *noun, masculine/feminine*
un publicitaire/une publicitaire = an
advertising executive

**publicité** *noun, feminine*
• la publicité = advertising
• une publicité = an advertisement, a
commercial

**publier** *verb* ②
= to publish

**puer** *verb* ①
= to stink
ça pue le poisson! = it stinks of fish!

**puis** *adverb*
= then
= next

**puisque** (**puisqu'** *before vowel or mute
h*) *conjunction*
= as
= since

**puissant/puissante** *adjective*
= powerful

**puisse** ▶ **pouvoir 2** 49

**puits** *noun, masculine* (❗ *never changes*)
un puits = a well

**pull** *noun, masculine*
un pull = a jumper, a sweater

**punaise** *noun, feminine*
• (*for pinning*)
une punaise = a drawing pin, a
thumbtack
• (*an insect*)
une punaise = a bug

**punir** *verb* ③
= to punish

**punition** *noun, feminine*
une punition = a punishment

**pur/pure** *adjective*
= pure
(*describing wine or spirits*) = neat

**purée** *noun, feminine*
• la purée (de pommes de terre) = mashed
potatoes
• la purée = puree

**PV**✻ *noun, masculine*
un PV✻ = a fine
= a parking ticket

**pyjama** *noun, masculine*
un pyjama = pyjamas, pajamas

**qu'** ▶ **que**

**quai** *noun, masculine*
un quai (*in a station*) = a platform
(*in a port*) = a quay
(*along a river*) = a bank
le navire est à quai = the ship has docked

**qualité** *noun, feminine*
• une qualité = a quality
• nom, prénom et qualité = surname, first
  name and occupation
  en sa qualité de représentant = in his/her
  capacity as a representative

**quand**
**1** *conjunction*
  = when
  quand il sera vieux = when he's old
  tu sortiras quand tu auras fini = you'll go
  out when you've finished
**2** *adverb*
  = when
  quand est-ce que vous partez? = when are
  you leaving?
  depuis quand est-il malade? = how long
  has he been ill?
**3 quand même** = still, even so

**quant à** *preposition*
  = as for

**quantité** *noun, feminine*
  une quantité = a quantity, an amount
  des quantités de = lots of

**quarante** *number*
  = forty

**quart** *noun, masculine*
  un quart = a quarter
  un quart d'heure = a quarter of an hour
  une heure moins le quart = a quarter to
  one
  une heure et quart = a quarter past one

**quartier** *noun, masculine*
• (*part of a town*)
  un quartier = an area, a district
  les gens du quartier = the locals
• (*a segment*)
  un quartier = a quarter
  le premier quartier de la lune = the moon's
  first quarter
**un quartier général** = headquarters

**quatorze** *number*
  = fourteen

**quatorzième** *number*
  = fourteenth

**quatre** *number*
  = quatre

**quatre-vingt(s)** *number*
  = eighty

**quatre-vingt-dix** *number*
  = ninety

**quatrième**
**1** *number*
  = fourth
**2** *noun, feminine*
  la quatrième *the class for secondary
  school students aged 13 to 14*

**que** (**qu'** *before vowel or mute h*)
  **!** *The construction* ne + verb + que *is
  treated under* ne.

**1** *conjunction*
• = that
  elle a dit qu'elle le ferait = she said that she
  would do it
  je veux que tu m'accompagnes = I want
  you to come with me
• = than, as
  plus gros que moi = fatter than me
  aussi fort que mon père = as strong as my
  father
  c'est le même que le mien = it's the same
  as mine
• = whether
  que tu le veuilles ou non = whether you
  like it or not
**2** *pronoun*
• = what
  que dire? = what can you say?
  je ne sais pas ce qu'il a dit = I don't know
  what he said
  qu'est-ce que c'est? = what's that?
• = that
  = who
  la voiture que tu as achetée = the car
  (that) you've bought
  l'ami que j'ai invité = the friend whom I
  invited
**3** *adverb*
  que c'est joli! = it's so pretty!

**québécois/québécoise** *adjective*
  = of Quebec
  = from Quebec

**quel/quelle**
**1** *determiner*
  = what
  = which
  quelle est la capitale du Togo? = what's
  the capital of Togo?
**2** *adjective*
• = what
  = which
  quelle heure est-il? = what time is it?
  quels disques as-tu achetés? = which
  records did you buy?
• quelle coïncidence! = what a coincidence!
• quel que soit le temps = whatever the
  weather
  quelles que soient leurs habitudes
  = whatever their habits

**quelque** *determiner*
• (*in the singular*) = some
  depuis quelque temps = for some time
• (*in the plural*) = some, a few
  = any
  quelques élèves = some pupils, a few
  pupils

**quelquefois** *adverb*
  = sometimes

**quelques-uns/quelques-unes**
*pronoun*
= some, a few

**quelqu'un** *pronoun*
= someone, somebody
= anyone, anybody

**quenelle** *noun, feminine*
une quenelle *a dumpling made of flour and egg, flavo(u)red with meat or fish*

**querelle** *noun, feminine*
une querelle = a quarrel

**question** *noun, feminine*
• (*a sentence asking something*)
une question = a question
poser une question à un élève = to ask a pupil a question
• (*something to be examined*)
une question = a matter
= an issue
c'est une question de vie ou de mort = it's a matter of life and death
pas question! = no way!

**questionnaire** *noun, masculine*
un questionnaire = a questionnaire

**questionner** *verb* 1
= to question

**quête** *noun, feminine*
une quête = a collection
faire la quête = to pass the hat around
= to collect for charity
= to take the collection

**queue** *noun, feminine*
• (*on an animal*)
une queue = a tail
• (*people or cars waiting*)
une queue = a queue, a line
faire la queue = to stand in a queue, to stand in line

**queue-de-cheval** *noun, feminine*
(*plural*) **queues-de-cheval**
une queue-de-cheval = a ponytail

**qui** *pronoun*
• = who
= whom
qui est-ce? = who is it?
l'homme à qui tu as parlé = the man to whom you spoke
à qui sont ces chaussures? = whose shoes are these?
• = who
= that
= which
qui que vous soyez = whoever you are
je n'ai jamais frappé qui que ce soit = I've never hit anybody

**quille** *noun, feminine*
une quille = a skittle

**quincaillerie** *noun, feminine*
une quincaillerie = a hardware shop, a hardware store

**quinzaine** *noun, feminine*
• une quinzaine = about fifteen
• une quinzaine (de jours) = a fortnight, two weeks

**quinze** *number*
= fifteen
quinze jours = fifteen days
= a fortnight, two weeks

**quinzième** *number*
= fifteenth

**quittance** *noun, feminine*
une quittance = a receipt
= a bill

**quitter** *verb* 1
**1** (! + *avoir*)
• = to leave
• ne quittez pas = hold the line please, hold on please
**2 se quitter** (! + *être*)
se quitter = to part

**quoi** *pronoun*
= what
quoi de neuf? = what's new?
je ne sais pas quoi faire = I don't know what to do
à quoi penses-tu? = what are you thinking about?
à quoi bon? = what's the point?
si je peux faire quoi que ce soit = if there's anything I can do
il n'y a pas de quoi = my pleasure, don't mention it
il n'y a pas de quoi s'inquiéter = there's nothing to worry about

**quotidien/quotidienne**
**1** *adjective*
= daily, everyday
**2 quotidien** *noun, masculine*
un quotidien = a daily (paper)

**rabais** *noun, masculine* (! *never changes*)
un rabais = a reduction

**raccompagner** *verb* 1
raccompagner quelqu'un = to take someone home

**raccourci** *noun, masculine*
un raccourci = a short cut

**raccourcir** *verb* 3
= to shorten

**raccrocher** *verb* 1
(*when telephoning*) = to hang up

**racine** noun, feminine
une racine = a root

**raconter** verb [1]
= to tell

**radar automatique** noun, masculine
le radar automatique = speed camera

**radiateur** noun, masculine
un radiateur = a radiator

**radin/radine**✻ adjective
= mean

**radio** noun, feminine
• (for broadcasts)
la radio = (the) radio
à la radio = on the radio
• (a medical examination)
une radio = an X-ray

**radis** noun, masculine (**!** never changes)
un radis = a radish

**radoucir: se radoucir** verb [3] (**!** + être)
se radoucir = to turn milder

**rafale** noun, feminine
une rafale de vent = a gust of wind

**raffiné/raffinée** adjective
= refined

**rafraîchir** verb [3]
**1** (**!** + avoir)
= to cool (down)
**2 se rafraîchir** (**!** + être)
• (if it's the weather)
se rafraîchir = to get cooler
• (if it's a person)
se rafraîchir = to freshen up, to wash up
= to have a drink

**rafraîchissement** noun, masculine
un rafraîchissement = a cold drink

**ragoût** noun, masculine
un ragoût = a stew

**raide** adjective
(describing a slope) = steep
(describing hair) = straight
(describing a collar, a person) = stiff

**raie** noun, feminine
• (in hair)
une raie = a parting, a part
• (a narrow band of colour)
une raie = a stripe

**rail** noun, masculine
un rail = a rail
les rails = the track(s)

**raisin** noun, masculine
le raisin = grapes
un grain de raisin = a grape
**les raisins de Corinthe** = currants
**les raisins secs** = raisins

**raison** noun, feminine
• une raison = a reason
• avoir raison = to be right

**raisonnable** adjective
= reasonable, moderate
= sensible

**ralenti** noun, masculine
le ralenti = slow motion
le moteur tourne au ralenti = the engine is
(just) ticking over

**ralentir** verb [3]
= to slow down

**ralentisseur** noun, masculine
un ralentisseur = a speed ramp

**râler**✻ verb [1]
= to moan

**ramasser** verb [1]
= to pick (up)
= to collect

**rame** noun, feminine
• une rame = an oar
• une rame de métro = a (metro) train

**ramer** verb [1]
= to row

**rampe** noun, feminine
une rampe (on a staircase) = a banister
**une rampe d'accès**
(to a motorway) = a sliproad, an entrance
ramp
(to a building) = a ramp

**ramper** verb [1]
= to crawl

**rance** adjective
= rancid

**rançon** noun, feminine
une rançon = a ransom

**randonnée** noun, feminine
• (a walk)
une randonnée = a ramble, a hike
• (an activity)
la randonnée = hiking
la randonnée à cheval = pony-trekking
la randonnée pédestre = rambling, hiking

**rang** noun, masculine
• (a line)
un rang = a row
se mettre en rangs = to get into line
• (a position)
un rang = a rank

**rangée** noun, feminine
une rangée = a row

**ranger** verb [13]
• = to put away
• = to tidy
= to sort out, to put in order

**râper** verb [1]
= to grate

---

✻ in informal situations

**rapide**
**1** *adjective*
= fast, quick
= prompt
**2** *noun, masculine*
• *(a train)*
un **rapide** = an express
• *(in a river)*
un **rapide** = rapids

**rapidement** *adverb*
= quickly, fast

**rappel** *noun, masculine*
un **rappel** = a reminder

**rappeler** *verb* 19
**1** (**!** + *avoir*)
• = to call back
• = to remind
**2 se rappeler** (**!** + *être*)
se **rappeler** = to remember

**rapport**
**1** *noun, masculine*
• *(an account)*
un **rapport** = a report
• *(a link)*
un **rapport** = a connection
**2 par rapport à** = compared with

**rapporter** *verb* 1
**1** (**!** + *avoir*)
= to take back, to bring back
**2 se rapporter à** (**!** + *être*)
se **rapporter à** = to relate to

**rapprocher** *verb* 1
= to move closer
= to bring closer

**raquette** *noun, feminine*
une **raquette** (*in tennis*) = a racket
(*in table tennis*) = a bat, a paddle

**rare** *adjective*
= rare
= scarce

**ras/rase** *adjective*
• des cheveux **ras** = close-cropped hair,
short hair
• une cuillère à café **rase** = a level
teaspoonful
plein à **ras** bord = full to the brim
• en **rase** campagne = in (the) open country

**raser**: **se raser** *verb* 1 (**!** + *être*)
se **raser** = to shave

**rasoir**
**1** *noun, masculine*
un **rasoir** = a razor
**2** *adjective*✗ (**!** *never changes*)
= boring

**rassembler** *verb* 1
**1** (**!** + *avoir*)
= to gather
= to bring together

**2 se rassembler** (**!** + *être*)
se **rassembler** = to gather
= to get together

**rassurer** *verb* 1
= to reassure

**rat** *noun, masculine*
un **rat** = a rat

**râteau** *noun, masculine*
(*plural*) **râteaux**
un **râteau** = a rake

**rater** *verb* 1
• = to miss
• = to fail

**rattraper** *verb* 1
• = to catch up with
**rattraper** un concurrent = to catch up with
a competitor
• = to make up for
**rattraper** le temps perdu = to make up for
lost time
• = to recapture, to catch

**ravin** *noun, masculine*
un **ravin** = a ravine

**ravissant/ravissante** *adjective*
= beautiful, delightful

**ravitailler** *verb* 1
**ravitailler** une ville = to provide a town
with fresh supplies
**ravitailler** un avion = to refuel a plane

**rayé/rayée** *adjective*
= striped

**rayer** *verb* 21
• = to cross out
• = to scratch

**rayon** *noun, masculine*
• *(of light)*
un **rayon** = a ray, a beam
• *(for books, goods)*
un **rayon** = a shelf
• *(of a circle)*
le **rayon** = the radius

**rayure** *noun, feminine*
• *(on material)*
une **rayure** = a stripe
• *(on glass, on metal)*
une **rayure** = a scratch

**réaction** *noun, feminine*
une **réaction** = a reaction

**réagir** *verb* 3
= to react

**réaliser** *verb* 1
**1** (**!** + *avoir*)
• *(to make something happen)*
**réaliser** son ambition = to achieve one's
ambition
• *(to understand)* = to realize

**R**

**2 se réaliser** (! + *être*)
se réaliser = to be fulfilled

**réaliste** *adjective*
= realistic

**réalité** *noun, feminine*
la réalité = reality

**réanimation** *noun, feminine*
la réanimation = resuscitation

**rebord** *noun, masculine*
le rebord de la fenêtre = the windowsill

**récemment** *adverb*
= recently

**récent/récente** *adjective*
= recent

**récepteur** *noun, masculine*
un récepteur = a (telephone) receiver

**recette** *noun, feminine*
• une recette = a recipe
• la recette = the takings

**recevoir** *verb* 5
• = to receive, to get
• = to receive, to welcome
• être reçu à un examen = to pass an exam

**rechange** *noun, masculine*
une pièce de rechange = a spare part

**recharge** *noun, feminine*
une recharge = a refill

**recharger** *verb*
= to recharge

**réchaud** *noun, masculine*
un réchaud = a (portable) stove

**réchauffement climatique** *noun, masculine*
le réchauffement climatique = global warming

**réchauffer** *verb* 1
• (*food*) = to reheat, to heat up
• (*person, part of the body*) = to warm up

**recherche** *noun, feminine*
• (*into a subject*)
la recherche = research
• (*looking for something*)
une recherche = a search

**récipient** *noun, masculine*
un récipient = a container

**récit** *noun, masculine*
un récit = a story

**réciter** *verb* 1
= to recite

**réclamation** *noun, feminine*
une réclamation = a complaint

**réclame** *noun, feminine*
• la réclame = publicity
• une réclame = an advertisement
• 'en réclame' = 'on offer', 'on sale'

**réclamer** *verb* 1
• = to ask for
• = to complain

**récolter** *verb* 1
= to harvest, to reap

**recommandé/recommandée** *adjective*
une lettre recommandée = a registered letter

**recommander** *verb* 1
• = to recommend
• = to advise

**recommencer** *verb* 12
= to start again, to start over

**récompense** *noun, feminine*
une récompense = a reward

**récompenser** *verb* 1
= to reward

**reconnaissance** *noun, feminine*
la reconnaissance = gratitude

**reconnaissant/reconnaissante** *adjective*
= grateful

**reconnaître** *verb* 63
• = to recognize
• = to admit
= to acknowledge

**recopier** *verb* 2
= to copy out
= to write out

**record** *noun, masculine*
le record du monde = the world record

**recouvrir** *verb* 32
= to cover

**récréation** *noun, feminine*
la récréation (*in school*) = break, recess

**reçu/reçue**
1 ▶ recevoir 5
2 reçu *noun, masculine*
un reçu = a receipt

**recueillir** *verb* 27
= to collect

**reculer** *verb* 1
• = to move back
= to reverse
• = to postpone

**reculons**: à reculons *adverb*
à reculons = backwards

**récupérer** *verb* 14
• (*after an illness*) = to recover
• (*having lost or lent something*) = to get back
= to collect
• (*in order to reuse*) = to salvage

**recyclage** *noun, masculine*
le recyclage (*of waste*) = recycling
(*of staff*) = retraining

**rédaction** *noun, feminine*
une rédaction = an essay, a theme

**redescendre** verb |6|
1 (! + *être*)
= to go down again, to come down again
2 (! + *avoir*)
= to take down again, to bring down
  again

**rediffusion** noun, feminine
une rediffusion = a repeat (broadcast)

**redoubler** verb |1|
redoubler (une classe) = to repeat a year

**redresser** verb |1|
• = to put up again
• = to straighten (up)

**réduction** noun, feminine
une réduction = a reduction, a discount

**réduire** verb |62|
= to reduce

**réduit/réduite**
1 ▶ réduire |62|
2 réduit noun, masculine
un réduit = a cubbyhole

**réel/réelle** adjective
= real

**réexpédier** verb |2|
• = to forward, to redirect
• = to send back

**refaire** verb |10|
= to do again
= to redo
= to make again

**réfectoire** noun, masculine
un réfectoire = a refectory, a dining hall

**refermer** verb |1|
= to close

**réfléchir** verb |3|
• = to reflect
  réfléchir la lumière = to reflect light
• réfléchir = to think

**reflet** noun, masculine
• (*an image*)
  un reflet = a reflection
• (*a flash of light*)
  un reflet = a glint
  = a shimmer
  cheveux châtain à reflets roux = brown
    hair with auburn highlights

**refléter** verb |14|
= to reflect

**réflexion** noun, feminine
• la réflexion = reflection
• une réflexion = a remark

**refrain** noun, masculine
• le refrain = the chorus
• c'est toujours le même refrain = it's the
  same old refrain

**refroidir** verb |3|
• = to cool down
• = to get cold

**refus** noun, masculine (! never changes)
un refus = a refusal

**refuser** verb |1|
= to refuse
= to turn down

**regagner** verb |1|
• = to get back to, to return to
• = to regain

**régaler: se régaler** verb |1| (! + *être*)
je me suis régalé = I really enjoyed that

**regard** noun, masculine
un regard = a look

**regarder** verb |1|
• = to look at
• = to watch
• = to concern
  ça ne te regarde pas = it's none of your
    business

**régime** noun, masculine
• (*what one eats*)
  un régime = a diet
• (*in politics*)
  un régime = a regime

**région** noun, feminine
une région = a region, an area

**règle**
1 noun, feminine
• (*for measuring*)
  une règle = a ruler
• (*to be obeyed*)
  une règle = a rule
2 règles noun, feminine plural
avoir ses règles = to have a period

**règlement** noun, masculine
le règlement = the regulations, the rules

**régler** verb |14|
• = to pay
• = to settle
• = to adjust

**réglisse** noun, feminine
la réglisse = liquorice, licorice

**règne** noun, masculine
un règne = a reign

**regretter** verb |1|
• = to be sorry
• = to regret
• = to miss

**régulier/régulière** adjective
• = regular
  un vol régulier = a scheduled flight
• = steady
  = even

**rein**
1 noun, masculine
un rein = a kidney

**R**

**2 reins** noun, masculine plural
les reins = the small of the back
avoir mal aux reins = to have (a) backache

**reine** noun, feminine
une reine = a queen

**rejoindre** verb 56
• = to join
• = to meet up with
• = to catch up with

**relais** noun, masculine (**!** never changes)
• (a place)
un relais = an inn
un relais routier = a roadside café, a truck stop
• (in sport)
un relais = a relay

**relever** verb 16
**1** (**!** + avoir)
• (after something has fallen) = to pick up
= to put back up
• (to become aware of) = to notice
**2 se relever** (**!** + être)
se relever (after a fall) = to get up

**relier** verb 2
• = to connect
• = to bind

**religieuse¹** noun, feminine
• ▶ religieux 2
• (a cake)
une religieuse = a round éclair

**religieux/religieuse²**
**1** adjective
= religious
**2** noun, masculine/feminine
un religieux/une religieuse = a monk/a nun

**relire** verb 41
= to read again
= to read over

**reliure** noun, feminine
une reliure = a binding

**remarier**: **se remarier** verb 2 (**!** + être)
se remarier = to remarry

**remarquer** verb 1
= to notice
faire remarquer = to point out

**rembourser** verb 1
= to reimburse, to pay back

**remède** noun, masculine
un remède = a medicine
= a cure

**remerciement** noun, masculine
des remerciements = thanks

**remercier** verb 2
= to thank

**remettre** verb 60
**1** (**!** + avoir)
• = to put back
remettre une lettre dans un tiroir = to put a letter back in a drawer
remettre son manteau = to put one's coat back on
• = to hand over, to give
je leur ai remis les clés = I handed the keys over to them
**2 se remettre** (**!** + être)
• se remettre = to recover
se remettre d'une maladie = to recover from an illness, to get over an illness
• se remettre à [travailler | marcher | pleurer …] = to start [working | walking | crying …] again

**remonter** verb 1
**1** (**!** + être)
• = to go back up(stairs), to come back up(stairs)
• remonter au dix-septième siècle = to go back to the seventeenth century
**2** (**!** + avoir)
• remonter les escaliers = to go back up the stairs
• remonter ses bagages = to take one's luggage back up(stairs)

**remorque** noun, feminine
une remorque = a trailer

**remplacer** verb 12
= to replace

**remplir** verb 3
= to fill

**remuer** verb 1
• = to move
= to wriggle
• = to stir

**renard** noun, masculine
un renard = a fox

**rencontre** noun, feminine
• une rencontre = an encounter
= a meeting
faire la rencontre d'un garçon = to meet a boy
• (in sport)
une rencontre (sportive) = a match, a game

**rencontrer** verb 1
= to meet
= to come across

**rendez-vous** noun, masculine (**!** never changes)
un rendez-vous = an appointment
= a date

**rendre** verb 6
**1** (**!** + avoir)
• = to give back, to return
• rendre visite à un ami = to visit a friend

**2 se rendre** (! + *être*)
* se rendre = to surrender
* se rendre à Paris = to go to Paris
* se rendre compte = to realize
  = to notice
* se rendre malade = to make oneself ill

**renne** *noun, masculine*
un renne = a reindeer

**renoncer** *verb* 12
renoncer à = to give up

**renouveler** *verb* 19
* = to renew
* = to replace

**rénover** *verb* 1
= to renovate

**renseignement**
**1** *noun, masculine*
un renseignement = (a piece of)
  information
des renseignements = information
**2 renseignements** *noun, masculine plural*
les renseignements (*on the telephone*)
  = directory enquiries, information
(*an office*) = enquiries, information

**renseigner** *verb* 1
**1** (! + *avoir*)
= to give information
être bien renseigné = to be well-informed
**2 se renseigner** (! + *être*)
se renseigner = to find out
= to enquire, to make enquiries

**rentrée** *noun, feminine*
la rentrée (scolaire *or* des classes) = the
  start of the school year

**rentrer** *verb* 1
**1** (! + *être*)
* = to go in, to come in
  rentrer dans une pièce = to go/come back
  into a room
* = to go home, to come home
* = to fit
  rentrer dans une boîte = to fit into a box
* rentrer dans un mur = to crash into a wall
**2** (! + *avoir*)
= to take in, to bring in

**renverser** *verb* 1
* = to spill
* = to knock over

**renvoyer** *verb* 24
* = to return
  = to throw back
  = to send back
* = to expel
  = to dismiss

**réparation** *noun, feminine*
une réparation = a repair

**réparer** *verb* 1
= to mend, to repair

**repas** *noun, masculine* (! *never changes*)
un repas = a meal

**repassage** *noun, masculine*
le repassage = ironing

**repasser** *verb* 1
**1** (! + *avoir*)
* repasser une jupe = to iron a skirt
* repasser un examen = to resit an exam
**2** (! + *être*)
* = to go past again
* = to call again

**répéter** *verb* 14
* = to repeat
* = to rehearse

**répétition** *noun, feminine*
* (*in a text*)
  une répétition = a repetition
* (*for actors*)
  une répétition = a rehearsal

**répondre** *verb* 6
= to answer, to reply

**réponse** *noun, feminine*
une réponse = an answer, a reply

**reportage** *noun, masculine*
un reportage = a report, an article

**repos** *noun, masculine* (! *never changes*)
le repos = rest
= relaxation
mon jour de repos = my day off

**reposer: se reposer** *verb* 1 (! + *être*)
se reposer = to rest

**reprendre** *verb* 52
* reprendre du pain = to have some more
  bread
* = to take back
* reprendre le travail = to go back to work
  reprendre ses études = to take up one's
  studies again
  reprendre la conversation = to continue
  the conversation
* = to start again
  l'école a repris = school has started again

**représentant/représentante** *noun,*
*masculine/feminine*
un représentant/une représentante = a
  representative

**représenter** *verb* 1
= to represent

**réprimander** *verb* 1
= to tell off

**repris/reprise ▶ reprendre** 52

**république** *noun, feminine*
une république = a republic

**requin** *noun, masculine*
un requin = a shark

R

**RER** noun, masculine
le RER a rapid-transit rail system in the Paris area

**réseau** noun, masculine
(plural) **réseaux**
un réseau = a network

**réservation** noun, feminine
une réservation = a reservation, a booking

**réserver** verb [1]
• = to reserve, to book
• = to put aside, to set aside

**résidence** noun, feminine
une résidence = a residence
= a place of residence
**une résidence secondaire** = a second home

**résolu/résolue**
1 ▶ résoudre [65]
2 adjective
= resolute, determined

**résoudre** verb [65]
= to solve, to resolve

**respecter** verb [1]
= to respect
= to treat with respect

**respiration** noun, feminine
la respiration = breathing

**respirer** verb [1]
= to breathe

**responsable**
1 adjective
= responsible
2 noun, masculine/feminine
• un responsable/une responsable = a person in charge
• le responsable de l'accident = the person responsible for the accident

**ressembler** verb [1]
1 (! + avoir)
ressembler à = to look like, to resemble
= to be like
2 se ressembler (! + être)
se ressembler = to look alike

**ressort** noun, masculine
un ressort = a spring

**reste** noun, masculine
• (the remaining part)
le reste = the rest
• (the remains of a meal)
les restes = the leftovers

**rester** verb [1] (! + être)
• = to stay
= to remain

---

• il me reste dix euros = I've got ten euros left
il ne reste que quelques personnes = there are only a few people left

**restituer** verb [1]
= to return, to hand back

**résultat** noun, masculine
le résultat = the result

**résumé** noun, masculine
un résumé = a summary

**rétablir** verb [3]
1 (! + avoir)
= to restore
2 se rétablir (! + être)
se rétablir = to recover

**retard** noun, masculine
un retard = a delay
avoir du retard = to be late
être en retard = to be late

**retarder** verb [1]
• = to be slow
• = to postpone, to put off
• = to delay, to hold up

**retenir** verb [36]
1 (! + avoir)
• = to reserve
retenir des places = to reserve seats
• = to hold (back)
retenir son souffle = to hold one's breath
• = to remember
2 se retenir (! + être)
• se retenir à une branche = to hold on to a branch
• se retenir de pleurer = to stop oneself from crying

**retenu/retenue¹** ▶ retenir [36]

**retenue²** noun, feminine
une retenue (in school) = a detention

**retirer** verb [1]
= to withdraw, to take out

**retour** noun, masculine
• le retour = the return
• le retour = the return journey
au retour = on the way back

**retourner** verb [1]
1 (! + avoir)
• = to turn over
= to turn inside out
= to turn upside down
• = to send back
2 (! + être)
= to go back, to return
3 se retourner (! + être)
se retourner = to turn around, to turn over

**retraite** noun, feminine
la retraite = retirement

**retraité/retraitée** noun,
masculine/feminine
un retraité/une retraitée = a retired person

**rétrécir** verb ③
= to shrink

**retrouver** verb ①
**1** (**!** + avoir)
• (after losing something) = to find
• (after arranging to get together) = to meet
• (after losing touch) = to see again
**2 se retrouver** (**!** + être)
• (by arrangement)
se retrouver = to meet
• (to end up)
se retrouver = to find oneself
se retrouver dans une situation difficile = to
find oneself in a difficult situation

**rétroviseur** noun, masculine
un rétroviseur = a rearview mirror

**réunion** noun, feminine
une réunion = a meeting

**réunir** verb ③
**1** (**!** + avoir)
• = to gather together
• = to collect
**2 se réunir** (**!** + être)
se réunir = to meet
= to get together

**réussir** verb ③
• = to succeed
= to be successful
• réussir à ouvrir la porte = to manage to
open the door
réussir à un examen = to pass an exam

**réussite** noun, feminine
• (an achievement)
une réussite = success
• (a game)
une réussite = patience, solitaire

**rêve** noun, masculine
un rêve = a dream

**réveil** noun, masculine
un réveil = an alarm clock

**réveiller** verb ①
**1** (**!** + avoir)
= to wake (up)
**2 se réveiller** (**!** + être)
se réveiller = to wake up

**réveillon** noun, masculine
le réveillon de Noël = Christmas Eve
celebrations
le réveillon du Nouvel An = New Year's Eve
celebrations

**révéler** verb ⑭
= to reveal
= to show

**revenir** verb ㊱ (**!** + être)
= to come back

**revenu/revenue**
**1** ▶ **revenir** ㊱
**2 revenu** noun, masculine
mon revenu = my income

**rêver** verb ①
= to dream

**réverbère** noun, masculine
un réverbère = a streetlamp

**rêveur/rêveuse** adjective
= dreamy

**réviser** verb ①
• = to revise
• réviser un moteur = to overhaul an engine

**revoir**
**1** verb ㊻
• = to see again
• = to go over
revoir un exercice = to go over an exercise
**2 au revoir** = goodbye

**revu/revue¹** ▶ **revoir 1** ㊻

**revue²** noun, feminine
• une revue = a magazine
• une revue = a show

**rez-de-chaussée** noun, masculine
(**!** never changes)
au rez-de-chaussée (in Britain) = on the
ground floor
(in the US) = on the first floor

**Rhin** noun, masculine
le Rhin = the Rhine

**rhum** noun, masculine
le rhum = rum

**rhume** noun, masculine
un rhume = a cold
**le rhume des foins** = hay fever

**riant** ▶ **rire 1** ㊸

**riche** adjective
= rich, wealthy

**ride** noun, feminine
une ride = a wrinkle

**rideau** noun, masculine
(plural) **rideaux**
un rideau = a curtain
des rideaux = curtains, drapes

**ridicule** adjective
= ridiculous

**rien** pronoun
= nothing
je ne veux rien = I don't want anything
ça ne fait rien = it doesn't matter
de rien = don't mention it

**rigoler*** verb ①
• = to laugh
• = to have fun
• = to joke

R

**rigolo/rigolote\*** adjective
= funny

**rimer** verb [1]
= to rhyme

**rinçage** noun, masculine
le rinçage = rinsing

**rincer** verb [12]
= to rinse

**rire**
1 verb [43]
• = to laugh
• = to have fun
il a dit ça pour rire = he said that as a joke
2 noun, masculine
un rire = a laugh, laughter

**risque** noun, masculine
un risque = a risk

**risquer** verb [1]
• = to risk
vos bagages ne risquent rien = your
luggage is quite safe
• = to venture
• tu risques de tomber = you might fall
il risque de faire froid = it might be cold
ça ne risque pas de se produire = there's
no chance of that happening

**rivage** noun, masculine
le rivage = the shore

**rive** noun, feminine
la rive (of a river) = the bank
(of a lake) = the shore

**rivière** noun, feminine
une rivière = a river

**riz** noun, masculine (**!** never changes)
le riz = rice

**robe** noun, feminine
une robe = a dress
**une robe de chambre** = a dressing gown,
a robe

**robinet** noun, masculine
un robinet = a tap, a faucet

**robuste** adjective
(describing a person) = robust, sturdy

**rocher** noun, masculine
un rocher = a rock

**rognon** noun, masculine
un rognon = a kidney

**roi** noun, masculine
un roi = a king

**rôle** noun, masculine
un rôle = a role
= a part

**romain/romaine** adjective
= Roman

**roman** noun, masculine
un roman = a novel
**un roman policier** = a detective novel, a
thriller

**romarin** noun, masculine
le romarin = rosemary

**ronce** noun, feminine
une ronce = a bramble

**rond/ronde**
1 adjective
• = round
• = chubby
2 **rond** noun, masculine
un rond = a circle
en rond = in a circle

**rondelle** noun, feminine
une rondelle = a slice

**rond-point** noun, masculine
(plural) **ronds-points**
un rond-point = a roundabout, a traffic
circle

**ronfler** verb [1]
= to snore

**ronger** verb [13]
1 (**!** + avoir)
= to gnaw
= to eat into
2 **se ronger** (**!** + être)
se ronger les ongles = to bite one's nails

**ronronner** verb [1]
= to purr

**rosbif** noun, masculine
un rosbif = a joint of beef, a roast of beef
= roast beef

**rose**
1 adjective
= pink
2 noun, feminine
une rose = a rose

**roseau** noun, masculine
(plural) **roseaux**
un roseau = a reed

**rosée** noun, feminine
la rosée = dew

**roseraie** noun, feminine
une roseraie = a rose garden

**rosier** noun, masculine
un rosier = a rose bush

**rossignol** noun, masculine
un rossignol = a nightingale

**rôti** noun, masculine
un rôti = a joint
= a roast

**roue** *noun, feminine*
une roue = a wheel
**une roue de secours** = a spare wheel, a
spare tire

**rouge**
**1** *adjective*
= red
**2** *noun, masculine*
le rouge = red
**le rouge à lèvres** = lipstick

**rouge-gorge** *noun, masculine*
(*plural*) **rouges-gorges**
un rouge-gorge = a robin

**rougeole** *noun, feminine*
la rougeole = measles

**rouille** *noun, feminine*
la rouille = rust

**rouleau** *noun, masculine*
(*plural*) **rouleaux**
un rouleau = a roll

**rouler** *verb* 1
• (*if it's a ball, a coin*) = to roll
• (*if it's a car*) = to go
  (*if it's a driver*) = to drive
• **rouler**✱ = to trick

**roumain/roumaine**
**1** *adjective*
= Romanian
**2 roumain** *noun, masculine*
le roumain = Romanian

**Roumanie** *noun, feminine*
la Roumanie = Romania

**rouspéter**✱ *verb* 14
= to grumble, to complain

**rousse** *adjective, feminine* ▶ **roux**

**route** *noun, feminine*
• une route = a road, a highway
• la route = the way
  **en (cours de) route** = on the way
  **se mettre en route** = to set off
  **en route!** = let's go!
  **il y a deux heures de route** = it's a two-
  hour drive
**une route départementale** = a
secondary road
**une route nationale** = a trunk road, a
national highway

**routier/routière**
**1** *adjective*
= road
**2 routier** *noun, masculine*
un routier = a lorry driver, a truck driver

**roux/rousse**
**1** *adjective*
= red
= red-haired
**2** *noun, masculine/feminine*
un roux/une rousse = a redhead

**Royaume-Uni** *noun, masculine*
le Royaume-Uni = the United Kingdom

**ruban** *noun, masculine*
un ruban = a ribbon

**ruche** *noun, feminine*
une ruche = a beehive

**rude** *adjective*
(*describing a task*) = hard, tough
(*describing a climate, a voice*) = harsh

**rue** *noun, feminine*
une rue = a street

**ruée** *noun, feminine*
une ruée = a rush
= a stampede

**ruelle** *noun, feminine*
une ruelle = an alley

**ruine** *noun, feminine*
• (*financial*)
  la ruine = ruin
• (*remains*)
  des ruines = ruins

**ruisseau** *noun, masculine*
(*plural*) **ruisseaux**
un ruisseau = a stream, a brook

**rumeur** *noun, feminine*
une rumeur (*gossip*) = a rumo(u)r
(*a noise*) = a rumble

**ruse** *noun, feminine*
• une ruse = a trick
• la ruse = cunning

**rusé/rusée** *adjective*
= cunning, crafty

**russe**
**1** *adjective*
= Russian
**2** *noun, masculine*
le russe = Russian

**Russie** *noun, feminine*
la Russie = Russia

**rustine** *noun, feminine*
une rustine = a patch

**rythme** *noun, masculine*
le rythme = (the) rhythm
= the rate, the pace

**R**

# Ss

**s'**
**1** *pronoun* ▶ **se**
**2** *conjunction* ▶ **si 2**

**sa** ▶ **son²**

**sable** *noun, masculine*
le sable = sand

**sac** *noun, masculine*
un sac = a bag
**un sac de couchage** = a sleeping bag
**un sac à dos** = a rucksack, a backpack
**un sac à main** = a handbag, a purse
**un sac à provisions** = a shopping bag, a
carry-all

**saccade** *noun, feminine*
une saccade = a jerk

**saccager** *verb* 13
= to wreck, to devastate
= to vandalize

**sache** ▶ **savoir** 47

**sachet** *noun, masculine*
un sachet = a packet
= a sachet
= a bag

**sacoche** *noun, feminine*
une sacoche = a bag
(*on a bicycle*) = a pannier, a saddlebag

**sacré/sacrée** *adjective*
= sacred, holy

**sage** *adjective*
• = good, well-behaved
• = wise

**Sagittaire** *noun, masculine*
le Sagittaire = Sagittarius

**saignant/saignante** *adjective*
(*describing steak*) = rare

**saigner** *verb* 1
= to bleed

**sain/saine** *adjective*
= healthy

**sais** ▶ **savoir** 47

**saisir** *verb* 3
• (*to catch hold of*) = to grab, to seize
saisir une balle au vol = to catch a ball
• (*to affect deeply*) = to grip
être saisi de panique = to be panic-
stricken
• (*to get the meaning*) = to understand

---
**✕** in informal situations

**saison** *noun, feminine*
une saison = a season
en cette saison = at this time of year
en toute saison = all year round

**saisonnier/saisonnière** *adjective*
= seasonal

**salade** *noun, feminine*
une salade = a (head of) lettuce
= a salad

**salaire** *noun, masculine*
un salaire = a salary, wages

**sale** *adjective*
= dirty

**salé/salée** *adjective*
= salty, salted
= savoury

**saler** *verb* 1
= to salt

**saleté** *noun, feminine*
• la saleté = dirtiness
= dirt, filth
• ramasser les saletés = to pick up the
rubbish, to pick up the trash

**salir** *verb* 3
**1** (**!** + *avoir*)
= to dirty, to soil
**2 se salir** (**!** + *être*)
se salir = to get dirty

**salle** *noun, feminine*
une salle = a room
= a hall
**une salle de bains** = a bathroom
**une salle de classe** = a classroom
**la salle d'embarquement** = the
departure lounge
**une salle à manger** = a dining room
**une salle de séjour** = a living room

**salon** *noun, masculine*
un salon = a lounge, a sitting room, a
parlor

**salopette** *noun, feminine*
une salopette = dungarees

**saluer** *verb* 1
• = to greet
• = to salute

**salut✕** *exclamation*
salut✕! = hi!
= goodbye!

**salutations** *noun, feminine plural*
des salutations = greetings
'sincères salutations' = 'yours sincerely'
= 'yours faithfully'

**samedi** *noun, masculine*
samedi = Saturday

**sang** *noun, masculine*
le sang = blood

**sang-froid** noun, masculine (**!** never changes)
le sang-froid = calm, composure

**sanglier** noun, masculine
un sanglier = a wild boar

**sangloter** verb **1**
= to sob

**sans** preposition
= without
sans doute = probably

**santé** noun, feminine
la santé = health
à votre santé! = cheers!

**santon** noun, masculine
un santon a Christmas crib figure

**saoul/saoule** adjective
= drunk

**sapin** noun, masculine
un sapin = a fir tree
**un sapin de Noël** = a Christmas tree

**satisfaire** verb **10**
= to satisfy

**satisfaisant/satisfaisante** adjective
• = satisfactory
• = satisfying

**satisfait/satisfaite** adjective
= satisfied

**sauce** noun, feminine
une sauce = a sauce
= gravy

**saucisse** noun, feminine
une saucisse = a sausage

**saucisson** noun, masculine
le saucisson ≈ salami

**sauf¹** preposition
= except
sauf si = unless

**sauf²/sauve** adjective
= safe
sain et sauf/saine et sauve = safe and sound

**saumon** noun, masculine
un saumon = a salmon

**saurai ▶ savoir** **47**

**saut** noun, masculine
un saut = a jump
**le saut en hauteur** = the high jump

**saute-mouton** noun, masculine
jouer à saute-mouton = to play leapfrog

**sauter** verb **1**
= to jump
= to skip
sauter à la corde = to skip, to jump rope

**sauterelle** noun, feminine
une sauterelle = a grasshopper

**sauvage** adjective
= wild

**sauve ▶ sauf 2**

**sauvegarder** verb **1**
= to save

**sauver** verb **1**
**1** (**!** + avoir)
= to save
= to rescue
**2 se sauver** (**!** + être)
se sauver = to escape
= to run away

**sauvetage** noun, masculine
un sauvetage = a rescue

**sauveteur** noun, masculine
un sauveteur = a rescuer

**savant/savante**
**1** adjective
• = learned
• les animaux savants = performing animals
**2** noun, masculine/feminine
un savant/une savante = a scholar
= a scientist

**saveur** noun, feminine
la saveur = the flavo(u)r

**savoir** verb **47**
• = to know
je n'en sais rien = I've no idea
• = to know how to

**savon** noun, masculine
le savon = soap

**savonnette** noun, feminine
une savonnette = a small bar of soap

**savoureux/savoureuse** adjective
= tasty

**scène** noun, feminine
• (in a theatre)
la scène = the stage
• (something seen)
une scène = a scene

**schéma** noun, masculine
un schéma = a diagram

**scie** noun, feminine
une scie = a saw

**science** noun, feminine
la science = science
les sciences (as a school subject)
= science

**scier** verb **2**
= to saw

**scintiller** verb **1**
= to twinkle, to sparkle, to glisten

**scolaire** adjective
= school

S

**Scorpion** noun, masculine
le Scorpion = Scorpion

**scotch** noun, masculine
(plural) **scotches**
• le scotch   = Sellotape   , Scotch tape
• le scotch = Scotch (whisky)

**scout/scoute** noun, masculine/feminine
un scout/une scoute = a boy scout/a girl
scout

**se** (**s'** before vowel or mute h) pronoun
• = oneself
   = himself/herself
   = itself
   = themselves
   se faire mal = to hurt oneself
   elles se sont fait mal = they hurt
      themselves
• = each other
   ils s'aimaient = they loved each other

**séance** noun, feminine
une séance = a session
(in a cinema) = a showing

**seau** noun, masculine
(plural) **seaux**
un seau = a bucket

**sec/sèche** adjective
• (without moisture) = dry
   des fruits secs = dried fruit
• (abrupt) = sharp

**sèche** ▶ sec

**sèche-cheveux** noun, masculine
(! never changes)
un sèche-cheveux = a hairdryer

**sèche-linge** noun, masculine (! never
changes)
un sèche-linge = a tumble dryer

**sécher** verb 14
= to dry (up)

**sécheresse** noun, feminine
la sécheresse = drought

**séchoir** noun, masculine
• un séchoir = a hairdryer
• un séchoir = a clothes horse, a drying rack
   = a rotary clothes dryer

**second/seconde¹** number
= second

**secondaire**
1 adjective
= secondary
2 noun, masculine
   le secondaire = secondary-school
   education, high-school education (for
   students aged 11 to 18)

**seconde²** noun, feminine
• (a unit of time)
   une seconde = a second
• (in school)
   la seconde the class for secondary school
   students aged 15 to 16
• (when travelling)
   voyager en seconde = to travel second
   class
   un billet de seconde = a second-class
   ticket

**secouer** verb 1
= to shake

**secourir** verb 26
= to rescue
= to help

**secours**
1 noun, masculine (! never changes)
   un secours = help
   au secours! = help!
   une sortie de secours = an emergency exit
2 noun, masculine plural
   des secours = rescuers
   = (relief) supplies

**secousse** noun, feminine
une secousse = a jolt

**secret/secrète**
1 adjective
   = secret
2 **secret** noun, masculine
   un secret = a secret

**secrétaire** noun, masculine/feminine
un secrétaire/une secrétaire = a secretary

**secrétariat** noun, masculine
le secrétariat = the secretary's office

**secrète** ▶ secret 1

**sectionner** verb 1
= to cut

**sécuriser** verb 1
= to reassure
= to give a feeling of security

**sécurité** noun, feminine
la sécurité = security
= safety
se sentir en sécurité = to feel safe
**la sécurité sociale** the French national
health and pensions organization

**séduisant/séduisante** adjective
= attractive

**seigneur** noun, masculine
un seigneur = a lord

**sein** noun, masculine
un sein = a breast

**seize** number
= sixteen

**seizième** number
= sixteenth

---

�910 in informal situations

**séjour** noun, masculine
* (a room)
  un séjour = a living room, a parlor
* (time spent somewhere)
  un séjour = a stay
  faire un séjour à l'étranger = to spend
    some time abroad
**un séjour linguistique** = a language-
  study holiday, a language-study vacation

**sel** noun, masculine
  le sel = salt

**sélectionner** verb [1]
  = to select

**selle** noun, feminine
  une selle = a saddle

**selon** preposition
* = according to
  selon moi = in my opinion
* = depending on
  selon le temps = depending on the
    weather

**semaine** noun, feminine
  une semaine = a week

**semblable** adjective
  = similar

**semblant** noun, masculine
  faire semblant [de dormir | d'être malade |
    d'avoir mal ...] = to pretend [to be asleep | to
    be ill | to be in pain ...]

**sembler** verb [1]
  = to seem
  il me semble que = it seems to me that
  il me semble qu'il pleut = I think it's
    raining

**semelle** noun, feminine
  une semelle = a sole

**semer** verb [1]
* = to sow
* = to scatter

**semoule** noun, feminine
  la semoule = semolina

**sens** noun, masculine (! never changes)
* un sens = a meaning
* le sens = sense
  le bon sens = common sense
  ça n'a pas de sens = it doesn't make sense
* le sens = the way
  = the direction
  plie-le dans l'autre sens = fold it the other
    way
  dans le sens de la flèche = in the
    direction of the arrow
  dans le sens des aiguilles d'une montre
    = clockwise
  une rue à sens unique = a one-way street
  'sens obligatoire' = 'one way'

**sensationnel/sensationnelle**
adjective
* (causing a stir) = sensational
* (very good)✗ = fantastic

**sensé/sensée** adjective
  = sensible

**sensible** adjective
  = sensitive

**senti ▶ sentir** [30]

**sentier** noun, masculine
  un sentier = a path
**un sentier de grande randonnée** = a
  long-distance footpath

**sentiment** noun, masculine
  un sentiment = a feeling

**sentir** verb [30]
**1** (! + avoir)
* = to feel
* = to sense
* = to smell
* = to smell of
  ça sent le brûlé = there's a smell of
    burning
**2 se sentir** (! + être)
  se sentir = to feel

**séparer** verb [1], **se séparer** (! + être)
  = to separate
  = to part
  = to divide

**sept** number
  = seven

**septante** number
  = seventy

**septembre** noun, masculine
  septembre = September

**septième** number
  = seventh

**serai ▶ être** [7]

**série** noun, feminine
* (a succession)
  une série = a series
* (a collection)
  une série = a set

**sérieux/sérieuse** adjective
* = serious
* = reliable

**seringue** noun, feminine
  une seringue = a syringe

**serpent** noun, masculine
  un serpent = a snake

**serre** noun, feminine
  une serre = a greenhouse

**serré/serrée** adjective
* (not big enough) = tight
* (too close together)
  être serrés = to be packed together

S

**serrer** verb [1]
**1** (**!** + *avoir*)
* = to grip
  = to squeeze
  **serrer la main d'un ami** = to shake hands with a friend
* = to tighten
  **serrer une ceinture** = to tighten a belt
* = to be too tight
  **ma jupe me serre à la taille** = my skirt is too tight around the waist
* (*on the road*)
  **'serrez à droite'** = 'keep to the right'
**2 se serrer** (**!** + *être*)
  **se serrer** = to squeeze up
  **je me suis serré contre elle** = I huddled up against her

**serrure** noun, feminine
  **une serrure** = a lock
  **le trou de la serrure** = the keyhole

**serrurier** noun, masculine
  **un serrurier** = a locksmith

**serveur/serveuse** noun, masculine/feminine
  **un serveur/une serveuse** = a waiter/a waitress

**servi/servie ▶ servir** [30]

**serviable** adjective
  = obliging

**service** noun, masculine
* **le service** = service
  **service compris** = service included
* **un service** = a favo(u)r
  **rendre service à un ami** = to be helpful to a friend, to do a friend a favo(u)r

**serviette** noun, feminine
* (*household linen*)
  **une serviette de toilette** = a towel
  **une serviette de table** = a napkin
* (*a kind of bag*)
  **une serviette** = a briefcase

**serviette-éponge** noun, feminine
(*plural*) **serviettes-éponges**
  **une serviette-éponge** = a terry(-cloth) towel

**servir** verb [30]
**1** (**!** + *avoir*)
* = to serve
  **qu'est-ce que je vous sers (à boire)?** = what would you like to drink?
* = to be of use
  = to come in handy
  **garde-le, ça peut servir** = keep it, it might come in handy
* **servir à quelque chose** = to be used for something
  **servir à quelqu'un** = to be used by someone
  **à quoi sert cet outil?** = what's this tool used for?
  **ça va me servir pour faire un coussin** = I'm going to use it to make a cushion
  **ça ne sert à rien de se mettre en colère** = there's no point in losing one's temper
  **j'ai écrit, mais ça n'a servi à rien** = I wrote, but it didn't do any good

* **servir de** = to serve as
  = to be used as
  **mon sac m'a servi d'oreiller** = I used my bag as a pillow
**2 se servir** (**!** + *être*)
* **se servir** = to help oneself
* **se servir de** = to use
  **il s'est servi d'un dictionnaire** = he used a dictionary

**ses ▶ son²**

**seuil** noun, masculine
  **le seuil** = the threshold

**seul/seule** adjective
* = alone, by oneself, on one's own
  **vivre seul** = to live alone
* = lonely
  **se sentir seul** = to feel lonely
* = single
  **pas un seul arbre** = not a single tree
  **une seule fois** = once only

**seulement** adverb
  = only

**sévère** adjective
  = strict, harsh
  = severe

**shampooing** noun, masculine
  **un shampooing** = a shampoo

**short** noun, masculine
  **un short** = shorts

**si**
**1** adverb
* = yes
  **'tu n'y vas pas?'—'si!'** = 'aren't you going?' —'yes I am!'
* = so
  **elle est si jolie!** = she's so pretty!
**2** conjunction (**s'** *before* **il** *or* **ils**)
* (*introducing a supposition*) = if
  **si j'étais riche** = if I were rich
  **si j'avais su** = if only I had known, if I'd only known
  **et s'il ne peut pas le réparer?** = and what if he can't repair it?
  **s'il vous plaît** = please
* (*introducing a suggestion*)
  **et si on allait en ville?** = how about going into town?

**sida** noun, masculine
  **le sida** = Aids

**siècle** noun, masculine
  **un siècle** = a century
  **au vingtième siècle** = in the twentieth century

**siège** noun, masculine
* (*a piece of furniture*)
  **un siège** = a seat
* (*a place*)
  **le siège (social)** = the headquarters, the head office

**sien/sienne** *pronoun*
le sien/la sienne = his/hers
les siens/les siennes = his/hers

**sieste** *noun, feminine*
une sieste = a siesta, a snooze, a nap

**siffler** *verb* 1
* = to whistle
* = to blow one's whistle
* = to boo

**sifflet** *noun, masculine*
un sifflet = a whistle
un coup de sifflet = a whistle blast, a
   whistle blow

**sigle** *noun, masculine*
un sigle = an acronym

**signalement** *noun, masculine*
un signalement = a description

**signaler** *verb* 1
* (*by informing*) = to report
   rien à signaler = nothing to report
* (*by drawing attention*) = to point out
   je vous signale qu'il est huit heures = may
      I point out that it's eight o'clock
* (*by means of a notice, a sign*) = to indicate
   = to signpost

**signalisation** *noun, feminine*
la signalisation = signs
la signalisation routière = road signs and
   markings

**signe** *noun, masculine*
un signe = a sign

**signer** *verb* 1
= to sign

**signifier** *verb* 2
= to mean

**silencieux/silencieuse** *adjective*
= silent
= quiet

**silhouette** *noun, feminine*
* (*a shape*)
   une silhouette = a silhouette
   = an outline
* (*a person*)
   une silhouette = a figure

**sillon** *noun, masculine*
un sillon = a furrow

**simple** *adjective*
* = simple
* = ordinary
   c'est une simple formalité = it's just a
      formality
* = single
   un aller simple = a single (ticket)

**singe** *noun, masculine*
un singe = a monkey

**sinistre**
**1** *adjective*
= sinister

**2** *noun, masculine*
un sinistre = a (natural) disaster
= a fire

**sinistré/sinistrée** *adjective*
= stricken
une région sinistrée = a disaster area

**sinon** *conjunction*
= otherwise

**sirène** *noun, feminine*
une sirène = a siren

**sirop** *noun, masculine*
un sirop = a syrup
un sirop (de fruits) = a (fruit) cordial
un sirop (pour la toux) = a cough mixture

**site** *noun, masculine*
un site = a site
* (*a place*)
**un site classé** = a conservation area
**un site pittoresque** = a beauty spot
**un site touristique** = a place of interest
* (*on the Internet*)
**un site web** = a website

**situation** *noun, feminine*
* (*a site*)
   la situation d'une ville = the location of a
      town
* (*the circumstances*)
   la situation est grave = the situation is
      serious
* (*a position*)
   une bonne situation = a good job

**situé/située** *adjective*
= situated, located
la ville est bien située = the town is in a
   good location

**situer: se situer** *verb* 1 (**!** + *être*)
* (*if it's a building, a town*)
   se situer = to be situated
* (*if it's an event*)
   se situer = to take place

**six** *number*
= six

**sixième**
**1** *number*
= sixth
**2** *noun, feminine*
la sixième *the class for secondary school
   students aged 11 to 12*

**ski** *noun, masculine*
* (*the equipment*)
   un ski = a ski
* (*the sport*)
   le ski = skiing
**le ski nautique** = water-skiing

**skier** *verb* 2
= to ski

**slip** *noun, masculine*
un slip (*for men*) = pants, shorts
   (*for women*) = knickers, panties

**S**

**slovaque**
**1** *adjective*
= Slovak
**2** *noun, masculine*
le slovaque = Slovak

**smoking** *noun, masculine*
un smoking = a dinner jacket, a tuxedo

**SNCF** *noun, feminine*
la SNCF *the French national railway*
*company*

**snob** *adjective*
= snobbish

**société** *noun, feminine*
• la société = society
• une société = a company

**soda** *noun, masculine*
le soda = soda water

**sœur** *noun, feminine*
une sœur = a sister

**soi** *pronoun*
= oneself
= itself

**soi-disant**
**1** *adjective* (**!** *never changes*)
= so-called
**2** *adverb*
= supposedly

**soie** *noun, feminine*
la soie = silk

**soif** *noun, feminine*
la soif = thirst
avoir soif = to be thirsty

**soigné/soignée** *adjective*
= meticulous, neat

**soigner** *verb* 1
**1** (**!** + *avoir*)
• = to treat
• = to look after
= to take care of
• = to take care over
**2 se soigner** (**!** + *être*)
se soigner = to look after oneself

**soigneusement** *adverb*
= carefully

**soi-même** *pronoun*
= oneself

**soin**
**1** *noun, masculine*
le soin = care
avec soin = carefully
**2 soins** *noun, masculine plural*
les soins = treatment
= care
donner les premiers soins aux blessés
= to give first aid to the injured

**soir** *noun, masculine*
un soir = an evening
à ce soir = see you tonight

**soirée** *noun, feminine*
• la soirée = the evening
• une soirée = a party

**soit**
**1** ▶ **être** 7
**2** *conjunction*
soit lundi soit mardi = either Monday or
Tuesday

**soixante** *number*
= sixty

**soixante-dix** *number*
= seventy

**soja** *noun, masculine*
le soja = soya

**sol** *noun, masculine*
le sol = the floor
= the ground
= the soil

**solaire** *adjective*
= sun
= suntan
= solar

**soldat** *noun, masculine*
un soldat = a soldier

**solde**
**1** *noun, masculine*
articles en solde = reduced items, sales
bargains, sale items
acheter une veste en solde = to buy a
jacket in a sale, to buy a jacket on sale
**2 soldes** *noun, masculine plural*
les soldes (*the event*) = the sales
(*the goods*) = sales goods, sale items

**soleil** *noun, masculine*
le soleil = the sun
au soleil = in the sun
il fait (du) soleil = it's sunny
un coup de soleil = sunburn
attraper un coup de soleil = to get
sunburned

**solennel/solennelle** *adjective*
= solemn

**solide** *adjective*
= solid, strong
= sturdy

**sombre** *adjective*
= dark
il fait sombre = it's dark

**sombrer** *verb* 1
= to sink

**somme**
**1** *noun, feminine*
une somme = a sum
**2** *noun, masculine*
un somme = a nap, a snooze

**sommeil** *noun, masculine*
le sommeil = sleep
avoir sommeil = to be sleepy

**sommes** ▶ **être** [7]

**sommet** *noun, masculine*
le sommet = the summit, the peak

**sommier** *noun, masculine*
un sommier = a (bed) base

**somnifère** *noun, masculine*
un somnifère = a sleeping pill

**son¹** *noun, masculine*
un son = a sound

**son²/sa** *determiner*
(*plural*) **ses**
= his/her
= its
son mari = her husband
sa femme = his wife
ses livres = his/her books
ses pattes = its paws

**sondage** *noun, masculine*
un sondage = a survey
= a(n opinion) poll

**sonner** *verb* [1]
= to ring
(*if it's a clock*) = to strike

**sonnerie** *noun, feminine*
• (*a noise*)
la sonnerie = the ringing
(*on a mobile or cell phone*) = the ringtone
• (*a mechanism*)
la sonnerie (*on an alarm clock*) = the alarm
(*on a door*) = the bell

**sonnette** *noun, feminine*
une sonnette = a bell

**sonore** *adjective*
• (*loud*) = resounding
• effets sonores = sound effects

**sont** ▶ **être** [7]

**sorcier** *noun, masculine/feminine*
un sorcier/une sorcière = a wizard/a witch

**sordide** *adjective*
= squalid
= sordid

**sort** *noun, masculine*
• le sort = fate
tirer au sort = to draw lots
• son sort = one's lot
être satisfait de son sort = to be satisfied
with one's lot
• un sort = a curse, a spell
jeter un sort à un ennemi = to put a curse
on an enemy

**sorte** *noun, feminine*
une sorte = a sort, a kind

**sortie** *noun, feminine*
• (*a way out*)
une sortie = an exit
• (*the action of leaving a place*)
il a été attaqué à sa sortie du bureau = he
was mugged as he left the office
se retrouver à la sortie de l'école = to meet
after school
• (*a trip*)
une sortie = an outing

**sortir** *verb* [30]
**1** (**!** + *être*)
• = to go out, to come out
• sortir de = to leave, to come out of
**2** (**!** + *avoir*)
= to take out
= to get out
sortir une lettre de sa poche = to take a
letter out of one's pocket
sors ton frère du lit! = get your brother out
of bed!

**sou** *noun, masculine*
• un sou ≈ a penny, a cent
• avoir des sous\* = to have money

**souci** *noun, masculine*
un souci = a worry
se faire du souci = to worry

**soucoupe** *noun, feminine*
une soucoupe = a saucer

**soudain/soudaine**
**1** *adjective*
= sudden
**2 soudain** *adverb*
= suddenly

**souffler** *verb* [1]
• = to blow
• = to prompt
on t'a soufflé la réponse = you were
prompted, you were told the answer
• = to breathe out
• = to get one's breath back

**souffrant/souffrante** *adjective*
= unwell

**souffrir** *verb* [4]
= to suffer
= to be in pain

**souhait** *noun, masculine*
un souhait = a wish

**souhaiter** *verb* [1]
= to wish
souhaite-moi bonne chance = wish me
luck
souhaiter la bienvenue à un visiteur = to
welcome a visitor
je souhaite qu'il ne fasse pas froid
= I hope that it won't be cold

**soûl/soûle** *adjective*
= drunk

**soulager** verb 13
= to relieve
le comprimé m'a soulagé = the pill made me feel better

**soulever** verb 16
= to lift
= to raise

**soulier** noun, masculine
un soulier = a shoe

**souligner** verb 1
* = to underline
* = to emphasize, to stress

**soupçon** noun, masculine
un soupçon = a suspicion

**soupçonner** verb 1
= to suspect

**soupe** noun, feminine
la soupe = soup

**souper**
1 noun, masculine
le souper = supper
2 verb 1
= to have supper

**soupir** noun, masculine
un soupir = a sigh

**soupirer** verb 1
= to sigh

**souple** adjective
* = supple
* = flexible

**source** noun, feminine
* (water)
une source = a spring
* (the origin or cause of something)
une source = a source

**sourcil** noun, masculine
un sourcil = an eyebrow

**sourd/sourde** adjective
* (unable to hear) = deaf
* (describing a noise, a pain) = dull

**souriant/souriante** adjective
= smiling

**sourire**
1 verb 43
= to smile
2 noun, masculine
un sourire = a smile

**souris** noun, feminine (**!** never changes)
une souris = a mouse

**sous**
1 preposition
= under, underneath
sous terre = underground
sous la pluie = in the rain
2 ▶ sou

---

**✗** in informal situations

**sous-marin/sous-marine**
(plural) **sous-marins/sous-marines**
1 adjective
= submarine, underwater
= deep-sea
2 **sous-marin** noun, masculine
un sous-marin = a submarine

**sous-sol** noun, masculine
(plural) **sous-sols**
le sous-sol = the basement

**sous-titre** noun, masculine
(plural) **sous-titres**
un sous-titre = a subtitle

**sous-vêtement** noun, masculine
(plural) **sous-vêtements**
des sous-vêtements = underwear

**soutenir** verb 36
= to support

**soutenu/soutenue** ▶ soutenir 36

**souterrain/souterraine**
1 adjective
= underground
2 **souterrain** noun, masculine
un souterrain = a subway, a pedestrian underpass

**soutien-gorge** noun, masculine
(plural) **soutiens-gorge**
un soutien-gorge = a bra

**souvenir**
1 noun, masculine
* (something remembered)
un souvenir = a memory
* (an object)
un souvenir = a souvenir
2 **se souvenir** verb 36 (**!** + être)
se souvenir de = to remember

**souvent** adverb
= often
le plus souvent = more often than not

**soyons** ▶ être 7

**spacieux/spacieuse** adjective
= spacious

**sparadrap** noun, masculine
le sparadrap = (sticking) plaster, surgical tape

**spatial/spatiale** adjective
(plural) **spatiaux/spatiales**
= space

**spécial/spéciale** adjective
(plural) **spéciaux/spéciales**
* (not ordinary) = special
* (strange) = odd

**spécialement** adverb
= specially
= especially

**spectacle** noun, masculine
* (in a theatre, a circus)
un spectacle = a show

- (*something seen*)
  un spectacle = a sight

**spectateur/spectatrice** *noun, masculine/feminine*
  un spectateur/une spectatrice = a member of the audience
  = a spectator

**spéléologie** *noun, feminine*
  la spéléologie = potholing, spelunking
  = speleology

**sponsoriser** *verb* 1
  = to sponsor

**sport** *noun, masculine*
  le sport = sport

**sportif/sportive**
1 *adjective*
- (*describing an event, a magazine*) = sports
- (*describing a person*)
  être sportif = to be the sporty type, to be athletic
2 *noun, masculine/feminine*
  un sportif/une sportive = a sportsman/a sportswoman

**square** *noun, masculine*
  un square = a small public garden

**squelette** *noun, masculine*
  le squelette = the skeleton

**squelettique** *adjective*
  = scrawny, thin as a rake

**stade** *noun, masculine*
  un stade = a stadium

**stage** *noun, masculine*
  un stage = a course
  = (a period of) work experience

**station** *noun, feminine*
- (*in a town*)
  une station de métro = a tube station, a subway station
  une station de taxis = a taxi rank, a taxi stand
- (*a town or a village*)
  une station balnéaire = a seaside resort
  une station de ski = a ski resort
  une station thermale = a spa

**stationnement** *noun, masculine*
  le stationnement = parking

**station-service** *noun, feminine*
(*plural*) **stations-service**
  une station-service = a service station, a gas station

**steak** *noun, masculine*
  un steak = a steak
  un steak haché = a beefburger

**sténodactylo**
1 *noun, masculine/feminine*
  un sténodactylo/une sténodactylo = a shorthand typist, a stenographer

2 *noun, feminine*
  la sténodactylo = shorthand typing, stenographing

**stop** *noun, masculine*
- un stop = a stop sign
- le stop* = hitch-hiking
  faire du stop* = to hitch-hike

**store** *noun, masculine*
  un store = a blind
  = an awning

**studio** *noun, masculine*
- (*accommodation*)
  un studio = a studio flat, a studio apartment
- (*a place of work*)
  un studio = a studio

**stupéfait/stupéfaite** *adjective*
  = astounded

**stylo** *noun, masculine*
  un stylo = a (fountain) pen
  **un stylo (à) bille** = a ball point pen, a biro
  **un stylo feutre** = a felt-tip pen

**su/sue** ▶ **savoir** 47

**subir** *verb* 3
  subir une opération = to undergo an operation
  subir des dégâts = to suffer damage

**subitement** *adverb*
  = suddenly

**succès** *noun, masculine* (**!** *never changes*)
  le succès = success

**sucer** *verb* 12
  = to suck

**sucette** *noun, feminine*
  une sucette = a lollipop, a lolly

**sucre** *noun, masculine*
  le sucre = sugar
  un sucre = a lump of sugar
  **le sucre d'orge** = barley sugar

**sucré/sucrée** *adjective*
  = sweet
  = sweetened

**sucrer** *verb* 1
  = to put sugar in
  = to sweeten

**sucreries** *noun, feminine plural*
  les sucreries = sweets, candies

**sud**
1 *noun, masculine*
  le sud = the south
2 *adjective* (**!** *never changes*)
  = south
  – southern

**Suède** *noun, feminine*
  la Suède = Sweden

**S**

**suédois/suédoise**
**1** *adjective*
= Swedish
**2 suédois** *noun, masculine*
le Suédois = Swedish

**sueur** *noun, feminine*
la sueur = sweat

**suffire** *verb* 39
• = to be enough
ça me suffit = that's enough for me
• il suffit de demander = all you have to do
is ask
il suffit d'une étincelle = one spark is
enough

**suffisamment** *adverb*
= enough

**suffisant/suffisante** *adjective*
= sufficient

**suis**
• ▶ être 7
• ▶ suivre 37

**suisse** *adjective*
= Swiss

**Suisse** *noun, feminine*
la Suisse = Switzerland

**suite**
**1** *noun, feminine*
• la suite = the rest
(*if it's another film or novel*) = the sequel
'suite page 45' = 'continued on page 45'
• une suite de = a succession of, a series of
**2 de suite** = in a row
à la suite de = following
trois jours de suite = three days in a row
**3 tout de suite** = straight away, right
away
**4 par la suite** = subsequently

**suivant/suivante**
**1** *adjective*
= next
= following
**2** *noun, masculine/feminine*
le suivant/la suivante = the next (one)
au suivant! = next!
**3 suivant** = according to

**suivi/suivie** ▶ suivre 37

**suivre** *verb* 37
= to follow
'à suivre' = 'to be continued'
faire suivre le courrier = to forward the
mail

**sujet** *noun, masculine*
un sujet = a subject

**super**
**1** *adjective*✱ (**!** *never changes*)
= great

**2** *noun, masculine*
le super ≈ 4-star (petrol), super

**superficie** *noun, feminine*
la superficie = the area

**supérieur/supérieure** *adjective*
• = upper, top
• = higher
• = superior

**supermarché** *noun, masculine*
un supermarché = a supermarket

**supplémentaire** *adjective*
= additional, extra

**supportable** *adjective*
= bearable

**supporter** *verb* 1
• = to support, to bear the weight of
• = to put up with, to bear

**supprimer** *verb* 1
= to remove
= to cancel
= to withdraw
= to do away with
= to cut

**sur** *preposition*
• = on
sur la table = on the table
• = over
un pont sur la rivière = a bridge over the
river
• = about
un livre sur la guerre = a book about war
• = out of
9 sur 20 = 9 out of 20
• = by
faire 10 mètres sur 15 = to measure 10
metres by 15

**sûr/sûre**
**1** *adjective*
• = sure, certain
c'est sûr = it's certain
j'en suis sûr = I'm sure of it
j'en étais sûr! = I knew it!
être sûr de soi = to be self-confident
• = safe
= reliable
un endroit sûr = a safe place
un homme sûr = a reliable man
**2 bien sûr** = of course

**sûreté** *noun, feminine*
la sûreté = safety
= security

**surf** *noun, masculine*
le surf = surfing
le surf des neiges = snowboarding

**surface** *noun, feminine*
la surface = the surface (area)

**surgelé/surgelée** *adjective*
= (deep-)frozen
les produits surgelés = frozen food

---

✱ in informal situations

**surligneur** *noun, masculine*
un surligneur = a highlighter

**surnaturel/surnaturelle** *adjective*
= supernatural

**surnom** *noun, masculine*
un surnom = a nickname

**surprenant/surprenante** *adjective*
= surprising
= amazing

**surprise** *noun, feminine*
une surprise = a surprise

**sursauter** *verb* 1
= to jump, to start

**surtout** *adverb*
= above all
= especially

**surveillant/surveillante** *noun,*
*masculine|feminine*
un surveillant/une surveillante (*in a*
*school*) = a supervisor
(*in a store*) = a store detective
(*in a prison*) = a warder, a guard

**surveiller** *verb* 1
• = to watch, to keep an eye on
• = to supervise

**survenir** *verb* 36
= to occur, to happen

**survêtement** *noun, masculine*
un survêtement = a tracksuit

**survivant/survivante** *noun,*
*masculine|feminine*
un survivant/une survivante = a survivor

**survoler** *verb* 1
= to fly over

**sus**: **en sus** *adverb*
en sus = in addition, on top

**svelte** *adjective*
= slender

**SVP** (*abbreviation of* **s'il vous plaît**)
SVP = please

**sympa**✻ *adjective* (! *never changes*)
= nice

**sympathie** *noun, feminine*
avoir de la sympathie pour quelqu'un = to
like someone

**sympathique** *adjective*
= nice, pleasant

**syndicat** *noun, masculine*
un syndicat = a trade union
**un syndicat d'initiative** = a tourist
information office

**synthétique** *adjective*
= man made

# Tt

**t'** ▶ **te**

**ta** ▶ **ton²**

**tabac** *noun, masculine*
• (*a substance*)
le tabac = tobacco
• (*a shop*)
un tabac = a tobacconist's, a smoke shop

**tabagisme** *noun, masculine*
le tabagisme = tobacco addiction

**table** *noun, feminine*
une table = a table
mettre la table = to set the table
se mettre à table = to sit down at the table
à table! = dinner is served!
**une table des matières** = a table of
contents
**une table de nuit** = a bedside table, a
night stand

**tableau** *noun, masculine*
(*plural*) **tableaux**
• (*ornamental*)
un tableau = a painting
= a picture
• (*a surface*)
un tableau = a board
**un tableau d'affichage** = a noticeboard,
a bulletin board
**le tableau de bord** = the dashboard
**le tableau (noir)** = the blackboard

**tablier** *noun, masculine*
un tablier = an apron

**tabouret** *noun, masculine*
un tabouret = a stool

**tache** *noun, feminine*
une tache = a stain

**tâche** *noun, feminine*
une tâche = a task, a job
les tâches ménagères = household chores

**tacher** *verb* 1
= to stain

**tâcher** *verb* 1
tâcher de = to try to

**taille** *noun, feminine*
• (*the middle of the body*)
la taille = the waist, the waistline
• (*overall dimensions*)
la taille = the size
quelle taille faites-vous? = what size do
you take?
taille unique = one size
• (*tallness*)
la taille = the height

T

**taille-crayon** noun, masculine
(plural) **taille-crayons**
  un taille-crayon = a pencil sharpener

**tailler** verb 1
  = to cut
  = to prune
  = to carve
  = to sharpen

**tailleur** noun, masculine
• (a garment)
  un tailleur = a (woman's) suit
• (a person)
  un tailleur = a tailor

**taire**: **se taire** verb 59 (**!** + être)
  se taire = to stop talking
  = to be silent, to fall silent
  taisez-vous! = be quiet!

**talent** noun, masculine
  le talent = talent
  un acteur de talent = a talented actor

**talkie-walkie** noun, masculine
(plural) **talkies-walkies**
  un talkie-walkie = a walkie-talkie

**talon** noun, masculine
  un talon = a heel

**talus** noun, masculine (**!** never changes)
  un talus = an embankment

**tambour** noun, masculine
  un tambour = a drum

**Tamise** noun, feminine
  la Tamise = the Thames

**tampon** noun, masculine
  un tampon (for documents) = a stamp

**tamponner** verb 1
**1** (**!** + avoir)
• (to put a mark on) = to stamp
• (to wipe) = to mop, to dab
**2 se tamponner** (**!** + être)
  se tamponner = to collide

**tandis que** (**tandis qu'** before vowel or
mute h) conjunction
  = while, whilst

**tant** adverb
• = so much
  il t'aime tant! = he loves you so much!
  tant mieux! = so much the better!
  tant mieux pour vous! = good for you!
  tant pis! = too bad!
• tant de = so much, so many
• tant que = as much as, as many as
  = as long as
  mange tant que tu veux = eat as much as
    you like
  il restera tant qu'il voudra = he'll stay as
    long as he likes

---

**✕** in informal situations

**tante** noun, feminine
  une tante = an aunt

**tapage** noun, masculine
  du tapage = a din, a racket

**taper** verb 1
• taper sur un clou = to hit a nail
  il m'a tapé sur l'épaule = he tapped me on
    the shoulder
• taper des mains = to clap one's hands
  taper du pied = to tap one's foot
  taper à la porte = to knock at the door
• taper (à la machine) = to type

**tapis** noun, masculine (**!** never changes)
  un tapis = a rug
  = a carpet

**tapisser** verb 1
• = to wallpaper
• = to line

**tapisserie** noun, feminine
• (woven or embroidered cloth)
  une tapisserie = a tapestry
• (paper)
  la tapisserie = the wallpaper

**taquiner** verb 1
  = to tease

**tard** adverb
  = late
  plus tard = later
  au plus tard = at the latest
  pas plus tard qu'hier = only yesterday

**tarder** verb 1
• tarder à arriver = to be a long time coming
  tes parents ne vont pas tarder = your
    parents won't be long
• tarder à répondre à une lettre = to take a
  long time replying to a letter
  = to put off replying to a letter
• il me tarde de les revoir = I'm longing to
  see them again, I can't wait to see them
  again

**tarif** noun, masculine
  le tarif = the price
  = the price list

**tarte** noun, feminine
  une tarte = a tart, a flan

**tartelette** noun, feminine
  une tartelette = a (small) tart

**tartine** noun, feminine
  une tartine = a slice of bread and butter

**tas** noun, masculine (**!** never changes)
  un tas = a pile, a heap
  en tas = in a pile, in a heap
• un (or des) tas✕ d'amis = loads of friends

**tasse** noun, feminine
  une tasse = a cup

**tâter** verb 1
  = to feel

**tâtonner** verb [1]
= to grope about

**tâtons**: **à tâtons** adverb
avancer à tâtons = to grope one's way
along

**taudis** noun, masculine (**!** never changes)
un taudis = a slum

**taupe** noun, feminine
une taupe = a mole

**taureau** noun, masculine
(plural) **taureaux**
un taureau = a bull

**Taureau** noun, masculine
le Taureau = Taurus

**taux** noun, masculine (**!** never changes)
le taux = the rate
= the level
le taux de change = the exchange rate

**tchèque**
**1** adjective
= Czech
**2** noun, masculine
le tchèque = Czech

**tchin(-tchin)**\* exclamation
tchin(-tchin)\*! = cheers!

**TD** noun, masculine plural ▶ travail

**te** (**t'** before vowel or mute h) pronoun
• = you
je te vois = I can see you
elle te l'a donné = she gave it to you
• = yourself
tu t'es fait mal? = did you hurt yourself?

**technicien/technicienne** noun,
masculine/feminine
un technicien/une technicienne = a
technician

**teindre** verb [55]
= to dye
= to stain

**teint/teinte¹**
**1** ▶ **teindre** [55]
**2 teint** noun, masculine
un teint = a complexion

**teinte²** noun, feminine
une teinte = a shade
= a colo(u)r

**teinture** noun, feminine
une teinture = a dye

**teinturerie** noun, feminine
une teinturerie = a dry cleaner's

**teinturier/teinturière** noun,
masculine/feminine
un teinturier/une teinturière = a dry cleaner

**tel/telle** adjective
= such
de telle sorte qu'il l'a cassé = in such a
way that he broke it
les pays tels que la France = countries
like France

**télé**\* noun, feminine
la télé\* = TV

**télécommandé/télécommandée**
adjective
= remote control

**télécopieur** noun, masculine
un télécopieur = a fax (machine)

**téléphérique** noun, masculine
un téléphérique = a cable car

**téléphone** noun, masculine
un téléphone = a (tele)phone
un téléphone portable = a mobile phone,
a cell phone, a cellular phone

**téléphoner** verb [1]
= to (tele)phone

**télésiège** noun, masculine
un télésiège = a chair lift

**téléski** noun, masculine
un téléski = a ski tow

**téléspectateur/téléspectatrice**
noun, masculine/feminine
un téléspectateur/une téléspectatrice = a
viewer

**téléviseur** noun, masculine
un téléviseur = a television (set)

**télévision** noun, feminine
la télévision = television, TV

**tellement** adverb
• = so (much)
il est tellement riche! = he's so rich!
c'est tellement mieux maintenant! = it's so
much better now!
• tellement de = so much, so many
elle a tellement de temps libre = she has so
much free time
il y avait tellement de monde que je suis
parti = there were so many people that I
left

**témoignage** noun, masculine
un témoignage = a personal account
(in court) = evidence

**témoin** noun, masculine
un témoin = a witness
être témoin d'un incident = to witness an
incident

**tempérament** noun, masculine
un tempérament = a disposition, a
temperament

**température** noun, feminine
la température = the temperature

T

**tempête** *noun, feminine*
une tempête = a storm
= a gale

**temporaire** *adjective*
= temporary

**temps** *noun, masculine* (**!** *never changes*)
* (*outside conditions*)
le temps = the weather
quel temps fait-il? = what's the weather
like?
il fait beau temps = the weather is fine
il a fait mauvais temps = the weather has
been bad
quel temps de chien! = what awful
weather!, it's terrible weather!
* (*as measured in hours*)
le temps = time
je n'ai pas le temps de me reposer = I
haven't got time to rest
il est grand temps de partir = it's high time
we left
ils ont fini à temps = they finished in time
de temps en temps = from time to time
pendant ce temps = meanwhile
* (*in grammar*)
un temps = a tense

**tenace** *adjective*
= stubborn, persistent

**tenir** *verb* 36
**1** (**!** + *avoir*)
* = to hold
* tiens!, tenez! (*when giving something*)
= here!
(*expressing surprise*) = hey!
**2 tenir à** (**!** + *avoir*)
tenir à sa famille = to be fond of one's
family
**3 se tenir** (**!** + *être*)
* se tenir = to hold on
se tenir à la rampe = to hold on to the
banister
* se tenir = to stand
se tenir droit (*if standing*) = to stand up
straight
se tenir tranquille = to keep still
* se tenir = to behave
tenez-vous bien! = behave yourselves!
* ils se tenaient par la main = they were
holding hands
**4** si cela ne tenait qu'à moi = if I had my way

**tennis** *noun, masculine* (**!** *never changes*)
* (*the sport*)
le tennis = tennis
* (*footwear*)
un tennis = a tennis shoe

**tentation** *noun, feminine*
la tentation = temptation

**tentative** *noun, feminine*
une tentative = an attempt

**tente** *noun, feminine*
une tente = a tent

**tenter** *verb* 1
* = to attempt
= to try
tenter sa chance = to try one's luck
* = to tempt
ça ne me tente guère = it doesn't appeal to
me very much

**tenu/tenue¹** ▶ **tenir** 36

**tenue²** *noun, feminine*
une tenue = an outfit, clothes
en tenue de soirée = in evening dress

**terminale** *noun, feminine*
la terminale *the class for secondary school
students aged 17 to 18*

**terminer** *verb* 1
**1** (**!** + *avoir*)
= to finish, to end
**2 se terminer** (**!** + *être*)
se terminer = end
se terminer par une bagarre = to end in a
fight

**terminus** *noun, masculine* (**!** *never
changes*)
le terminus (*for a train*) = the end of the
line
(*for a bus*) = the terminus

**terne** *adjective*
= dull

**terrain** *noun, masculine*
* (*a site*)
un terrain = a piece of land
(*used for sport*) = a pitch, a ground
* (*the surface underfoot*)
le terrain = the ground
**un terrain d'atterrissage** = a landing
strip
**un terrain à bâtir** = a building plot
**un terrain de camping** = a campsite
**un terrain de jeux** = a playground
**un terrain de sports** = a sports ground, a
sports field
**un terrain vague** = a piece of wasteland

**terrasse** *noun, feminine*
une terrasse = a terrace
= a flat roof
s'asseoir à la terrasse d'un café = to sit at
a table outside a café

**terre** *noun, feminine*
* (*the surface underfoot*)
la terre = the ground
sous terre = underground
par terre = on the ground, on the floor
* (*the substance*)
la terre = the earth, the soil
(*as opposed to the sea*) = land
aller à terre = to go ashore
* (*a type of clay*)
un pot en terre = an earthenware pot

- (an area in private ownership)
  une terre = a piece of land
  des terres = land

**Terre** noun, feminine
  la Terre = Earth

**terrestre** adjective
  (describing plants or animals) = land
  (relating to the Earth) = of the Earth

**terrible** adjective
- = terrible
- (excellent)✖ = terrific
  le livre n'est pas terrible✖ = it's not a great book

**tes** ▶ **ton²**

**testament** noun, masculine
  un testament = a will

**tester** verb [1]
  = to test

**tête** noun, feminine
- (part of the body)
  la tête = the head
  se laver la tête = to wash one's hair
- (the front part of the head)
  la tête = the face
  tu fais une drôle de tête = you look funny
  faire la tête = to sulk
  n'en faire qu'à sa tête = to get one's way
- (as opposed to the end)
  la tête = the front
  = the head
  être en tête = to be at the front
  une tête en l'air = a scatterbrain

**têtu/têtue** adjective
  = stubborn, obstinate

**texte** noun, masculine
  un texte = a text

**texto** noun, masculine
  un texto = a text message

**TGV** noun, masculine
  un TGV = a high speed train

**thé** noun, masculine
- le thé = tea
- un thé = a cup of tea

**théâtre** noun, masculine
  un théâtre = a theatre, a theater
  faire du théâtre = to be an actor/an actress, to act

**théière** noun, feminine
  une théière = a teapot

**thème** noun, masculine
- le thème = the theme
- (a translation)
  un thème = a prose

**thermal/thermale** adjective
(plural) **thermaux/thermales**
  une source thermale = a thermal spring
  une station thermale = a spa

**thermos** noun, masculine (! never changes)
  un thermos = a (vacuum) flask

**thon** noun, masculine
  le thon = tuna

**thym** noun, masculine
  le thym = thyme

**tibia** noun, masculine
  le tibia = the shin

**ticket** noun, masculine
  un ticket = a ticket

**tiède** adjective
  = warm
  = lukewarm, tepid

**tien/tienne**: pronoun
  le tien/la tienne = yours
  les tiens/les tiennes = yours

**tiens** ▶ **tenir** [36]

**tiers** noun, masculine (! never changes)
  un tiers = one third

**tiers-monde** noun, masculine
  le tiers-monde = the Third World

**tige** noun, feminine
  une tige = a stem

**tigre** noun, masculine
  un tigre = a tiger

**tilleul** noun, masculine
- un tilleul = a lime tree
- le tilleul = lime tea

**timbre** noun, masculine
  un timbre = a (postage) stamp

**timbrer** verb [1]
  = to put a stamp on

**timide** adjective
  = shy

**timidité** noun, feminine
  la timidité = shyness

**tir** noun, masculine
- le tir (in an attack) = firing
  (as a sport) = shooting
- le tir à l'arc = archery

**tirage** noun, masculine
- (in a lottery)
  le tirage (au sort) = the draw
- (for a newspaper)
  le tirage = the circulation

**tire-bouchon** noun, masculine
(plural) **tire-bouchons**
  un tire-bouchon = a corkscrew

**tirelire** noun, feminine
  une tirelire = a piggy bank

**tirer** verb [1]
- = to pull
- = to draw

**T**

* = to fire
= to shoot
* tirer au sort = to draw lots

**tiroir** noun, masculine
un tiroir = a drawer

**tiroir-caisse** noun, masculine
(plural) **tiroirs-caisses**
un tiroir-caisse = a cash register

**tisane** noun, feminine
la tisane = herbal tea

**tisser** verb 1
= to weave

**tissu** noun, masculine
le tissu = material, fabric

**titre** noun, masculine
un titre = a title

**toc** exclamation
toc toc! = knock! knock!

**toi** pronoun
= you
plus jeune que toi = younger than you
toi, tu as de la chance = you're lucky, you
   are
ce livre est à toi = this book belongs to
   you, this book is yours
à toi (de jouer)! = it's your turn (to play)!
allons chez toi = let's go to your house
lève-toi! = get up!

**toile** noun, feminine
* (material)
la toile = cloth
= canvas
* (in art)
une toile = a canvas
**une toile d'araignée** = a cobweb, a
   spider's web
**une toile cirée** = an oilcloth

**toilette**
**1** noun, feminine
faire sa toilette = to have a wash
**2 toilettes** noun, feminine plural
les toilettes (in a house) = the toilet, the
   bathroom
(in a public place) = the toilets

**toi-même** pronoun
= yourself

**toise** noun, feminine
une toise = a height gauge

**toit** noun, masculine
un toit = a roof
**un toit ouvrant** = a sunroof

**tôle** noun, feminine
la tôle = sheet metal
**la tôle ondulée** = corrugated iron

**tomate** noun, feminine
une tomate = a tomato

**tombe** noun, feminine
une tombe = a grave

**tomber** verb 1 (**!** + être)
* = to fall
= to fall over
c'est tombé de ma poche = it fell out of
   my pocket
il est tombé de l'arbre = he fell off the tree
tomber en panne = to break down
* laisser tomber = to drop
* (to see or meet by chance)
tomber sur = to come across
= to run into
* (to happen)
ça tombe bien, moi aussi je suis libre
   = that's good, I'm free too

**ton¹** noun, masculine
* (a way of speaking)
un ton = a tone
d'un ton sec = drily
* (a colour)
un ton = a shade

**ton²/ta** determiner
(plural) **tes**
= your

**tonalité** noun, feminine
la tonalité = the dialling tone, the dial
   tone

**tondeuse** noun, feminine
une tondeuse (à gazon) = a lawnmower

**tondre** verb 6
tondre le gazon = to mow the grass
tondre un mouton = to shear a sheep
tondre quelqu'un = to shave someone's
   head

**tondu/tondue** ▶ tondre 6

**tonneau** noun, masculine
(plural) **tonneaux**
un tonneau = a barrel

**tonnerre**
**1** noun, masculine
le tonnerre = thunder
un coup de tonnerre = a clap of thunder
**2 du tonnerre✗** = fabulous

**torchon** noun, masculine
un torchon = a tea towel, a dish towel

**tordre** verb 6
**1** (**!** + avoir)
= to twist
= to wring
= to bend
**2 se tordre** (**!** + être)
se tordre la cheville = to twist one's ankle

**tordu/tordue** adjective
**1** ▶ tordre 6
**2** adjective
= crooked
= twisted

---

✗ in informal situations

**tornade** *noun, feminine*
une tornade = a tornado

**torrent** *noun, masculine*
un torrent = a torrent
pleuvoir à torrents = to rain very heavily

**torse** *noun, masculine*
le torse = the chest

**tort** *noun, masculine*
avoir tort = to be wrong

**tortue** *noun, feminine*
une tortue = a tortoise, a turtle

**tôt** *adverb*
= early
tôt le matin = early in the morning
le plus tôt possible = as soon as possible

**toucher** *verb* [1]
* = to touch
* = to get
toucher un salaire = to get a wage
* = to cash

**touffe** *noun, feminine*
une touffe (of hair, grass) = a tuft

**toujours** *adverb*
* (all the time) = always
il est toujours en retard = he's always late
* (showing that something is continuing)
= still
tu habites toujours Paris? = are you still
living in Paris?
il n'est toujours pas levé = he's still not up
elle est toujours aussi jolie = she's as pretty
as ever

**tour**
**1** *noun, feminine*
* (a building)
une tour = a tower
= a tower block, a high rise
* (in chess)
une tour = a rook, a castle
**2** *noun, masculine*
* (a turning movement)
un tour = a turn
faire un tour de manège = to have a go on
a fairground ride
faire le tour du lac (on foot) = to walk
round the lake
faire le tour du monde en bateau = to sail
round the world
* (in a game, a rota)
un tour = a turn
à tour de rôle = in turn
* (an outing)
(aller) faire un tour = to go for a stroll
aller faire un tour à Rome = to go to Rome
* (a piece of mischief)
un tour = a trick
jouer un tour à un ami = to play a trick on
a friend
* (a size)
un tour = a measurement
mon tour de taille = my waist
measurement

**tourbillon** *noun, masculine*
un tourbillon = a whirlpool
un tourbillon (de vent) = a whirlwind
un tourbillon de poussière = a whirl of
dust

**tourisme** *noun, masculine*
le tourisme = tourism

**touristique** *adjective*
= tourist
un endroit touristique = a popular tourist
spot

**tournée** *noun, feminine*
* une tournée (for a postman) = a round
(for a singer, a theatre company) = a tour
* (in a café)
une tournée = a round (of drinks)

**tourner** *verb* [1]
**1** (**!** + avoir)
* = to turn
* tourner un film = to shoot a film
**2 se tourner** (**!** + être)
se tourner = to turn around

**tournoi** *noun, masculine*
un tournoi = a tournament

**tous** ▶ tout 1, 2

**Toussaint** *noun, feminine*
la Toussaint = All Saints' Day

**tousser** *verb* [1]
= to cough

**tout/toute**
(plural) **tous/toutes**
**1** *adjective*
* = all
= every
il a plu toute la journée = it rained all day
(long)
c'est tout ce que tu veux? = is that all you
want?
tout le reste = everything else
tout le monde = everyone
tous les jours = every day
tous les deux ans = every other year
ils sont venus tous les deux = they both
came
* tout un/tout une = a whole
manger tout un pain = to eat a whole loaf
* = any
à toute heure = at any time
de toute façon = in any case
**2** *pronoun*
= everything
= anything
= all
il a tout oublié = he's forgotten everything
tout peut arriver = anything can happen
100 euros en tout = 100 euros in all
tous ensemble = all together

**T**

**3** *adverb*
- = quite
  = very
  c'est tout naturel = it's quite natural
  c'est tout près d'ici = it's very near
  être tout seul = to be all by oneself
  continuer tout droit = to carry straight on
  tout neuf/toute neuve = brand-new
  des rideaux tout faits = ready-made
    curtains
- tout en [marchant | travaillant | écoutant la
  radio …] = while [walking | working | listening
  to the radio …]
- (*in some phrases*)
  tout à coup = suddenly
  tout à fait = quite
  tout à l'heure = in a moment
  à tout à l'heure! = see you later!
  tout de même = all the same, even so
  tout de suite = at once
**4 tout** *noun, masculine*
- le tout = the lot
- pas du tout = not at all

**toux** *noun, feminine* (**!** *never changes*)
  une toux = a cough

**TP** *noun, masculine plural* ▶ **travail**

**tracasser** *verb* 1
  = to bother

**trace** *noun, feminine*
- une trace = a trail, a track
- une trace = a mark, a trace
  des traces de pas = footprints
  des traces de doigts = fingermarks

**tracer** *verb* 12
  = to draw
  = to write

**traduire** *verb* 62
  = to translate

**trafic** *noun, masculine*
  le trafic = traffic

**trafiquant/trafiquante** *noun,*
*masculine/feminine*
  un trafiquant/une trafiquante = a
    trafficker, a dealer

**train**
**1** *noun, masculine*
  un train = a train
**2 en train de** = in the process of
  être en train de [travailler | dormir | se
  doucher …] = to be [working | sleeping |
  having a shower …]

**traîneau** *noun, masculine*
(*plural*) **traîneaux**
  un traîneau = a sledge

**traîner** *verb* 1
- = to drag (along)

- traîner dans les rues = to hang around
  (on) the streets
- (*to be scattered*) = to be lying around
  laisser traîner ses affaires = to leave one's
    things lying around

**trait**
**1** *noun, masculine*
  un trait = a line
**2 traits** *noun, masculine plural*
  des traits (*of a face*) = features

**traitement** *noun, masculine*
  un traitement = a treatment

**traiter** *verb* 1
  = to treat

**trajet** *noun, masculine*
  un trajet = a journey

**tranche** *noun, feminine*
  une tranche (*of cheese, bread*) = a slice

**tranquille** *adjective*
  = quiet
  = calm, peaceful

**tranquillité** *noun, feminine*
  la tranquillité = peace and quiet

**transmettre** *verb* 60
- = to broadcast
- = to pass on, to convey
- = to transmit

**transpirer** *verb* 1
  = to sweat, to perspire

**transport** *noun, masculine*
- le transport = transport, transportation
- les transports en commun = public
  transport

**transporter** *verb* 1
  = to carry

**travail**
(*plural*) **travaux**
**1** *noun, masculine*
- le travail = work
- un travail = a job
**2 travaux** *noun, masculine plural*
  des travaux = work
  = roadwork(s)
  les travaux ménagers = housework
  **les travaux dirigés, TD** = practicals
  **les travaux manuels** = handicrafts
  **les travaux pratiques, TP** = practical
    work
  **les travaux publics** = civil engineering

**travailler** *verb* 1
  = to work
  = to practise

**travailleur/travailleuse**
**1** *adjective*
  = hardworking
**2** *noun, masculine/feminine*
  un travailleur/une travailleuse = a worker

---

**✗** in informal situations

**travaux ▶ travail**

**travers** noun, masculine
**1 à travers** = through
= across
**2 de travers**
ta cravate est de travers = your tie is crooked
boutonné de travers = buttoned up wrongly
j'ai avalé de travers = it went down the wrong way
**3 en travers de**
= across

**traversée** noun, feminine
une traversée = a crossing

**traverser** verb [1]
• = to cross
• = to go through

**traversin** noun, masculine
un traversin = a bolster

**trèfle** noun, masculine
• (a plant)
le trèfle = clover
• (at cards)
trèfle = clubs

**treille** noun, feminine
une treille = a climbing vine

**treize** number
= thirteen

**treizième** number
= thirteenth

**tremblement** noun, masculine
un tremblement = a tremor
**un tremblement de terre** = an earthquake

**trembler** verb [1]
= to shake
= to tremble, to quiver

**trempé/trempée** adjective
= soaked, sodden, soaking wet
trempé jusqu'aux os = soaked to the skin

**tremper** verb [1]
• = to soak
• = to dip

**trente** number
= thirty

**très** adverb
= very
avoir très faim = to be very hungry
très volontiers = gladly

**trésor** noun, masculine
un trésor = a treasure

**tresse** noun, feminine
une tresse = a plait, a braid

**tribu** noun, feminine
une tribu = a tribe

**tribune** noun, feminine
la tribune (in a stadium) = the grandstand

**tricher** verb [1]
= to cheat

**tricolore** adjective
le drapeau tricolore = the French flag

**tricot** noun, masculine
• (a craft)
le tricot = knitting
• (a knitted garment)
un tricot = a jumper, a sweater

**tricoter** verb [1]
= to knit

**trier** verb [2]
• = to sort (out)
• = to select

**trimestre** noun, masculine
un trimestre = a term

**triste** adjective
= sad

**tristesse** noun, feminine
la tristesse = sadness

**trois** number
= three

**troisième**
**1** number
= third
**2** noun, feminine
la troisième the class for secondary school students aged 14 to 16

**trombone** noun, masculine
• (an instrument)
un trombone = a trombone
• (for fastening papers)
un trombone = a paper clip

**trompe** noun, feminine
une trompe d'éléphant = an elephant trunk

**tromper** verb [1]
**1** (! + avoir)
= to deceive
**2 se tromper** (! + être)
• se tromper = to make a mistake
se tromper de bus = to take the wrong bus
se tromper de date = to get the date wrong
• se tromper = to be mistaken

**trompette** noun, feminine
une trompette = a trumpet

**tronc** noun, masculine
un tronc = a trunk

**trop**
**1** adverb = too
= too much
c'est trop petit = it's too small
tu parles trop = you talk too much
**2 trop de** = too much, too many

**T**

**trottoir** *noun, masculine*
un trottoir = a pavement, a sidewalk
le bord du trottoir = the kerb, the curb

**trou** *noun, masculine*
* un trou = a hole
  (*in a hedge*) = a gap
* (*a small town*)✘
  un trou✘ (perdu) = a dump

**troupeau** *noun, masculine*
(*plural*) **troupeaux**
un troupeau = a herd
= a flock

**trousse** *noun, feminine*
une trousse = a (small) case
= a kit
**une trousse d'écolier** = a pencil case
**une trousse de secours** = a first-aid kit
**une trousse de toilette** = a toilet bag

**trouver** *verb* [1]
**1** (**!** + *avoir*)
* = to find
* = to think
  je trouve qu'il a raison = I think he's right
  comment trouves-tu mon copain? = what
  do you think of my friend?
**2 se trouver** (**!** + *être*)
* se trouver = to be
  se trouver à Nice = to be in Nice
* se trouver = to find
  se trouver une excuse = to find an excuse
* je me trouve bien ici = I like it here
  se trouver mal = to pass out, to faint

**truc** *noun, masculine*
* (*when referring vaguely to something*)
  un truc = a thing
* (*a clever way*)✘
  un truc✘ = a trick
  = a knack

**truffe** *noun, feminine*
une truffe = a truffle

**truite** *noun, feminine*
une truite = a trout

**TTC** (*abbreviation of* **toutes taxes
comprises**)
TTC = inclusive of tax

**tu** *pronoun*
= you

**tube** *noun, masculine*
* un tube = a tube, a pipe
* (*a song*)✘
  un tube✘ = a hit

**tuer** *verb* [1]
= to kill

**tue-tête**: **à tue-tête** *adverb*
chanter à tue-tête = to sing at the top of
one's voice

**tuile** *noun, feminine*
une tuile = a tile

**Tunisie** *noun, feminine*
la Tunisie = Tunisia

**tunisien/tunisienne** *adjective*
= Tunisian

**tunnel** *noun, masculine*
un tunnel = a tunnel
le tunnel sous la Manche = the Channel
Tunnel

**turc/turque**
**1** *adjective*
= Turkish
**2 turc** *noun, masculine*
le turc = Turkish

**Turquie** *noun, feminine*
la Turquie = Turkey

**tutoyer** *verb* [23]
tutoyer quelqu'un = to address someone
using the 'tu' form

**tuyau** *noun, masculine*
(*plural*) **tuyaux**
un tuyau = a pipe
**un tuyau d'arrosage** = a hosepipe
**le tuyau d'échappement** = the exhaust

**TVA** *noun, feminine*
la TVA = VAT

**type** *noun, masculine*
* (*a sort*)
  un type = a type, a kind
* (*a man*)✘
  un type✘ = a bloke, a guy

**typique** *adjective*
= typical

# Uu

**ULM** *noun, masculine* (**!** *never changes*)
* (*the equipment*)
  un ULM = a microlight
* (*the sport*)
  l'ULM = microlighting

**un/une**
**1** *number*
= one
trente et un jours = thirty-one days
une fois = once
un jour sur deux = every other day
**2** *determiner*
(*plural*) **des**
= a(n)
un chat = a cat
des enfants = children

**3** *pronoun*
*(plural)* **uns/unes**
(l')un/(l')une = one
les uns/les unes = some
l'un d'entre vous = one of you
pourquoi les uns et pas les autres? = why
some and not others?

**uni/unie** *adjective*
• *(not at odds)* = united
= close-knit
• *(not patterned)* = plain

**unique** *adjective*
• = only
être fils/fille unique = to be an only child
• = unique
une occasion unique = a unique
opportunity

**uniquement** *adverb*
= only

**unir** *verb* ③
= to unite

**unité** *noun, feminine*
• une unité = a unit
• l'unité = unity

**univers** *noun, masculine* (**!** *never
changes*)
l'univers = the universe

**universitaire** *adjective*
= university

**université** *noun, feminine*
l'université = university, college

**uns/unes** ▶ **un 3**

**urbain/urbaine** *adjective*
= urban
la vie urbaine = city life

**urbanisme** *noun, masculine*
l'urbanisme = town planning, city
planning

**urgence** *noun, feminine*
• l'urgence = the urgency
téléphonez d'urgence = phone
immediately
des mesures d'urgence = emergency
measures
on l'a transporté d'urgence à l'hôpital = he
was rushed to the hospital
• *(in a hospital)*
une urgence = an emergency
le service des urgences = the casualty
department, the accident and
emergency department

**urticaire** *noun, feminine*
l'urticaire = nettle rash

**usage** *noun, masculine*
l'usage = the use
'à usage externe' = 'for external use only'

**usager** *noun, masculine*
un usager *(of a service)* = a user
les usagers de la route = road users

**usé/usée** *adjective*
= worn

**user** *verb* ①
**1** (**!** + *avoir*)
= to wear out
= to wear down
**2 s'user** (**!** + *être*)
s'user = to wear out

**usine** *noun, feminine*
une usine = a factory

**ustensile** *noun, masculine*
un ustensile = a utensil

**utile** *adjective*
= useful

**utiliser** *verb* ①
= to use

**va** ▶ **aller 1** ⑨

**vacances** *noun, feminine plural*
des vacances = holidays, a vacation
être en vacances = to be on holiday, to be
on vacation

**vacancier/vacancière** *noun,
masculine/feminine*
un vacancier/une vacancière = a
holidaymaker, a vacationer

**vache** *noun, feminine*
une vache = a cow

**vagabonder** *verb* ①
= to wander

**vague**
**1** *adjective*
= vague
**2** *noun, masculine*
il regardait dans le vague = he was staring
into space
**3** *noun, feminine*
• une vague = a wave
• une vague de froid = a cold spell

**vaincre** *verb* ⑤⑦
= to defeat
= to overcome

**vaincu/vaincue**
**1** ▶ **vaincre** ⑤⑦
**2** *noun, masculine/feminine*
les vaincus = the losers

**V**

**vainqueur** *noun, masculine*
  un vainqueur = a winner
  = a victor

**vais** ▶ **aller 1** ⑨

**vaisselle** *noun, feminine*
  la vaisselle = crockery, dishes
  faire la vaisselle = to do the dishes

**valable** *adjective*
  = valid

**valet** *noun, masculine*
• (*a person*)
  un valet = a manservant
• (*at cards*)
  un valet = a jack

**valeur** *noun, feminine*
  la valeur (*in terms of money*) = value
  (*in terms of merit*) = worth
  les objets de valeur = valuables
  sans valeur = worthless

**valise** *noun, feminine*
  une valise = a suitcase
  faire ses valises = to pack

**vallée** *noun, feminine*
  une vallée = a valley

**valoir** *verb* 45
• = to be worth
  = to cost
  ça en vaut la peine = it's worth it
• il vaut mieux partir tôt = it's better to leave
  early
  il vaut mieux que tu y ailles = you'd better
  go

**valu** ▶ **valoir** 45

**vanille** *noun, feminine*
  la vanille = vanilla

**vapeur**
**1** *noun, feminine*
  la vapeur = steam
  un bateau à vapeur = a steamboat
  faire cuire des légumes à la vapeur = to
  steam vegetables
**2 vapeurs** *noun, feminine plural*
  des vapeurs = fumes

**vaporisateur** *noun, masculine*
  un vaporisateur = a spray

**vaporiser** *verb* 1
  = to spray
  = to vaporize

**varappe** *noun, feminine*
  la varappe = rock-climbing

**variable** *adjective*
• = variable
• = changeable, unpredictable

**variante** *noun, feminine*
  une variante = a variation

**varié/variée** *adjective*
  = varied
  = various
  'sandwichs variés' = 'a selection of
  sandwiches'

**variété**
**1** *noun, feminine*
• la variété = variety
• une variété = a variety
**2 variétés** *noun, feminine plural*
  un spectacle de variétés = a variety show

**vas** ▶ **aller 1** ⑨

**vase**
**1** *noun, masculine*
  un vase = a vase
**2** *noun, feminine*
  la vase = mud

**vaste** *adjective*
  = vast, huge
  = large

**vaudrait** ▶ **valoir** 45

**vaut** ▶ **valoir** 45

**vautour** *noun, masculine*
  un vautour = a vulture

**veau** *noun, masculine*
(*plural*) **veaux**
• (*the animal*)
  un veau = a calf
• (*the meat*)
  le veau = veal

**vécu/vécue**
**1** ▶ **vivre** 38
**2** *adjective*
  = real-life

**vedette** *noun, feminine*
• (*a person*)
  une vedette = a star
• (*a boat*)
  une vedette = a motor launch

**véhicule** *noun, masculine*
  un véhicule = a vehicle

**veille** *noun, feminine*
  la veille = the day before
  la veille au soir = the night before

**veiller** *verb* 1
• (*to remain awake*) = to stay up
• (*to be alert*) = to be watchful

**veilleur** *noun, masculine*
  un veilleur de nuit = a night watchman

**veilleuse** *noun, feminine*
  une veilleuse = a night light
  = a pilot light

**veine** *noun, feminine*
• une veine = a vein
• la veine✘ = luck
  avoir de la veine✘ = to be lucky

---

✘ in informal situations

**vélo** noun, masculine
un vélo = a bike
un vélo tout terrain = a mountain bike
faire du vélo = to cycle

**vélomoteur** noun, masculine
un vélomoteur = a moped

**velours** noun, masculine (! never changes)
le velours = velvet
= corduroy

**venais** ▶ venir ᴈ6

**vendanges** noun, feminine plural
les vendanges = the grape harvest

**vendeur/vendeuse** noun, masculine/feminine
un vendeur/une vendeuse = a seller, a vendor
= a shop assistant
= a salesman/a saleswoman

**vendre** verb ⑥
**1** (! + avoir)
= to sell
'à vendre' = 'for sale'
**2 se vendre** (! + être)
se vendre = to be sold
ça se vend bien = it sells well

**vendredi** noun, masculine
vendredi = Friday
le vendredi = on Fridays

**vendu/vendue** ▶ vendre ⑥

**vénéneux/vénéneuse** adjective
= poisonous

**vengeance** noun, feminine
la vengeance = revenge

**venger** verb ⑬
**1** (! + avoir)
= to avenge
**2 se venger** (! + être)
se venger = to get one's revenge

**venir** verb ᴈ6 (! + être)
• = to come
viens déjeuner = come for lunch
faire venir un plombier = to call a plumber
ça ne m'est jamais venu à l'idée = it never crossed my mind
• venir de faire = to have just done

**vent** noun, masculine
le vent = the wind
il y a du vent, il fait du vent = it's windy

**vente** noun, feminine
une vente = a sale
des médicaments en vente libre = drugs available over the counter
**la vente par correspondance** = mail-order selling
**une vente aux enchères** = an auction

**ventre** noun, masculine
le ventre (a person's) = the stomach
(an animal's) = the (under)belly

**venu/venue** ▶ venir ᴈ6

**ver** noun, masculine
un ver = a worm
= a maggot
**un ver de terre** = an earthworm

**verbe** noun, masculine
un verbe = a verb

**verdure** noun, feminine
la verdure = greenery

**verger** noun, masculine
un verger = an orchard

**verglacé/verglacée** adjective
= icy

**verglas** noun, masculine (! never changes)
le verglas = black ice

**vérifier** verb ②
= to check

**véritable** adjective
= real, true, genuine

**vérité** noun, feminine
la vérité = the truth

**vernis** noun, masculine (! never changes)
le vernis = varnish
= glaze
du vernis à ongles = nail polish

**verrai** ▶ voir ᴈ6

**verre** noun, masculine
• (a substance)
le verre = glass
• (a container)
un verre = a glass
un verre à vin = a wine glass
un verre de vin = a glass of wine
aller prendre un verre = to go for a drink
• (on spectacles)
un verre = a lens
**des verres de contact** = contact lenses

**vers**
**1** noun, masculine (! never changes)
un vers = a line (of verse)
des vers = poetry
**2** preposition
• = toward(s)
rouler vers Paris = to go toward(s) Paris
vers le soir = toward(s) evening
• = about
vers six heures = at about six o'clock

**Verseau** noun, masculine
le Verseau = Aquarius

**verser** verb ①
• = to pour
• = to pay

**V**

**version** *noun, feminine*
• (*an exercise*)
une version = a translation (*into one's own language*)
• (*an account, an adaptation*)
une version = a version
un film en version originale = a film in the original language

**vert/verte** *adjective*
= green

**vertèbre** *noun, feminine*
une vertèbre = a vertebra
se déplacer une vertèbre = to slip a disc

**vertical/verticale** *adjective*
(*plural*) **verticaux/verticales**
= vertical
= upright

**verticalement** *adverb*
• = vertically
• (*in a crossword*) = down

**vertige** *noun, masculine*
le vertige = dizziness
= vertigo
avoir le vertige = to feel dizzy

**veste** *noun, feminine*
une veste = a jacket

**vestiaire** *noun, masculine*
un vestiaire (*in a gym*) = a changing room
(*in a theatre, a museum*) = a cloakroom

**vestibule** *noun, masculine*
un vestibule = a hall
= a foyer, a lobby

**veston** *noun, masculine*
un veston = a (man's) jacket

**vêtement** *noun, masculine*
un vêtement = a garment
des vêtements = clothes, clothing
'vêtements pour hommes' = 'menswear'

**vétérinaire** *noun, masculine/feminine*
un vétérinaire/une vétérinaire = a veterinary surgeon, a veterinarian

**vêtu/vêtue** *adjective*
= dressed
elle était vêtue d'une robe noire = she was wearing a black dress

**veuf/veuve**
**1** *adjective*
= widowed
**2** *noun, masculine/feminine*
un veuf/une veuve = a widower/a widow

**veuille** ▶ **vouloir** 48

**veulent** ▶ **vouloir** 48

**veuve** ▶ **veuf**

**veux** ▶ **vouloir** 48

**vexer** *verb* 1
**1** (**!** + *avoir*)
= to offend, to upset

**2 se vexer** (**!** + *être*)
se vexer = to take offence, to get upset

**viande** *noun, feminine*
la viande = meat
de la viande de bœuf = beef

**victime** *noun, feminine*
une victime = a victim
= a casualty

**victoire** *noun, feminine*
une victoire = a victory

**vide**
**1** *adjective*
= empty, vacant
= blank
**2** *noun, masculine*
• (*a space*)
un vide = a gap
• (*absence of air*)
le vide = a vacuum
emballé sous vide = vacuum-packed
• sauter dans le vide = to jump

**vidéothèque** *noun, feminine*
une vidéothèque = a video library
= a video collection

**vider** *verb* 1
**1** (**!** + *avoir*)
= to empty
**2 se vider** (**!** + *être*)
se vider = to empty

**vie** *noun, feminine*
la vie = life
être en vie = to be alive
la vie active = working life
la vie est chère = the cost of living is high

**vieil** ▶ **vieux 1**

**vieillard/vieillarde** *noun,*
*masculine/feminine*
un vieillard/une vieillarde = an old man/an old woman
les vieillards = old people

**vieille** ▶ **vieux**

**vieillir** *verb* 3
= to get old(er)
= to age

**viendrai** ▶ **venir** 36

**viens** ▶ **venir** 36

**vierge** *adjective*
= virgin
= blank
= new

**Vierge** *noun, feminine*
• la Vierge = Virgo
• la (Sainte) Vierge = the (Blessed) Virgin

**vietnamien/vietnamienne**
**1** *adjective*
= Vietnamese

**2 vietnamien** noun, masculine
le vietnamien = Vietnamese

**vieux/vieille**
(plural) **vieux/vieilles**
**1** adjective
= old

> ! **vieil** is used instead of **vieux** before
> masculine nouns that begin with a vowel
> or a mute h. The plural of **vieil** is **vieux**.

un vieil homme = an old man
de vieilles photos = old photographs
**2** noun, masculine/feminine
un vieux/une vieille = an old man/an old
woman
les vieux = old people

**vif/vive¹** adjective
* (describing a person) = lively
* (describing a pace, a movement) = brisk
rouler à vive allure = to drive at high speed
* (describing a light, a colour) = bright
* (describing the cold, the wind) = biting
* (describing a pain) = sharp

**vigne** noun, feminine
la vigne – vine
une vigne = a vineyard
**la vigne vierge** = Virginia creeper

**vigneron/vigneronne** noun,
masculine/feminine
un vigneron/une vigneronne = a
winegrower

**vignette** noun, feminine
une vignette = a label
(on a car) = a tax disc

**vignoble** noun, masculine
un vignoble = a vineyard

**vilain/vilaine** adjective
* = naughty, nasty
* = ugly

**villa** noun, feminine
une villa = a detached house
= a villa

**village** noun, masculine
un village = a village

**ville** noun, feminine
une ville = a town, a city
aller en ville = to go into town

**vin** noun, masculine
le vin = wine

**vinaigre** noun, masculine
le vinaigre = vinegar

**vinaigrette** noun, feminine
la vinaigrette = vinaigrette, oil and vinegar
dressing

**vingt** number
= twenty

**vingtaine** noun, feminine
une vingtaine = about twenty
= twenty

**vingt et un/vingt et une** number
= twenty-one

**vingt et unième** number
= twenty-first

**vingtième** number
= twentieth

**violent/violente** adjective
= violent

**violet/violette¹** adjective
= purple

**violette²** noun, feminine
une violette = a violet

**violon** noun, masculine
un violon = a violin

**violoncelle** noun, masculine
un violoncelle = a cello

**vipère** noun, feminine
une vipère = an adder, a viper

**virage** noun, masculine
un virage = a bend

**virgule** noun, feminine
une virgule = a comma
= a decimal point

**vis**
**1 ▸ vivre** 38
**2** noun, feminine (! never changes)
une vis = a screw

**visage** noun, masculine
le visage = the face

**viser** verb 1
* = to aim at
* = to be aimed at

**visite** noun, feminine
une visite = a visit
= a call
rendre visite à un ami = to pay a visit to a
friend
avoir de la visite = to have visitors
**une visite médicale** = a medical
examination

**visiter** verb 1
visiter une ville = to visit a town
visiter un appartement = to view a flat, to
look at an apartment

**visser** verb 1
= to screw on

**vite** adverb
= quickly, fast
vite! = quick!
j'ai parlé trop vite = I spoke too hastily

**vitesse** noun, feminine
* la vitesse = speed
en vitesse = quickly
à toute vitesse = at top speed
* une vitesse = a gear

**V**

**vitre** *noun, feminine*
  une vitre = a windowpane
  = a pane of glass
  les vitres d'une voiture = the windows of a
    car

**vitrine** *noun, feminine*
* (*in a shop*)
  une vitrine = a (shop) window
  faire les vitrines = to go window shopping
* (*in a museum*)
  une vitrine = a display cabinet, a curio
    cabinet

**vivant/vivante** *adjective*
* = alive, living
  être vivant = to be alive
  les êtres vivants = living creatures
* = lively

**vive²**
**1** *adjective, feminine* ▶ **vif**
**2** *verb* ▶ **vivre** 38

**vivre** *verb* 38
  = to live
  se laisser vivre = to take things easy

**vocabulaire** *noun, masculine*
  le vocabulaire = vocabulary

**vœu** *noun, masculine*
(*plural*) **vœux**
  un vœu = a wish
  meilleurs vœux = best wishes
  les vœux du Nouvel An = New Year's
    greetings

**voici** *preposition*
  = here is, this is
  = here are, these are
  me voici = here I am
  voici un mois = a month ago

**voie** *noun, feminine*
* (*for traffic*)
  une voie = a road
  = a street
  la voie publique = the public highway
  une voie sans issue = a dead end
* (*part of a road*)
  une voie = a lane
* (*for a train*)
  une voie = a track
* en voie de = in the process of
  un pays en voie de développement = a
    developing country
  une espèce en voie de disparition = an
    endangered species
  **la voie ferrée** = the railway track, the
    railroad track

**voilà** *preposition*
  = here is, this is
  = here are, these are
  te voilà enfin! = here you are at last!
  voilà tout = that's all
  voilà un mois = a month ago

**voile**
**1** *noun, feminine*
* une voile = a sail
* la voile = sailing
**2** *noun, masculine*
  un voile = a veil

**voir** *verb* 46
**1** (**!** + *avoir*)
* = to see
  on verra = we'll see
  un film à voir = a film worth seeing
  faire voir quelque chose à quelqu'un = to
    show someone something
* = to be able to see
  je ne vois rien, je n'y vois rien = I can't see
    a thing
* (*to be connected*)
  ça n'a rien à voir = that's got nothing to do
    with it
* (*when encouraging someone*)
  voyons, soyez sages! = come on, be good!
**2 se voir** (**!** + *être*)
* (*to be visible*)
  se voir = to show
  ça se voit de loin = it can be seen from a
    distance
* (*to meet*)
  se voir = to see each other

**voisin/voisine**
**1** *adjective*
  = neighbo(u)ring
  = nearby
**2** *noun, masculine/feminine*
  un voisin/une voisine = a neighbo(u)r

**voiture** *noun, feminine*
  une voiture = a car, an automobile
  = a carriage, a car
  en voiture! = all aboard!

**voix** *noun, feminine* (**!** *never changes*)
* (*the way one speaks*)
  une voix = a voice
  à voix basse = in a low voice
  à haute voix = out loud
* (*in an election*)
  une voix = a vote

**vol** *noun, masculine*
* (*through the air*)
  un vol = a flight
  à vol d'oiseau = as the crow flies
* (*an offence*)
  un vol = a theft, a robbery
  un vol à main armée = an armed robbery
  **le vol à voile** = gliding

**volaille** *noun, feminine*
  la volaille = poultry

**volant/volante**
**1** *adjective*
  = flying
**2 volant** *noun, masculine*
* (*in a car*)
  un volant = a steering wheel
  donner un coup de volant = to turn the
    wheel sharply

* (in badminton)
  un volant = a shuttlecock
* (on a skirt)
  un volant = a flounce

**volcan** noun, masculine
un volcan = a volcano

**voler** verb 1
* = to steal
  il **s'est fait voler sa voiture** = he had his car stolen
* voler un passant = to rob a passer-by
* = to fly

**volet** noun, masculine
un volet (on a window) = a shutter

**voleur/voleuse** noun, masculine/feminine
un voleur/une voleuse = a thief

**volontaire**
1 adjective
 = deliberate
2 noun, masculine/feminine
un volontaire/une volontaire = a volunteer

**volonté** noun, feminine
la volonté = will
= will-power

**volontiers** adverb
= gladly, willingly
= with pleasure

**vomir** verb 3
* = to vomit, to bring up
* = to be sick, to throw up

**vont** ▶ aller 1 9

**vos** ▶ votre

**voter** verb 1
= to vote

**votre** determiner
(plural) **vos**
= your

**vôtre** pronoun
le vôtre/la vôtre/les vôtres = yours
à la vôtre! = cheers!

**voudrais** ▶ vouloir 48

**vouloir** verb 48
* (expressing determination) = to want
  je veux partir = I want to leave
  il ne voulait pas que tu viennes = he didn't want you to come
* (expressing a wish, a polite request)
  que veux-tu boire?, que voulez-vous boire? = what would you like to drink?
  je voudrais des poires = I'd like pears
  comme tu veux = as you wish
  veuillez vous asseoir = please sit down
* vouloir dire = to mean
  qu'est-ce que ça veut dire? = what does it mean?

**voulu/voulue**
1 ▶ vouloir 48

---

2 adjective
* = required
* = deliberate, planned

**vous** pronoun
* = you
  vous avez gagné = you've won
  à cause de vous = because of you
  la voiture est à vous = the car is yours
* = yourself
* = yourselves
  soignez-vous = look after yourself
  = look after yourselves
  allez vous laver les mains = go and wash your hands
* = each other
  vous vous aimez? = do you love each other?

**vous-même** pronoun
(plural) **vous-mêmes**
= yourself
= yourselves

**vouvoyer** verb 23
vouvoyer quelqu'un = to address someone using the "vous" form

**voyage** noun, masculine
un voyage = a trip, a journey
aimer les voyages = to love travel(l)ing
**un voyage de noces** = a honeymoon
**un voyage organisé** = a package tour

**voyager** verb 13
= to travel

**voyageur/voyageuse** noun, masculine/feminine
un voyageur/une voyageuse = a passenger
= a travel(l)er

**voyant/voyante**
1 adjective
= loud
2 noun, masculine/feminine
un voyant/une voyante = a clairvoyant
3 **voyant** noun, masculine
un voyant lumineux = a warning light

**voyelle** noun, feminine
une voyelle = a vowel

**voyons** ▶ voir 46

**voyou** noun, masculine
un voyou = a lout
= a rascal

**vrai/vraie**
1 adjective
= true
= real, genuine
2 **vrai** noun, masculine
le vrai = the truth
à vrai dire = to tell the truth
pour de vrai = for real

**vraiment** adverb
= really

**V**

**vrombir** verb ③
= to roar

**VTT** noun, masculine
un VTT = a mountain bike

**vu/vue¹**
**1 ▶ voir** 46
**2** adjective
• être bien vu = to be well thought of
  ce serait plutôt mal vu = it wouldn't go
  down well
• bien vu! = good point!
• c'est tout vu = my mind is made up
**3 vu** = in view of

**vue²** noun, feminine
• la vue = sight
  avoir une bonne vue = to have good
  eyesight
  je la connais de vue = I know her to see
  perdre un ami de vue = to lose touch with
  a friend
  à vue d'œil = visibly
• une vue = a view
  avoir vue sur le lac = to look out onto the
  lake

**wagon** noun, masculine
un wagon = a wagon, a car
= a carriage, a car

**wagon-lit** noun, masculine
(plural) **wagons-lits**
un wagon-lit = a sleeper, a sleeping car

**wagon-restaurant** noun, masculine
(plural) **wagons-restaurants**
un wagon-restaurant = a restaurant car, a
dining car

**WC** noun, masculine plural
les WC = the toilet, the bathroom

**Web** noun, masculine
le Web = the Web

**y** pronoun
• = it
  j'y pense souvent = I often think about it
  il s'y attendait = he was expecting it
  tu n'y peux rien = you can't do anything
  about it

---

**\*** in informal situations

elle n'y arrivera jamais = she'll never
  manage it
je n'y comprends rien = I don't understand
  a thing
• = there
j'y mange parfois = I sometimes eat there
j'y vais = I'm going
• il y a = there is
= there are
il n'y en a plus = there's none left
= there aren't any left

**yaourt** noun, masculine
un yaourt = a yogurt

**yeux ▶ œil**

**yoga** noun, masculine
le yoga = yoga

**Zz**

**zapper\*** verb ①
= to flick through the TV channels

**zèbre** noun, masculine
un zèbre = a zebra

**zéro**
**1** number
= zero
**2** noun, masculine
zéro (in school) = nought, zero
(in a match) = nil, nothing
il est zéro heure quinze = it's a quarter
  past midnight
trois (buts) à zéro = three nil, three
  nothing
avoir le moral à zéro\* = to feel very down
repartir à zéro = to start all over again

**zeste** noun, masculine
un zeste de citron = the zest of a lemon

**zigzag** noun, masculine
un zigzag = a zigzag
une route en zigzag = a winding
  road

**zodiaque** noun, masculine
le zodiaque = the zodiac

**zone** noun, feminine
une zone = a zone, an area
**une zone industrielle** = an industrial
estate, an industrial park

**zoo** noun, masculine
un zoo = a zoo

**zoologique** adjective
= zoological

**zut\*** exclamation
= blast!
= oh dear!

# Dictionary know-how

This section contains a number of short exercises which will help you to use your dictionary more effectively. You will find answers to all of the exercises at the end of the section p. 182.

## 1 Identifying French nouns and adjectives

Here is an extract from a French advertisement for a gas oven. See if you can find fourteen different nouns and underline them, and six different adjectives and circle them (or make two lists). If you are not sure of some words, look them up in the French-English half of the dictionary and see if the term 'noun' or 'adjective' is used to describe them.

---

### GAZ DE FRANCE, LE CHOIX DE LA QUALITÉ

Pourquoi les Français préfèrent-ils le gaz naturel?

Si vous venez dîner chez moi, vous verrez un magnifique objet, écran plat, coins carrés, dont la beauté luisante saute aux yeux

Un poste de télévision? Non, non, ce n'est pas mon téléviseur, c'est mon nouveau four au gaz naturel.

---

The publishers would like to thank Gaz de France for permission to reproduce copyright material.

## 2 Checking the gender of French nouns

Here are some English nouns which appear in the English-French half of the dictionary. Find out what their French equivalents are and make two separate lists, masculine nouns and feminine nouns.

| | | | |
|---|---|---|---|
| bag | hippopotamus | magic | saddle |
| cake shop | island | oyster | thunderstorm |
| doorbell | jumper | peach | waitress |
| felt-tip pen | library | raincoat | worm |

# 3 Identifying French and English pronouns

Each of the following phrases appears in the French–English half of this dictionary in entries where a pronoun is the headword. In each one, underline the pronoun(s) and give the English equivalent(s).

ça ne fait rien

c'est un cadeau

ce sont des détails sans importance

il l'a invitée

elle ne me parle pas

donne-la-moi

je lui ai prêté ma robe

elles se sont fait mal

il vous l'a prêté

donne-nous l'adresse

# 4 Recognizing French verbs

Underline the verb in each sentence.

Pierre descend la rue sur son vélo.

Sophie ne connaît pas le nom du magasin.

Les sapeurs pompiers arriveront dans cinq minutes.

Chaque année nous passons nos vacances d'été en France.

Ma sœur a un bassin avec des poissons dans son jardin.

# 5 Identifying French adverbs

Here is a list of twelve French words. Eight of them are adverbs and four are not. Underline the ones which are not, or make a list, and say what they are. If you are not sure of some of them, look them up in the French–English half of the dictionary.

| | | |
|---|---|---|
| **absolument** | **enseignement** | **seulement** |
| **certainement** | **facilement** | **stationnement** |
| **directement** | **heureusement** | **vêtement** |
| **énormément** | **médicament** | **vraiment** |

## 6 Identifying subjects and objects

We have left out the subjects and objects from this French newspaper report. Choose suitable words from the list below in order to complete it. When you have finished, list the subjects and objects separately.

---

# L'OURS FÉLIX ATTAQUE

......................................... a dévoré ...................................................

depuis son arrivée dans les Pyrénées. Hier, ..................................... ,

transplanté des forêts de Slovénie, a entièrement dévoré

............................................. qui se trouvait près de Portet-d'Aspet en

Haute-Garonne. ............................................... a aussitôt

compensé ..................................... de la perte de sa bête.

............................................. est de 200 pour l'attaque, qui ne sont versés

qu'une seule fois, puis de 300 par mouton. Pourtant, .....................................

devraient se rassurer. ..................................... sont toujours plus

prédateurs que les vieux. Avec le temps, .................... perdra

............................................. pour la chasse.

---

| | | |
|---|---|---|
| l'animal | Le département | Félix |
| le berger | les jeunes ours | sa passion |
| les bergers | neuf moutons | Le 'tarif' |
| une brebis | L'ours Félix | |

The publishers would like to thank *Libération* for permission to use copyright material.

---

## 7 Word search

Here is a grid in which are hidden eleven French words: 3 masculine nouns, 3 feminine nouns, 2 adjectives, 2 verbs and 1 pronoun. They may appear horizontally or vertically, and in either direction. When you have found them, circle them. If you are not sure of any of them, look them up in the French–English section of the dictionary.

| | | | | | | | | | |
|---|---|---|---|---|---|---|---|---|---|
| B | G | R | A | N | D | K | Y | S | T |
| H | O | E | P | M | Q | C | E | L | A |
| S | T | N | D | N | O | R | U | I | V |
| Z | E | N | X | A | K | E | B | F | C |
| D | F | O | G | H | J | S | K | L | P |
| M | R | D | E | N | T | U | A | P | Q |
| M | O | N | D | E | P | C | O | A | D |
| P | G | A | W | C | U | X | V | R | N |
| C | U | B | A | G | U | E | T | T | E |
| R | H | A | N | F | Q | E | M | T | K |

**abandonner**
**baguette**
**cela**
**dent**
**excuser**
**fils**
**grand**
**monde**
**noz**
**part**
**rond**

## 8 Accents are important!

Here is part of a letter typed by somebody who does not know how to find the accents on a word processor. Use your dictionary as necessary to help you put them in:

> Ma chere Louise,
>
> Merci pour ta lettre que j'ai reçue hier. Ce matin, comme
> d'habitude, je suis allee faire mes courses au marche ou j'ai
> rencontre Madame Bonnard, que tu connais tres bien, je crois. Elle
> m'a dit que sa fille ainee, Sandrine, a fini ses etudes et qu'elle part
> en Grece faire un stage de six mois dans un hotel. Ça devrait etre
> amusant, non? Qu'est-ce que tu comptes faire toi-meme cet ete? Est-
> ce que tu restes en France ou esperes-tu toujours visiter la Norvege?
> Moi, je vais passer deux semaines dans la maison de campagne de
> mon frere a Gaillac...

## 9 Using page headings

In order to help you find what you are looking for quickly, every page of the main section of the dictionary has a word at the top which identifies the first entry on that page. In this exercise the left-hand column contains a list of entries and the right-hand column a selection of page headings. Choose the page where you would expect to find the entry you are looking for.

| Entry | Page headings |
|---|---|
| **encourager** | énerver \| enseigne   en \| énervé |
| **historique** | hâte \| histoire   historique \| hôtesse |
| **liquide** | librairie \| loge   logé \| luge |
| **mener** | mélanger \| mesure   mesurer \| million |
| **renseigner** | reine \| rendre   renne \| requin |
| **sérieux** | séjour \| serré   serrer \| siège |
| **vieil** | version \| vietnamien   vieux \| vitesse |

# 10 Masculine or feminine?

Some French nouns can be both masculine and feminine, and change their meaning accordingly. Use your dictionary to find the following nouns and list them with their different meanings in two columns, masculine and feminine, e.g.

*un* livre = ......................   *une* livre = ......................

livre
manche
mode
moule
poêle
tour
vase
voile

# 11 Which preposition, à or de?

Many verbs in French take a preposition, either *à* or *de*, before an infinitive e.g. *il m'a demandé de venir demain*; *elle a réussi à ouvrir la porte*. In the following extract, all of the prepositions have been left out. Use your dictionary to check what they should be.

Jean-Pierre a longtemps refusé . . . accepter la proposition de son ami, Michel, mais finalement il a décidé . . . dire oui. Michel avait envie . . . faire une randonnée de plusieurs semaines à vélo à travers l'Europe et avait tout fait pour convaincre son ami . . . venir avec lui. A vrai dire, Jean-Pierre préférait passer son temps . . . se faire bronzer sur la plage, mais il essayait toujours . . . faire plaisir à son copain et c'est pour cette raison que Michel est parvenu . . . le persuader. Bien entendu, c'est Michel qui s'est chargé . . . faire tous les préparatifs du voyage, alors que Jean-Pierre a commencé . . . tracer l'itinéraire sur la carte.

## 12 Find the verb

Some words in English can be both nouns and verbs e.g. race. In this exercise, you have to find the following English words in the English–French half of the dictionary and then give the French for the verb only.

| | | |
|---|---|---|
| aim | iron | question |
| block | joke | sail |
| camp | kiss | train |
| dance | milk | welcome |
| finish | paint | yell |

## 13 Choosing the right word

Very often you cannot use a word exactly as it is given in the dictionary. In the case of adjectives with an irregular feminine form, for example, you have to make sure that you select the form which is appropriate to the noun you are using. Use your dictionary to find the correct form of the adjective to match the nouns in the following sentences.

Elle a de .................... yeux et de .................... dents. (*beautiful*)

Notre .......................... maison était très .................. . (*former*) (*old*)

C'est une très ..................... idée. (*good*)

La .......................... chose à faire est de trouver l'entrée .......................... .
(*first*) (*secret*)

Elles sont si ........................................ . (*happy*)

La neige est ................................... . (*white*)

Il a une ................................... voiture. (*new*)

Mon père est .................., mais ma mère est ....................................... .
(*Italian*) (*Norwegian*)

# 14 Which part of speech?

Use your dictionary to help you arrange these words in separate lists according to their parts of speech (masculine noun, feminine noun, adjective etc). Some words may belong to more than one category and will therefore appear in more than one list.

| | | |
|---|---|---|
| **chasse** | **inscrire** | **pâle** |
| **dessous** | **juste** | **que** |
| **en** | **mouche** | **relire** |
| **facilement** | **notre** | **toi-même** |
| **gendre** | **ouest** | **vers** |

# 15 Translating phrasal verbs

Use your dictionary to find the correct translation for the following English sentences containing phrasal verbs.

The button's **come off**.

The dustmen have **taken** the rubbish **away**.

She is **bringing up** her children on her own.

They've **given up** smoking.

I'm going to **take** my shoes **off**.

# 16 Find the plural

Use your dictionary as necessary to find the plural of the following nouns (be careful, some of them are exceptions to the general guidelines):

un bijou, des .....................................

un cas, des .....................................

un cheval, deux .............................

un cheveu, mes .............................

une croix, deux .............................

un manteau, deux .....................................

un pneu, quatre .........................................

du travail, des .........................................

un trou, deux .........................................

un vieux, des .........................................

# 17 **Faux amis**

Some French words look the same as, or similar to English words, but in fact have a different meaning. These are known as *faux amis* or false friends. Use your dictionary to find the meanings of the following French words:

| | |
|---|---|
| actuellement | éventuellement |
| un bonnet | gentil |
| un car | le matériel |
| une cave | le pétrole |
| une course | un pin |
| décevoir | sale |
| délivrer | sensible |
| un engin | |

# 18 **False friends**

Now use your dictionary to find a French meaning for each of these English 'lookalikes'.

| | |
|---|---|
| actually | eventually |
| a bonnet | gentle |
| a car | material |
| a cave | petrol |
| a course | a pin |
| to deceive | a sale |
| to deliver | sensible |
| an engine | |

# 19 Male or female?

Some French masculine nouns also have a feminine form. This is particularly true of words denoting an occupation un commerçant, une commerçante. Some simply add -e to the masculine form but many do not. Use your dictionary to find the feminine form of the following nouns:

| | |
|---|---|
| un astronaute | un piéton |
| un conseiller | un religieux |
| un enquêteur | un scout |
| un jongleur | un skieur |
| un musicien | un téléspectateur |

# 20 Which meaning?

Some words have more than one meaning and it's important to check that you have chosen the right one. In this dictionary different meanings of a word are marked by a bullet point (•). We have given you one meaning of the French words below. Use your dictionary to find another one.

| | | |
|---|---|---|
| une baie | • a bay | • ................................... |
| blanc | • white | • ................................... |
| un centimètre | • a centimetre | • ................................... |
| enlever | • to remove | • ................................... |
| un gorille | • a gorilla | • ................................... |
| le jour | • the day | • ................................... |
| mauvais | • bad | • ................................... |
| noir | • black | • ................................... |
| un pépin | • a pip | • ................................... |
| une radio | • a radio | • ................................... |
| un tailleur | • a tailor | • ................................... |
| voler | • to steal | • ................................... |

# 21 **Mots croisés**

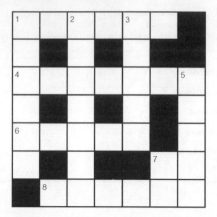

**Across**

1 avoid (*verb*) (6)
4 washing (*noun*) (7)
6 stadium (*noun*) (5)
7 him (*pronoun*) (2)
8 studies (*plural noun*) (6)

**Down**

1 church (*noun*) (6)
2 moment (*noun*) (7)
3 thorn (*noun*) (5)
5 they (*pronoun*) (5)
7 the (*determiner*) (2)

# 22 **Odd one out**

Hidden in this list of nouns is a verb. See if you can find it, then use your dictionary to check whether you are right.

abattoir        givre

bagarre        injure

colorier        lecture

enfer          ordre

foudre         sentier

# 23 **Filling in the gaps**

Here is a dialogue between a market stall holder and someone shopping for fruit and vegetables. Use your dictionary to help you fill in the names of the things she buys.

| | |
|---|---|
| CLIENTE: | Bonjour, monsieur. |
| MARCHAND: | Bonjour, madame. Que voulez-vous aujourd'hui? |
| CLIENTE: | Eh bien, nous avons des invités ce soir et j'ai besoin de plusieurs choses. Pour commencer je voudrais un kilo de belles (*tomatoes*), s'il vous plaît, et deux bottes de (*radishes*). C'est tellement bon, les (*radishes*) au beurre. |
| MARCHAND: | Très bien, et avec ça? |
| CLIENTE: | J'ai besoin d'une (*lettuce*), une grosse. |
| MARCHAND: | Voilà. Il y a autre chose? |
| CLIENTE: | Oui, oui. Je voudrais, deux kilos de (*potatoes*), une livre d'(*onions*), une livre de (*carrots*), un (*cauliflower*) et un (*cucumber*). |
| MARCHAND: | Et avec ça? |
| CLIENTE: | Les (*peaches*) sont bonnes aujourd'hui? |
| MARCHAND: | Oui, elles sont très bonnes. |
| CLIENTE: | Donnez-m'en un kilo et puis avec ça une livre de (*plums*) et une barquette de (*raspberries*). |
| MARCHAND: | Bien, madame. Ce sera tout? |
| CLIENTE: | Oui, merci, c'est tout pour aujourd'hui. |

# 24 **French reflexive verbs**

Use your dictionary to find the French equivalents of the following English sentences:

(a) I'm going to get changed.

(b) We argue about money.

(c) He easily gets bored.

(d) She always parks near the office.

(e) Sometimes I get impatient.

(f) What's happening?

(g) I always wake up at 7 o'clock.

(h) The war's coming to an end.

(i) Stamps are sold in the cafés.

(j) She's great fun.

## Answers

**1**
**Nouns:** gaz, France, choix, qualité, Français, objet, écran, coins, beauté, yeux, poste, télévision, téléviseur, four.
**Adjectives:** naturel, magnifique, plat, carrés, luisante, nouveau.

**2**
**Masculine nouns:** sac, feutre, hippopotame, pull, imperméable, orage, ver.
**Feminine nouns:** pâtisserie, sonnette, île, bibliothèque, magie, huître, pêche, selle, serveuse.

**3**
**ça** ne fait rien (*it doesn't matter*)
**c'**est un cadeau (*it's a present*)
**ce** sont des détails sans importance (*these are unimportant details*)
il **l'**a invitée (*he invited her*)
elle ne **me** parle pas (*she won't speak to me*)
donne-**la**-**moi** (*give it to me*)
je **lui** ai prêté ma robe (*I lent her my dress*)
elles **se** sont fait mal (*they hurt themselves*)
il **vous l'**a prêté (*he lent it to you*)
donne-**nous** l'adresse (*give us the address*)

**4**
Pierre **descend** la rue sur son vélo.
Sophie ne **connaît** pas le nom du magasin.
Les sapeurs pompiers **arriveront** dans cinq minutes.
Chaque année nous **passons** nos vacances d'été en France.
Ma sœur **a** un bassin avec des poissons dans son jardin.

**5**
enseignement, médicament, stationnement, vêtement (*all masculine nouns*).

**6**
**L'ours Félix** a dévoré **neuf moutons** depuis son arrivée dans les Pyrénées. Hier, **l'animal** (*or* **Félix**), transplanté des forêts de Slovénie, a entièrement dévoré une brebis qui se trouvait près de Portet-d'Aspet en Haute-Garonne. **Le département** a aussitôt compensé **le berger** de la perte de sa bête. **Le 'tarif'** est de 600F pour l'attaque, qui ne sont versés qu'une seule fois, puis de 800F par mouton. Pourtant, **les bergers** devraient se rassurer: **les jeunes ours** sont toujours plus prédateurs que les vieux. Avec le temps, **Félix** (*or* **l'animal**) perdra **sa passion** pour la chasse.
**Subjects:** l'ours Félix, l'animal, le département, le 'tarif', les bergers, les jeunes ours, Félix.
**Objects:** neuf moutons, une brebis, le berger, sa passion.

**7**

**8**
Ma chère Louise,
Merci pour ta lettre que j'ai reçue hier. Ce matin, comme d'habitude, je suis allée faire mes courses au marché où j'ai rencontré Madame Bonnard, que tu connais très bien, je crois. Elle m'a dit que sa fille aînée, Sandrine, a fini ses études et qu'elle part en Grèce faire un stage de six mois dans un hôtel. Ça devrait être amusant, non? Qu'est-ce que tu comptes faire toi-même cet été? Est-ce que tu restes en France ou espères-tu toujours visiter la Norvège? Moi, je vais passer deux semaines dans la maison de campagne de mon frère à Gaillac . . .

**9**
encourager **en** | énerver
horreur **historique** | hôtesse
liquide **librairie** | loge
mener **mélanger** | mesure
renseigner **renne** | requin
sérieux **séjour** | serré
vieil **version** | vietnamien

**10**
un livre = *a book*
une livre = *a pound*

un manche = *a handle*
une manche = *a sleeve*

un mode (de vie) = *a (life)style*
une mode = *a fashion*

un moule = *a mould*
une moule = *a mussel*

un poêle = *a stove*
une poêle = *a frying pan*

un tour = *a trick, a turn*
une tour = *a tower*

un vase = *a vase*
la vase = *mud*

un voile = *a veil*
une voile = *a sail*

## 11

Jean-Pierre a longtemps refusé d'accepter la proposition de son ami, Michel, mais finalement il a décidé de dire oui. Michel avait envie **de** faire une randonnée de plusieurs semaines à vélo à travers l'Europe et avait tout fait pour convaincre son ami **de** venir avec lui. A vrai dire, Jean-Pierre préférait passer son temps à se bronzer sur la plage, mais il essayait toujours **de** faire plaisir à son copain et c'est pour cette raison que Michel est parvenu à le persuader. Bien entendu, c'est Michel qui s'est chargé **de** faire tous les préparatifs du voyage, alors que Jean-Pierre a commencé à tracer l'itinéraire sur la carte.

## 12

to aim *viser*; to block *bloquer*; to camp *camper*; to dance *danser*; to finish *finir*; to iron *repasser*; to joke *plaisanter*; to kiss *embrasser*; to milk *traire*; to paint *peindre*; to question *interroger*; to sail *voyager en bateau*; to train *former, entraîner*; to welcome *accueillir*; to yell *crier*.

## 13

Elle a de **beaux** yeux et de **belles** dents.

Notre **ancienne** maison était très **vieille**.

C'est une très **bonne** idée.

La **première** chose à faire est de trouver l'entrée **secrète**.

Elles sont si **heureuses**.

La neige est **blanche**.

Il a une **nouvelle** voiture.

Mon père est **italien**, mais ma mère est **norvégienne**.

## 14

**Masculine noun:** dessous, gendre, ouest, vers.

**Feminine noun:** chasse, mouche.

**Pronoun:** en, que, toi-même.

**Adjective:** juste, ouest, pâle.

**Preposition:** en, vers.

**Verb:** inscrire, relire.

**Adverb:** dessous, facilement, juste, que.

**Determiner:** notre.

**Conjunction:** que.

## 15

Le bouton s'est détaché.
Les éboueurs ont enlevé les déchets.
Elle élève ses enfants toute seule.
Ils ont cessé de fumer.
Je vais enlever mes chaussures.

## 16

bijoux, cas, chevaux, cheveux, croix, manteaux, pneus, travaux, trous, vieux

## 17

*actuellement* currently, at the moment
*un bonnet* a cap, a hat
*un car* a coach, bus
*une cave* a cellar
*une course* a race, an errand
*décevoir* to disappoint
*délivrer* to free, to issue
*un engin* a device, a vehicle
*éventuellement* possibly, if necessary
*gentil* kind, nice
*le matériel* the equipment
*le pétrole* oil, petroleum
*un pin* a pine
*sale* dirty
*sensible* sensitive

## 18

actually *en fait, vraiment, exactement*
a bonnet *un capot*
a cap *une casquette, un capuchon, une capsule*
a car *une voiture*
a cave *une grotte*
a course *un cours, un plat*
to deceive *tromper*
to deliver *livrer*
an engine *un moteur, une locomotive*
eventually *finalement*
gentle *doux*
material *la documentation* (a material *une matière, une substance, un tissu, une étoffe*)
petrol *l'essence*
a pin *une épingle*
a sale *une solde*
sensible *raisonnable, judicieux, pratique*

## 19

une astronaute
une conseillère
une enquêtrice
une jongleuse
une musicienne
une piétonne
une religieuse
une scoute
une skieuse
une téléspectatrice

## 20

| *une baie* | • a bay | • a berry |
|---|---|---|
| *blanc* | • white | • blank |
| *un centimètre* | • a centimetre | • a tape measure |
| *enlever* | • to remove | • to kidnap |
| *un gorille* | • a gorilla | • a bodyguard |
| *le jour* | • the day | • daylight |
| *mauvais* | • bad | • wrong |
| *noir* | • black | • dark |
| *un pépin* | • a pip | • a slight problem |
| *une radio* | • a radio | • an X-ray |
| *un tailleur* | • a tailor | • a (woman's) suit |
| *voler* | • to steal | • to fly |

**21**

|   |   |   |   |   |   |   |
|---|---|---|---|---|---|---|
| ¹É | V | ²I | T | ³E | R |   |
| G |   | N |   | P |   |   |
| ⁴L | E | S | S | I | V | ⁵E |
| I |   | T |   | N |   | L |
| ⁶S | T | A | D | E |   | L |
| E |   | N |   |   | ⁷L | E |
|   | ⁸É | T | U | D | E | S |

**22**

The verb is *colorier*.

**23**

tomates, radis, salade (*or* laitue), pommes de terre, oignons, carottes, chou-fleur, concombre, pêches, prunes, framboises

**24**

(a) Je vais **me changer**.

(b) Nous **nous disputons** pour des questions d'argent.

(c) Il **s'ennuie** facilement.

(d) Elle **se gare** toujours près du bureau.

(e) Parfois je **m'impatiente**.

(f) Qu'est-ce qui **se passe**?

(g) Je **me réveille** toujours à sept heures.

(h) La guerre **se termine**.

(i) Les timbres **se vendent** dans les cafés.

(j) On **s'amuse** bien avec elle.

**a, an** *determiner*
a, an = un/une
a dog = un chien
an exhibition = une exposition
my mother's a doctor = ma mère est
médecin

**able** *adjective*
* (*having the possibility*)
to be able to [walk | travel | sleep …]
= pouvoir [marcher | voyager | dormir …]
* (*having the skill or knowledge*)
to be able to [drive | read | type …] = savoir
[conduire | lire | taper à la machine …]

**aboard** *adverb*
to go aboard = monter à bord

**about**

! Often about occurs in combinations with
verbs, for example: bring about, run about
etc. To find the correct translations for this
type of verb, look up the separate
dictionary entries at bring, run etc.

**1** *preposition*
it's a book about France = c'est un livre
sur la France
I need some information about the town
= j'ai besoin de renseignements sur la
ville
**2** *adverb*
= environ
I have about 200 euros left = il me reste
environ 200 euros
Oxford is about 40 km from here = Oxford
est à environ 40 km d'ici
we arrived at about midnight = nous
sommes arrivés vers minuit
**3 to be about to** = être sur le point de
to be about to [leave | cry | fall asleep …]
= être sur le point de [partir | pleurer |
s'endormir …]

**above**
**1** *preposition*
= au-dessus de
their apartment is above the shop = leur
appartement se trouve au-dessus de la
boutique
there is a shelf above it = il y a une
étagère au-dessus
**2 above all** = surtout

**abroad** *adverb*
= à l'étranger
to go abroad = aller à l'étranger

**absent** *adjective*
= absent/absente

**accent** *noun*
an accent = un accent

**accept** *verb*
= accepter

**accident** *noun*
* (*causing injury or damage*)
an accident = un accident
a car accident = un accident de voiture
* I heard about it by accident = je l'ai appris
par hasard

**accommodation** *noun*
to look for accommodation = chercher un
logement

**accompany** *verb*
= accompagner

**account** *noun*
* (*in a bank or post office*)
an account = un compte
there's money in my account = il y a de
l'argent sur mon compte
* to take travelling expenses into account
= tenir compte des frais de voyage

**accountant** *noun* ▶ 315|
an accountant = un comptable/une
comptable

**accuse** *verb*
to accuse someone of cheating = accuser
quelqu'un de tricher

**across** *preposition*
* to go across the street = traverser la rue
to run across the street = traverser la rue
en courant
to swim across the Channel = traverser la
Manche à la nage
a journey across the desert = un voyage à
travers le désert
* (*on the other side of*) = de l'autre côté de
he lives across the street = il habite de
l'autre côté de la rue

**act** *verb*
* (*to do something*) = agir
* (*to play a role*) = jouer

**activity** *noun*
an activity = une activité
sports activities = les activités sportives

**actor** *noun* ▶ 315|
an actor = un acteur

**actress** *noun* ▶ 315|
an actress = une actrice

**actually** *adverb*

! Note that actually is not translated by
actuellement.

actually, she's a very good athlete = en
fait, c'est une très bonne athlète
what actually happened? = qu'est-ce qui
s'est passé exactement?

**adapt** *verb*
= s'adapter (**!** + *être*)

**add** *verb*
* (*to put in*) = ajouter
* (*in arithmetic*) = additionner

**address** *noun*
an address = une adresse

**admire** *verb*
= admirer

**admit** *verb*
* (*to recognize as being true*) = reconnaître
* (*to own up*) = avouer
did she admit that she'd stolen the money? = est-ce qu'elle a avoué avoir volé l'argent?
* to be admitted to (the) hospital = être hospitalisé/hospitalisée

**adolescent** *noun*
an adolescent = un adolescent/une adolescente

**adopt** *verb*
= adopter

**adult** *noun*
an adult = un adulte/une adulte

**advantage** *noun*
* (*a positive point*)
an advantage = un avantage
* to take advantage of a situation = profiter d'une situation

**adventure** *noun*
an adventure = une aventure

**advertisement** *noun*
* (*on TV, in the cinema*)
an advertisement = une publicité
* (*in a newspaper*)
an advertisement = une (petite) annonce
to answer job advertisements = répondre aux offres d'emploi

**advertising** *noun*
advertising = la publicité

**advice** *noun*
a piece of advice = un conseil
advice = des conseils

**advise** *verb*
to advise someone to rest = conseiller à quelqu'un de se reposer
I've been advised not to go there = on m'a déconseillé d'y aller

**aerial** *noun*
an aerial = une antenne

**aerobics** *noun* ▶ 248 |
aerobics = l'aérobic (*masculine*)

**affect** *verb*
the farmers have been affected by the drought = les fermiers ont été touchés par la sécheresse
the war is bound to affect tourism = la guerre va sûrement avoir des conséquences pour le tourisme

**afford** *verb*
to be able to afford a car = avoir les moyens d'acheter une voiture

**afraid** *adjective*
to be afraid = avoir peur
to be afraid of spiders = avoir peur des araignées
to be afraid to go out = avoir peur de sortir

**Africa** *noun* ▶ 218 |
Africa = l'Afrique (*feminine*)

**African** ▶ 275 |
**1** *adjective*
= africain/africaine
**2** *noun*
the Africans = les Africains (*masculine*)

**after**
**1** *preposition*
= après
we'll leave after breakfast = nous partirons après le petit déjeuner
the day after tomorrow = après-demain
**2** *conjunction*
after we had eaten, we went for a walk = après avoir mangé, nous sommes allés nous promener
they went in after the film had started = ils sont entrés après le début du film
**3 after all** = après tout

**afternoon** *noun* ▶ 211 |, ▶ 356 |
an afternoon = un après-midi, une après-midi

**afterwards**, **afterward** (*US English*)
*adverb*
* (*after*) = après
* (*later*) = plus tard

**again** *adverb*
= encore
are you going camping again this year? = est-ce que vous allez encore camper cette année?

**!** *Note that there will very often be a specific French verb to translate the idea of doing something again—to start again = recommencer, to do the work again = refaire le travail, to see someone again = revoir quelqu'un.*

**against** *preposition*
= contre

**age** *noun* ▶ 187 |
age = l'âge (*masculine*)
he's my age, he's the same age as me = il a mon âge

**aged** *adjective*
= âgé de/âgée de
a boy aged 13 = un garçon âgé de 13 ans

**ago** *adverb*
two weeks ago = il y a deux semaines
long ago = il y a longtemps

# Age

Note that, where English says **to be X years old**, French says **avoir X ans** (*to have X years*).

## How old?

| | |
|---|---|
| *how old **are you**?* | = quel âge **as-tu**? |
| *what age **is she**?* | = quel âge **a-t-elle**? |

The word **ans** (*years*) is never dropped:

| | |
|---|---|
| *he is forty-one (years old)* | = il a quarante et un **ans** |
| *the house is a hundred years old* | = la maison a cent **ans** |
| *a man of fifty* | = un homme de cinquante **ans** |

Note the use of **de** after **âgé**:

| | |
|---|---|
| *a woman aged thirty* | = une femme âgée **de** trente ans |

## Comparing ages

| | |
|---|---|
| *I'm older **than** you* | = je suis plus âgé **que** toi |
| *she's younger **than** him* | = elle est plus jeune **que** lui |
| *Anne's two years **younger*** | = Anne a deux ans **de moins** |
| *Tom's five years **older than** Jo* | = Tom a cinq ans **de plus que** Jo |

## Approximate ages

| | |
|---|---|
| *he is **about** fifty* | = il a **environ** cinquante ans |
| *she's **just over** sixty* | = elle **vient** d'avoir soixante ans |
| *games for **the under** twelves* | = jeux pour **les moins de** douze ans |
| *only for **the over** eighteens* | = seulement pour **les plus de** dix-huit ans |

---

**agree** *verb*
- (*to have the same opinion*) = être d'accord
  **I don't agree with you** = je ne suis pas d'accord avec toi
- (*to be ready*)
  **to agree to come a week later** = accepter de venir une semaine plus tard
- (*to reach a decision*) = se mettre d'accord
  (**!** + *être*)

**agriculture** *noun*
  **agriculture** = l'agriculture (*feminine*)

**ahead** *adverb*
  **to go on ahead** = partir en avant

**Aids** *noun* ▶ 266 |
  **Aids** = le sida

**aim**
**1** *noun*
  **an aim** = un but
**2** *verb*
- (*to be directed at*)
  **to be aimed at young people** = viser les jeunes
- (*when using a weapon*)
  **to aim a rifle at someone** = braquer un fusil sur quelqu'un

**air** *noun*
  **air** = l'air (*masculine*)
  **to throw a ball up into the air** = lancer un ballon en l'air
  **to let the air out of a tyre** = dégonfler un pneu

**air force** *noun*
  **the air force** = l'armée de l'air
  | **!** Note that **armée** is feminine.

**air hostess** *noun* ▶ 315 | (*British English*)
  **an air hostess** = une hôtesse de l'air

**airmail** *noun*
  **to send a letter by airmail** = envoyer une lettre par avion

**airport** *noun*
  **an airport** = un aéroport

**alarm clock** *noun*
  **an alarm clock** = un réveil

**alcohol** *noun*
  **alcohol** = l'alcool (*masculine*)

**alive** *adjective*
  = vivant/vivante

**all**
**1** *determiner*
  = tout/toute (+ *singular*)
  = tous/toutes (+ *plural*)
  **I spent all week working** = j'ai passé toute la semaine à travailler
  **all the men have left** = tous les hommes sont partis
**2** *pronoun*
  = tout
  **that's all** = c'est tout
  **after all we've done** = après tout ce que nous avons fait

**3** *adverb*
to be all alone = être tout seul/toute seule
all along the street = tout le long de la rue

**allow** *verb*
to allow someone to [work | play | leave ...]
= permettre à quelqu'un de [travailler |
jouer | partir ...]
they don't allow me to smoke at home
= on ne me permet pas de fumer à la
maison
smoking is not allowed = il est interdit de
fumer

**all right** *adjective*
• (*when giving your opinion*) = pas mal✶
the film was all right = le film n'était pas
mal✶
• (*when talking about health*)
are you all right? = ça va?
• (*when asking someone's opinion*)
is it all right if I come later? = est-ce que ça
va si je viens plus tard?
come at about nine, all right? = viens vers
neuf heures, d'accord?
• (*when agreeing*) = d'accord

**almond** *noun*
an almond = une amande

**almost** *adverb*
= presque
we're almost there = nous sommes
presque arrivés
I almost forgot = j'ai failli oublier

**alone**
**1** *adjective*
= seul/seule
to be all alone = être tout seul/toute seule
leave me alone! = laisse-moi tranquille!
**2** *adverb*
[to work | to live | to travel ...] alone
= [travailler | vivre | voyager ...] seul/seule

**along** *preposition*
= le long de
there are seats all along the canal = il y a
des bancs tout le long du canal

**aloud** *adverb*
to read aloud = lire à haute voix

**already** *adverb*
= déjà
it's ten o'clock already = il est déjà dix
heures
have you finished already? = tu as déjà
fini?

**also** *adverb*
= aussi

**although** *conjunction*
= bien que
although she's strict, she's fair = bien
qu'elle soit sévère, elle est juste

---

**✶** in informal situations

**!** *Note that the subjunctive is used after*
bien que.

**always** *adverb*
= toujours
I always go to France in (the) summer = je
vais toujours en France en été

**amazed** *adjective*
= stupéfait/stupéfaite

**amazing** *adjective*
= extraordinaire

**ambition** *noun*
an ambition = une ambition

**ambitious** *adjective*
= ambitieux/ambitieuse

**ambulance** *noun*
an ambulance = une ambulance

**America** *noun* ▶ 218|
America = l'Amérique (*feminine*)

**American** ▶ 275|
**1** *adjective*
= américain/américaine
**2** *noun*
the Americans = les Américains
(*masculine*)

**among, amongst** *preposition*
• (*in the middle of*) = parmi
the ruins are hidden among the trees = les
ruines sont cachées parmi les arbres
• (*in a particular group*) = chez
unemployment among young people = le
chômage chez les jeunes

**amount** *noun*
an amount = une quantité

**amusement arcade** *noun*
an amusement arcade = une salle de jeux
électroniques

**amusement park** *noun*
an amusement park = un parc
d'attractions

**an** ▶ a

**ancestor** *noun*
an ancestor = un ancêtre/une ancêtre

**and** *conjunction*
• and = et
a red and white sweater = un pull rouge
et blanc
she stood up and went out = elle s'est
levée et elle est sortie
to go faster and faster = aller de plus en
plus vite
• (*in numbers, and is not translated*)
three hundred and sixty-five = trois cent
soixante-cinq

**anger** *noun*
anger = la colère

**A**

**angry** *adjective*
to be angry = être en colère
to be angry with someone = être en colère
contre quelqu'un

**animal** *noun*
an animal = un animal
farm animals = les animaux de la ferme

**ankle** *noun* ▶ 201 |
the ankle = la cheville

**announcement** *noun*
an announcement = une annonce

**annoy** *verb*
= agacer

**annoyed** *adjective*
to be annoyed with someone = être
fâché/fâchée contre quelqu'un

**another**
1 *determiner*
• another = un autre/une autre, encore
un/une
another cup of coffee? = encore un café?
I'll buy another ticket for Alison = je vais
acheter un autre billet pour Alison
• (*different*) = un autre/une autre
there's another way of doing it = il y a une
autre façon de le faire
she's got another boyfriend now = elle a
un nouveau copain maintenant
2 *pronoun*
there are some pears left—would you like
another? = il reste des poires—est-ce que
tu en veux encore une?

! Note that it is necessary to use en,
which might be translated as 'of it' or 'of
them', with pronouns like another. See
also any, a few, a lot etc for this use of en.

**answer**
1 *noun*
an answer = une réponse
did you get an answer? = est-ce que tu as
eu une réponse?
there's no answer (*at the door*) = il n'y a
personne
(*on the phone*) = ça ne répond pas
2 *verb*
= répondre
to answer a question = répondre à une
question
to answer the phone = répondre au
téléphone
**answer back** = répondre

**answering machine** *noun*
an answering machine = un répondeur
(téléphonique)

**ant** *noun*
an ant = une fourmi

**antique** *noun*
an antique = un objet ancien

**antique shop** *noun*
an antique shop = un magasin
d'antiquités

**anxious** *adjective*
= inquiet/inquiète, anxieux/anxieuse
then I started to get anxious = j'ai
commencé à m'inquiéter à ce moment-
là

**any**
1 *determiner*
• (*in questions*) = du/de la (! de l' + *vowel or
mute h*)
= des (+ *plural*)
is there any tea? = est-ce qu'il y a du thé?
is there any tart left? = est-ce qu'il reste de
la tarte?
have you got any money? = est-ce que
vous avez de l'argent?
• (*with the negative*) = de (! d' + *vowel or
mute h*)
we don't have any bread = nous n'avons
pas de pain
I didn't have any friends = je n'avais pas
d'amis
• (*whatever*)
take any cup you like = prenez n'importe
quelle tasse
2 *pronoun*
= en
do you have any? = est-ce que vous en
avez?
he doesn't have any = il n'en a pas

! Note that it is necessary to use en,
which might be translated as 'of it' or 'of
them', with pronouns like any. See also
another, a few, a lot etc for this use of en.

**anyone** *pronoun* (*also* **anybody**)
• (*in questions*) = quelqu'un
do you know anyone who could help us?
= est-ce que tu connais quelqu'un qui
pourrait nous aider?
• (*with the negative*) = personne
there isn't anyone in the house = il n'y a
personne dans la maison
• (*everyone*)
anyone could do it = n'importe qui
pourrait le faire

**anything** *pronoun*
• (*in questions*) = quelque chose
can I do anything to help? = est-ce que je
peux faire quelque chose pour vous
aider?
• (*with the negative*) = rien
she didn't say anything = elle n'a rien dit
there isn't anything to do here = il n'y a
rien à faire ici
• (*everything*) = tout
I like anything to do with sports = j'aime
tout ce qui a rapport au sport

**anyway** *adverb*
= de toute façon
I didn't want to go there anyway = de
toute façon je ne voulais pas y aller

**anywhere** *adverb*
* (*in questions*) = quelque part
  can you see a phone booth anywhere?
  = est-ce que tu vois une cabine
  téléphonique quelque part?
* (*with the negative*) = nulle part
  you can't go anywhere = on ne peut aller
  nulle part
* (*any place*)
  we can meet anywhere you like = nous
  pouvons nous retrouver où tu veux

**apart**
**1** *adjective*
  they don't like being apart = ils n'aiment
  pas être séparés
**2 apart from** = à part

**apartment** *noun*
  an apartment = un appartement

**apartment block** *noun*
  an apartment block = un immeuble

**apologize** *verb*
  = s'excuser (**!** + *être*)

**apology** *noun*
  an apology = des excuses (*feminine plural*)

**appear** *verb*
* (*to seem*)
  to appear happy = avoir l'air
  heureux/heureuse
* (*to come into view*) = apparaître (**!** + *être*)

**appetite** *noun*
  the appetite = l'appétit (*masculine*)
  to have a good appetite = avoir bon
  appétit

**apple** *noun*
  an apple = une pomme

**apple juice** *noun*
  apple juice = le jus de pomme

**appliance** *noun*
  an appliance = un appareil

**application** *noun*
  an application = une candidature

**apply** *verb*
  to apply for a job = poser sa candidature
  pour un emploi
  to apply for a passport = faire une
  demande de passeport

**appointment** *noun*
  an appointment = un rendez-vous
  to make an appointment = prendre
  rendez-vous

**appreciate** *verb*

  **!** *Note that* apprécier *usually means to
  like.*

  I'd appreciate it if you could let me know
  = je vous serais reconnaissant de
  m'informer

**approach** *verb*
  = s'approcher de (**!** + *être*)

**approve** *verb*
  to approve of someone = apprécier
  quelqu'un

**apricot** *noun*
  an apricot = un abricot

**April** *noun* ▶ **222** |
  April = avril (*masculine*)

**Aquarius** *noun*
  Aquarius = Verseau (*masculine*)

**architect** *noun* ▶ **315** |
  an architect = un architecte/une
  architecte

**area** *noun*
  an area (*of a country*) = une région
  (*of a city*) = un quartier
  in the poorer areas of Paris = dans les
  quartiers plus défavorisés de Paris

**area code** *noun* (*US English*)
  an area code = un indicatif

**argue** *verb*
* (*to quarrel*) = se disputer (**!** + *être*)
  to argue about money = se disputer pour
  des questions d'argent
* (*to discuss a subject*) = discuter
  to argue about politics = discuter de
  politique

**argument** *noun*
  an argument = une dispute
  to have an argument with someone = se
  disputer avec quelqu'un

**Aries** *noun*
  Aries = Bélier (*masculine*)

**arm** *noun* ▶ **201** |
  the arm = le bras
  she's hurt her arm = elle s'est fait mal au
  bras

**armchair** *noun*
  an armchair = un fauteuil

**armed** *adjective*
  = armé/armée

**arms** *noun*
  arms = les armes (*feminine*)

**army** *noun*
  an army = une armée
  to join the army = s'engager (**!** + *être*)

**around**

  **!** *Often* around *occurs in combinations
  with verbs, for example:* run around, turn
  around *etc. To find the correct
  translations for this type of verb, look up
  the separate dictionary entries at* run, turn
  *etc.*

**1** *preposition*
= autour de
there are trees all around the garden = il y
a des arbres tout autour du jardin
the people around me were speaking
French = les gens autour de moi
parlaient français
to go around the world = faire le tour du
monde
**2** *adverb*
= environ
it costs around £200 = ça coûte environ
200 livres sterling
we'll be there at around four o'clock
= nous serons là vers quatre heures

**arrange** *verb*
to arrange a break in Italy = organiser des
vacances en Italie
to arrange to have lunch together
= s'arranger pour déjeuner ensemble

**arrest** *verb*
= arrêter

**arrive** *verb*
= arriver (**!** + être)
we arrived at the station at noon = nous
sommes arrivés à la gare à midi

**arrow** *noun*
an arrow = une flèche

**art** *noun*
• art = l'art (*masculine*)
• (*as a school subject*)
art = le dessin

**art gallery** *noun*
an art gallery = un musée d'art

**artificial** *adjective*
= artificiel/artificielle

**artist** *noun* ▶ **315**
an artist = un artiste/une artiste

**arts and crafts** *noun*
arts and crafts = les travaux manuels
**!** *Note that* travaux *is masculine plural.*

**as**
**1** *conjunction*
• as = comme
as you know, we're leaving = comme vous
le savez, nous partons
• (*at the time when*)
the phone rang as I was getting out of the
bath = le téléphone a sonné au moment
où je sortais du bain
I used to live there as a child = j'habitais
là quand j'étais enfant
• (*British English*) (*because, since*) = comme
as you were out, I left a message
= comme tu étais sorti j'ai laissé un
message
• (*when used with* the same)
my coat is the same as yours = j'ai le
même manteau que toi

**2** *preposition*
she's got a job as a teacher = elle a trouvé
un poste d'enseignante
he was dressed as a sailor = il était
habillé en marin
**3** *adverb*
as [intelligent | rich | strong ...] as = aussi
[intelligent | riche | fort ...] que
go there as fast as you can = vas-y aussi
vite que possible
I have as much work as you = j'ai autant
de travail que toi
he plays the piano as well as his sister
= il joue du piano aussi bien que sa sœur
**4 as usual** = comme d'habitude

**ashamed** *adjective*
to be ashamed = avoir honte

**ashes** *noun*
ashes = les cendres (*feminine*)

**ashtray** *noun*
an ashtray = un cendrier

**Asia** *noun* ▶ **218**
Asia = l'Asie (*feminine*)

**Asian** *adjective* ▶ **275**
(*from China, Japan*) = asiatique

**ask** *verb*
• to ask = demander
he asked me my name = il m'a demandé
mon nom
to ask someone to [phone | take a message |
do the shopping ...] = demander à
quelqu'un de [téléphoner | prendre un
message | faire les courses ...]
I'll ask them if they want to come = je vais
leur demander s'ils veulent venir
to ask for money = demander de l'argent
to ask to speak to someone = demander à
parler à quelqu'un
to ask a question = poser une question
• (*to invite*) = inviter
to ask some friends to dinner = inviter des
amis à dîner
he asked her out = il l'a invitée à sortir
avec lui
• (*to look for information*) = se renseigner
(**!** + être)
did you ask about the tickets? = est-ce que
tu t'es renseigné pour les billets?

**asleep** *adjective*
to be asleep = dormir
to fall asleep = s'endormir (**!** + être)

**assemble** *verb*
= se rassembler (**!** + être)

**assistant** *noun*
an assistant = un assistant/une assistante

**asylum seeker** *noun*
an asylum seeker = un demandeur d'asile/une
demandeuse d'asile

**at** *preposition*

  **!** *There are many verbs which involve the use of* at, *like* look at, laugh at, point at *etc. For translations,* look up the entries at look, laugh, point *etc.*

- (*when talking about a position or place*) = à
  **we met at a concert** = nous nous sommes
  rencontrés à un concert
  **he's not at his desk** = il n'est pas à son
  bureau
  **at the** = au/à la (**!** à l' + *vowel or mute h*)
  = aux (+ *plural*)
  **they're at the clinic** = ils sont à la clinique
  **to be** [at home | at school | at work ...] = être [à
  la maison | à l'école | au travail ...]
- (*at the house, shop, practice of*) = chez
  **we'll be at Nathalie's** = nous serons chez
  Nathalie
  **he's got an appointment at the dentist's**
  = il a rendez-vous chez le dentiste
- (*when talking about time*) = à
  **the film starts at nine o'clock** = le film
  commence à neuf heures
- (*when talking about age*) = à
  **she was able to read at four years of age**
  = elle savait lire à l'âge de quatre ans

**athlete** *noun* ▶ 315 |
  **an athlete** = un athlète/une athlète

**athletics** *noun* ▶ 248 |
  **athletics** (*in Britain*) = l'athlétisme
  (*masculine singular*)
  (*in the US*) = les sports (*masculine*)

**Atlantic** *noun*
  **the Atlantic** = l'Atlantique (*masculine*)

**atmosphere** *noun*
- (*the air*)
  **the atmosphere** = l'atmosphère (*feminine*)
- (*a mood, a feeling*)
  **an atmosphere** = une ambiance

**at sign** *noun*
  **an at sign** = un arobas(e)

**attach** *verb*
  = attacher
  **to be attached to the wall** = être fixé/fixée
  au mur

**attachment** *noun*
  (*in an email*)
  **an attachment** = une pièce jointe

**attack** *verb*
  **to attack a town** = attaquer une ville
  **to attack someone in the street** = agresser
  quelqu'un dans la rue

**attempt**
**1** *verb*
  **to attempt to break the record** = tenter de
  battre le record
**2** *noun*
  **an attempt** = une tentative

**attend** *verb*
  **to attend the village school** = fréquenter
  l'école du village
  **to attend evening classes** = suivre des
  cours du soir

**attention** *noun*
  **attention** = l'attention (*feminine*)
  **to get someone's attention** = attirer
  l'attention de quelqu'un
  **to pay attention to the teacher** = écouter
  le professeur

**attic** *noun*
  **an attic** = un grenier

**attitude** *noun*
  **an attitude** = une attitude
  **he has a strange attitude toward(s)**
  **people** = il a une attitude bizarre envers
  les gens

**attract** *verb*
  = attirer

**attractive** *adjective*
  **to be attractive** = être
  séduisant/séduisante

**auburn** *adjective* ▶ 213 |
  = auburn (**!** *never changes*)

**audience** *noun*
  **an audience** = un public

**August** *noun* ▶ 222 |
  **August** = août (*masculine*)

**aunt** *noun*
  **an aunt** = une tante

**au pair** *noun*
  **an au pair** = une jeune fille au pair

**Australia** *noun* ▶ 218 |
  **Australia** = l'Australie (*feminine*)

**Australian** ▶ 275 |
**1** *adjective*
  = australien/australienne
**2** *noun*
  **the Australians** = les Australiens
  (*masculine*)

**Austria** *noun* ▶ 218 |
  **Austria** = l'Autriche (*feminine*)

**Austrian** ▶ 275 |
**1** *adjective*
  = autrichien/autrichienne
**2** *noun*
  **the Austrians** = les Autrichiens
  (*masculine*)

**author** *noun* ▶ 315 |
  **an author** = un écrivain

**automatic** *adjective*
  = automatique

**autumn** *noun*
  **autumn** = l'automne (*masculine*)
  **in (the) autumn** = en automne

**available** *adjective*
- (*on sale*)
  **tickets for the concert are still available**
  = il reste encore des billets pour le
  concert

**Bb**

* (fine) = disponible
are you available? = est-ce que vous êtes
disponible?

**average** *adjective*
= moyen/moyenne
the average teenager = l'adolescent
moyen

**avoid** *verb*
• (*to prevent*) = éviter
to avoid spending money = éviter de
dépenser de l'argent
• (*to stay away from*) = éviter

**awake** *adjective*
to be awake (*having slept*) = être
réveillé/réveillée
to stay awake = rester éveillé/éveillée
to keep someone awake = empêcher
quelqu'un de dormir

**award** *noun*
an award = un prix
she got the award for best actress = elle a
reçu le prix de la meilleure actrice

**aware** *adjective*
to be aware of the [problem | danger | risk ...]
= être conscient/consciente du [problème |
danger | risque ...]

**away** *adverb*
• (*absent*)
to be away = être absent/absente
she's away on business = elle est en
voyage d'affaires
• (*when talking about distances*)
to be far away = être loin
London is 40 km away = Londres est à 40
km d'ici

**awful** *adjective*
• (*no good*) = épouvantable
I thought the film was awful = j'ai trouvé le
film épouvantable
• (*causing shock*) = terrible
• I feel awful = je ne me sens pas bien du
tout

**awkward** *adjective*
(*describing a situation, a problem*)
= délicat/délicate
I feel awkward about telling him = ça me
gêne de le lui dire

**axe, ax** (*US English*) *noun*
an axe = une hache

**baby** *noun*
a baby = un bébé

**babysit** *verb*
= faire du babysitting

**back**

> **!** Often back occurs in combinations with
> verbs, for example: come back, get back,
> give back etc. To find the correct
> translations for this type of verb, look up
> the separate dictionary entries at come,
> get, give etc.

**1** *noun*
• (*part of the body*) ▶ **201**
the back = le dos
I've hurt my back = je me suis fait mal au
dos
• (*the rear*)
at the back of the supermarket = derrière
le supermarché
to sit in the back of the car = s'asseoir à
l'arrière de la voiture
**2** *adverb*
• to be back = être de retour
I'll be back in five minutes = je serai de
retour dans cinq minutes
• (*before in time*)
back in January = en janvier

**back door** *noun*
the back door = la porte de derrière

**background** *noun*
• (*of a person*)
a background = un milieu
• (*of a picture*)
the background = l'arrière-plan
(*masculine*)
in the background = à l'arrière-plan

**backpack** *noun*
a backpack = un sac à dos

**back seat** *noun*
the back seat = le siège arrière

**back to front** *adverb*
= sens devant derrière
to put a sweater on back to front = mettre
un pull sens devant derrière

**backwards, backward** (*US English*)
*adverb*
= en arrière

**bacon** *noun*
bacon = le bacon

**bad** *adjective*
* bad = mauvais/mauvaise (**!** *before the noun*)
  a bad film = un mauvais film
  a bad idea = une mauvaise idée
  I have some bad news = j'ai une mauvaise nouvelle
  to be bad [at maths | at tennis | at chess ...] = être mauvais/mauvaise [en maths | au tennis | aux échecs ...]
  it's a bad time to go on holiday = ce n'est pas le bon moment pour partir en vacances
  'was the film good?'—'not bad' = 'est-ce que le film était bien?'—'pas mal✶'
  smoking is bad for you = fumer est mauvais pour ta santé
* (*serious*) = grave
  a bad accident = un accident grave
* (*when talking about food*) = mauvais/mauvaise (**!** *before the noun*)
* (*not kind, not honest*) = méchant/méchante
  to feel bad = culpabiliser
* (*severe*)
  to have a bad cold = avoir un gros rhume

**badger** *noun*
  a badger = un blaireau

**badly** *adverb*
* (*not well*) = mal
  she slept badly = elle a mal dormi
* (*seriously*) = gravement
  he was badly injured = il a été gravement blessé

**badminton** *noun* ▶ 248 |
  badminton = le badminton

**bad-tempered** *adjective*
  to be bad-tempered = avoir mauvais caractère

**bag** *noun*
  a bag = un sac

**baggage** *noun*
  baggage = les bagages (*masculine plural*)

**bake** *verb*
* (*to prepare bread or cakes*) (*bread*) = faire du pain
  (*cakes*) = faire des gâteaux
* (*to be cooked in the oven*) = cuire (au four)

**baker** *noun* ▶ 315 |
  a baker = un boulanger/une boulangère

**bakery** *noun* ▶ 315 |
  a bakery = une boulangerie

**balance** *noun*
  balance = l'équilibre (*masculine*)
  to lose one's balance = perdre l'équilibre

**balcony** *noun*
  a balcony = un balcon

**bald** *adjective*
  = chauve

**ball** *noun*
  a ball (*in football, rugby or basketball*) = un ballon
  (*in tennis, golf or cricket*) = une balle
  (*in billiards*) = une bille
  to play ball = jouer au ballon

**ballet** *noun*
  ballet = le ballet

**balloon** *noun*
  a balloon = un ballon en baudruche

**ban** *verb*
  = interdire

**banana** *noun*
  a banana = une banane

**band** *noun*
  a band = un groupe
  a rock band = un groupe de rock

**bandage** *noun*
  a bandage = un bandage

**bang**
**1** *noun*
* (*a loud noise*)
  a bang = une détonation
* (*US English*) (*a fringe*)
  bangs = une frange
**2** *verb*
* (*to close with a bang*) = claquer
* (*to hurt*)
  to bang one's head on the wall = se cogner la tête contre le mur
* (*to hit*)
  to bang one's fist on the table = taper du poing sur la table

**bank** *noun*
  a bank = une banque

**bank account** *noun*
  a bank account = un compte bancaire

**bank holiday** *noun* (*British English*)
  a bank holiday = un jour férié

**bank manager** *noun* ▶ 315 |
  a bank manager = un directeur de banque

**bar** *noun*
* (*a place*)
  a bar = un bar
  to go to a bar = aller dans un bar
* (*a piece of metal*)
  a bar = une barre
* (*on a cage or window*)
  a bar = un barreau
* (*other uses*)
  a bar of soap = une savonnette
  a bar of chocolate = une tablette de chocolat

**barbecue** *noun*
  a barbecue = un barbecue

---

✶ in informal situations

**barely** adverb
= à peine
he was barely able to walk = il pouvait à
peine marcher

**bargain** noun
a bargain = une affaire

**bark** verb
= aboyer

**barn** noun
a barn = une grange

**barrel** noun
a barrel = un tonneau

**base** verb
to be based in London = être basé/basée à
Londres
to be based on a true story = être
basé/basée sur une histoire vécue

**baseball** noun ▶ 248 |
baseball = le base-ball

**basement** noun
a basement = un sous-sol

**basically** adverb
= au fond

**basin** noun
a basin = une cuvette

**basket** noun
a basket = un panier

**basketball** noun ▶ 248 |
basketball = le basket

**bat** noun
• (in cricket or baseball)
a bat = une batte
• (an animal)
a bat = une chauve-souris

**bath** noun
• to have a bath = prendre un bain
he's in the bath = il est dans son bain
• (a bathtub)
a bath = une baignoire

**bathroom** noun
• a bathroom = une salle de bains
• (US English) (the toilet)
to go to the bathroom = aller aux toilettes

**battery** noun
a battery (for a torch) = une pile
(for a car) = une batterie

**battle** noun
a battle = une bataille

**bay** noun
a bay = une baie

**be** verb
▶ 196 | See the boxed note on be for more
information and examples.

• to be – être
to be intelligent = être
intelligent/intelligente
he is tall = il est grand
we are rich = nous sommes riches
be polite! = sois poli!
It's a girl = c'est une fille
it's Monday = c'est lundi
it's past midnight = il est minuit passé
it's late = il est tard
the house has been sold = la maison a été
vendue
he'll be famous = il sera célèbre
• (when talking about jobs) ▶ 315 |
she is a lawyer = elle est avocat
he is a good doctor = c'est un bon
médecin
• (when describing a physical or mental
state)
to be [cold | hungry | afraid ...] = avoir [froid |
faim | peur ...]
my feet are cold = j'ai froid aux pieds
I am 18 = j'ai 18 ans
• (when describing the weather)
the weather is [fine | awful | cold ...] = il fait
[beau | mauvais | froid ...]
it's not too hot = il ne fait pas trop chaud
it's raining = il pleut
• (when talking about travelling)
I've never been to Spain = je ne suis
jamais allé en Espagne
have you ever been to Africa? = est-ce que
tu es déjà allé en Afrique?
• (when talking about health)
how are you? = comment allez-vous?,
comment vas tu?
I'm very well = je vais très bien
how is your mother? = comment va ta
mère?
• (in continuous tenses)
I'm coming = j'arrive
it was snowing = il neigeait
he is reading = il lit, il est en train de lire
• (in questions and short answers)
it's a lovely house, isn't it? = c'est une
belle maison, n'est-ce-pas?
'he's not here'—'yes he is' = 'il n'est pas
là'—'si'

**beach** noun
a beach = une plage

**beak** noun
a beak = un bec

**beam** noun
a beam = une poutre

**bean** noun
a bean = un haricot

**bear**
**1** noun
a bear = un ours
**2** verb
= supporter

**beard** noun
a beard = une barbe

# be

## As an ordinary verb

When **be** is used as a simple verb in *subject + verb* sentences, it is generally translated by **être**:

| | |
|---|---|
| *I am tired* | = je **suis** fatigué |
| *Paul is a doctor* | = Paul **est** médecin |

## As an auxiliary verb in progressive tenses

In English, **be** can be used in combination with another verb to form a progressive tense which allows us to express *an idea of duration, of something happening over a period of time.*

### The present

French uses the present tense to translate both forms of the English present tense, the simple and the progressive:

| | |
|---|---|
| *I work in London* | = je travaille à Londres |
| *I am working in London* | = je travaille à Londres |

To emphasize the idea of duration, **être en train de** + *infinitive* can be useful:

| | |
|---|---|
| *I'm working* | = je suis **en train de** travailler |
| *he's reading the paper* | = il est **en train de** lire le journal |

### The future

By using the progressive form of the present tense, you can also refer to the future:

| | |
|---|---|
| *we're going to Paris next week* | = nous allons à Paris la semaine prochaine |

### The past

To express the difference between *she watched TV* and *she was watching TV*, French uses the perfect and the imperfect tenses:

| | |
|---|---|
| *she **watched** TV* | = elle a **regardé** la télévision |
| *she **was watching** TV* | = elle **regardait** la télévision |

Again, to emphasize the idea of an activity happening over a period of time, the phrase **être en train de** + *infinitive* is useful:

| | |
|---|---|
| *she **was watching** TV when I phoned her* | = elle **était en train de regarder** la télévision quand je lui ai téléphoné |

## As part of the passive

In French, as in English, the passive is formed in exactly the same way using **être**:

| | |
|---|---|
| *the rabbit **was killed by** a fox* | = le lapin **a été tué** par un renard |
| *the window **has been fixed*** | = la fenêtre **a été réparée** |

However, in spoken French, the impersonal pronoun **on** is often used to translate the passive if there is a person clearly involved:

| | |
|---|---|
| *the window has been fixed* | = **on** a réparé la fenêtre |

## In short questions

With questions like *aren't you?, wasn't she?*, the general French phrase **n'est-ce pas?** can be useful in specific cases:

| | |
|---|---|
| *you're a doctor, **aren't you?*** | = vous êtes médecin, **n'est-ce pas?** |

With negative questions, **par hasard** can be useful:

| | |
|---|---|
| *he's not there, **is he?*** | = il n'est pas là **par hasard?** |

## In short answers

There is no French equivalent for the verb in short answers such as *no, he's not, yes, we were* etc.

| | |
|---|---|
| *'is he around?' — 'no, he's not'* | = 'est-ce qu'il est là?' — 'non' |
| *'are you coming?'— 'yes, I am'* | = 'est-ce que tu viens?' — 'oui' |

If answering 'yes' to contradict a negative statement, the most useful translation is **si**:

| | |
|---|---|
| *'you're **not** coming, are you?' — '**yes, I am'*** | = 'tu **ne** viens pas?' — '**si**' |

**beat** *verb*
- (*to hit hard*) = battre
- (*in cooking*) = battre
- (*to win against*) = battre
  Scotland beat England two nil = l'Écosse a battu l'Angleterre deux à zéro
**beat up** = battre

**beautiful** *adjective*
= beau/belle (**!** *before the noun*)

> **!** *Note that* **bel** *is used instead of* **beau** *before masculine nouns beginning with a vowel (*endroit*) or a mute h (*hôtel*). The plural of* **beau** *and* **bel** *is* **beaux**.

a beautiful garden = un beau jardin
a beautiful girl = une belle fille
a beautiful place = un bel endroit
they are beautiful cities = ce sont de belles villes

**beauty** *noun*
beauty = la beauté

**because**
**1** *conjunction*
= parce que
he did it because it was necessary = il l'a fait parce que c'était nécessaire
**2 because of** = à cause de
we didn't go out because of the rain = nous ne sommes pas sortis à cause de la pluie

**become** *verb*
= devenir
to become an adult = devenir adulte

**bed** *noun*
a bed = un lit
to go to bed = se coucher (**!** + *être*)

**bedroom** *noun*
a bedroom = une chambre

**bee** *noun*
a bee = une abeille

**beef** *noun*
beef = le bœuf
roast beef = le rosbif

**beer** *noun*
- (*the product*)
  beer = la bière
- (*a glass of beer*)
  a beer = une bière

**beet, beetroot** (*British English*) *noun*
a beet(root) = une betterave

**before**
**1** *preposition*
= avant
before the holidays = avant les vacances
the day before yesterday = avant-hier
the day before the exam = la veille de l'examen

**2** *adjective*
= précédent/précédente, d'avant
the week before = la semaine précédente, la semaine d'avant
the day before = la veille
**3** *adverb*
= avant
two months before = deux mois avant
have you been to Paris before? = est-ce que tu es déjà allé à Paris?
**4** *conjunction*
I'd like to see him before I go = j'aimerais le voir avant de partir
I'd like to see him before he goes = j'aimerais le voir avant son départ

**beg** *verb*
= mendier

**beggar** *noun*
a beggar = un mendiant/une mendiante

**begin** *verb*
= commencer
to begin [working | laughing | raining ...] = commencer à [travailler | rire | pleuvoir ...]

**beginner** *noun*
a beginner = un débutant/une débutante

**beginning** *noun*
the beginning = le début
in the beginning = au début
at the beginning of May = début mai

**behave** *verb*
= se conduire (**!** + *être*)
he behaved badly = il s'est mal conduit
to be well behaved = être sage
behave yourself! = tiens-toi bien!

**behaviour** (*British English*), **behavior** (*US English*) *noun*
behaviour = la conduite

**behind** *preposition*
= derrière
I looked behind me = j'ai regardé derrière moi

**Belgian** ▶ 275 |
**1** *adjective*
= belge
**2** *noun*
the Belgians = les Belges (*masculine*)

**Belgium** *noun* ▶ 218 |
Belgium = la Belgique

**believe** *verb*
= croire

**bell** *noun*
- (*in a church*)
  a bell = une cloche
- (*on a door or bicycle*)
  a bell = une sonnette

**belong** verb
* (to be the property of)
  to belong to someone = appartenir à
  quelqu'un
  that book belongs to me = ce livre
  m'appartient
* (to be a member of)
  to belong to a club = faire partie d'un club

**belongings** noun
  belongings = les affaires (feminine)

**below** preposition
  = au-dessous de
  the kitchen is below my bedroom = la
  cuisine se trouve au-dessous de ma
  chambre
  there's a cupboard below it = il y a un
  placard au-dessous

**belt** noun
  a belt = une ceinture

**bench** noun
  a bench = un banc

**bend**
1 verb
* (to lean, to move) = se pencher (**!** + être)
  to bend one's head = pencher la tête
  to bend one's knees = plier les genoux
* (to make crooked) = tordre
2 noun
  a bend = un tournant, un virage
**bend down** = se pencher (**!** + être)

**beneath** preposition
  = sous

**beside** preposition
  = à côté de
  he is sitting beside me = il est assis à côté
  de moi
  to live beside the sea = habiter au bord de
  la mer

**best**
1 noun
  the best = le meilleur/la meilleure
  to be the best at French = être le
  meilleur/la meilleure en français
  who is the best at drawing? = qui dessine
  le mieux?
  to do one's best = faire de son mieux
2 adjective
  = meilleur/meilleure
  the best hotel in town = le meilleur hôtel
  de la ville
  she speaks the best French = c'est elle
  qui parle le mieux français
  my best friend = mon meilleur ami/ma
  meilleure amie
  the best book I've ever read = le meilleur
  livre que j'aie jamais lu

  | **!** Note that the subjunctive is used after
  the superlative le meilleur... que.

  the best thing to do would be to phone
  him = le mieux serait de lui téléphoner

3 adverb
  = le mieux
  the best dressed man = l'homme le
  mieux habillé
  I like tennis best = le tennis est mon sport
  préféré

**bet** verb
  = parier

**better**
1 adjective
  = meilleur/meilleure
  her new film is better than the others
  = son nouveau film est meilleur que les
  précédents
  he is better at sports than me = il est
  meilleur en sport que moi
  the weather is going to get better = le
  temps va s'améliorer
  he was ill but now he's better = il était
  malade mais maintenant il va mieux
2 adverb
  = mieux
  he speaks French better than I do = il
  parle mieux le français que moi
  we'd better go = nous ferions mieux de
  partir
  it's better to [phone | write | check ...] = il
  vaut mieux [téléphoner | écrire | vérifier ...]

**between**
1 preposition
  = entre
  there is a wall between the two gardens
  = il y a un mur entre les deux jardins
  between now and next year = d'ici l'année
  prochaine
2 **in between** = au milieu

**beyond** preposition
  = au-delà de
  beyond the village = au-delà du village

**bicycle** noun
  a bicycle = un vélo

**big** adjective
* (large) = grand/grande (**!** before the noun)
  a big garden = un grand jardin
  a big party = une grande fête
  they have big houses = ils ont de grandes
  maisons
  a big car = une grosse voiture
* (heavy, thick) = gros/grosse (**!** before the
  noun)
  a big parcel = un gros paquet
  a big book = un gros livre
* (important, serious) = gros/grosse (**!** before
  the noun)
  a big salary = un gros salaire
  to make a big mistake = faire une grave
  erreur

**bike** noun
  a bike = un vélo

**bill** noun
* (for gas, electricity, telephone)
  a bill = une facture

**B**

* (in a restaurant)
a bill = une addition
could we have the bill please?
= l'addition, s'il vous plaît
* (in a hotel)
a bill = une note
* (US English) (money)
a bill = un billet de banque

**billiards** noun ▶ 248 |
billiards = le billard

**bin** noun (British English)
a bin = une poubelle

**biology** noun
biology = la biologie

**bird** noun
a bird = un oiseau

**biro** noun (British English)
a biro = un stylo-bille

**birth** noun
a birth = une naissance
a place of birth = un lieu de naissance

**birthday** noun
a birthday = un anniversaire
Happy birthday! = Bon anniversaire!

**biscuit** noun (British English)
a biscuit = un gâteau sec, un biscuit

**bit**
1 noun
(of cheese, bread, wood) = un morceau
(of string, paper) = un bout
2 **a bit** (British English)
a bit [early | nasty | odd …] = un peu [tôt |
méchant | bizarre …]

**bite** verb
= mordre
to bite one's nails = se ronger les ongles

**bitter** adjective
= amer/amère

**black** adjective ▶ 213 |
= noir/noire

**blackberry** noun
a blackberry = une mûre

**blackboard** noun
a blackboard = un tableau noir

**blackcurrants** noun
blackcurrants = le cassis (singular)

**blade** noun
* (of a knife, a sword)
a blade = une lame
* a blade of grass = un brin d'herbe

**blame**
1 verb
to blame someone = en vouloir à
quelqu'un
2 noun
to take the blame = prendre la
responsabilité

**blank** adjective
(describing a page) = blanc/blanche
(describing a cassette) = vierge

**blanket** noun
a blanket = une couverture

**blaze** verb
= être en flammes

**bleed** verb
= saigner
my nose is bleeding = je saigne du nez

**blind**
1 adjective
= aveugle
2 verb
* (destroy someone's sight) = aveugler
* (to dazzle) = éblouir
3 noun
a blind = un store

**blink** verb
= cligner des yeux

**blister** noun
a blister = une ampoule

**block**
1 noun
* (a building)
a block of apartments = un immeuble
* (a group of houses)
a block of houses = une pâté de maisons
* (a large piece)
a block = un bloc
a block of ice = un bloc de glace
2 verb
= bloquer
to block a road = bloquer une route

**blond, blonde** adjective ▶ 213 |
= blond/blonde
he has blond hair = il a les cheveux blonds
my sister's blonde = ma sœur est blonde

**blood** noun
blood = le sang

**blouse** noun
a blouse = un chemisier

**blow**
1 verb
* (if it's the wind) = souffler
the wind blew the door shut = un coup de
vent a fermé la porte
* (if it's a person) = souffler
to blow a whistle = donner un coup de
sifflet
to blow one's nose = se moucher
(! + être)
to blow bubbles = faire des bulles
* (if it's a light bulb) = sauter
2 noun
a blow = un coup
**blow away**
to be blown away = être
emporté/emportée par le vent

**blow down**
   to be blown down = être abattu/abattue
      (par le vent)
**blow out** = souffler
   to blow out a candle = souffler une bougie
**blow up**
• (*to destroy*) = faire sauter
   to blow up a car = faire sauter une voiture
• (*to be destroyed*) = sauter
• (*to put air into*) = gonfler

**blue** *adjective* ▶ 213 |
   = bleu/bleue

**blush** *verb*
   = rougir

**board**
**1** *noun*
• (*a piece of wood*)
   a board = une planche
• (*for games*)
   a board (*in chess*) = un échiquier
   (*in draughts, checkers*) = un damier
• (*a blackboard*)
   a board = un tableau noir
**2** *verb*
   to board a ship = monter à bord d'un
      navire
**3 on board** = à bord

**boarding school** *noun*
   a boarding school = une pension

**boast** *verb*
   = se vanter (**!** + *être*)

**boat** *noun*
   a boat = un bateau

**body** *noun*
   the body = le corps
   a dead body = un cadavre

**boil** *verb*
• (*if it's a person*)
   to boil water = faire bouillir de l'eau
   to boil an egg = faire cuire un œuf
• (*if it's water, milk*) = bouillir

**boiled egg** *noun*
   a boiled egg = un œuf à la coque

**boiler** *noun*
   a boiler = une chaudière

**boiling** *adjective*
   = bouillant/bouillante

**bomb**
**1** *noun*
   a bomb = une bombe
**2** *verb*
   = bombarder

**bone** *noun* ▶ 201 |
   a bone (*in the body, in meat*) = un os
   (*in fish*) = une arête

───────
**✕** in informal situations

**bonnet** *noun* (*British English*)
   the bonnet (*in a car*) = le capot

**book**
**1** *noun*
   a book = un livre
**2** *verb*
   = réserver
   to book a room = réserver une chambre
   the flight is fully booked = le vol est
      complet

**booking** *noun*
   a booking = une réservation

**bookshop, bookstore** *noun* ▶ 315 |
   a bookshop, a bookstore = une librairie

**boot** *noun*
• (*worn on the feet*)
   a boot = une botte
• (*British English*) (*of a car*)
   the boot = le coffre

**border** *noun*
   a border = une frontière
   to cross the border = passer la frontière

**bore** *verb*
   = ennuyer

**bored** *adjective*
   to be bored, to get bored = s'ennuyer
      (**!** + *être*)

**boring** *adjective*
   = ennuyeux/ennuyeuse

**born** *adjective*
   to be born = naître (**!** + *être*)
   he was born in February = il est né au
      mois de février
   she was born in Italy = elle est née en
      Italie

**borrow** *verb*
   = emprunter
   to borrow some money from someone
      = emprunter de l'argent à quelqu'un

**boss** *noun*
   the boss = le patron/la patronne

**both**
**1** *determiner*
   both girls are blonde = les deux filles sont
      blondes
   both my sons = mes deux fils
   both Anne and Brian came = Anne et
      Brian sont venus tous les deux
**2** *pronoun*
   = tous les deux/toutes les deux
   you are both wrong, both of you are
      wrong = vous avez tort tous les
      deux/toutes les deux

**bother** *verb*
• (*to take the trouble*)
   don't bother calling back = ce n'est pas la
      peine de rappeler
• (*to worry, to upset*) = tracasser

# The human body

Note the use of **le**, **la**, **l'** or **les** in French where English uses a possessive adjective:

| | |
|---|---|
| he raised **his** hand | = il a levé **la** main |
| she closed **her** eyes | = elle a fermé **les** yeux |
| **my** eye hurts | = j'ai mal à **l'**œil |

For expressions such as *he hurt his foot* or *she brushed her teeth*, where the action involves more than the simple movement of a body part, use a reflexive verb in French:

| | |
|---|---|
| *she has broken* her leg | = **elle s'est cassé** la jambe |
| *he was washing* his hands | = **il se lavait** les mains |

Note also the following:

| | |
|---|---|
| *she broke his* nose | = **elle lui a cassé** le nez (literally *she broke to him the nose*) |

## Describing people

Here are some ways of describing people in French:

| | |
|---|---|
| *his hair is long* | = il a les cheveux longs |
| *he has long hair* | = il a les cheveux longs |
| *a boy with long hair* | = un garçon aux cheveux longs |
| *her eyes are blue* | = elle a les yeux bleus |
| *she has blue eyes* | = elle a les yeux bleus |
| *the girl with blue eyes* | = la fille aux yeux bleus |
| *his nose is red* | = il a le nez rouge |
| *he has a red nose* | = il a le nez rouge |
| *a man with a red nose* | = un homme au nez rouge |

▶ For other expressions with terms relating to parts of the body, ▶ **266** .

---

- (*in polite apologies*) = déranger
  **I'm sorry to bother you** = je suis désolé de vous déranger

**bottle** *noun*
  a bottle = une bouteille

**bottle-opener** *noun*
  a bottle-opener = un décapsuleur

**bottom**
1 *noun*
- (*the lowest part*)
  **the bottom of the hill** = le pied de la colline
  **at the bottom of** [the page | the stairs | the street ...] = en bas [de la page | de l'escalier | de la rue ...]
  **at the bottom** [of the lake | of the sea | of the garden ...] = au fond [du lac | de la mer | du jardin ...]
- (*at the lowest level*)
  **to be bottom of the class** = être dernier/dernière de la classe
- (*part of the body*) ▶ **201** 
  **the bottom** = le derrière✶
2 *adjective*
  **the bottom** [shelf | drawer | cupboard ...] = [l'étagère | le tiroir | le placard ...] du bas

**bound: to be bound to** *verb*
  **it's bound to create problems** = ça va sûrement créer des problèmes
  **she's bound to complain** = elle va sûrement se plaindre
  **it was bound to happen** = cela devait arriver

**bow¹** *noun*
- (*a knot*)
  a bow = un nœud
- (*a weapon*)
  a bow = un arc

**bow²** *verb*
  = saluer
  **to bow one's head** = baisser la tête

**bowl** *noun*
  a bowl = un bol
  (*shallow*) = une assiette

**bowling** *noun* ▶ **248** 
  bowling = le bowling

**box** *noun*
  a box = une boîte
  (*when moving*) = un carton

**boxing** *noun* ▶ **248** 
  boxing = la boxe

**boy** *noun*
  a boy = un garçon

**boyfriend** *noun*
  a boyfriend = un copain

**bra** *noun*
  a bra = un soutien-gorge

**bracelet** *noun*
  a bracelet = un bracelet

**braid** *noun* (*US English*)
  a braid = une natte, une tresse

**brain** *noun* ▶ 201 |
  the brain = le cerveau

**brake** *noun*
  a brake = un frein

**branch** *noun*
  a branch = une branche

**brand-new** *adjective*
  = tout neuf/toute neuve

**brandy** *noun*
  brandy = le cognac

**brave** *adjective*
  = courageux/courageuse

**Brazil** *noun* ▶ 218 |
  Brazil = le Brésil

**bread** *noun*
  bread = le pain

**break**
**1** *verb*
* (*to be damaged*) = se casser (**!** + *être*)
  the chair broke = la chaise s'est cassée
* (*to crack, to smash or damage*) = casser
  to break an egg = casser un œuf
* (*to injure*)
  to break one's leg = se casser la jambe
  she broke her arm = elle s'est cassé le bras
* (*not to keep*)
  to break a promise = manquer à une
    promesse
  to break the rules = enfreindre le
    règlement
**2** *noun*
* a break (*a short rest*) = une pause
  (*at school*) = une récréation
  to take a break = faire une pause
* (*a holiday*)
  a break = des vacances (*feminine plural*)
**break down**
* (*if it's a TV, a car*) = tomber en panne
  (**!** + *être*)
* (*to get upset*) = s'effondrer (**!** + *être*)
**break into** = cambrioler
  to be broken into = être
    cambriolé/cambriolée
**break out**
  (*if it's a fire*) = se déclarer (**!** + *être*)
  (*if it's violence*) = éclater
**break up**
* (*if it's a crowd*) = se disperser (**!** + *être*)
* (*if it's a couple*) = se séparer (**!** + *être*)
  to break up with someone = rompre avec
    quelqu'un
* (*to put an end to*) = mettre fin à
  the police broke up the demonstration
    = la police a mis fin à la manifestation

**breakfast** *noun*
  breakfast = le petit déjeuner
  to have breakfast = prendre le petit
    déjeuner

---

**×** in informal situations

**breast** *noun* ▶ 201 |
  a breast = un sein

**breath** *noun*
  breath = le souffle
  to be out of breath = être hors d'haleine
  to hold one's breath = retenir sa
    respiration

**breathe** *verb*
  = respirer
**breathe in** = inspirer
**breathe out** = expirer, souffler

**breeze** *noun*
  a breeze = une brise

**brick** *noun*
  a brick = une brique

**bride** *noun*
  a bride = une mariée

**bridegroom** *noun*
  a bridegroom = un marié

**bridge** *noun*
  a bridge = un pont

**brief** *adjective*
  = bref/brève (**!** *before the noun*)

**bright** *adjective*
* (*describing colours, light*) = vif/vive
  a bright yellow dress = une robe jaune vif
* (*having plenty of light, sun*) = clair/claire
  this room is not very bright = cette pièce
    n'est pas très claire
  a bright spell = une belle éclaircie
  to get brighter = s'éclaircir (**!** + *être*)
* (*intelligent*) = intelligent/intelligente

**brilliant** *adjective*
* (*very intelligent*) = brillant/brillante
* (*British English*) (*used for emphasis*)
  = génial/géniale×

**bring** *verb*
* to bring = apporter
  to bring someone a present = apporter un
    cadeau à quelqu'un
  it will bring us good luck = ça va nous
    porter chance
* (*to be accompanied by*) = amener
  he brought his sister to the party = il a
    amené sa sœur à la soirée
**bring about**
  to bring about a change = provoquer un
    changement
**bring back** = rapporter
  he brought me back some perfume = il
    m'a rapporté du parfum
**bring up** = élever
  to bring up a child = élever un enfant

**Britain** *noun* ▶ 218 |
  Britain = la Grande-Bretagne

**British** ▶ 275 |
**1** *adjective*
  = britannique

**2** *noun*
the British = les Britanniques (*masculine plural*)

**broad** *adjective*
= large

**broadband** *noun*
broadband = le haut débit

**broadcast** *verb*
= diffuser

**brochure** *noun*
a brochure = une brochure

**broke** *adjective*
= fauché/fauchée✶

**broken** *adjective*
= cassé/cassée

**bronze** *noun*
bronze = le bronze

**brother** *noun*
a brother = un frère

**brother-in-law** *noun*
a brother-in-law = un beau-frère

**brown** *adjective* ▶ 213 |
* (*in colour*) = marron (**!** *never changes*)
to have brown eyes = avoir les yeux marron
* (*describing hair*) = châtain (**!** *never changes*)
* to go brown = bronzer

**bruise** *noun* ▶ 266 |
a bruise = un bleu

**brush**
**1** *noun*
* (*for hair, teeth, clothes or shoes*)
a brush = une brosse
* (*for sweeping up*)
a brush = un balai
* (*for painting*)
a brush = un pinceau
**2** *verb*
to brush one's hair = se brosser les cheveux
to brush one's teeth = se brosser les dents

**Brussels** *noun* ▶ 218 |
Brussels = Bruxelles

**bubble** *noun*
a bubble = une bulle

**bucket** *noun*
a bucket = un seau

**budgerigar, budgie** *noun*
a budgerigar = une perruche

**build** *verb*
= construire
to build a house = construire une maison

**building** *noun*
a building = un bâtiment

**Bulgaria** *noun* ▶ 218 |
Bulgaria = la Bulgarie

**bull** *noun*
a bull = un taureau

**bullet** *noun*
a bullet = une balle

**bulletin** *noun*
a (news) bulletin = un bulletin (d'informations)

**bully** *verb*
= tyranniser

**bump** *verb*
to bump one's head = se cogner la tête
**bump into**
* (*to hit*) = rentrer dans (**!** + *être*)
* (*to meet*) = tomber sur (**!** + *être*)

**bunch** *noun*
a bunch of flowers = un bouquet de fleurs
a bunch of grapes = une grappe de raisins
a bunch of keys = un trousseau de clés

**burger** *noun*
a burger = un hamburger

**burglar** *noun*
a burglar = un cambrioleur/une cambrioleuse

**burglar alarm** *noun*
a burglar alarm = une sirène d'alarme

**burglary** *noun*
a burglary = un cambriolage

**burn**
**1** *verb*
* (*to destroy, to get rid of*) = brûler
to burn rubbish = brûler des ordures
* (*to injure*)
to burn oneself = se brûler (**!** + *être*)
to burn one's finger = se brûler le doigt
* (*to be on fire*) = brûler
* (*when cooking*) = laisser brûler
* (*in the sun*)
to burn easily = attraper facilement des coups de soleil
**2** *noun*
a burn = une brûlure
**burn down** = brûler

**burner** *noun*
(*for CDs, DVDs*)
a burner = une graveur

**burst** *verb*
* (*if it's a balloon, a pipe*) = éclater
* (*if it's a river*)
to burst its banks = déborder
**burst into**
to burst into tears = fondre en larmes
**burst out**
to burst out laughing = éclater de rire

**bury** *verb*
= enterrer

**bus** *noun*
a bus = un bus

**bus conductor** *noun* ▶ 315 |
a bus conductor = un receveur/une
receveuse d'autobus

**bus driver** *noun* ▶ 315 |
a bus driver = un conducteur/une
conductrice d'autobus

**bush** *noun*
a bush = un buisson

**business** *noun*
• (*commercial activities*)
business = les affaires (*feminine plural*)
to go to London on business = aller à
Londres pour affaires
• (*a company*)
a business = une entreprise
• (*when protecting one's privacy*)
that's my business = ça me regarde
it's none of your business = ça ne te
regarde pas

**businessman** *noun* ▶ 315 |
a businessman = un homme d'affaires

**businesswoman** *noun* ▶ 315 |
a businesswoman = une femme d'affaires

**bus station** *noun*
a bus station = une gare routière

**bus stop** *noun*
a bus stop = un arrêt d'autobus

**busy** *adjective*
= occupé/occupée
to be busy packing = être occupé à faire
ses valises
to have a busy day = avoir une journée
chargée
to lead a busy life = mener une vie
active

**but** *conjunction*
= mais
he understands French but he doesn't
speak it = il comprend le français mais
il ne le parle pas

**butcher** *noun* ▶ 315 |
a butcher = un boucher

**butter** *noun*
butter = le beurre

**butterfly** *noun*
a butterfly = un papillon

**button** *noun*
a button = un bouton

**buy** *verb*
= acheter
to buy a present for someone = acheter
un cadeau à quelqu'un
she bought herself a new coat = elle s'est
acheté un nouveau manteau

**buzz** *verb*
= bourdonner

**by** *preposition*

• by = par
by accident = accidentellement
by chance = par hasard
by mistake = par erreur
one by one = un par un/une par une
he was bitten by a dog = il a été mordu
par un chien
• (*on one's own*)
by oneself = tout seul/toute seule
• (*using*)
to travel by bus = voyager en bus
we went there by bicycle = nous y
sommes allés à bicyclette
to pay by cheque = payer par chèque
to book by phone = réserver par
téléphone
to come in by the back door = entrer par
la porte de derrière
• (*as a result of*)
he succeeded by working hard = il a
réussi en travaillant beaucoup
• (*beside*)
by the sea = au bord de la mer
by the side of the road = au bord de la
route
• (*indicating the author or painter*) = de
a book by Charles Dickens = un livre de
Charles Dickens
a painting by Chagall = un tableau de
Chagall
• (*when talking about time*)
by next Thursday = d'ici jeudi prochain
he should be here by now = il devrait
déjà être là
• (*when talking about figures, rates*)
to increase by 20% = augmenter de 20%
to be paid by the hour = être payé/payée à
l'heure
8 metres by 4 metres = 8 mètres sur 4

# Cc

**cab** *noun*
a cab = un taxi

**cabbage** *noun*
cabbage = le chou

**cable car** *noun*
a cable car = un téléphérique

**café** *noun*
a café = un café

**cake** *noun*
a cake = un gâteau

**cake shop** *noun* ▶ 315 |
a cake shop = une pâtisserie

**calculator** *noun*
a calculator = une calculatrice, une
calculette

**calendar** *noun*
a calendar = un calendrier

**calf** *noun*
* (*the animal*)
a calf = un veau
* (*part of the leg*) ▶ 201 |
the calf = le mollet

**call** *verb*
* (*to name*) = appeler
he's called Michael = il s'appelle Michael
it's called 'un robinet' in French = en
français ça s'appelle 'un robinet'
* (*to describe as*)
to call someone a coward = traiter
quelqu'un de lâche
* (*to call out (to*)) = appeler
the teacher is calling us = le professeur
nous appelle
* (*to phone*) = appeler
who's calling? = qui est à l'appareil?
* (*to get to come*) = appeler
to call the doctor = faire venir le médecin
* (*to wake*) = réveiller
* (*to pay a visit*) = passer (! + *être*)
they called yesterday = ils sont passés
hier

**call back**
* (*to come back*) = repasser (! + *être*)
* (*to phone back*) = rappeler
**call off** = annuler
**call out**
to call out the numbers for the lottery
= annoncer les numéros gagnants du
loto
**call up** = appeler

**call centre** *noun*
a call centre = un centre d'appels

**calm**
**1** *adjective*
= calme
**2** *verb*
= calmer
**calm down** = se calmer (! + *être*)

**camcorder** *noun*
a camcorder = un caméscope

**camel** *noun*
a camel = un chameau

**camera** *noun*
a camera (*for taking photos*) = un appareil
photo
(*in a studio, for videos*) = une caméra

**camp**
**1** *noun*
a summer camp = un camp de vacances
**2** *verb*
= camper
to go camping = faire du camping

**camping** *noun*
camping = le camping

**campsite** *noun*
a campsite = un camping

**can¹** *verb*
* (*to have the possibility*)
can you come? = est-ce que tu peux
venir?
where can I buy stamps? = où est-ce que
je peux acheter des timbres?
he can't sleep when it's hot = il ne peut
pas dormir quand il fait chaud
* (*when talking about seeing, hearing,
understanding, you don't usually translate
can*)
I can hear you better now = je t'entends
mieux maintenant
can they see us? = est-ce qu'ils nous
voient?
he can't understand Japanese = il ne
comprend pas le japonais
* (*to be allowed to*)
can I smoke? = est-ce que je peux fumer?
we can't turn right here = nous ne
pouvons pas tourner à droite ici
* (*to know how to*)
she can swim = elle sait nager
he can't drive yet = il ne sait pas encore
conduire
can you speak French? = est-ce que tu
parles français?
* (*when asking, offering or suggesting*)
can we borrow your car? = est-ce que
nous pouvons emprunter ta voiture?
can I help you? = est-ce que je peux vous
aider?
you can phone back later if you like
= vous pouvez rappeler plus tard si vous
voulez

**can²** *noun*
a can = une boîte

**Canada** *noun* ▶ 218 |
Canada = le Canada

**Canadian** ▶ 275 |
**1** *adjective*
= canadien/canadienne
**2** *noun*
the Canadians = les Canadiens
(*masculine*)

**canal** *noun*
a canal = un canal

**cancel** *verb*
= annuler

**cancer** *noun* ▶ 266 |
cancer = le cancer

**candle** *noun*
a candle (*in a room, on a cake*) = une
bougie
(*in a church*) = un cierge

**candy** *noun* (*US English*)
* candy = la confiserie
* (*a sweet*)
a candy = un bonbon

**canoe** *noun*
a canoe = un canoë, un canoë-kayak

**canoeing** noun ▶ 248 |
canoeing = le canoë-kayak

**can-opener** noun
a can-opener = un ouvre-boîtes

**canteen** noun
a canteen = une cantine

**cap** noun
a cap = une casquette
a baseball cap = une casquette de base-ball

**capable** adjective
* to be capable of looking after oneself
= être capable de se débrouiller tout seul
* (having ability, skill)
= compétent/compétente

**capital**
**1** noun
the capital = la capitale
Paris is the capital of France = Paris est la capitale de la France
**2** adjective
= majuscule
capital P = P majuscule

**captain** noun
a captain = un capitaine

**car** noun
a car = une voiture

**caravan** noun (British English)
a caravan = une caravane

**card** noun
* (for sending to someone)
a card = une carte
* (for playing games)
a card = une carte (à jouer)
to play cards = jouer aux cartes

**cardphone** noun
a cardphone = un téléphone à carte

**care**
**1** noun
* (to take care) = faire attention
to take care crossing the street = faire attention en traversant la rue
* to take care of someone = s'occuper de quelqu'un
**2** verb
I don't care = ça m'est égal
to care about the environment
= s'intéresser à l'environnement

**career** noun
a career = une carrière

**careful** adjective
to be careful = faire attention
to be careful crossing the street = faire attention en traversant la rue
to be careful not to make mistakes = faire attention de ne pas faire d'erreurs

**careless** adjective
to be careless = être négligent/négligente

**car ferry** noun
a car ferry = un ferry, un transbordeur

**carnival** noun
* (British English) (a festival)
a carnival = un carnaval
* (US English) (a fair)
a carnival = une fête foraine

**car park** noun (British English)
a car park = un parking, un parc de stationnement

**carpet** noun
carpet = la moquette

**car phone** noun
a car phone = un téléphone de voiture

**carrot** noun
a carrot = une carotte

**carry** verb
* (to hold) = porter
I can't carry the shopping = je ne peux pas porter les courses
* (to move)
to carry the baggage upstairs = monter les bagages
to carry the boxes downstairs = descendre les cartons
**carry on** = continuer

**cartoon** noun
a cartoon (a comic strip) = une bande dessinée, une BD
(a film) = un dessin animé

**case¹**: **in case** conjunction
= au cas où
keep the bike in case you need it = garde le vélo au cas où tu en aurais besoin
**!** Note that the conditional is used after au cas où.

**case²** noun
a case = une valise

**cash**
**1** noun
cash = l'argent liquide
**!** Note that argent is masculine.

I don't have any cash = je n'ai pas d'argent liquide
to pay in cash = payer en espèces
**2** verb
= encaisser

**cash dispenser** noun
a cash dispenser = un distributeur automatique de billets

**cassette** noun
a cassette = une cassette

**cassette player** noun
a cassette player = un lecteur de cassettes

**castle** noun
a castle = un château

**cat** noun
a cat = un chat/une chatte

**catch** verb
* (to capture) = attraper
to catch a fish = attraper un poisson
* (to take hold of) = attraper
* (to pinch, to stick)
he caught his finger in the door = il s'est pris le doigt dans la porte
my shirt got caught in the thorns = ma chemise s'est prise dans les ronces
* he was running to catch his train = il courait pour attraper son train
* (to take by surprise)
to catch someone stealing = surprendre quelqu'un en train de voler
to get caught = se faire prendre (! + être)
* (to become ill with)
to catch flu = attraper la grippe
to catch a cold = s'enrhumer (! + être), attraper un rhume
* to catch fire = prendre feu

**catch up**
to catch up with someone = rattraper quelqu'un

**caterpillar** noun
a caterpillar = une chenille

**cathedral** noun
a cathedral = une cathédrale

**cauliflower** noun
cauliflower = le chou-fleur

**cause** verb
the storm will cause damage = l'orage va causer des dégâts
it's going to cause delays = ça va provoquer des retards

**cautious** adjective
= prudent/prudente

**cave** noun
a cave = une grotte

**CD** noun
a CD = un disque compact, un CD

**CD player** noun
a CD player = une platine laser

**ceiling** noun
the ceiling = le plafond

**celebrate** verb
= faire la fête

**celery** noun
celery = le céleri

**cell** noun
a cell = une cellule

**cellar** noun
a cellar = une cave

**cello** noun ▶ 290 |
a cello = un violoncelle

**cell phone, cellular phone**
(US English) noun
a cell phone = un téléphone portable

**cement** noun
cement = le ciment

**cemetery** noun
a cemetery = un cimetière

**cent** noun
* (of euro)
a cent = un centime (d'euro)
* (of dollar)
a cent = un cent

**centimetre** (British English),
**centimeter** (US English) noun ▶ 285 |
a centimetre = un centimètre

**central heating** noun
central heating = le chauffage central

**centre** (British English), **center** (US English) noun
* (a place for activities, meetings)
a centre = un centre
a leisure centre = un centre de loisirs
* (the middle)
the centre = le centre
near the centre of London = près du centre de Londres

**century** noun ▶ 356 |
a century = un siècle

**certain** adjective
= certain/certaine

**certainly** adverb
= certainement

**chain** noun
a chain = une chaîne

**chair** noun
a chair = une chaise

**chalk** noun
chalk = la craie

**champagne** noun
champagne = le champagne

**champion** noun
a champion = un champion/une championne
a tennis champion = un champion/une championne de tennis

**chance** noun
* (when talking about a possibility)
there is a chance that she'll have a job in Paris = il est possible qu'elle ait un travail à Paris

! Note that the subjunctive is used after il est possible que.

* (an opportunity)
a chance = une occasion
to have a chance to meet people = avoir l'occasion de rencontrer des gens
* by chance = par hasard

**change**
**1** noun
* a change = un changement

C

- (*a different experience*)
  it makes a change from homework = ça
     change des devoirs
  let's go to the beach for a change = allons
     à la plage pour changer
- (*cash*)
  change = la monnaie
  have you got change for 20 euros?
     = pouvez-vous me faire la monnaie de
     20 euros?

**2** *verb*
- (*to become different, to make different*)
  = changer
  the town has changed a lot = la ville a
     beaucoup changé
  I've changed my mind = j'ai changé d'avis
- (*to replace*) = changer
  to change a wheel = changer une roue
- (*to exchange in a shop*) = échanger
  change a shirt for a smaller size
     = échanger une chemise pour une taille
     plus petite
- (*to switch*) = changer de
  to change places with someone
     = changer de place avec quelqu'un
  she keeps changing channels = elle
     n'arrête pas de changer de chaîne
- (*when talking about one's clothes*) = se
  changer (**!** + *être*)
  to get changed = se changer (**!** + *être*)
- (*when using transport*) = changer
- to change dollars into euros = changer des
  dollars en euros

**changing room** *noun*
  a changing room = un vestiaire

**channel** *noun*
  a TV channel = une chaîne de télévision

**Channel** *noun*
  the (English) Channel = la Manche

**chapter** *noun*
  a chapter = un chapitre

**charge**
**1** *verb*
  to charge someone for the damage = faire
     payer les dégâts à quelqu'un
  they'll charge you for the electricity = ils
     te feront payer l'électricité
**2** *noun*
- (*a price, a fee*)
  a charge = des frais (*masculine plural*)
  there's no charge = c'est gratuit
**3 in charge** = responsable
  to be in charge of the money = être
     responsable de l'argent

**charming** *adjective*
  = charmant/charmante

**chase** *verb*
  (*on foot*) = courir après
  (*in a car*) = poursuivre

---

**×** in informal situations

**chase away** = chasser

**chat**
**1** *verb*
  = bavarder, discuter
**2** *noun*
  a chat = une conversation
**chat up** (*British English*) = draguer×

**cheap** *adjective*
- (*not expensive*) = bon marché (**!** *never
  changes*)
  it's cheap = c'est bon marché, ça ne coûte
     pas cher
  it's cheaper to take the bus = ça coûte
     moins cher de prendre le bus
- (*of poor quality*) = de mauvaise qualité

**cheat** *verb*
  = tricher

**check**
**1** *verb*
- (*to make sure*) = vérifier
  you should check whether it's true = tu
     devrais vérifier si c'est vrai
- (*to inspect*) = contrôler
  they didn't even check our passports = ils
     n'ont même pas contrôlé nos passeports
**2** *noun*
- (*US English*) (*a bill*)
  a check = une addition
- (*US English*) (*a cheque*)
  a check = un chèque
**check in** = se présenter à l'enregistrement
**check out** = partir (**!** + *être*)

**checkbook** *noun* (*US English*)
  a checkbook = un carnet de chèques, un
     chéquier

**checkers** *noun* ▶ **248** | (*US English*)
  checkers = les dames (*feminine*)

**check-in** *noun*
  the check-in = l'enregistrement
     (*masculine*)

**checkout** *noun*
  a checkout = une caisse

**cheek** *noun* ▶ **201** |
  the cheek = la joue

**cheeky** *adjective*
  = effronté/effrontée, insolent/insolente

**cheerful** *adjective*
  = gai/gaie

**cheese** *noun*
  cheese = le fromage

**chef** *noun* ▶ **315** |
  a chef = un chef cuisinier

**chemist** *noun* ▶ **315** |
- (*in a shop*)
  a chemist = un pharmacien/une
     pharmacienne
- (*in a laboratory*)
  a chemist = un chimiste/une chimiste

**chemistry** *noun*
chemistry = la chimie

**cheque** *noun* (*British English*)
a cheque = un chèque
to write a cheque for £50 = faire un
 chèque de 50 livres

**cheque book** *noun* (*British English*)
a cheque book = un carnet de chèques,
 un chéquier

**cherry** *noun*
a cherry = une cerise

**chess** *noun* ▶ 248 |
chess = les échecs (*masculine plural*)

**chest** *noun* ▶ 201 |
the chest = la poitrine

**chestnut**
**1** *noun*
a chestnut = un marron, une châtaigne
**2** *adjective*
= châtain (! *never changes*)
to have chestnut hair = avoir les cheveux
 châtain

**chew** *verb*
(*if it's a person*) = mâcher
(*if it's an animal*) = ronger

**chewing gum** *noun*
chewing gum = le chewing-gum

**chicken** *noun*
• (*the bird*)
 a chicken = une poule
• (*the meat*)
 chicken = le poulet

**child** *noun*
a child = un enfant/une enfant

**chilly** *adjective*
it's chilly = il fait froid

**chimney** *noun*
a chimney = une cheminée

**chin** *noun* ▶ 201 |, ▶ 237 |
the chin = le menton

**China** *noun* ▶ 218 |
China = la Chine

**Chinese** ▶ 275 |
**1** *adjective*
= chinois/chinoise
**2** *noun*
• (*the people*)
 the Chinese = les Chinois (*masculine
 plural*)
• (*the language*)
 Chinese = le chinois

**chips** *noun*
• (*British English*) (*French fries*)
 chips = les frites (*feminine*)
• (*US English*) (*crisps*)
 (*potato*) chips = les chips (*feminine*)

**chocolate** *noun*
chocolate = le chocolat
a box of chocolates = une boîte de
 chocolats

**choice** *noun*
a choice = un choix
we had no choice = nous n'avions pas le
 choix

**choir** *noun*
a choir = une chorale

**choke** *verb*
= s'étouffer (! + *être*)

**choose** *verb*
= choisir

**chore** *noun*
a chore = une tâche
to do the chores = faire le ménage

**Christian** *adjective*
= chrétien/chrétienne

**Christian name** *noun*
a Christian name = un nom de baptême

**Christmas** *noun*
Christmas (Day) = (le jour de) Noël
Merry Christmas!, Happy Christmas!
 = Joyeux Noël!

**Christmas carol** *noun*
a Christmas carol = un chant de Noël

**Christmas cracker** *noun* (*British
English*)
a Christmas cracker = un diablotin

**Christmas Eve** *noun*
Christmas Eve = la veille de Noël

**Christmas tree** *noun*
a Christmas tree = un sapin de Noël

**church** *noun*
a church (*Catholic or Anglican*) = une
 église
(*Protestant*) = un temple

**cider** *noun*
cider = le cidre

**cigar** *noun*
a cigar = un cigare

**cigarette** *noun*
a cigarette = une cigarette

**cigarette lighter** *noun*
a cigarette lighter = un briquet

**cinema** *noun* (*British English*)
a cinema = un cinéma

**circle** *noun*
a circle = un cercle
we were sitting in a circle = nous étions
 assis en cercle

**circus** *noun*
a circus = un cirque

**citizen** noun
* (of a country)
  a citizen = un citoyen/une citoyenne
* (of a city or town)
  a citizen = un habitant/une habitante

**city** noun
  a city = une (grande) ville

**city centre** (British English), **city center** (US English) noun
  the city centre = le centre-ville

**civilized** adjective
  = civilisé/civilisée

**civil servant** noun ▶ 315 |
  a civil servant = un fonctionnaire/une fonctionnaire

**clap** verb
  = applaudir

**clarinet** noun ▶ 290 |
  a clarinet = une clarinette

**class** noun
* (a group of students)
  a class = une classe
* (a lesson)
  a class = un cours
  a history class = un cours d'histoire
* (a social group)
  a (social) class = une classe (sociale)

**classical music** noun
  classical music = la musique classique

**classmate** noun
  a classmate = un camarade/une camarade de classe

**classroom** noun
  a classroom = une salle de classe

**clean**
**1** adjective
* (not dirty) = propre
  my hands are clean = j'ai les mains propres
  to keep the house clean = tenir la maison propre
* (not polluted) = pur/pure
**2** verb
  = nettoyer
  to have a jacket cleaned = faire nettoyer une veste

**clear**
**1** adjective
* (easy to understand, making sense) = clair/claire
  is that clear? = est-ce que c'est clair?
* (obvious)
  it is clear that no-one is happy = il est clair que personne n'est content
* (easy to see or hear, distinct)
  a clear voice = une voix claire
  your writing must be clear = votre écriture doit être lisible
* (with no rain or cloud) = clair/claire
  on a clear day = par temps clair

**2** verb
* (to empty, to remove from)
  to clear the table = débarrasser la table
  to clear the building = évacuer le bâtiment
  to clear the snow off the road = dégager la neige de la route
* (if it's fog, mist) = se dissiper (**!** + être)

**clever** adjective
* (intelligent) = intelligent/intelligente
  to be clever at mathematics = être doué/douée pour les mathématiques
* (smart) = astucieux/astucieuse

**cliff** noun
  a cliff = une falaise

**climate** noun
  a climate = un climat

**climb** verb
* to climb (up) a tree = grimper à un arbre
  to climb a mountain = faire l'ascension d'une montagne
  to climb over a wall = passer par-dessus un mur
* (to rise higher) = monter (**!** + être)

**climbing** noun ▶ 248 |
  climbing = l'escalade (feminine)

**clinic** noun
  a clinic = un centre médical

**cloakroom** noun
  a cloakroom = un vestiaire

**clock** noun
  a clock (on a building, in a classroom) = une horloge
  (smaller, as an ornament) = une pendule
  (in sporting events) = un chronomètre

**close¹**
**1** adjective
* (near) = proche
  the station is quite close = la gare est assez proche
  is the house close to the school? = est-ce que la maison est près de l'école?
* (as a friend or relation) = proche
**2** adverb
  to live close (by) = habiter tout près
  to come closer = s'approcher (**!** + être)

**close²** verb
  = fermer
  close your eyes = ferme les yeux
  the shop closes at noon = le magasin ferme à midi
  the door closed suddenly = tout d'un coup, la porte s'est fermée
**close down** = fermer définitivement

**closed** adjective
  = fermé/fermée

**cloth** noun
* (material)
  cloth = le tissu

# The clock

## What time Is it?

*what time Is it?* = quelle heure est-il?
*could you tell me the time?* = pouvez-vous me donner l'heure?
*it's exactly four o'clock* = il est exactement quatre heures

| It is ... | Il est ... | say |
|---|---|---|
| 4 o'clock | 4 heures | |
| | 4 h | quatre heures |
| 4 o'clock in the morning / 4 am | 4 h 00 | quatre heures du matin |
| 4 o'clock in the afternoon / 4 pm | 16 h 00 | quatre heures de l'après-midi |
| | | seize heures* |
| 4.10 / ten past four | 4 h 10 | quatre heures dix |
| 4.15 | 4 h 15 | quatre heures quinze |
| a quarter past four | 4 h 15 | quatre heures et quart |
| 4.20 | 4 h 20 | quatre heures vingt |
| 4.25 | 4 h 25 | quatre heures vingt-cinq |
| 4.30 | 4 h 30 | quatre heures trente |
| half past four | 4 h 30 | quatre heures et demie† |
| 4.35 | 4 h 35 | quatre heures trente-cinq |
| twenty-five to five | 4 h 35 | cinq heures moins vingt-cinq |
| 4.40 | 4 h 40 | quatre heures quarante |
| twenty to five | 4 h 40 | cinq heures moins vingt |
| 4.45 / a quarter to five | 4 h 45 | cinq heures moins le quart |
| 4.50 | 4 h 50 | quatre heures cinquante |
| ten to five | 4 h 50 | cinq heures moins dix |
| 4.55 | 4 h 55 | quatre heures cinquante-cinq |
| five to five | 4 h 55 | cinq heures moins cinq |
| 5 o'clock | 5 h 00 | cinq heures |
| 16.15 | 16 h 15 | seize heures quinze |
| 8 o'clock in the evening | 8 h du soir | huit heures du soir |
| 8 pm | 20 h 00 | vingt heures |
| 12.00 | 12 h 00 | douze heures |
| noon / 12 noon | 12 h 00 | midi |
| midnight / 12 midnight | 24 h 00 | minuit |

\* In timetables etc. the twenty-four hour clock is used, so that **4 pm** is **seize heures**. In ordinary usage, one says **quatre heures (de l'après-midi)**.

† Note that **demi** agrees with the noun it follows:

une heure et demie
un jour et demi
minuit et demi
midi et demi

Note also that, when it comes before the noun, **demi** is hyphenated and does not change:

une **demi**-journée
les **demi**-heures.

## When?

French never drops the word **heures**: *at five* is **à cinq heures** and so on:

French always uses **à**, whether or not English includes the word *at*. The only exception is when there is another preposition present, as in **vers cinq heures** (*about five o'clock*), **avant cinq heures** (*before five o'clock*) etc:

*what time did it happen?* = **à quelle** heure cela s'est-il passé?
*what time will he come at?* = **à quelle** heure va-t-il venir?
*it happened at two o'clock* = c'est arrivé **à** deux heures
*he'll come at four* = il viendra **à** quatre heures
*at about five* = **vers** cinq heures / **à** cinq heures **environ**
*it must be ready by ten* = il faut que ce soit prêt **avant** dix heures
*closed from 1 to 2 pm* = fermé **de** treize **à** quatorze heures
*every hour on the hour* = toutes les heures **à** l'heure juste

• a cloth (for dusting) = un chiffon
   (for the floor) = une serpillière
   (for dishes) = un torchon

**clothes** noun
   clothes = les vêtements (masculine)
   to put on one's clothes = s'habiller
      (! + être)
   to take off one's clothes = se déshabiller
      (! + être)
   to have no clothes on = être tout nu/toute
      nue

**cloud** noun
   a cloud = un nuage

**clown** noun
   a clown = un clown

**club** noun
• a club = un club
   a tennis club = un club de tennis
   to be in a club = faire partie d'un club
• (a nightclub)
   a club = une boîte de nuit

**clue** noun
• (in an investigation)
   a clue = un indice
• (in a crossword)
   a clue = une définition

**clumsy** adjective
   = maladroit/maladroite

**coach**
1 noun (British English)
• (a bus)
   a coach = un car
• (of a train)
   a coach = un wagon
2 verb
   = entraîner

**coach station** noun
   a coach station = une gare routière

**coal** noun
   coal = le charbon

**coast** noun
   the coast = la côte

**coat** noun
• a coat = un manteau
• (of an animal)
   the coat (of a dog) = le poil
   (of a cat) = la fourrure

**coat hanger** noun
   a coat hanger = un cintre

**cobweb** noun
   a cobweb = une toile d'araignée

**cock** noun
   a cock = un coq

**cocoa** noun
• (the drink)
   cocoa = le chocolat
• (the product)
   cocoa = le cacao

**coconut** noun
   a coconut = une noix de coco

**cod** noun
   cod = le cabillaud

**coffee** noun
• (the product)
   coffee = le café
• (a cup of coffee)
   a coffee = un café

**coffee machine** noun
   a coffee machine (an appliance) = une
      cafetière électrique
   (a machine) = une machine à café

**coin** noun
   a coin = une pièce
   a two-euro coin = une pièce de deux euros

**coincidence** noun
   a coincidence = une coïncidence

**cold**
1 adjective
   = froid/froide
   to be cold, to feel cold = avoir froid
   I'm very cold = j'ai très froid
   it's cold in the classroom = il fait froid
      dans la salle de classe
   you'll get cold = tu vas prendre froid
   to go cold = refroidir
   a cold meal = un repas froid
2 noun
• (the lack of heat)
   the cold = le froid
• (a common illness)
   a cold = un rhume

**collapse** verb
   (if it's a building, a chair) = s'effondrer
      (! + être)
   (if it's a wall) = s'écrouler (! + être)

**collar** noun
• (on a shirt or jacket)
   a collar = un col
• (for a pet)
   a collar = un collier

**colleague** noun
   a colleague = un collègue/une collègue

**collect** verb
• (to gather) = ramasser
   to collect the exercise books = ramasser
      les cahiers
• (to make a collection of) = collectionner
   he collects stamps = il collectionne les
      timbres
• (to take away)
   to collect the post = faire la levée du
      courrier
   to collect the rubbish = ramasser les
      ordures

───────────────

**✕** in informal situations

# Colours

Most colour adjectives agree with the noun they are describing:

| | |
|---|---|
| a blue coat | = un manteau bleu |
| a blue dress | = une robe bleue |

There are exceptions, labelled (**!** *never changes*) in the dictionary. Even with a plural noun, this type of adjective remains the same:

| | |
|---|---|
| brown shoes | = des chaussures marron |
| orange curtains | = des rideaux orange |

This rule also applies to shades of colour:

| | |
|---|---|
| a dark blue dress | = une robe bleu foncé |
| pale blue curtains | = des rideaux bleu pâle |

### Describing the colour of something

| | |
|---|---|
| what colour is your car? | = ta voiture est de quelle couleur? |
| | (*more formally*) de quelle couleur est ta voiture? |
| it's green | = elle est verte |
| to paint something green | = peindre quelque chose en vert |

### Describing people

Note the use of **les**:

| | |
|---|---|
| to have brown eyes | = avoir **les** yeux marron |

Note the use of **à**:

| | |
|---|---|
| the girl with the blond hair | = la fille **aux** cheveux blonds |

---

**collection** *noun*
- (*a set*)
  a collection = une collection
  she has a great collection of posters
  = elle a une super\* collection d'affiches
- (*money collected*)
  a collection = une collecte

**college** *noun*
  a college = un établissement
  d'enseignement supérieur
  to go to college, to be at college = faire
  des études supérieures

**colour** (*British English*), **color** (*US English*)
**1** *noun*
  a colour = une couleur
  what colour is the car? = de quelle
  couleur est la voiture?
**2** *verb*
  to colour the drawings (in) = colorier les
  dessins

**colourful** (*British English*), **colorful** (*US English*) *adjective*
  a colourful shirt = une chemise aux
  couleurs vives

**colour television** (*British English*), **color television** (*US English*) *noun*
  a colour television = une télévision (en)
  couleur

**comb**
**1** *noun*
  a comb = un peigne
**2** *verb*
  to comb one's hair = se peigner (**!** + *être*)

**come** *verb*
- to come = venir (**!** + *être*)
  she's coming today = elle vient
  aujourd'hui
  come to Paris with us = viens avec nous à
  Paris
  we came by bike = nous sommes venus à
  bicyclette
  come and see! = venez voir!
  I'm coming! = j'arrive!
  is the bus coming? = est-ce que le bus
  arrive?
  be careful when you come down the
  stairs = faites attention en descendant
  l'escalier
  he won't come into the house = il ne veut
  pas entrer dans la maison
  to come through the city centre = passer
  par le centre-ville
- (*to call around*) = passer (**!** + *être*)
- (*to reach*)
  turn left when you come to the traffic
  lights = tournez à gauche quand vous
  arriverez aux feux
- (*to attend*) = venir (**!** + *être*)
  will you be able to come to the meeting?
  = est-ce que tu pourras venir à la
  réunion?

* (to be a native or a product of)
  **she comes from Italy** = elle est italienne
  **the strawberries all come from Spain**
  = toutes les fraises viennent d'Espagne
* (in a contest)
  **to come first** = arriver premier/première
**come around** ▶ **come round**
**come back** = revenir (**!** + être)
  **to come back home** = rentrer (**!** + être)
**come in**
* (to enter) = entrer (**!** + être)
* (if it's a plane, a train) = arriver (**!** + être)
* **the tide's coming in** = la marée monte
**come off**
  (if it's a cover, a lid) = s'enlever (**!** + être)
  (if it's a button, a label) = se détacher
  (**!** + être)
**come on**
* (to start to work) (if it's heating) = se mettre
  en marche
  (if it's a light) = s'allumer (**!** + être)
* (when encouraging someone)
  **come on, hurry up!** = allez, dépêchez-
  vous!
  **come on, you can do better than that!**
  = allez, tu peux faire mieux!
**come on to** (US English)
  **to come on to someone** = draguer
  quelqu'un**\***
**come out**
* (to leave a place) = sortir (**!** + être)
  **I saw him as I was coming out of the shop**
  = je l'ai vu en sortant du magasin
* (to become available)
  (if it's a film) = sortir (**!** + être)
  (if it's a book) = paraître (**!** + être)
* (to wash out) = s'en aller (**!** + être)
* (if it's a photo)
  **the photo didn't come out** = la photo est
  ratée
* (if it's smoke, fire)
  **there are flames coming out of the**
  **windows** = il y a des flammes qui
  sortent par les fenêtres
**come round**
* (to visit) = venir (**!** + être)
* (after a faint) = reprendre connaissance
**come to**
  **the meal came to 25 euros** = le repas a
  coûté 25 euros
  **how much does it come to?** = ça fait
  combien?
**come up**
* (to be discussed)
  **to come up in conversation** = être
  abordé/abordée dans la conversation
* (if it's the sun) = se lever (**!** + être)

**comfortable** adjective
* (if it's a chair, a bed) = confortable
  **are you comfortable?** = êtes-vous bien
  installés?
* (relaxed) = à l'aise
* (having enough money) = aisé/aisée

**comforter** noun (US English)
  **a comforter** = une couette

**comic strip** noun
  **a comic strip** = une bande dessinée, une
  BD

**commercial**
**1** adjective
  = commercial/commerciale
**2** noun
  **a commercial** = une publicité

**commit** verb
  **to commit a crime** = commettre un crime

**common** adjective
  = courant/courante

**communicate** verb
  = communiquer

**community** noun
  **a community** = une communauté

**company** noun
* (a business)
  **a company** = une société
* (a group of actors)
  **a theatre company** = une troupe de
  théâtre
* (other people)
  **company** = la compagnie
  **to keep someone company** = tenir
  compagnie à quelqu'un
  **to keep bad company** = avoir de
  mauvaises fréquentations

**company secretary** noun ▶ **315**
  **a company secretary** = un secrétaire
  général

**compare** verb
  = comparer
  **to compare France with Italy** = comparer
  la France à l'Italie
  **she compares herself to her older sister**
  = elle se compare à sa sœur aînée

**compass** noun
  **a compass** = une boussole

**competition** noun
* **competition** = la concurrence
  **there's a lot of competition between the**
  **schools** = il y a beaucoup de
  concurrence entre les écoles
* (a contest)
  **a competition** = un concours
  **a drawing competition** = un concours de
  dessin

**competitive** adjective
  **to be competitive** = avoir l'esprit de la
  compétition

**complain** verb
  = se plaindre (**!** + être)
  **to complain about the food** = se plaindre
  de la nourriture

**complete**
**1** adjective
it was a complete disaster = c'était un désastre total
this is a complete waste of time = c'est vraiment du temps perdu
**2** verb
= terminer
to complete a training course = terminer un stage de formation

**completely** adverb
= complètement

**complicate** verb
= compliquer

**complicated** adjective
= compliqué/compliquée

**compliment**
**1** noun
a compliment = un compliment
**2** verb
to compliment someone = faire des compliments à quelqu'un

**comprehensive** noun (British English)
a comprehensive = une école (publique) secondaire

**compulsory** adjective
= obligatoire

**computer** noun
a computer = un ordinateur

**computer game** noun
a computer game (the game) = un jeu électronique
(the software) = un logiciel de jeu

**computer programmer** noun ▶ 315 |
a computer programmer = un programmeur/une programmeuse

**computer scientist** noun ▶ 315 |
a computer scientist = un informaticien/une informaticienne

**computer studies** noun
computer studies = l'informatique (feminine)

**concentrate** verb
= se concentrer (! + être)

**concert** noun
a concert = un concert
in concert at Wembley = en concert à Wembley

**concert hall** noun
a concert hall = une salle de concert

**concrete** noun
concrete = le béton

**condemn** verb
to condemn someone to death = condamner quelqu'un à mort

**condition**
**1** noun
a condition = un état
in a terrible condition = dans un état lamentable
the car is in good condition = la voiture est en bon état
**2 on condition that** = à condition que
you can go on condition that her parents drive you home = tu peux y aller à condition que ses parents te ramènent
**!** Note that the subjunctive is used after à condition que.

**condom** noun
a condom = un préservatif

**conductor** noun ▶ 315 |
a conductor = un chef d'orchestre

**cone** noun
a cone = un cornet

**conference** noun
a conference = une conférence

**confidence** noun
• confidence = l'assurance (feminine)
• (trust)
to have confidence in someone = avoir confiance en quelqu'un

**confident** adjective
= sûr de soi
she's a confident girl = c'est une fille sûre d'elle

**confidential** adjective
= confidentiel/confidentielle

**confiscate** verb
= confisquer

**conflict** noun
a conflict = un conflit

**confused** adjective
to get confused = s'embrouiller (! + être)

**congratulate** verb
= féliciter

**congratulations** noun (also exclamation)
congratulations! = félicitations!

**connection** noun
a connection = un rapport
it has no connection with the strike = cela n'a aucun rapport avec la grève

**conscientious** adjective
= consciencieux/consciencieuse

**conscious** adjective
• (aware) = conscient/consciente
• (after an operation) = réveillé/réveillée

**construct** verb
= construire

**consult** verb
= consulter

C

## contact
**1** *noun*
to be in contact with someone = être en contact avec quelqu'un
to lose contact = perdre contact
**2** *verb*
= contacter

## contact lens *noun*
a contact lens = une lentille de contact

## contain *verb*
= contenir

## content *adjective*
= content/contente

## contest *noun*
a contest = un concours
the Eurovision song contest = le concours Eurovision de la chanson

## continent *noun*
• (*a large mass of land*)
a continent = un continent
• (*British English*) (*Europe*)
the Continent = l'Europe continentale

## continental quilt *noun* (*British English*)
a continental quilt = une couette

## continue *verb*
= continuer
to continue to talk, to continue talking = continuer à parler
to continue down the street = continuer à descendre la rue

## continuous *adjective*
= incessant/incessante
the continuous noise of the traffic = le bruit incessant de la circulation

## contraception *noun*
contraception = la contraception

## contract *noun*
a contract = un contrat
to have a two-year contract = avoir un contrat de deux ans

## contradict *verb*
= contredire

## contradiction *noun*
a contradiction = une contradiction

## contrast *noun*
a contrast = un contraste

## contribute *verb*
• (*to give money*) = donner (de l'argent)
• to contribute to a discussion = participer à une discussion

## control
**1** *noun*
to take control of a situation = prendre une situation en main
to lose control of a car = perdre le contrôle d'une voiture

**2** *verb*
to control a region = contrôler une région
to control traffic = diriger la circulation

## convenient *adjective*
• (*useful, practical*) = pratique
it's more convenient to take the bus = il est plus pratique de prendre le bus
• (*suitable*) = pratique
it's a convenient place to meet = c'est un endroit pratique pour se retrouver
it's not convenient for me = ça ne me convient pas

## conversation *noun*
a conversation = une conversation
to make conversation = faire la conversation

## convince *verb*
= convaincre

## cook
**1** *verb*
• (*to prepare food*) = faire la cuisine, cuisiner
to cook a meal = préparer un repas
to cook vegetables = faire cuire des légumes
• (*to be cooked in the oven*) = cuire
**2** *noun* ▶ **315** |
a cook = un cuisinier/une cuisinière

## cooker *noun* (*British English*)
a cooker = une cuisinière

## cookie *noun* (*US English*)
a cookie = un gâteau sec, un biscuit

## cooking *noun*
cooking = la cuisine
to do the cooking = faire la cuisine

## cool *adjective*
• (*fresh, not hot*) = frais/fraîche
a cool drink = une boisson fraîche
it's much cooler today = il fait beaucoup plus frais aujourd'hui
• (*calm*) = calme
• (*fashionable*) = branché/branchée✖
• (*relaxed*) = décontracté/décontractée

## cool down
• (*to get colder*) = refroidir
• (*to calm down*) = se calmer (**!** + *être*)

## cooperate *verb*
= coopérer

## cope *verb*
• (*to manage*) = se débrouiller (**!** + *être*)
• to cope with pain = supporter la douleur

## copper *noun*
copper = le cuivre

## copy
**1** *noun*
a copy = une copie
**2** *verb*
= copier
to copy in an exam = copier à un examen

---

✖ in informal situations

**copy down, copy out** = recopier

**cork** noun
• a cork = un bouchon
• cork = le liège

**corkscrew** noun
a corkscrew = un tire-bouchon

**corner** noun
• (of a street, a building)
the corner = l'angle (masculine)
= le coin
the shop on the corner = le magasin qui
fait l'angle
to go around the corner = tourner au coin
de la rue
• (in football, hockey)
a corner = un corner

**correct**
**1** adjective
= bon/bonne (**!** before the noun),
correct/correcte
the correct answer = la bonne réponse, la
réponse correcte
that is correct = c'est exact
**2** verb
= corriger

**correction** noun
a correction = une correction

**corridor** noun
a corridor = un couloir

**cost** verb
= coûter
how much does it cost? = ça coûte
combien?
it costs a lot of money = ça coûte très cher

**costume** noun
a costume = un costume

**cosy** adjective (British English)
a cosy room = une pièce confortable

**cot** noun (British English)
a cot = un lit de bébé

**cottage** noun
a cottage = une petite maison

**cotton** noun
• (the material)
cotton = le coton
• (the thread)
cotton = le fil de coton

**cotton wool** noun (British English)
cotton wool = le coton hydrophile

**couch** noun
a couch = un canapé

**cough** verb
= tousser

**could** verb
• (had the possibility)
I couldn't move = je ne pouvais pas
bouger
he couldn't sleep for weeks = il n'a pas pu
dormir pendant des semaines

• (knew how to)
she could read at the age of three = elle
savait lire à l'âge de trois ans
he couldn't type = il ne savait pas taper à
la machine
I couldn't speak any German = je ne
parlais pas allemand
• (when talking about seeing, hearing,
understanding, you don't translate could)
I couldn't see a thing = je n'y voyais rien
he could hear them = il les entendait
they couldn't understand me = ils ne me
comprenaient pas
• (when implying that something did not
happen)
she could have become a doctor = elle
aurait pu devenir médecin
you could have apologized! = tu aurais
pu t'excuser!
• (when indicating a possibility)
they could be wrong = ils se trompent
peut-être
a bike could be useful = un vélo pourrait
être utile
• (when asking, offering or suggesting)
could I speak to Annie? = est-ce que je
pourrais parler à Annie?
could you take a message? = est-ce que
vous pourriez prendre un message?
we could ask Gary = nous pourrions
demander à Gary

**count** verb
= compter
**count on**
to count on someone = compter sur
quelqu'un

**counter** noun
a counter (in a shop) = un comptoir
(in a bank, a post office) = un guichet
(in a bar) = un bar, un comptoir

**country** noun
• (a state)
a country = un pays
• (the countryside)
the country = la campagne
to live in the country = vivre à la
campagne

**countryside** noun
the countryside = la campagne

**couple** noun
• a couple of days (two days) = deux jours
(a few days) = deux ou trois jours
• (two people)
a couple = un couple

**courage** noun
courage = le courage

**courageous** adjective
= courageux/courageuse

**course**
**1** noun
• (a series of lessons or lectures)
a course = un cours

# Countries, cities, and continents

## Countries and continents

Most countries and all continents are used with the definite article in French:

| | |
|---|---|
| *I like France | Canada* | = j'aime **la** France / **le** Canada |
| *to visit the United States* | = visiter **les** États-Unis |

All the continent names are feminine in French. Generally, the names of countries ending in **e** are feminine and the rest are mostly masculine. Some names of countries are plural, eg **les États-Unis**.

## In, to, and from somewhere

With continent names and feminine singular names of countries, for **in** and **to** use **en**, and for **from** use **de** (or **d'** before a vowel or mute 'h'):

| | |
|---|---|
| *to go **to** Europe | **to** France* | = aller **en** Europe / **en** France |
| *to come **from** France | **from** Germany* | = venir **d'**Europe / **d'**Allemagne |

With masculine names of countries beginning with a consonant, use **au** for **in** and **to**, and **du** for **from** and with masculine names of countries beginning with a vowel use **en** for **in** and **to**, and **d'** for from

| | |
|---|---|
| *to live **in** Canada | **in** Iraq* | = vivre **au** Canada / **en** Irak |
| *to come **from** Japan | **from** Iraq* | = venir **du** Japon / **d'**Irak |

With plurals, use **aux** for **in** and **to**, and **des** for **from**

| | |
|---|---|
| *to live **in the** United States* | = vivre **aux** États-Unis |
| *to come **from the** United States* | = venir **des** États-Unis |

## Towns and cities

For **in** and **to** with the name of a town, use **à** in French; if the French name includes the definite article, **à** will become **au**, **à la**, **à l'** or **aux**.

| | |
|---|---|
| *to live **in** Toulouse | **in le** Havre |* | = vivre **à** Toulouse / **au** Havre / |
| ***in la** Rochelle | **in les** Arcs* | **à la** Rochelle / **aux** Arcs |

Similarly, **from** is **de**, becoming **du**, **de la**, **de l'** or **des** when it combines with the definite article in town names:

| | |
|---|---|
| *to come **from** Toulouse | **from le** Havre |* | = venir **de** Toulouse / **du** Havre / |
| ***from la** Rochelle | **from les** Arc* | **de la** Rochelle / **des** Arcs |

---

a language course = un cours de langue
* (*part of a meal*)
  a course = un plat
  **what's the main course?** = qu'est-ce qu'il y a comme plat principal?
**2 of course** = bien sûr
  of course not! = bien sûr que non!

**court** *noun*
* (*of law*)
  a court = une cour, un tribunal
  to go to court = aller devant les tribunaux
* (*for playing sports*)
  a tennis court = un court de tennis
  a basketball court = un terrain de basket

**court case** *noun*
  a court case = un procès

**cousin** *noun*
  a cousin = un cousin/une cousine

**cover**
**1** *verb*
  to cover = couvrir
  to be covered in spots = être couvert/couverte de boutons
**2** *noun*
* (*a lid*)
  a cover = un couvercle
* (*for a cushion, a quilt*)
  a cover = une housse
* (*a blanket*)
  a cover = une couverture
* (*on a book, a magazine, an exercise book*)
  the cover = la couverture

**coverage** *noun*
  (*of mobile phone reception*)
  coverage = la couverture

**cow** *noun*
  a cow = une vache

**coward** *noun*
  a coward = un lâche/une lâche

**cowboy** noun
a cowboy = un cowboy

**cozy** adjective (US English)
a cozy room = une pièce confortable

**crab** noun
a crab = un crabe

**crack** verb
* (to damage) = fêler
* (to get damaged) = se fêler (! + être)
* (to get broken) = se casser (! + être)

**cradle** noun
a cradle = un berceau

**cramp** noun
a cramp = une crampe

**crash**
1 noun
a crash = un accident
a car crash = un accident de voiture
2 verb
to crash into a tree = rentrer dans un arbre
the plane crashed = l'avion s'est écrasé

**crayon** noun
a crayon = une craie grasse

**crazy** adjective
= fou/folle

**cream** noun
cream = la crème

**create** verb
= créer
to create employment = créer des emplois

**credit** noun
credit = le crédit
they don't give credit = ils ne font pas crédit

**credit card** noun
a credit card = une carte de crédit

**cricket** noun ▶ 248
cricket = le cricket

**crime** noun
* (a criminal act)
a crime (serious) = un crime
(minor) = un délit
* (in general)
crime = la criminalité

**criminal**
1 noun
a criminal = un criminel/une criminelle
2 adjective
= criminel/criminelle

**crisis** noun
a crisis = une crise

**crisps** noun (British English)
crisps = les chips (feminine)

**critical** adjective
= critique

**criticize** verb
= critiquer

**crocodile** noun
a crocodile = un crocodile

**crooked** adjective
a crooked line = une ligne brisée
the picture is crooked = le tableau est de travers

**cross**
1 verb
* (to go across)
to cross the road = traverser la rue
to cross the Channel = traverser la Manche
to cross the border = passer la frontière
to cross into Italy = passer en Italie
* (other uses)
to cross one's legs = croiser les jambes
our letters crossed = nos lettres se sont croisées
2 noun
a cross = une croix
3 adjective
= fâché/fâchée
to get cross = se fâcher (! + être)
**cross out** = rayer

**crossroads** noun
a crossroads = un carrefour

**crossword puzzle** noun
a crossword puzzle = des mots croisés
! Note that mots is masculine plural.

**crow** noun
a crow = un corbeau

**crowd** noun
* (a large number of people)
a crowd = une foule
crowds of people = une foule de gens
* (watching a game)
the crowd = les spectateurs (masculine plural)

**crown** noun
a crown = une couronne

**cruel** adjective
= cruel/cruelle

**cruelty** noun
cruelty = la cruauté

**cruise** noun
a cruise = une croisière

**crush** verb
= écraser

**crutch** noun
a crutch = une béquille

**cry**
1 verb
= pleurer
2 noun
a cry = un cri

**cub** *noun*
a cub = un petit

**cuckoo** *noun*
a cuckoo = un coucou

**cucumber** *noun*
a cucumber = un concombre

**cuddle** *noun*
a cuddle = un câlin
to give someone a cuddle = faire un câlin
à quelqu'un

**culprit** *noun*
a culprit = un coupable/une coupable

**cultural** *adjective*
= culturel/culturelle

**culture** *noun*
culture = la culture

**cunning** *adjective*
(*describing a person*) = rusé/rusée
(*describing a plan*) = habile

**cup** *noun*
• a cup = une tasse
a cup of coffee = une tasse de café
• (*in sport*)
a cup = une coupe

**cupboard** *noun*
a cupboard = un placard

**curb** *noun* (*US English*)
the curb = le bord du trottoir

**cure**
**1** *verb*
= guérir
**2** *noun*
a cure = un traitement

**curious** *adjective*
= curieux/curieuse

**curly** *adjective*
= frisé/frisée
to have curly hair = avoir les cheveux
frisés

**currency** *noun*
a currency = une monnaie
foreign currency = les devises étrangères
| **!** *Note that* **devises** *is feminine plural.*

**curry** *noun*
a curry = un curry

**curtain** *noun*
a curtain = un rideau
to draw the curtains = tirer les rideaux

**cushion** *noun*
a cushion = un coussin

**custard** *noun* (*British English*)
custard ≈ la crème anglaise

**custom** *noun*
a custom = une coutume

**customer** *noun*
a customer = un client/une cliente

**customs** *noun*
customs = la douane
to go through customs = passer à la
douane

**customs officer** *noun* ▶ 315 |
a customs officer = un douanier/une
douanière

**cut**
**1** *verb*
= couper
to cut an apple in half = couper une
pomme en deux
to cut [one's fingers | one's knee | one's foot ...]
= se couper [les doigts | le genou | le pied ...]
she cut herself = elle s'est coupée
to have one's hair cut = se faire couper les
cheveux
I got my hair cut = je me suis fait couper
les cheveux
**2** *noun*
a cut = une coupure
**cut down** = abattre
**cut out**
to cut a photo out of a magazine
= découper une photo dans un
magazine
**cut up** = couper

**cute** *adjective*
= mignon/mignonne

**CV** *noun*
a CV = un CV, un curriculum vitae

**cycle** *verb*
to cycle to school = aller à l'école à vélo
to go cycling = faire du vélo

**cycle lane**, **cycle path** *noun*
a cycle lane = une piste cyclable

**cycling** *noun* ▶ 248 |
cycling = le cyclisme

**cyclist** *noun*
a cyclist = un cycliste/une cycliste

**cynical** *adjective*
= cynique

**Czech Republic** *noun* ▶ 218 |
the Czech Republic = la République
tchèque

# Dd

**dad, Dad** *noun*
   a dad = un papa

**daffodil** *noun*
   a daffodil = une jonquille

**daisy** *noun*
   a daisy = une pâquerette

**damage**
**1** *verb*
   to damage = abîmer
   the building was damaged by the fire = le
      bâtiment a été endommagé par
      l'incendie
   (*to harm*) = nuire à
   it can damage your health = cela nuit à la
      santé
**2** *noun*
   damage = les dégâts (*masculine plural*)
   to cause damage = faire des dégâts

**damp** *adjective*
   = humide

**dance**
**1** *verb*
   = danser
**2** *noun*
   a dance = une danse

**dancer** *noun* ▶ 315 |
   a dancer = un danseur/une danseuse

**dancing** *noun*
   dancing = la danse

**danger** *noun*
   danger = le danger
   to be in danger = être en danger

**dangerous** *adjective*
   = dangereux/dangereuse

**Danish** ▶ 275 |
**1** *adjective*
   = danois/danoise
**2** *noun*
   Danish = le danois

**dare** *verb*
   (*to have the courage*) = oser
   (*when testing someone*)
   to dare someone to play a trick = défier
      quelqu'un de jouer un tour
   (*when expressing anger*)
   don't dare speak to me like that! = je
      t'interdis de me parler sur ce ton!

**dark**
**1** *adjective*
   (*lacking light*) = sombre
   it's getting dark = il commence à faire
      nuit

(*describing a colour, clothes*) ▶ 213 |
   = sombre
   he always wears dark clothes = il porte
      toujours des vêtements sombres
   a dark blue dress = une robe bleu foncé
   (*describing a person*) = brun/brune
**2** *noun*
   the dark = le noir, l'obscurité (*feminine*)

**darts** *noun* ▶ 248 |
   darts = les fléchettes (*feminine*)

**date** *noun* ▶ 222 |
   (*in a calendar*)
   a date = une date
   what date is today? = quelle est la date
      aujourd'hui?
   (*with a friend*)
   a date = un rendez-vous
   to go out on a date with someone = sortir
      avec quelqu'un

**daughter** *noun*
   a daughter = une fille

**daughter-in-law** *noun*
   a daughter in law = une belle-fille

**dawn** *noun*
   dawn = l'aube (*feminine*)
   at dawn = à l'aube

**day** *noun* ▶ 356 |

   **!** *Note that* day *is usually translated by*
   jour *in French. However it is sometimes
   translated by* journée, *when there is an
   emphasis on the idea of duration.*

   a day = un jour
   what day is it today? = quel jour sommes-
      nous aujourd'hui?
   during the day = pendant la journée
   we had a very nice day = nous avons
      passé une journée très agréable
   the next day, the day after = le lendemain
   the day before = la veille

**daylight** *noun*
   daylight = le jour, la lumière du jour

**dazzle** *verb*
   = éblouir

**dead** *adjective*
   = mort/morte
   he is dead = il est mort

**deaf** *adjective*
   = sourd/sourde

**deal**
**1** *noun*
   a deal (*in business*) = une affaire
   (*with a friend*) = un marché
   a great deal [of money | of time | of energy ...]
   = beaucoup [d'argent | de temps | d'énergie ...]
**2** *verb*
   to deal the cards = distribuer les cartes
**deal with** = s'occuper de (**!** + *être*)
   to deal with a problem = s'occuper d'un
      problème

# Dates, days, and months

## The days of the week

Note that French uses lower-case letters for the names of days.
Write the names of days in full; do not abbreviate as in English (*Tues, Sat* and so on).

| | |
|---|---|
| *Monday* | = lundi |
| *Tuesday* | = mardi |
| *Wednesday* | = mercredi |
| *Thursday* | = jeudi |
| *Friday* | = vendredi |
| *Saturday* | = samedi |
| *Sunday* | = dimanche |

**lundi** in the notes below stands for any day; they all work the same way. Note the use of **le** for regular occurrences, and no article for single ones. (*Remember: do not translate* **on**.)

| | |
|---|---|
| *on Monday* | = lundi |
| *on Mondays* | = le lundi |
| *Monday afternoon* | = lundi après-midi |
| *last / next Monday* | = lundi dernier / prochain |
| *last Monday night* | = la nuit de lundi dernier |
| | (*if evening*) lundi dernier dans la soirée |
| *early on Monday* | = lundi matin de bonne heure |
| *late on Monday* | = lundi soir tard |
| *a month from Monday* | = dans un mois lundi |
| *from Monday on* | = à partir de lundi |

## The months of the year

As with the days of the week, do not use capitals to spell the names of the months in French, and do not abbreviate as in English ( *Jan, Feb* and so on).

| | | | | |
|---|---|---|---|---|
| *January* | = janvier | *July* | = juillet |
| *February* | = février | *August* | = août |
| *March* | = mars | *September* | = septembre |
| *April* | = avril | *October* | = octobre |
| *May* | = mai | *November* | = novembre |
| *June* | = juin | *December* | = décembre |

**May** in the notes below stands for any month; they all work the same way.

| | |
|---|---|
| *in May* | = en mai / au mois de mai |
| *next May* | = en mai prochain |
| *last May* | = l'année dernière en mai |
| *in early / late May* | = début / fin mai |

## Dates

French has only one generally accepted way of writing dates: **le 10 mai** (say **le dix mai**).
If the days of the week is included, put it after the **le**:

| | |
|---|---|
| *Monday, May 1st 1901* | = le lundi 1er mai 1901 |
| *what's the date?* | = quel jour sommes-nous? |
| *it's the tenth of May* | = nous sommes le 10 mai / on est le 10 mai |
| *in 1968* | = en 1968 |
| *in the year 2000* | = en l'an 2000 |
| *in the seventeenth century* | = au dix-septième siècle |

| | Write | Say |
|---|---|---|
| *May 1* | le 1er mai | le premier mai |
| *May 2* | le 2 mai | le deux mai |
| *from 4th to 16th May* | du 4 au 16 mai | du quatre au seize mai |
| *May 6 1968* | le 6 mai 1968 | le six mai mille neuf cent soixante-huit |
| *in the 1980s* | dans les années 80 | dans les années quatre-vingt |
| *the 16th century* | le XVIe siècle | le seizième siècle |

**dear**
**1** *adjective*
(*in letters*) = cher/chère
Dear Anne = Chère Anne
Dear Anne and Paul = Chers Anne et Paul
Dear Sir/Madam = Monsieur, Madame
(*expensive*) = cher/chère
**2** *exclamation* ▶ 237 |
oh dear! = oh mon Dieu!

**death** *noun*
death = la mort

**death penalty** *noun*
the death penalty = la peine de mort

**debate** *noun*
a debate = un débat

**debt** *noun*
a debt = une dette
to be in debt = avoir des dettes

**decade** *noun*
a decade = une décennie

**decaffeinated** *adjective*
= décafféiné/décafféinée

**deceive** *verb*
= tromper

**December** *noun* ▶ 222 |
December = décembre (*masculine*)

**decide** *verb*
= décider
he decided [to accept | to stay | to get
married…] = il a décidé [d'accepter | de
rester | de se marier…]

**decision** *noun*
a decision = une décision
to make a decision = prendre une
décision

**deck** *noun*
a deck = un pont
on deck = sur le pont

**deckchair** *noun*
a deckchair = une chaise longue

**decorate** *verb*
(*with ornaments*) = décorer
(*with wallpaper*) = tapisser
(*to paint*) = peindre

**decoration** *noun*
a decoration = une décoration

**deed** *noun*
(*of a house*)
a deed = un acte de propriété

**deep** *adjective* ▶ 285 |
= profond/profonde
how deep is the lake? = quelle est la
profondeur du lac?

**deer** *noun*
a deer (*male*) = un cerf
(*female*) = une biche

**defeat**
**1** *verb*
to defeat an enemy = vaincre un ennemi
the team was defeated = l'équipe a été
battue
**2** *noun*
a defeat = une défaite

**defence** (*British English*), **defense** (*US
English*) *noun*
defence = la défense

**defend** *verb*
= défendre

**definite** *adjective*
(*describing a decision*) = ferme
(*describing a plan*) = précis/précise
nothing is definite = rien n'est sûr
(*obvious, visible*) = net/nette
a definite improvement = une nette
amélioration

**definitely** *adverb*
= sans aucun doute
they're definitely lying = ils mentent sans
aucun doute
I'm definitely coming = c'est décidé, je
viens
'definitely!' = 'absolument!'

**defy** *verb*
= défier

**degree** *noun*
(*from a university*)
a degree = un diplôme universitaire
(*in measurements*)
a degree = un degré

**delay**
**1** *verb*
= retarder
**2** *noun*
a delay = un retard

**deliberate** *adjective*
= délibéré/délibérée

**deliberately** *adverb*
= exprès
he did it deliberately = il l'a fait exprès

**delicious** *adjective*
= délicieux/délicieuse

**delighted** *adjective*
= ravi/ravie
to be delighted with a present = être
ravi/ravie d'un cadeau

**deliver** *verb*
= livrer
to deliver goods = livrer des marchandises
to deliver mail = distribuer le courrier

**demand** *verb*
= exiger

**demolish** *verb*
= démolir

**D**

**demonstration** *noun*
a demonstration = une manifestation

**denim jacket** *adjective*
a denim jacket = un blouson en jean

**Denmark** *noun* ▶ 218 |
Denmark = le Danemark

**dentist** *noun* ▶ 315 |
a dentist = un dentiste/une dentiste

**deny** *verb*
= nier

**department** *noun*
a department (*in a firm*) = un service
(*in a large store*) = un rayon
(*in a school*) = une section
(*in a university*) = un département

**department store** *noun*
a department store = un grand magasin

**depend** *verb*
= dépendre
to depend on someone = dépendre de
quelqu'un
it depends on you = cela dépend de toi
it depends = ça dépend

**depressed** *adjective*
= déprimé/déprimée

**depressing** *adjective*
= déprimant/déprimante

**deprive** *verb*
= priver

**depth** *noun* ▶ 285 |
depth = la profondeur

**describe** *verb*
= décrire

**description** *noun*
a description = une description

**desert** *noun*
a desert = un désert

**deserve** *verb*
= mériter
he deserves to be punished = il mérite
d'être puni

**design**
**1** *verb*
(*to plan*) = concevoir
the house was designed for a hot climate
= la maison a été conçue pour un climat
chaud
(*in fashion*)
to design clothes = créer des vêtements
**2** *noun*
(*a subject of study*)
(fashion) design = le stylisme
(*a pattern*)
a design = un motif

**desk** *noun*
a desk = un bureau

**desperate** *adjective*
= désespéré/désespérée

**dessert** *noun*
a dessert = un dessert

**destroy** *verb*
= détruire

**detail** *noun*
a detail = un détail
to go into details = entrer dans les détails

**detective** *noun* ▶ 315 |
a detective = un inspecteur de police
a private detective = un détective

**detective story** *noun*
a detective story = un roman policier

**determined** *adjective*
= déterminé/déterminée
to be determined to go = être
décidé/décidée à y aller

**develop** *verb*
= développer

**development** *noun*
a development = un développement

**diagram** *noun*
a diagram = un schéma

**dial** *verb*
to dial a number = composer un numéro

**dialling code** *noun* (*British English*)
a dialling code = un indicatif

**dialling tone** (*British English*), **dial
tone** (*US English*) *noun*
a dialling tone = une tonalité

**diamond** *noun*
a diamond = un diamant

**diary** *noun*
(*for personal thoughts*)
a diary = un journal
(*for appointments*)
a diary = un agenda

**dice** *noun*
a dice = un dé

**dictionary** *noun*
a dictionary = un dictionnaire

**die** *verb*
to die = mourir (**!** + *être*)
he died in the war = il est mort à la guerre
to be dying of cancer = être
atteint/atteinte d'un cancer incurable
(*used for emphasis*)
I'm dying to go on holiday = je meurs
d'envie de partir en vacances

**diet** *noun*
a diet = un régime
to go on a diet = se mettre au régime

**difference** noun
a difference = une différence
I can't tell the difference = je ne vois pas la différence
it won't make any difference = ça ne changera rien

**different** adjective
= différent/différente

**difficult** adjective
= difficile
Spanish is not difficult to learn = l'espagnol n'est pas difficile à apprendre
to be difficult to get along with = être difficile à vivre

**difficulty** noun
a difficulty = une difficulté, un problème
to have difficulty concentrating = avoir du mal à se concentrer

**dig** verb
= creuser

**dig up**
(when gardening) = bêcher
(to find what was buried) = déterrer

**digital** adjective
= numérique

**dim** adjective
(describing a light) = faible
(describing a room) = sombre

**diner** noun (US English)
a diner = un café-restaurant

**dinghy** noun
a dinghy = un dériveur

**dining room** noun
a dining room = une salle à manger

**dinner** noun
a dinner = un dîner
dinner's ready! = à table!

**dip** verb
= tremper

**direct**
1 adjective
= direct/directe
2 verb
(when talking about directions)
could you direct me to the station? = pourriez-vous m'indiquer le chemin pour aller à la gare?
(in cinema or theatre)
to direct a film = réaliser un film
to direct a play = mettre en scène une pièce

**direction** noun
a direction = une direction, un sens
is this the right direction? = est-ce que c'est la bonne direction?
they were going in the other direction = ils allaient dans l'autre sens

**directions** noun
directions = les indications (feminine)
to give someone directions = donner des indications à quelqu'un
to ask someone for directions = demander le chemin à quelqu'un

**director** noun ▶ 315|
(of a film or play)
a director = un metteur en scène
(of a company)
a director = un directeur/une directrice

**dirt** noun
dirt = la saleté

**dirty**
1 adjective
= sale
to get dirty = se salir (! + être)
2 verb
= salir

**disabled** adjective
= handicapé/handicapée

**disadvantage** noun
a disadvantage = un désavantage

**disagree** verb
= ne pas être d'accord
I disagree with you = je ne suis pas d'accord avec toi

**disappear** verb
= disparaître

**disappoint** verb
= décevoir

**disappointed** adjective
= déçu/déçue

**disappointing** adjective
= décevant/décevante

**disappointment** noun
disappointment = la déception

**disapprove** verb
to disapprove of someone = ne pas apprécier quelqu'un

**disaster** noun
a disaster = une catastrophe, un désastre

**discipline** noun
discipline = la discipline

**disco** noun
a disco = une discothèque

**disconnect** verb
(to pull out a plug) = débrancher
(to cut off) = couper

**discourage** verb
= décourager

**discover** verb
= découvrir

**discovery** noun
a discovery = une découverte

D

**discreet** *adjective*
= discret/discrète

**discrimination** *noun*
discrimination = la discrimination

**discuss** *verb*
= discuter de
to discuss politics = discuter de politique

**discussion** *noun*
a discussion = une discussion

**disease** *noun* ▶ 266 |
a disease = une maladie

**disguise**
**1** *noun*
a disguise = un déguisement
to wear a disguise = être déguisé/déguisée
**2** *verb*
to disguise oneself as a woman = se
déguiser en femme

**disgusting** *adjective*
= dégoûtant/dégoûtante

**dish** *noun*
(*food*)
a dish = un plat
the dishes = la vaisselle (*singular*)
to wash the dishes = faire la vaisselle

**dishonest** *adjective*
= malhonnête

**dishwasher** *noun*
a dishwasher = un lave-vaisselle

**dislike** *verb*
= ne pas aimer
I dislike him = je ne l'aime pas

**dismiss** *verb*
= renvoyer

**disobedient** *adjective*
= désobéissant/désobéissante

**disobey** *verb*
to disobey someone = désobéir à
quelqu'un

**display** *noun*
a display = un étalage
a window display = une vitrine

**dispute** *noun*
a dispute (*between individuals*) = une
dispute
(*between groups*) = un conflit

**disqualify** *verb*
= disqualifier

**disrupt** *verb*
= perturber

**dissatisfied** *adjective*
= mécontent/mécontente

**distance** *noun*
a distance = une distance
in the distance = au loin
to keep one's distance = garder ses
distances

**distinct** *adjective*
(*easy to see, to hear*) = distinct/distincte
(*definite*) = net/nette (**!** *before the noun*)

**distinguish** *verb*
= distinguer
to distinguish between truth and lies
= faire la distinction entre la vérité et les
mensonges

**distract** *verb*
= distraire
to distract someone from working
= empêcher quelqu'un de travailler

**distressed** *adjective*
= bouleversé/bouleversée

**distribute** *verb*
= distribuer

**disturb** *verb*
= déranger

**disturbing** *adjective*
= troublant/troublante

**dive** *verb* ▶ 248 |
= plonger
to go diving = faire de la plongée

**divide** *verb*
(*in arithmetic*) = diviser
(*to share*) = partager

**diving board** *noun*
a diving board = un plongeoir

**divorce**
**1** *noun*
a divorce = un divorce
**2** *verb*
= divorcer

**DIY** *noun* (*British English*)
DIY = le bricolage

**dizzy** *adjective*
to feel dizzy = avoir la tête qui tourne

**do** *verb* ▶ 237 |
▶ 227 | *See the boxed note on* **do** *for more
information and examples.*
to do = faire
to do the cooking = faire la cuisine
to do one's homework = faire ses devoirs
what has he done with the newspaper?
= qu'est-ce qu'il a fait du journal?
what has she done to her hair? = qu'est-ce
qu'elle a fait à ses cheveux?
do as you're told = fais ce qu'on te dit
(*in questions, negatives*)
do you like cats? = est-ce que tu aimes les
chats?
I don't like cats = je n'aime pas les chats
I didn't do anything = je n'ai rien fait
don't shout! = ne crie pas!

# do

## As an ordinary verb

Usually, the French equivalent of the verb to do is **faire**:

| | |
|---|---|
| *she is **doing** her homework* | = elle **fait** ses devoirs |
| *what **has** he **done** with the newspaper?* | = qu'est-ce qu'il **a fait** du journal? |

## As an auxiliary verb

### In questions

In French there is no auxiliary verb in questions equivalent to **do** in English.

When the subject is a pronoun, use either of these structures: *verb + hyphen + subject* or, less formally, **est-ce que** + *subject + verb*:

| | |
|---|---|
| ***do** you like Mozart?* | = aimes-tu Mozart? |
| | = **est-ce que** tu aimes Mozart? |

When the subject is a noun, there are again two possibilities:

| | |
|---|---|
| ***did** your sister ring?* | = **est-ce que** ta sœur a téléphoné? |
| | = ta sœur a-t-elle téléphoné? |

### In negatives

Equally, auxiliaries are not used in negatives in French:

| | |
|---|---|
| *I **don't** like Mozart* | = je n'aime pas Mozart. |

### In emphatic uses

There is no verbal equivalent for the use of **do** in such expressions as *I do like your dress*. In emphatic uses, French may use an adverb like *beaucoup, vraiment*:

| | |
|---|---|
| *I **do** like your dress* | = j'aime **beaucoup** ta robe |
| *I **do** think you should go* | = je pense **vraiment** que tu devrais y aller |

### When referring back to another verb

In this case the verb **to do** is not translated at all:

| | |
|---|---|
| *I live in Oxford and so **does** Lily* | = j'habite à Oxford et Lily aussi |
| *she gets paid more than I **do*** | = elle est payée plus que moi |
| *'I don't like carrots' — 'neither **do** I'* | = 'je n'aime pas les carottes' — 'moi non plus' |

### In polite requests

In polite requests the phrase *je vous en prie* or *je t'en prie* is useful.

| | |
|---|---|
| ***do** sit down* | = asseyez-vous, **je vous en prie** |

### In imperatives

In French there is no use of an auxiliary verb in imperatives:

| | |
|---|---|
| ***don't** shut the door* | = ne ferme pas la porte |
| ***do** be quiet* | = tais-toi! |

### In short questions

With questions like **doesn't he?** or **didn't he?**, there is a general French phrase question **n'est-ce pas?** which will work in many cases:

| | |
|---|---|
| *you like fish, **don't you?*** | = tu aimes les poisson, **n'est-ce pas?** |

With positive tag questions **par hasard** can often be used as a translation:

| | |
|---|---|
| *Lola didn't phone, **did she?*** | = Lola n'a pas téléphoné **par hasard?** |

### In short answers

There is no direct French equivalent for the verb such as *no, he doesn't, yes, we did* etc.

| | |
|---|---|
| *'does he play tennis?' — '**no, he doesn't**'* | = 'est-ce qu'il joue au tennis?' — '**non**' |
| *'do you like strawberries?' —'**yes I do**'* | = 'aimez-vous les fraises?' — '**oui**' |

If answering 'yes' to contradict a negative statement, the most useful translation is **si**:

| | |
|---|---|
| *'Marion didn't say that' —'**yes she did**'* | = 'Marion n'a pas dit ça' — '**si**' |

▶ For more examples, see the entry **do**.

*(in short answers and tag questions)*
'**do you like strawberries?**'—'**yes, I do**'
  = 'est-ce que tu aimes les fraises?'—'oui'
'**I never said I liked him**'—'**yes, you did**'
  = 'je n'ai jamais dit que je l'aimais'—'si,
  tu l'as dit'
'**I love chocolate**'—'**so do I!**' = 'j'adore le
  chocolat'—'moi aussi!'
'**who wrote it?**'—'**I did**' = 'qui l'a écrit?'
  —'moi'
**he lives in London, doesn't he?** = il habite
  à Londres, n'est-ce-pas?
**Martine didn't phone, did she?** = Martine
  n'a pas téléphoné, par hasard?
'**may I sit down?**'—'**yes, please do**'
  = 'puis-je m'asseoir?'—'je t'en prie'
*(to be enough)* = suffire
**ten pounds will do** = dix livres suffiront
**that box will do** = cette boîte fera l'affaire
*(to perform)*
**he did well** = il s'est bien débrouillé
**he did badly** = il s'est mal débrouillé
**do up** *(British English)*
  **to do up one's buttons** = se boutonner
    (**!** + *être*)
  **to do up a house** = refaire une maison
**do with**
  **it's got something to do with computers**
    = ça a quelque chose à voir avec
    l'informatique
  **it has nothing to do with him** = ça n'a rien
    à voir avec lui
**do without** = se passer de (**!** + *être*)
  **I can do without a television** = je peux me
    passer de télévision

**dock** *noun*
  **a dock** = un dock

**doctor** *noun* ▶ 315 |
  **a doctor** = un médecin

**document** *noun*
  **a document** = un document

**documentary** *noun*
  **a documentary** = un documentaire

**dog** *noun*
  **a dog** = un chien

**doll** *noun*
  **a doll** = une poupée

**dollar** *noun*
  **a dollar** = un dollar

**dolphin** *noun*
  **a dolphin** = un dauphin

**dominoes** *noun* ▶ 248 |
  **dominoes** = les dominos *(masculine)*

**donkey** *noun*
  **a donkey** = un âne

**door** *noun*
  **a door** = une porte

**doorbell** *noun*
  **a doorbell** = une sonnette

**dormitory** *noun*
  **a dormitory** = un dortoir

**dose** *noun*
  **a dose** = une dose

**double**
**1** *adjective*
  *(of an amount)* = double
  **a double helping of strawberries** = une
    double portion de fraises
  *(when spelling or giving a number)*
  **Annie is spelled with a double 'n'** = Annie
    s'écrit avec deux 'n'
  **three double five** *(British English)* = trois
    cent cinquante cinq
**2** *verb*
  = doubler

**double bass** *noun* ▶ 290 |
  **a double bass** = une contrebasse

**double bed** *noun*
  **a double bed** = un grand lit

**double-decker** *noun*
  **a double-decker** = un autobus à impériale

**double room** *noun*
  **a double room** = une chambre pour deux
    personnes

**doubt**
**1** *noun*
  **a doubt** = un doute
  **there's no doubt that he is innocent** = son
    innocence ne fait aucun doute
  **I've no doubt that it's true** = je suis certain
    que c'est vrai
**2** *verb*
  = douter
  **I doubt if she'll come** = je doute qu'elle
    vienne
  | **!** *Note that the subjunctive is used after*
  | *douter que.*

**dough** *noun*
  **dough** = la pâte

**doughnut**, **donut** *(US English) noun*
  **a doughnut** = un beignet

**down**
  | **!** *Often* down *occurs in combinations with*
  | *verbs, for example:* calm down, let down,
  | slow down *etc. To find the correct*
  | *translations for this type of verb, look up*
  | *the separate dictionary entries at* calm,
  | let, slow *etc.*

**1** *preposition*
  **to go down the street** = descendre la rue
  **he walked down the corridor** = il a
    descendu le couloir
  **he ran down the hill** = il a descendu la
    colline en courant
  **the kitchen is down those stairs** = la
    cuisine est en bas de cet escalier

**2** *adverb*
  she's down in the cellar = elle est dans la cave
  down in Brighton = à Brighton
  to go down to the country = aller à la campagne
  to go down = descendre (**!** + *être*)
  to fall down – tomber (**!** + *être*)
  down there = là-bas

**downstairs** *adverb*
  = en bas
  to go downstairs = descendre (l'escalier)
  to bring the boxes downstairs = descendre les cartons

**dozen** *noun* ▶ 317 |
  a dozen = une douzaine
  a dozen eggs = une douzaine d'œufs

**draft** *noun* (*US English*)
  a draft = un courant d'air

**drag** *verb*
  = traîner

**drain** *verb*
  (*when cooking*) = égoutter
  (*if it's water*)
  to drain (away) – s'écouler (**!** + *être*)

**drama** *noun*
  (*a play, an event*)
  a drama = un drame
  (*theatre*)
  drama = le théâtre

**dramatic** *adjective*
  = spectaculaire

**drapes** *noun* (*US English*)
  drapes = les rideaux (*masculine*)

**draught** *noun* (*British English*)
  a draught = un courant d'air

**draughts** *noun* ▶ 248 | (*British English*)
  draughts = les dames (*feminine*)

**draw**
**1** *verb*
  (*with a pen or pencil*) = dessiner
  to draw a rabbit = dessiner un lapin
  to draw a picture = faire un dessin
  to draw a line = tracer une ligne
  she drew his portrait = elle a fait son portrait
  (*to pull*) = tirer
  to draw the curtains = tirer les rideaux
  (*to take out*) = sortir
  to draw a knife = sortir un couteau
  (*in a lottery*)
  to draw a ticket = tirer un ticket au sort
  (*to attract*) = attirer
  the circus drew a large crowd = le cirque a attiré beaucoup de monde
  (*British English*) (*in sport*) – faire match nul
  Christmas is drawing near = Noël approche

**2** *noun*
  (*in sport*)
  a draw = un match nul
  (*in a lottery*)
  a draw = un tirage au sort

**draw aside**
  to draw someone aside = prendre quelqu'un à part

**draw back**
  to draw back the curtains = ouvrir les rideaux

**draw up**
  to draw up a list = dresser une liste

**drawer** *noun*
  a drawer = un tiroir

**drawing** *noun*
  drawing = le dessin

**dread** *verb*
  = appréhender

**dreadful** *adjective*
  = épouvantable

**dream**
**1** *noun* ▶ 237 |
  a dream = un rêve
  to have a dream = faire un rêve
**2** *verb*
  = rêver
  to dream of going to Japan = rêver d'aller au Japon

**dress**
**1** *noun*
  a dress = une robe
**2** *verb*
  (*to put one's own clothes on*) = s'habiller (**!** + *être*)
  (*to put clothes on someone*) = habiller

**dress up**
  (*in good clothes*) = s'habiller (**!** + *être*)
  (*in a disguise*) = se déguiser (**!** + *être*)
  she dressed up as a clown = elle s'est déguisée en clown

**dressing gown** *noun*
  a dressing gown = une robe de chambre

**drill**
**1** *noun*
  a drill = une perceuse
**2** *verb*
  to drill a hole = percer un trou
  to drill through the wall = percer un trou dans le mur

**drink**
**1** *verb*
  = boire
**2** *noun*
  a drink = une boisson
  a drink of water = un verre d'eau

D

## drive
**1** *verb*
(*in a car*) = conduire
**to learn to drive** = apprendre à conduire
**he drives to work** = il va au travail en voiture
**to drive someone home** = ramener quelqu'un en voiture
(*to make*)
**to drive someone mad** = rendre quelqu'un fou/folle
**2** *noun*
**a drive** = un tour (en voiture)
**to go for a drive** = aller faire un tour (en voiture)
**drive away**
(*in a car*) = démarrer
(*to chase away*) = chasser
**drive back** = rentrer (en voiture) (**!** + *être*)

## driver *noun*
**a driver** = un conducteur/une conductrice

## driver's license (*US English*), driving licence (*British English*) *noun*
**a driver's license** = un permis de conduire

## drizzle *verb*
= bruiner

## drop
**1** *verb*
(*to come down*) = baisser
**the temperature has dropped** = la température a baissé
(*to let fall*) = laisser tomber
**she dropped her suitcase** = elle a laissé tomber sa valise
(*to fall*) = tomber (**!** + *être*)
**2** *noun*
(*a fall*)
**a drop** = une baisse
**a drop in temperature** = une baisse de température
(*of liquid*)
**a drop** = une goutte
**drop in** = passer (**!** + *être*)
**he dropped in to see me** = il est passé me voir
**drop off** = déposer
**could you drop me off at the station?** = est-ce que tu pourrais me déposer à la gare?
**drop out**
**to drop out of school** = abandonner ses études
**to drop out of a race** = se retirer d'une course

## drought *noun*
**a drought** = une sécheresse

## drown *verb*
= se noyer (**!** + *être*)

## drug
**1** *noun*
(*for illegal use*)
**a drug** = une drogue

**to be on drugs** = se droguer (**!** + *être*)
(*for medical use*)
**a drug** = un médicament
**2** *verb*
**to drug someone** = droguer quelqu'un

## drug addict *noun*
**a drug addict** = un toxicomane/une toxicomane

## drum *noun* ▶ 290 ⏐
**a drum** = un tambour
**to play drums** = jouer de la batterie

## drunk *adjective*
= ivre

## dry
**1** *adjective*
= sec/sèche
**a dry day** = une journée sans pluie
**2** *verb*
**to dry clothes** = faire sécher des vêtements
**to dry oneself** = se sécher (**!** + *être*)
**he dried his hands** = il s'est séché les mains
**to dry the dishes** = essuyer la vaisselle

## duck
**1** *noun*
**a duck** = un canard
**2** *verb*
= baisser la tête

## due
**1 due to** = à cause de
**the game was cancelled due to bad weather** = le match a été annulé à cause du mauvais temps
**2** *adjective*
(*expected*)
**the train is due (in) at two o'clock** = le train doit arriver à deux heures
(*owed*) = dû/due
**the amount due** = la somme due

## dull *adjective*
(*describing a person or book*) = terne
(*describing a colour*) = terne
(*describing the weather or a landscape*) = morne

## dumb *adjective*
(*unable to speak*) = muet/muette
(*stupid*) = bête

## dump
**1** *verb*
= jeter
**2** *noun*
**a dump** = une décharge

## during *preposition*
= pendant
**during the summer** = pendant l'été

## dust
**1** *noun*
**dust** = la poussière

**2** *verb*
= épousseter

**dustbin** *noun* (*British English*)
a dustbin = une poubelle

**dustman** *noun* (*British English*)
a dustman = un éboueur

**dustpan** *noun*
a dustpan = une pelle (à poussière)

**Dutch ▶ 275|**
**1** *adjective*
= hollandais/hollandaise
**2** *noun*
the Dutch = les Hollandais (*masculine plural*)

**duty** *noun*
• (*a task, part of one's job*)
a duty = une fonction
to take up one's duties = prendre ses fonctions
• (*of a soldier, a nurse*)
to be on duty = être de service
• (*what one must do*)
duty = le devoir
• (*a tax*)
customs duties = les droits de douane
❗ *Note that* droits *is masculine.*

**DVD** *noun*
a DVD = un DVD (❗ *never changes*)

**DVD player** *noun*
a DVD player = un lecteur DVD

**dye** *verb*
= teindre
to dye one's hair = se teindre les cheveux

**each**
**1** *determiner*
= chaque
each time I see him = chaque fois que je le vois
**2** *pronoun*
= chacun/chacune
each of the boys = chacun des garçons
each of them has a car = ils ont chacun/elles ont chacune une voiture

**each other** *pronoun*
❗ *Note that* each other *is very often translated by using a reflexive pronoun like* se, s', nous *or* vous.

they know each other already = ils se connaissent déjà
we write to each other every year = nous nous écrivons tous les ans

**eager** *adjective*
= enthousiaste

**eagle** *noun*
an eagle = un aigle

**ear** *noun* **▶ 201|**
an ear = une oreille

**early** *adverb*
• early = tôt
to get up early = se lever tôt
early in the afternoon = en début d'après-midi
• (*ahead of time*) = en avance
to arrive early = arriver en avance

**earn** *verb*
to earn lots of money = gagner beaucoup d'argent

**earring** *noun*
an earring = une boucle d'oreille

**earth** *noun*
• (*the planet*)
the earth = la terre
• (*soil*)
earth = la terre

**easily** *adverb*
= facilement

**east**
**1** *noun*
the east = l'est (*masculine*)
in the east of France = dans l'est de la France
**2** *adverb*
to go east = aller vers l'est
to live east of Paris = vivre à l'est de Paris
**3** *adjective*
= est (❗ *never changes*)
to work in east London = travailler dans l'est de Londres

**Easter** *noun*
Easter = Pâques (*feminine plural*)
Happy Easter! = Joyeuses Pâques!

**Easter egg** *noun*
an Easter egg = un œuf de Pâques

**easy** *adjective*
= facile
it's easy to fix = c'est facile à réparer
it's not easy to find work there = il n'est pas facile d'y trouver du travail

**eat** *verb*
= manger
**eat out** = manger au restaurant

**EC** *noun*
the EC = la Communauté Européenne

**echo** *noun*
an echo = un écho

**economic** *adjective*
= économique

**economics** *noun*
economics = les sciences économiques
! *Note that* sciences *is feminine plural.*

**economy** *noun*
the economy = l'économie (*feminine*)

**edge** *noun*
* (*of a road, table, an object*)
the edge = le bord
the edge of the lake = le bord du lac
at the edge of the town = aux abords de la ville
* (*of a forest, a wood or field*)
the edge = la lisière
* (*of a blade or knife*)
the edge = le tranchant

**educate** *verb*
= instruire
he was educated in Paris = il a fait ses études à Paris

**education** *noun*
education = l'instruction (*feminine*)
to get a good education = recevoir une bonne instruction

**effect** *noun*
an effect = un effet

**effective** *adjective*
= efficace

**efficient** *adjective*
= efficace

**effort** *noun*
an effort = un effort
to make an effort = faire un effort

**egg** *noun*
an egg = un œuf

**eggcup** *noun*
an eggcup = un coquetier

**eight** *number* ▶ 187 |, ▶ 211 |
eight = huit
eight apples = huit pommes
I've got eight (of them) = j'en ai huit

**eighteen** *number* ▶ 187 |, ▶ 211 |
eighteen = dix-huit

**eighteenth** *number*
* (*in a series*) = dix-huitième
* (*in dates*) ▶ 222 |
the eighteenth of August = le dix-huit août

**eighth** *number*
* (*in a series*) = huitième
* (*in dates*) ▶ 222 |
the eighth of August = le huit août

**eighty** *number* ▶ 187 |
eighty = quatre-vingts

**either**
**1** *conjunction*
they're coming on either Tuesday or Wednesday = ils viendront soit mardi, soit mercredi
he didn't contact either Helen or Paul = il n'a contacté ni Helen ni Paul
**2** *pronoun*
take either (of them) = prends l'un ou l'autre/l'une ou l'autre
I don't know either (of them) = je ne connais ni l'un ni l'autre/l'une ni l'autre
**3** *determiner*
take either road = prenez l'une ou l'autre route
I don't want to live in either country = je ne veux habiter dans aucun des deux pays
**4** *adverb*
= non plus
she can't do it either = elle ne peut pas le faire non plus

**elbow** *noun* ▶ 201 |
the elbow = le coude

**elder** *adjective*
= aîné/aînée

**elderly** *adjective*
= âgé/âgée

**eldest** *adjective*
= aîné/aînée
the eldest daughter = l'aînée

**elect** *verb*
= élire

**election** *noun*
an election = une élection
to win an election = remporter les élections

**electric** *adjective*
= électrique

**electrician** *noun* ▶ 315 |
an electrician = un électricien/une électricienne

**electricity** *noun*
electricity = l'électricité (*feminine*)

**elegant** *adjective*
= élégant/élégante

**elephant** *noun*
an elephant = un éléphant

**elevator** *noun* (*US English*)
an elevator = un ascenseur

**eleven** *number* ▶ 187 |, ▶ 211 |
eleven = onze
eleven apples = onze pommes
I've got eleven (of them) = j'en ai onze

**eleventh** *number*
* (*in a series*) = onzième
* (*in dates*) ▶ 222 |
the eleventh of May = le onze mai

**else**
**1** adverb
= d'autre
someone else = quelqu'un d'autre
nothing else = rien d'autre
what else did he say? = qu'est-ce qu'il a
   dit d'autre?
something else = autre chose
everything else = tout le reste
**2 or else** = sinon
be quiet or else! = taisez-vous sinon!

**elsewhere** adverb
= ailleurs

**email** noun
an email = un email, un mél
an email address = une adresse
   électronique

**embarrassed** adjective
= gêné/gênée

**embarrassing** adjective
= gênant/gênante

**embassy** noun
an embassy = une ambassade

**emergency** noun
an emergency = une urgence
in an emergency = en cas d'urgence

**emergency exit** noun
an emergency exit = une sortie de secours

**emigrate** verb
= émigrer

**emotion** noun
an emotion = une émotion

**emotional** adjective
• (describing a scene or moment)
= émouvant/émouvante
• (describing a person) = émotif/émotive

**emperor** noun
an emperor = un empereur

**employ** verb
= employer

**employed** adjective
to be employed = avoir un emploi

**employee** noun
an employee = un employé/une employée

**employer** noun
an employer = un employeur

**employment** noun
employment = le travail, l'emploi
   (masculine)

**empty**
**1** adjective
= vide
**2** verb
= vider

**encourage** verb
= encourager

**end**
**1** noun
• (the final part)
the end = la fin
at the end of May = fin mai
in the end = finalement
• (the furthest part)
the end = le bout
at the end of the street = au bout de la rue
**2** verb
• (to come to an end) = se terminer
   (! + être)
• (to put an end to) = mettre fin à
• (to finish) = terminer

**end up**
to end up in London = se retrouver à
   Londres
to end up going abroad = finir par aller à
   l'étranger

**ending** noun
the ending = la fin

**enemy** noun
an enemy = un ennemi/une ennemie

**energetic** adjective
= énergique

**energy** noun
energy = l'énergie (feminine)

**engaged** adjective
• to get engaged = se fiancer (! + être)
to be engaged = être fiancé/fiancée
• (British English) (describing a phone, toilet)
= occupé/occupée

**engine** noun
• (of a car)
an engine = un moteur
• (for a train)
an engine = une locomotive

**engineer** noun ▶ 315 |
an engineer = un ingénieur

**England** noun ▶ 218 |
England = l'Angleterre (feminine)

**English** ▶ 275 |
**1** adjective
= anglais/anglaise
**2** noun
• (the people)
the English = les Anglais (masculine
   plural)
• (the language)
English = l'anglais (masculine)

**enjoy** verb
• (to like) = aimer
he enjoys fishing = il aime la pêche
did you enjoy your holiday? = est-ce que
   tu as passé de bonnes vacances?
• (to have a good time) ▶ 237 |
to enjoy oneself = s'amuser (! + être)

**enjoyable** adjective
= agréable

E

**enormous** *adjective*
= énorme

**enough**
**1** *determiner*
= assez de
I don't have enough [time | friends …] = je n'ai pas assez [de temps | d'amis …]
there's enough room for everyone = il y a assez de place pour tout le monde
**2** *adverb*
= assez
is it big enough? = est-ce que c'est assez grand?
you're not old enough = tu n'es pas assez grand
**3** *pronoun*
= assez
we have enough to eat = nous avons assez à manger
I've had enough = j'en ai assez
that's enough = ça suffit

**enquire** *verb*
= se renseigner (! + *être*)
I'll enquire about the price = je vais me renseigner sur le prix

**enter** *verb*
• (*to go into*) = entrer dans (! + *être*)
• (*to take part in*) = participer à

**entertain** *verb*
= divertir

**entertaining** *adjective*
= divertissant/divertissante

**entertainment** *noun*
entertainment = le divertissement, les distractions (*feminine plural*)

**enthusiasm** *noun*
enthusiasm = l'enthousiasme (*masculine*)

**enthusiastic** *adjective*
= enthousiaste

**entrance** *noun*
an entrance = une entrée
the entrance to the castle = l'entrée du château

**envelope** *noun*
an envelope = une enveloppe

**environment** *noun*
the environment = l'environnement (*masculine*)

**envy**
**1** *noun*
envy = l'envie (*feminine*)
**2** *verb*
= envier

**episode** *noun*
an episode = un épisode

**equal**
**1** *adjective*
= égal/égale
to fight for equal rights = lutter pour l'égalité des droits
**2** *verb*
= égaler
six and four equals ten = six et quatre égalent dix

**equality** *noun*
equality = l'égalité (*feminine*)

**equator** *noun*
the equator = l'équateur (*masculine*)

**equipment** *noun*
equipment (*in an office, a laboratory, a factory*) = le matériel
(*for an activity*) = l'équipement (*masculine*)

**eraser** *noun*
an eraser = une gomme

**escalator** *noun*
an escalator = un escalier mécanique

**escape** *verb*
• (*to get away*) = s'échapper (! + *être*)
he escaped from prison = il s'est échappé de prison
• (*to avoid*) = échapper à
to escape death = échapper à la mort

**especially** *adverb*
= surtout

**essay** *noun*
an essay (*by a pupil*) = une rédaction
(*by a student*) = une dissertation

**essential** *adjective*
= essentiel/essentielle

**ethnic** *adjective*
= ethnique

**euro** *noun*
a euro = un euro

**eurocheque** *noun*
a eurocheque = un Eurochèque

**Europe** *noun* ▶ **218**
Europe = l'Europe (*feminine*)

**European** *adjective* ▶ **275**
= européen/européenne

**European Union** *noun*
the European Union = l'Union européenne
| ! *Note that* **Union** *is feminine.*

**evacuate** *verb*
= évacuer

**even**[1]
**1** *adverb*
• (*when expressing surprise*) = même
he didn't even try = il n'a même pas essayé
she even works on weekends = elle travaille même le week-end
• (*in comparisons*) = encore
it's even colder today = il fait encore plus froid aujourd'hui

**2 even though** = bien que
he's bored even though he's with other
people = bien qu'il soit avec d'autres
personnes, il s'ennuie
! Note that the subjunctive is used after
bien que.

**even²** adjective
• (flat, smooth) = régulier/régulière
• (when talking about numbers)
an even number = un nombre pair

**evening** noun ▶ 211|, ▶ 356|
! Note that evening is usually translated
by soir in French. However it is sometimes
translated by soirée, when there is an
emphasis on the idea of duration.

an evening = un soir
at eight o'clock in the evening = à huit
heures du soir
to spend the evening at home = passer la
soirée à la maison

**event** noun
an event = un événement

**eventually** adverb
! Note that eventually is never translated
by éventuellement.

= finalement

**ever** adverb
• (at any time)
nothing ever happens here = il ne se
passe jamais rien ici
no-one will ever know = personne ne le
saura jamais
have you ever been to Greece? = est-ce
que tu es déjà allé en Grèce?
I hardly ever go there = je n'y vais presque
jamais
• (always)
he's as lazy as ever = il est toujours aussi
paresseux

**every** determiner ▶ 356|
= tous les/toutes les
every time I meet her = toutes les fois que
je la rencontre
every day = tous les jours
every second day, every other day = tous
les deux jours
two out of every three people = deux
personnes sur trois

**everyone** pronoun (also **everybody**)
= tout le monde
everyone else = tous les autres

**everything** pronoun
= tout

**everywhere** adverb
= partout
everywhere else = partout ailleurs

**evidence** noun
a piece of evidence = une preuve
to give evidence = témoigner

**evil** noun
evil = le mal

**exact** adjective
= exact/exacte

**exactly** adverb
= exactement

**exaggerate** verb
= exagérer

**exam** noun
an exam = un examen
to pass an exam = réussir à un examen
to take an exam = passer un examen

**examine** verb
= examiner

**example** noun
an example = un exemple
for example = par exemple

**excellent** adjective
= excellent/excellente

**except** preposition
= sauf

**exchange** verb
= échanger
to exchange a hat for a scarf = échanger
un chapeau contre une écharpe

**exchange rate** noun
the exchange rate = le taux de change

**excited** adjective
= excité/excitée

**exciting** adjective
= passionnant/passionnante

**exclude** verb
= exclure

**excuse**
**1** noun
an excuse = une excuse
to make excuses = trouver des excuses
**2** verb
= excuser
excuse me! = excusez-moi!

**exercise** noun
• (to keep fit)
an exercise = un exercice
to take exercise, to do exercise = faire de
l'exercice
• (a piece of work)
an exercise = un exercice

**exercise book** noun
an exercise book = un cahier

**exhausted** adjective
= épuisé/épuisée

**exhibition** noun
an exhibition = une exposition

**exit** noun
an exit = une sortie

E

**expect** verb
- (to be prepared for) = s'attendre à (**!** + être)
  **to expect bad news** = s'attendre à de mauvaises nouvelles
  **they expect to win** = ils s'attendent à gagner
- (to wait for) = attendre
- (to want) = vouloir
  **they expect us to do the work** = ils veulent que nous fassions le travail
  **!** Note that the subjunctive is used after vouloir que.

**expenses** noun
  **expenses** = les frais (masculine)

**expensive** adjective
  = cher/chère

**experience** noun
  **an experience** = une expérience

**experienced** adjective
  = expérimenté/expérimentée

**experiment**
1 noun
  **an experiment** = une expérience
2 verb
  = expérimenter

**expert** noun
  **an expert** = un spécialiste/une spécialiste
  **a computer expert** = un spécialiste/une spécialiste en informatique

**explain** verb
  = expliquer
  **to explain a rule to someone** = expliquer une règle à quelqu'un

**explanation** noun
  **an explanation** = une explication

**explode** verb
  = exploser

**exploit** verb
  = exploiter

**explosion** noun
  **an explosion** = une explosion

**export** verb
  = exporter

**express**
1 verb
  **to express oneself** = s'exprimer (**!** + être)
2 adverb
  **to send a letter express** = envoyer une lettre en exprès

**expression** noun
  **an expression** = une expression

**express train** noun
  **an express train** = un rapide

**extinct** adjective
  (describing an animal) = disparu/disparue
  (describing a volcano) = éteint/éteinte

**extra**
1 adjective
  = supplémentaire
  **an extra bed** = un lit supplémentaire
  **to pay an extra ten pounds** = payer dix livres de plus
2 adverb
  **to pay extra** = payer un supplément

**extraordinary** adjective
  = extraordinaire

**extreme** adjective
  = extrême

**extremely** adverb
  = extrêmement

**eye** noun ▶ 201 |
  **an eye** = un œil
  **to have green eyes** = avoir les yeux verts

**eyebrow** noun ▶ 201 |
  **an eyebrow** = un sourcil

**eyelash** noun ▶ 201 |
  **an eyelash** = un cil

**eyelid** noun ▶ 201 |
  **an eyelid** = une paupière

**eye shadow** noun
  **eye shadow** = le fard à paupières

**eyesight** noun
  **eyesight** = la vue
  **to have good eyesight** = avoir une bonne vue

# Ff

**face**
1 noun
  **the face** = le visage, la figure
  **to make a face** = faire une grimace
2 verb
  (to be opposite) = être face à
  **she was facing me** = elle était face à moi
  (to have to deal with) = confronter
  **I can't face seeing them again** = je n'ai pas le courage de les revoir
  (to look toward(s))
  **my room faces the sea** = ma chambre donne sur la mer
**face up to** = faire face à

**fact**
1 noun
  **a fact** = un fait
2 **in fact** = en fait

**factory** noun
  **a factory** = une usine

# Useful everyday expressions in spoken French

### When things are going well

| | | | |
|---|---|---|---|
| *well done!* | = bravo! | *congratulations!* | = félicitations! |
| | = chapeau**\***! | *good luck!* | = bonne chance! |
| | (*I take my hat* | *way to go! (US English)* | = bravo! |
| | *off to him / you etc*) | *wow!* | = super**\***!, génial**\***! |

### When things are not so good

| | | | |
|---|---|---|---|
| *hard luck!* | = pas de chance! | *good luck! (you'll need it)* | – bon courage! |
| *too bad !* | = tant pis! | *ouch!* | = aïe!, ouïlle! |
| *cheer up!, chin up!* | = courage! | *shit!* | = merde**♦\***! |
| *oh dear!* | = oh là là**\***! | *yuck!, ugh!* | = beurk**\***! |
| | = ça alors! | *phew! (that was close)* | = ouf! |
| *damn!* | = ah, mince**\***! | *get well soon!* | = bon rétablissement!, |
| *blast!* | = zut**\***! | | remets-toi vite! |

### Coming

| | |
|---|---|
| *welcome!* | = bienvenue! |
| *nice to meet you, pleased to meet you* | = enchanté/enchantée de faire votre connaissance |
| *hello!* | = bonjour! (*face to face*) |
| | = allô, bonjour! (*on the phone*) |
| *hi!* | = salut**\***! |
| *hi again!* | = rebonjour**\***! |

### Going

| | |
|---|---|
| *goodbye!* | = au revoir! |
| *bye!* | = salut**\***! tchao**\***! |
| *cheers! (British English)* | = salut**\***! |
| *see you soon / later / next week!* | = à bientôt! / plus tard! / la semaine prochaine! |
| *see you around!* | = à un de ces jours! |
| *(have a) safe journey!* | = bon voyage! |
| *all the best!* | = bonne continuation! |

### Wishing someone well

| | |
|---|---|
| *have a nice day!* | = bonne journée! |
| *have a good weekend!* | = bon week-end! |
| *have a great holiday or vacation!* | = bonnes vacances! |
| *have a good time!, enjoy yourself!* | = amuse-toi bien!, amusez-vous bien! |
| *have a good trip!* | = bon voyage! |

### Special greetings

| | | | |
|---|---|---|---|
| *Happy birthday!* | = Bon anniversaire! | *Happy New Year!* | = Bonne année! |
| *Happy Christmas!* | = Joyeux Noël! | *April fool!* | = poisson d'avril! |

### In reply to: 'Would you like ...?'

| | |
|---|---|
| *yes, please* | – volontiers |
| | = oui, je veux bien! |
| | = pourquoi pas? |

### In reply to: 'Thank you'

| | |
|---|---|
| *you're very welcome* | = je t'en prie, je vous en prie |
| *don't mention it* | = (il n'y a) pas de quoi |
| *no problem, not at all* | = de rien |

### Eating and drinking

| | |
|---|---|
| *enjoy your meal!* | = bon appétit! |
| *cheers!* | = santé!, à la tienne!, à la vôtre!, tchin! tchin! |

### Sleeping

| | | | |
|---|---|---|---|
| *good night!* | = bonne nuit! | *sweet dreams!* | = fais de beaux rêves! |
| *sleep well!* | = dors bien! | | |

**\*** in informal situations   **♦\*** may be considered offensive

**fade** *verb*
  (*if it's a material*) = se décolorer (**!** + *être*)
  (*if it's a colour*) = passer (**!** + *être*)

**fail** *verb*
  = échouer
  **to fail an exam** = échouer à un examen

**failure** *noun*
  **a failure** (*an event, an attempt*) = un échec
  (*a person*) = un raté/une ratée

**faint** *verb*
  = s'évanouir (**!** + *être*)

**fair**
**1** *adjective*
  (*just*) = juste
  **it's not fair** = ce n'est pas juste
  (*in colour*)
  **to have fair hair** = avoir les cheveux
    blonds
  **to have fair skin** = avoir le teint clair
**2** *noun*
  (*British English*) (*a funfair*)
  **a fair** = une fête foraine
  (*a display of goods*)
  **a (trade) fair** = une foire

**fairly** *adverb*
  = assez

**faith** *noun*
  **to have faith in someone** = avoir
    confiance en quelqu'un

**faithful** *adjective*
  = fidèle

**fall**
**1** *verb*
  (*if it's a person*) = tomber (**!** + *être*)
  **she fell to the ground** = elle est tombée
    par terre
  (*to come down, to be reduced*) = baisser
  (*other uses*)
  **to fall asleep** = s'endormir (**!** + *être*)
  **to fall ill** = tomber malade (**!** + *être*)
  **to fall in love with someone** = tomber
    amoureux/amoureuse de quelqu'un
**2** *noun*
  (*in prices, temperature*)
  **a fall** = une baisse
  **a fall in prices** = une baisse des prix
  (*US English*) (*autumn*)
  **fall** = l'automne (*masculine*)
**fall down**
  (*if it's a person*) = tomber (**!** + *être*)
  (*if it's a building*) = s'effondrer (**!** + *être*)
**fall off** = tomber (**!** + *être*)
  **to fall off a chair** = tomber d'une chaise
**fall out**
  (*from somewhere*) = tomber (**!** + *être*)
  **the letter fell out of his pocket** = la lettre
    est tombée de sa poche
  (*to quarrel*) = se brouiller (**!** + *être*)

**fall over** = tomber (par terre) (**!** + *être*) .
**fall through** = tomber à l'eau

**false** *adjective*
  = faux/fausse

**false teeth** *noun*
  **false teeth** = un dentier (*singular*)

**familiar** *adjective*
  = familier/familière

**family** *noun*
  **a family** = une famille

**famous** *adjective*
  = célèbre

**fan** *noun*
  (*of a pop star, an actor, a sport*)
  **a fan** = un fan/une fan
  (*for cooling*)
  **a fan** (*electric*) = un ventilateur
  (*hand-held*) = un éventail

**fancy dress party** *noun* (*British
English*)
  **a fancy dress party** = une soirée costumée

**fantastic** *adjective*
  = formidable, super**✶**

**far**
**1** *adverb*
  ▶ **285** |
  **far (away)** = loin
  **how far is it to London?** = Londres est à
    combien de kilomètres?
  **how far is Oxford from London?** = Oxford
    est à quelle distance de Londres?
  **we went as far as the coast** = nous
    sommes allés jusqu'à la côte
  (*in time*)
  **as far back as 1950** = déjà en 1950
  (*very much*) = beaucoup
  **you're eating far too much bread** = tu
    manges beaucoup trop de pain
  **we know far fewer people here** = on
    connaît beaucoup moins de monde ici
**2** *adjective*
  = autre (**!** *before the noun*)
  **at the far side of the room** = de l'autre côté
    de la pièce
**3 so far** = jusqu'ici

**fare** *noun*
  **the fare** (*on a bus or the underground*) = le
    prix du ticket
  (*on a train or plane*) = le prix du billet

**farm** *noun*
  **a farm** = une ferme

**farmer** *noun* ▶ **315** |
  **a farmer** = un fermier

**fascinating** *adjective*
  = fascinant/fascinante

**fashion** *noun*
  **fashion** = la mode
  **to be in fashion** = être à la mode
  **to go out of fashion** = se démoder
    (**!** + *être*)

---

**✶** in informal situations

**fashionable** adjective
= à la mode

**fast**
**1** adjective
(describing movement) = rapide
to be fast = avancer
my watch is ten minutes fast = ma montre
avance de dix minutes
**2** adverb
= vite, rapidement

**fasten** verb
to fasten a seatbelt = attacher une
ceinture de sécurité

**fast-forward** verb
to fast-forward a cassette = faire avancer
rapidement une cassette

**fat** adjective
= gros/grosse (**!** before the noun)
to get fat = grossir

**fatal** adjective
= mortel/mortelle

**father** noun
a father = un père

**Father Christmas** noun (British
English)
Father Christmas = le père Noël

**father-in-law** noun
a father-in-law = un beau-père

**faucet** noun (US English)
a faucet = un robinet

**fault** noun
to be someone's fault = être (de) la faute
de quelqu'un
it's not my fault = ce n'est pas (de) ma
faute
whose fault was it? = à qui la faute?

**favour** (British English), **favor** (US
English)
**1** noun
a favour = un service
to do someone a favour = rendre (un)
service à quelqu'un
to ask someone a favour = demander un
service à quelqu'un
**2 in favour of**
to be in favour of a change in the law
= être pour un changement de la loi

**favourite** (British English), **favorite** (US
English) adjective
= préféré/préférée
it's my favourite film = c'est mon film
préféré

**fax** noun
a fax = un fax

**fear** noun
fear = la peur

**feather** noun
a feather = une plume

**February** noun ▶ 222
February = février (masculine)

**fed up** adjective
to be fed up = en avoir marre✶

**fee** noun
a fee (to attend an event, a show) = un
droit d'entrée
(to join a club, a union) = une cotisation

**feeble** adjective
= faible

**feed** verb
= nourrir
I must feed the children = je dois donner à
manger aux enfants

**feel** verb
(referring to an emotion, an impression)
to feel happy = être heureux/heureuse
he's feeling uncomfortable = il se sent
mal à l'aise
to feel afraid = avoir peur
I feel as if I'm being followed = j'ai
l'impression qu'on me suit
it feels like winter = on se croirait en hiver
it feels good to be back home = ça fait du
bien d'être chez soi
(referring to a physical feeling)
to feel [hot | cold | sleepy…] = avoir [chaud |
froid | sommeil…]
to feel ill = se sentir malade
to feel a draught = sentir un courant d'air
I don't feel a thing = je ne sens rien
(describing how something seems)
the box felt very heavy = la boîte était
lourde
the room feels very cold = la pièce est très
froide
(to touch) = tâter, toucher
to feel like [going out | eating | dancing…]
= avoir envie de [sortir | manger | danser…]
I don't feel like it = je n'en ai pas envie

**feeling** noun
(emotional)
a feeling = un sentiment
to hurt someone's feelings = blesser
quelqu'un
(physical)
a feeling = une sensation
I have a feeling he's right = j'ai
l'impression qu'il a raison

**felt-tip pen** noun
a felt-tip pen = un crayon feutre

**female** adjective
(in biology) = femelle
(relating to women) = féminin/féminine

**feminine** adjective
= féminin/féminine

**fence** noun
a fence = une clôture

**fencing** noun ▶ 248
fencing = l'escrime (feminine)

F

**festival** noun
a festival = une fête

**fetch** verb
= aller chercher
go and fetch some water = va chercher de
l'eau

**fever** noun
to have a fever = avoir de la fièvre

**few** ▶ 317 |
**1 a few**
a few [people | houses | books ...] = quelques
[personnes | maisons | livres ...]
a few of the houses were burned down
= quelques-unes des maisons ont été
brûlées
a few of them speak Greek = quelques-
uns d'entre eux parlent grec
I would like a few more = j'en voudrais
quelques-uns/quelques-unes de plus

! Note that it is necessary to use en,
which may be translated as 'of them', with
phrases like a few. See also another, a lot,
none etc for this use of en.

**2** determiner
(not many) = peu de
few [visitors | letters | meals ...] = peu de
[visiteurs | lettres | repas ...]
(several)
the first few weeks = les premières
semaines
**3** pronoun
= peu
few of us succeeded = peu d'entre nous
ont réussi
there are so few of them (of people) = ils
sont si peu nombreux
(of things) = il y en a tellement peu

**fewer** ▶ 317 |
**1** determiner
= moins de
fewer shops = moins de magasins
**2** pronoun
= moins
fewer than ten people = moins de dix
personnes

**fewest**
**1** determiner
the fewest = le moins de
they have the fewest advantages = ce
sont eux qui ont le moins d'avantages
**2** pronoun
the fewest = le moins

**field** noun
a field = un champ

**fifteen** number ▶ 187 |, ▶ 211 |
fifteen = quinze

**fifteenth** number
(in a series) = quinzième
(in dates) ▶ 222 |
the fifteenth of May = le quinze mai

**fifth** number
(in a series) = cinquième
(in dates) ▶ 222 |
the fifth of June = le cinq juin

**fifty** number ▶ 187 |, ▶ 211 |
fifty = cinquante

**fight**
**1** verb
to fight (against) prejudice = lutter contre
les préjugés
to fight for justice = lutter pour la justice
(in war) = se battre (! + être)
to fight the enemy = combattre l'ennemi
(physically) = se battre (! + être)
(to quarrel) = se disputer (! + être)
**2** noun
(a campaign)
a fight = une lutte
(physical)
a fight = une bagarre
**fight back** = se défendre (! + être)

**figure** noun
(a number)
a figure = un chiffre
to have a good figure = être bien fait/bien
faite

**file** noun
a file (for documents) = un dossier
(in a computer) = un fichier
in single file = en file indienne

**fill** verb
(to make full) = remplir
(to become full) = se remplir (! + être)
**fill in** = remplir

**film**
**1** noun
(in cinema or on TV)
a film = un film
(for a camera)
a film = une pellicule
**2** verb
= filmer

**filthy** adjective
= sale

**final**
**1** adjective
= dernier/dernière (! before the noun)
**2** noun
a final = une finale

**finally** adverb
= finalement

**find** verb
= trouver
**find out**
to find out the truth = découvrir la vérité
if he ever finds out he'll be furious = si
jamais il l'apprend il sera furieux

**fine**
**1** adjective
(very good, excellent) = beau/belle
(! before the noun)
the weather is fine = il fait beau

*(in good health)*
I feel fine = je me sens très bien
*(expressing agreement)*
(that's) fine = d'accord
**2** *noun*
a fine = une amende

**finger** *noun* ▶ 201 |
a finger = un doigt

**finish**
**1** *verb*
*(to end)* = finir
to finish writing a letter = finir d'écrire
   une lettre
*(to come to an end)* = finir
**2** *noun*
the finish *(in a race)* = l'arrivée *(feminine)*

**Finland** *noun* ▶ 218 |
Finland = la Finlande

**fire**
**1** *noun*
fire = le feu
a fire *(for heat)* = un feu
*(causing damage)* = un incendie
to catch fire = prendre feu
to be on fire = être en feu
**2** *verb*
*(to shoot)* = tirer
*(to dismiss)* = renvoyer

**fire alarm** *noun*
a fire alarm = une sonnerie d'alarme
   incendie

**fire brigade** *(British English)*, **fire
department** *(US English)* noun
the fire brigade = les pompiers *(masculine
   plural)*

**fire engine** *noun*
a fire engine = une voiture de pompiers

**fireman** *noun* ▶ 315 |
a fireman = un pompier

**fire station** *noun*
a fire station = une caserne de pompiers

**fireworks display** *noun*
a fireworks display = un feu d'artifice

**firm**
**1** *noun*
a firm = une entreprise
**2** *adjective*
= ferme

**first**
**1** *adjective*
= premier/première *(! before the noun)*
the first time = la première fois
the first three weeks = les trois premières
   semaines
**2** *adverb*
*(to begin with)* = d'abord
first of all = tout d'abord
*(for the first time)* = pour la première fois

to arrive first = arriver le premier/la
   première
**3** *noun*
*(in a series or group)*
the first = le premier/la première
he was the first to congratulate us = il a
   été le premier à nous féliciter
*(in dates)* ▶ 222 |
the first of June = le premier juin
**4 at first** = au début

**first aid** *noun*
first aid = les premiers soins
  | **!** *Note that* soins *is masculine plural.*

**first class** *adverb*
to travel first class = voyager en première
   classe

**first floor** *noun*
the first floor *(in Britain)* = le premier étage
*(in the US)* = le rez-de-chaussée

**first name** *noun*
a first name = un prénom

**fish**
**1** *noun*
a fish = un poisson
**2** *verb*
to go fishing = aller à la pêche

**fisherman** *noun* ▶ 315 |
a fisherman = un pêcheur

**fishing** *noun* ▶ 248 |
fishing = la pêche

**fishing rod** *noun*
a fishing rod = une canne à pêche

**fist** *noun* ▶ 201 |
the fist = le poing

**fit**
**1** *verb*
the shoes don't fit me = les chaussures ne
   me vont pas
the photo won't fit into the envelope = la
   photo ne rentre pas dans l'enveloppe
will the table fit here? = est-ce qu'il y a de
   la place pour la table ici?
**2** *adjective*
*(suitable, capable)*
the house isn't fit to live in = la maison
   n'est pas habitable
to be fit to drive = être en état de conduire
he's not fit to be a minister = il n'est pas
   capable d'être ministre
*(healthy)*
to be fit = être en forme
**fit in**
*(in a room or car)*
can you all fit in? = est-ce qu'il y a de la
   place pour vous tous?
*(in a group or team)* = s'intégrer *(! + être)*

**fitness** *noun*
*(physical)* fitness = la forme *(physique)*

**F**

**five** *number* ▶ **187 |**, ▶ **211 |**
　five = cinq
　five apples = cinq pommes
　I've got five (of them) = j'en ai cinq

**fix** *verb*
　(*to decide on, to set*) = fixer
　(*to repair*) = réparer
　to get a watch fixed = faire réparer une
　　montre
　(*to prepare*) = préparer

**flag** *noun*
　a flag = un drapeau

**flame** *noun*
　a flame = une flamme
　to go up in flames = s'enflammer
　　(**!** + *être*)

**flash**
**1** *noun*
　a flash (*for a camera*) = un flash
**2** *verb*
　to flash (on and off) = clignoter

**flashlight** *noun*
　a flashlight = une lampe de poche

**flask** *noun*
　a flask = un thermos

**flat**
**1** *noun* (*British English*)
　a flat = un appartement
**2** *adjective*
　= plat/plate
　to have a flat tyre = avoir un pneu à plat

**flavour** (*British English*), **flavor** (*US English*) *noun*
　a flavour (*of food*) = une saveur, un goût
　(*of ice cream, yogurt*) = un parfum

**flea** *noun*
　a flea = une puce

**flight** *noun*
　a flight = un vol

**flight attendant** *noun* ▶ **315 |**
　a flight attendant = un steward/une
　　hôtesse de l'air

**float** *verb*
　= flotter
　to float up into the air = s'envoler (**!** + *être*)

**flock** *noun*
　(*of sheep, goats, geese*)
　a flock = un troupeau
　(*of birds*)
　a flock = une volée

**flood** *noun*
　a flood = une inondation

**floor** *noun*
　(*a surface*)
　a floor = un plancher
　to sit on the floor = s'asseoir par terre
　(*a storey*)
　a floor = un étage

**florist** *noun* ▶ **315 |**
　a florist = un fleuriste/une fleuriste

**flour** *noun*
　flour = la farine

**flow** *verb*
　(*if it's a liquid*) = couler
　(*if it's traffic*) = circuler

**flower**
**1** *noun*
　a flower = une fleur
**2** *verb*
　= fleurir

**flu** *noun* ▶ **266 |**
　flu = la grippe

**fluently** *adverb*
　= couramment

**flush** *verb*
　to flush the toilet = tirer la chasse d'eau

**flute** *noun* ▶ **290 |**
　a flute = une flûte

**fly**
**1** *noun*
　a fly = une mouche
**2** *verb*
　(*if it's a bird, a kite, a plane, an insect*)
　　= voler
　(*if it's a passenger*) = prendre l'avion
　to fly from London to Paris = aller de
　　Londres à Paris en avion
　to fly a plane = piloter un avion
　(*if it's a flag*) = flotter
　fly away = s'envoler (**!** + *être*)

**fog** *noun*
　fog = le brouillard

**fold** *verb*
　to fold a shirt = plier une chemise
　to fold one's arms = croiser les bras

**folder** *noun*
　a folder (*for work*) = une chemise
　(*in computing*) = un dossier

**follow** *verb*
　(*to go or come after*) = suivre
　(*to use, to look at*) = suivre
　I followed the signposts = j'ai suivi les
　　panneaux indicateurs

**following** *adjective*
　= suivant/suivante

**fond** *adjective*
　I'm very fond of you = je t'aime beaucoup

**food** *noun*
　food = la nourriture

**fool** *verb*
　= tromper, duper

**foot** *noun*
　(*part of the leg*) ▶ **201 |**
　the foot = le pied
　on foot = à pied

(of a rabbit, a cat, a dog, a cow)
**the foot** = la patte
(in measurements) ▶ **285**
**a foot** = un pied
! Note that a foot = 30.48 cm.

**football** noun ▶ **248**
**football** (soccer) = le football
(American football) = le football américain
(a ball)
**a football** = un football

**footballer** (British English), **football player** (US English) noun ▶ **315**
**a footballer** = un joueur/une joueuse de football

**footprint** noun
**a footprint** = une trace de pas

**footstep** noun
**a footstep** = un pas

**for** preposition
▶ **244** See the boxed note on for for more information and examples.
for = pour
**the letter is for you** = la lettre est pour toi
**to work for a company** = travailler pour une entreprise
**he cooked dinner for us** = il nous a préparé à manger
(when talking about time)
**we've been living here for two years** = on habite ici depuis deux ans, ça fait deux ans qu'on habite ici
**he's going to Paris for a year** = il va à Paris pour un an
**she read for two hours** = elle a lu pendant deux heures
**I've been waiting for three hours** = ça fait trois heures que j'attends
**he won't arrive for another two weeks** = il ne va pas arriver avant deux semaines
(when talking about distance) = pendant
**we drove for 80 kilometres** = nous avons roulé pendant 80 kilomètres
(when talking about money)
**he bought it for £50** = il l'a acheté pour 50 livres
**a cheque for £20** = un chèque de 20 livres
(in favour (of)) = pour
**say hello to her for me** = donne-lui le bonjour de ma part
(other uses)
**T for Tom** = T comme Tom
**the Minister for Education** = le ministre de l'éducation
**what is the French for 'badger'?**
= comment dit-on 'badger' en français?
**we went** [for a swim | for a run | for a walk ...]
= nous sommes allés [nager | courir | nous promener ..]

**forbid** verb
= interdire
**to forbid someone to go out** = interdire à quelqu'un de sortir
**smoking is forbidden** = il est interdit de fumer

**force**
**1** verb
= forcer
**to force someone to leave** = forcer quelqu'un à partir
**2** noun
**force** = la force
**by force** = de force

**forecast** noun
**the forecast** = les prévisions (feminine plural)
**the forecast is for rain** = la météo prévoit de la pluie

**forehead** noun ▶ **201**
**the forehead** = le front

**foreign** adjective
= étranger/étrangère

**foreigner** noun
**a foreigner** = un étranger/une étrangère

**forest** noun
**a forest** = une forêt

**forever, for ever** adverb
= pour toujours

**forget** verb
= oublier
**to forget about someone** = oublier quelqu'un
**to forget** [to do the shopping | to eat | to call ...]
= oublier [de faire les courses | de manger | de téléphoner ...]

**forgive** verb
**to forgive someone** = pardonner à quelqu'un

**fork** noun
**a fork** = une fourchette

**form**
**1** noun ▶ **245**
(a shape)
**a form** = une forme
(a document)
**a form** = un formulaire
(referring to mood or fitness)
**to be in good form** = être en bonne forme
(British English) (a class)
**a form** = une classe
**to be in the sixth form** = être en terminale
**2** verb
(to create, to make) = former
**to form a circle** = former un cercle
(to start, to set up) = créer

**formal** adjective
(describing language) = soutenu/soutenue
**to wear formal clothes** (for the evening)
= être en tenue de soirée
(official) = officiel/officielle

**former** adjective
= ancien/ancienne (! before the noun)

**fortnight** noun ▶ **356** (British English)
**a fortnight** = quinze jours (masculine plural)

# for

## Some general uses

for is generally translated by **pour**:

| | |
|---|---|
| *for my sister* | = **pour** ma sœur |
| *for me* | = **pour** moi |

When **for** followed by a verb is used to explain the purpose of something, it is translated by **pour** + *infinitive*:

| | |
|---|---|
| *a product for losing weight* | = un produit **pour** maigrir |

## When talking about time

for in time expressions may be translated by **depuis**, **pendant** or **pour**. The following examples are designed to show you which translation to choose. Note that tense is very important in distinguishing between them.

● When **for** is used to express the time period of something that started in the past and is still going on, French uses either *present tense* + **depuis** or ça fait✱ ... **que** + *present tense*:

| | |
|---|---|
| *I have been waiting for three hours* | = j'attends **depuis** trois heures |
| (and I am still waiting) | = **ça fait✱** trois heures **que** j'attends |
| *we've been together for two years* | = nous sommes ensemble **depuis** deux ans |
| (and we're still together) | = **ça fait✱** deux ans **que** nous sommes ensemble |

When **for** is used after a verb in the past perfect tense placing an event even further back in time, French uses either *imperfect* + **depuis** or ça faisait✱ ... **que** + *imperfect*:

| | |
|---|---|
| *I had been waiting for two hours* | = j'attendais **depuis** deux heures |
| (and was still waiting) | = **ça faisait✱** deux heures **que** j'attendais |

● When **for** is used in negative sentences with the present perfect tense to express the time that has elapsed since something has happened, French uses the same tense as English, either *perfect* + **depuis** or ça fait✱ ... **que** + *perfect*:

| | |
|---|---|
| *I haven't seen him for ten years* | = je ne l'ai pas vu **depuis** dix ans |
| (and I still haven't seen him) | = **ça fait✱** dix ans que je ne l'ai pas vu |

When **for** is used in negative sentences after a verb in the past perfect tense, again placing events further back in time, French uses either *past perfect* + **depuis** or ça faisait✱ ... **que** + *past perfect*:

| | |
|---|---|
| *I hadn't seen him for ten years* | = je ne l'avais pas vu **depuis** dix ans |
| | = **ça faisait✱** dix ans que je ne l'avais pas vu |

● When **for** is used to express the time period of something that happened in the past and is no longer going on, French uses *present perfect* + **pendant**:

| | |
|---|---|
| *last Sunday I read for two hours* | = dimanche dernier j'ai lu **pendant** deux heures |

● When **for** is used to express a time period in the future, French uses *present* or *future* + **pour**:

| | |
|---|---|
| *I'm going to Montreal for six weeks* | = je vais à Montréal **pour** six semaines |
| *I will go to Montreal for six weeks* | = j'irai à Montréal **pour** six semaines |

● When the verb **to be** is used in the future with **for** to emphasize the period of time, French uses *future* + **pendant**:

| | |
|---|---|
| *I will be in Brussels for six weeks* | = je serai à Bruxelles **pendant** six semaines |

✱ in informal situations

---

**fortunately** *adverb*
= heureusement

**fortune** *noun*
a fortune = une fortune
to make a fortune = faire fortune
to tell someone's fortune = dire la bonne
aventure à quelqu'un

**forty** *number* ▶ **187 |**, ▶ **211 |**
forty = quarante

**forward**
**1** *adverb*
= en avant
to step forward = faire un pas en
avant

# Forms of address (Miss, Mr, Mrs)

### When speaking to someone

Where English puts the surname after the title, French normally uses the title alone:

| | |
|---|---|
| *Good morning,* **Miss Jones** | = bonjour, **Mademoiselle** |
| *Good evening,* **Mr Halpin** | = bonsoir, **Monsieur** |
| *Good morning,* **Mrs Davies** | = bonjour, **Madame** |

### When speaking about someone

In this case, French and English behave the same:

*Miss Jones | Mr Halpin | Mrs Davies* = Mademoiselle Jones / Monsieur Halpin /
*is here*                              Madame Davies est là

### When writing to someone

When starting a letter, translations will differ according to the degree of formality involved:

| | formal | less formal |
|---|---|---|
| *Dear Miss Jones* | = Mademoiselle | = Chère Mademoiselle |
| *Dear Mr Halpin* | = Monsieur | = Cher Monsieur |
| *Dear Mrs Davies* | = Madame | = Chère Madame |

▶ There is no French equivalent of **Ms** but one can use **Madame** in similar circumstances.

---

**2** *verb*
to forward a letter to someone = faire
suivre une lettre à quelqu'un

**found** *verb*
= fonder

**fountain** *noun*
a fountain = une fontaine

**four** *number* ▶ **187 |**, ▶ **211 |**
four = quatre
four apples = quatre pommes
I've got four (of them) = j'en ai quatre

**fourteen** *number* ▶ **187 |**, ▶ **211 |**
fourteen = quatorze

**fourteenth** *number*
(*in a series*) = quatorzième
(*in dates*) ▶ **222 |**
the fourteenth of July = le quatorze juillet

**fourth** *number*
(*in a series*) = quatrième
(*in dates*) ▶ **222 |**
the fourth of July = le quatre juillet

**fox** *noun*
a fox = un renard

**fragile** *adjective*
= fragile

**frame** *noun*
a frame = un cadre

**France** *noun* ▶ **218 |**
France = la France

**frank** *adjective*
= franc/franche

**freckle** *noun*
a freckle = une tache de rousseur

**free**
**1** *adjective*
(*costing nothing*) = gratuit/gratuite
(*independent, able to come and go*) = libre
he is free to do what he likes = il est libre
de faire ce qu'il veut
(*not occupied, available*) = libre
are you free on Monday? = est-ce que tu
es libre lundi?
**2** *verb*
= libérer
**3** *adverb*
= gratuitement

**freedom** *noun*
freedom = la liberté

**freeway** *noun* (*US English*)
a freeway = une autoroute

**freeze** *verb*
(*in cold weather*) = geler
the river froze = la rivière a gelé
the ground was frozen = le sol était gelé
(*in a freezer*) = congeler
to freeze to death = mourir de froid

**freezer** *noun*
a freezer = un congélateur

**freezing** *adjective*
  it's freezing = il fait un temps glacial
  this room is freezing = cette pièce est
    glaciale
  to be freezing *(if it's a person)* = être
    gelé/gelée

**French** ▶ 275 |
**1** *adjective*
  = français/française
**2** *noun*
  *(the people)*
  the French = les Français *(masculine plural)*
  *(the language)*
  French = le français

**French fries** *noun*
  French fries = les frites *(feminine)*

**fresh** *adjective*
  = frais/fraîche

**Friday** *noun* ▶ 222 |
  Friday = vendredi *(masculine)*

**fridge** *noun*
  a fridge = un frigo✖

**fried** *adjective*
  = frit/frite

**fried egg** *noun*
  a fried egg = un œuf sur le plat

**friend** *noun*
  a friend = un ami/une amie
  to make friends = se faire des amis
  to make friends with someone = devenir
    ami/amie avec quelqu'un

**friendly** *adjective*
  = gentil/gentille

**fright** *noun*
  to get a fright = avoir peur
  to give someone a fright = faire peur à
    quelqu'un

**frightened** *adjective*
  to be frightened = avoir peur

**fringe** *noun* *(British English)*
  a fringe = une frange

**frog** *noun*
  a frog = une grenouille

**from** *preposition*

  ┌─────────────────────────────────────────┐
  │ **!** *There are many verbs which involve the*
  │ *use of* from, *like* borrow from, escape from
  │ *etc. For translations, look up the entries at*
  │ borrow, escape *etc.*
  └─────────────────────────────────────────┘

**from** = de (**!** d' + *vowel or mute h*)
  the boy from London = le garçon (qui
    vient) de Londres
  where is she from? = d'où vient-elle?
  to come back from the office = rentrer du
    bureau
  to return from a holiday = rentrer de
    vacances
  there's a message from Paul = il y a un
    message de Paul
  the train from Oxford is late = le train en
    provenance d'Oxford est en retard
  we live ten minutes from the city centre
    = nous habitons à dix minutes du
    centre-ville
  *(when talking about time)* = de, à partir de
  the shop is open from eight to six = le
    magasin est ouvert de huit heures à
    dix-huit heures
  from Monday to Saturday = du lundi au
    samedi
  from April on = à partir du mois d'avril
  from then on = à partir de ce moment-là
  fifty years from now = d'ici cinquante ans
  *(British English)* *(in arithmetic)*
  5 from 8 leaves 3 = 5 ôté de 8, il reste 3

**front**
**1** *noun*
  *(of a building)*
  the front of a house = la façade d'une
    maison
  the front of a shop = la devanture d'un
    magasin
  my room is at the front of the house = ma
    chambre est sur le devant de la maison
  *(of a car, a train or queue)*
  at the front of the bus = à l'avant du bus
  at the front of the queue = au début de la
    queue
**2 in front of** = devant

**front door** *noun*
  the front door = la porte d'entrée

**front page** *noun*
  the front page = la première page

**front seat** *noun*
  the front seat = le siège avant

**frost** *noun*
  frost = le givre, la gelée

**frozen** *adjective*
  = congelé/congelée

**fruit** *noun*
  a piece of fruit = un fruit
  he likes fruit = il aime les fruits

**frustrated** *adjective*
  = frustré/frustrée

**fry** *verb*
  to fry potatoes = faire frire des pommes de
    terre

**frying pan** *noun* *(British English)*
  a frying pan = une poêle

---

✖ in informal situations

**full** *adjective*
(*not empty*) = plein/pleine
the streets were full of people = les rues
  étaient pleines de monde
(*describing a flight, a hotel*)
= complet/complète
(*maximum*)
to travel at full speed = rouler à toute
  vitesse
to get full marks = obtenir la note
  maximale
(*complete*)
to pay the full fare = payer plein tarif
his full name = ses nom et prénom

**full-time** *adverb*
= à plein temps
to work full-time = travailler à plein temps

**fumes** *noun*
fumes = les fumées (*feminine*)

**fun** *noun*
It's fun = c'est amusant
skiing is fun = c'est amusant de faire du
  ski
to have fun = s'amuser (**!** + *être*)
she's fun = on s'amuse bien avec elle

**function** *verb*
= fonctionner

**funeral** *noun*
a funeral = un enterrement

**funfair** *noun* (*British English*)
a funfair = une fête foraine

**funny** *adjective*
(*amusing*) = drôle, amusant/amusante
(*odd*) = drôle, bizarre

**fur** *noun*
fur (*an animal's coat*) = les poils (*masculine
  plural*)
(*on a garment*) = la fourrure

**furious** *adjective*
= furieux/furieuse

**furniture** *noun*
a piece of furniture = un meuble
furniture = les meubles

**further** *adverb*
= plus loin
he lives further away from the school = il
  habite plus loin de l'école
how much further is it? = c'est encore
  loin?

**fuss** *noun*
a fuss = des histoires (*feminine plural*)

**future**
**1** *noun*
the future = l'avenir (*masculine*)
in the future = dans l'avenir
in future, let us know = à l'avenir, préviens
  nous
**2** *adjective*
= futur/future

**gallery** *noun*
a gallery = un musée

**game** *noun*
a game = un jeu
a game of football = un match de football
a game of tennis = une partie de tennis

**games** *noun* (*British English*)
games = le sport

**game show** *noun*
a game show = un jeu télévisé

**gang** *noun*
a gang (*a group of friends, young people*)
  = une bande
(*of criminals*) = un gang

**gap** *noun*
a gap (*in a fence or hedge*) = un trou
(*between buildings, cars*) = un espace
(*a period of time*)
a gap = un intervalle

**garage** *noun*
a garage = un garage

**garbage** *noun* (*US English*)
garbage = les ordures (*feminine plural*)

**garden**
**1** *noun*
a garden = un jardin
**2** *verb*
= faire du jardinage

**gardener** *noun* ▶ 315|
a gardener = un jardinier/une jardinière

**gardening** *noun*
gardening = le jardinage

**garlic** *noun*
garlic = l'ail (*masculine*)

**gas** *noun*
(*for cooking, heating*)
gas = le gaz
(*US English*) (*gasoline*)
gas = l'essence (*feminine*)

**gas station** *noun* (*US English*)
a gas station = une station-service

**gate** *noun*
a gate (*to a garden, a town, a prison*) = une
  porte
(*to a field*) = une barrière

**gather** *verb*
(*to come together*) = se rassembler
(**!** + *être*)

G

# Games and sports

## With or without the definite article?

French normally uses **le**, **la**, **l'** or **les** with names of games and sports:

| | |
|---|---|
| *football* | = le football |
| *chess* | = les échecs (*masculine plural*) |
| *to play football* | = jouer au football |
| *to play tennis* | = jouer au tennis |
| *to play chess* | = jouer aux échecs |
| *to go climbing* | = faire de l'escalade |
| *to beat somebody at tennis* | = battre quelqu'un au tennis |
| *to win at chess* | = gagner aux échecs |
| *to lose at marbles* | = perdre aux billes |

## Players and events

| | |
|---|---|
| *a tennis player* | = un joueur de tennis |

but

| | |
|---|---|
| *I'm not a tennis player* | = je ne joue pas au tennis |
| *he's a good tennis player* | = il joue bien au tennis |
| *a game of tennis* | = une partie de tennis |
| *a tennis champion* | = un champion de tennis |
| *the French tennis champion* | = le champion de France de tennis |
| *a tennis championship* | = un championnat de tennis |
| *the rules of tennis* | = les règles du tennis |

---

- (*to collect*)
  **to gather wood** = ramasser du bois
  **to gather fruit** = cueillir des fruits

**gay** *adjective*
  = homosexuel/homosexuelle

**gear** *noun*
- (*in a car or bus, on a bike*)
  **a gear** = une vitesse
- (*equipment*)
  **gear** = le matériel
  **fishing gear** = le matériel de pêche
- (*clothes*)
  **my football gear** = ma tenue de football
  **your swimming gear** = tes affaires pour la piscine

**Gemini** *noun*
  Gemini = Gémeaux (*masculine*)

**general**
**1** *noun*
  **a general** = un général
**2** *adjective*
  = général/générale
**3 in general** = en général

**generation** *noun*
  **a generation** = une génération

**generous** *adjective*
  = généreux/généreuse

**Geneva** *noun* ▶ **218** |
  Geneva = Genève

**genius** *noun*
  **a genius** = un génie

**gentle** *adjective*
  = doux/douce

**gentleman** *noun*
  **a gentleman** = un monsieur

**geography** *noun*
  geography = la géographie

**germ** *noun*
  **a germ** = un microbe

**German** ▶ **275** |
**1** *adjective*
  = allemand/allemande
**2** *noun*
- (*the people*)
  **the Germans** = les Allemands (*masculine*)
- (*the language*)
  **German** = l'allemand (*masculine*)

**Germany** *noun* ▶ **218** |
  Germany = l'Allemagne (*feminine*)

**get** *verb*
  ▶ *See the boxed note on* **get** *for more information and examples.*
**get away**
- (*to escape*) = s'échapper (**!** + *être*)
- **he won't get away with it** = il ne va pas s'en tirer comme ça
**get back**
- (*to return*) = revenir (**!** + *être*)
- (*to have back*) = récupérer
  **I got my bike back** = j'ai récupéré mon vélo
  **he'll get his money back** = il va être remboursé

# get

## A multi-purpose verb

The word **get** is extremely common in English and does not have a multi-purpose French equivalent.

However, it is helpful to try to find a synonym (a word which has the same sense) and from there, a suitable translation:

| | |
|---|---|
| *he's gone to get* (or *fetch*) *help* | = il est parti **chercher** de l'aide |
| *I'll call when we get* (or *arrive*) *there* | = j'appellerai quand nous arriverons |

## Main senses

### When changing from one state (of mind) to another

French very often has a specific verb for the various combinations of **to get** + *adjective*:

| | |
|---|---|
| *to get old | angry | worried* | = vieillir / se fâcher / s'inquiéter |

**devenir** + *adjective* is also useful:

| | |
|---|---|
| *to get jealous* | = **devenir** jaloux / jalouse |

### When asking, telling or persuading

The translations **dire (à quelqu'un)** and **demander (à quelqu'un)** are helpful:

| | |
|---|---|
| *get him to call me* | = **dis-lui** de m'appeler |
| *I'll get her to help me* | = je lui **demanderai** de m'aider |

### When getting things done by someone else

The construction **faire** + *infinitive verb* is useful here:

| | |
|---|---|
| *to get the car cleaned* | = **faire nettoyer** la voiture |
| *to get a TV repaired* | = **faire réparer** une télévision |
| *to get one's hair cut* | = **se faire couper** les cheveux |

### When to get means to obtain

| | |
|---|---|
| *to get* (or *buy*) *someone a present* | = **acheter** un cadeau à quelqu'un |
| *I got* (or *found*) *a job in Paris* | = j'ai **trouvé** un travail à Paris |

### When to get means to receive

The best translation is **recevoir**:

| | |
|---|---|
| *we got a letter from Mark* | = nous **avons reçu** une lettre de Mark |

but

| | |
|---|---|
| *to get good grades* | = **avoir** de bonnes notes |

### When cooking

A translation which will work well is **préparer**:

| | |
|---|---|
| *to get dinner* | = **préparer** le déjeuner |

### With illnesses:

In this context **attraper** is useful:

| | |
|---|---|
| *to get measles* | = **attraper** la rougeole |
| *to get a cold* | = **s'enrhumer** (+ *être*) |

### When using transport

The most reliable translation is **prendre**:

| | |
|---|---|
| *we can get the bus* | = on peut **prendre** le bus |
| *to get a taxi to the station* | = **prendre** un taxi pour aller à la gare |

▶ To find translations for other expressions using get—to get sick, to get a surprise, to get **better**, etc. —look up the entries at **sick**, **surprise**, **better**, etc.

▶ You will also find translations for *phrasal verbs* using get (**get down**, **get away**, **get on**, **get up**) listed separately in the dictionary.

**get down**
- (*to come or go down*) = descendre
  (**!** + *être*)
  can he get down from the tree? = est-ce
  qu'il peut descendre de l'arbre?
- (*to take down*) = descendre (**!** + *avoir*)
  I got the box down from the shelf = j'ai
  descendu la boîte de l'étagère
- (*to depress*) = déprimer
  it gets him down = ça le déprime
**get in** = entrer (**!** + *être*)
**get off**
- (*to leave a bus or train*) = descendre
  (**!** + *être*)
  I'm getting off at the next stop = je
  descends au prochain arrêt
  he fell as he was getting off the train = il
  est tombé en descendant du train
- (*to remove*) = enlever
  to get a stain off = enlever une tache
**get on**
- (*to climb on board a bus or train*) = monter
  (**!** + *être*)
  to get on the bus = monter dans le bus
- to get on well = bien s'entendre (**!** + *être*)
  I get on well with her = je m'entends bien
  avec elle
- (*in polite enquiries*)
  how did you get on? = comment est-ce
  que ça s'est passé?
  how is she getting on at school? = et ses
  études, ça marche✴?
**get out**
- (*to leave*) = sortir (**!** + *être*)
  she got out of the building = elle est sortie
  du bâtiment
- (*to take out*) = sortir (**!** + *avoir*)
  to get the furniture out of the house
  = sortir les meubles de la maison
**get over**
  to get over a shock = se remettre d'un
  choc
**get through to**
  to get through to someone = avoir
  quelqu'un au téléphone
**get together** = se réunir (**!** + *être*)
**get up** = se lever (**!** + *être*)

**ghost** *noun*
  a ghost = un fantôme

**gift** *noun*
- (*a present*)
  a gift = un cadeau
- (*an ability*)
  a gift = un don
  to have a gift for languages = avoir le don
  des langues

**ginger** *adjective* ▶ 213 |
  = roux/rousse
  to have ginger hair (*British English*) = avoir
  les cheveux roux

**girl** *noun*
  a girl = une fille

**girlfriend** *noun*
  a girlfriend (*in a couple*) = une (petite)
  amie
  (*a female friend*) = une amie

**give** *verb*

> **!** *For translations of expressions like to*
> *give someone a lift, to give someone an*
> *injection, to give someone a fright etc,*
> *look up the entries* lift, injection, fright.

- to give = donner
  to give someone a book = donner un livre
  à quelqu'un
  I gave him the photos = je lui ai donné les
  photos
  give me the newspapers = donne-moi les
  journaux
  give them to me = donne-les-moi
  to give someone a drink = donner à boire
  à quelqu'un
  to give one's seat to someone = laisser sa
  place à quelqu'un
- (*to offer*) = offrir
  he gave us one of his pictures = il nous a
  offert un de ses tableaux
  to give someone a present = faire un
  cadeau à quelqu'un
- to give someone a message = transmettre
  un message à quelqu'un
**give away**
- (*to make a present of*) = donner
- to give away a secret = révéler un secret
**give back** = rendre
**give in** = céder
**give off**
  to give off fumes = dégager des vapeurs
**give out**
  to give out the exercise books
  = distribuer les cahiers
**give up**
- (*to stop*)
  to give up smoking = cesser de fumer
  to give up the idea of working abroad
  = renoncer à l'idée de travailler à
  l'étranger
- to give oneself up to the police = se livrer à
  la police

**glad** *adjective*
  = content/contente

**glass** *noun*
  a glass = un verre

**glasses** *noun*
  glasses = les lunettes (*feminine*)

**glove** *noun*
  a glove = un gant

**glow** *verb*
  = luire

**glue**
**1** *noun*
  glue = la colle

---

✴ in informal situations

**2** verb
= coller

**go** verb
▶ **253** See the boxed note on **go** for more information and examples.

**go across** = traverser
**go after** = poursuivre
**go ahead**
- (if it's an event) = avoir lieu
  the concert's going ahead after all = le concert aura finalement lieu
- (if it's a person)
  go ahead, there's no-one there = vas-y, il n'y a personne
**go around** ▶ **go round**
**go around with** ▶ **go round with**
**go away** = partir (! + être)
  go away! = allez-vous-en!, va-t'en!
**go back** = retourner (! + être)
  Gary went back to Paris = Gary est retourné à Paris
  to go back to school = reprendre les cours
  to go back to work = reprendre le travail
  to go back to sleep = se rendormir (! + être)
**go by** = passer (! + être)
**go down**
- (if it's quality, a price, a salary) = baisser
- (if it's a person) = descendre
  she went down into the basement = elle est descendue au sous-sol
  we went down the hill = nous avons descendu la pente
- (if it's the sun) = se coucher (! + être)
- (if it's a computer) = tomber en panne (! + être)
**go in**
- (to enter) = entrer (! + être)
- (to return inside) = rentrer (! + être)
**go off**
- (to explode) = exploser
- (to ring) (if it's an alarm clock) = sonner
  (if it's an alarm) = se déclencher (! + être)
- (to leave) = partir (! + être)
- the milk will go off = le lait va tourner
- (to be switched off) = s'éteindre (! + être)
**go on**
- (to continue) = continuer
  to go on talking = continuer à parler
- (to happen)
  what's going on? = qu'est-ce qui se passe?
- (to keep talking)
  he goes on (and on) about his work = il n'arrête pas de parler de son travail
- (to be switched on) (if it's a light) = s'allumer (! + être)
  (if it's heating, a machine) = se mettre en marche (! + être)
**go out**
- (to leave the house) = sortir (! + être)
  are you going out this evening? = est-ce que tu sors ce soir?
- (as a boyfriend, a girlfriend)
  to go out with someone = sortir avec quelqu'un
- (to be switched off, to stop burning) = s'éteindre (! + être)
- the tide's going out = la marée descend
**go over**
- (to check)
  to go over some grammar = vérifier quelques points de grammaire
- (to revise) = revoir
**go round**
- (British English) (to call on) = passer (! + être)
  to go round to see someone = passer voir quelqu'un
- (to walk around, to visit) = visiter
  to go round the museums = visiter les musées
  to go round the shops = faire les magasins
- (to be enough)
  is there enough bread to go round? = est-ce qu'il y a assez de pain pour tout le monde?
**go round with**
- (British English) (to spend time with) = fréquenter
**go through**
- (to have, to live through)
  to go through a difficult time = traverser une période difficile
  I don't want to go through that again = je ne voudrais pas revivre ça
- (to search) = fouiller
- (to check) = examiner
**go together** = aller ensemble
  the skirt and blouse go well together = la jupe et la chemise vont bien ensemble
**go up**
- (if it's a person) = monter
  he went up to bed = il est monté se coucher
  he went up the stairs = il a monté l'escalier
  to go up to the top of the hill = monter jusqu'en haut de la colline
  to go up to the top floor = monter jusqu'au dernier étage
- (if it's a price, a salary) = augmenter
**go with** = aller avec (! + être)
  the trousers don't really go with your jacket = le pantalon ne va pas très bien avec ta veste

**goal** noun
  a goal = un but

**goalkeeper** noun
  a goalkeeper = un gardien de but

**goat** noun
  a goat = une chèvre

**god** noun
  a god = un dieu
  God = Dieu

**goddaughter** noun
  a goddaughter = une filleule

**godfather** noun
  a godfather = un parrain

**G**

**godmother** noun
a godmother = une marraine

**godson** noun
a godson = un filleul

**going**: to be going to
= aller
I'm going to [leave | go to Ireland | learn to drive …] = je vais [partir | aller en Irlande | apprendre à conduire …]
we were going to phone you = on allait te téléphoner

**gold**
**1** noun
gold = l'or (masculine)
**2** adjective
= en or
a gold ring = une bague en or

**goldfish** noun
a goldfish = un poisson rouge

**golf** noun ▶ 248 |
golf = le golf

**golf course** noun
a golf course = un terrain de golf

**good**
**1** adjective
• good = bon/bonne (**!** before the noun)
a good book = un bon livre
a good party = une bonne soirée
we've got some good news = nous avons de bonnes nouvelles
to have good eyesight = avoir une bonne vue
to be good [at chemistry | at drawing | at chess …] = être bon/bonne [en chimie | en dessin | aux échecs …]
it's a good time to visit Paris = c'est le bon moment pour visiter Paris
exercise is good for you = ça fait du bien de faire de l'exercice
to look good (healthy) = avoir bonne mine
I don't feel too good = je ne me sens pas très bien
I had a good time = je me suis bien amusé
• (talking about food) = bon/bonne (**!** before the noun)
• (obedient) = sage
• (kind) = gentil/gentille
it's very good of you to let me know = c'est très gentil de votre part de me prévenir
**2** noun
it's no good shouting = ça ne sert à rien de crier
to be no good at Latin = être nul/nulle✱ en latin
the change will do you good = le changement te fera du bien
**3** exclamation
• (when pleased)
good = c'est bien

• (when relieved)
'he's much better'—'good' = 'il va beaucoup mieux'—'tant mieux'
• (when praising)
good! = très bien!
**4 for good** = pour toujours

**good afternoon** noun (also exclamation)
good afternoon (when meeting) = bonjour
(when leaving) = au revoir

**goodbye** noun (also exclamation)
goodbye = au revoir

**good evening** noun (also exclamation)
good evening = bonsoir

**good-looking** adjective
= beau/belle (**!** before the noun)

**good morning** noun (also exclamation)
good morning (when meeting) = bonjour
(when leaving) = au revoir

**goodnight** noun (also exclamation)
goodnight = bonne nuit

**goods** noun
goods = la marchandise (singular)

**goose** noun
a goose = une oie

**gooseberry** noun
a gooseberry = une groseille à maquereau

**gorilla** noun
a gorilla = un gorille

**gossip** verb
• (to chat) = bavarder
• (to talk in a harmful way) = faire des commérages

**got**: to have got verb
▶ See the boxed note on got for more information and examples.
• (to have) = avoir
I've got work to do = j'ai du travail
have you got a cold? = est-ce que tu as un rhume?
• (to be obliged to)
to have got to = devoir
I've got to [go | work | get dressed …] = je dois [partir | travailler | m'habiller …], il faut que [je parte | je travaille | je m'habille …]
**!** Note that the subjunctive is used after il faut que.

**government** noun
a government = un gouvernement

**GP** noun ▶ 315 | (British English)
a GP = un médecin, un généraliste

**grab** verb
to grab someone by the arm = saisir quelqu'un par le bras
he tried to grab my handbag = il a essayé d'arracher mon sac à main

---

✱ in informal situations

# go

▶ You will find translations for phrasal verbs like **go away**, **go back**, **go round**, etc listed separately in the dictionary.

▶ For translations of expressions like **I'm going to leave / go to London / learn to drive**, see the entry **going**.

## Getting from A to B

Generally **go** is translated by **aller** (**!** + *être*):

| | |
|---|---|
| *we went to the cinema* | = nous sommes allés au cinéma |
| *to go to town / to school / to the market* | = aller en ville / à l'école / au marché |
| *to go to Brussels / to Germany / to Japan* | = aller à Bruxelles / en Allemagne / au Japon |
| *to go to the dentist's / the doctor's / the chemist's* | = aller chez le dentiste / le médecin / le pharmacien |
| *to go for a swim / for a coffee / for a walk* | = aller nager / prendre un café / se promener |

G

## Translating verbs of movement in French

Moving in, out, back, away etc is usually translated using a single verb in French which takes **être**:

| | |
|---|---|
| *to go into a room* | = entrer dans une pièce |
| *to go away on vacation* | = partir en vacances |
| *to go back to work in France* | = retourner travailler en France |
| *to go home* | = rentrer |
| *to go outside* | = sortir |
| *to go upstairs* | = monter |

See also the phrasal verbs listed separately for further translations.

## *go* meaning *to become*

There is often a single French verb to translate the structure **to go** + *adjective*:

| | |
|---|---|
| *to go pale* | = pâlir |
| *to go red* | = rougir |
| but | |
| *the light went red* | = le feu est passé au rouge |

**devenir** + *adjective* is a useful alternative:

| | |
|---|---|
| *to go crazy* | = devenir fou / folle |
| *to go blind* | = devenir aveugle |

## In polite inquiries

| | |
|---|---|
| *how's it going?* | = comment ça va? |
| *everything's going very well* | = tout va très bien |
| *how did the exam go?* | = comment s'est passé l'examen? |

## Talking about time, money, food ...

| | |
|---|---|
| *the time goes so quickly* | = le temps passe si vite |
| *50 euros won't go far here* | = on n'ira pas loin avec 50 euros ici |
| *the money's / bread's / petrol's gone* | = il n'y a plus d'argent / de pain / d'essence |

## Describing how (and if) something works

| | |
|---|---|
| *is the car going?* | = est-ce que la voiture marche? |
| *it's still not going* | = ça ne marche toujours pas |
| *to get the heating going* | = mettre le chauffage en marche |

**grade** noun
• (a mark)
  a grade = une note
• (US English) (a class)
  a grade = une classe
  he's in the eighth grade = il est en
    quatrième

**grade school** noun (US English)
  grade school = l'école primaire
  **!** Note that école is feminine.

**gradually** adverb
  = peu à peu

**gram(me)** noun ▶ 285 |
  a gram = un gramme

**grammar** noun
  grammar = la grammaire

**grandchild** noun
  a grandchild = un petit-fils/une petite-
    fille
  the grandchildren = les petits-enfants

**granddaughter** noun
  a granddaughter = une petite-fille

**grandfather** noun
  a grandfather = un grand-père

**grandmother** noun
  a grandmother = une grand-mère

**grandparents** noun
  grandparents = les grands-parents
    (masculine)

**grandson** noun
  a grandson = un petit-fils

**grapefruit** noun
  a grapefruit = un pamplemousse

**grapes** noun
  grapes = le raisin (singular)
  a bunch of grapes = une grappe de raisin

**grass** noun
  grass = l'herbe (feminine)
  (in gardens) = la pelouse
  to cut the grass = tondre la pelouse

**grasshopper** noun
  a grasshopper = une sauterelle

**grateful** adjective
  = reconnaissant/reconnaissante
  I would be grateful if you could let me
    know = je vous serais reconnaissant de
    me prévenir

**grave** noun
  a grave = une tombe

**gray** (US English) ▶**grey**

**grease** noun
  grease = la graisse

**greasy** adjective
  = gras/grasse

**great** adjective
• (stressing size, amount, importance)
  = grand/grande (**!** before the noun)
  a great improvement = une grande
    amélioration
  to have great difficulty reading = avoir
    beaucoup de mal à lire
  the guide book was a great help = le
    guide a été très utile
• (showing enthusiasm)
  that's great! = c'est formidable!, c'est
    génial**✶**!
  I had a great time = je me suis bien amusé

**Great Britain** noun ▶ 218 |
  Great Britain = la Grande-Bretagne

**great grandfather** noun
  a great grandfather = un arrière-grand-
    père

**great grandmother** noun
  a great grandmother = une arrière-grand-
    mère

**Greece** noun ▶ 218 |
  Greece = la Grèce

**greedy** adjective
  = gourmand/gourmande

**Greek** ▶ 275 |
**1** adjective
  = grec/grecque
**2** noun
• (the people)
  the Greeks = les Grecs (masculine)
• (the language)
  Greek = le grec

**green** adjective ▶ 213 |
  = vert/verte

**greenhouse** noun
  a greenhouse = une serre

**grey** (British English), **gray** (US English)
adjective ▶ 213 |
  = gris/grise
  to have grey hair = avoir les cheveux gris

**grill** verb
  = faire griller

**grin** verb
  = sourire

**grocer** noun ▶ 315 |
  a grocer = un épicier/une épicière

**grocery** noun ▶ 315 |
  a grocery = une épicerie

**ground** noun
• the ground = le sol
  the ground is hard in winter = le sol est
    dur en hiver
  to throw papers on the ground = jeter des
    papiers par terre
  to get up off the ground = se lever
    (**!** + être)

---

**✶** in informal situations

- (*land used for sports*)
  a sports ground = un terrain de sport

**ground floor** *noun* (*British English*)
  the ground floor = le rez-de-chaussée

**group** *noun*
- (*a number of people*)
  a group = un groupe
- (*a band*)
  a (rock) group = un groupe (de rock)

**grow** *verb*
- (*to get big, strong*) (*if it's a person, an animal*) = grandir
  (*if it's a plant*) = pousser
- (*as a gardener, a farmer*) = cultiver
  to grow vegetables = cultiver des légumes
- (*to get long*) = pousser
  she's decided to let her hair grow = elle a décidé de se laisser pousser les cheveux
- (*to let grow*)
  to grow a beard = se laisser pousser la barbe
- (*to become*) = devenir (**!** + *être*)
  she's grown more cynical = elle est devenue plus cynique
  to grow old = vieillir
- (*to increase in size*)
  the population will grow = la population va augmenter
**grow up** = grandir
  when I grow up, I want to be a doctor = je veux être médecin quand je serai grand

**grumble** *verb*
  = ronchonner

**guard** *noun*
- (*in a prison, at a bank*)
  a guard = un gardien/une gardienne
- (*in the army*)
  a guard = un garde
  to be on guard = être de garde

**guard dog** *noun*
  a guard dog = un chien de garde

**guess** *verb*
  = deviner

**guest** *noun*
- (*a person invited to stay*)
  a guest = un invité/une invitée
- (*at a hotel*)
  a guest = un client/une cliente

**guesthouse** *noun*
  a guesthouse = une pension de famille

**guide**
**1** *noun*
- (*a person*)
  a (tour) guide = un guide
- (*British English*) (*a Girl Guide*)
  a guide = une guide
**2** *verb*
  = guider

**guide book** *noun*
  a guide book = un guide

**guided tour** *noun*
  a guided tour = une visite guidée

**guilty** *adjective*
  = coupable
  to feel guilty = culpabiliser

**guinea pig** *noun*
  a guinea pig = un cochon d'Inde

**guitar** *noun* ▶ 290 |
  a guitar = une guitare

**gum** *noun*
  the gum = la gencive

**gun** *noun*
  a gun (*a weapon*) = une arme à feu
  (*a rifle*) = un fusil
  (*a revolver*) = un revolver

**gym** *noun*
  a gym = une salle de gym*

**gymnasium** *noun*
  a gymnasium = un gymnase

**gymnastics** *noun* ▶ 248 |
  gymnastics = la gymnastique

**gypsy** *noun*
  a gypsy = un gitan/une gitane

**H**

# Hh

**habit** *noun*
  a habit = une habitude

**hail** *noun*
  hail = la grêle

**hair** *noun*
  hair (*on the head*) = les cheveux (*masculine plural*)
  (*on the body*) = les poils (*masculine plural*)

**hairbrush** *noun*
  a hairbrush = une brosse à cheveux

**hairdresser** *noun* ▶ 315 |
  a hairdresser = un coiffeur/une coiffeuse

**hairdryer** *noun*
  a hairdryer = un sèche-cheveux

**hairstyle** *noun*
  a hairstyle = une coiffure

**half** ▶ 317 |
**1** *noun*
- a half = une moitié
  to cut a melon in half = couper un melon en deux
- (*in a game*)
  the first half = la première mi-temps

**2** *adjective*
a half-litre of milk, half a litre of milk = un demi-litre de lait
**3** *pronoun*
* (*when talking about quantities, numbers*)
to spend half of one's pocket money = dépenser la moitié de son argent de poche
half the pupils speak French = la moitié des élèves parlent français
* (*when talking about time, age*) ▶ **211 |**, ▶ **187 |**
an hour and a half = une heure et demie
he's three and a half = il a trois ans et demi
it's half (past) three (*British English*) = il est trois heures et demie
**4** *adverb*
Sam's half French half Irish = Sam est moitié français moitié irlandais

**half hour** *noun* ▶ **356 |**
a half hour = une demi-heure

**half term** *noun* (*British English*)
half term = les vacances de la mi-trimestre
**!** *Note that* **vacances** *is feminine plural.*

**hall** *noun*
* (*in a house, an apartment*)
a hall = une entrée
* (*for public events*)
a hall = une grande salle

**ham** *noun*
ham = le jambon

**hamburger** *noun*
a hamburger = un hamburger

**hammer** *noun*
a hammer = un marteau

**hamster** *noun*
a hamster = un hamster

**hand** *noun*
* (*the part of the body*) ▶ **201 |**
the hand = la main
he had a pencil in his hand = il avait un crayon à la main
to hold someone's hand = tenir quelqu'un par la main
* (*help*)
a hand = un coup de main
* (*on a clock or watch*)
a hand = une aiguille
* (*when judging a situation or subject*)
on the one hand..., on the other... = d'un côté..., d'un autre côté...

**handbag** *noun*
a handbag = un sac à main

**handball** *noun* ▶ **248 |**
handball = le handball

**handicapped** *adjective*
= handicapé/handicapée

**handkerchief** *noun*
a handkerchief = un mouchoir

**handle** *noun*
a handle = une poignée

**handsome** *adjective*
= beau/belle (**!** *before the noun*)
a handsome man = un bel homme

**handwriting** *noun*
handwriting = l'écriture (*feminine*)

**handy** *adjective*
* (*practical*) = pratique
* (*helpful*) = utile

**hang** *verb*
* (*on a hook, a coat hanger, a line*)
to hang a picture (up) on the wall = accrocher un tableau au mur
to hang clothes (up) in a wardrobe = suspendre des vêtements dans une armoire
to hang clothes on a line = étendre du linge
* (*to be attached*)
the portrait hangs over the piano = le portrait est accroché au-dessus du piano
to be hanging from the ceiling = être suspendu/suspendue au plafond
* (*to kill*) = pendre
**hang around**
* (*to wait*) = attendre
* (*to waste time, to do nothing*) = traîner
**hang on to** = s'agripper à (**!** + *être*)
she was hanging on to the rope = elle s'agrippait à la corde
**hang up**
* (*on a hook, a coat hanger, a line*)
to hang up one's coat = accrocher son manteau
to hang clothes up to dry = mettre des vêtements à sécher
* your coat's hanging up in the hall = ton manteau est suspendu dans l'entrée
* (*when phoning*) = raccrocher

**hang-gliding** *noun* ▶ **248 |**
hang-gliding = le deltaplane

**happen** *verb*
* (*to occur*) = se passer (**!** + *être*), arriver (**!** + *être*)
what happened? = qu'est-ce qui s'est passé?, qu'est-ce qui est arrivé?
the accident happened last week = l'accident est arrivé la semaine dernière
to happen again = se reproduire (**!** + *être*)
* (*to affect someone*)
what happened to you? = qu'est-ce qui t'est arrivé?
something odd happened to me = il m'est arrivé quelque chose de bizarre

**happy** *adjective*
- (*content*) = heureux/heureuse
  to make someone happy = rendre
  quelqu'un heureux
  they were happy to hear from you = ils
  ont été heureux d'avoir de tes nouvelles
  he's happy with the language course = le
  cours de langue lui plaît
- (*in greetings*)
  Happy birthday! = Bon anniversaire!
  Happy New Year! = Bonne année!

**hard**
**1** *adjective*
- (*firm, stiff*) = dur/dure
  the ground is hard = le sol est dur
- (*difficult*) = difficile
  a hard question = une question difficile
  it's hard to understand = c'est difficile à
  comprendre
  I find it hard to concentrate = j'ai du mal à
  me concentrer
- (*harsh, tough*)
  a hard winter = un hiver rude
  to be having a hard time = traverser une
  période difficile
- (*severe*) = dur/dure, sévère
**2** *adverb*
  to work hard = travailler dur
  they hit him hard = ils l'ont frappé fort
  to try hard to concentrate = faire
  beaucoup d'efforts pour se concentrer

**hard disk** *noun*
  a hard disk = un disque dur

**hardly** *adverb*
  = à peine
  I hardly know them = je les connais à
  peine

**hardware** *noun*
  hardware (*for computers*) = le matériel
  (informatique)

**hard-working** *adjective*
  = travailleur/travailleuse

**hare** *noun*
  a hare = un lièvre

**harm** *verb*
  to harm someone = faire du mal à
  quelqu'un
  to harm the environment = nuire à
  l'environnement

**harmful** *adjective*
  = nocif/nocive

**harmless** *adjective*
  = inoffensif/inoffensive

**harp** *noun* ▶ 290
  a harp = une harpe

**harvest** *noun*
  the harvest (*of wheat*) = la moisson
  (*of fruit*) = la récolte
  (*of grapes*) = la vendange

**hat** *noun*
  a hat = un chapeau

**hate** *verb*
- (*to feel a strong dislike for*)
  to hate someone = détester quelqu'un
- (*to feel hatred for*) = haïr

**hatred** *noun*
  hatred = la haine

**have**
**1** *verb*
▶ 258 | *See the boxed note on* **have** *for more
information and examples.*
- (*to eat, to drink*)
  to have a sandwich = manger un
  sandwich
  to have a glass of wine = boire un verre de
  vin
  to have dinner = dîner
- (*to get*)
  I had a letter from Bob yesterday = j'ai
  reçu une lettre de Bob hier
  I'll let you have the money soon = je te
  donnerai l'argent bientôt
- (*to hold or organize*)
  to have a party = faire une fête
  to have a competition = organiser un
  concours
- (*to spend*) ▶ 237 |
  we had a nice day at the beach = nous
  avons passé une journée agréable à la
  plage
  I'll have a good time in Paris = je
  m'amuserai bien à Paris
- (*to suffer*)
  to have [flu | a headache | a toothache ...]
  = avoir [la grippe | mal à la tête | mal aux
  dents ...]
- (*to get something done*)
  to have the house painted = faire peindre
  la maison
  she had her hair cut = elle s'est fait couper
  les cheveux
- to have a baby = avoir un enfant
**2** *auxiliary verb*

> **!** *For a detailed note on the use of* **have** *as
> an auxiliary verb, see the boxed note on*
> **have**. *All verbs which don't take* avoir *as
> an auxiliary verb are marked (***!** + être) *in
> this dictionary.*

  you've seen her, haven't you? = tu l'as
  vue, n'est-ce pas?
  he hasn't called, has he? = il n'a pas
  téléphoné, par hasard?
  'I've no money'—'yes you have!' = 'je n'ai
  pas d'argent'—'mais si tu en as!'
**3 to have to** = devoir
  I have to [study | pay | go home ...] = je dois
  [étudier | payer | rentrer ...]
  you don't have to go back to France = tu
  n'es pas obligé de retourner en France

**hay** *noun*
  hay = le foin

# have

## As an ordinary verb

- When **have** or **have got** is used as a verb meaning *possess*, it can generally be translated by **avoir**:

| | |
|---|---|
| *I have (got) a car* | = j'**ai** une voiture |
| *she has (got) a good memory* | = elle **a** une bonne mémoire |
| *they have (got) problems* | = ils **ont** des problèmes |

For examples and particular usages see the entry **have**; see also the entry **got**.

- **have** is also used with certain noun objects where the whole expression is equivalent to a verb: *to have dinner* = to dine; *to have a walk* = to walk; *to have a swim* = to swim. In such cases, the phrase is very often translated by the equivalent verb in French (*dîner, se promener, se baigner*).

## As an auxiliary verb

- When used as an auxiliary in present perfect and past perfect tenses, **have** is normally translated by **avoir**:

| | |
|---|---|
| *I have seen* | = j'**ai** vu |
| *I had seen* | = j'**avais** vu |

- However, some verbs in French, especially verbs of movement and change of state (*aller, venir, descendre, mourir*), always take **être** in these tenses:

| | |
|---|---|
| *he has left* | = il **est** parti |
| *she's fallen* | = elle **est** tombée |

In this case, remember the past participle agrees with the subject of the verb:

| | |
|---|---|
| *she has gone* | = elle **est** allée |
| *they had come back* | = ils **étaient** revenus |
| *we had stayed at home* | = nous **étions** restés chez nous |

If you are in doubt as to whether a verb conjugates with **être** or **avoir**, consult the French entry, where verbs taking **être** will be indicated like this: (**!** + *être*).

- Reflexive verbs (*se lever, se coucher*) always conjugate with **être**:

| | |
|---|---|
| *she has fainted* | = elle **s'est** évanouie |
| *have you had a rest?* | = est-ce que tu **t'es** reposé? |
| *he had fallen asleep* | = il **s'était** endormi |
| *I had changed my clothes* | = je **m'étais** changé |

In this case, the past participle agrees with the reflexive pronoun only when the pronoun is a direct object. Otherwise there is no agreement:

| | |
|---|---|
| *she has hurt herself* | = elle **s'est** fait mal |
| *I've washed my hair* | = je **me suis** lavé les cheveux |
| *he's broken his leg* | = il **s'est** cassé la jambe |

## to have (got) to

- **to have (got) to** meaning *must* is translated by either **devoir** or the impersonal construction **il faut que** + *subjunctive*:

| | |
|---|---|
| *I have to leave now* | = je **dois** partir maintenant |
| | = **il faut que** je parte maintenant |
| *you've got to understand* | = tu **dois** comprendre |
| | = **il faut que** tu comprennes |

- In negative sentences, **not to have to** is usually translated by **ne pas être obligé / obligée de**:

| | |
|---|---|
| *you don't have to go* | = tu **n'es pas obligé** d'y aller |
| *we don't have to accept* | = nous **ne sommes pas obligés** d'accepter |

▶ For **have** used with illnesses, see usage note **Illnesses, aches, and pains ▶ 266 |**.

**hazel** *adjective* ▶ **213** |
= noisette (**!** *never changes*)

**hazelnut** *noun*
a hazelnut = une noisette

**he** *pronoun*
he = il
he's coming next week = il vient la semaine prochaine
there he is = le voilà!
HE didn't write the letter = ce n'est pas lui qui a écrit la lettre
I work in London but he doesn't = je travaille à Londres mais lui non
he's a strange man = c'est un homme bizarre

**head**
**1** *noun*
• (*the part of the body*) ▶ **201** |
the head = la tête
• (*the mind*)
he's got it into his head that he's ugly = il s'est mis dans la tête qu'il était laid
• a head of cabbage = un chou
a head of lettuce = une laitue
• (*the person in charge*)
the head = le responsable/la responsable, le directeur/la directrice
a head of State = un chef d'État
**2** *verb*
• (*to be in charge of*)
to head a team = être à la tête d'une équipe
• (*in soccer*)
to head the ball = faire une tête
**head for** = se diriger vers (**!** + *être*)

**headache** *noun* ▶ **266** |
to have a headache = avoir mal à la tête
my headache's gone = mon mal de tête est passé

**headlamp, headlight** *noun*
a headlamp = un phare

**headline** *noun*
a headline = un gros titre
to hit the headlines = faire la une des journaux
the news headlines = les grands titres de l'actualité

**headquarters** *noun*
the headquarters (*of a company, a business*) = le siège social
(*of an army*) = le quartier général

**headteacher** *noun* ▶ **315** |
a headteacher = un directeur/une directrice

**health** *noun*
health = la santé

**healthy** *adjective*
• (*in good health*) = en bonne santé
• (*good for the health*) = sain/saine

**hear** *verb*
• to hear = entendre
he can't hear anything = il n'entend rien
I heard someone coming in = j'ai entendu quelqu'un entrer
you can hear him practising the piano = on l'entend qui travaille le piano
• (*to learn, to discover*)
to hear the news = apprendre la nouvelle
I've heard about that school = j'ai entendu parler de cette école
we've heard a lot about you = nous avons beaucoup entendu parler de vous
• (*to listen to*) = écouter
**hear from** = avoir des nouvelles de
have you heard from Cathy? = est-ce que tu as eu des nouvelles de Cathy?
**hear of** = entendre parler de
I've never heard of the place = je n'ai jamais entendu parler de cet endroit

**heart** *noun*
• (*part of the body*) ▶ **201** |
the heart = le cœur
• (*the centre*)
right in the heart of London = en plein cœur de Londres
• by heart = par cœur

**heart attack** *noun* ▶ **266** |
a heart attack = une crise cardiaque

**heat**
**1** *verb*
= chauffer
**2** *noun*
• the heat = la chaleur
I can't stand the heat = je ne supporte pas la chaleur
• (*on a cooker*)
to cook at a low heat = faire cuire à feu doux
• (*in a sporting contest*)
a heat = une épreuve éliminatoire
**heat up**
• (*to cook*) = faire chauffer
• (*to warm up again*) = réchauffer

**heater** *noun*
a heater = un appareil de chauffage

**heating** *noun*
heating = le chauffage

**heatwave** *noun*
a heatwave = une vague de chaleur

**heaven** *noun*
heaven = le paradis

**heavy** *adjective*
• (*in weight*) ▶ **285** | = lourd/lourde
• (*in quantity, intensity*)
the traffic is very heavy = il y a beaucoup de circulation
to be a heavy smoker = beaucoup fumer
to have a heavy cold = avoir un gros rhume
• (*describing food*) = lourd/lourde

H

- it's very heavy today = il fait très lourd aujourd'hui

**hedge** noun
a hedge = une haie

**hedgehog** noun
a hedgehog = un hérisson

**heel** noun ▶ 201|
the heel = le talon

**height** noun ▶ 285|
height (of a person) = la taille
(of a building, a tree) = la hauteur
to be afraid of heights = avoir le vertige

**helicopter** noun
a helicopter = un hélicoptère

**hell** noun
hell = l'enfer

**hello** noun (also exclamation) ▶ 237|
hello! (when greeting someone) = bonjour!
(on the phone) = allô!

**helmet** noun
a helmet = un casque

**help**
**1** verb
- to help = aider
  to help someone to [walk | do the housework | escape ...] = aider quelqu'un à [marcher | faire le ménage | s'échapper ...]
  the medicine helps to cure the illness = le médicament aide à guérir la maladie
  to help each other = s'aider, s'entraider (**!** + être)
- (at a meal)
  to help oneself = se servir (**!** + être)
  help yourselves! = servez-vous!
- I can't help thinking about it = je ne peux pas m'empêcher d'y penser
**2** exclamation
help! = au secours!
**3** noun
help (a helping hand) = l'aide (feminine)
(urgent assistance) = le secours
to ask someone for help = demander de l'aide à quelqu'un
to shout for help = crier au secours
**help out** = donner un coup de main

**helpful** adjective
- (ready to help) = serviable, aimable
- (useful) = utile

**helping** noun
a helping = une portion

**helpless** adjective
- (having no power)
  = impuissant/impuissante
- (because of weakness, ill health)
  = impotent/impotente

**hen** noun
a hen = une poule

**her**
**1** pronoun

> **!** Note that there is a boxed usage note at them. The entries me, him, her and us are modelled on this note where you will find detailed grammatical information and fuller explanations.

- her = la (**!** l' + vowel or mute h)
  I know her = je la connais
  I don't know her = je ne la connais pas
  do I know her? = est-ce que je la connais?
- he's seen her = il l'a vue
  he hasn't seen her = il ne l'a pas vue
  has he seen her? = est-ce qu'il l'a vue?
- catch her! = attrape-la!
  help her! = aide-la!
  don't help her! = ne l'aide pas!
  don't hit her! = ne la frappe pas!
- I gave the book to her = je lui ai donné le livre
  I didn't give the book to her = je ne lui ai pas donné le livre
  did I give the book to her? = est-ce que je lui ai donné le livre?
- her = lui
  write to her! = écris-lui!
  say it to her! = dis-le-lui!
  don't show it to her! = ne le lui montre pas!
- her = elle
  he did it for her = il l'a fait pour elle
  it's her = c'est elle
  stand in front of her = mets-toi devant elle
**2** determiner
her = son/sa (+ singular)
= ses (+ plural)

> **!** Note that sa becomes son before a vowel or mute h.

I hate her dog = je déteste son chien
what do you think of her house? = qu'est-ce que tu penses de sa maison?
she licked her plate = elle a léché son assiette
did you see all her CDs? = est-ce que tu as vu tous ses disques compacts?
she broke her leg = elle s'est cassé la jambe

> **!** Note that, when talking about parts of the body, son, sa, ses are not used. See the usage note on The human body ▶ 201| for further examples.

**herd** noun
a herd = un troupeau

**here** adverb
- (when talking about location) = ici
  is it far from here? = est-ce que c'est loin d'ici?
  I'm up here = je suis là

- *(when drawing attention)*
  here's the post office = voici la poste
  here they are = les voici
  here's my telephone number = voici mon
    numéro de téléphone
  here comes the train = voilà le train
  here—take my pencil = tiens—prends mon
    crayon
- *(in general statements)* = là
  tell him I'm not here = dis-lui que je ne
    suis pas là
  we're here to help you = nous sommes là
    pour vous aider

**hers** *pronoun*
  the green pen is hers = le stylo vert est à
    elle
  which bag is hers? = lequel de ces sacs est
    le sien?
  my jacket is red but hers is green = ma
    veste est rouge mais la sienne est verte
  my parents are younger than hers = mes
    parents sont plus jeunes que les siens

  **!** *Note that, when comparing objects,
  people, etc, one of the following
  translations—le sien, la sienne, les siens
  or les siennes—will be used. To know
  which one to use, find out whether the
  object, person, etc being described is
  masculine or feminine, singular or plural.*

**herself** *pronoun*
- *(when used as a reflexive pronoun)*
  she wants to enjoy herself = elle veut
    s'amuser
  she's cut herself with a knife = elle s'est
    coupée avec un couteau
- *(when used for emphasis)*
  she said it herself = elle l'a dit elle-même
  she did it all by herself = elle l'a fait toute
    seule

**hesitate** *verb*
  = hésiter

**hi** *exclamation*
  hi! = salut\*!

**hiccups** *noun*
  to have hiccups = avoir le hoquet

**hidden** *adjective*
  = caché/cachée

**hide** *verb*
- *(to avoid showing)* = cacher
  to hide documents from the police
    = cacher des documents à la police
- *(to avoid being seen)* = se cacher (**!** + *être*)

**hi-fi** *noun*
  a hi-fi = une chaîne hi-fi

**high**
**1** *adjective* ▶ 285 |
- *(having a great height)* = haut/haute
  the mountains are high = les montagnes
    sont hautes
- *(describing a level, a price, a speed)*
  = élevé/élevée
  prices are high = les prix sont élevés
  the train travels at high speed = le train
    roule très vite

- *(describing a standard, grade)*
  the standard is high = le niveau est élevé
  to get high grades = avoir de très bonnes
    notes
- *(describing a voice)* = aigu/aiguë
**2** *adverb*
  don't go any higher = ne montez pas plus
    haut

**high rise block** *noun*
  a high rise block = une tour d'habitation

**high school** *noun*
  a high school *(in the US)* = un
    établissement secondaire
  *(in Britain)* = un lycée

**hijack** *verb*
  = détourner

**hike** *verb*
  to go hiking = faire de la randonnée

**hiking** *noun* ▶ 248 |
  hiking = la randonnée

**hill** *noun*
  a hill = une colline
  *(a rise in the road)* = une pente

**him** *pronoun*

  **!** *Note that there is a boxed usage note at
  them. The entries me, him, her and us are
  modelled on this note where you will find
  detailed grammatical information and
  fuller explanations.*

- him = le (**!** l' + *vowel or mute* h)
  I know him = je le connais
  I don't know him = je ne le connais pas
  do I know him? = est-ce que je le connais?
- she's seen him = elle l'a vu
  she hasn't seen him = elle ne l'a pas vu
  has she seen him? = est-ce qu'elle l'a vu?
- catch him! = attrape-le!
  help him! = aide-le!
  don't help him! = ne l'aide pas!
  don't hit him! = ne le frappe pas!
- I gave the book to him = je lui ai donné le
    livre
  I didn't give the book to him = je ne lui ai
    pas donné le livre
  did I give the book to him? = est-ce que je
    lui ai donné le livre?
- him = lui
  write to him! = écris-lui!
  say it to him! = dis-lui!
  don't show it to him! = ne le lui montre
    pas!
- him = lui
  he did it for him = il l'a fait pour lui
  it's him = c'est lui
  stand in front of him = mets-toi devant lui

**himself** *pronoun*
- *(when used as a reflexive pronoun)*
  he wants to enjoy himself = il veut
    s'amuser
  he's cut himself with a knife = il s'est
    coupé avec un couteau

- (*when used for emphasis*)
  he said it himself = il l'a dit lui-même
  he did it all by himself = il l'a fait tout seul

**hip** *noun* ▶ **201**
the hip = la hanche

**hippopotamus**, **hippo** *noun*
a hippopotamus = un hippopotame

**hire** *verb*
- (*to employ*) = embaucher
- (*British English*) (*to rent*) = louer
  to hire a car = louer une voiture
- (*to lend for a fee*) = louer
  they hire (out) the skates = ils louent les
  patins

**his**
**1** *determiner*
his = son/sa (+ *singular*)
= ses (+ *plural*)

> **!** *Note that* sa *becomes* son *before a
> vowel or mute h.*

I hate his dog = je déteste son chien
what do you think of his house? = qu'est-
  ce que tu penses de sa maison?
he licked his plate = il a léché son assiette
did you see all his CDs? = est-ce que tu as
  vu tous ses disques compacts?
he broke his arm = il s'est cassé le bras

> **!** *Note that, when talking about parts of
> the body,* son, sa, ses *are not used. See
> the usage note on* **The human body**
> ▶ **201** *for further examples.*

**2** *pronoun*
the blue pen is his = le stylo bleu est à lui
which house is his? = laquelle de ces
  maisons est la sienne?
my shirt is white but his is yellow = ma
  chemise est blanche mais la sienne est
  jaune
my brother is taller than his = mon frère
  est plus grand que le sien

> **!** *Note that, when comparing objects,
> people, etc, one of the following
> translations—*le sien, la sienne, les siens
> *or* les siennes—*will be used. To know
> which one to use, find out whether the
> object, person, etc which is being
> described is masculine or feminine,
> singular or plural.*

**history** *noun*
history = l'histoire (*feminine*)

**hit**
**1** *verb*
- (*to strike*) = frapper
  to hit someone on the head = frapper
    quelqu'un à la tête
  to hit one's head on a chair = se cogner la
    tête contre une chaise

- (*to crash into*)
  to hit a wall = heurter un mur
  to hit a pedestrian = renverser un piéton
**2** *noun*
a hit (*a song*) = un tube✶
(*a film, a play*) = un succès
**hit back** = riposter
to hit someone back = rendre un coup à
  quelqu'un

**hitchhike** *verb*
= faire de l'auto-stop, faire du stop✶

**hitchhiker** *noun*
a hitchhiker = un auto-stoppeur/une auto-
  stoppeuse

**hoarse** *adjective*
to be hoarse = être enroué/enrouée

**hobby** *noun*
a hobby = un passe-temps

**hockey** *noun* ▶ **248**
hockey = le hockey

**hold**
**1** *verb*
- to hold = tenir
  he held some coins in his hand = il avait
    quelques pièces dans la main
- (*to arrange*)
  to hold a competition = organiser un
    concours
  the party will be held in the school = la
    fête aura lieu dans l'école
- (*to keep or hide*) = détenir
  to hold someone hostage = garder
    quelqu'un en otage
- (*to keep back*) = garder
  to hold a seat for someone = garder une
    place pour quelqu'un
- (*other uses*)
  to hold the world record = détenir le
    record mondial
  to hold someone responsible = tenir
    quelqu'un pour responsable
  to hold, to hold the line = patienter
**2** *noun*
- to get hold of the ball = attraper le ballon
- to get hold of someone (*to find*) = trouver
    quelqu'un
  (*by phone*) = joindre quelqu'un
**hold on**
- (*to wait*) = attendre
- hold on tight! = tiens-toi bien!
**hold on to** = s'agripper à (**!** + *être*)
**hold up**
- (*to raise*) = lever
  to hold up one's hand ≈ lever le doigt
- (*to delay*)
  to hold someone up = retarder quelqu'un
  to hold up the traffic = ralentir la
    circulation
- (*to rob*) = attaquer

**hole** *noun*
a hole = un trou

---

✶ in informal situations

**holiday** noun
* (British English) (a vacation)
a holiday = des vacances (feminine plural)
to go on holiday = partir en vacances
* (a national or religious festival)
a (public) holiday = un jour férié
* (British English) (time taken off work)
a day's holiday = un jour de congé
to take two weeks' holiday = prendre
quinze jours de congé

**Holland** noun ▶ 218 |
Holland = la Hollande

**holly** noun
holly = le houx

**home**
**1** noun
* a home (a place to live) = un logement
(a house) = une maison
to leave home = quitter la maison
to work from home = travailler à domicile
* (for elderly, ill or disabled people)
a home for handicapped children = un
établissement pour enfants handicapés
an old people's home = une maison de
retraite
**2** adverb

> ! Note that chez soi changes to chez moi,
> chez lui, chez eux, etc depending on the
> person whose home is being talked
> about.

to go home (to one's house) = retourner à
la maison, rentrer (chez soi)
(to one's home country) = rentrer (dans son
pays)
on my way home = en rentrant chez moi
to be home (from school, work) = être
rentré/rentrée
I can take you home = je peux te
raccompagner chez toi
**3 at home**
* (in one's house) = à la maison, chez soi
she's working at home = elle travaille à la
maison, elle travaille chez elle
he lives at home = il habite chez ses
parents
* to feel at home = se sentir à l'aise
make yourselves at home = faites comme
chez vous
* (when talking about a sports team) = à
domicile

**homeless** adjective
to be homeless = être sans abri, être sans
logement

**homesick** adjective
to be homesick (when abroad) = avoir le
mal du pays

**homework** noun
homework = les devoirs (masculine plural)

**homosexual** noun
a homosexual = un homosexuel/une
homosexuelle

**honest** adjective
* honest = honnête
* (frank, sincere) = franc/franche
to be honest, I'd rather stay here = à vrai
dire, je préfère rester ici

**honestly** adverb
= franchement, honnêtement

**honey** noun
honey = le miel

**honeymoon** noun
a honeymoon = un voyage de noces

**hood** noun
* (to cover the head)
a hood = un capuchon
* (US English) (of a car)
the hood = le capot

**hoof** noun
a hoof = un sabot

**hook** noun
* (for hanging clothes, pictures)
a hook = un crochet
* (for fishing)
a hook = un hameçon

**hooligan** noun
a hooligan = un voyou, un vandale
a football hooligan = un hooligan

**hoover** verb (British English)
to hoover the house = passer l'aspirateur
dans la maison

**hop** verb
= sauter à cloche-pied

**hope**
**1** verb
= espérer
I hope you don't mind = j'espère que cela
ne vous dérange pas
I hope she remembers to come = j'espère
qu'elle pensera à venir

> ! Note that, when talking about the future,
> espérer que is followed by the future
> tense.

we hope to meet lots of people = nous
espérons rencontrer beaucoup de
monde
I hope so = j'espère que oui
**2** noun
hope = l'espoir (masculine)
to give up hope = abandonner tout espoir

**hopeless** adjective
* (without hope of success)
= désespéré/désespérée
* (without any ability) = nul/nulle
to be hopeless at cooking = être
incapable de faire la cuisine

**horn** noun
* (on a car, a bus)
a horn = un klaxon
to blow a horn = klaxonner

H

- (of an animal)
  a horn = une corne
- (an instrument) ▶ 290 |
  a horn = un cor

**horoscope** noun
  the horoscope = l'horoscope (masculine)

**horrible** adjective
  = affreux/affreuse

**horror film** noun
  a horror film = un film d'épouvante

**horse** noun
  a horse = un cheval
  he likes horses = il aime les chevaux

**horseracing** noun ▶ 248 |
  horseracing = les courses (feminine plural)

**horseriding** noun ▶ 248 |
  horseriding = l'équitation (feminine)

**hospital** noun
  a hospital = un hôpital
  he's still in (the) hospital = il est toujours
    à l'hôpital
  to be taken to (the) hospital = être
    hospitalisé/hospitalisée

**host** noun
  a host = un hôte

**hostage** noun
  a hostage = un otage

**hostel** noun
  a hostel = un foyer

**hostess** noun
  a hostess = une hôtesse

**hot** adjective
- (very warm) = chaud/chaude
  to be hot, to feel hot = avoir chaud
  I'm very hot = j'ai très chaud
  it's too hot in the office = il fait trop chaud
    au bureau
  a hot meal = un repas chaud
- (strong, with a lot of spices)
  a hot mustard = une moutarde forte
  a very hot dish = un plat très épicé

**hot air balloon** noun
  a hot air balloon = une montgolfière

**hot dog** noun
  a hot dog = un hot dog

**hotel** noun
  a hotel = un hôtel

**hour** noun ▶ 211 |, ▶ 356 |
  an hour = une heure
  I earn two pounds an hour = je gagne
    deux livres (de) l'heure

**house** noun
  a house = une maison
  to go to someone's house = aller chez
    quelqu'un
  the bike is at my house = le vélo est chez
    moi

**housewife** noun ▶ 315 |
  a housewife = une femme au foyer

**housework** noun
  to do the housework = faire le ménage

**housing estate** (British English),
**housing development** (US English)
noun
  a housing estate = une cité (ouvrière)

**hovercraft** noun
  a hovercraft = un aéroglisseur

**how** adverb
- (in what way) = comment
  how did you find us? = comment est-ce
    que tu nous as trouvés?
  I know how [to swim | to ride a horse | to cook
    a curry ...] = je sais [nager | monter à cheval |
    préparer un curry ...]
- (in polite questions)
  how are you? = comment allez-vous?,
    comment vas-tu?
  how is your sister? = comment va ta sœur?
  how was your holiday? = est-ce que tes
    vacances se sont bien passées?
- (in questions requiring specific information)
  how long will it take? = combien de temps
    faudra-t-il?
  how tall are you? = combien mesures-tu?
  how old is he? = quel âge a-t-il?
- (when making a suggestion)
  how would you like to eat out? = est-ce
    que ça te dirait d'aller au restaurant?
  how about going to the cinema tonight?
    = et si on allait au cinéma ce soir?

**however** adverb
- (nevertheless) = toutefois, cependant
- however hard I try, I can't understand
  grammar = j'ai beau essayer, je ne
    comprends pas la grammaire

**how many** ▶ 317 |
**1** pronoun
  = combien
  how many do you want? = combien en
    voulez-vous?
  how many of you are there? = combien
    êtes-vous?
**2** determiner
  = combien de
  how many children are going on the trip?
    = combien d'enfants vont participer à
    l'excursion?

**how much** ▶ 317 |
**1** pronoun
  = combien
  how much does it come to? = ça fait
    combien?
  how much is the jacket? = combien coûte
    la veste?
**2** determiner
  = combien de
  how much money do you have left?
    = combien d'argent est-ce qu'il te reste?

**huge** *adjective*
= énorme

**human being** *noun*
a human being = un être humain

**humour** (*British English*), **humor** (*US English*) *noun*
humour = l'humour (*masculine*)
to have a sense of humour = avoir le sens de l'humour

**hundred** *number* ▶ 187 |
one hundred, a hundred = cent
three hundred = trois cents
five hundred and fifty euros = cinq cent cinquante euros
about a hundred people = une centaine de personnes

**Hungary** *noun* ▶ 218 |
Hungary = la Hongrie

**hungry** *adjective*
to be hungry = avoir faim
I'm very hungry = j'ai très faim

**hunt** *verb* ▶ 248 |
= chasser
to go hunting = aller à la chasse

**hurdles** *noun* ▶ 248 |
the hurdles = la course de haies

**hurrah, hurray** *noun* (*also exclamation*)
hurrah! = hourra!

**hurry**
**1** *verb*
• = se dépêcher (**!** + *être*)
hurry home! = dépêche-toi de rentrer!
• to hurry someone = bousculer quelqu'un
**2** *noun*
to be in a hurry = être pressé/pressée
there's no hurry = ça ne presse pas
**hurry up** = se dépêcher (**!** + *être*)

**hurt** *verb*
• (*to injure*)
to hurt oneself = se faire mal (**!** + *être*)
to hurt one's leg = se faire mal à la jambe
• (*to be painful*)
my throat hurts = j'ai mal à la gorge
that hurts = ça fait mal
• (*to upset*) = blesser
to hurt someone's feelings = blesser quelqu'un

**husband** *noun*
a husband = un mari

# I i

**I** *pronoun*
I = je (**I** j' + *vowel or mute h*)
I've got to go = je dois m'en aller
here I am = me voilà
I didn't do it = ce n'est pas moi qui l'ai fait
I'm the one who does all the work = c'est moi qui fais tout le travail
she drives but I don't = elle conduit mais moi non

**ice** *noun*
• (*frozen water*)
ice = la glace
• (*on roads*)
ice = le verglas
• (*in a drink*)
ice = des glaçons (*masculine plural*)

**ice cream** *noun*
ice cream = la glace
an ice cream = une glace

**ice hockey** *noun* ▶ 248 |
ice hockey = le hockey sur glace

**ice rink** *noun*
an ice rink = une patinoire

**ice-skate** *noun*
an ice-skate = un patin à glace

**ice-skating** *noun* ▶ 248 |
ice-skating = le patin à glace

**icing** *noun*
icing = le glaçage

**idea** *noun*
an idea = une idée
what a good idea! = quelle bonne idée!
I've no idea how much it costs = je ne sais pas du tout combien ça coûte

**identity card** *noun*
an identity card = une carte d'identité

**idiot** *noun*
an idiot = un idiot/une idiote

**if** *conjunction*
= si
if you like = si tu veux
if it rains, we won't go = s'il pleut, nous n'irons pas
if I were rich, I would travel = si j'étais riche, je voyagerais
I wonder if they'll come = je me demande s'ils vont venir
if I were you, I'd refuse = à ta place, je refuserais

# Illnesses, aches, and pains

## Where does it hurt?

*where does it hurt?* = où est-ce que ça vous fait mal?
*his leg hurts* = il a mal à la jambe

(Do not confuse, **faire mal à quelqu'un** with **faire du mal à quelqu'un**, which means *to harm somebody*.)

Note that with **avoir mal à** French uses the definite article (**le, la, les,** or **l'**) with the part of the body, where English has a possessive, hence:

*he **has a pain in** his leg* = il **a mal à la** jambe
*his head **was hurting*** = il **avait mal à la** tête

## Accidents

*she broke **her** leg* = elle s'est cassé **la** jambe
*I twisted **my** ankle* = je me suis foulé **la** cheville

## Being ill

French mostly uses the definite article with the name of an illness:

*to have flu | measles* = avoir **la** grippe / **la** rougeole
but
*to have cancer* = avoir **un** cancer

## Falling ill

French has no general equivalent of **to get**. However, where English can use **catch**, French can use **attraper**:

*to **catch** measles* = **attraper** la rougeole
*to **catch** a cold* = **attraper** un rhume

## Treatment

*to be treated for rabies* = **se faire soigner contre** la rage
*to take tablets for indigestion* = **prendre des comprimés contre** l'indigestion
*to be operated on for cancer* = **être opéré d'**un cancer

---

**ignore** *verb*
  to ignore a person = faire semblant de ne pas voir quelqu'un
  to ignore a problem = ne prêter aucune attention à un problème

**ill** *adjective*
  = malade

**illegal** *adjective*
  = illégal/illégale

**illness** *noun*
  an illness = une maladie

**imagination** *noun*
  imagination = l'imagination (*feminine*)
  to have imagination = avoir de l'imagination

**imagine** *verb*
  = imaginer

**imitate** *verb*
  = imiter

**immediately** *adverb*
  = immédiatement

**impatient** *adjective*
  = impatient/impatiente
  to get impatient = s'impatienter (**!** + *être*)

**import** *verb*
  = importer

**important** *adjective*
  = important/importante
  it is important to eat well = il est important de bien manger

**impossible** *adjective*
  = impossible
  it's impossible to argue with him = c'est impossible de discuter avec lui

**impress** *verb*
  = impressionner

**impression** *noun*
  an impression = une impression
  to make a good impression = faire bonne impression

**improve** verb
- (to make better) = améliorer
  to improve living conditions = améliorer
  les conditions de vie
  to improve one's French = se
  perfectionner en français
- (to get better) = s'améliorer (! + être)

**improvement** noun
  an improvement = une amélioration

**in**

> ! Often in occurs in combinations with
> verbs, for example: drop in, fit in, move in
> etc. To find the correct translations for this
> type of verb, look up the separate
> dictionary entries at drop, fit, move etc.

**1** preposition
- (inside) = dans
  in the house = dans la maison
  I read it in the newspaper = je l'ai lu dans
  le journal
  there's a letter in the envelope = il y a une
  lettre dans l'enveloppe
  there's a letter in it = il y a une lettre
  dedans
  the woman in the photograph = la femme
  sur la photo
- (at) = à
  I learned German in school = j'ai fait de
  l'allemand à l'école
  in the countryside = à la campagne
- (when talking about countries or cities)
  to live [in Ireland | in Japan | in Paris …]
  = vivre [en Irlande | au Japon | à Paris …]
- (dressed in) = en
  in a skirt = en jupe
  to be dressed in black = être
  habillé/habillée en noir
- (showing the way in which something is
  done) = en
  written in French = écrit en français
  we paid in cash = nous avons payé en
  espèces
  they were sitting in a circle = ils étaient
  assis en cercle
  in ink = à l'encre
- (during)
  in October = en octobre
  in the night = pendant la nuit
  in the morning = le matin
- (within)
  I'll be ready in ten minutes = je serai prêt
  en dix minutes
  she'll be back in half an hour = elle sera de
  retour dans une demi-heure
- (other uses)
  to stay in the rain = rester sous la pluie
  she's in her twenties = elle a entre vingt
  et trente ans
  one in ten = un sur dix
  to cut an apple in two = couper une
  pomme en deux

**2** adverb
- (at home, available) = là
  tell her I'm not in = dis-lui que je ne suis
  pas là
- (arrived)
  the train is in = le train est en gare
  the tide is in = c'est la marée haute

**inch** noun ▶ 285 |
  an inch = un pouce
  | ! Note that an inch = 2.54 cm.

**include** verb
  = comprendre
  service is included in the bill = le service
  est compris dans la note

**including** preposition
  = y compris
  they were all invited, including the
  children = ils étaient tous invités, y
  compris les enfants

**income** noun
  an income = un revenu

**income tax** noun
  income tax = l'impôt sur le revenu
  | ! Note that impôt is masculine.

**inconvenient** adjective
  it's an inconvenient place to meet = c'est
  un endroit peu pratique pour se
  retrouver
  an inconvenient time = un moment
  inopportun
  I hope that's not inconvenient for you
  = j'espère que cela ne vous dérange pas

**increase**
**1** verb
  = augmenter
  to increase in value = augmenter de
  valeur
  to increase by 10% = augmenter de 10%
**2** noun
  an increase = une augmentation

**incredible** adjective
  = incroyable

**independent** adjective
  = indépendant/indépendante

**India** noun ▶ 218 |
  = l'Inde (feminine)

**Indian** ▶ 275 |
**1** adjective
  = indien/indienne
**2** noun
- (from India)
  the Indians = les Indiens (masculine)
- (from North America)
  the Indians = les Indiens d'Amérique

**indicate** verb
  = indiquer

**indifferent** adjective
  = indifférent/indifférente

**indigestion** *noun* ▶ 266 |
  to have indigestion = avoir mal à
    l'estomac

**individual**
**1** *adjective*
  = individuel/individuelle
**2** *noun*
  an individual = un individu

**indoor** *adjective*
  = couvert/couverte
  an indoor swimming pool = une piscine
    couverte

**indoors** *adverb*
  = à l'intérieur

**industrial** *adjective*
  = industriel/industrielle

**industry** *noun*
  industry = l'industrie (*feminine*)

**inevitable** *adjective*
  = inévitable

**infant school** *noun* (*British English*)
  an infant school = une école maternelle

**infection** *noun*
  an infection = une infection

**influence**
**1** *noun*
  an influence = une influence
  to have influence = avoir de l'influence
**2** *verb*
• (*to persuade*) = influencer
• (*to make a strong impression on*)
  to influence someone = avoir une
    influence sur quelqu'un
  to be too influenced by someone = se
    laisser trop influencer par quelqu'un

**inform** *verb*
  to inform the police of an accident
    = signaler un accident à la police
  to keep someone informed = tenir
    quelqu'un au courant

**informal** *adjective*
• (*describing a person, a person's manner*)
  = simple
• (*describing a word, a language*)
  = familier/familière
• (*describing a discussion or an interview*)
  = informel/informelle

**information** *noun*
  a piece of information = un
    renseignement
  information = des renseignements

**information desk** *noun*
  the information desk = l'accueil
    (*masculine*)

**information technology** *noun*
  information technology = l'informatique
    (*feminine*)

**ingredient** *noun*
  an ingredient = un ingrédient

**inhabitant** *noun*
  an inhabitant = un habitant/une habitante

**inheritance tax** *noun*
  inheritance tax = les droits de
    succession
  **!** *Note that* **droits** *is masculine plural.*

**injection** *noun*
  an injection = une piqûre
  to give someone an injection = faire une
    piqûre à quelqu'un

**injured** *adjective*
  = blessé/blessée

**injury** *noun*
  an injury = une blessure

**ink** *noun*
  ink = l'encre (*feminine*)

**innocent** *adjective*
  = innocent/innocente

**inquiry** *noun*
  an inquiry = une enquête

**insect** *noun*
  an insect = un insecte

**inside**
**1** *preposition*
  = à l'intérieur de
  inside the house = à l'intérieur de la
    maison
**2** *adverb*
  = à l'intérieur
  he's inside = il est à l'intérieur
  let's bring the chairs inside = rentrons les
    chaises
**3** *noun*
  the inside = l'intérieur (*masculine*)
  the inside of the palace = l'intérieur du
    palais
**4** *adjective*
  = intérieur/intérieure
**5 inside out** = à l'envers
  to put one's shirt on inside out = mettre sa
    chemise à l'envers

**inspect** *verb*
• (*if it's an official*) = inspecter
• (*if it's a conductor*) = contrôler

**inspector** *noun*
• (*on a bus, a train*)
  an inspector = un contrôleur/une
    contrôleuse
• (*in the police*)
  a police inspector = un inspecteur de
    police

**instantly** *adverb*
  = immédiatement

**instead**
**1 instead of**
- (rather than) = au lieu de
  he hired a van instead of a car = il a loué
  une camionnette au lieu d'une voiture
  instead of working he watched TV = au
  lieu de travailler il a regardé la
  télévision
- (in place of) = à la place de
  use oil instead of butter = utilisez de
  l'huile à la place du beurre
  his wife came instead of him = sa femme
  est venue à sa place
**2** adverb
  I don't feel like going to the cinema—let's
  stay at home instead = je n'ai pas envie
  d'aller au cinéma—restons plutôt à la
  maison

**instruction** noun
  an instruction = une instruction
  to give someone instructions to check the
  baggage = donner l'ordre à quelqu'un
  de vérifier les bagages
  the instructions for use = le mode
  d'emploi

**instrument** noun ▶ 290 |
  an instrument = un instrument
  to play an instrument = jouer d'un
  instrument

**insult** verb
  = insulter

**insurance** noun
  insurance = l'assurance (feminine)

**insure** verb
  = assurer
  to insure a car against theft = assurer une
  voiture contre le vol

**intelligent** adjective
  = intelligent/intelligente

**intend** verb
  he intends [to leave | to learn Spanish ...] = il
  a l'intention [de partir | d'apprendre
  l'espagnol ...]

**intense** adjective
  = intense

**intensive care** noun
  to be in intensive care = être en soins
  intensifs

**interest**
**1** noun
- (enthusiasm)
  interest = l'intérêt (masculine)
  to have an interest in music = s'intéresser
  à la musique
- (financial)
  interest = l'intérêt (masculine)
**2** verb
  = intéresser

**interested** adjective
  = intéressé/intéressée
  to be interested [in politics | in sport | in
  painting ...] = s'intéresser [à la politique | au
  sport | à la peinture ...]
  are you interested? = ça t'intéresse?

**interesting** adjective
  = intéressant/intéressante

**interfere** verb
- (to get involved in)
  to interfere in someone's business = se
  mêler des affaires de quelqu'un
- (to have a bad effect on)
  it's going to interfere with his work = ça va
  l'empêcher de travailler

**intermission** noun
  an intermission = un entracte

**international** adjective
  = international/internationale

**Internet** noun
  the Internet = l'Internet, le Net

**interpreter** noun ▶ 315 |
  an interpreter = un interprète/une
  interprète

**interrupt** verb
  = interrompre

**interval** noun
- (in time or at a location)
  an interval = un intervalle
  at regular intervals = à intervalles
  réguliers
- (British English) (during a play, a show)
  an interval = un entracte

**interview**
**1** noun
  an interview (for a job) = un entretien
  (with a journalist) = une interview
**2** verb
  to interview someone (if it's an employer)
  = faire passer un entretien à quelqu'un
  (if it's a journalist) = interviewer quelqu'un
  (if it's the police) = interroger quelqu'un

**intimidate** verb
  = intimider

**into** preposition
- (when talking about a location) = dans
  to go into the garden = aller dans le jardin
  to get into bed = se mettre au lit
- (indicating a change) = en
  to translate a letter into French = traduire
  une lettre en français
  to turn someone into a frog = transformer
  quelqu'un en grenouille

**introduce** verb
- (to bring in) = introduire
  to introduce a law = introduire une loi
- (when people meet) = présenter
  he introduced me to Peter = il m'a
  présenté à Peter

# it

- When **it** is used as a subject pronoun to stand for a specific object (or animal), **il** or **elle** is used in French depending on whether the object referred to is masculine or feminine:

  'where is the book | chair?' — 'it's    = 'où est le livre | la chaise?' — 'il | **elle** est
  in the kitchen'               dans la cuisine'

- When **it** is used as an object pronoun, it is translated by **le** or **la** (**l'** before a vowel or mute h) depending on whether the object referred to is masculine or feminine:

  it's my book | my chair and I want **it** = c'est mon livre | ma chaise et je **le** | **la** veux

  Note that the object pronoun normally comes before the verb in French and that in tenses like the perfect and the past perfect, the past participle agrees with it:

  I liked his shirt, did you notice **it**?    = sa chemise m'a plu, est-ce que tu **l'**as remarquée?
                                       sa chemise m'a plu, **l'**as-tu remarquée?

  In imperatives the pronoun comes after the verb:

  it's my book, give **it** to me    = c'est mon livre, donne-**le**-moi*
  * Note the hyphens.

  However, in negative commands, the pronoun comes before the verb:

  it's my book, don't give **it** to him!    = c'est mon livre, ne **le** lui donne pas!

- When **it** is used after a preposition in English, the two words (preposition + **it**) are often translated by one word in French. If the preposition would normally be translated by **de** in French (**of**, **about**, **from** etc), the preposition + **it** = **en**:

  we talked a lot about **it**    = on **en** a beaucoup parlé
  have you heard of **it**?    = est-ce que tu **en** as entendu parler?

  If the preposition would normally be translated by **à** in French (**to**, **in**, **at** etc), the preposition + **it** = **y**:

  they went to **it**    = ils **y** sont allés

  For translations of **it** following prepositions not normally translated by **de** or **à** (above, under, over, etc) consult the entry for the preposition.

- When **it** is used in expressions like it's raining, it will snow etc, the translation will always be **il**: **il** pleut, **il** va neiger. See the entry for the verb in question.

▶ For translations of it's Friday, it's five o'clock etc, consult the usage notes on **Dates, days, and months** and **The clock**.

---

- (on radio or television) = présenter
  **to introduce a programme** = présenter
  une émission

**invade** verb
= envahir

**invent** verb
= inventer

**invention** noun
an invention = une invention

**investigate** verb
to investigate a crime = enquêter sur un
crime

**investigation** noun
an investigation = une enquête

**invisible** adjective
= invisible

**invitation** noun
an invitation = une invitation

**invite** verb
= inviter
**to invite someone to a party** = inviter
quelqu'un à une fête

**involved** adjective
**to be involved in an accident** = avoir un
accident
**to get involved in someone's problems**
= se mêler des problèmes de quelqu'un

**Ireland** noun ▶ 218 |
Ireland = l'Irlande (feminine)

**Irish** ▶ 275 |
**1** adjective
= irlandais/irlandaise
**2** noun
- (the people)
  **the Irish** = les Irlandais (masculine
  plural)
- (the language)
  **Irish** = l'irlandais (masculine)

**iron**
**1** *noun*
- iron = le fer
- an iron = un fer à repasser
**2** *verb*
  = repasser

**island** *noun*
  an island = une île

**it** *pronoun*
▶ 270 | *See the boxed note on* it *for more information and examples.*
  where is it? (*if it's an object*) = où est-il/elle?
  (*if it's a place*) = où est-ce?
  who is it? = qui est-ce?
  it's me = c'est moi
  it's a nice house = c'est une jolie maison
  it is [difficult | easy | complicated ...] = c'est [difficile | facile | compliqué...]
  it doesn't matter = ça ne fait rien
  it's easy to make a mistake = il est facile de se tromper
  it's [cold | warm | mild ...] = il fait [froid | chaud | doux...]
  I've heard about it = j'en ai entendu parler
  did you go to it? = est-ce que tu y es allé?

**Italian** ▶ 275 |
**1** *adjective*
  = italien/italienne
**2** *noun*
- (*the people*)
  the Italians = les Italiens (*masculine*)
- (*the language*)
  Italian = l'italien (*masculine*)

**Italy** *noun* ▶ 218 |
  Italy = l'Italie (*feminine*)

**itchy** *adjective*
  my leg is itchy = j'ai la jambe qui me démange

**its** *determiner*
  its = son/sa (+ *singular*)
  = ses (+ *plural*)
  ! *Note that* sa *becomes* son *before a vowel or mute h.*

  its nose = son nez
  its tail = sa queue
  its ear = son oreille
  its eyes = ses yeux

**itself** *pronoun*
- (*when used as a reflexive pronoun*)
  the cat's going to hurt itself = le chat va se faire mal
- (*when used for emphasis*)
  the car itself was not damaged = la voiture elle-même n'a pas été endommagée
  the heating comes on by itself = le chauffage se met en marche tout seul

# Jj

**jacket** *noun*
  a jacket = une veste
  (*gathered at the waist*) = un blouson

**jail** *noun*
  a jail = une prison

**jam** *noun* (*British English*)
  jam = la confiture

**Jamaica** *noun* ▶ 218 |
  Jamaica = la Jamaïque

**January** *noun* ▶ 222 |
  January = janvier (*masculine*)

**Japan** *noun* ▶ 218 |
  Japan = le Japon

**Japanese** ▶ 275 |
**1** *adjective*
  = japonais/japonaise
**2** *noun*
  (*the people*)
  the Japanese = les Japonais (*masculine plural*)
  (*the language*)
  japanese = le japonais

**jaw** *noun* ▶ 201 |
  the jaw = la mâchoire

**jazz** *noun*
  jazz = le jazz

**jealous** *adjective*
  = jaloux/jalouse
  he is jealous of her = il est jaloux d'elle

**jeans** *noun*
  jeans = un jean (*singular*)

**jeer** *verb*
  to jeer someone = se moquer de quelqu'un

**jelly** *noun*
  (*US English*) (*jam*)
  jelly = la confiture
  (*British English*) (*a dessert*)
  jelly = la gelée de fruits

**Jesus** *noun*
  Jesus = Jésus

**jet** *noun*
  a jet = un jet, un avion à réaction

**jewellery** (*British English*), **jewelry** (*US English*) *noun*
  a piece of jewellery = un bijou
  jewellery = les bijoux (*plural*)

**Jewish** *adjective*
  = juif/juive

**jigsaw puzzle** *noun*
  a jigsaw puzzle = un puzzle

**job** *noun*
  (*work*)
  a job = un emploi
  to look for a job = chercher un emploi
  (*a task*)
  a job = un travail, une tâche

**jogging** *noun* ▶ 248 |
  jogging = le jogging

**join** *verb*
  (*meet up with*) = rejoindre
  I'll join you in half an hour = je vous
    rejoins dans une demi-heure
  (*become a member of*)
  to join a club = s'inscrire dans un club
  to join a company = entrer dans une
    entreprise
**join in**
  to join in a game = participer à un jeu

**joke**
  **1** *noun*
  a joke = une plaisanterie, une blague✱
  **2** *verb*
  = plaisanter

**journalist** *noun* ▶ 315 |
  a journalist = un journaliste/une
    journaliste

**journey** *noun*
  a journey = un voyage
  to go on a journey = partir en voyage

**joy** *noun*
  joy = la joie

**judge**
  **1** *noun* ▶ 315 |
  a judge = un juge
  **2** *verb*
  = juger

**judo** *noun* ▶ 248 |
  judo = le judo

**jug** *noun*
  a jug = un pichet

**juice** *noun*
  juice = le jus
  fruit juice = le jus de fruits

**July** *noun* ▶ 222 |
  July = juillet (*masculine*)

**jump** *verb*
  = sauter
  the children were jumping on the bed
    = les enfants sautaient sur le lit
  to jump across the stream = franchir le
    ruisseau d'un bond
  to jump rope = sauter à la corde
  to jump out of the window = sauter par la
    fenêtre

  to jump the queue (*British English*) = passer
    devant tout le monde

**jumper** *noun* (*British English*)
  a jumper = un pull

**June** *noun* ▶ 222 |
  June = juin (*masculine*)

**junior high school** *noun* (*US English*)
  a junior high school ≈ un collège

**junior school** *noun* (*British English*)
  a junior school = une école primaire

**jury** *noun*
  the jury = le jury

**just¹** *adverb*
  (*very recently*)
  I have just [arrived | seen her | received the
    letter ...] = je viens [d'arriver | de la voir | de
    recevoir la lettre ...]
  I had just turned on the TV = je venais
    d'allumer la télévision
  (*at this or that very moment*) = juste
  I was just about to phone you = j'étais
    juste sur le point de t'appeler, j'allais
    t'appeler
  you've just missed him = il vient juste de
    partir
  I arrived just as he was leaving = je suis
    arrivé juste au moment où il partait
  (*only*) = juste
  just two days ago = il y a juste deux jours
  he's just a child = ce n'est qu'un enfant
  (*barely*) = tout juste
  I got there just in time = je suis arrivé juste
    à temps
  she's just 18 = elle a tout juste 18 ans
  (*when comparing*)
  she is just as intelligent as he is = elle est
    tout aussi intelligente que lui
  (*immediately*) = juste
  just before the weekend = juste avant le
    week-end

**just²** *adjective*
  = juste

**justice** *noun*
  justice = la justice

# Kk

**kangaroo** *noun*
  a kangaroo = un kangourou

**karate** *noun* ▶ 248 |
  karate = le karaté

---

**keen** *adjective*
  a keen student = un étudiant/une
    étudiante enthousiaste
  to be keen on swimming = aimer la
    natation

**keep** *verb*
  – garder
  to keep someone in (the) hospital
    = garder quelqu'un à l'hôpital
  we keep the wine in the cellar = nous
    gardons le vin dans la cave
  this sweater will keep you warm = ce pull
    te tiendra chaud
  to keep someone waiting = faire attendre
    quelqu'un
  (*to delay*) = retenir
  what kept you? = qu'est-ce qui t'a retenu?
  I won't keep you long = je n'en ai pas pour
    longtemps
  (*to put*) = ranger
  where do you keep the cups? = où est-ce
    que tu ranges les tasses?
  (*not to break, not to reveal*)
  to keep a promise = tenir une promesse
  to keep a secret = garder un secret
  (*to continue*)
  to keep [walking | talking | running …]
    = continuer à [marcher | parler | courir …]
  to keep going = continuer
  to keep calm = rester calme
  (*if it's food*) = se conserver (**!** + *être*)
**keep away** = ne pas s'approcher (**!** + *être*)
  keep away from the fire! = ne t'approche
    pas du feu!
**keep back** = retenir
  he kept the children back after school = il
    a retenu les enfants après l'école
**keep on**
  to keep on [talking | walking | singing …]
    = continuer à [parler | marcher | chanter …]
**keep out**
  to keep out of the sun = ne pas se mettre
    au soleil
  to keep the rain out = empêcher la pluie
    d'entrer
**keep up** = suivre
  to keep up with the other pupils = suivre
    en classe

**kerb** *noun* (*British English*)
  the kerb = le bord du trottoir

**kettle** *noun*
  a kettle = une bouilloire

**key** *noun*
  a key = une clé

**keyhole** *noun*
  a keyhole = un trou de serrure

**kick** *verb*
  to kick someone = donner un coup de
    pied à quelqu'un
  he kicked the ball = il a donné un coup de
    pied dans le ballon
**kick off** = donner le coup d'envoi

**kick out**
  to kick someone out = mettre quelqu'un à
    la porte

**kid** *noun*
  (*a child*)
  a kid = un enfant/une enfant, un
    gamin/une gamine*
  (*a young goat*)
  a kid = un chevreau

**kidnap** *noun*
  = enlever

**kill** *verb*
  = tuer
  to kill oneself = se suicider (**!** + *être*)

**kilo** *noun* ▶ 285 |
  a kilo = un kilo

**kilogram(me)** *noun* ▶ 285 |
  a kilogram = un kilogramme

**kilometre** (*British English*), **kilometer**
(*US English*) *noun* ▶ 285 |
  a kilometre = un kilomètre

**kind**
**1** *noun*
  It's a kind of [fish | novel | hotel …] = c'est
    une sorte [de poisson | de roman | d'hôtel …]
  what kind of film is it? = c'est quel genre
    de film?
  what kind of car is it? = qu'est-ce que c'est
    comme voiture?
**2** *adjective*
  = gentil/gentille

**king** *noun*
  a king = un roi

**kingdom** *noun*
  a kingdom = un royaume

**kiss**
**1** *verb*
  to kiss someone = embrasser quelqu'un
  to kiss (each other) = s'embrasser
    (**!** + *être*)
**2** *noun*
  a kiss = un baiser

**kitchen** *noun*
  a kitchen = une cuisine

**kite** *noun*
  a kite = un cerf-volant

**kitten** *noun*
  a kitten = un chaton

**knee** *noun* ▶ 201 |
  the knee = le genou

**kneel down** *verb*
  = se mettre à genoux (**!** + *être*)

**knife** *noun*
  a knife = un couteau

**knit** *verb*
  = tricoter

**K**

**knock**
**1** *verb*
to knock on the door = frapper à la porte
**2** *noun*
a knock = un coup
to get a knock on the head = recevoir un
coup sur la tête
**knock down**
(*in an accident*) = renverser
(*to demolish*) = démolir
**knock out**
(*to make unconscious*) = assommer
(*in a contest*) = éliminer
**knock over** = renverser

**knot** *noun*
a knot = un nœud

**know** *verb*
(*when talking about facts, information*)
= savoir
he thinks he knows everything = il croit
tout savoir
I know why he phoned = je sais pourquoi
il a téléphoné
she knows how to swim = elle sait nager
I don't know the French word for it = je ne
sais pas comment ça se dit en français
let me know = tenez-moi au courant
does he know about the party? = est-ce
qu'il est au courant pour la soirée?
to know all about art = s'y connaître en art
(*when talking about people, places*)
= connaître
do you know Paris? = est-ce que tu
connais Paris?
to get to know someone = faire la
connaissance de quelqu'un

**knowledge** *noun*
knowledge = les connaissances (*feminine
plural*)

# L1

**laboratory** *noun*
a laboratory = un laboratoire

**lace** *noun*
(*the material*)
lace = la dentelle
(*for shoes*)
a lace = un lacet
to tie one's laces = lacer ses chaussures

**lack**
**1** *noun*
a lack [of food | of money | of interest …] = un
manque [de nourriture | d'argent | d'intérêt …]

**2** *verb*
= manquer de
he lacks confidence = il manque
d'assurance

**ladder** *noun*
a ladder = une échelle

**lady** *noun*
a lady = une dame

**lake** *noun*
a lake = un lac

**lamb** *noun*
a lamb = un agneau

**lamp** *noun*
a lamp = une lampe

**lampshade** *noun*
a lampshade = un abat-jour

**land**
**1** *noun*
(*for farming, as opposed to the sea*)
land = la terre
(*property*)
a piece of land = un terrain
to own land = posséder des terres
(*the countryside*)
the land = la campagne
**2** *verb*
(*to fall*) = tomber (**!** + *être*)
(*if it's a plane*) = atterrir
(*if it's a passenger*) = débarquer

**land registry** *noun*
the land registry = le cadastre

**landscape** *noun*
a landscape = un paysage

**language** *noun*
a language = une langue
foreign languages = les langues
étrangères
bad language = le langage grossier

**laptop** *noun*
a laptop = un portable

**large** *adjective*
(*big*) = grand/grande (**!** *before the noun*)
a large garden = un grand jardin
a large house = une grande maison
(*when talking about numbers*) = gros/grosse
(**!** *before the noun*)
a large sum of money = une grosse
somme
a large population = une forte population
(*bulky*) = gros/grosse (**!** *before the noun*)
a large parcel = un gros paquet

**last**
**1** *adjective*
= dernier/dernière
last week = la semaine dernière
that's the last time I saw her = c'est la
dernière fois que je l'ai vue
**2** *adverb*
(*most recently*)
when I was last here = la dernière fois que
je suis venu ici

# Languages and nationalities

## Languages

The names of languages in French are always written with a small letter, not a capital as in English. French almost always uses the definite article **le** or **l'** with languages:

*to learn French* = apprendre **le** français

except after **en**:

*to translate a word into French* = traduire un mot **en** français

and it may be omitted with **parler**:

*to speak French* = parler français / parler **le** français

but

*to speak in French* = parler **en** français

When **French** means **in French** or **of the French**, it is translated by **français**:

*the French language* = la langue **française**

If you want to make it clear you mean **in French** and not **from France**, use **en français**:

*a French book* = un livre **en français**

When **French** means **relating to French** or **about French**, it is translated by **de français**:

*a French class* = une classe **de français**

## Nationalities

Adjectives indicating nationality **never** have capitals in French:

*a French student* = un étudiant **français** / une étudiante **française**

Nouns have capitals in French when they mean *a person of a specific nationality*:

*a Frenchman | a Frenchwoman* = un **Français** / une **Française**
*French people or the French* = les **Français** (*masculine plural*)

English sometimes has a special word for a person *of a specific nationality*; in French, the same word is almost always either an adjective (no capitals) or a noun (with capitals):

*Spanish* = **espagnol**
*a Spaniard* = un **Espagnol** / une **Espagnole**
*the Spaniards* = les **Espagnols** (*masculine plural*)

You can use either the adjective or the noun to refer to nationality:

*he | she is French* = il est **français** / elle est **française**
= c'est un **Français** / c'est une **Française**

---

(*at the end*) = en dernier
**I'll do the dishes last (of all)** = je ferai la
   vaisselle en dernier
(*in final position*)
**he came last in the race** = il est arrivé
   dernier dans la course
**3** *pronoun*
**the last** = le dernier/la dernière
**they were the last to arrive** = ils ont été les
   derniers à arriver
**the night before last** = avant-hier soir
**4** *verb*
= durer
**the film lasts two hours** = le film dure
   deux heures

## late
**1** *adverb*
(*far into the day or night*) = tard
**late in the afternoon** = tard dans l'après-
   midi
**it's getting late** = il se fait tard

(*not on time*) = en retard
**to arrive half an hour late** = arriver avec
   une demi-heure de retard
**2** *adjective*
= en retard
**to be late for work** = arriver en retard au
   travail
**the train was two hours late** = le train a eu
   deux heures de retard
**to make someone late** = retarder
   quelqu'un

**later** *adverb*
= plus tard
**I'll call back later** = je rappellerai plus tard
**see you later!** = à plus tard!

## latest
**1** *adjective*
= dernier/dernière (**!** *before the noun*)
**the latest news** = les dernières nouvelles
**2 at the latest** = au plus tard

**Latin** noun
Latin = le latin

**laugh**
**1** verb
= rire
to laugh at a joke = rire d'une plaisanterie
to make someone laugh = faire rire
quelqu'un
to laugh at someone = se moquer de
quelqu'un
**2** noun
a laugh = un rire

**laundry** noun
the laundry = le linge (sale)
to do the laundry = faire la lessive

**law** noun
(a set of rules in a country)
the law = la loi
to obey the law = respecter la loi
it's against the law = c'est interdit par la
loi
(a rule)
a law = une loi
(as a subject)
law = le droit

**lawn** noun
a lawn = une pelouse

**lawnmower** noun
a lawnmower = une tondeuse à gazon

**lawyer** noun ▶ 315 |
a lawyer = un avocat/une avocate

**lay** verb
(to put) = poser, mettre
lay some newspapers on the floor = mets
des journaux par terre
to lay the table = mettre le couvert
(of a chicken)
to lay an egg = pondre un œuf
**lay down** = poser, mettre
he laid the tray down on the table = il a
posé le plateau sur la table
**lay off** = licencier

**lazy** adjective
= paresseux/paresseuse

**lead¹** verb
(to guide) = mener, conduire
this road will lead you to the village
= cette route vous mènera au village
(in a match) = mener
(in a race) = être en tête
to lead a busy life = mener une vie active
(to have as a result)
to lead to an accident = entraîner un
accident

**lead²** noun
lead = le plomb

**leader** noun
a leader (of a political party) = un leader,
un dirigeant
(of a state) = un chef d'État

**leaf** noun
a leaf = une feuille

**leak** verb
(if it's a container) = fuir
the pipe leaks = il y a une fuite dans le
tuyau
(if it's a boat, shoes) = prendre l'eau

**lean**
**1** verb
(to support oneself)
to lean against the wall = s'appuyer contre
le mur
(to put)
to lean a bicycle against the wall
= appuyer un vélo contre le mur
to lean out of the window = se pencher par
la fenêtre
**2** adjective
= maigre
**lean back** = se pencher en arrière
(**!** + être)
**lean forward** = se pencher en avant
(**!** + être)
**lean on** = s'appuyer sur (**!** + être)

**learn** verb
= apprendre
to learn how to drive = apprendre à
conduire

**leash** noun
a leash = une laisse

**least**
**1** determiner
the least
= le moins de
they have the least money = ce sont eux
qui ont le moins d'argent
**2** pronoun
it was the least I could do! = c'était la
moindre des choses!
**3** adverb
the least = le moins/la moins (+ singular)
= les moins (+ plural)
the least expensive shop = le magasin le
moins cher
the least difficult question = la question la
moins difficile
**4** at least
(at the minimum) = au moins
he's at least thirty = il a au moins trente
ans
(when expressing some doubt) = du moins
he's gone out—at least, I think so = il est
sorti—du moins, il me semble

**leather** noun
leather = le cuir

**leave** verb
(to go away from) = quitter
to leave school = quitter l'école
she left her husband = elle a quitté son
mari

(*to go away*) = partir (**!** + *être*)
he left the next day = il est parti le
  lendemain
(*to go out of*) = sortir de (**!** + *être*)
she left the room = elle est sortie de la
  pièce
(*to allow to remain*) = laisser
leave your coat here = laisse ton manteau
  ici
(*to put, to give*) = laisser
he didn't leave a message = il n'a pas
  laissé de message
she left him some money = elle lui a laissé
  de l'argent
(*to put off*) = laisser
leave it until tomorrow = laisse ça pour
  demain
(*to remain*)
there's nothing left = il ne reste rien
we've got ten minutes left = il nous reste
  dix minutes
(*other uses*)
I left them to clean the windows = je les ai
  laissés nettoyer les fenêtres
**leave behind** = laisser
he left his belongings behind = il a laissé
  ses affaires
**leave out**
(*not to show or talk about*) (*by accident*)
  = oublier
(*deliberately*) = omettre
(*to exclude*) = exclure
to feel left out = se sentir exclu/exclue
**leave over**
there was not much left over = il ne restait
  plus grand-chose
there is some food left over = il reste un
  peu de nourriture

**lecture** *noun*
a lecture (*to students*) = un cours
  magistral
(*to the public*) = une conférence

**left**
**1** *noun*
the left = la gauche
the first street on the left = la première rue
  à gauche
**2** *adjective*
= gauche
his left hand = sa main gauche
**3** *adverb*
= à gauche
to turn left = tourner à gauche

**left-click** *verb*
= cliquer à gauche

**leg** *noun*
(*of a person*) ▶ **201** |
the leg = la jambe
(*of animals*)
the leg = la patte
(*of meat*)
a leg of lamb = un gigot d'agneau

**legal** *adjective*
= légal/légale

**leisure** *noun*
leisure = les loisirs (*masculine plural*)

**leisure centre** (*British English*),
**leisure center** (*US English*) *noun*
a leisure centre = un centre de loisirs

**lemon** *noun*
a lemon = un citron

**lemonade** *noun*
lemonade = la limonade

**lend** *verb*
= prêter
to lend someone money = prêter de
  l'argent à quelqu'un

**length** *noun* ▶ **285** |
(*in measurements*)
length = la longueur
length (*of a book, a film, a list*) = la
  longueur
(*of an event*) = la durée

**leopard** *noun*
a leopard = un léopard

**less** ▶ **317** |
**1** *determiner*
= moins de
less [money | food | time ...] = moins
  [d'argent | de nourriture | de temps ...]
I have less work than he does = j'ai moins
  de travail que lui
**2** *pronoun*
= moins
to cost less = coûter moins cher
he reads less than she does = il lit moins
  qu'elle
they have less than you – ils en ont
  moins que toi

  **!** *Note that it is necessary to use* en,
  *which might be translated as 'of it', with*
  *pronouns like* less. *See also* another, a
  few, a lot *etc for this use of* en.

**3** *adverb*
= moins
we travel less in winter = nous voyageons
  moins l'hiver
**4** *preposition*
(*minus*) = moins
**5 less and less** = de moins en moins
less and less often = de moins en moins
  souvent
**6 less than** = moins de
in less than half an hour = en moins d'une
  demi-heure

**lesson** *noun*
a lesson = un cours
a riding lesson = une leçon d'équitation

**let¹** *verb*
(*when making suggestions*)
let's go home = rentrons
let's go! = allons-y!

L

(*to allow*) = laisser
**to let someone in** = laisser entrer
  quelqu'un
**he let me help him** = il m'a laissé l'aider
**she lets him do what he likes** = elle le
  laisse faire ce qu'il veut
**he's letting his hair grow** = il se laisse
  pousser les cheveux
**let down** = décevoir
**let go**
  (*to stop holding*) = lâcher prise
  **he let go of me** = il m'a lâché
  (*to release*) = relâcher
  **he let the prisoners go** = il a relâché les
    prisonniers
**let in**
  (*to a room or house*) = faire entrer
  **he let me in** = il m'a fait entrer
  **to let in the rain** = laisser entrer la pluie
**let out**
  (*to allow to go out*) = laisser sortir
  **let me out!** = laisse-moi sortir!
  **to let out a scream** = laisser échapper un
    cri
**let through**
  **to let someone through** = laisser passer
    quelqu'un

**let²** *verb* (*British English*)
  = louer

**letter** *noun*
  **a letter** = une lettre

**letter box** *noun* (*British English*)
  **a letter box** = une boîte aux lettres

**lettuce** *noun*
  **a lettuce** = une laitue

**level**
**1** *noun*
  **a level** = un niveau
**2** *adjective*
  = plat/plate

**library** *noun*
  **a library** = une bibliothèque

**licence** (*British English*), **license** (*US
English*) *noun*
  **a licence** = un permis

**license plate** *noun* (*US English*)
  **a license plate** = une plaque
    minéralogique

**lick** *verb*
  = lécher

**lid** *noun*
  **a lid** = un couvercle

**lie**
**1** *verb*
  (*on the ground, on a bed*) = s'allonger
  (**!** + *être*)
  **he lay down on the sofa** = il s'est allongé
    sur le canapé
  **he was lying on the sofa** = il était allongé
    sur le canapé

(*to be situated*) = se trouver (**!** + *être*)
  (*not to tell the truth*) = mentir
**2** *noun*
  **a lie** = un mensonge
  **to tell a lie** = mentir
**lie around** = traîner
  **he always leaves his keys lying around**
    = il laisse toujours traîner ses clés
**lie down** = s'allonger (**!** + *être*)

**life** *noun*
  **life** = la vie
  **a way of life** = un mode de vie

**lifestyle** *noun*
  **a lifestyle** = un style de vie

**lift**
**1** *verb*
  **to lift one's arm** = lever le bras
  **to lift a lid** = soulever un couvercle
**2** *noun*
  (*British English*) (*an elevator*)
  **a lift** = un ascenseur
  (*in a car*)
  **to give someone a lift to the station**
    = conduire quelqu'un à la gare
**lift up** = soulever

**light**
**1** *noun*
  (*from the sun, moon*)
  **light** = la lumière
  (*in a room, on a machine*)
  **a light** = une lumière
  **to switch on a light** = allumer
  (*for traffic*)
  **the lights are green** = le feu est au vert
  (*in a street*)
  **a light** = un réverbère
  **have you got a light?** = est-ce que vous
    avez du feu?
**2** *adjective*
  (*not dark*) ▶ **213** | = clair/claire
  **it's still light outside** = il fait encore jour
    dehors
  **a light blue dress** = une robe bleu clair
  (*not heavy*) = léger/légère
**3** *verb*
  = allumer
  **he lit a cigarette** = il a allumé une
    cigarette
  **to light a fire** = faire un feu

**light bulb** *noun*
  **a light bulb** = une ampoule

**lighthouse** *noun*
  **a lighthouse** = un phare

**lightning** *noun*
  **a flash of lightning** = un éclair

**like¹** *preposition*
  = comme
  **people like you and me** = des gens comme
    toi et moi
  **what's it like?** = c'est comment?

**like²** verb
(when expressing an interest) = aimer
I like [swimming | reading | dancing ...]
  = j'aime (bien) [nager | lire | danser ...]
I like it! = ça me plaît!
how do you like America? = est-ce que
  l'Amérique te plaît?
(when expressing a wish) = vouloir, aimer
I'd like coffee please = je voudrais un café
  s'il vous plaît
I'd like to live here = j'aimerais vivre ici

**limit** noun
a limit = une limite

**line**
1 noun
a line = une ligne
a straight line = une ligne droite
(US English) (a queue)
a line = une queue
to stand in line = faire la queue
(a row)
a line = une rangée
the line is bad = la ligne est mauvaise
2 verb
to be lined with trees = être bordé/bordée
  d'arbres

**link** verb
(by train) = relier
to link Paris to Brussels = relier Paris à
  Bruxelles
(to make a connection between) = lier
the two murders are linked = les deux
  meurtres sont liés

**lion** noun
a lion = un lion

**lip** noun
a lip = une lèvre

**lipstick** noun
lipstick = le rouge à lèvres

**list** noun
a list = une liste

**listen** verb
= écouter
to listen to someone = écouter quelqu'un

**litre** (British English), **liter** (US English)
noun
a litre = un litre

**little¹**
1 determiner
= peu de
little [food | wine | money ...] = peu [de
  nourriture | de vin | d'argent ...]
there is very little time = il y a très peu de
  temps
2 pronoun
a little = un peu
I only ate a little = je n'en ai mangé qu'un
  peu

! Note that it is necessary to use en,
which might be translated as 'of it', with
pronouns like a little. See also a lot, more,
none, etc for this use of en.

3 adverb
= peu
4 a little (bit) = un peu
5 little by little = peu à peu

**little²** adjective
= petit/petite (! before the noun)

**live¹** verb
(to have one's home) = vivre, habiter
he lives in London = il habite à Londres, il
  vit à Londres
(to be alive) = vivre
that's not enough to live on = ça ne suffit
  pas pour vivre

**live²** adjective
(alive) = vivant/vivante
(of a match, a show) = en direct

**lively** adjective
= vivant/vivante

**living room** noun
a living room = une salle de séjour

**load** noun
(on a truck, being carried)
a load = un chargement
loads of money = beaucoup d'argent

**loaf** noun
a loaf (of bread) = un pain

**loan** noun
a loan (money lent) = un prêt
(money borrowed) = un emprunt

**lobster** noun
a lobster = un homard

**local** adjective
a local newspaper = un journal local
the local people = les gens du coin

**lock**
1 verb
= fermer à clé
she locked the door = elle a fermé la porte
  à clé
2 noun
a lock = une serrure
a bicycle lock = un antivol
**lock in**
to lock someone in = enfermer quelqu'un
to lock oneself in = s'enfermer (! + être)

**locker** noun
a locker = un casier

**logical** adjective
= logique

**London** noun ▶ 218 |
  – Londres

**lonely** adjective
= seul/seule

**L**

## long

**1** *adjective* ► 285 |
= long/longue
a long letter = une longue lettre
to have long hair = avoir les cheveux longs
the film is two hours long = le film dure
deux heures
I haven't seen him for a long time = ça fait
longtemps que je ne l'ai pas vu
**2** *adverb*
= longtemps
long ago = il y a longtemps
you can stay as long as you like = tu peux
rester aussi longtemps que tu veux
I won't be long = je n'en ai pas pour
longtemps
**3 as long as** = à condition que
as long as the weather is nice = à
condition qu'il fasse beau

! *Note that the subjunctive is used after* à
condition que.

## look

**1** *verb*
= regarder
to look at a picture = regarder un tableau
to look out of the window = regarder par
la fenêtre
(*to appear*)
to look tired = avoir l'air fatigué/fatiguée
to look well = avoir bonne mine
he looks young = il fait jeune
she looks like her mother = elle ressemble
à sa mère
what does he look like? = il est comment?
**2** *noun*
a look = un regard
**look after** = s'occuper de (**!** + *être*)
to look after a child = s'occuper d'un
enfant
**look down**
(*to lower one's eyes*) = baisser les yeux
to look down on someone = regarder
quelqu'un de haut
**look for** = chercher
he is looking for a job = il cherche un
emploi
**look forward to**
I am looking forward to meeting her
= j'attends avec impatience le plaisir de
faire sa connaissance
**look onto** = donner sur
my bedroom looks onto the garden = ma
chambre donne sur le jardin
**look out** = faire attention
**look through**
to look through a book = feuilleter un
livre
**look up**
to look up a word in a dictionary
= chercher un mot dans un dictionnaire
(*to raise one's eyes*) = lever les yeux

**loose** *adjective*
(*describing clothes*) = ample
(*describing a screw*) = desserré/desserrée

**lorry** *noun* (*British English*)
a lorry = un camion

**lose** *verb*
= perdre

**lost** *adjective*
= perdu/perdue
to get lost = se perdre (**!** + *être*)

**lot** *pronoun* ► 317 |
a lot = beaucoup
he eats a lot = il mange beaucoup
a lot [of money | of time | of books ...]
= beaucoup [d'argent | de temps | de livres ...]
there's not a lot left = il n'en reste pas
beaucoup

! *Note that it is necessary to use* en,
*which may be translated as* 'of it' *or* 'of
them', *with pronouns like* a lot. *See also*
another, a few, any *etc for this use of* en.

**lottery** *noun*
a lottery = une loterie

**loud** *adjective*
= fort/forte
to talk in a loud voice = parler fort

**loudspeaker** *noun*
a loudspeaker = un haut-parleur

**lounge** *noun*
a lounge = un salon

## love

**1** *verb*
(*when talking about people*) = aimer
to love each other = s'aimer (**!** + *être*)
(*when talking about things, activities*)
= adorer
**2** *noun*
love = l'amour (*masculine*)
to be in love = être amoureux/amoureuse
to make love = faire l'amour

**lovely** *adjective*
(*beautiful*) = beau/belle (**!** *before the noun*)
a lovely apartment = un bel appartement
you've got lovely eyes = tu as de beaux
yeux
(*very nice, kind*) = charmant/charmante

## low

**1** *adjective*
= bas/basse
to speak in a low voice = parler à voix
basse
**2** *adverb*
= bas
to turn the lights down low = baisser les
lumières

**lower** *verb*
= baisser

**loyal** *adjective*
= loyal/loyale

---

**✗** in informal situations

**loyalty card** *noun*
a loyalty card = une carte de fidélité

**luck** *noun* ▶ 237 |
luck = la chance
good luck! = bonne chance!
to bring someone (good) luck = porter
bonheur à quelqu'un

**lucky** *adjective*
to be lucky = avoir de la chance

**lunch** *noun*
lunch = le déjeuner

**lung** *noun*
the lung = le poumon

**Luxembourg** *noun* ▶ 218 |
Luxembourg = le Luxembourg

**luxury**
**1** *noun*
luxury = le luxe
**2** *adjective*
a luxury hotel = un hôtel de luxe

# Mm

**machine** *noun*
a machine = une machine

**mad** *adjective*
• (*crazy*) = fou/folle
to go mad = devenir fou/folle
• (*very angry*) = furieux/furieuse

**magazine** *noun*
a magazine = un magazine

**magic** *adjective*
= magique

**maiden name** *noun*
a maiden name = un nom de jeune fille

**mail**
**1** *noun*
• (*the postal system*)
the mail = la poste
• (*letters*)
mail = le courrier
**2** *verb* (*US English*)
to mail a letter to someone = envoyer une
lettre à quelqu'un

**mailbox** *noun* (*US English*)
a mailbox = une boîte aux lettres

**mailman** *noun* ▶ 315 | (*US English*)
a mailman = un facteur

**main** *adjective*
= principal/principale

**main course** *noun*
a main course = un plat principal

**major**
**1** *adjective*
= majeur/majeure
a major event = un événement majeur
**2** *noun*
a major = un commandant

**majority** *noun*
a majority = une majorité

**make** *verb*
! Note that the word make can often be
translated by faire. This entry covers the
most frequent uses of make but to find
translations for other expressions like to
make a mess, to make a mistake, to make
sure etc, look up the entries at mess,
mistake, sure etc.

• to make = faire
to make [the bed | a film | some coffee ...]
= faire [le lit | un film | du café ...]
to make room = faire de la place
to make a phone call = passer un coup de
fil
to make friends = se faire des amis
(! + *être*)
to make breakfast = préparer le petit
déjeuner
to be made of [gold | metal | wood ...] = être
en [or | métal | bois ...]
to be made in France = être
fabriqué/fabriquée en France
• (*to cause a particular reaction*)
to make someone [happy | ill | jealous ...]
= rendre quelqu'un [heureux | malade |
jaloux ...]
to make someone [annoyed | tired |
sleepy ...] = [agacer | fatiguer | endormir ...]
quelqu'un
to make someone [cry | laugh | eat ...]
= faire [pleurer | rire | manger ...] quelqu'un
• to make someone wait = faire attendre
quelqu'un
• (*to earn*)
to make a lot of money = gagner
beaucoup d'argent
to make a living = gagner sa vie
to make a profit = faire un bénéfice
**make do** = faire avec
**make out** = faire
to make out a list = faire une liste
to make a cheque out to someone = faire
un chèque à quelqu'un
**make up**
• (*to be friends again*) = se réconcilier
(! + *être*)
• to make up an excuse = inventer un
prétexte
• to make up a parcel = faire un paquet

**make-up** *noun*
make-up = le maquillage
to wear make-up = se maquiller (! + *être*)

**male** *adjective*
• (*in biology*) = mâle
• (*relating to men*) = masculin/masculine

M

**man** *noun*
• a man = un homme
  a single man = un célibataire
• man = l'homme

**manage** *verb*
• (*to run*) = gérer
• to manage to finish one's homework
  = réussir à finir ses devoirs

**manager** *noun* ▶ 315 |
  a manager (*of a company, a bank, a
    project*) = un directeur/une directrice
  (*of a shop*) = un gérant/une gérante
  (*of a football team*) = un manager

**manner** *noun*
  a manner = une attitude

**manners** *noun*
  manners = les manières (*feminine*)
  it's bad manners not to say hello = c'est
    impoli de ne pas dire bonjour

**manufacture** *verb*
  = fabriquer

**many** ▶ 317 |
**1** *determiner*
• (*a lot of*) = beaucoup de
  were there many tourists? = est-ce qu'il y
    avait beaucoup de touristes?
  there weren't many people there = il n'y
    avait pas beaucoup de monde
• (*when used with* how, too, so, as)
  how many cases have you got?
    = combien de valises avez-vous?
  you eat too many chips = tu manges trop
    de frites
  there are so many things to do here = il y
    a tant de choses à faire ici
  I got as many presents as you did = j'ai
    reçu autant de cadeaux que toi
**2** *pronoun*
  are there many left? = est-ce qu'il en reste
    beaucoup?
  I've got too many = j'en ai trop
  take as many as you like = prends-en
    autant que tu veux

  ! *Note that it is necessary to use* en,
  *which might be translated as 'of them',
  with pronouns like* many. *See also*
  another, a few, a lot *etc for this use of* en.

  many (of them) speak English = beaucoup
    (d'entre eux) parlent anglais

**map** *noun*
  a map (*of a country or region*) = une carte
  (*of a town or a transport system*) = un plan

**marble** *noun*
  marble = le marbre

**marbles** *noun* ▶ 248 |
  marbles = les billes (*feminine*)

**march** *verb*
• (*in the army*) = marcher au pas
• (*in a demonstration*) = manifester

**March** *noun* ▶ 222 |
  March = mars (*masculine*)

**margarine** *noun*
  margarine = la margarine

**mark**
**1** *noun*
• a mark (*on a surface*) = une tache
  (*on a person's body*) = une marque
  to leave marks on the table = laisser des
    taches sur la table
• (*British English*) (*a grade*)
  a mark = une note
  to get good marks = avoir de bonnes
    notes
**2** *verb*
• (*to stain*) = tacher
• to mark the homework = corriger les
    devoirs
• (*to indicate*) = indiquer

**marker** *noun*
  a marker (*a pen*) = un marqueur
  (*a felt-tip pen*) = un feutre

**market** *noun*
• (*the place*)
  a market = un marché
  a flea market = un marché aux puces
• (*the system*)
  the market = le marché
  the job market = le marché du travail

**marmalade** *noun*
  marmalade = la confiture d'oranges

**marriage** *noun*
  marriage = le mariage

**married** *adjective*
  = marié/mariée
  to be married to someone = être
    marié/mariée à quelqu'un

**marry** *verb*
  to marry someone = se marier avec
    quelqu'un (! + *être*)

**marsh** *noun*
  a marsh = un marécage

**masculine** *adjective*
  = masculin/masculine

**mashed potatoes** *noun*
  mashed potatoes = la purée de pommes
    de terre

**mask** *noun*
  a mask = un masque

**mat** *noun*
  a mat = un (petit) tapis

---

✗ in informal situations

## match
**1** noun
- (British English) (a game)
  a match = un match
  a football match = un match de football
- (a matchstick)
  a match = une allumette

**2** verb
the shoes match the belt = les chaussures
sont assorties à la ceinture

**mate** noun (British English)
a mate = un copain/une copine

**material** noun
a material = un tissu, une étoffe

**math** (US English), **maths** (British
English) noun
math(s) = les maths (feminine plural)

**mathematics** noun
mathematics = les mathématiques
(feminine plural)

## matter
**1** noun
what's the matter? = qu'est-ce qu'il y a?
what's the matter with her? = qu'est-ce
qu'elle a?

**2** verb
does it really matter? = est-ce que c'est
vraiment important?
it doesn't matter = ça ne fait rien, ça n'a
pas d'importance

## maximum
**1** adjective
the maximum price = le prix maximum
a maximum temperature of 80 degrees
= une température maximale de 80
degrés

**2** noun
the maximum = le maximum

**may** verb
- (when talking about a possibility)
  they may be able to come = ils pourront
  peut-être venir
  she may not have seen him = elle ne l'a
  peut-être pas vu
  it may rain = il risque de pleuvoir
- (when asking for or giving permission)
  may I come in? = est-ce que je peux
  entrer?, puis-je entrer?
  you may sit down = vous pouvez vous
  asseoir

**May** noun ▶ 222 |
May = mai (masculine)

**maybe** adverb
= peut-être

**mayor** noun ▶ 315 |
a mayor = un maire

## me pronoun
> **!** Note that there is a boxed usage note at
> them. The entries me, him, her and us are
> modelled on this note where you will find
> detailed grammatical information and
> fuller explanations.

- me = me (**!** m' + vowel or mute h)
  they know me = ils me connaissent
  they don't know me = ils ne me
  connaissent pas
  do they know me? = est-ce qu'ils me
  connaissent?
- he's seen me = il m'a vu
  he hasn't seen me = il ne m'a pas vu
  has he seen me? = est-ce qu'il m'a vu?
- help me! = aide-moi!
  hold me! = tiens-moi!
  don't bother me! = ne m'embête pas!
  don't hit me! = ne me frappe pas!
- she gave the book to me = elle m'a donné
  le livre
  she didn't give the book to me = elle ne
  m'a pas donné le livre
  did she give the book to me? = est-ce
  qu'elle m'a donné le livre?
- write to me! = écris-moi!
  say it to me! = dis-le-moi!
  don't show it to me! = ne me le montre
  pas!
- me = moi
  he did it for me = il l'a fait pour moi
  it's me = c'est moi
  stand in front of me = mets-toi devant moi

**meal** noun
a meal = un repas

## mean
**1** verb
- to mean = vouloir dire
  what does that mean? = qu'est-ce que ça
  veut dire?
  what does the word 'bête' mean? = que
  veut dire le mot 'bête'?
- (to have as a result)
  it means giving up my job = ça veut dire
  que je dois abandonner mon travail
- (to intend)
  I meant to order a pizza = je voulais
  commander une pizza
  she didn't mean to upset you = elle ne
  voulait pas te faire de la peine
  he meant it as a joke = il voulait
  plaisanter
- (to intend to say) = vouloir dire
  what do you mean? = qu'est-ce que tu
  veux dire?
- her work means a lot to her = son travail
  compte beaucoup pour elle
  money doesn't mean much to him
  = l'argent n'a pas beaucoup
  d'importance pour lui

**2** adjective
- (British English) (not generous) = avare,
  radin/radine**✱**

**M**

- to be mean to someone = être méchant/méchante avec quelqu'un

**meaning** *noun*
a meaning = un sens

**means** *noun*
a means = un moyen
a means of transport = un moyen de transport
a means of earning money = un moyen de gagner de l'argent

**meant**: **to be meant to** *verb*
to be meant to = être censé/censée
I'm meant to be at my parents' house = je suis censé être chez mes parents

**meanwhile** *adverb*
= pendant ce temps

**measles** *noun* ▶ 266 |
measles = la rougeole

**measure** *verb*
= mesurer

**meat** *noun*
meat = la viande

**mechanic** *noun* ▶ 315 |
a mechanic = un mécanicien/une mécanicienne

**medal** *noun*
a medal = une médaille
the gold medal = la médaille d'or

**media** *noun*
the media = les médias (*masculine*)

**medical** *adjective*
= médical/médicale
to have medical treatment = suivre un traitement médical

**medicine** *noun*
a medicine = un médicament

**Mediterranean** *noun*
the Mediterranean = la (mer) Méditerranée

**medium** *adjective*
= moyen/moyenne

**meet** *verb*
- (*by accident or appointment*) = rencontrer
she met him at the butcher's = elle l'a rencontré à la boucherie
can we meet (up) next week? = est-ce qu'on peut se voir la semaine prochaine?
to meet again = se revoir (**!** + *être*)
- (*to be introduced to*) ▶ 237 | = faire la connaissance de
she met him at a wedding = elle a fait sa connaissance à un mariage
have you met Tom? = est-ce que vous connaissez Tom?

- (*to fetch*)
I can meet you at the station = je peux aller te chercher à la gare
can you meet me at the station? = peux-tu venir me chercher à la gare?
- (*to have a meeting*) = se réunir (**!** + *être*)

**meeting** *noun*
a meeting = une réunion

**melon** *noun*
a melon = un melon

**melt** *verb*
- the snow is starting to melt = la neige commence à fondre
- the salt will melt the ice = le sel fera fondre le verglas

**member** *noun* ▶ 315 |
a member = un membre
a member of staff = un membre du personnel

**memory** *noun*
- memory = la mémoire
to have a good memory = avoir bonne mémoire
he's got a bad memory = il n'a pas de mémoire
- (*of a person, a place or time*)
a memory = un souvenir

**memory stick** *noun*
a memory stick = une carte mémoire

**mend** *verb*
- (*to fix*) = réparer
- (*by sewing*) = raccommoder

**mental** *adjective*
= mental/mentale

**menu** *noun*
a menu = un menu

**mess** *noun*
a mess = le désordre
your room is in a mess = ta chambre est en désordre
to make a mess in the kitchen = mettre du désordre dans la cuisine

**message** *noun*
a message = un message

**metal** *noun*
a metal = un métal

**method** *noun*
a method = une méthode

**metre** (*British English*), **meter** (*US English*) *noun* ▶ 285 |
a metre = un mètre

**Mexico** *noun* ▶ 218 |
Mexico = le Mexique

**microphone** *noun*
a microphone = un microphone

**microwave** *noun*
a microwave = un four à micro-ondes

# Length and weight measurements

## Length measurements

Note that French has a *comma* where English has a *decimal point*:

| | |
|---|---|
| *1 inch* = 2,54 cm | *1 yard* = 91,44 cm |
| *1 foot* = 30,48 cm | *1 mile* = 1,61 km (kilomètres) |

## Length

| | |
|---|---|
| *how long is the rope?* | = quelle est la longueur de la corde? |
| *it's ten metres long* | = elle fait dix mètres |
| *the rope is three metres too short* | = la corde est trop courte de trois mètres |

## Height

| | | |
|---|---|---|
| People | *how tall is he?* | = combien mesure-t-il? |
| | *he's six feet tall* | = il mesure un mètre quatre-vingts |
| | *Tom is taller | smaller than Jane* | = Tom est plus grand | plus petit que Jane |
| Things | *how high is the tower?* | = quelle est la hauteur de la tour? |
| | *it's 100 metres high* | = elle fait cent mètres de† haut / de† hauteur |
| | *A is higher | lower than B* | = A est plus haut / moins haut que B |

## Distance

| | |
|---|---|
| *how far is it from Paris to Nice?* | = quelle distance y a-t-il entre Paris et Nice? |
| *it's about 800 kilometres* | = il y a environ 800 kilomètres |

M

## Width / breadth

| | |
|---|---|
| *how wide is the river?* | = quelle est la largeur de la rivière? |
| *it's seven metres wide* | = elle fait sept mètres de† large / de† largeur |

## Depth

| | |
|---|---|
| *how deep is the lake?* | = quelle est la profondeur du lac? |
| *it's four metres deep* | = il fait quatre mètres de† profondeur |

Note the French construction with **de**, coming after the noun it describes:

| | |
|---|---|
| *a street two kilometres long* | = une rue **de** deux kilomètres de† long |
| *a 100-metre-high tower* | = une tour **de** cent mètres de† haut |
| *a ten-kilometre walk* | = une promenade **de** dix kilomètres |
| *a river 50 metres wide* | = une rivière **de** 50 mètres de† largeur |

## Weight measurements

Again, note that French has a *comma* where English has a *decimal point*:

| | |
|---|---|
| *1 ounce* = 28,35 g (grammes) | *1 stone* = 6,35 kg (kilos) |
| *1 pound* * = 453,60 g | *1 ton* = 1 014,60 kg |

**\* a pound** (£1) is translated by **une livre** in French, but the French **livre** = 500 grammes (half a kilo).

| | | |
|---|---|---|
| People | *how much does he weigh?* | = combien pèse-t-il? |
| | *he weighs 10st | 140 lbs* | = il pèse 63 kg 500 (soixante-trois kilos cinq cents) |
| Things | *what does the parcel weigh?* | = combien pèse le colis? |
| | *how heavy is it?* | = quel est son poids? |
| | *it weighs 10 kilos* | = il pèse 10 kilos |
| | *A weighs more than B* | = A pèse plus lourd que B |
| | *sold by the kilo* | = vendu au kilo |

† The use of **de** is obligatory in these constructions.

**midday** noun ▶ 211 |, ▶ 356 |
midday = midi (*masculine*)
at midday = à midi

**middle** noun
the middle = le milieu
in the middle of the road = au milieu de la route
to be in the middle of cooking a meal = être en train de préparer un repas

**middle-aged** adjective
= d'âge mûr (**!** *never changes*)

**midnight** noun ▶ 211 |, ▶ 356 |
midnight = minuit (*masculine*)
at midnight = à minuit

**might** verb
• (*when talking about a possibility*)
she might be right = elle a peut-être raison
they might have got lost = ils se sont peut-être perdus
'will you come?'—'I might' = 'est-ce tu viendras?'—'peut-être'
we might miss the plane = nous risquons de rater l'avion
he said he might not come = il a dit qu'il ne viendrait peut-être pas
• (*when implying something didn't happen*)
you might have been killed! = tu aurais pu te faire tuer!
she might have warned us = elle aurait pu nous prévenir
• (*when making suggestions*)
you might try leaving a message = vous pourriez laisser un message
it might be better to wait = ce serait peut-être mieux d'attendre

**mild** adjective
= doux/douce
the weather's mild, it's mild = il fait doux

**mile** noun ▶ 285 |
a mile = un mile
**!** *Note that a* **mile** = *1609 m.*

**military** adjective
= militaire

**milk**
**1** noun
milk = le lait
**2** verb
= traire

**milkman** noun ▶ 315 |
a milkman = un laitier

**million** number
one million, a million = un million
three million dollars = trois millions de dollars
a million inhabitants = un million d'habitants

**mind**
**1** noun
• the mind = l'esprit (*masculine*)
to have a logical mind = avoir l'esprit logique
I have a lot on my mind = j'ai beaucoup de soucis
• to make up one's mind to change jobs = se décider à changer de travail
to change one's mind = changer d'avis
**2** verb
• (*when expressing an opinion*)
'where shall we go?'—'I don't mind' = 'où irons-nous?'—'ça m'est égal'
she doesn't mind the heat = la chaleur ne la dérange pas
I wouldn't mind some cake = je prendrais volontiers du gâteau
• (*in polite questions or requests*)
do you mind if I smoke? = est-ce que cela vous dérange si je fume?
would you mind coming? = est-ce que ça vous ennuierait de venir?
• (*to be careful*)
mind the steps! = fais attention aux marches!
mind you don't break the plates = fais attention de ne pas casser les assiettes
• (*to take care of*) = s'occuper de (**!** + *être*)
• never mind, she'll get the next train = ne t'en fais pas, elle prendra le train suivant

**mine¹** pronoun
the green pen is mine = le stylo vert est à moi
guess which house is mine = devine laquelle de ces maisons est la mienne
her coat is brown but mine is dark green = son manteau est marron mais le mien est vert foncé
his sister's the same age as mine = sa sœur a le même âge que la mienne
**!** *Note that, when comparing objects, people, etc, one of the following translations—*le mien, la mienne, les miens *or* les miennes—*will be used. To know which one to use, find out whether the object, person, etc which is being described is masculine or feminine, singular or plural.*

**mine²** noun
a mine = une mine

**miner** noun ▶ 315 |
a miner = un mineur

**mineral water** noun
a mineral water = une eau minérale

**minimum**
**1** adjective
the minimum price = le prix minimum
a minimum temperature of 15 degrees = une température minimale de 15 degrés
**2** noun
the minimum = le minimum

**minister** noun ▶ 315 |
- (in government)
  à minister = un ministre
  the minister for Education = le ministre de
  l'Éducation
- (in religion)
  a minister = un ministre du culte

**minor** adjective
  = mineur/mineure
  a minor injury = une blessure légère

**minority** noun
  a minority = une minorité

**minus** preposition
  = moins
  it's minus four outside = il fait moins
  quatre dehors

**minute** noun ▶ 211 |, ▶ 356 |
  a minute = une minute
  they'll be here any minute now = ils vont
  arriver d'une minute à l'autre

**mirror** noun
  a mirror (on a wall) = un miroir, une glace
  (on a car) = un rétroviseur

**miserable** adjective
  = malheureux/malheureuse
  to feel miserable = avoir le cafard

**miss** verb
- to miss the target = manquer la cible
  the stone just missed his head = la pierre
  lui a frôlé la tête
- (to fail to see) = rater
  you can't miss it = tu ne peux pas le rater
- to miss an opportunity = laisser passer une
  occasion
- (to feel sad not to see)
  I miss you = tu me manques
  we'll miss Oxford = Oxford va nous
  manquer
- (other uses)
  don't miss this film = ne rate pas ce film
  she missed her plane = elle a raté son
  avion
  to miss school (due to illness) = manquer
  l'école
  (by skipping classes) = sauter les cours

**Miss** noun
▶ See the boxed note on Forms of address.
  Miss = mademoiselle (feminine)

**missing** adjective
  to be missing = manquer
  there's a book missing = il manque un
  livre

**mist** noun
  mist = la brume

**mistake** noun
  a mistake = une erreur

a spelling mistake = une faute
  d'orthographe
  to make a mistake = se tromper (! + être)

**mistletoe** noun
  mistletoe = le gui

**mix** verb
- (to put together) = mélanger
- (to go together) = se mélanger (! + être)
- to mix with the other students = fréquenter
  les autres étudiants
  **mix up** = confondre
  to get the two languages mixed up
  = confondre les deux langues
  I'm always mixing him up with his brother
  = je le confonds toujours avec son frère

**mixture** noun
  a mixture = un mélange

**mobile phone** noun
  a mobile phone = un téléphone portable,
  un portable

**model** noun
- (of a train, a car, a building)
  a model = un modèle réduit, une
  maquette
- ▶ 315 |
  a (fashion) model = un mannequin

**modern** adjective
  = moderne

**Mohammed** noun
  Mohammed = Mahomet

**mom, Mom** noun (US English)
  a mom = une maman

**moment** noun
  a moment = un instant
  there's no-one there at the moment = il
  n'y a personne en ce moment

**Monday** noun ▶ 222 |
  Monday = lundi (masculine)

**money** noun
  money = l'argent (masculine)

**monkey** noun
  a monkey = un singe

**month** noun ▶ 356 |
  a month = un mois
  he'll be back in two months' time = il sera
  de retour dans deux mois

**Montreal** noun ▶ 218 |
  Montreal = Montréal

**monument** noun
  a monument = un monument

**mood** noun
  to be in a good mood = être de bonne
  humeur
  I'm in a very bad mood = je suis de très
  mauvaise humeur

M

**moon** *noun*
the moon = la lune

**moped** *noun*
a moped = un vélomoteur

**moral** *adjective*
= moral/morale

**more** ▶ 317 |
**1** *determiner*
= plus de
more [friends | books | CDs …] = plus [d'amis | de livres | de disques compacts …]
more [money | food | time …] = plus [d'argent | de nourriture | de temps …]
I have more work than him = j'ai plus de travail que lui
there's no more bread = il n'y a plus de pain
there's more tea = il y a encore du thé
would you like more coffee? = voulez-vous encore du café?
he bought two more tickets = il a acheté deux billets de plus
**2** *pronoun*
= plus
to cost more = coûter plus cher
I did more than you = j'en ai fait plus que toi
I can't tell you any more = je ne peux pas t'en dire plus
we need more (of them) = il nous en faut plus
we need more (of it) = il nous en faut davantage

! Note that *it is necessary to use* en, *which might be translated as 'of it' or 'of them', with pronouns like* more. *See also* another, a few, a lot *etc for this use of* en.

**3** *adverb*
• *(when comparing)* = plus
it's more complicated than that = c'est plus compliqué que ça
• *(when talking about time)*
he doesn't live there any more = il n'habite plus là
**4 more and more** = de plus en plus
more and more expensive = de plus en plus cher
**5 more or less** = plus ou moins
**6 more than** = plus de
there were more than 20 people there = il y avait plus de 20 personnes

**morning** *noun* ▶ 211 |, ▶ 356 |

! Note that morning *is usually translated by* matin *in French. However it is sometimes translated by* matinée, *when there is an emphasis on the idea of duration.*

a morning = un matin
at three o'clock in the morning = à trois heures du matin
to spend the morning reading the paper = passer la matinée à lire le journal

**mosquito** *noun*
a mosquito = un moustique

**most**
**1** *determiner*
• *(the majority of)* = la plupart de
most schools will be closed = la plupart des écoles seront fermées
• *(in superlatives)*
the most = le plus de
who has the most money? = qui a le plus d'argent?
**2** *pronoun*
= la plupart de
most of the time they phone each other = la plupart du temps ils se téléphonent
most (of them) speak Greek = la plupart (d'entre eux) parlent grec
**3** *adverb*
the most
= le plus/la plus (+ *singular*)
= les plus (+ *plural*)
the most expensive shop in London = le magasin le plus cher de Londres
the most beautiful town in France = la plus belle ville de France
**4 at (the) most** = au maximum, au plus
**5 most of all** = par-dessus tout

**mostly** *adverb*
= pour la plupart

**mother** *noun*
a mother = une mère

**mother-in-law** *noun*
a mother-in-law = une belle-mère

**motor** *noun*
a motor = un moteur

**motorbike** *noun*
a motorbike = une moto

**motorcyclist** *noun*
a motorcyclist = un motocycliste/une motocycliste

**motorist** *noun*
a motorist = un automobiliste/une automobiliste

**motor racing** *noun* ▶ 248 |
motor racing = la course automobile

**motorway** *noun* (*British English*)
a motorway = une autoroute

**mountain** *noun*
a mountain = une montagne
in the mountains = en montagne

**mountain bike** *noun*
a mountain bike = un vélo tout terrain, un VTT

**mountain climbing** *noun* ▶ 248 |
mountain climbing = l'alpinisme (*masculine*)

**mouse** *noun*
(*animal and for computer*)
a mouse = une souris

**moustache, mustache** (US English)
noun
a moustacho = une moustache

**mouth** noun ▶ 201 |
• (of a person)
the mouth = la bouche
to have a big mouth = avoir une grande
gueule✗
• (of an animal)
the mouth = la gueule
• (of a river)
the mouth = l'embouchure (feminine)

**move** verb
• (to make a movement) = bouger
don't move! = ne bouge pas!
the train's starting to move = le train
démarre
• (to put elsewhere) = déplacer
to move the car = déplacer la voiture
to move a chair (out of the way)
= déplacer une chaise
• (to make a movement with) = bouger
I couldn't move my leg = je n'arrivais pas à
bouger la jambe
don't move the camera = ne bouge pas
l'appareil photo
• (to act) = agir
• to move (house) = déménager
to move to Paris = déménager à Paris
**move away**
• (to live elsewhere) = déménager
• (to make a movement away) = s'éloigner
(! + être)
to move away from the window
= s'éloigner de la fenêtre
**move back** = reculer
**move forward** = s'avancer (! + être)
**move in** = emménager
to move in with friends = s'installer avec
des amis
**move out** = déménager
**move over** = se pousser (! + être)
move over please = pousse-toi s'il te plaît

**movement** noun
a movement = un mouvement

**movie** noun (US English)
a movie = un film

**movies** noun (US English)
the movies = le cinéma

**movie theater** noun (US English)
a movie theater = un cinéma

**moving** adjective
= émouvant/émouvante

**mow** verb
to mow the lawn = tondre le gazon

**MP** noun ▶ 315 | (British English)
an MP = un député

**Mr** noun
▶ See the boxed note on Forms of address.
Mr = monsieur (masculine)

**Mrs** noun
▶ See the boxed note on Forms of address
Mrs = madame (feminine)

**much** ▶ 317 |
**1** adverb
• (a lot) = beaucoup
her work is much more tiring = son travail
est beaucoup plus fatigant
he doesn't read much = il ne lit pas
beaucoup
• (often) = beaucoup
they don't go out much = ils ne sortent
pas beaucoup
• (when used with very, too or so)
he misses her very much = elle lui
manque beaucoup
you talk too much = tu parles trop
she loves him so much = elle l'aime
tellement
**2** pronoun
(in questions) = beaucoup
(in negative statements) = grand-chose
is there much to be done? = est-ce qu'il y a
beaucoup à faire?
he didn't eat much = il n'a pas mangé
grand-chose
**3** determiner
• (a lot of) = beaucoup de
I haven't got much time = je n'ai pas
beaucoup de temps
do you have much work? = est-ce que
vous avez beaucoup de travail?
• (when used with how, very, too, so or as)
how much money have you got?
= combien d'argent as-tu?
she doesn't eat very much meat = elle ne
mange pas beaucoup de viande
I spent too much money – j'ai dépensé
trop d'argent
don't use so much salt = ne mets pas tant
de sel
she has as much work as me = elle a
autant de travail que moi

**mud** noun
mud = la boue

**mug**
**1** noun
a mug = une grande tasse
**2** verb
to be mugged = se faire agresser (! + être)

**multiply** verb
= multiplier

**mum, Mum** noun (British English)
a mum = une maman

**mumps** noun ▶ 266 |
mumps = les oreillons (masculine plural)

**murder**
**1** noun
a murder = un meurtre

M

# Musical instruments

## Playing an instrument

Note the use of **de** with **jouer**:

| | |
|---|---|
| *to play the piano* | = **jouer du** piano |
| *to play the flute* | = **jouer de la** flûte |

but

| | |
|---|---|
| *to learn the piano* | = **apprendre le** piano |
| *to learn the guitar* | = **apprendre la** guitare |

## Players

English **-ist** is very often French **-iste**. The gender will reflect the sex of the player:

| | |
|---|---|
| *a pianist* | = **un** pian**iste** / **une** pian**iste** |
| *a violonist* | = **un** violon**iste** / **une** violon**iste** |

But note the French when these words are used with **good** and **bad** like this:

| | |
|---|---|
| *he's a good pianist* | = **il joue bien du** piano |
| *he's a bad pianist* | = **il joue mal du** piano |

## Use with another noun

**de** is usually correct:

| | |
|---|---|
| *to take piano lessons* | = prendre des leçons **de** piano |
| *a guitar solo* | = un solo **de** guitare |
| *a piano teacher* | = un professeur **de** piano |

---

**2** *verb*
= assassiner

**murderer** *noun*
a murderer = un meurtrier

**muscle** *noun*
a muscle = un muscle

**museum** *noun*
a museum = un musée

**mushroom** *noun*
a mushroom = un champignon

**music** *noun*
music = la musique

**musical** *noun*
a musical = une comédie musicale

**musical instrument** *noun*
a musical instrument = un instrument de
musique

**musician** *noun* ▶ 315 |
a musician = un musicien/une
musicienne

**Muslim** *adjective*
= musulman/musulmane

**mussel** *noun*
a mussel = une moule

**must** *verb*

> **!** *The verbs* **devoir** *and* **falloir** *are used to
> translate* **must**. *Note that the subjunctive
> is used after* **il faut que**.

- (*when stressing the importance of
something*)
**you must go to the doctor** = il faut que tu
ailles chez le médecin
**we mustn't tell anyone** = il ne faut en
parler à personne
- (*when talking about a rule*)
**she must take the exam in June** = elle
doit passer l'examen au mois de
juin
**visitors must go to (the) reception** = les
visiteurs doivent se présenter au bureau
d'accueil
- (*when assuming that something is
true*)
**it must be nice to live there** = ça doit être
agréable de vivre là-bas
**you must be David's sister** = tu dois être
la sœur de David
**they must have been bored** = ils ont dû
s'ennuyer

**mustard** *noun*
mustard = la moutarde

**mutton** *noun*
mutton = le mouton

# Using the subjunctive

There are a number of examples in this dictionary which use the subjunctive. They are highlighted in the text with a note. The type of examples generating the subjunctive fall into three main categories. They are examples which contain:

- certain verbs, mainly:
  - falloir
  - vouloir

- certain conjunctions:
  - bien que ...
  - jusqu'à ce que ...
  - à condition que ...
  - pour que ...
  - à moins que ...

- certain phrases, often expressing a personal opinion:
  - il est bizarre que ...
  - c'est dommage que ...
  - je suis content que ...
  - je doute que ...

## Verbs

- *falloir* is by far the most common verb requiring the subjunctive in this dictionary. The impersonal form **il faut que** is most often used to translate **must**.

  | | |
  |---|---|
  | I **must** go | = il **faut que** je m'en aille |
  | you **must** come | = il **faut que** tu viennes |

- *vouloir*, meaning **to want**, requires the subjunctive in specific cases. Compare:

  | | |
  |---|---|
  | I want **to come** | = je veux **venir** |
  | I want you **to come** | = je veux que **tu viennes** |

  The second example uses the subjunctive because there are two 'subjects' involved, I and you. In the first example, there is only one subject, which means that no subjunctive is required.

## Conjunctions

The most common conjunctions requiring the subjunctive in French in this dictionary are:

- **bien que** (= *although, even though, though*)

  **although** she's quite old, she has lots of energy = **bien qu'**elle soit assez âgée, elle a beaucoup d'énergie

- **jusqu'à ce que** (= *until*)

  let's watch television **until** they arrive = regardons la télévision **jusqu'à ce qu'**ils arrivent

- **à condition que** (= *provided, on condition that, as long as*)

  you can go out with them **provided** they bring you home = tu peux sortir avec eux **à condition qu'**ils te ramènent

- **pour que** (= *so that*)

  be quiet **so that** I can sleep = tais-toi **pour que** je puisse dormir!

- **à moins que** (= *unless*)

  I am not going **unless** you come with me = je n'y vais pas **à moins que** tu viennes avec moi

## Phrases

When stating an opinion, the subjunctive is always used with the following phrases:

| | |
|---|---|
| it's strange that she's never there | = il est bizarre qu'elle ne soit jamais là |
| it's a pity we can't go there | = c'est dommage qu'on ne puisse pas y aller |
| I'm glad he has lots of friends | = je suis content qu'il ait beaucoup d'amis |
| I doubt if he'll come | = je doute qu'il vienne |

## Superlatives

| | |
|---|---|
| it's the best book (that) I have ever read | = c'est le meilleur livre **que j'aie jamais lu** |
| it's the most expensive watch (that) he's seen | = c'est la montre la plus chère **qu'il ait vue** |

In French, the subjunctive is always used in clauses with **que** following a superlative adjective like *le meilleur* / *la meilleure*, *le plus mauvais* / *la plus mauvaise* etc.

▶ For more information on the subjunctive forms of French verbs, see the **verb tables ▶ 381 **.

▶ For information on grammar terms used in this note, see the **glossary page x**.

**my** *determiner*
  my = mon/ma (+ *singular*)
    = mes (+ *plural*)
    **!** *Note that* ma *becomes* mon *before a vowel or mute h.*

  they hate my dog = ils détestent mon chien
  what do you think of my house? = qu'est-ce que tu penses de ma maison?
  he's my age = il a mon âge
  I sold all my CDs = j'ai vendu tous mes disques compacts
  I broke my leg = je me suis cassé la jambe
    **!** *Note that, when talking about parts of the body,* mon, ma *and* mes *are not used. See the usage note on* The human body ▶ 201 | *for further examples.*

**myself** *pronoun*
• (*when used as a reflexive pronoun*)
  I want to enjoy myself = je veux m'amuser
  I didn't hurt myself = je ne me suis pas fait mal
• (*when used for emphasis*)
  I told them myself = je le leur ai dit moi-même
  I did it all by myself = je l'ai fait tout seul

**mystery** *noun*
  a mystery = un mystère

# Nn

**nail** *noun* ▶ 201 |
• (*for use in attaching, repairing*)
  a nail = un clou
• (*on the fingers or toes*)
  a nail = un ongle

**nail polish** *noun*
  nail polish = le vernis à ongles

**naked** *adjective*
  = nu/nue

**name** *noun*
• (*of a person*)
  a name = un nom
  what's your name? = comment t'appelles-tu?, comment vous appelez-vous?
  my name is Louis = je m'appelle Louis
• (*of a book, a play or film*)
  a name = un titre

**narrow** *adjective*
  = étroit/étroite

**nasty** *adjective*
• (*mean, unkind*) = méchant/méchante
• (*unpleasant*) = désagréable

**national** *adjective*
  = national/nationale

**native** *adjective*
  a native language = une langue maternelle
  a native French speaker = une personne de langue maternelle française

**natural** *adjective*
  = naturel/naturelle
  it's natural to be disappointed = c'est normal d'être déçu

**naturally** *adverb*
  = naturellement

**nature** *noun*
  nature = la nature

**naughty** *adjective*
  = vilain/vilaine

**navy** *noun*
  the navy = la marine

**navy blue** *adjective* ▶ 213 |
  = bleu marine (**!** *never changes*)

**near**
**1** *preposition*
  = près de
  he was sitting near us = il était assis près de nous
**2** *adverb*
  they live quite near = ils habitent tout près

**3** adjective
= proche
the school is quite near = l'école est assez
  proche
the nearest shops are several miles away
  = les magasins les plus proches sont à
  plusieurs kilomètres d'ici

**nearby** adverb
= à proximité

**nearly** adverb
= presque
we're nearly there = nous sommes
  presque arrivés
I nearly [forgot | gave up | fell asleep …] = j'ai
  failli [oublier | abandonner | m'endormir …]

**neat** adjective
(in one's habits) = ordonné/ordonnée
(in how one looks) = net/nette
(describing work, handwriting)
  = soigné/soignée

**necessary** adjective
= nécessaire

**neck** noun ▶ 201 |
the neck = le cou

**necklace** noun
a necklace = un collier

**need** verb
- ((to) have to)
  you don't need to ask permission = tu
    n'es pas obligé de demander la
    permission
  they'll need to come early = il va falloir
    qu'ils viennent de bonne heure

  **!** Note that the subjunctive is used after
  falloir que.

- (to want) = avoir besoin de
  they need [money | help | friends …] = ils ont
    besoin [d'argent | d'aide | d'amis …]
  we need to see the doctor = nous avons
    besoin de voir le médecin
  everything you need = tout ce qu'il vous
    faut

**needle** noun
a needle = une aiguille

**negative**
**1** adjective
- (pessimistic) = négatif/négative
- (harmful) = néfaste
**2** noun
a negative = un négatif

**neighbour** (British English), **neighbor**
(US English) noun
a neighbour = un voisin/une voisine

**neither**
**1** conjunction
- (in neither… nor sentences) = ni… ni

she speaks neither French nor English
  = elle ne parle ni français ni anglais
I have neither the time nor the energy to
  argue = je n'ai ni le temps ni la force de
  discuter
- (nor)
  'I can't sleep'—'neither can I' = 'je
    n'arrive pas à dormir'—'moi non plus'
**2** determiner
= aucun des deux/aucune des deux
neither girl answered = aucune des deux
  filles n'a répondu
**3** pronoun
= ni l'un/l'une ni l'autre
neither of them is coming = ni l'un ni
  l'autre ne vient

**!** Note that, in sentences with a verb, the
negative ne or n' (before a vowel or mute
h) is used together with ni… ni,
aucun/aucune des deux and ni l'un/l'une
ni l'autre to translate neither. Remember
that ne comes before the verb or the
auxiliary verb.

**nephew** noun
a nephew = un neveu

**nerves** noun
nerves = les nerfs (masculine)
to get on someone's nerves = énerver
  quelqu'un

**nervous** adjective
- (frightened)
  to be nervous = avoir peur
- (anxious) = angoissé/angoissée
  to feel nervous = être angoissé/angoissée

**nest** noun
a nest = un nid

**net** noun
- (for fishing)
  a net = un filet
- (in sport)
  the net (in football) = les filets (masculine
    plural)
  (in tennis) = le filet

**Netherlands** noun ▶ 218 |
the Netherlands = les Pays-Bas (masculine
  plural)

**network** noun
a network = un réseau

**neutral** adjective
= neutre

**never** adverb
**!** Note that, in sentences with a verb, the
negative ne or n' (before a vowel or mute
h) is used together with jamais to
translate never. Remember that ne comes
before the verb or the auxiliary verb.

- (*not ever*) = jamais
  **they never come to see us** = ils ne
  viennent jamais nous voir
  **she has never been to the opera** = elle
  n'est jamais allée à l'opéra
  **I'll never go back there again** = je n'y
  retournerai plus jamais
- (*when used for emphasis*)
  **she never even apologized** = elle ne s'est
  même pas excusée

**nevertheless** *adverb*
= pourtant, néanmoins

**new** *adjective*
= nouveau/nouvelle (**!** *before the noun*)

> **!** *Note that* **nouvel** *is used instead of*
> **nouveau** *before masculine nouns*
> *beginning with a vowel* (**endroit, ordina-**
> **teur**) *or a mute h* (**hôtel**)*. The plural of*
> **nouveau** *and* **nouvel** *is* **nouveaux**.

**a new bike** = un nouveau vélo
**a new car** = une nouvelle voiture
**a new computer** = un nouvel ordinateur
**new dresses** = de nouvelles robes

**newborn baby** *noun*
**a newborn baby** = un nouveau-né

**news** *noun*
- **a piece of news** = une nouvelle
  **have you heard the news?** = est-ce que tu
  connais la nouvelle?
  **that's good news** = c'est une bonne
  nouvelle
  **have you any news of John?** = est-ce que
  tu as des nouvelles de John?
- (*on radio, TV*)
  **the news** = le journal (*singular*)= , les
  informations (*feminine*)

**newsagent's** *noun* ▶ 315 | (*British
English*)
**a newsagent's** = un magasin de journaux

**newspaper** *noun*
**a newspaper** = un journal

**New Year** *noun*
**the New Year** = le nouvel an
**Happy New Year!** = Bonne année!

**New Year's Day**, **New Year's** (*US
English*) *noun*
**New Year's (Day)** = le jour de l'an

**New Year's Eve** *noun*
**New Year's Eve** = la Saint-Sylvestre

**New Zealand** *noun* ▶ 218 |
**New Zealand** = la Nouvelle-Zélande

**next**
**1** *adjective*
- (*when talking about what is still to come*)
  = prochain/prochaine

---

**I'll take the next train to London** = je
prendrai le prochain train pour Londres
**he'll be here next week** = il sera là la
semaine prochaine
- (*when talking about what followed*)
  = suivant/suivante
  **I took the next train** = j'ai pris le train
  suivant
  **they arrived the next day** = ils sont arrivés
  le lendemain
- (*in a queue*)
  **'who's next?'** = 'à qui le tour?'
  **'I'm next'** = 'c'est mon tour'
**2** *adverb*
- (*in the past*) = ensuite
  **what happened next?** = qu'est-ce qui s'est
  passé ensuite?
- (*now*) = maintenant
  **what'll we do next?** = qu'est-ce qu'on fait
  maintenant?
- (*in the future*)
  **when you next go to Paris, give Gary a
  call** = la prochaine fois que tu iras à
  Paris, passe un coup de fil à Gary
**3 next to** = à côté de

**next door** *adverb*
= à côté

**nice** *adjective*
- (*enjoyable*) = agréable
  **it's nice to be able to relax** = c'est agréable
  de pouvoir se détendre
- (*kind, friendly*) = sympathique, sympa**✗**
  **to be nice to someone** = être
  gentil/gentille avec quelqu'un
- (*attractive*) = beau/belle (**!** *before the noun*)

**nickname** *noun*
**a nickname** = un surnom

**niece** *noun*
**a niece** = une nièce

**night** *noun* ▶ 356 |
- (*as opposed to day*)
  **a night** = une nuit
  **I didn't sleep last night** = je n'ai pas dormi
  cette nuit
  **he stayed out all night** = il n'est pas rentré
  de la nuit
- (*evening*)
  **a night** = un soir
  **last night** = hier soir
  **a night at the cinema** = une soirée au
  cinéma

> **!** *See the note at* **evening** *for information
> on* **soir** *and* **soirée**.

**nightclub** *noun*
**a nightclub** = une boîte de nuit

**nightdress** *noun*
**a nightdress** = une chemise de nuit

---

**nightmare** noun
a nightmare = un cauchemar
to have a nightmare = faire un cauchemar

**nil** noun
nil = zéro

**nine** number ▶ 187 |, ▶ 211 |
nine = neuf
nine books = neuf livres
I have nine (of them) = j'en ai neuf

**nineteen** number ▶ 187 |, ▶ 211 |
nineteen = dix-neuf

**nineteenth** number
• (in a series) = dix-neuvième
• (in dates) ▶ 222 |
the nineteenth of July = le dix-neuf juillet

**ninety** number ▶ 187 |
ninety = quatre-vingt-dix

**ninth** number
• (in a series) = neuvième
• (in dates) ▶ 222 |
the ninth of December = le neuf décembre

**no**
**1** adverb
• no = non
no thanks = non merci
• he no longer works here = il ne travaille
plus ici
**2** determiner
• (not any)
we have no money = nous n'avons pas
d'argent
there are no trains = il n'y a pas de trains
• (when refusing permission)
no smoking = défense de fumer
no talking! = silence!
• (when used for emphasis)
this is no time to argue = ce n'est pas le
moment de discuter
it's no problem = ce n'est pas du tout un
problème

**nobody** ▶ no-one

**noise** noun
noise = le bruit
to make noise = faire du bruit

**noisy** adjective
= bruyant/bruyante

**none** pronoun

> ! Note that, when there is a verb in the
> sentence, the negative ne or n' (before a
> vowel or mute h) is used together with
> aucun/aucune to translate none.
> Remember that ne comes before the verb
> or the auxiliary verb.

none = aucun/aucune
none of the girls went to the class
= aucune des filles n'est allée au cours
none of [us | you | them ...] can speak
German = aucun [de nous | de vous | d'entre
eux ...] ne parle allemand
there's none left = il n'y en a plus
I've got none, I have none = je n'en ai pas

> ! Note that it is necessary to use en which
> might be translated as 'of it' or 'of them',
> with pronouns like none. See also another,
> a few, a lot etc for this use of en.

**nonsense** noun
that's nonsense! = c'est absurde!

**noon** noun ▶ 211 |, ▶ 356 |
noon = midi (masculine)
at noon = à midi

**no-one** pronoun (also **nobody**)

> ! Note that, when there is a verb in the
> sentence, the negative ne or n' (before a
> vowel or mute h) is used together with
> personne to translate no-one. Remember
> that ne comes before the verb or the
> auxiliary verb.

no-one = personne
no-one tells me anything = personne ne
me dit rien
no-one saw him = personne ne l'a vu
there's no-one else in the office = il n'y a
personne d'autre au bureau

**nor** conjunction

> ! For translations of nor when used in
> combination with neither, look at the entry
> for neither in this dictionary.

'I don't like him'—'nor do I' = 'je ne l'aime
pas'—'moi non plus'

**normal** adjective
= normal/normale

**normally** adverb
= normalement

**north**
**1** noun
the north = le nord
in the north of France = dans le nord de la
France
**2** adverb
to go north = aller vers le nord
to live north of Paris = vivre au nord de
Paris
**3** adjective
= nord (! never changes)
to work in north London = travailler dans
le nord de Londres

**North America** noun ▶ 218 |
North America = l'Amérique du Nord
| ! Note that **Amérique** is feminine.

**northeast** noun
the northeast = le nord-est

**Northern Ireland** noun ▶ 218 |
Northern Ireland = l'Irlande du Nord
| ! Note that **Irlande** is feminine.

**northwest** noun
the northwest = le nord-ouest

**Norway** noun ▶ 218 |
Norway = la Norvège

**N**

# not

## Used without a verb

When **not** is used without a verb before an adjective, a noun, an adverb, a verb or a pronoun it is translated by **pas**:

| | |
|---|---|
| *not at all* | = **pas** du tout |
| *not bad* | = **pas** mal |
| *it's a cat not a dog* | = c'est un chat **pas** un chien |
| *you should walk, not run* | = il faut marcher, **pas** courir |
| *she should apologise, not me* | = c'est elle qui devrait s'excuser, **pas** moi |

## Used with a verb

When **not** is used with the verbs *be, do, have, will* and *would*, the translation is **ne … pas** (**n'** before a vowel or mute h): **ne** comes before the verb or the auxiliary, and **pas** comes after the verb or auxiliary:

| | |
|---|---|
| *it's not a cat* | = ce n'est **pas** un chat |
| *he doesn't like oranges* | = il n'aime **pas** les oranges |
| *I haven't seen him* | = je ne l'ai **pas** vu |
| *she hasn't arrived yet* | = elle n'est **pas** encore arrivée |
| *she won't come by car* | = elle ne viendra **pas** en voiture |
| *it wouldn't matter* | = ce ne serait **pas** grave |

When used with a verb in the infinitive, **ne** and **pas** are placed together before the verb:

| | |
|---|---|
| *he decided not to go* | = il a décidé de **ne pas** y aller |
| *you were wrong not to tell her* | = tu as eu tort de **ne pas** le lui dire |

## Used in short questions

When **not** is used in short questions, the whole question can usually be translated by the French **n'est-ce pas**:

| | |
|---|---|
| *she bought it, didn't she?* | = elle l'a acheté, **n'est-ce pas**? |
| *you were there too, weren't you?* | = tu y étais aussi, **n'est-ce pas**? |
| *they're living in Germany, aren't they?* | = ils habitent en Allemagne, **n'est-ce pas**? |
| *he's got a lot of money, hasn't he?* | = il a beaucoup d'argent, **n'est-ce pas**? |
| *you'll come too, won't you?* | = vous viendrez vous aussi, **n'est-ce pas**? |
| *he likes fish, doesn't he?* | = il aime le poisson, **n'est-ce pas**? |

▶ For more examples, see the entry **not**.

---

**Norwegian** ▶ 275 |
**1** *adjective*
= norvégien/norvégienne
**2** *noun*
the Norwegians = les Norvégiens

**nose** *noun* ▶ 201 |
the nose = le nez

**not**
▶ *See the boxed note on* not *for more information and examples*
**1** *adverb*
= ne… pas (**!** n' + *vowel or mute h…* pas)

> **!** *Remember that* ne *or* n' *(before a vowel or mute h) comes before the verb or auxiliary verb and* pas *after.*

she's not at home = elle n'est pas chez elle
hasn't he phoned you? = il ne t'a pas téléphoné?
I hope not = j'espère que non

we're going to go out whether it rains or not = qu'il pleuve ou non, nous allons sortir
not everyone likes football = le football ne plaît pas à tout le monde
**2 not at all**
• (*in no way*) = pas du tout
he's not at all worried = il n'est pas du tout inquiet
• 'thanks a lot'—'not at all' = 'merci beaucoup'—'de rien'

**note**
**1** *noun*
• (*to remind oneself*)
a note = une note
• (*a message*)
a note = un mot
I left you a note = je t'ai laissé un mot
• (*British English*) (*money*)
a note = un billet
a 50-euro note = un billet de 50 euros

- *(in music)*
  **a note** = une note
**2** *verb*
  **to note (down)** = noter

**notebook** *noun*
  **a notebook** = un carnet

**nothing** *pronoun*
  **nothing** = rien

  **!** Note that, when there is a verb in the sentence, the negative ne or n' (before a vowel or mute h) is used together with rien to translate nothing. Remember that ne or n' comes before the verb or the auxiliary verb.

  **nothing has changed** = rien n'a changé
  **there's nothing left** = il ne reste rien
  **she said nothing** = elle n'a rien dit
  **I knew nothing about it** = je n'en savais rien
  **there's nothing we can do about it** = nous n'y pouvons rien
  **I had nothing to do with it!** = je n'y étais pour rien!
  **it's nothing to do with us** = ça ne nous regarde pas

**notice**
**1** *verb*
  = remarquer
**2** *noun*
- *(a written sign)*
  **a notice** = une pancarte
- *(warning people)*
  **notice** = le préavis
  **a month's notice** = un mois de préavis
  **to be cancelled at short notice** = être annulé/annulée à la dernière minute
- **don't take any notice, take no notice** = ne fais pas attention

**novel** *noun*
  **a novel** = un roman

**November** *noun* ▶ 222 |
  **November** = novembre *(masculine)*

**now**
**1** *adverb*
  = maintenant
  **we have to do it now** = il faut le faire maintenant
  **I'm phoning her now** = je suis en train de lui téléphoner
  **do it right now** = fais-le tout de suite
  **now is the time to contact them** = c'est le moment de les contacter
  **I should have told you before now** = j'aurais dû te le dire avant
  **it hasn't been a problem until now** = ça n'a pas posé de problème jusqu'à présent
  **between now and next Monday** = d'ici lundi prochain
  **from now on** = à partir de maintenant
**2 now and again, now and then** = de temps en temps

**nowhere** *adverb*
  = nulle part
  **I go nowhere without my dog** = je ne vais nulle part sans mon chien
  **there's nowhere to sit** = il n'y a pas d'endroit pour s'asseoir

**nuclear** *adjective*
  = nucléaire

**nuisance** *noun*
  **to be a nuisance** = être pénible
  **it's a nuisance having to pay in cash** = c'est agaçant de devoir payer en espèces

**numb** *adjective*
- **to go numb** = s'engourdir (**!** + être)
  **my hands are numb** = j'ai les mains engourdies
- *(before an operation)* = insensible

**number**
**1** *noun*
- **a number** *(a figure)* = un chiffre
  *(of a house, a bus, a telephone, a passport)* = un numéro
  **to dial the wrong number** = faire un faux numéro
- *(when talking about quantities)* ▶ 317 |
  **a number of** [demonstrations | people | times ...] = un certain nombre de [manifestations | personnes | fois ...]
  **a small number of tourists** = quelques touristes
**2** *verb*
  = numéroter

**numberplate** *noun* *(British English)*
  **a numberplate** = une plaque minéralogique

**nun** *noun* ▶ 315 |
  **a nun** = une religieuse

**nurse** *noun* ▶ 315 |
  **a nurse** = un infirmier/une infirmière

**nursery** *noun*
  **a nursery** = une crèche

**nursery school** *noun*
  **a nursery school** = une école maternelle

**nut** *noun*
  **a nut** *(a walnut)* = une noix

**nylon** *noun*
  **nylon** = le nylon

**N**

# Oo

**oak** *noun*
an oak = un chêne

**oar** *noun*
an oar = une rame

**obedient** *adjective*
= obéissant/obéissante

**obey** *verb*
= obéir
to obey someone = obéir à quelqu'un
to obey the law = se conformer à la loi

**object**
**1** *noun*
an object = un objet
**2** *verb*
= soulever des objections

**oblige** *verb*
to be obliged to leave = être obligé/obligée
de partir
to oblige someone = rendre service à
quelqu'un

**obtain** *verb*
= obtenir

**obvious** *adjective*
= évident/évidente

**obviously** *adverb*
= manifestement

**occasion** *noun*
an occasion = une occasion
on special occasions = dans les grandes
occasions

**occasionally** *adverb*
= de temps à autre

**occupy** *verb*
(*to take over*) = occuper
(*to keep busy*)
to keep oneself occupied = s'occuper
(**!** + *être*)
to keep the children occupied = occuper
les enfants

**occur** *verb*
= se produire (**!** + *être*)

**ocean** *noun*
the ocean = l'océan (*masculine*)

**o'clock** *adverb* ▶ 211 |
it's five o'clock = il est cinq heures
at one o'clock = à une heure

**October** *noun* ▶ 222 |
October = octobre (*masculine*)

**octopus** *noun*
an octopus = une pieuvre

**odd** *adjective*
(*strange*) = bizarre
(*not matching*) = dépareillé/dépareillée
(*when talking about numbers*)
an odd number = un nombre impair

**odour** (*British English*), **odor** (*US English*)
*noun*
an odour = une odeur

**of** *preposition*
of = de (**!** d' + *vowel or mute h*)
the sound of an engine = le bruit d'un
moteur
it's in the centre of Paris = c'est au centre
de Paris
a photo of the dog = une photo du chien
half of the salad = la moitié de la salade
at the top of the stairs = en haut de
l'escalier
the names of the pupils = le nom des
élèves
(*when talking about quantities*) ▶ 317 |
of = de (**!** d' + *vowel or mute h*)
a kilo of potatoes = un kilo de pommes
de terre
a bottle of mineral water = une bouteille
d'eau minérale
two cans of beer = deux cannettes de
bière
the flowers are lovely so we bought some
of them = les fleurs sont belles alors
nous en avons acheté
have you heard of it? = est-ce que tu en as
entendu parler?
there are six of them in the family = ils
sont six dans la famille
there were too many of them = ils étaient
trop nombreux

**!** *Note that* en *is used to translate* 'of it' *or*
'of them' *when talking about things, but*
*not usually when referring to people.*

**off**

**!** *Often* off *occurs in combinations with*
*verbs, for example:* get off, go off, take off
*etc. To find the correct translations for this*
*type of verb, look up the separate*
*dictionary entries at* get, go, take *etc.*

**1** *adverb*
(*leaving*)
I'm off (*British English*) = je m'en vais
they're off to Italy tomorrow = ils partent
pour l'Italie demain
(*away*)
the coast is a long way off = la côte est
loin d'ici
we could see them from a long way off
= on les voyait de loin
(*free*)
to take a day off = prendre un jour de
congé
today's her day off = elle ne travaille pas
aujourd'hui

(not working, switched off)
the lights are all off = toutes les lumières
sont éteintes
**2** adjective
the milk is off = le lait a tourné

**offence** (British English), **offense** (US
English) noun
(a crime)
an offence = un délit
to take offence = s'offenser (**!** + être)

**offend** verb
= vexer

**offer** verb
to offer someone a job = offrir un emploi
à quelqu'un
to offer to water the plants = se proposer
pour arroser les plantes

**office** noun
an office = un bureau

**office block** noun (British English)
an office block = un immeuble de
bureaux

**officer** noun
an officer (in the army or navy) = un
officier
(in the police) = un policier

**office worker** noun ▶ 315 |
an office worker = un employé/une
employée de bureau

**official** adjective
= officiel/officielle

**often** adverb
= souvent

**oil** noun
(for heating, energy)
oil = le pétrole
(for a car)
oil = l'huile (feminine)
(for cooking, for health)
oil = l'huile (feminine)

**okay, OK**
**1** adjective
(when asking or giving opinions)
is it okay if I come later? = est ce que je
peux venir plus tard?
it's okay to invite them = on peut les
inviter
(when talking about health)
to feel okay = aller bien
are you okay? = ça va?
**2** adverb
okay = d'accord

**old** adjective
(not new, not young) = vieux/vieille
(**!** before the noun)

**!** Note that vieil is used instead of vieux
before masculine nouns beginning with a
vowel (ordinateur) or a mute h (hôtel). The
plural of vieux and vieil is vieux.

an old oak = un vieux chêne
an old woman = une vieille femme
an old man = un vieil homme
old houses = de vieilles maisons
old people = les personnes âgées
(when talking about a person's age) ▶ 187 |
how old are you? = quel âge as-tu?
a three-year old girl = une fillette de trois
ans
I'm as old as he is = j'ai le même âge que
lui
she's eight years older than her brother
= elle a huit ans de plus que son frère
to be the oldest = être l'aîné/l'aînée
to be old enough to go out at night = être
en âge de sortir le soir
(previous) = ancien/ancienne (**!** before the
noun)
that's my old address = c'est mon
ancienne adresse
in the old days = autrefois

**old-fashioned** adjective
(describing attitudes, ideas)
= démodé/démodée
(describing people) = vieux jeu (**!** never
changes)

**olive**
**1** noun
an olive = une olive
**2** adjective ▶ 213 |
= vert olive (**!** never changes)

**olive oil** noun
olive oil = l'huile d'olive
**!** Note that huile is feminine.

**Olympic Games** noun
the Olympic Games = les Jeux olympiques
**!** Note that Jeux is masculine plural.

**omelette** noun
an omelette = une omelette

**on**
**!** Often on occurs in combinations with
verbs, for example: count on, get on, keep
on etc. To find the correct translations for
this type of verb, look up the separate
dictionary entries for count, get, keep etc.

**1** preposition
on = sur
it's on the table = c'est sur la table
it's on top of the wardrobe = c'est sur
l'armoire
you've got a spot on your nose = tu as un
bouton sur le nez
there's a stain on it = il y a une tache
dessus
to fall on the floor = tomber par terre
I like the picture on the wall = j'aime le
tableau qui est au mur
to live on Park Avenue = habiter Park
Avenue

*(when talking about transport)*
**to travel on the bus** = voyager en bus
**I'm on my bike today** = je suis à vélo aujourd'hui
*(about)* = sur
**it's a book on Africa** = c'est un livre sur l'Afrique
**a programme on primary schools** = une émission sur les écoles primaires
*(when talking about time)*
**she was born on the sixth of December** = elle est née le six décembre
**I'll be there on Saturday** = j'y serai samedi
**we went there on my birthday** = nous y sommes allés le jour de mon anniversaire
*(when talking about the media)*
**on television** = à la télévision
**I saw it on the news** = je l'ai vu aux informations
**is the film out on video?** = est-ce que le film est sorti en vidéo?
*(using)*
**to be on drugs** = se droguer (**!** + *être*)
**2** *adverb*
*(when talking about what one wears)*
**to have a sweater on** = porter un pull
**to have make-up on** = être maquillé/maquillée
*(working, switched on)*
**why are all the lights on?** = pourquoi est-ce que toutes les lumières sont allumées?
**the radio was on all evening** = la radio a marché toute la soirée
*(showing)*
**what's on?** *(on TV)* = qu'est-ce qu'il y a à la télévision?
*(in the cinema)* = qu'est-ce qu'on joue (au cinéma)?
*(when talking about time)*
**from Tuesday on, I'll be here** = à partir de mardi, je serai là
**a little later on** = un peu plus tard

## once
**1** *adverb*
*(one time)* = une fois
**once a day** = une fois par jour
*(in the old days)* = autrefois
**2** *conjunction*
= une fois que
**it'll be easier once we've found a house** = ce sera plus facile une fois que nous aurons trouvé une maison
**3 at once** = tout de suite

## one
**1** *number* ▶ **187 |**, ▶ **211 |**
**one** = un/une
**one child** = un enfant/une enfant
**one of my colleagues** = un/une de mes collègues
**one hundred** = cent

**2** *determiner*
*(the only)*
**she's the one person who can help him** = c'est la seule personne capable de l'aider
**it's the one thing that annoys me** = c'est la seule chose qui m'agace
*(the same)*
**to take three exams in the one day** = passer trois examens dans la même journée
**3** *pronoun*
*(when referring to something generally)*
**I need an umbrella—have you got one?** = j'ai besoin d'un parapluie—est-ce que tu en as un?

**!** *Note that it is necessary to use* en, *which might be translated as 'of them', with pronouns like* one. *See also* any, a few, many *etc for this use of* en.

*(when referring to a specific person or thing)*
**he's the one who told me to be quiet** = c'est lui qui m'a dit de me taire
**which one?** = lequel/laquelle?
**this one** = celui-ci/celle-ci
*(when used to mean 'you' or 'people')*
**one never knows** = on ne sait jamais
**4 one by one** = un par un/une par une

## one another *pronoun*
**!** *Note that* one another *is very often translated by using a reflexive pronoun like* se, s', nous *or* vous.

**to love one another** = s'aimer (**!** + *être*)
**we don't like being apart from one another** = nous n'aimons pas être séparés (l'un de l'autre)

## oneself *pronoun*
= se (**!** *s'* + vowel or mute h)
**to enjoy oneself** = s'amuser (**!** + *être*)
**to hurt oneself** = se blesser (**!** + *être*)

## onion *noun*
**an onion** = un oignon

## online *adjective*
= en ligne

## only
**1** *adverb*

**!** *Note that in sentences with a verb, the negative* ne *is often used together with* que *to translate* only. *Remember that* ne *comes before the verb or the auxiliary verb.*

**only** = ne... que
**it's only a game** = ce n'est qu'un jeu
**you only have to ask** = vous n'avez qu'à demander
**they've only met once** = ils ne se sont rencontrés qu'une fois
**he only hit his elbow** = il s'est juste cogné le coude

**2** *adjective*
= seul/seule (**!** *before the noun*)
she was the only one who didn't speak
French = elle était la seule à ne pas
parler français
the only problem is that I can't drive = le
seul problème c'est que je ne conduis
pas
an only daughter = une fille unique
**3 only just**
I've only just [arrived | heard the news | moved
house...] = je viens juste [d'arriver |
d'apprendre la nouvelle | de déménager...]
she had only just bought a car = elle
venait d'acheter une voiture

**onto** *preposition*
= sur

**open**
**1** *verb*
to open = ouvrir
to open a letter = ouvrir une lettre
what time do you open? = à quelle heure
est-ce que vous ouvrez?
the shop opens at eight = le magasin
ouvre à huit heures
the door opens very easily = la porte
s'ouvre facilement
(*to start*) (*when talking about a film*) = sortir
(**!** + *être*)
(*when talking about a play*) = commencer
**2** *adjective*
(*not closed*) = ouvert/ouverte
leave the door open = laisse la porte
ouverte
the pool isn't open = la piscine n'est pas
ouverte
(*frank*) = franc/franche
**3** *noun*
out in the open = dehors, en plein air

**opener** *noun*
an opener (*for bottles*) = un décapsuleur
(*for cans*) = un ouvre-boites

**open-minded** *adjective*
to be open-minded = avoir l'esprit ouvert

**opera** *noun*
an opera = un opéra

**operate** *verb*
(*to make something work*) = faire marcher
(*to carry out an operation*) = opérer
to operate on someone = opérer
quelqu'un
to operate on someone's leg = opérer
quelqu'un à la jambe

**operation** *noun*
an operation = une opération
to have an operation = se faire opérer
(**!** + *être*)

**operator** *noun* ▶ 315 |
an operator = un standardiste/une
standardiste

**opinion** *noun*
an opinion (*a point of view*) = un avis
(*when judging a person, a situation*) = une
opinion
in my opinion, they're lying = à mon avis,
ils mentent

**opponent** *noun*
an opponent = un adversaire/une
adversaire

**opportunity** *noun*
an opportunity = une occasion
to take the opportunity to visit Paris
= profiter de l'occasion pour visiter Paris

**oppose** *verb*
to oppose a plan = s'opposer à un projet
to be opposed to nuclear weapons = être
contre les armes nucléaires

**opposite**
**1** *preposition*
= en face de
she was sitting opposite me = elle était
assise en face de moi
**2** *adjective*
the opposite sex = le sexe opposé
he was walking in the opposite direction
= il allait dans l'autre sens
**3** *adverb*
= en face
**4** *noun*
the opposite = le contraire
it's the exact opposite = c'est tout le
contraire

**optician** *noun* ▶ 315 |
an optician = un opticien/une opticienne

**optimist** *noun*
an optimist = un optimiste/une optimiste

**optimistic** *adjective*
= optimiste

**or** *conjunction*
or = ou
once or twice a week = une ou deux fois
par semaine
we'll stay either here or at Martine's
= nous resterons soit ici soit chez
Martine
do you have any brothers or sisters?
= est-ce que tu as des frères et sœurs?
(*in negative sentences*)
I can't come today or tomorrow = je ne
peux venir ni aujourd'hui ni demain
don't tell Mum or Dad = ne le dis ni à
maman ni à papa
(*otherwise*) = sinon
be careful or you'll break the cups = fais
attention sinon tu vas casser les tasses

**oral** *adjective*
= oral/orale

**orange**
**1** *noun*
an orange = une orange

**O**

**2** *adjective* ▶ **213** |
= orange (**!** *never changes*)

**orange juice** *noun*
orange juice = le jus d'orange

**orchard** *noun*
an orchard = un verger

**orchestra** *noun*
an orchestra = un orchestre

**order**
**1** *verb*
(*to tell*)
to order someone to leave = ordonner à
quelqu'un de partir
(*to ask for*) = commander
to order goods from a magazine
= commander des articles dans un
magazine
**2** *noun*
(*an instruction*)
an order = un ordre
to give orders = donner des ordres
the right order = le bon ordre
the list is in alphabetical order = la liste
est dans l'ordre alphabétique
**3 in order to** = pour
I phoned them in order to change the date
= je leur ai téléphoné pour changer la
date

**ordinary** *adjective*
(*not unusual*) = ordinaire
an ordinary family = une famille ordinaire
(*average*) = moyen/moyenne

**organ** *noun*
(*the musical instrument*) ▶ **290** |
an organ = un orgue
(*a part of the body*)
an organ = un organe

**organization** *noun*
an organization = une organisation

**organize** *verb*
= organiser
to get organized = s'organiser (**!** + *être*)

**original** *adjective*
(*first*) = original/originale
(*true, real*) = originel/originelle
(*new, fresh*) = original/originale

**ornament** *noun*
an ornament = un bibelot

**orphan** *noun*
an orphan = un orphelin/une orpheline

**ostrich** *noun*
an ostrich = une autruche

**other**
**1** *adjective*
= autre (+ *singular*)
= autres (+ *plural*)
not that dress, the other one = pas cette
robe-là, l'autre
they sold the other car = ils ont vendu
l'autre voiture
to annoy the other pupils = embêter les
autres élèves

some people like driving, other people
hate it = certains aiment conduire,
d'autres détestent ça
every other Saturday = un samedi sur
deux
**2** *pronoun*
he makes the others laugh = il fait rire les
autres
some students learn French easily,
others have problems = certains élèves
apprennent le français facilement,
d'autres ont des problèmes
they came in one after the other = ils sont
entrés l'un après l'autre

**otherwise** *conjunction*
= sinon
it's not dangerous, otherwise I wouldn't
go = ce n'est pas dangereux, sinon je
n'irais pas

**otter** *noun*
an otter = une loutre

**ought** *verb*
(*when talking about what should be done*)
you ought not to say things like that = tu
ne devrais pas dire des choses pareilles
(*when making a polite suggestion*)
you ought to be in bed = tu devrais être au
lit
(*when saying something may happen*)
they ought to arrive tomorrow = ils
devraient arriver demain
(*when saying something didn't happen*)
someone ought to have gone with them
= quelqu'un aurait dû les accompagner

**our** *determiner*
our = notre (+ *singular*)
= nos (+ *plural*)
he ran over our dog = il a écrasé notre
chien
what do you think of our house? = qu'est-
ce que tu penses de notre maison?
all our CDs have been stolen = on a volé
tous nos disques compacts

**ours** *pronoun*
the grey car is ours = la voiture grise est à
nous
which case is ours? = laquelle de ces
valises est la nôtre
their garden is bigger than ours = leur
jardin est plus grand que le nôtre
their children are younger than ours
= leurs enfants sont plus jeunes que les
nôtres

**!** *Note that, when comparing objects,
people, etc, one of the following
translations—le nôtre, la nôtre or les
nôtres—will be used. To know which one
to use, find out whether the object,
person etc which is being described is
masculine singular, feminine singular or
just plural.*

**ourselves** pronoun
> (when used as a reflexive pronoun)
> **we want to enjoy ourselves** = nous
> voulons nous amuser, on veut s'amuser
> **we didn't hurt ourselves** = nous ne nous
> sommes pas fait mal, on ne s'est pas fait
> mal
>
> ! Note that on is more usual in spoken
> French.
>
> (when used for emphasis)
> **we organized everything ourselves**
> = nous avons tout organisé nous-mêmes
> **we like to be by ourselves** = nous aimons
> être seuls

**out**

> ! Often out occurs in combinations with
> verbs, for example: blow out, come out,
> find out, give out etc. To find the correct
> translations for this type of verb, look up
> the separate dictionary entries at blow,
> come, find, give etc.

**1** adverb
> (outside) = dehors
> **they're out there** = ils sont dehors
> **to stay out in the rain** = rester dehors sous
> la pluie
> **she's out in the garden** = elle est dans le
> jardin
> **I'm looking for the way out** = je cherche la
> sortie
> (absent)
> **to be out** = être sorti/sortie
> **someone called while you were out**
> = quelqu'un a téléphoné pendant que tu
> étais sorti
> (not lighting, not on)
> **to be out** = être éteint/éteinte
> **all the lights were out** = toutes les
> lumières étaient éteintes

**2 out of**
> **to walk out of the building** = sortir du
> bâtiment
> **to get out of the city** = sortir de la ville
> **to take a pencil out of the drawer**
> = prendre un crayon dans le tiroir

**outdoor** adjective
> = en plein air
> **an outdoor swimming pool** = une piscine
> en plein air

**outdoors** adverb
> = dehors

**outer space** noun
> **outer space** = l'espace (masculine)

**outside**
**1** preposition
> (in front of) = devant
> **to wait outside the school** = attendre
> devant l'école
> (beyond)
> **outside the city** = en dehors de la ville

**2** adverb
> = dehors
> **let's go outside** = allons dehors
> **let's bring the chairs outside** = sortons les
> chaises
**3** noun
> **the outside** = l'extérieur (masculine)
> **the outside of the building** = l'extérieur du
> bâtiment
**4** adjective
> = extérieur/extérieure

**oven** noun
> **an oven** = un four

**over**

> ! Often over occurs in combinations with
> verbs, for example: get over, move over
> etc. To find the correct translations for this
> type of verb, look up the separate
> dictionary entries at get, move etc.

**1** preposition
> **over** = par-dessus
> **to climb over a wall** = passer par-dessus un
> mur
> **we climbed over it** = nous sommes passés
> par-dessus
> (across)
> **it's somewhere over there** = c'est quelque
> part par là
> **come over here** = viens par ici
> (above) = au-dessus de
> **the picture over the piano** = le tableau au-
> dessus du piano
> **young people over 18** = les jeunes de plus
> de 18 ans
> (during)
> **we saw them over the weekend** = nous les
> avons vus pendant le week-end
> (everywhere)
> **I've looked all over the house for my keys**
> = j'ai cherché mes clés partout dans la
> maison
**2** adverb
> (finished)
> **the term is over** = le trimestre est terminé
> **is the film over?** = est-ce que le film est
> fini?
> (to one's home)
> **to ask someone over** = inviter quelqu'un
> **to start over again** = recommencer à zéro

**overdose** noun
> **an overdose** = une surdose

**overtake** verb
> = dépasser

**overweight** adjective
> = trop gros/trop grosse

**owe** verb
> = devoir
> **to owe money to someone** = devoir de
> l'argent à quelqu'un

**owl** noun
> **an owl** = un hibou, une chouette

## own
**1** *adjective*
= propre (**!** *before the noun*)
you should clean your own room = tu devrais ranger ta propre chambre
he'd like his own car = il voudrait une voiture à lui, il voudrait sa propre voiture
**2** *pronoun*

> **!** *Note that, when comparing objects, people etc, the translations given for the pronouns* mine, yours, his, hers, ours *or* theirs *work for* my own, your own *etc.*

I didn't use his pencil—I've got my own = je n'ai pas utilisé son crayon—j'ai le mien
they have a house of their own = ils ont une maison à eux, ils ont leur propre maison
**3** *verb*
= avoir
he owns a shop in town = il a un magasin en ville
who owns that dog? = à qui est ce chien?
**4 on one's own** = tout seul/toute seule
**own up** = avouer

## owner *noun*
an owner = un propriétaire/une propriétaire

## ox *noun*
an ox = un bœuf

## oxygen *noun*
oxygen = l'oxygène (*masculine*)

## oyster *noun*
an oyster = une huître

# Pp

## Pacific *noun*
the Pacific = le Pacifique

## pack
**1** *verb*
= faire ses bagages
I've got to pack my suitcase = je dois faire ma valise
**2** *noun*
a pack = un paquet
a pack of cigarettes = un paquet de cigarettes
a pack of cards = un jeu de cartes
**pack up** = faire ses bagages
to pack up one's belongings = emballer ses affaires

## package *noun*
a package = un paquet, un colis

## packed *adjective*
(*describing a room*) = plein/pleine à craquer
(*describing a train, a bus*) = bondé/bondée

## packet *noun*
a packet = un paquet

## page *noun*
a page = une page
on page six = (à la) page six

## pain *noun*
pain = la douleur
I've got a pain in my back = j'ai mal au dos
to be in pain = souffrir

## painful *adjective*
= douloureux/douloureuse

## paint
**1** *noun*
paint = la peinture
**2** *verb*
= peindre

## paintbrush *noun*
a paintbrush = un pinceau

## painter *noun* ▶ 315 |
a painter = un peintre

## painting *noun*
• (*a picture*)
a painting = un tableau
• (*the activity*)
painting = la peinture

## pair *noun*
a pair = une paire
a pair of shoes = une paire de chaussures

## pajamas *noun* (*US English*)
pajamas = un pyjama (*singular*)

## Pakistan *noun* ▶ 218 |
Pakistan = le Pakistan

## palace *noun*
a palace = un palais

## pale *adjective*
= pâle
to go pale, to turn pale = pâlir

## pancake *noun*
a pancake = une crêpe

## panic *verb*
= s'affoler (**!** + *être*)

## pants *noun*
• (*British English*) (*underwear*)
pants = un slip (*singular*)
• (*US English*) (*trousers*)
pants = un pantalon (*singular*)

## pantyhose *noun* (*US English*)
pantyhose = un collant

## paper *noun*
• (*for writing or drawing on*)
paper = le papier
a piece of paper = un bout de papier

- (a newspaper)
  a paper = un journal

**parachuting** noun ▶ 248 |
parachuting = le parachutisme

**parade** noun
a parade = un défilé

**paragliding** noun ▶ 248 |
paragliding = le parapente

**Paralympic Games** noun
the Paralympic Games = les Jeux
paralympiques

**paralysed** (British English), **paralyzed**
(US English) adjective
= paralysé/paralysée

**parcel** noun
a parcel = un paquet, un colis

**parents** noun
parents = les parents (masculine)

**Paris** noun ▶ 218 |
Paris = Paris

**park**
1 noun
a park = un jardin public, un parc
2 verb
to park a car = garer une voiture
to park near the office = se garer près du
bureau

**parking lot** noun (US English)
a parking lot = un parking, un parc de
stationnement

**parking meter** noun
a parking meter = un parcmètre

**parliament** noun
a parliament = un parlement

**parrot** noun
a parrot = un perroquet

**part**
- (a part) = une partie
  part of the [book | film | time ...] = une partie
  du [livre | film | temps ...]
  it's part of the job = ça fait partie du
  travail
  in this part of the country = dans cette
  région
- (a piece for a machine, a car)
  a part = une pièce
- (a role)
  a part = un rôle
  to play the part of Tommy = jouer le rôle
  de Tommy

**participate** verb
= participer

**particular**
1 adjective
= particulier/particulière
2 in particular = en particulier

**partner** noun
- (in a relationship)
  a partner = un compagnon/une compagne
- (in dancing, sport)
  a partner = un partenaire/une partenaire

**part-time** adverb
= à temps partiel
to work part-time = travailler à temps
partiel

**party** noun
- (a social event)
  a party = une fête
  (held in the evening) = une soirée
  a birthday party = une fête d'anniversaire,
  un anniversaire
  a children's party = un goûter d'enfants
- a political party = un parti politique

**pass** verb
- (to go past) = passer (! + être)
  to let someone pass = laisser passer
  quelqu'un
  to pass the school = passer devant l'école
  to pass a car = dépasser une voiture
  to pass someone in the street = croiser
  quelqu'un dans la rue
- (to give) = passer
  pass me the salt, please = passe-moi le
  sel, s'il te plaît
  to pass the ball to someone = passer le
  ballon à quelqu'un
- (to spend) = passer
  to pass the time [reading | painting | listening
  to the radio ...] = passer le temps [en lisant |
  en faisant de la peinture | en écoutant la
  radio ...]
- (to succeed in an exam) = réussir
  to pass an exam = réussir un examen
**pass around**
to pass around the biscuits = faire passer
les biscuits
**pass on** = transmettre
to pass on a message to someone
= transmettre un message à quelqu'un

**passage** noun
a passage (indoors) = un couloir
(outdoors) = un passage

**passenger** noun
a passenger = un passager/une passagère

**passport** noun
a passport = un passeport

**past**
1 noun
the past = le passé
in the past = dans le passé
2 adjective
= dernier/dernière (! before the noun)
the past few days have been difficult = ces
derniers jours ont été difficiles
3 preposition
- (when talking about time) ▶ 211 |
  it's twenty past four = il est quatre heures
  vingt
  it's past midnight = il est minuit passé

P

- (by)
  to go past someone = passer devant
    quelqu'un
  she ran past me = elle est passée devant
    moi en courant
- (beyond) = après
  it's just past the traffic lights = c'est juste
    après les feux
4 adverb
  to go past, to walk past = passer (**!** + être)

**pasta** noun
  pasta = les pâtes (feminine)

**pastry** noun
- (for baking)
  pastry = la pâte
  to make pastry = faire de la pâte
- (a cake)
  a pastry = une pâtisserie, un gâteau

**patch** noun
- (on a garment)
  a patch = une pièce
- (on a tyre)
  a patch = une rustine

**path** noun
  a path = un chemin
  (narrower) = un sentier
  (in a garden) = une allée

**patience** noun
  patience = la patience
  to lose patience with someone = perdre
    patience avec quelqu'un

**patient**
1 noun
  a patient = un patient/une patiente
2 adjective
  = patient/patiente

**patrol car** noun
  a patrol car = une voiture de police

**pattern** noun
- (a design)
  a pattern = un dessin, un motif
- (when making garments)
  a pattern (for knitting) = un modèle
  (for sewing) = un patron

**pavement** noun (British English)
  a pavement = un trottoir

**paw** noun
  a paw = une patte

**pay**
1 verb
- to pay = payer
  to pay the bills = payer les factures
  to pay for the shopping = payer les
    courses
  he paid for my meal = il a payé mon repas
- (when talking about wages)
  the work doesn't pay very well = le travail
    est mal payé
  I'm paid eight pounds an hour = je suis
    payé huit livres de l'heure

- (to give)
  to pay attention to the teacher = écouter
    le professeur
  to pay someone a visit = rendre visite à
    quelqu'un
  to pay someone a compliment = faire des
    compliments à quelqu'un
2 noun
  pay = le salaire
  the pay is very good = c'est très bien payé
**pay back** = rembourser

**PE** noun
  PE = l'éducation physique
  | **!** Note that éducation is feminine.

**pea** noun
  a pea = un petit pois

**peace** noun
  peace = la paix

**peach** noun
  a peach = une pêche

**peacock** noun
  a peacock = un paon

**peanut** noun
  a peanut = une cacahuète

**pear** noun
  a pear = une poire

**pearl** noun
  a pearl = une perle

**pebble** noun
  a pebble (on a beach) = un galet

**pedestrian** noun
  a pedestrian = un piéton

**pedestrian crossing** noun
  a pedestrian crossing = un passage pour
    piétons

**peel** verb
  = éplucher

**pen** noun
  a pen = un stylo

**penalty** noun
  a penalty (in soccer) = un tir de
    réparation, un penalty
  (in rugby) = une pénalité

**pencil** noun
  a pencil = un crayon

**pencil case** noun
  a pencil case = une trousse à crayons

**pencil sharpener** noun
  a pencil sharpener = un taille-crayon

**penfriend** (British English), **penpal**
noun
  a penfriend = un correspondant/une
    correspondante

**penguin** noun
  a penguin = un pingouin

**penknife** noun
a penknife = un canif

**pensioner** noun
a pensioner = un retraité/une retraitée

**people** noun
people (in general) = les gens (masculine plural)
(if counting) = les personnes (feminine plural)
we met very nice people = nous avons fait la connaissance de gens très sympathiques
most people don't know what's going on = la plupart des gens ne savent pas ce qui se passe
there were three people at the meeting = il y avait trois personnes à la réunion
there are too many people here = il y a trop de monde ici
to help other people = aider les autres

**pepper** noun
• (the spice)
pepper = le poivre
• (the vegetable)
a pepper = un poivron

**per** preposition
per person = par personne

**per cent**, **percent** (US English) noun
per cent = pour cent, %

**perfect** adjective
= parfait/parfaite
to speak perfect French = parler un français parfait
it's the perfect place for a picnic = c'est l'endroit idéal pour un pique-nique

**perform** verb
• (to do)
to perform a task = exécuter une tâche
• (to act, to play) = jouer

**perfume** noun
perfume = le parfum
to wear perfume = mettre du parfum

**perhaps** adverb
= peut-être

**period** noun
• (in time)
a period = une période
a trial period = une période d'essai
• (in history)
a period = une époque
• (for women)
a period = des règles (feminine plural)
to have one's period = avoir ses règles
• (a school lesson)
a period = un cours

**permanent** adjective
= permanent/permanente

**permission** noun
permission = la permission
to get permission = obtenir la permission

**person** noun
a person = une personne
an old person = une personne âgée
to be a kind person = être gentil/gentille
he's not a very patient person = il n'est pas très patient

**personal** adjective
= personnel/personnelle

**personal computer** noun
a personal computer = un ordinateur personnel

**personality** noun
a personality = une personnalité

**perspire** verb
= transpirer

**persuade** verb
= persuader
to persuade someone to buy a car = persuader quelqu'un d'acheter une voiture

**pessimist** noun
a pessimist = un pessimiste/une pessimiste

**pessimistic** adjective
= pessimiste

**pet** noun
a pet = un animal de compagnie
do you have any pets? = est-ce que tu as des animaux?

**petrol** noun (British English)
petrol = l'essence (feminine)
to run out of petrol = tomber en panne d'essence

**petrol station** noun (British English)
a petrol station = une station d'essence

**pet shop** noun ▶ 315 |
a pet shop = une animalerie

**phone**
**1** noun
a phone = un téléphone
the phone's ringing = le téléphone sonne
to answer the phone = répondre au téléphone
he's on the phone = il est au téléphone
**2** verb
= téléphoner
to phone someone = téléphoner à quelqu'un, passer un coup de fil à quelqu'un

**phone book** noun
a phone book = un annuaire téléphonique

**phone booth** noun
a phone booth = une cabine téléphonique

P

**phone call** *noun*
  a phone call = un coup de fil, un appel
    téléphonique
  to receive a phone call = recevoir un
    appel téléphonique, recevoir un coup
    de fil
  to make a phone call = téléphoner, passer
    un coup de fil

**phone card** *noun*
  a phone card = une télécarte

**phone number** *noun*
  a phone number = un numéro de
    téléphone

**photo** *noun*
  a photo = une photo

**photocopier** *noun*
  a photocopier = une photocopieuse

**photocopy** *noun*
  a photocopy = une photocopie

**photograph** *noun*
  a photograph = une photo
  to take a photograph of someone
    = prendre quelqu'un en photo

**photographer** *noun* ▶ 315 |
  a photographer = un photographe/une
    photographe

**physical** *adjective*
  = physique

**physics** *noun*
  physics = la physique

**piano** *noun* ▶ 290 |
  a piano = un piano

**pick** *verb*
* (*to choose*) = choisir
  to pick a number = choisir un chiffre
* (*to collect*) = cueillir
  to pick blackberries = cueillir des mûres
* (*to take*)
  to pick a book off the shelf = prendre un
    livre sur l'étagère
**pick on** = s'en prendre à (**!** + *être*)
  he's always picking on me = il s'en prend
    toujours à moi
**pick out** = choisir
**pick up**
* (*to lift*) = ramasser
  to pick the clothes up off the floor
    = ramasser les vêtements par terre
  to pick a baby up = prendre un bébé dans
    ses bras
  to pick up the phone = décrocher le
    téléphone
* (*to collect*)
  to pick up passengers = prendre des
    passagers
  he's coming to pick me up = il vient me
    chercher

* (*to buy*) = prendre
  I stopped to pick up some milk = je me
    suis arrêté pour prendre du lait
* (*to learn*)
  to pick up a little German = apprendre un
    peu d'allemand

**picnic** *noun*
  a picnic = un pique-nique
  to go on a picnic = aller faire un pique-
    nique

**picture** *noun*
* a picture (*painted*) = une peinture, un
    tableau
  (*drawn*) = un dessin
  to paint someone's picture = faire le
    portrait de quelqu'un
* (*a photograph*)
  a picture = une photo
* the pictures = le cinéma (*singular*)

**piece** *noun*
* (*a bit*)
  a piece = un morceau
  a piece of cheese = un morceau de
    fromage
  a piece of string = un bout de ficelle
* (*a part of a machine*)
  a piece = une pièce
* (*a broken part*)
  a piece = un morceau
  to fall to pieces = tomber en morceaux
* (*a coin*)
  a 50-pence piece = une pièce de 50 pence
* (*other uses*)
  a piece of furniture = un meuble
  a piece of information = un
    renseignement
  a piece of advice = un conseil

**pierce** *verb*
  = percer

**pig** *noun*
  a pig = un porc, un cochon

**pigeon** *noun*
  a pigeon = un pigeon

**pile**
* a pile = une pile
  (*untidy*) = un tas
  a pile of old shoes = un tas de vieilles
    chaussures
* (*lots*)
  piles of [toys | records | books ...] = des tas**✽**
    de [jouets | disques | livres ...]

**pill** *noun*
* (*a tablet*)
  a pill = un comprimé
* (*a method of contraception*)
  the pill = la pilule

**pillow** *noun*
  a pillow = un oreiller

**pilot** *noun* ▶ 315 |
  a pilot = un pilote

---

**pin**
**1** *noun*
a pin = une épingle
**2** *verb*
= accrocher

**PIN** *noun*
a PIN = un code confidentiel
(d'identification)

**pinball** *noun* ▶ 248 |
pinball = le flipper

**pinch** *verb*
• to pinch = pincer
he pinched my arm = il m'a pincé le bras
• (*to hurt by being too tight*) = serrer
my shoes are pinching = mes chaussures
me serrent

**pineapple** *noun*
a pineapple = un ananas

**pine tree** *noun*
a pine tree = un pin

**pink** *adjective* ▶ 213 |
= rose

**pint** *noun*
• (*the quantity*)
a pint ≈ un demi-litre

> **!** *Note that a pint = 0.57 l in Britain and
> 0.47 l in the US.*

a pint of milk ≈ un demi-litre de lait
• (*British English*) (*a drink*)
to go for a pint = aller boire une bière

**pipe** *noun*
• (*for gas, water*)
a pipe = un tuyau
• (*for smoking*)
a pipe = une pipe

**pirate** *noun*
a pirate = un pirate

**Pisces** *noun*
Pisces = Poissons (*masculine plural*)

**pitch** *noun* (*British English*)
a (football) pitch = un terrain (de football)

**pity**
**1** *noun*
• pity = la pitié
• (*when expressing regret*)
what a pity! = quel dommage!
it's a pity you can't come = c'est dommage
que tu ne puisses pas venir

> **!** *Note that the subjunctive is used after*
> c'est dommage que.

**2** *verb*
= plaindre

**pizza** *noun*
a pizza = une pizza

**place** *noun*
• a place = un endroit
it's the best place to buy salmon = c'est le
meilleur endroit pour acheter du
saumon
Oxford is a nice place = Oxford est une
belle ville
they come from all over the place = ils
viennent de partout
this place is dirty = c'est sale ici
• (*a home*)
at Alison's place = chez Alison
I'd like a place of my own = j'aimerais
avoir un chez-moi
• (*in a queue, on a bus, in a car park, at
table*)
a place = une place
is this place free? = est-ce que cette place
est libre?
to take someone's place = prendre la
place de quelqu'un
to find a place to park = trouver une place
pour se garer
• (*on a team, a course, in a firm*)
a place = une place
to get a place on a course = obtenir une
place dans un cours
• (*in a contest*)
a place = une place
to win first place = gagner la première
place

**plain**
**1** *adjective*
• (*simple*) = simple
a plain dress = une robe simple
• (*not good-looking*) = quelconque
**2** *noun*
a plain = une plaine

**plait** *noun* (*British English*)
a plait = une natte, une tresse

**plan**
**1** *noun*
• (*what one intends to do*)
a plan = un plan
we need a plan = il nous faut un plan
• (*what one has arranged to do*)
a plan = un projet
do you have any plans for the future?
= est-ce que tu as des projets pour
l'avenir?
I don't have any plans for tonight = je n'ai
rien de prévu pour ce soir
**2** *verb*
• (*to prepare, to organize*)
to plan [a trip | a school timetable | a
meeting.. ] = organiser [un voyage | un
emploi du temps | une réunion ...]
• (*to intend*) = avoir l'intention de
I'm planning to visit Scotland = j'ai
l'intention de visiter l'Écosse

**plane** *noun*
a plane = un avion

**P**

**planet** *noun*
a planet = une planète

**plant**
**1** *noun*
a plant = une plante
**2** *verb*
= planter

**plaster** *noun (British English)*
a plaster = un pansement adhésif

**plastic**
**1** *noun*
plastic = le plastique
**2** *adjective*
= en plastique

**plate** *noun*
a plate = une assiette

**platform** *noun*
a platform = un quai
on platform 4 = au quai numéro 4

**play**
**1** *verb*
• *(to have fun)* = jouer
to play with friends = jouer avec des amis
to play a trick on someone = jouer un
tour à quelqu'un
to play cards = jouer aux cartes
• *(when talking about sports)* ▶ **248** = jouer
to play [football | cricket | tennis…] = jouer
[au football | au cricket | au tennis…]
France is playing (against) Ireland = la
France joue contre l'Irlande
• *(when talking about music)* ▶ **290** = jouer
to play [the piano | the flute | drums…] = jouer
[du piano | de la flûte | de la batterie…]
• *(to put on)* = mettre
to play [a video | a CD | a record…] = mettre
[une cassette vidéo | un disque compact | un
disque…]
• *(when talking about theatre, cinema)*
to play the role of Richard II = jouer le rôle
de Richard II
the film will be playing at the Phoenix = le
film va passer au Phoenix
**2** *noun*
a play = une pièce
**play around** = faire l'imbécile
**play back**
to play back a tape = repasser une cassette

**player** *noun* ▶ **248**
a player = un joueur/une joueuse
a tennis player = un joueur/une joueuse
de tennis

**playground** *noun*
a playground = une aire de jeu
the school playground = la cour de
récréation

**please** *adverb*
*(formal, to several people)* = s'il vous plaît
*(informal)* = s'il te plaît
please come in = entrez, je vous en prie
'more cake?'—'yes please' = 'encore du
gâteau?'—'oui, je veux bien'

**pleased** *adjective*
= content/contente
I was very pleased with myself = j'étais
très content de moi
pleased to meet you = enchanté

**plenty** *pronoun*
to have plenty [of time | of money | of
friends…] = avoir beaucoup [de temps |
d'argent | d'amis…]

**plot** *noun*
• *(a plan)*
a plot = un complot
• *(the story in a film, a novel, a play)*
a plot = une intrigue

**plug** *noun*
• *(on an appliance)*
a plug = une prise
to pull out the plug = débrancher la prise
• *(in a sink or bath)*
a plug = une bonde
**plug in** = brancher

**plum** *noun*
a plum = une prune

**plumber** *noun* ▶ **315**
a plumber = un plombier

**plus** *preposition*
= plus
three plus three are six = trois plus trois
font six

**pocket** *noun*
a pocket = une poche

**pocketbook** *noun (US English)*
a pocketbook = un sac à main

**pocket money** *noun*
pocket money = l'argent de poche
| **!** Note that **argent** is masculine.

**poem** *noun*
a poem = un poème

**point**
**1** *noun*
• *(a statement in a discussion)*
a point = une remarque
to make a point = faire une remarque
• *(the most important idea)*
the point = le point essentiel
that's not the point = là n'est pas la
question
• *(use)*
there's no point in shouting = ça ne sert à
rien de crier
• *(when talking about time)*
to be on the point of [moving | leaving |
selling the house…] = être sur le point de
[déménager | partir | vendre la maison…]
• *(the sharp end)*
the point = la pointe
the point of a pencil = la pointe d'un
crayon
• *(in a contest, a game)*
a point = un point

**2** *verb*
* (*to indicate*)
  to point (one's finger) at someone
  = montrer quelqu'un du doigt
  to point at a house = indiquer une maison
  to point the way to the station = indiquer
  la direction de la gare
* (*to aim*)
  to point a gun at someone = braquer un
  pistolet sur quelqu'un
  **point out** = montrer
  can you point them out to me? = est-ce
  que tu peux me les montrer?

**poison**
**1** *noun*
  poison = le poison
**2** *verb*
  = empoisonner

**Poland** *noun* ▶ **218** |
  Poland = la Pologne

**pole** *noun*
  a pole = une perche

**police** *noun*
  the police = la police

**policeman** *noun* ▶ **315** |
  a policeman = un policier

**police station** *noun*
  a police station = un poste de police

**policewoman** *noun* ▶ **315** |
  a policewoman = une femme policier

**polish** *verb*
  to polish shoes = cirer des chaussures
  to polish the car = lustrer la voiture

**polite** *adjective*
  = poli/polie

**political** *adjective*
  = politique

**politician** *noun* ▶ **315** |
  a politician = un homme/une femme
  politique

**politics** *noun*
  politics = la politique

**pollute** *verb*
  = polluer

**pollution** *noun*
  pollution = la pollution

**pond** *noun*
  a pond (*large*) = un étang
  (*smaller*) = une mare
  (*in a garden*) = un bassin

**pony** *noun*
  a pony = un poney

**ponytail** *noun*
  a ponytail = une queue de cheval

**pool** *noun*
* (*a swimming pool*)
  a pool = une piscine

* (*on the ground, the floor*)
  a pool of water = une flaque d'eau
* (*the game*) ▶ **248** |
  pool = le billard américain

**poor** *adjective*
* (*not wealthy*) – pauvre
* (*not satisfactory*) = mauvais/mauvaise
  (**!** *before the noun*)
  to be poor at languages = être faible en
  langues
* (*expressing sympathy*) = pauvre (**!** *before
  the noun*)
  the poor boy is exhausted = le pauvre
  garçon est épuisé

**popular** *adjective*

> **!** Note that popular is not usually
> translated by populaire.

  a popular hobby = un passe-temps
  répandu
  she's very popular = elle a beaucoup
  d'amis
  to be popular with the girls = avoir du
  succès auprès des filles

**population** *noun*
  a population – une population

**pork** *noun*
  pork = le porc

**port** *noun*
  a port = un port

**portrait** *noun*
  a portrait = un portrait

**Portugal** *noun* ▶ **218** |
  Portugal = le Portugal

**Portuguese** ▶ **275** |
**1** *adjective*
  = portugais/portugaise
**2** *noun*
* (*the people*)
  the Portuguese = les Portugais (*masculine
  plural*)
* (*the language*)
  Portuguese = le portugais

**positive** *adjective*
  = positif/positive

**possibility** *noun*
  a possibility = une possibilité

**possible** *adjective*
  = possible
  they came as quickly as possible = ils
  sont venus le plus vite possible
  I did as much as possible = j'ai fait tout ce
  que j'ai pu

**post** (*British English*)
**1** *noun*
  the post (*the system*) = la poste
  (*the letters*) = le courrier
  has the post come yet? = est-ce que le
  courrier est arrivé?

**P**

**2** *verb*
  to post a letter = poster une lettre

**postbox** *noun* (*British English*)
  a postbox = une boîte aux lettres

**postcard** *noun*
  a postcard = une carte postale

**postcode** *noun* (*British English*)
  a postcode = un code postal

**poster** *noun*
  a poster (*giving information*) = une affiche
  (*used as a picture*) = un poster

**postman** *noun* ▶ 315 ⎮ (*British English*)
  a postman = un facteur

**post office** *noun*
  a post office = un bureau de poste

**postpone** *verb*
  to postpone a concert = reporter un
    concert
  let's postpone the party until next week
    = reportons la fête à la semaine
    prochaine

**pot** *noun*
• (*a container*)
  a pot = un pot
  to make a pot of tea = faire du thé
• (*a saucepan*)
  a pot = une casserole

**potato** *noun*
  a potato = une pomme de terre

**pottery** *noun*
  pottery = la poterie

**pound** *noun*
• (*the currency*)
  a pound = une livre
• (*the measurement*)
  a pound ≈ une livre
  | **!** Note that a pound = 453.6 g.

  two pounds of apples ≈ un kilo de
    pommes

**pour** *verb*
• (*from a container*) = verser
  to pour milk into a bowl = verser du lait
    dans un bol
• (*to serve*) = servir
  to pour someone a vodka = servir une
    vodka à quelqu'un
• (*to flow*) = couler (à flots)
  the water was pouring into the kitchen
    = l'eau coulait dans la cuisine
• (*to escape*)
  there is smoke pouring out of the window
    = il y a de la fumée qui sort par la
    fenêtre
• (*to rain*)
  it's pouring (with rain) = il pleut à verse

• (*to enter or leave in large numbers*)
  to pour into the city = affluer dans la ville
  to pour out of the stadium = sortir en
    grand nombre du stade

**powder** *noun*
  a powder = une poudre

**power** *noun*
• (*control*)
  power = le pouvoir
  to be in power = être au pouvoir
• (*influence*)
  to have great power = avoir une grande
    influence
• (*electricity*)
  power = le courant

**practical** *adjective*
  = pratique

**practise** (*British English*), **practice** (*US
English*) *verb*
  (*at the piano, guitar*) = s'exercer (**!** + *être*)
  (*at a sport*) = s'entraîner (**!** + *être*)
  (*for a play, a concert*) = répéter
  to practise [the violin | one's French | a
    song …] = travailler [le violon | son français |
    une chanson …]

**praise** *verb*
  to praise someone (*when talking to
    someone else*) = faire l'éloge de
    quelqu'un
  (*when talking directly to someone*)
    = féliciter quelqu'un

**prawn** *noun* (*British English*)
  a prawn = une crevette rose

**prayer** *noun*
  a prayer = une prière

**precaution** *noun*
  a precaution = une précaution

**precious** *adjective*
  = précieux/précieuse

**precise** *adjective*
  = précis/précise

**prefer** *verb*
  = préférer, aimer mieux
  to prefer chocolate to vanilla = mieux
    aimer le chocolat que la vanille
  I'd prefer to phone = j'aimerais mieux
    téléphoner

**pregnant** *adjective*
  = enceinte

**prejudice** *noun*
  a prejudice = un préjugé

**prepare** *verb*
• (*to get something or someone ready*)
  = préparer
  to prepare pupils for an exam = préparer
    des élèves à un examen

- (to get ready)
  to prepare for [an exam | a trip | a party …]
  = se préparer pour [un examen | un voyage |
  une fête …]

**prepared** adjective
- (willing)
  to be prepared to wait = être prêt/prête à
  attendre
- (ready)
  to be prepared for an exam = être
  prêt/prête pour un examen

**prescription** noun
  a prescription = une ordonnance

**present**
**1** noun
- (a gift)
  a present = un cadeau
  to give someone a present = offrir un
  cadeau à quelqu'un
- (now)
  the present = le présent
  I'm staying here for the present = je reste
  ici pour l'instant
**2** verb
- (to give)
  to present a prize to someone = remettre
  un prix à quelqu'un
- (on radio or TV)
  to present a programme = présenter une
  émission

**president** noun ▶ 315 |
  a president = un président/une présidente

**press**
**1** verb
  = appuyer sur
  to press the bell = appuyer sur la sonnette
  to press (oneself) against the wall = se
  plaquer contre le mur
**2** noun
  the press = la presse

**pressure** noun
  pressure = la pression
  to put pressure on someone = faire
  pression sur quelqu'un

**pretend** verb
  = faire semblant
  he's pretending to be annoyed = il fait
  semblant d'être vexé

**pretty**
**1** adjective
  = joli/jolie
**2** adverb
  = assez
  that's pretty good = ce n'est pas mal du
  tout*

**prevent** verb
  to prevent a war = éviter une guerre
  to prevent someone from [working | having
  fun | sleeping …] = empêcher quelqu'un
  de [travailler | s'amuser | dormir …]

**previous** adjective
  = précédent/précédente

**price** noun
  a price = un prix

**pride** noun
- pride = la fierté
- (self-respect)
  pride = l'amour-propre (masculine)

**priest** noun ▶ 315 |
  a priest = un prêtre

**primary school** noun
  a primary school = une école primaire

**primary school teacher** noun ▶ 315 |
  a primary school teacher = un
  instituteur/une institutrice

**prime minister** noun ▶ 315 |
  the prime minister = le premier ministre

**prince** noun
  a prince = un prince

**princess** noun
  a princess = une princesse

**principal** noun
  a principal (in a senior school) = un
  proviseur
  (in a junior school) = un directeur/une
  directrice

**print**
**1** verb
  = imprimer
  to print a book = imprimer un livre
**2** noun
- (of a photo)
  a print = une épreuve
- (of a finger, a foot)
  a print = une empreinte

**printer** noun
  a printer = un imprimeur

**priority** noun
  a priority = une priorité

**prison** noun
  a prison = une prison
  to put someone in prison = mettre
  quelqu'un en prison

**prisoner** noun
  a prisoner = un prisonnier/une
  prisonnière
  to be taken prisoner = être fait
  prisonnier/faite prisonnière

**private**
**1** adjective
- (personal) = privé/privée
  my private life = ma vie privée
- (not run by the state) = privé/privée
  a private school = une école privée
**2 in private** = en privé

**prize** noun
  a prize = un prix

**probably** adverb
  = probablement

P

**problem** *noun*
  a problem = un problème
  to cause a problem = poser un problème

**process** *noun*
  a process = un processus
  to be in the process of writing a letter
    = être en train d'écrire une lettre

**produce**
**1** *verb*
• (*to make*) = produire
• (*to create*)
  to produce a film = produire un film
  to produce a play = mettre en scène une
    pièce
**2** *noun*
  produce = les produits (*masculine plural*)

**product** *noun*
  a product = un produit

**production** *noun*
  production (*of food*) = la production
  (*of machinery, cars*) = la fabrication

**profession** *noun*
  a profession = une profession

**professional** *adjective*
  = professionnel/professionnelle

**professor** *noun* ▶ 315 |
  a professor = un professeur d'université

**profit** *noun*
  a profit = un bénéfice

**program**
**1** *noun*
• (*for a computer*)
  a program = un programme
• (*US English*) ▶ **programme**
**2** *verb*
  = programmer

**programme** (*British English*), **program**
(*US English*)
**1** *noun*
• (*on radio, TV*)
  a programme = une émission
  a programme about China = une émission
    sur la Chine
• (*for a play, a concert*)
  a programme = un programme
**2** *verb*
  = programmer

**progress** *noun*
  progress = le progrès
  to make progress = faire des progrès

**project** *noun*
  a project (*at school*) = un dossier

**promise**
**1** *verb*
  = promettre
  to promise [to write | to repay a loan | to say
    nothing ...] = promettre [d'écrire | de
    rembourser un prêt | de ne rien dire ...]

**2** *noun*
  a promise = une promesse

**pronounce** *verb*
  = prononcer

**proof** *noun*
  proof = une preuve

**properly** *adverb*
  = correctement

**property** *noun*
  property = la propriété

**protect** *verb*
  = protéger
  to protect oneself = se protéger (**!** + *être*)

**protest** *verb*
• (*to complain*) = protester
• (*to demonstrate*) = manifester

**protester** *noun*
  a protester = un manifestant/une
    manifestante

**proud** *adjective*
  = fier/fière
  she's proud of her work = elle est fière de
    son travail

**prove** *verb*
  = prouver

**provide** *verb*
  to provide meals = fournir des repas
  to provide work for people = fournir du
    travail aux gens
  to provide a transport service = assurer
    un service de transport

**provided** *conjunction*
  I'll lend you my car provided you pay me
    = je te prête ma voiture à condition que
    tu me paies
  **!** *Note that the subjunctive is used after* à
  condition que.

**psychiatrist** *noun* ▶ 315 |
  a psychiatrist = un psychiatre/une
    psychiatre

**psychologist** *noun* ▶ 315 |
  a psychologist = un psychologue/une
    psychologue

**pub** *noun* (*British English*)
  a pub = un pub

**public**
**1** *noun*
  the public = le public
**2** *adjective*
  a public park = un jardin public
  a public library = une bibliothèque
    municipale
**3 in public** = en public

**public holiday** *noun*
  a public holiday = un jour férié

# Shops, trades, and professions

## Work and Jobs

| | |
|---|---|
| *what does she do?* | = qu'est-ce qu'elle fait comme métier? |
| *what do you do for a living?* | = qu'est-ce que vous faites dans la vie? |

- There are various ways of saying what someone works at in French. In this area, the major difference between the two languages is the *absence of article* in French, whereas in the singular English always has **a**.

Note the following examples:

| | |
|---|---|
| *he's got a job as **a** mechanic* | = il travaille comme mécanicien |
| *to work as **a** translator* | = travailler comme traducteur / traductrice |
| *Paul is **a** dentist* | = Paul est dentiste |
| *I want to be **a** policeman* | = je voudrais devenir agent de police |

- The only case where you would use the article **un / une** or **des** in the plural would be in combination with **c'est** or **ce sont**, so:

| | |
|---|---|
| *she is a teacher* | = elle est professeur |
| but | = **c'est** un professeur* |
| *she's a judge* | = elle est juge |
| but | = **c'est** un juge* |
| *they are all doctors* | = ils sont tous médecins |
| but | = **ce sont** tous **des** médecins* |

- When using an adjective to describe what kind of doctor / teacher / worker a person is, you must use **c'est un / une** ...

| | |
|---|---|
| *she's a good journalist* | = c'est une bonne journaliste |
| *he's a bad teacher* | = c'est un mauvais professeur |
| *he's an excellent chef* | = c'est un chef excellent |

* Note that some professions do not have a feminine form and the article will always be masculine as in the examples using **professeur, juge, médecin, ministre,** ...

## Shops

In English you can say *at the baker's* or *at the baker's shop*, French also has this possibility but the translation for *at* will also differ depending on what follows:

| | |
|---|---|
| *at the baker's* | = **chez** le boulanger |
| *at the baker's shop* | = à la boulangerie |

**chez** means *at the house or premises of* and is used with the French word for the particular tradesman or professional:

| | |
|---|---|
| *I'm going to the chemist's* | = je vais **chez** le pharmacien |
| *she's gone to the hairdresser's* | = elle est allée **chez** le coiffeur |
| *I've got an appointment at the dentist's* | = j'ai rendezvous **chez** le dentiste |
| *is he at the doctor's?* | = est-ce qu'il est **chez** le médecin? |

However you can also use **à la / au** (or **à l'** + *vowel or mute h*) with the French word for a shop:

| | |
|---|---|
| *I'm going to the chemist's* | = je vais **à la** pharmacie |
| *he's at the grocer's* | = il est **à l'**épicerie |
| *they've gone to the baker's* | = ils sont allés **à la** boulangerie |

So in French you could have translations using either **à la** or **chez** in the following example:

| | |
|---|---|
| *go to the butcher's* | = va **à la** boucherie |
| | = va **chez** le boucher |

---

**public transport** *noun*
public transport = les transports en commun

❗ *Note that* transports *is masculine plural.*

**pudding** *noun* (British English)
a pudding = un dessert

**puddle** *noun*
a puddle = une flaque

**pull** *verb*
* to pull = tirer
  to pull someone's hair = tirer les cheveux
  de quelqu'un
  to pull (on) a rope = tirer sur une corde
* (*to move*)
  to pull the piano into the hall = traîner le
  piano dans l'entrée
  to pull someone away from the door
  = éloigner quelqu'un de la porte
* (*to take out*)
  to pull a handkerchief out of one's pocket
  = tirer un mouchoir de sa poche
  to pull someone out of the river = sortir
  quelqu'un de la rivière
* to pull a face (*British English*) = faire une
  grimace
**pull down**
* (*to knock down*) = démolir
* (*to lower*) = baisser
**pull out**
  to pull a tooth out = arracher une dent
**pull up**
* (*to stop*) = s'arrêter (**!** + *être*)
* (*to remove*)
  to pull up the flowers = arracher les fleurs
* to pull up one's socks = remonter ses
  chaussettes

**pullover** *noun*
  a pullover = un pull

**pump** *noun*
  a pump = une pompe
  a bicycle pump = une pompe à bicyclette
**pump up** = gonfler

**pumpkin** *noun*
  a pumpkin = une citrouille

**punch** *verb*
  = donner des coups de poing
  she punched him in the face = elle lui a
  donné un coup de poing dans la figure

**puncture** *noun*
  a puncture = une crevaison

**punish** *verb*
  = punir

**pupil** *noun*
  a pupil = un élève/une élève

**puppet** *noun*
  a puppet = une marionnette

**puppy** *noun*
  a puppy = un chiot

**pure** *adjective*
  = pur/pure

**purple** *adjective* ▶ **213**
  = violet/violette

**purpose**
**1** *noun*
  a purpose = un but
**2 on purpose** = exprès
  you did it on purpose! = tu l'as fait exprès!

**purse** *noun*
* (*for money*)
  a purse = un porte-monnaie
* (*US English*) (*a handbag*)
  a purse = un sac à main

**push** *verb*
* to push = pousser
  to push a car = pousser une voiture
  to push someone down the stairs
  = pousser quelqu'un dans l'escalier
  to push someone out of the way = écarter
  quelqu'un
  to push past someone = bousculer
  quelqu'un
* (*to sell*) = vendre
  to push drugs = vendre de la drogue

**pushchair** *noun* (*British English*)
  a pushchair = une poussette

**pusher** *noun*
  a pusher = un revendeur/une revendeuse
  de drogue

**put** *verb*
  = mettre
  to put the cards on the table = mettre les
  cartes sur la table
  don't put sugar in my coffee = ne mets pas
  de sucre dans mon café
  to put someone in prison = mettre
  quelqu'un en prison
  to put someone in a bad mood = mettre
  quelqu'un de mauvaise humeur
**put away** = ranger
**put back**
* (*to return to its place*) = remettre
  to put a book back on a shelf = remettre
  un livre sur une étagère
* (*to change the time*)
  to put the clocks back = retarder les
  pendules
**put down**
* (*on a surface*) = poser
  put your cases down here, Laurence
  = pose tes valises ici, Laurence
* (*when phoning*)
  to put the phone down = raccrocher
* (*British English*) (*to give an injection to*)
  = piquer
  our dog had to be put down = on a dû
  faire piquer notre chien
**put forward** = avancer
  to put the clocks forward = avancer les
  pendules
**put off**
* (*to delay*)
  we'll have to put the party off till next
  week = il va falloir reporter la fête à la
  semaine prochaine
* (*to switch off*) = éteindre
**put on**
* (*when dressing*) = mettre
  to put jeans on = mettre un jean

# Quantities

Note the use of **en** (*of it* or *of them*) in the following examples. This word must be included when the thing you are talking about is not expressed. However, **en** is not needed when the commodity is specified (*there is a lot of butter* = il y a beaucoup de beurre):

## How much?

| | |
|---|---|
| *how much is there?* | = combien y **en** a-t-il? |
| *there's a lot* | = il y **en** a beaucoup |
| *there's not much* | = il n'y **en** a pas beaucoup |
| *there's two kilos* | = il y **en** a deux kilos |
| *how much sugar have you?* | = combien de sucre as-tu? |
| *I've got a lot* | = j'**en** ai beaucoup |
| *I haven't got (very) much* | = je n'**en** ai pas beaucoup |
| *I've got two kilos* | = j'**en** ai deux kilos |

## How many?

| | |
|---|---|
| *how many are there?* | = combien y **en** a-t-il?* |
| *there are a lot* | = il y **en** a beaucoup* |
| *there aren't many* | = il n'y **en** a pas beaucoup* |
| *there are twenty* | = il y **en** a vingt |
| *how many apples have you?* | = combien de pommes as-tu?* |
| | tu as combien de pommes? |
| *I've got a lot* | = j'**en** ai beaucoup |
| *I haven't got many* | = je n'**en** ai pas beaucoup |

## Comparisons

| | |
|---|---|
| *I've got twenty* | = j'**en** ai vingt |
| *Tim has got more than Tom* | = Tim **en** a plus que Tom |
| *Tim has got more money than Tom* | = Tim a plus d'argent que Tom |
| *much more than* | = beaucoup plus que |
| *a little more than* | = un peu plus que |
| *Tim has got more apples than Tom* | = Tim a plus de pommes que Tom |
| *many more apples than Tom* | = beaucoup plus de pommes que Tom |
| *a few more apples than Tom* | = quelques pommes de plus que Tom |
| *a few more people than yesterday* | = quelques personnes de plus qu'hier |
| *Tom has got less than Tim* | = Tom **en** a moins que Tim |
| *Tom has got less money than Tim* | = Tom a moins d'argent que Tim |
| *much less than* | = beaucoup moins que |
| *a little less than* | = un peu moins que |
| *Tom has got fewer than Tim* | = Tom **en** a moins que Tim |
| *Tom has got fewer apples than Tim* | = Tom a moins de pommes que Tim |
| *many fewer than* | = beaucoup moins que |

## Relative quantities

| | |
|---|---|
| *how many are there to the kilo?* | = combien y **en** a-t-il au kilo?* |
| *there are ten to the kilo* | = il y **en** a dix au kilo* |
| *how many do you get for ten euros?* | = combien peut-on **en** avoir pour dix euros? |
| *you get five for ten euros* | = il y **en** a cinq pour dix euros |
| *how much does it cost a litre?* | = combien coûte le litre? |
| *it costs £5 a litre* | = ça coûte cinq livres le litre |
| *how much do apples cost a kilo?* | = combien coûte le kilo de pommes? |
| *how many glasses do you get to the bottle?* | = combien y a-t-il de verres par bouteille? |
| *you get six glasses to the bottle* | = il y a six verres par bouteille |

* Note the use of a singular verb in French in these examples.

- (*to switch on*)
  to put the heating on = allumer le
      chauffage
  to put the kettle on = mettre la bouilloire à
      chauffer
  to put a CD on = mettre un disque
      compact
- to put on weight = prendre du poids
- (*to organize, to produce*) = monter
  to put on a play = monter une pièce

**put out**
- to put out a cigarette = éteindre une
      cigarette
- (*to take out*) = sortir
  to put the bins out = sortir les
      poubelles

**put up**
- (*to lift*)
  to put one's hair up = remonter ses
      cheveux
  to put up one's hand (*in class*) ≈ lever le
      doigt
- (*to attach*)
  to put a sign up = mettre une pancarte
- (*when camping*)
  to put up a tent = planter une tente
- (*British English*) (*to raise*) = augmenter
  to put the rent up = augmenter le loyer
- (*to give someone a place to stay*)
  = héberger

**put up with** = supporter

**puzzle** *noun*
  a puzzle = un casse-tête

**pyjamas** *noun* (*British English*)
  pyjamas = un pyjama (*singular*)

**qualified** *adjective*
- (*having studied*) = diplômé/diplômée
- (*having experience, skills*)
  = qualifié/qualifiée

**quality** *noun*
  quality = la qualité

**quantity** *noun* ▶ 317 |
  a quantity = une quantité

**quarrel**
**1** *noun*
  a quarrel = une dispute
**2** *verb*
  = se disputer (**!** + *être*)

---

**✗** in informal situations

**quarter**
**1** *noun*
  a quarter = un quart
  a quarter of an hour = un quart d'heure
  to cut the tomatoes in quarters = couper
      les tomates en quatre
**2** *pronoun*
- (*when talking about quantities,
  numbers*) ▶ 317 |
  a quarter of the population can't read
      = un quart de la population ne sait pas
      lire
- (*when talking about time*) ▶ 211 |
  an hour and a quarter = une heure et
      quart
  it's (a) quarter past five = il est cinq
      heures et quart

**quay** *noun*
  a quay = un quai

**queen** *noun*
  a queen = une reine

**question**
**1** *noun*
- (*a request for information*)
  a question = une question
  to ask someone a question = poser une
      question à quelqu'un
- (*a problem, a matter*)
  a question = un problème
**2** *verb*
  = interroger

**queue** (*British English*)
**1** *noun*
  a queue (*of people*) = une queue, une file
      d'attente
  (*of cars, trucks*) = une file
  to join the queue = se mettre à la queue
**2** *verb*
  = faire la queue

**quick** *adjective*
  = rapide
  a quick answer = une réponse rapide
  it's quicker to go by train = c'est plus
      rapide d'y aller en train
  it's the quickest way [to get to London | to
  save money | to make friends ...] = c'est le
  moyen le plus rapide [d'aller à Londres | de
  gagner de l'argent | de se faire des amis ...]

**quickly** *adverb*
  = vite, rapidement

**quiet**
**1** *adjective*
- (*silent*) = silencieux/silencieuse
  to keep quiet = garder le silence
  to go quiet = se taire (**!** + *être*)
  be quiet! = taisez-vous!
- (*not talkative*) = réservé/réservée
- (*calm*) = tranquille
  it's a quiet little village = c'est un petit
      village tranquille

**2** *noun*
quiet = le silence
quiet please! = silence, s'il vous plaît!

**quietly** *adverb*
to speak quietly = parler doucement
to [play | sit | read ...] quietly = [jouer |
s'asseoir | lire ...] en silence

**quit** *verb*
• *(to resign)* = démissionner
• *(US English) (to give up)*
to quit [smoking | drinking | working ...]
= arrêter de [fumer | boire | travailler ...]

**quite** *adverb*
• *(rather)* = assez
they go back to France quite often = ils
rentrent assez souvent en France
I quite like Chinese food = j'aime assez la
cuisine chinoise
she earns quite a lot of money = elle
gagne pas mal* d'argent
• *(completely)*
I'm not quite ready yet = je ne suis pas
encore tout à fait prêt
you're quite right = vous avez entièrement
raison
are you quite sure? = en êtes-vous
certain?
• *(exactly)*
'is it true?'—'not quite' = 'est-ce que c'est
vrai?'—'pas exactement'
I don't quite know what he does = je ne
sais pas exactement ce qu'il fait

**quiz** *noun*
a quiz = un jeu de questions-réponses

# Rr

**rabbit** *noun*
a rabbit = un lapin

**rabies** *noun* ▶ 266 |
rabies = la rage

**race**
**1** *noun*
*(a contest)*
a race = une course
to have a race = faire une course
*(for horse-racing)*
the races = les courses *(feminine)*
**2** *verb*
*(to compete with)*
to race (against) someone = faire la
course avec quelqu'un
I'll race you to the car = on fait la course
jusqu'à la voiture
*(to take part in a contest)* = courir

**racehorse** *noun*
a racehorse = un cheval de course

**racetrack** *noun*
a racetrack *(for horses)* = un champ de
courses
*(for cars)* = un circuit

**racism** *noun*
racism = le racisme

**racket, racquet** *noun*
a racket = une raquette

**radiator** *noun*
a radiator = un radiateur

**radio** *noun*
a radio = une radio
on the radio = à la radio

**radio station** *noun*
a radio station = une station de radio

**rage** *noun*
rage = la rage, la colère
to fly into a rage = se mettre en colère

**raid** *verb*
to raid a bank = attaquer une banque
the police raided the building = la police a
fait une descente dans le bâtiment

**rail** *noun*
*(for holding on to)*
a rail = une rampe, une main courante
*(for trains)*
rails = les rails *(masculine)*

**railway** *(British English)*, **railroad** *(US
English) noun*
*(a track)*
a railway = une voie ferrée
*(the rail system)*
the railway = le chemin de fer

**railway line** *noun (British English)*
a railway line = une ligne de chemin de
fer

**railway station** *noun (British English)*
a railway station = une gare

**rain**
**1** *noun*
rain = la pluie
to stand in the rain = rester sous la pluie
**2** *verb*
= pleuvoir
it's raining = il pleut

**rainbow** *noun*
a rainbow = un arc-en-ciel

**raincoat** *noun*
a raincoat = un imperméable

**raise** *verb*
*(to lift)* = lever
*(to increase)* = augmenter
to raise prices = augmenter les prix
*(in anger)*
to raise one's voice = hausser le ton

**R**

*(to talk about)*
**to raise a subject** = soulever une question
*(to bring up)*
**to raise children** = élever des enfants

**range** *noun*
*(a selection)*
**a range** *(of goods, prices)* = une gamme
*(of activities, school subjects)* = un grand choix
*(of mountains)*
**a range** = une chaîne
*(US English) (for cooking)*
**a range** = une cuisinière

**rare** *adjective*
*(not common)* = rare
*(very slightly cooked)* = saignant/saignante

**rarely** *adverb*
= rarement

**rasher** *noun (British English)*
**a rasher (of bacon)** = une tranche (de bacon)

**raspberry** *noun*
**a raspberry** = une framboise

**rat** *noun*
**a rat** = un rat

**rather** *adverb*
*(when saying what one would prefer)*
**I'd rather** [leave | stay here | read the paper …] = j'aimerais mieux [partir | rester ici | lire le journal …]
**I'd rather you came with me** = j'aimerais mieux que tu viennes avec moi
**!** *Note that the subjunctive is used after j'aimerais mieux que.*

*(quite)* = plutôt
**I think he's rather nice** = je le trouve plutôt sympathique

**raw** *adjective*
= cru/crue

**razor** *noun*
**a razor** = un rasoir

**razor blade** *noun*
**a razor blade** = une lame de rasoir

**reach** *verb*
*(to arrive at)* = atteindre
**they reached the town at midnight** = ils ont atteint la ville à minuit
*(to be delivered to)* = parvenir à (**!** + *être*)
**the letter never reached him** = la lettre ne lui est pas parvenue
*(by stretching)*
**to reach up** = lever le bras
**I can't reach the shelf** = je n'arrive pas à atteindre l'étagère
*(to come to)* = arriver à (**!** + *être*)
**to reach a decision** = arriver à une décision
*(to contact by phone)* = joindre
**I can be reached at this number** = on peut me joindre à ce numéro

**reach out** = tendre le bras

**react** *verb*
= réagir

**read** *verb*
= lire
**the writing is difficult to read** = l'écriture est difficile à lire
**to read to someone** = faire la lecture à quelqu'un

**read out**
**to read out the names** = lire les noms à haute voix

**read through** *(once)* = lire
*(a second time)* = relire

**reading** *noun*
**reading** = la lecture

**ready** *adjective*
*(prepared)* = prêt/prête
**are you ready to leave?** = est-ce que vous êtes prêts à partir?
**to get ready** = se préparer (**!** + *être*)
**to get a meal ready** = préparer le repas
*(happy)* = prêt/prête
**I'm ready to help them** = je suis prêt à les aider

**real** *adjective*
*(not imagined)* = réel/réelle
*(not artificial)* = vrai/vraie (**!** *before the noun*)
**are they real diamonds?** = est-ce que ce sont de vrais diamants?
**it's a real shame** = c'est vraiment dommage

**reality** *noun*
**reality** = la réalité

**realize** *verb*
= se rendre compte (**!** + *être*)
**I didn't realize (that) he was your boss** = je ne me suis pas rendu compte que c'était ton patron

**really** *adverb*
= vraiment
**it's really easy to make** = c'est vraiment facile à faire
**what really happened?** = qu'est-ce qui s'est réellement passé?
**really?** = c'est vrai?

**rear**
**1** *noun*
**the rear** = l'arrière *(masculine)*
**2** *verb*
= élever

**reason** *noun*
**a reason** = une raison
**that's a good reason to learn French** = c'est une bonne raison d'apprendre le français
**is there any reason why you shouldn't drive?** = pourquoi est-ce que vous ne devriez pas conduire?
**tell me the reason why** = dis-moi pourquoi

**reassure** verb
= rassurer

**receipt** noun
a receipt = un reçu
a till receipt = un ticket de caisse

**receive** verb
(to get) = recevoir
we received a letter from the teacher
= nous avons reçu une lettre du
professeur
(to meet) = accueillir, recevoir
to be well received = être bien reçu/reçue

**recent** adjective
= récent/récente

**recently** adverb
= récemment

**reception** noun
(in a hotel, a hospital, a company)
the reception = la réception
ask at (the) reception = adressez-vous à la
réception
(a formal event)
a reception = une réception

**receptionist** noun ▶ 315 |
a receptionist = un réceptionniste/une
réceptionniste

**recharge** verb
= recharger

**recipe** noun
a recipe = une recette

**recognize** verb
= reconnaître

**recommend** verb
= recommander

**record**
**1** noun
(information)
the records (historical, public) = les
archives (feminine)
(personal, medical) = le dossier (singular)
(for playing music)
a record = un disque
(in sport)
a record = un record
to break the world record = battre le
record du monde
**2** verb
= enregistrer

**recorder** noun ▶ 290 |
a recorder = une flûte à bec

**recover** verb
= se remettre (! + être)
to recover from an illness = se remettre
d'une maladie

**recycle** verb
= recycler

**red** adjective ▶ 213 |
= rouge
to go red, to turn red = rougir
to have red hair = avoir les cheveux roux

**red-haired** adjective
= roux/rousse

**reduce** verb
to reduce prices = baisser les prix
to reduce the number of employees
= réduire le nombre d'employés
to reduce speed = ralentir

**reduction** noun
a reduction = une réduction

**redundant** adjective (British English)
to be made redundant = être
licencié/licenciée pour raisons
économiques

**referee** noun ▶ 315 |
a referee = un arbitre

**reflection** noun
a reflection = un reflet

**refreshing** adjective
= rafraîchissant/rafraîchissante

**refrigerator** noun
a refrigerator = un réfrigérateur, un
frigidaire

**refugee** noun
a refugee = un réfugié/une réfugiée

**refuse¹** verb
= refuser
to refuse [to listen | to stop | to pay …]
= refuser [d'écouter | de s'arrêter | de payer …]

**refuse²** noun (British English)
refuse = les ordures (feminine plural)

**regards** noun
give her my regards = transmettez-lui
mes amitiés

**region** noun
a region = une région

**regional** adjective
= régional/régionale

**register** noun
the register = le cahier d'appel
to take the register = faire l'appel

**regret** verb
= regretter
I regret changing my mind = je regrette
d'avoir changé d'avis
he regrets that he can't come = il regrette
de ne pas pouvoir venir
I regret that he can't come = je regrette
qu'il ne puisse pas venir
! Note that the subjunctive is used after
regretter que.

**regular** adjective
regular = régulier/régulière

**R**

**regularly** adverb
= régulièrement

**rehearsal** noun
a rehearsal = une répétition

**rehearse** verb
= répéter

**reject** verb
to reject someone's advice = rejeter les
conseils de quelqu'un
to reject a candidate = refuser un
candidat

**relationship** noun
a relationship = une relation, des relations
(plural)
to have a good relationship = bien
s'entendre (**!** + être)
she has a good relationship with her
parents = elle s'entend bien avec ses
parents

**relative** noun
a relative = un parent/une parente
my relatives = ma famille

**relax** verb
= se détendre (**!** + être)

**relaxed** adjective
= détendu/détendue,
décontracté/décontractée

**relay race** verb
a relay race = une course de relais

**release** verb
= libérer

**reliable** adjective
a reliable person = une personne digne de
confiance
a reliable car = une voiture fiable

**relieved** adjective
= soulagé/soulagée

**religion** noun
religion = la religion

**religious education, RE** (British
English) noun
religious education = l'instruction
religieuse
| **!** Note that instruction is feminine.

**rely** verb
(to depend on) = dépendre de
(to count on) = compter sur
can we rely on you? = est-ce qu'on peut
compter sur toi?

**remain** verb
= rester

**remark** noun
a remark = une remarque, une réflexion

**remarkable** adjective
= remarquable

**remember** verb
= se souvenir (**!** + être)
do you remember her? = est-ce que tu te
souviens d'elle?
I remember writing down the address = je
me souviens d'avoir noté l'adresse
to remember to [write the letter | water the
plants | turn off the lights …] = penser à
[écrire la lettre | arroser les plantes | éteindre les
lumières …]

**remind** verb
= rappeler
to remind someone to buy milk = rappeler
à quelqu'un d'acheter du lait
she reminds me of my sister = elle me
rappelle ma sœur

**remote control** noun
a remote control = une télécommande

**remove** verb
= enlever
to remove the stains from a carpet
= enlever les taches d'une moquette

**rent**
**1** verb
= louer
to rent an apartment = louer un
appartement
**2** noun
a rent = un loyer
**rent out** = louer

**repair** verb
= réparer
to have a bicycle repaired = faire réparer
un vélo

**repeat** verb
(to say again) = répéter
to repeat a year = redoubler une classe

**replace** verb
= remplacer
they replaced the fence with a wall = ils
ont remplacé la clôture par un mur

**reply**
**1** verb
= répondre
to reply to a letter = répondre à une lettre
**2** noun
a reply = une réponse

**report**
**1** verb
(to tell about) = signaler
to report an accident = signaler un
accident
(in the news)
to report on an event = faire un reportage
sur un événement
(to complain about)
to report the noise = se plaindre du bruit
**2** noun
(in the news)
a report = un communiqué
(longer) = un reportage

(an official document)
a report = un rapport
(British English) (from school)
a (school) report = un bulletin scolaire

**report card** noun (US English)
a report card = un bulletin scolaire

**reporter** noun ▶ 315 |
a reporter = un journaliste/une
journaliste, un reporter

**represent** verb
= représenter

**republic** noun
a republic = une république

**request** noun
a request = une demande

**rescue** verb
(from danger) = sauver

**resemble** verb
= ressembler à
to resemble each other = se ressembler
(! + être)

**resent** verb
to resent someone = en vouloir à
quelqu'un
he resents her for winning = il lui en veut
d'avoir gagné

**reservation** noun
a reservation = une réservation

**reserve** verb
= réserver

**resign** verb
= démissionner

**resist** verb
= résister

**respect**
1 verb
= respecter
2 noun
respect = le respect
out of respect = par respect

**responsibility** noun
responsibility = la responsabilité

**responsible** adjective
(the cause of) = responsable
to be responsible for the damage = être
responsable des dégâts
(in charge) = responsable
to be responsible for organizing a trip
= être chargé/chargée d'organiser une
sortie

**rest**
1 noun
(what is left)
the rest = le reste
we spent the rest of the day in the garden
= on a passé le reste de la journée dans
le jardin

(time to recover)
rest = le repos
to need rest = avoir besoin de repos
(a break)
a rest = une pause
to have a rest = se reposer (! + être)
2 verb
= se reposer (! + être)

**restaurant** noun
a restaurant = un restaurant

**result** noun
a result = un résultat
the exam results = les résultats des
examens
as a result of an accident = à la suite d'un
accident

**résumé** noun (US English)
a résumé = un CV, un curriculum vitae

**retire** verb
= prendre sa retraite

**return** verb
(to go back) = retourner (! + être)
(to come back) = revenir (! + être)
(from abroad, to one's home) = rentrer
(! + être)
(to give back) = rendre
can you return my book? = est-ce que tu
peux me rendre mon livre?
(to send back) = renvoyer
to return goods = renvoyer des articles
(to start again)
to return to work = reprendre le travail
to return to school = reprendre l'école

**return ticket** noun
a return ticket = un billet aller-retour

**reveal** verb
to reveal a secret = révéler un secret

**revenge** noun
revenge = la vengeance
to get one's revenge = se venger (! + être)

**revolution** noun
a revolution = une révolution

**reward**
1 noun
a reward = une récompense
2 verb
= récompenser

**rewind** verb
= rembobiner

**rhinoceros, rhino** noun
a rhinoceros = un rhinocéros

**rhythm** noun
rhythm = le rythme

**rib** noun ▶ 201 |
a rib = une côte

**rice** noun
rice = le riz

**R**

**rich** *adjective*
= riche
to get rich = s'enrichir (**!** + *être*)

**rid**: **to get rid of** *verb*
= se débarrasser de (**!** + *être*)

**ride**
**1** *verb* ▶ **248**|
to ride, to go riding = faire du cheval
to ride a horse = monter à cheval
to be riding a bike = rouler à vélo
**2** *noun*
to go for a ride (*in a car, on a bike*) = aller
faire un tour
(*on a horse*) = aller faire une promenade à
cheval

**ridiculous** *adjective*
= ridicule

**rifle** *noun*
a rifle = un fusil

**right**
**1** *adjective*
(*not left*) = droit/droite
his right hand = sa main droite
(*honest, good*) = bien
it's not right to steal = ce n'est pas bien de
voler
to do the right thing = faire ce qu'il faut
(*correct*) = bon/bonne (**!** *before the noun*)
the right answer = la bonne réponse
is this the right direction? = est-ce que
c'est la bonne direction?
you're right = tu as raison
that's right = c'est ça
**2** *noun*
(*the direction*)
the right = la droite
the first street on the right = la première
rue à droite
(*what one is entitled to*)
a right = un droit
to have a right to education = avoir droit à
l'instruction
human rights = les droits de l'homme
**3** *adverb*
= à droite
to turn right = tourner à droite

**right-click** *verb*
= cliquer à droite

**ring**
**1** *verb*
(*British English*) (*to phone*) = appeler
to ring for a taxi = appeler un taxi
(*to make a sound*) = sonner
to ring the bell = sonner
the doorbell rang = on a sonné à la porte
**2** *noun*
(*a piece of jewellery*)
a ring = une bague
a wedding ring = une alliance
(*a circle*)
a ring = un cercle
(*in a circus*)
the ring = la piste

**ringtone** *noun*
a ringtone = une sonnerie

**rinse** *verb*
= rincer

**ripe** *adjective*
= mûr/mûre

**rise** *verb*
(*if it's smoke, water*) = monter (**!** + *être*)
(*if it's a price*) = augmenter
(*if it's a plane*) = s'élever (**!** + *être*)
(*if it's the sun or moon*) = se lever (**!** + *être*)

**risk**
**1** *noun*
a risk = un risque
**2** *verb*
= risquer
to risk losing one's job = risquer de perdre
son travail

**river** *noun*
a river = une rivière
(*flowing into the sea*) = un fleuve

**riverbank** *noun*
a riverbank = une berge

**road** *noun*
a road = une route
the road to London = la route de Londres

**road sign** *noun*
a road sign = un panneau de signalisation

**roadworks** *noun*
roadworks = les travaux (*masculine*)

**roar** *verb*
(*if it's a lion*) = rugir
(*if it's a person*) = hurler
(*if it's an engine*) = vrombir

**roast**
**1** *verb*
= rôtir
**2** *adjective*
= rôti/rôtie
to eat roast beef = manger du rôti de bœuf
**3** *noun*
a roast = un rôti

**rob** *verb*
to rob someone = voler quelqu'un
to rob a bank = dévaliser une banque

**robbery** *noun*
a robbery = un vol

**robin** *noun*
a robin = un rouge-gorge

**robot** *noun*
a robot = un robot

**rock** *noun*
(*the material*)
rock = la roche
(*a large stone*)
a rock = un rocher
(*music*)
rock = le rock

**rock climbing** *noun* ▶ 248 |
rock climbing = la varappe

**rocket** *noun*
a rocket = une fusée

**role** *noun*
a role = un rôle

**roll**
**1** *verb*
= rouler
the ball rolled under a car = le ballon a
roulé sous une voiture
to roll the pastry into a ball = faire une
boule de la pâte
**2** *noun*
(*of paper, cloth, plastic*)
a roll = un rouleau
a roll of film = une pellicule
(*bread*)
a roll = un petit pain
(*US English*) (*at school*)
to call the roll = faire l'appel
**roll about, roll around** (*if it's an object*)
= rouler
**roll over** = se retourner (**!** + *être*)
**roll up** = enrouler
to roll up a newspaper = rouler un journal

**roller coaster** *noun*
a roller coaster = des montagnes russes
**!** *Note that* montagnes *is feminine plural.*

**roller-skate** *noun*
a roller-skate = un patin à roulettes

**roller-skating** *noun* ▶ 248 |
roller-skating = le patin à roulettes

**Romania** *noun* ▶ 218 |
Romania = la Roumanie

**romantic** *adjective*
= romantique

**roof** *noun*
a roof = un toit

**room** *noun*
a room = une pièce
(*for sleeping*) = une chambre
(*for working*) = un bureau
(*for teaching, holding meetings*) = une salle
(*space*)
room = la place
to make room = faire de la place
is there room? = est-ce qu'il y a de la
place?

**root** *noun*
a root = une racine

**rope** *noun*
a rope = une corde

**rose** *noun*
a rose = une rose

**rosy** *adjective*
= rose
to have rosy cheeks = avoir les joues roses

**rotten** *adjective*
= pourri/pourrie

**rough** *adjective*
(*not smooth*) = rugueux/rugueuse
to have rough skin = avoir la peau
rugueuse
(*not gentle*) = brutal/brutale
(*tough*) = dur/dure
to live in a rough area = habiter un
quartier dur
(*not exact, precise*)
a rough figure = un chiffre approximatif
(*difficult*) = dur/dure, difficile
to have a rough time = traverser une
période difficile
(*caused by bad weather*)
a rough sea = une mer agitée

**round**

**!** *Often* round *occurs in combinations with*
*verbs. For more information, see the note*
*at* around.

**1** *preposition*
= autour de
to be sitting round a table = être
assis/assises autour d'une table
to sail round the world = faire le tour du
monde en bateau
to go round Oxford = visiter Oxford
**2** *adverb*
to go round and round = tourner en rond
to go round to John's = passer chez John
to invite someone round = inviter
quelqu'un chez soi
**3** *noun*
a round (*in a quiz*) = une manche
(*in showjumping*) = un parcours
(*in boxing*) = un round
(*in an election*) = un tour
**4** *adjective*
= rond/ronde

**roundabout** *noun*
(*British English*) (*in a fair*)
a roundabout = un manège
(*for traffic*)
a roundabout = un rond-point

**route** *noun*
a route = un itinéraire
a bus route = une ligne d'autobus

**routine** *noun*
a routine = une routine

**row¹**
**1** *noun*
a row (*of people, trees*) = un rang
(*of houses, seats*) = une rangée
(*of cars*) = une file
the pupils were sitting in rows = les élèves
étaient assis en rangs
(*when talking about frequency*)
to be absent five days in a row = être
absent/absente cinq jours de suite

R

**2** *verb*
  (*as an activity*) = ramer
  (*as a sport*) ▶ **248** | = faire de l'aviron
  to row across a lake = traverser un lac à la
    rame

**row²** *noun* (*British English*)
  a row = une dispute
  to have a row with someone = se disputer
    avec quelqu'un

**rowing** *noun* ▶ **248** |
  rowing = l'aviron (*masculine*)

**rowing boat** (*British English*),
**rowboat** (*US English*) *noun*
  a rowing boat = un bateau à rames

**royal** *adjective*
  = royal/royale

**rub** *verb*
  to rub a stain = frotter une tache
  to rub one's eyes = se frotter les yeux
**rub out** (*British English*) = s'effacer
(**!** + *être*)
  to rub out a mistake = effacer une erreur

**rubber** *noun*
  (*the material*)
  rubber = le caoutchouc
  (*British English*) (*an eraser*)
  a rubber = une gomme

**rubbish** *noun* (*British English*)
  (*refuse*)
  rubbish (*household*) = les ordures
    (*feminine plural*)
  (*in the street, in a dump*) = les déchets
    (*masculine plural*)
  (*poor quality goods*)
  rubbish = la camelote✱

**rubbish bin** *noun* (*British English*)
  a rubbish bin = une poubelle

**rucksack** *noun*
  a rucksack = un sac à dos

**rude** *adjective*
  (*not polite*) = impoli/impolie
  to be rude to someone = être
    impoli/impolie envers quelqu'un
  (*vulgar*) = grossier/grossière
  a rude word = un gros mot

**rug** *noun*
  a rug = un tapis

**rugby** *noun* ▶ **248** |
  rugby = le rugby

**ruin**
**1** *verb*
  (*to spoil*) = gâcher
  to ruin a meal = gâcher un repas
  (*to damage*) = abîmer
  you'll ruin your shoes = tu vas abîmer tes
    chaussures

**2** *noun*
  a ruin = une ruine

**rule**
**1** *noun*
  a rule (*of a game, a language*) = une règle
  (*in a school, an organization*) = un
    règlement
  it's against the rules = c'est contraire au
    règlement
**2** *verb*
  (*if it's a leader*) = gouverner
  (*if it's a king, queen*) = régner sur
  (*if it's a party*) = diriger

**ruler** *noun*
  a ruler = une règle

**rumour** (*British English*), **rumor** (*US
English*) *noun*
  a rumour = une rumeur

**run**
**1** *verb*
  to run = courir
  to run after someone = courir après
    quelqu'un
  to run across the street = traverser la rue
    en courant
  to run a race = faire une course
  (*from danger*) = fuir, s'enfuir (**!** + *être*)
  (*to manage*) = diriger
  (*to work, to operate*) = marcher
  the car runs on unleaded petrol = la
    voiture marche à l'essence sans plomb
  the system is running well = le système
    marche bien
  (*to organize*) = organiser
  to run a competition = organiser un
    concours
  (*when talking about transport*) = circuler
  the buses don't run after midnight = les
    bus ne circulent pas après minuit
  (*to flow*) = couler
  (*to fill with water*)
  to run a bath = faire couler un bain
  (*to come off*) (*when talking about dyes*)
    = déteindre
  (*when talking about make-up*) = couler
  (*in an election*)
  to run for president = être
    candidat/candidate à la présidence
  (*other uses*)
  to be running late = être en retard
  to be running a temperature = avoir de la
    fièvre
**2** *noun*
  a run = une course
  to go for a run = aller courir
**run about, run around** = courir
**run away** = s'enfuir (**!** + *être*)
**run off** = partir en courant (**!** + *être*)

**runner** *noun*
  a runner = un coureur/une coureuse (à
    pied)

---
✱ in informal situations

## rush
**1** *verb*
- *(to hurry)* = se dépêcher (**!** + *être*)
  to rush to finish one's homework = se
  dépêcher de finir ses devoirs
  to rush into a shop = se précipiter dans un
  magasin
  to rush out of the house = se précipiter
  hors de la maison
  to be rushed to the hospital = être
  emmené/emmenée d'urgence à l'hôpital
- *(to put pressure on)* = bousculer
**2** *noun*
  to be in a rush = être pressé/pressée
  to do one's homework in a rush = faire ses
  devoirs à la va-vite

## rush hour *noun*
  the rush hour = les heures de pointe
  **!** *Note that* heures *is feminine plural.*

## Russia *noun* ▶ 218 |
  Russia = la Russie

## Russian ▶ 275 |
**1** *adjective*
  = russe
**2** *noun*
- *(the people)*
  the Russians = les Russes (*masculine*)
- *(the language)*
  Russian = le russe

## rusty *adjective*
  = rouillé/rouillée

# Ss

## sad *adjective*
  = triste

## saddle *noun*
  a saddle = une selle

## safe ▶ 237 |
**1** *adjective*
- *(without risk)* = sûr/sûre
  a safe place = un endroit sûr
  it's not safe for children = c'est dangereux
  pour les enfants
  is it safe to go there? = est-ce qu'on peut y
  aller sans danger?
- *(free from danger)*
  to feel safe = se sentir en sécurité
  your car is safe here = ici, votre voiture ne
  risque rien
- *(out of danger)* = sain et sauf/saine et
  sauve
**2** *noun*
  a safe = un coffre-fort

## safety *noun*
  safety = la sécurité

## Sagittarius *noun*
  Sagittarius = Sagittaire (*masculine*)

## sail
**1** *noun*
  a sail = une voile
  to set sail = prendre la mer
**2** *verb*
  to sail around the world = faire le tour du
  monde en bateau
  to go sailing = faire de la voile

## sailing *noun* ▶ 248 |
  sailing = la voile

## sailing boat (*British English*), **sailboat**
(*US English*) *noun*
  a sailing boat = un bateau à voiles

## sailor *noun* ▶ 315 |
  a sailor = un marin

## saint *noun*
  a saint = un saint/une sainte

## salad *noun*
  a salad = une salade

## salary *noun*
  a salary = un salaire

## sale *noun*
- to be on sale (*British English*) = être en
  vente
  for sale = à vendre
- the sales = les soldes (*masculino*)

## sales assistant *noun* ▶ 315 | (*British
English*)
  a sales assistant = un vendeur/une
  vendeuse

## salmon *noun*
  a salmon = un saumon

## salt *noun*
  salt = le sel

## same
**1** *adjective*
  = même
  she's got the same coat as me = elle a le
  même manteau que moi
  they go to the same school = ils vont à la
  même école
  it's the same as the car I had before
  = c'est la même voiture que celle que
  j'avais avant
  it's all the same to me = ça m'est
  complètement égal
  the houses all look the same = les
  maisons sont toutes pareilles
  people are the same everywhere = les
  gens sont partout pareils
  things aren't the same without them = ce
  n'est pas la même chose sans eux
  it's the same as ever = c'est toujours la
  même chose

S

**2** *pronoun*
the same = la même chose
I'll have the same = je prendrai la même
chose
to do the same as the others = faire
comme les autres
'Happy New Year!'—'the same to you!'
= 'Bonne année!'—'à toi de même!'

**sand** *noun*
sand = le sable

**sandal** *noun*
a sandal = un nu-pied

**sandwich** *noun*
a sandwich = un sandwich
a ham sandwich = un sandwich au
jambon

**Santa (Claus)** *noun*
Santa (Claus) = le Père Noël

**sardine** *noun*
a sardine = une sardine

**satellite TV** *noun*
satellite TV = la télévision par satellite

**satisfactory** *adjective*
= satisfaisant/satisfaisante

**satisfied** *adjective*
= satisfait/satisfaite

**Saturday** *noun* ▶ 222 ǀ
Saturday = samedi (*masculine*)

**sauce** *noun*
a sauce = une sauce

**saucepan** *noun*
a saucepan = une casserole

**saucer** *noun*
a saucer = une soucoupe

**sausage** *noun*
a sausage = une saucisse

**save** *verb*
• (*to rescue*) = sauver
they saved his life = ils lui ont sauvé la vie
• (*to avoid spending*)
to save (up) = faire des économies
to save money = mettre de l'argent de
côté
• (*to avoid wasting*)
to save [time | energy | money ...]
= économiser [du temps | de l'énergie | de
l'argent ...]
• (*to keep*) = garder
to save a piece of cake for someone
= garder un morceau de gâteau pour
quelqu'un
to save a file = sauvegarder un fichier
• (*to spare*)
to save someone a lot of work = éviter
beaucoup de travail à quelqu'un
it will save us from having to drive all
night = ça nous évitera de conduire
toute la nuit

**savings** *noun*
savings = les économies (*feminine*)

**saw** *noun*
a saw = une scie

**saxophone** *noun* ▶ 290 ǀ
a saxophone = un saxophone

**say** *verb*
= dire
to say goodbye = dire au revoir
she says (that) she can't go out tonight
= elle dit qu'elle ne peut pas sortir ce
soir
he said to wait here = il a dit d'attendre ici
they say she's very rich = on dit qu'elle
est très riche
I can't say who did it = je ne peux pas dire
qui a fait ça
she wouldn't say = elle n'a pas voulu le
dire
I said to myself that you'd like that = je me
suis dit que ça te ferait plaisir
what does the message say? = que dit le
message?
it says here that smoking is not allowed
= il est dit ici qu'on n'a pas le droit de
fumer
I'd say she was forty = je lui donne
quarante ans
let's say there are twenty people at the
party = supposons qu'il y ait vingt
personnes à la fête
❗ Note that the subjunctive is used after
supposer que.

**scandal** *noun*
a scandal = un scandale

**scare** *verb*
= faire peur à
you scared me! = tu m'as fait peur!
**scare away** = faire fuir

**scared** *adjective*
to be scared = avoir peur

**scarf** *noun*
a scarf (*long*) = une écharpe
(*square*) = un foulard

**scenery** *noun*
scenery = le paysage

**school**
**1** *noun*
a school = une école
to be at school = être à l'école
**2** *adjective*
= scolaire
a school bus = un car de ramassage
scolaire

**schoolbag** *noun*
a schoolbag = un cartable

**schoolboy** *noun*
a schoolboy = un élève

**schoolgirl** noun
  a schoolgirl = une élève

**science** noun
  science = la science
  to study science = étudier les sciences

**scientist** noun ▶ 315 |
  a scientist = un scientifique/une
    scientifique

**scissors** noun
  scissors = les ciseaux (*masculine*)
  a pair of scissors = une paire de ciseaux

**score** verb
  to score a goal = marquer un but

**Scorpio** noun
  Scorpio = Scorpion (*masculine*)

**Scotland** noun ▶ 218 |
  Scotland = l'Écosse

**Scottish** adjective ▶ 275 |
  = écossais/écossaise

**scratch** verb
• (*when itchy*) = se gratter (**!** + *être*)
  to scratch one's arm = se gratter le bras
• (*if it's a person or an animal*) = griffer
  (*if it's a bush, thorns*) = égratigner
• (*to mark, to damage*) = érafler

**scream** verb
  = hurler

**screen** noun
  a screen = un écran

**screw** noun
  a screw = une vis

**scroll** verb
  (*on a computer*)
  to scroll up/down = défiler vers le haut/le bas

**sea** noun
  a sea = une mer
  beside the sea, by the sea = au bord de la
    mer

**seagull** noun
  a seagull = une mouette

**seal** verb
  a seal = un phoque

**search** verb
• to search = chercher
  to search for someone = chercher
    quelqu'un
• (*to examine a place, a person*) = fouiller
  they searched me at the airport = on m'a
    fouillé à l'aéroport

**seashell** noun
  a seashell = un coquillage

**seasick** adjective
  to be seasick, to get seasick = avoir le
    mal de mer

**seaside** noun
  at the seaside = au bord de la mer
  to go to the seaside = aller à la mer

**season** noun
  a season = une saison
  strawberries are in season = c'est la
    saison des fraises

**seat** noun
• (*a chair, a bench*)
  a seat = un siège
  have a seat = asseyez-vous
• (*on transport, in a theatre*)
  a seat = une place

**seatbelt** noun
  a seatbelt = une ceinture de sécurité

**second**
**1** adjective
  = deuxième, second/seconde
  it's the second time I've called her = c'est
    la deuxième fois que je l'appelle
  every second Monday = un lundi sur
    deux
**2** noun
• (*in a series*)
  the second = le deuxième/la deuxième, le
    second/la seconde
• (*in time*)
  a second = une seconde
  (*a very short time*) = un instant
• (*in dates*) ▶ 222 |
  the second of May = le deux mai
**3** adverb
  = deuxième
  to come second = arriver deuxième

**secondary school** noun
  a secondary school = une école
    secondaire

**second-hand** adjective
  a second-hand [car | coat | book ...] = [une
    voiture | un manteau | un livre ...] d'occasion

**secret**
**1** adjective
  = secret/secrète
**2** noun
  a secret = un secret
  to tell someone a secret = confier un
    secret à quelqu'un
**3 in secret** = en secret

**secretary** noun ▶ 315 |
  a secretary = un secrétaire/une secrétaire

**see** verb ▶ 237 |
• to see = voir
  what can you see? = qu'est-ce que tu vois?
  I can't see them = je ne les vois pas
  he saw the people running = il a vu les
    gens qui couraient
  do they see each other often? = est-ce
    qu'ils se voient souvent?
  see you tomorrow! = à demain!
  I'll go and see = je vais voir
• (*to accompany*)
  I'll see you home = je vais te
    raccompagner chez toi

S

**seem** *verb*
- (*to appear*)
  she seems [happy | annoyed | tired ...] = elle a l'air [contente | vexée | fatiguée ...]
  they seem to be looking for someone = on dirait qu'ils cherchent quelqu'un
- (*when talking about one's impressions*) = sembler
  it seems (that) there are a lot of problems = il semble qu'il y ait beaucoup de problèmes
  it seems strange (to me) = ça (me) paraît bizarre

**seldom** *adverb*
= rarement

**self-confident** ▶ **confident**

**selfish** *adjective*
= égoïste

**sell** *verb*
= vendre
to sell books to the students = vendre des livres aux étudiants
he sold me his car = il m'a vendu sa voiture
water is sold in bottles = l'eau se vend en bouteilles

**send** *verb*
= envoyer
to send help = envoyer des secours
to send a package to someone = envoyer un paquet à quelqu'un
he sent her a letter = il lui a envoyé une lettre
to send someone to post a letter = envoyer quelqu'un mettre une lettre à la poste
to send a pupil home from school = renvoyer un élève chez lui/une élève chez elle
**send away** = faire partir
**send back** = renvoyer
**send for** = faire venir
to send for the doctor = faire venir le médecin
**send off**
to send a player off = expulser un joueur
**send on**
to send on baggage = expédier des bagages à l'avance
to send on post = faire suivre du courrier

**senior high school** (*US English*),
**senior school** (*British English*) *noun*
a senior (high) school ≈ un lycée

**sense** *noun*
- (*common*) sense = le bon sens
  to have the sense to go home = avoir le bon sens de rentrer chez soi
- (*allowing one to see, hear, smell etc*)
  a sense = un sens
  the sense of taste = le goût
- (*a meaning*)
  a sense = un sens
  it doesn't make sense = ça n'a pas de sens
  it makes sense to check first = c'est une bonne idée de vérifier d'abord

**sensible** *adjective*

> **!** Note that **sensible** in English is never translated by **sensible** in French.

(*describing a person*) = raisonnable
(*describing a decision*) = judicieux/judicieuse
(*describing clothes*) = pratique

**sensitive** *adjective*
(*describing a person*) = sensible
(*describing a situation*) = délicat/délicate

**sentence**
**1** *noun*
- (*in grammar*)
  a sentence = une phrase
- (*for a crime*)
  a (prison) sentence = une peine (de prison)
**2** *verb*
to sentence someone to one year in prison = condamner quelqu'un à un an de prison

**separate**
**1** *adjective*
a separate room = une pièce à part
the children have separate rooms = les enfants ont chacun leur chambre
there are two separate problems = il y a deux problèmes différents
**2** *verb*
- to separate = séparer
- (*if it's a couple*) = se séparer (**!** + *être*)

**separated** *adjective*
= séparé/séparée

**separately** *adverb*
= séparément

**September** *noun* ▶ **222** |
September = septembre (*masculine*)

**serial** *noun*
a serial = un feuilleton
a TV serial = un feuilleton télévisé

**series** *noun*
a series = une série

**serious** *adjective*
- (*causing worry*) = grave
  a serious accident = un accident grave
- (*describing a personality*) = sérieux/sérieuse
- to be serious about football = prendre le football au sérieux
  to be serious about going to college = avoir vraiment l'intention d'aller à l'université

**serve** verb
* (in a shop) = servir
  **are you being served?** = est-ce qu'on
  s'occupe de vous?
* (at table) = faire le service
  **to serve the soup** = servir la soupe
* (in sport) = servir

**service** noun
* (which people need or find useful)
  **a service** = un service
* (in a shop, a restaurant)
  **service** = le service
* (in a church)
  **a service** = un office

**service station** noun
  **a service station** = une station-service

**set**
**1** noun
* (a collection)
  **a set of keys** = un jeu de clés
  **a set of stamps** = une série de timbres
* (in tennis)
  **a set** = un set
**2** verb
* (to decide on) = fixer
  **to set** [a date | a price | a goal ...] = fixer [une
  date | un prix | un but ...]
* (for a particular time)
  **to set an alarm clock** = mettre un réveil
  **to set a video** (British English)
  = programmer un magnétoscope
* (in school)
  **to set homework** = donner des devoirs
  **to set an exam** = préparer les sujets d'un
  examen
* (to be responsible for)
  **to set a record** = établir un record
  **to set a good example to someone**
  = montrer le bon exemple à quelqu'un
* (when talking about a story, a film)
  **the film is set in Paris** = le film se passe à
  Paris
* (when talking about the sun) = se coucher
  (**!** + être)
* (other uses)
  **to set the table** = mettre la table
  **to set fire to a house** = mettre le feu à une
  maison
  **to set someone free** = libérer quelqu'un
**set off**
* (to leave) = partir (**!** + être)
* (to cause to go off)
  **to set off fireworks** = faire partir un feu
  d'artifice
  **to set off a bomb** = faire exploser une
  bombe
  **to set off a burglar alarm** = déclencher
  une sirène d'alarme
**set up** = monter (**!** + avoir)
  **to set up a company** = monter une
  entreprise

**settle** verb
* (to end)
  **to settle an argument** = mettre fin à une
  dispute

* (to decide on) = fixer
  **nothing is settled yet** = rien n'est encore
  fixé
* (to make one's home) = s'installer
  (**!** + être)
**settle down**
* (to get comfortable) = s'installer (**!** + être)
* (to marry) = se ranger (**!** + être)
**settle in** = s'adapter (**!** + être)

**seven** number ► **187**|, ► **211**|
  **seven** = sept
  **seven exams** = sept examens
  **I've got seven (of them)** = j'en ai sept

**seventeen** number ► **187**|, ► **211**|
  **seventeen** = dix-sept

**seventeenth** number
* (in a series) = dix-septième
* (in dates) ► **222**|
  **the seventeenth of May** = le dix-sept mai

**seventh** number
* (in a series) = septième
* (in dates) ► **222**|
  **the seventh of July** = le sept juillet

**seventy** number ► **187**|
  **seventy** = soixante-dix

**several** determiner
  = plusieurs

**severe** adjective
* (serious) = grave
* (harsh) = sévère

**sew** verb
  = coudre

**sewing** noun
  **sewing** = la couture

**sewing machine** noun
  **a sewing machine** = une machine à
  coudre

**sex** noun
  **sex** = le sexe
  **to have sex** = avoir des rapports sexuels

**shade** noun
* (out of the sun)
  **shade** = l'ombre (feminine)
  **to sit in the shade** = s'asseoir à l'ombre
* (a colour)
  **a shade** = un ton
* (for a lamp)
  **a shade** = un abat-jour

**shadow** noun
  **a shadow** = une ombre

**shake** verb
* **to shake** = secouer
  **the earthquake shook the building** = le
  tremblement de terre a ébranlé le
  bâtiment
  **to shake a bottle** = agiter une bouteille
  **to shake hands with someone** = serrer la
  main de quelqu'un

**S**

- (*when saying no*)
  to shake one's head = faire non de la tête
- (*with cold, fear, shock*) = trembler
  he was shaking with fear = il tremblait de peur
- (*during an explosion, an earthquake*) = trembler

## shall *verb*

> **!** Note that, when referring to the future, French uses the future tense of the verb to translate **shall** + *verb*: I shall leave = je partirai.

- (*when talking about the future*)
  I shall see you next Tuesday = je te verrai mardi prochain
- (*when making suggestions*)
  shall I set the table? = est-ce que je mets la table?
  shall we go to the cinema? = et si nous allions au cinéma?

## shame *noun*

- shame = la honte
  shame on you! = tu devrais avoir honte!
- (*when expressing regret*)
  that's a shame = c'est dommage

## shampoo *noun*

shampoo = le shampooing

## shape *noun*

- (*a form*)
  a shape = une forme
  a square shape = une forme carrée
  in the shape of a square = en forme de carré
- (*when talking about health*)
  to be in good shape = être en forme
  to get in shape = se mettre en forme

## share

**1** *verb*
= partager
to share a house = partager une maison
**2** *noun*
a share = une part
to pay one's fair share = payer sa part
**share out** (*British English*) (*amongst others*) = répartir
(*within a group*) = partager

## shark *noun*

a shark = un requin

## sharp *adjective*

- (*used for cutting*) = tranchant/tranchante
- (*with a point*) = pointu/pointue
- (*sudden*) = brusque
  a sharp bend = un virage serré
- (*intelligent*) = vif/vive
- (*aggressive*) = acerbe
- (*in taste*) = acide

## shave *verb*

= se raser (**!** + *être*)

## she *pronoun*

she = elle
she'll be there too = elle sera là aussi
there she is! = la voilà!
SHE didn't say it = ce n'est pas elle qui l'a dit
he works in London but she doesn't = il travaille à Londres mais elle non
she's an intelligent girl = c'est une fille intelligente

## sheep *noun*

a sheep = un mouton
(*female*) = une brebis

## sheet *noun*

- (*for a bed*)
  a sheet = un drap
- (*a piece*)
  a sheet (*of paper*) = une feuille
  (*of glass*) = une plaque

## shelf *noun*

a shelf (*for books, ornaments*) = une étagère
(*in a shop*) = un rayon
a set of shelves = une étagère

## shell *noun*

a shell (*of an egg, a nut, a snail*) = une coquille
(*of a crab, a tortoise*) = une carapace

## shelter

**1** *noun*
- (*from rain, danger*)
  a shelter = un abri
- (*for homeless people*)
  a shelter = un refuge
**2** *verb*
- (*to take shelter*) = se mettre à l'abri
- (*to help*) = donner refuge à

## shin *noun* ▶ 201 |

the shin = le tibia

## shine *verb*

- (*to give out light*) = briller
  the light is shining in my eyes = j'ai la lumière dans les yeux
- (*to point*)
  to shine a torch at someone = braquer une lampe sur quelqu'un
- (*to reflect light*) = reluire

## ship *noun*

a ship (*large*) = un navire
(*smaller*) = un bateau
a passenger ship = un paquebot

## shirt *noun*

a shirt = une chemise

## shiver *verb*

(*with cold*) = grelotter
(*with fear*) = trembler

## shock
**1** *noun*
- *(an upsetting experience)*
  a shock = un choc
  to get a shock = avoir un choc
  to give someone a shock = faire un choc à quelqu'un
- *(the medical state)*
  to be in shock = être en état de choc
- *(from electricity)*
  a shock = une décharge
  to get a shock = recevoir une décharge
**2** *verb*
- *(to upset)* = consterner
- *(to cause a scandal)* = choquer

**shoe** *noun*
  a shoe *(for a person)* = une chaussure
  *(for a horse)* = un fer

**shoot** *verb*
- *(using a weapon)* = tirer
  to shoot someone = tirer sur quelqu'un
  they shot him in the leg = ils lui ont tiré dans la jambe
  to shoot someone dead = abattre quelqu'un
- *(to move very fast)*
  to shoot past = passer en trombe
- *(to make)*
  to shoot a film = tourner un film

## shop
**1** *noun*
  a shop = un magasin
  *(small, fashionable)* = une boutique
**2** *verb*
  to go shopping = aller faire des courses

**shop assistant** *noun* ▶ 315 | *(British English)*
  a shop assistant = un vendeur/une vendeuse

**shopkeeper** *noun* ▶ 315 |
  a shopkeeper = un commerçant/une commerçante

**shopping** *noun*
  shopping = les courses *(feminine plural)*
  to do the shopping = faire les courses

**shopping cart** *noun* *(US English)*
  a shopping cart = un caddie

**shopping centre** *(British English)*,
**shopping mall** *(US English)* *noun*
  a shopping centre, a shopping mall = un centre commercial

**shopping trolley** *noun* *(British English)*
  a shopping trolley = un caddie

**shop window** *noun*
  a shop window = une vitrine

**shore** *noun*
- *(the edge of the sea)*
  the shore = la côte, le rivage
- *(dry land)*
  the shore = la terre

## short
**1** *adjective*
- *(not lasting long)* = court/courte *(! before the noun)*
  to go for a short walk = faire une petite promenade
  a short speech = un bref discours
  the days are getting shorter = les jours diminuent
- *(not long)* = court/courte
  a short skirt = une jupe courte
  to have short hair = avoir les cheveux courts
- *(not tall)* = petit/petite *(! + être)*
- to be short of [money | food | ideas ...] = être à court [d'argent | de nourriture | d'idées ...]
**2** **in short** = bref

**short cut** *noun*
  a short cut = un raccourci

**shortly** *adverb*
- *(soon)* = bientôt
- *(not long)* = peu de temps
  shortly before we left = peu de temps avant notre départ

**shorts** *noun*
  shorts = un short *(singular)*

**shot** *noun*
- *(from a gun)*
  a shot = un coup (de feu)
  to fire a shot at someone = tirer sur quelqu'un
- *(in sports)* ▶ 248 |
  a shot *(in football)* = un tir
  *(in tennis, golf, cricket)* = un coup

**should** *verb*

> **!** *Note that, in general, should is translated by devoir in the conditional, either present* (you shouldn't smoke = tu ne devrais pas fumer) *or past* (he shouldn't have left = il n'aurait pas dû partir)*.*

- *(when talking about what is right, what one ought to do)*
  she should learn to drive = elle devrait apprendre à conduire
  shouldn't he be at school? = est-ce qu'il ne devrait pas être à l'école?
  you shouldn't have said that! = tu n'aurais pas dû dire ça!
- *(when saying something may happen)*
  we should be there by midday = nous devrions être là vers midi
  it shouldn't be too difficult = cela ne devrait pas être trop difficile
- *(when implying that something, though likely, didn't happen)*
  the letter should have arrived yesterday = la lettre aurait dû arriver hier
- *(when asking for advice or permission)*
  should I call the doctor? = est-ce que je devrais appeler le médecin?

S

**shoulder** *noun* ▶ **201** ⎸
  the shoulder = l'épaule
  to wear a sweater over one's shoulders
    = porter un pull sur les épaules
  to have round shoulders = avoir le dos
    rond

**shout**
**1** *verb*
  = crier
  to shout at someone = crier après
    quelqu'un
**2** *noun*
  a shout = un cri
**shout out** = pousser un cri

**shovel** *noun*
  a shovel = une pelle

**show**
**1** *verb*
• (*to let someone see*) = montrer
  to show someone a photo = montrer une
    photo à quelqu'un
  I'll show you how it works = je vais te
    montrer comment ça marche
• (*to go with*)
  I'll show you to your room = je vais vous
    accompagner à votre chambre
• (*to point to, to indicate*) = indiquer
  to show someone where to go = indiquer
    à quelqu'un où aller
  there's a sign showing the way to the
    pool = il y a un panneau qui indique la
    direction de la piscine
• (*to be on TV, at the cinema*) = passer
  (**!** + *être*)
  the film is showing at the Phoenix = le
    film passe au Phoenix
  to be shown on TV = passer à la télévision
**2** *noun*
• a show (*on a stage*) = un spectacle
  (*on TV, radio*) = une émission
• (*an exhibition*)
  a show = une exposition
**show off** = faire le fier/la fière
**show round**
  to show someone around the town = faire
    visiter la ville à quelqu'un
**show up** = se pointer✗ (**!** + *être*)

**shower** *noun*
• (*for washing*)
  a shower = une douche
  to have a shower = prendre une douche
• (*rain*)
  a shower = une averse

**showjumping** *noun* ▶ **248** ⎸
  showjumping = le saut d'obstacles

**shrimp** *noun*
  a shrimp = une crevette grise

**shrink** *verb*
  = rétrécir

─────────────
✗ in informal situations

**shut**
**1** *adjective*
  = fermé/fermée
  my eyes were shut = j'avais les yeux
    fermés
**2** *verb*
  = fermer
  to shut the windows = fermer les fenêtres
  the door doesn't shut properly = la porte
    ne ferme pas bien
**shut down** = fermer
  the factory shut down in May = l'usine a
    fermé au mois de mai
**shut out**
  to shut someone out = laisser quelqu'un
    dehors
**shut up**
• (*to be quiet*) = se taire (**!** + *être*)
  shut up! = tais-toi!
• (*to lock inside*) = enfermer

**shy** *adjective*
  = timide

**sick** *adjective*
• (*ill*) = malade
  to get sick = tomber malade (**!** + *être*)
  to feel sick = avoir mal au cœur
  to be sick (*British English*) (*to vomit*)
    = vomir
• (*fed up*)
  he's sick of the neighbours = il en a
    marre✗ des voisins

**sickness** *noun*
  a sickness = une maladie

**side** *noun*
• a side = un côté
  it's an apartment block with shops on
    either side = c'est un immeuble avec des
    magasins de chaque côté
  to be driving on the wrong side of the
    road = rouler du mauvais côté de la
    route
  by the side of the river = au bord de la
    rivière
  the north side of the city = le nord de la
    ville
  he works on the other side of London = il
    travaille à l'autre bout de Londres
• (*of a person's body*)
  the side = le côté
  to be lying on one's side = être
    allongé/allongée sur le côté
  on my right side = à ma droite
• (*in a conflict, a contest*)
  a side = un camp
• (*a team*)
  a side = une équipe
**side with** = se mettre du côté de

**sidewalk** *noun* (*US English*)
  a sidewalk = un trottoir

**sigh** *verb*
  = soupirer

**sight** noun
sight = la vue
to have good sight = avoir une bonne vue
to be out of sight = être caché/cachée

**sightseeing** noun
sightseeing = le tourisme

**sign**
1 noun
• (a mark)
  a sign = un signe
  the dollar sign = le symbole du dollar
• (for traffic, for advertising)
  a sign = un panneau
• (a notice)
  a sign = une pancarte
2 verb
  = signer
**sign on** (British English) = pointer au chômage

**signal**
1 noun
  a signal = un signal
2 verb
• (to make signs) = faire des signes
  to signal to someone to come = faire
  signe à quelqu'un de venir
• (when driving) = mettre son clignotant

**signature** noun
  a signature = une signature

**signpost** noun
  a signpost = un panneau indicateur

**silence** noun
  silence = le silence

**silent** adjective
• (quiet) = silencieux/silencieuse
• (without sound or words) = muet/muette

**silk** noun
  silk = la soie

**silly** adjective
  = idiot/idiote

**silver**
1 noun
  silver = l'argent (masculine)
2 adjective
  = en argent
  a silver ring = une bague en argent

**SIM card** noun
  a SIM card = une carte SIM

**simple** adjective
  = simple

**since**
1 preposition
  ! Note that, when since is used to
  describe an event or an action that is still
  going on, rather than an event or an
  action that belongs to the past and has
  finished, the present tense + depuis is
  used in French. In the same way, if the
  event or action has its starting point
  further back in the past, in French the
  imperfect tense + depuis is used.

= depuis
I haven't seen him since yesterday = je ne
  l'ai pas vu depuis hier
I haven't been feeling well since Monday
  – je ne me sens pas bien depuis lundi
she had been living in France since 1988
  = elle vivait en France depuis 1988
2 conjunction
• (from the time when) = depuis que
  since she left = depuis qu'elle est partie,
  depuis son départ
  I've lived here since I was ten = j'habite
  ici depuis l'âge de dix ans
  it's ten years since she died = cela fait dix
  ans qu'elle est morte
• (because) = comme
  since she was ill, she couldn't go
  = comme elle était malade, elle ne
  pouvait pas y aller
3 adverb
  = depuis

**sincere** adjective
  – sincère

**sincerely** adverb
  = sincèrement
  Yours sincerely (British English),
  Sincerely yours (US English) = Veuillez
  agréer, Monsieur/Madame, l'expression
  de mes sentiments les meilleurs
  (less formal) = Meilleures salutations

**sing** verb
  = chanter

**singer** noun ▶ 315
  a singer = un chanteur/une chanteuse

**singing** noun
  singing = le chant

**single** adjective
• (one) = seul/seule (! before the noun)
  we visited three towns in a single day
  = nous avons visité trois villes en une
  seule journée
• (when used for emphasis)
  every single day = tous les jours sans
  exception
  I didn't see a single person = je n'ai vu
  absolument personne
• (without a partner) = célibataire

**single bed** noun
  a single bed = un lit pour une personne

**single room** noun
  a single room = une chambre à une
  personne

**single ticket** noun (British English)
  a single ticket = un aller simple

**sink**
1 noun
  a sink = un évier
2 verb
  = couler

S

**sister** *noun*
a sister = une sœur

**sister-in-law** *noun*
a sister-in-law = une belle-sœur

**sit** *verb*
• (*to take a seat*) = s'asseoir (**!** + *être*)
to be sitting on the floor = être assis/assise
par terre
• (*British English*) (*to take*)
to sit an exam = passer un examen
**sit down** = s'asseoir (**!** + *être*)
to be sitting down = être assis/assise
**sit up** = se redresser (**!** + *être*)
sit up straight! = tiens-toi droit!

**sitting room** *noun*
a sitting room = un salon

**situated** *adjective*
= situé/située
situated near the town centre
= situé/située près du centre-ville

**situation** *noun*
a situation = une situation

**six** *number* ▶ **187** |, ▶ **211** |
six = six
six weeks = six semaines
I've got six (of them) = j'en ai six

**sixteen** *number* ▶ **187** |, ▶ **211** |
sixteen = seize

**sixteenth** *number*
• (*in a series*) = seizième
• (*in dates*) ▶ **222** |
the sixteenth of July = le seize juillet

**sixth** *number*
• (*in a series*) = sixième
• (*in dates*) ▶ **222** |
the sixth of February = le six février

**sixty** *number* ▶ **187** |
sixty = soixante

**size** *noun*
• (*when talking about a person*)
a size = une taille
she's about your size = elle est à peu près
de ta taille
• (*when talking about clothes*)
a size (*of garment*) = une taille
(*of shoe*) = une pointure
I'd like this in a smaller size = je voudrais
ce modèle en plus petit
what size do you take? (*in clothes*)
= quelle taille faites-vous?
(*in shoes*) = vous chaussez du combien?
• (*when talking about how big something is*)
the size (*of a building, a region*) = la
grandeur
(*of an apple, a parcel*) = la grosseur

**skateboard** *noun* ▶ **248** |
a skateboard = un skateboard, une
planche à roulettes

**skating** *noun* ▶ **248** |
skating = le patin

**skating rink** *noun*
a skating rink (*for ice-skating*) = une
patinoire
(*for roller-skating*) = une piste de patin à
roulettes

**sketch** *noun*
• (*a drawing*)
a sketch = un croquis
• (*a funny scene*)
a sketch = un sketch

**ski**
**1** *noun*
a ski = un ski
**2** *verb*
to go skiing = faire du ski

**skiing** *noun* ▶ **248** |
skiing = le ski

**skilful** (*British English*), **skillful** (*US
English*) *adjective*
= habile, adroit/adroite

**skill** *noun*
• (*the quality*)
skill (*mental*) = l'habileté (*feminine*)
(*physical*) = la dextérité
• (*a particular ability*)
a skill (*learned*) = une compétence
(*natural*) = une aptitude

**skin** *noun*
the skin = la peau

**skinny** *adjective*
= maigre

**skip** *verb*
• (*to give little jumps*) = sautiller
• (*with a rope*) = sauter à la corde
• to skip classes = sauter les cours

**ski resort** *noun*
a ski resort = une station de ski

**skirt** *noun*
a skirt = une jupe

**sky** *noun*
the sky = le ciel
a clear sky = un ciel dégagé

**skydiving** *noun* ▶ **248** |
skydiving = le parachutisme (en chute
libre)

**slap** *verb*
to slap someone = donner une tape à
quelqu'un
(*across the face*) = gifler quelqu'un

**sled**, **sledge** (*British English*)
**1** *noun*
a sled (*for fun*) = une luge
(*for transport*) = un traîneau
**2** *verb*
to go sledging (*British English*) = faire de
la luge

**sleep**
**1** *noun*
sleep = le sommeil
to go to sleep = s'endormir (**!** + *être*)
to go back to sleep = se rendormir
(**!** + *être*)
to put someone to sleep = endormir
quelqu'un
**2** *verb*
• (*to be asleep*) = dormir
• to sleep with someone = coucher avec
quelqu'un
**sleep in** = faire la grasse matinée

**sleeping bag** *noun*
a sleeping bag = un sac de couchage

**sleepy** *adjective*
to be sleepy, to feel sleepy = avoir
sommeil, avoir envie de dormir

**sleet** *noun*
sleet = la neige fondue

**sleeve** *noun*
a sleeve = une manche
to roll up one's sleeves = retrousser ses
manches

**slice**
**1** *noun*
a slice (*of bread, meat*) = une tranche
(*of lemon, cucumber*) = une rondelle
**2** *verb*
to slice bread = couper du pain en
tranches

**slide**
**1** *verb*
= glisser
the plates slid off the table = les assiettes
ont glissé de la table
**2** *noun*
• (*an image*)
a slide = une diapositive
• (*in a playground*)
a slide = un toboggan

**slim**
**1** *adjective*
= mince
**2** *verb* (*British English*)
= maigrir

**slip** *verb*
• (*to slide*) = glisser
• the glass slipped out of my hands = le
verre m'a échappé des mains

**slipper** *noun*
a slipper = une pantoufle

**slippery** *adjective*
= glissant/glissante

**slot machine** *noun*
a slot machine = une machine à sous

**Slovakia** *noun* ▶ 218
Slovakia = la Slovaquie

**slow** *adjective*
• (*not fast*) = lent/lente
to make slow progress = avancer
lentement
• (*not bright*) = lent/lente (d'esprit)
• (*describing a watch, a clock*)
to be slow = retarder
the clock is 20 minutes slow = la pendule
retarde de 20 minutes
**slow down** = ralentir

**slowly** *adverb*
= lentement

**sly** *adjective*
= rusé/rusée

**small** *adjective*
= petit/petite (**!** before the noun)
a small car = une petite voiture
a small quantity = une faible quantité

**small ad** *noun* (*British English*)
a small ad = une petite annonce

**smart** *adjective*
• (*British English*) (*elegant*)
= élégant/élégante
• (*intelligent*) = intelligent/intelligente
• (*expensive*) = chic (**!** never changes)

**smash** *verb*
• (*to break*) = briser, fracasser
• (*to get broken*) = se briser, se fracasser
(**!** + *être*)
**smash up** = démolir

**smell**
**1** *noun*
• (*an odour*)
a smell = une odeur
• (*the sense*)
the sense of smell = l'odorat (*masculine*)
**2** *verb*
= sentir
that smells nice = ça sent bon
I can smell burning = ça sent le brûlé

**smile**
**1** *verb*
= sourire
to smile at someone = sourire à quelqu'un
**2** *noun*
a smile = un sourire

**smoke**
**1** *noun*
smoke = la fumée
**2** *verb*
= fumer

**smooth** *adjective*
(*not rough*) = lisse
a smooth road = une route plane
a smooth crossing = une traversée sans
heurts

**smother** *verb*
= étouffer

**snack** *noun*
a snack = un casse-croûte

**snail** *noun*
a snail = un escargot

**snake** *noun*
a snake = un serpent

**sneaker** *noun*
a sneaker (*high*) = une basket
(*low*) = un tennis

**sneeze** *verb*
= éternuer

**snobbish** *adjective*
= snob

**snooker** *noun* ▶ 248 |
snooker = le billard anglais

**snore** *verb*
= ronfler

**snow**
**1** *noun*
snow = la neige
**2** *verb*
= neiger
it's snowing = il neige

**snowball** *noun*
a snowball = une boule de neige

**snowboarding** *noun*
snowboarding = le surf des neiges

**snowman** *noun*
a snowman = un bonhomme de neige

**so**
**1** *adverb*
• so = si, tellement
he's so [happy | stupid | smart ...] = il est si
  [content | bête | malin ...]
they speak so fast = ils parlent si vite, ils
  parlent tellement vite
it's so much easier = c'est tellement plus
  facile
she has so many clothes = elle a tant de
  vêtements
I've so much work to do = j'ai tant de
  travail à faire
• (*also*)
I'm fifteen and so is he = j'ai quinze ans et
  lui aussi
if you go, so will I = si tu y vas, j'y vais
  aussi
• (*other uses*)
I think so = je pense que oui
I'm afraid so = j'ai bien peur que oui
I told you so = je te l'avais bien dit
who says so? = qui dit ça?
so what? = et alors?
and so on = et ainsi de suite
**2 so (that)** = pour que
be quiet so I can work = tais-toi pour que
  je puisse travailler

> ! *Note that the subjunctive is used after*
> pour que.

**3 so as** = pour
we left early so as not to miss the train
  = nous sommes partis tôt pour ne pas
  rater le train

**soap** *noun*
• (*for washing*)
soap = le savon
• (*on TV*)
a soap = un feuilleton

**soccer** *noun* ▶ 248 |
soccer = le football
= sociable

**social** *adjective*
= social/sociale

**social studies** *noun*
social studies = l'instruction civique

> ! *Note that* instruction *is feminine.*

**social worker** *noun* ▶ 315 |
a social worker = un travailleur social/une
  travailleuse sociale

**sock** *noun*
a sock = une chaussette

**sofa** *noun*
a sofa = un canapé

**soft** *adjective*
• (*not hard or tough*) = doux/douce
to have soft skin = avoir la peau douce
the ground is soft here = la terre est
  meuble ici
a soft toffee = un caramel mou
• (*not harsh or severe*) = doux/douce
• (*not strict*) = indulgent/indulgente

**software** *noun*
a software = un logiciel

**soldier** *noun* ▶ 315 |
a soldier = un soldat

**sole** *noun*
• the sole (*of the foot*) = la plante du pied
• (*of a shoe*)
a sole = une semelle

**solicitor** *noun* ▶ 315 | (*British English*)
a solicitor (*for documents*) ≈ un notaire
(*for court work*) ≈ un avocat/une avocate

**solution** *noun*
a solution = une solution

**solve** *verb*
= résoudre
to solve a problem = résoudre un
  problème

## some

**1** *determiner*
* *(an amount or a number of)* = du/de la (**!** de l' + *vowel or mute* h)
  = des (+ *plural*)
  I have to buy some bread = je dois acheter du pain
  have some water = prenez de l'eau
  we bought some beer = nous avons acheté de la bière
  she ate some strawberries = elle a mangé des fraises
  we visited some beautiful towns = nous avons visité des villes superbes
* *(certain)* = certains/certaines
  some people don't like travelling by plane = certaines personnes n'aiment pas voyager en avion

**2** *pronoun*
* *(an amount or a number of)* = en
  I know where you can find some = je sais où tu peux en trouver
  have some more! = reprenez-en!

  **!** *Note that it is necessary to use* on, *which might be translated as* 'of it' *or* 'of them', *with pronouns like* some. *See also* any, a few, a lot *etc for this use of* en.

* *(certain people or things)*
  some are quite expensive = certains sont assez chers/certaines sont assez chères
  some (of them) are French = certains d'entre eux sont français/certaines d'entre elles sont françaises

## someone *pronoun* (also **somebody**)
= quelqu'un
someone famous = quelqu'un de célèbre

## something *pronoun*
= quelque chose
I saw something interesting = j'ai vu quelque chose d'intéressant
there's something odd about him = il a quelque chose de bizarre

## sometimes *adverb*
= quelquefois, parfois

## somewhere *adverb*
= quelque part
they live somewhere in Ireland = ils habitent quelque part en Irlande
let's go somewhere else = allons ailleurs

## son *noun*
a son = un fils

## song *noun*
a song = une chanson

## son-in-law *noun*
a son-in-law = un gendre

## soon *adverb*
* *(in a short time)* = bientôt
  see you soon! = à bientôt!

* *(early)*
  the sooner the better = le plus tôt sera le mieux
  as soon as possible = dès que possible
  come as soon as you can = viens dès que tu pourras

  **!** *Note that, if talking about future time, the future tense is used after* dès que.

## sore *adjective*
to have a sore [throat | leg | back ...] = avoir mal [à la gorge | à la jambe | au dos ...]
it's very sore = ça fait très mal

## sorry

**1** *exclamation*
* *(when apologizing)*
  sorry! = pardon!, désolé/désolée!
* *(when asking someone to repeat)*
  sorry? = pardon?

**2** *adjective*
* *(when apologizing)* = désolé/désolée
  I'm sorry I'm late = je suis désolé d'être en retard
  to say sorry = s'excuser (**!** + *être*)
* *(when expressing regret)*
  I'm sorry you can't come = je suis désolé que tu ne puisses pas venir

  **!** *Note that the subjunctive is used after* être désolé que.

* *(to feel pity for)*
  to feel sorry for someone = plaindre quelqu'un
  to feel sorry for oneself = s'apitoyer sur son sort

## sort

**1** *noun*
it's a sort of [bird | computer | loan ..] = c'est une sorte [d'oiseau | d'ordinateur | de prêt ...]
I don't like that sort of thing = je n'aime pas ce genre de choses
he's not that sort of person = ce n'est pas son genre

**2** *verb*
to sort files = classer des dossiers
to sort the books into piles = ranger les livres en piles

## sort out
* *(to solve)* = régler
  to sort out a problem = régler un problème
* *(to deal with)* = s'occuper de (**!** + *être*)
  I'll sort it out = je m'en occuperai
* *(to organize)* = classer
  to sort out the documents = classer les documents
* *(to pick out, to choose)*
  to sort out the photos = trier les photos
  to sort out the old clothes from the new = séparer les vieux vêtements des neufs

## sound

**1** *noun*
* a sound *(a noise)* = un bruit
  *(of an instrument, a bell)* = un son

S

I heard the sound of voices = j'ai entendu un bruit de voix
• (of a radio, a television)
the sound = le son
to turn the sound up = monter le son
**2** verb
it sounds [dangerous | odd | interesting ...] = ça a l'air [dangereux | bizarre | intéressant ...]
it sounds like a piano = on dirait un piano

**soup** noun
a soup = une soupe, un potage

**sour** adjective
= aigre
to go sour = tourner

**south**
**1** noun
the south = le sud
in the south of France = dans le sud de la France
**2** adverb
to go south = aller vers le sud
to live south of Paris = vivre au sud de Paris
**3** adjective
= sud (**!** never changes)
to work in south London = travailler dans le sud de Londres

**South Africa** noun ▶ 218 |
South Africa = l'Afrique du Sud
**!** Note that Afrique is feminine.

**South America** noun ▶ 218 |
South America = l'Amérique du Sud
**!** Note that Amérique is feminine.

**southeast** noun
the southeast = le sud-est

**southwest** noun
the southwest = le sud-ouest

**souvenir** noun
a souvenir = un souvenir

**space** noun
• (room)
space = la place
to take up space = prendre de la place
• (an area of land)
an open space = un espace libre
• (outer space)
space = l'espace (masculine)
• (a gap)
a space = un espace

**Spain** noun ▶ 218 |
Spain = l'Espagne (feminine)

**Spanish** ▶ 275 |
**1** adjective
= espagnol/espagnole
**2** noun
Spanish = l'espagnol (masculine)

**spare** adjective
• (extra) = en plus
I've got a spare ticket = j'ai un billet en plus
• (available) = disponible
are there any spare seats? = est-ce qu'il y a des places disponibles?

**spare part** noun
a spare part = une pièce de rechange

**spare room** noun
a spare room = une chambre d'amis

**spare time** noun
spare time = les loisirs (masculine plural)

**speak** verb
= parler
to speak German = parler (l')allemand
they're not speaking (to each other) = ils ne se parlent pas
who's speaking, please? = qui est à l'appareil?
generally speaking = en règle générale
**speak up** = parler plus fort

**special** adjective
= spécial/spéciale
**!** Note that spécial can also mean odd or strange in French: il est assez spécial = he's rather strange.

a special offer = une offre spéciale

**speciality** (British English), **specialty** (US English) noun
a speciality = une spécialité

**specially** adverb
= spécialement

**spectator** noun
a spectator = un spectateur/une spectatrice

**speech** noun
a speech = un discours

**speed**
**1** noun
speed = la vitesse
**2** verb
• to speed away = s'éloigner à toute allure
• (to drive too fast) = conduire trop vite
**speed up** = accélérer

**speed camera** noun
a speed camera = un radar automatique

**speed limit** noun
a speed limit = une limitation de vitesse

**spell** verb
(when speaking) = épeler
(when writing) = écrire
how do you spell it? = comment ça s'écrit?

**spelling** noun
spelling = l'orthographe (feminine)

**spend** verb
• (to pay money) = dépenser

- *(to pass)*
  **to spend (some) time** [reading | painting | writing letters …] = passer du temps [à lire | à faire de la peinture | à écrire des lettres …]

**spider** *noun*
  **a spider** = une araignée

**spill** *verb*
- *(if it's a person)* = renverser
  **don't spill the milk** = ne renverse pas le lait
- *(if it's a liquid)* = se répandre (**!** + *être*)

**spinach** *noun*
  **spinach** = les épinards *(masculine plural)*

**spit** *verb*
  = cracher

**spite**: **in spite of** *preposition*
  = malgré
  **we went out in spite of the weather** = nous sommes sortis malgré le temps

**spiteful** *adjective*
  = méchant/méchante

**spoil** *verb*
- *(to take away from)* = gâcher
  **to spoil the evening** = gâcher la soirée
- *(to ruin, to damage)* = abîmer
- *(as a parent)* = gâter
  **to spoil a child** = gâter un enfant

**sponge** *noun*
  **a sponge** = une éponge

**spoon** *noun*
  **a spoon** = une cuillère

**sport** *noun* ▶ **248** |
  **a sport** = un sport
  **to be good at sports** = être bon/bonne en sport

**sports centre** *(British English)*, **sports center** *(US English)* *noun*
  **a sports centre** = un centre sportif

**sports club** *noun*
  **a sports club** = un club sportif

**spot**
**1** *noun*
- *(on an animal)*
  **a spot** = une tache
- *(British English)* *(on the face or body)*
  **a spot** = un bouton
- *(a place)*
  **a spot** = un endroit
  **on the spot** *(there and then)* = sur-le-champ
**2** *verb*
- *(to see)* = apercevoir
- *(to recognize)* = repérer

**sprain** *verb*
  **to sprain one's wrist** = se fouler le poignet

**spring** *noun*
  **spring** = le printemps
  **in spring** = au printemps

**spy** *noun*
  **a spy** = un espion/une espionne

**square**
**1** *noun*
- *(the shape)*
  **a square** = un carré
- *(in a town)*
  **a square** = une place
**2** *adjective*
  = carré/carrée

**squash**
**1** *noun* ▶ **248** |
  **squash** = le squash
**2** *verb*
  = écraser

**squeak** *verb*
  *(if it's a door, a wheel)* = grincer
  *(if it's a shoe, a chair)* = craquer

**squeeze** *verb*
  **to squeeze a lemon** = presser un citron
  **to squeeze someone's hand** = serrer la main de quelqu'un

**squirrel** *noun*
  **a squirrel** = un écureuil

**stable** *noun*
  **a stable** = une écurie

**stadium** *noun*
  **a stadium** = un stade

**staff** *noun*
  **the staff** *(of a company)* = le personnel
  *(of a school, a college)* = le personnel enseignant

**stage** *noun*
  **a stage** = une scène

**stain**
**1** *noun*
  **a stain** = une tache
**2** *verb*
  = tacher

**stairs** *noun*
  **the stairs** = l'escalier *(masculine singular)*
  **to fall down the stairs** = tomber dans l'escalier

**stamp** *noun*
- *(for an envelope)*
  **a stamp** = un timbre
  **a 0·46 euro stamp** = un timbre à 0,46 euros
- *(on a document, a passport)*
  **a stamp** = un cachet

**stamp-collecting** *noun*
  **stamp-collecting** = la philatélie

**stand** *verb*
- **to be standing** = être debout
  **to stay standing, to remain standing** = rester debout (**!** + *être*)
  **to be able to stand** = tenir debout
  **you're standing in my way** = tu me bloques le passage

**S**

* (*to put*)
  to stand a vase on a table = mettre un
    vase sur une table
* (*to step*)
  to stand on a nail = marcher sur un clou
* (*to bear*)
  I can't stand French = je déteste le
    français
  he can't stand playing football = il déteste
    jouer au football
* (*other uses*)
  to stand for election (*British English*) = se
    présenter aux élections
  to stand trial = passer en jugement
**stand back** = reculer
**stand for**
* (*to represent*) = représenter
* (*to mean*) = vouloir dire
**stand out**
  (*if it's a person*) = sortir de l'ordinaire
**stand up**
* to stand up = se lever (**!** + *être*)
* to stand someone up = poser un lapin**✶** à
    quelqu'un
**stand up for** = défendre
  to stand up for oneself = se défendre
    (**!** + *être*)
**stand up to** = tenir tête à
  to stand up to someone = tenir tête à
    quelqu'un

**star** *noun*
* (*in space*)
  a star = une étoile
* (*a famous person*)
  a star = une vedette, une star

**stare** *verb*
  to stare at someone = dévisager
    quelqu'un

**start**
**1** *verb*
* (*to begin*) = commencer
  to start [working | writing | running …]
    = commencer à [travailler | écrire | courir …]
  you should start by phoning them = tu
    devrais commencer par leur téléphoner
* (*to begin one's working life*)
  to start (out) as a teacher = débuter
    comme professeur
* (*to set up*) = lancer
  to start a fashion = lancer une mode
* (*to cause*) = déclencher
  to start a war = déclencher une guerre
* (*to begin working*) = démarrer
  the car won't start = la voiture ne veut pas
    démarrer
* (*to put into action*)
  to start a car = faire démarrer une voiture
  to start a machine = mettre une machine
    en marche

**2** *noun*
  a start = un début
  at the start of the week = au début de la
    semaine
**start off** = commencer
**start over** (*US English*) = recommencer
**starter** *noun* (*British English*)
  a starter = un hors-d'œuvre
**state** *noun*
* (*a country, part of a country*)
  a state = un état
* (*a government*)
  the State = l'État
* (*a condition*)
  a state = un état
  to be in a bad state (of repair) = être en
    mauvais état
  she's in no state to work = elle n'est pas
    en état de travailler

**statement** *noun*
  a statement = une déclaration
  (*official*) = un communiqué

**station** *noun*
* (*for trains*)
  a station = une gare
* (*on TV*)
  a station = une chaîne

**statue** *noun*
  a statue = une statue

**stay**
**1** *verb*
* (*to remain*) = rester (**!** + *être*)
  we stayed there for a week = nous
    sommes restés là une semaine
* (*to have accommodation*) = loger
  to stay with friends = loger chez des amis
**2** *noun*
  a stay = un séjour
**stay away from** = éviter
  to stay away from school = ne pas aller à
    l'école
**stay in** = rester à la maison
**stay out**
  to stay out late = rentrer tard
**stay up** (*to wait*) = veiller
  (*to keep late hours*) = se coucher tard

**steady** *adjective*
* (*continuous*)
  to make steady progress = faire des
    progrès réguliers
* (*not likely to move*) = stable

**steak** *noun*
  a steak = un steak

**steal** *verb*
  = voler
  to steal from someone = voler quelqu'un
  to steal money from someone = voler de
    l'argent à quelqu'un

**steam** *noun*
  steam = la vapeur

**✶** in informal situations

**steel** *noun*
steel = l'acier (*masculine*)

**steep** *adjective*
= raide

**steering wheel** *noun*
a steering wheel = un volant

**step**
**1** *noun*
• (*when walking*)
a step = un pas
to take a step = faire un pas
• (*in stairs, at a door*)
a step = une marche
• (*a series of actions*)
to take steps = prendre des mesures
**2** *verb*
to step in a puddle = marcher dans une
flaque
**step aside** = s'écarter (**!** + *être*)

**stepbrother** *noun*
a stepbrother = un demi-frère

**stepfather** *noun*
a stepfather = un beau-père

**stepmother** *noun*
a stepmother = une belle-mère

**stepsister** *noun*
a stepsister = une demi-sœur

**stereo** *noun*
a stereo = une chaîne stéréo

**stewardess** *noun* ▶ 315 |
a stewardess = une hôtesse de l'air

**stick**
**1** *verb*
• (*using glue or tape*) = coller
• (*to become attached*) = coller
• (*to get blocked*) = se coincer (**!** + *être*)
the door is stuck = la porte est coincée
**2** *noun*
• (*a piece of wood*)
a stick = un bâton
• (*for walking*)
a stick = une canne
**stick at**
to stick at a task = persévérer dans une
tâche
**stick out** = dépasser
there's a nail sticking out = il y a un clou
qui dépasse
his ears stick out = il a les oreilles
décollées

**sticky tape** *noun* (*British English*)
sticky tape = le scotch    , le ruban adhésif

**stiff** *adjective*
• (*not soft, not supple*) = raide
to have stiff legs (*after sport, walking*)
= avoir des courbatures dans les jambes
• (*not easy to use*)
to be stiff (*if it's a door, a drawer*) = être
dur/dure à ouvrir

(*if it's a handle*) = être dur/dure à tourner

**still**[1] *adverb*
• (*when there has been no change*)
= toujours
does she still play the piano? = est-ce
qu'elle joue toujours du piano?
I still don't understand why you left = je
ne comprends toujours pas pourquoi tu
es parti
• (*when referring to the future*) = encore
she could still win = elle pourrait encore
gagner

**still**[2]
**1** *adverb*
to sit still = se tenir tranquille
**2** *adjective*
= calme

**sting** *verb*
= piquer

**stir** *verb*
= remuer

**stomach** *noun* ▶ 201 |, ▶ 266 |
the stomach = l'estomac (*masculine*)
to have a pain in one's stomach = avoir
mal au ventre

**stone** *noun*
a stone = une pierre
(*a pebble*) = un caillou

**stop**
**1** *verb*
• (*to put an end to*) = arrêter
to stop [smoking | laughing | working…]
= arrêter de [fumer | rire | travailler…]
stop it! = arrête!
• (*to prevent*)
to stop someone from [leaving | winning |
talking…] = empêcher quelqu'un de
[partir | gagner | parler…]
• (*to come to a halt*) = s'arrêter (**!** + *être*)
the bus didn't stop = le bus ne s'est pas
arrêté
• (*when talking about machines, noise,
weather*) = s'arrêter (**!** + *être*)
suddenly the noise stopped = tout à
coup, le bruit s'est arrêté
it's stopped raining = il s'est arrêté de
pleuvoir, la pluie s'est arrêtée
**2** *noun*
a (bus) stop = un arrêt (de bus)
to miss one's stop = rater son arrêt

**store** *noun*
a store = un magasin
(*smaller*) = une boutique

**storey** (*British English*), **story** (*US
English*) *noun*
a storey = un étage

**storm** *noun*
a storm = une tempête
(*with thunder*) = un orage

**S**

**story** noun
* a story = une histoire
  a true story = une histoire vécue
  a ghost story = une histoire de fantômes
* (in a newspaper)
  a story = un article
* (a rumour)
  a story = une rumeur
* (US English) ▶ **storey**

**stove** noun (US English)
  a stove = une cuisinière

**straight**
**1** adjective
* straight = droit/droite
  a straight line = une ligne droite
* (not curly) = raide
  to have straight hair = avoir les cheveux raides
* (in the right position) = bien droit/droite
  the picture isn't straight = le tableau est de travers
* (honest) = honnête, droit/droite
**2** adverb
* straight = droit
  to stand up straight = se tenir droit
  to go straight ahead = aller tout droit
* (without delay) = directement
  to go straight home = rentrer directement

**strange** adjective
* (odd) = bizarre
  it's strange that she doesn't come any more = il est bizarre qu'elle ne vienne plus

  ! Note that the subjunctive is used after il est bizarre que.

* (unknown) = inconnu/inconnue

**stranger** noun
  a stranger = un inconnu/une inconnue
  (a foreigner) = un étranger/une étrangère

**straw** noun
* (for feeding animals)
  straw = la paille
* (for drinking)
  a straw = une paille

**strawberry** noun
  a strawberry = une fraise

**stream** noun
  a stream = un ruisseau

**street** noun
  a street = une rue

**streetlamp** noun
  a streetlamp = un réverbère

**strength** noun
  strength = la force

**stressful** adjective
= stressant/stressante

**stretch** verb
= s'étirer (! + être)
to stretch one's arms = s'étirer les bras

**strict** adjective
= strict/stricte

**strike** noun
  a strike = une grève
  to go on strike = se mettre en grève

**string** noun
  string = la ficelle
  a piece of string = un bout de ficelle

**striped** adjective
= rayé/rayée

**stroke** verb
= caresser

**stroller** noun (US English)
  a stroller = une poussette

**strong** adjective
* (having physical, mental strength)
  = fort/forte
  she's strong = elle a de la force, elle est forte
* (not easily damaged) = solide
* (having force, power) = fort/forte
  a strong wind = un vent fort
  it's strong tea = c'est du thé fort
* (obvious, noticeable) = fort/forte (! before the noun)
  a strong German accent = un fort accent allemand
  a strong smell of garlic = une forte odeur d'ail
* (having military power)
  = puissant/puissante

**stubborn** adjective
= entêté/entêtée

**student** noun ▶ 315 |
  a student (at university) = un étudiant/une étudiante
  (at school) = un élève/une élève

**study**
**1** verb
  to study history = étudier l'histoire, faire des études d'histoire
  to study to be a teacher = faire des études pour être professeur
  to study for an exam = réviser pour un examen
**2** noun
  a study = un bureau

**stuff**
**1** noun
  stuff (things) = les choses (feminine plural)
  (belongings) = les affaires (feminine plural)
**2** verb
  to stuff a suitcase with clothes = bourrer une valise de vêtements
  to stuff oneself = s'empiffrer✶ (! + être)

**stuffing** noun
  a stuffing = une farce

---

✶ in informal situations

**stupid** *adjective*
= bête, stupide

**style** *noun*
• (*a way of dressing, behaving*)
**style** = la classe
**to have style** = avoir de la classe
• (*a design, a type*)
**a style** (*of car, garment*) = un modèle
(*of building*) = un type
• (*a fashion*)
**a style** = une mode

**stylish** *adjective*
= élégant/élégante

**subject** *noun*
• (*of a conversation*)
**a subject** = un sujet
**to change the subject** = parler d'autre
chose
• (*being studied*)
**a subject** (*at school, college*) = une
matière
(*for an essay, a report*) = un sujet

**suburb** *noun*
the suburbs = la banlieue (*singular*)

**subway** *noun*
• (*US English*) (*the underground*)
**the subway** = le métro
• (*British English*) (*an underground passage*)
**a subway** = un passage souterrain

**succeed** *verb*
= réussir

**success** *noun*
**success** = le succès, la réussite
**to be a success** (*if it's a party*) = être
réussi/réussie
(*if it's a film, a book*) = avoir du succès

**successful** *adjective*
**to be successful** (*in an attempt*) = réussir
(*describing a film, a book*) = avoir du
succès

**such**
**1** *determiner*
**there's no such thing** = ça n'existe pas
**2** *adverb*
**they have such a lot of money** = ils ont
tant d'argent
**she's such a strange person** = elle est si
bizarre
**I've never seen such a mess** = je n'ai
jamais vu une pagaille* pareille

**suddenly** *adverb*
= tout à coup

**suffer** *verb* ▶ **266**
= souffrir

**sugar** *noun*
**sugar** = le sucre

**suggestion** *noun*
**a suggestion** = une suggestion

**suicide** *noun*
**to commit suicide** = se suicider (**!** + être)

**suit**
**1** *noun*
**a suit** (*a man's*) = un costume
(*a woman's*) = un tailleur
**2** *verb*
• (*to be convenient*) = convenir
**to suit someone** = convenir à quelqu'un
**does Friday suit you?** = est-ce que
vendredi te convient?
• (*to look well on*)
**the hat suits you** = le chapeau te va bien

**suitable** *adjective*
**a suitable present** = un cadeau approprié
**to be suitable for children** = convenir aux
enfants

**suitcase** *noun*
**a suitcase** = une valise

**sum** *noun*
• **a sum of money** = une somme d'argent
• **a sum** = un calcul
**to be good at sums** = être bon/bonne en
calcul
**sum up** = récapituler

**summer** *noun*
**summer** = l'été (*masculine*)
**in summer** = en été

**summer holiday** (*British English*),
**summer vacation** (*US English*) *noun*
**the summer holiday** = les vacances d'été
(*from school*) = les grandes vacances
**!** *Note that vacances is feminine plural.*

**sun** *noun*
**the sun** = le soleil
**to sit in the sun** = s'asseoir au soleil

**sunbathe** *verb*
= se faire bronzer (**!** + être)

**sunburn** *noun*
**sunburn** = un coup de soleil

**sunburned** *adjective*
**to get sunburned** = attraper un coup de
soleil

**Sunday** *noun* ▶ **222**
**Sunday** = dimanche (*masculine*)

**sunglasses** *noun*
**sunglasses** = les lunettes de soleil
**!** *Note that lunettes is feminine plural.*

**sunny** *adjective*
= ensoleillé/ensoleillée
**it's going to be sunny** = il va faire du soleil

**sunset** *noun*
**sunset** = le coucher du soleil

**sunshade** *noun*
**a sunshade** = un parasol

**sunshine** *noun*
**sunshine** = le soleil

S

**suntan** *noun*
a suntan = un bronzage
to get a suntan = bronzer

**suntan oil** *noun*
a suntan oil = une huile solaire

**supermarket** *noun*
a supermarket = un supermarché

**supper** *noun*
a supper (*an evening meal*) = un dîner
(*after a show*) = un souper

**support** *verb*
• (*to agree with, to help*) = soutenir
to support the strike = soutenir la grève
• (*to keep*)
to support a family = subvenir aux besoins
d'une famille
to support oneself = subvenir à ses
propres besoins
• (*to hold, to help physically*) = soutenir

**supporter** *noun*
a supporter (*of a team*) = un supporter
(*of a party*) = un sympathisant/une
sympathisante

**suppose** *verb*
• (*to imagine*) = supposer
I don't suppose you know yet? = je
suppose que tu n'es pas encore au
courant?
• (*to be meant to*)
to be supposed to = être censé/censée
I'm supposed to pay for the shopping = je
suis censé payer les courses

**sure** *adjective*
• (*certain*) = sûr/sûre
I'm sure he said nine o'clock = je suis sûr
qu'il a dit neuf heures
are you sure? = est-ce que tu en es sûr?
I'm not sure if she's coming = je ne sais
pas trop si elle vient
to make sure that the door is closed
= s'assurer que la porte est fermée
• (*bound*)
he's sure to win = il va sûrement gagner
• sure of oneself = sûr/sûre de soi

! *Note that* soi *will change to* moi, lui, elle,
eux *etc, depending on the person or
people being described.*

she's sure of herself = elle est sûre d'elle

**surf** *verb* ▶ 248 |
to go surfing = faire du surf

**surface**
**1** *noun*
a surface = une surface
**2** *verb*
= remonter à la surface

**surfboard** *noun*
a surfboard = une planche de surf

**surgeon** *noun* ▶ 315 |
a surgeon = un chirurgien

**surgery** *noun*
• to have surgery = se faire opérer (! + *être*)
• (*British English*) (*the place*)
a surgery = un cabinet médical

**surname** *noun*
a surname = un nom de famille

**surprise**
**1** *noun*
• (*an event, a gift*)
a surprise = une surprise
• (*being amazed*)
surprise = la surprise, l'étonnement
(*masculine*)
to take someone by surprise = prendre
quelqu'un au dépourvu
**2** *verb*
= surprendre

**surprised** *adjective*
= étonné/étonnée
I'm not surprised = ça ne m'étonne pas

**surrender** *verb*
= se rendre (! + *être*)

**surround** *verb*
= entourer
to be surrounded by trees = être
entouré/entourée d'arbres

**surroundings** *noun*
the surroundings (*of a town*) = les
environs (*masculine*)

**survey** *noun*
a survey = un sondage

**survive** *verb*
= survivre
to survive the winter = survivre à l'hiver
to survive an accident = réchapper d'un
accident

**suspect**
**1** *verb*
= soupçonner
she's suspected of stealing money = elle
est soupçonnée d'avoir volé de l'argent
**2** *noun*
a suspect = un suspect/une suspecte

**suspicious** *adjective*
= méfiant/méfiante
to be suspicious of someone = se méfier
de quelqu'un

**swan** *noun*
a swan = un cygne

**swap** *verb*
= échanger

**sweat** *verb*
= transpirer

**sweater** *noun*
a sweater = un pull

**sweatshirt** *noun*
a sweatshirt = un sweatshirt

**Sweden** *noun* ▶ 218 |
Sweden = la Suède

**Swedish** ▶ 275 |
**1** *adjective*
= suédois/suédoise
**2** *noun*
Swedish = le suédois

**sweep** *verb*
= balayer

**sweet**
**1** *adjective*
• sweet (*tasting of sugar*) = sucré/sucrée
(*not bitter or dry*) = doux/douce
to have a sweet tooth = aimer les
sucreries
• (*describing a smell*) = bon/bonne (**!** *before
the noun*)
• (*kind, gentle*) = gentil/gentille
• (*cute*) = mignon/mignonne
**2** *noun* (*British English*)
a sweet = un bonbon

**swim**
**1** *verb*
= nager
to swim across a lake = traverser un lac à
la nage
**2** *noun*
a swim = une baignade
to go for a swim (*in the sea*) = aller se
baigner (**!** + *être*)

**swimming** *noun* ▶ 248 |
swimming = la natation

**swimming pool** *noun*
a swimming pool = une piscine

**swimsuit** *noun*
a swimsuit = un maillot de bain

**swing**
**1** *verb*
• (*to move back and forth*) = se balancer
(**!** + *être*)
to swing on a gate = se balancer sur un
portillon
• (*to move something back and forth*)
= balancer
to swing one's legs = balancer les jambes
**2** *noun*
a swing = une balançoire

**Swiss** ▶ 275 |
**1** *adjective*
= suisse
**2** *noun*
the Swiss = les Suisses (*masculine plural*)

**switch**
**1** *noun*
a switch (*for a light*) = un interrupteur
(*on a radio, an appliance*) = un bouton
**2** *verb*
= changer
to switch seats = changer de place
to switch from English to French = passer
de l'anglais au français

**switch off** = éteindre
to switch off the light = éteindre la
lumière
**switch on** = allumer
to switch the radio on = allumer la radio

**Switzerland** *noun* ▶ 218 |
Switzerland = la Suisse

**sympathetic** *adjective*
(*showing pity*)
= compatissant/compatissante
(*showing understanding*)
= compréhensif/compréhensive

**syringe** *noun*
a syringe = une seringue

**system** *noun*
a system = un système

# T t

**table** *noun*
a table = une table

**tablet** *noun*
a tablet = un comprimé

**table tennis** *noun* ▶ 248 |
table tennis = le tennis de table, le ping-
pong

**tail** *noun*
a tail = une queue

**take** *verb*
**!** *See the usage note on* Talking about
time ▶ 356 | *for more information and
examples.*
• (*to take hold of*) = prendre
to take someone by the hand = prendre
quelqu'un par la main
• (*to carry with one*) = emporter, prendre
I took my umbrella = j'ai emporté mon
parapluie
I'll take the letters to Jack = je vais porter
les lettres à Jack
• (*to accompany, to bring*) = emmener
to take the children for a walk = emmener
les enfants faire une promenade
to take someone home = raccompagner
quelqu'un
• (*to remove*) = prendre
to take a book off the shelf = prendre un
livre sur l'étagère
• (*to steal*) = prendre, voler
• (*to cope with, to bear*) = supporter
he can't take the pain = il ne supporte pas
la douleur
I can't take any more = je n'en peux plus

T

- (*when talking about what is necessary*)
  **it takes** [time | courage | patience ...] = il faut [du temps | du courage | de la patience ...]
  **it takes two hours to get to Paris** = il faut deux heures pour aller à Paris
  **to take a long time to do one's homework** = mettre longtemps pour faire ses devoirs
  **it won't take long** = ça ne prendra pas longtemps
- (*to accept*) = accepter
- (*to react to*) = prendre
  **he took the news badly** = il a mal pris la nouvelle
- (*to use when travelling*) = prendre
  **to take a taxi** = prendre un taxi
  **take the first turn on the right** = prenez la première rue à droite
- (*to do*)
  **to take exams** = passer des examens
- (*to have*) = prendre
  **to take** [a vacation | a shower | driving lessons ...] = prendre [des vacances | une douche | des leçons de conduite ...]
  **I don't take sugar** = je ne prends pas de sucre
- (*to wear*)
  **to take a size 10** (*in clothes*) = s'habiller en 38
  **to take a size 5** (*in shoes*) = chausser du 38

**take apart** = démonter
**take away**
  **to take away the rubbish** = enlever les déchets
  **to take someone away** = emmener quelqu'un
**take back** = rapporter
  **I had to take the dress back** = j'ai dû rapporter la robe
**take down**
- (*to remove*)
  **to take a poster down** = enlever une affiche
  **to take down a tent** = démonter une tente
- (*to write down*) = noter
**take hold of** = prendre
**take off**
- (*from an airport*) = décoller
- (*to remove*) = enlever
  **I took off my shoes** = j'ai enlevé mes chaussures
  **to take off one's clothes** = se déshabiller (**!** + *être*)
**take out**
- (*from a box, a pocket, a bag*) = sortir
  **he took a pen out of his pocket** = il a sorti un stylo de sa poche
- (*from a bank account*) = retirer
  **to take money out** = retirer de l'argent
- (*to be nasty to*)
  **to take it out on someone** = s'en prendre à quelqu'un

**take part**
  **to take part in a game** = participer à un jeu
**take place** = avoir lieu
**take up**
- (*as a hobby*)
  **to take up windsurfing** = se mettre à faire de la planche à voile
- (*to use up*) = prendre
  **to take up space** = prendre de la place

**talented** *adjective*
  = doué/douée

**talk**
**1** *verb*
- (*to speak*) = parler
  **to talk on the phone** = parler au téléphone
  **to talk in French** = parler en français
  **to talk to someone** = parler à quelqu'un
  **I talked to them about the trip** = je leur ai parlé de la sortie
  **they were talking about you** = ils parlaient de toi
  **to talk to oneself** = parler tout seul/toute seule
- (*to chat*) = bavarder
**2** *noun*
- (*a conversation*)
  **a talk** = une conversation
- (*about a special subject*)
  **a talk** (*in class*) = un exposé
  (*to a club, a group*) = une causerie
- (*discussions*)
  **talks** = les négociations (*feminine*)

**talkative** *adjective*
  = bavard/bavarde

**tall** *adjective* ▶ **285**
  (*describing a person*) = grand/grande
  (**!** *before the noun*)
  (*describing a building, a tree*) = haut/haute
  **to be six feet tall** ≈ mesurer un mètre quatre-vingts
  **to get tall** = grandir

**tan** *noun*
  **a tan** = un bronzage
  **to get a tan** = bronzer

**tanned** *adjective*
  = bronzé/bronzée

**tap**
**1** *noun* (*British English*)
  **a tap** = un robinet
  **to turn the tap off** = fermer le robinet
**2** *verb*
  **to tap on the door** = frapper à la porte

**tape**
**1** *noun*
- **a tape** (*for a tape recorder*) = une cassette
  (*for a video*) = une cassette vidéo
- (*for repairs, for sticking*)
  **tape** = le scotch
**2** *verb*
  = enregistrer

---

**✗** in informal situations

**tape recorder** *noun*
a tape recorder = un magnétophone

**target**
**1** *noun*
a target = une cible
**2** *verb*
= viser

**tart** *noun (British English)*
a tart = une tarte
an apple tart = une tarte aux pommes

**task** *noun*
a task = une tâche

**taste**
**1** *noun*
* (*when eating, drinking*)
a taste = un goût
* (*when talking about preferences*)
taste = le goût
to have good taste = avoir du goût
**2** *verb*
* (*when describing a flavour*)
to taste good = être bon/bonne
to taste awful = avoir mauvais goût
it tastes like cabbage = ça a le goût du chou
* (*when eating, drinking*) = goûter

**Taurus** *noun*
Taurus = Taureau (*masculine*)

**tax** *noun*
a tax (*on income, profits*) = un impôt
(*on goods, property*) = une taxe

**taxi** *noun*
a taxi = un taxi

**taxi rank** (*British English*), **taxi stand**
(*US English*) *noun*
a taxi rank = une station de taxis

**tea** *noun*
* (*the product*)
tea = le thé
* (*a cup of tea*)
a tea = un thé
* (*British English*) (*a meal*)
tea (*in the afternoon*) = le thé
(*in the evening*) = le dîner

**teach** *verb*
* (*to help someone to learn skills*)
to teach someone [to read | to drive | to ride a horse ...] = apprendre à quelqu'un à [lire | conduire | monter à cheval ...]
* (*to work as a teacher*) = enseigner
to teach French to adults = enseigner le français à des adultes

**teacher** *noun* ▶ 315 |
a teacher = un enseignant/une enseignante
(*in a primary school*) = un professeur des écoles, un instituteur/une institutrice
(*in a secondary school*) = un professeur

**team** *noun*
a team = une équipe

**teapot** *noun*
a teapot = une théière

**tear**¹ *verb*
* (*to cause damage to*) = déchirer
to tear a page out of a book = arracher une page d'un livre
* (*to get damaged*) = se déchirer (**!** + *être*)
**tear off** = détacher
**tear up** = déchirer

**tear**² *noun*
a tear = une larme
to burst into tears = fondre en larmes

**tease** *verb*
= taquiner

**teaspoon** *noun*
a teaspoon = une petite cuillère

**technical** *adjective*
= technique

**teenager** *noun*
a teenager = un adolescent/une adolescente

**telephone** *noun*
a telephone = un téléphone

**telephone directory** *noun*
a telephone directory = un annuaire

**telescope** *noun*
a telescope = un télescope

**television** *noun*
a television = un téléviseur
I saw the film on television = j'ai vu le film à la télévision

**tell** *verb*
* (*to say to*) = dire à
did you tell your parents? – est-ce que tu l'as dit à tes parents?
to tell someone about a problem = parler d'un problème à quelqu'un
* (*for interest, fun*) = raconter
to tell jokes = raconter des blagues✱
* (*when giving orders or instructions*)
to tell someone to leave the classroom = dire à quelqu'un de quitter la salle de classe
to tell someone not to smoke = interdire à quelqu'un de fumer
* (*to work out, to know*)
I can tell (that) she's disappointed = je vois bien qu'elle est déçue
you can tell he's lying = on voit bien qu'il ment
* (*when making distinctions*)
to tell the twin brothers apart = distinguer les jumeaux
I can't tell which is which = je n'arrive pas à les distinguer
* (*to reveal*) = répéter
don't tell anyone = ne le répète pas
**tell off**
to tell someone off = réprimander quelqu'un

T

**temper** *noun*
to be in a temper = être en colère
to lose one's temper = se mettre en colère

**temperature** *noun* ▶ **266** |
the temperature = la température
to have a temperature = avoir de la
température, avoir de la fièvre

**temporary** *adjective*
(*describing a job*) = temporaire
(*describing accommodation*) = provisoire

**ten** *number* ▶ **187** |, ▶ **211** |
ten = dix
ten houses = dix maisons
I've got ten (of them) = j'en ai dix

**tennis** *noun* ▶ **248** |
tennis = le tennis

**tense** *adjective*
= tendu/tendue

**tent** *noun*
a tent = une tente

**tenth** *number*
• (*in a series*) = dixième
• (*in dates*) ▶ **222** |
the tenth of December = le dix décembre

**term** *noun*
a term = un trimestre

**terrible** *adjective*
• (*expressing shock*) = épouvantable
• (*used for emphasis*) = affreux/affreuse

**terrified** *adjective*
= terrifié/terrifiée

**terror** *noun*
terror = la terreur

**terrorist** *noun*
a terrorist = un terroriste/une terroriste

**test**
**1** *verb*
• (*to try out*) = essayer, tester
• (*in exams*) = contrôler
**2** *noun*
• a test = un test
(*in school, college*) (*written*) = un contrôle
(*oral*) = un contrôle oral
a driving test = un examen du permis de
conduire
• to have an eye test = se faire faire un
examen de la vue

**text**
**1** *verb*
= envoyer un texto à quelqu'un
**2** *noun*
• a text (message) = un texto
• a text = un texte

**than**
**1** *preposition*
• (*in comparisons*) = que
to be [stronger | more intelligent ...] than
= être [plus fort | plus intelligent ...] que
I've got more money than you = j'ai plus
d'argent que toi

• (*when talking about quantities*) ▶ **317** | = de
more than half of the pupils are absent
= plus de la moitié des élèves sont
absents
it's worth less than £100 = ça vaut moins
de 100 livres
**2** *conjunction*
= que
he's older than Al = il est plus âgé qu'Al

**thank** *verb*
= remercier

**thanks**
**1** *adverb* = merci
**2 thanks to** = grâce à

**thank you** *adverb*
= merci
thank you for coming = merci d'être venu

**that** *pronoun*
▶ **351** | *See the boxed note on* that *for more
information and examples.*
what's that? = qu'est-ce que c'est?
who's that? = qui est-ce?
is that Louis? = c'est Louis?
that's how they make butter = c'est
comme ça qu'on fait le beurre
that's not true = ce n'est pas vrai
that's the kitchen = ça, c'est la cuisine

**the** *determiner*
▶ **352** | *See the boxed note on* the *for
detailed information and examples.*

**theatre** (*British English*), **theater** (*US
English*) *noun*
a theatre = un théâtre

**their** *determiner*
their = leur (+ *singular*)
= leurs (+ *plural*)
I don't like their house = je n'aime pas
leur maison
they're selling their CDs = ils vendent
leurs disques compacts

**theirs** *pronoun*
the new house is theirs = la nouvelle
maison est à eux
which car is theirs? = laquelle est leur
voiture?
my car is red but theirs is green = ma
voiture est rouge mais la leur est verte
our parents are younger than theirs = nos
parents sont plus jeunes que les leurs

! *Note that, when comparing objects,
people etc, one of the following
translations—*le leur, la leur *or* les
leurs—*will be used. To know which one to
use, find out whether the object, person
etc. being described is masculine
singular, feminine singular or just plural.*

# that

## As a determiner

In French, determiners agree with the noun that follows; so **that** is translated as follows:

| | | | |
|---|---|---|---|
| **ce** or **cet** | + | *masculine singular noun* | **ce** monsieur, **cet** homme |
| **cette** | + | *feminine singular noun* | **cette** femme |
| **ces** | + | *noun plural* | **ces** livres, **ces** histoires |

Note, however, that the above translations are also used for the English **this** (plural *these*). So when it is necessary to insist on **that** as opposed to another or others of the same sort, the adverbial tag **-là** is added to the noun:

*I prefer **that** colour* = je préfère **cette** couleur**-là**

## As a pronoun

- In French, pronouns reflect the gender and number of the noun they are standing for.

  So **that** (meaning *that one*) is translated by

  | **celui-là** | *for a masculine noun* |
  |---|---|
  | **celle-là** | *for a feminine noun* |

  and **those** (meaning *those ones*) is translated by

  | **ceux-là** | *for a masculine noun* |
  |---|---|
  | **celles-là** | *for a feminine noun* |

  *all the dresses are nice but*
  *I like **that** best* = toutes les robes sont jolies mais
  je préfère **celle-là**

- When used as a relative pronoun, **that** is translated by **qui** when it is the subject of the verb and by **que** when it is the object:

  *the man **that** stole the car* = l'homme **qui** a volé la voiture
  *the film **that** I saw* = le film **que** j'ai vu

  Remember that in the present perfect and past perfect tenses, the past participle agrees with the noun that **que** is referring back to:

  *the girl **that** I met* = la fille **que** j'ai rencontrée
  *the apples **that** I bought* = les pommes **que** j'ai achetées

- When that is used as a relative pronoun with a preposition, it is translated by **lequel** when standing for a masculine singular noun, by **laquelle** when standing for a feminine singular noun, by **lesquels** when standing for a masculine plural noun, and by **lesquelles** when standing for a feminine plural noun:

  *the chair that I was sitting on* = la chaise sur **laquelle** j'étais assis
  *the children that I bought the* = les enfants pour **lesquels** j'ai acheté les livres
  *books for*

  If the preposition would normally be translated by **à** in French (**to**, **at** etc), the translation of the whole (*preposition + relative pronoun*) will be:

  | **auquel** | *for a masculine noun* |
  |---|---|
  | **à laquelle** | *for a feminine noun* |
  | **auxquels** | *for a masculine plural noun* |
  | **auxquelles** | *for a feminine plural noun* |

  *the girls **that** I was talking to* = les filles **auxquelles** je parlais

  If the preposition used would normally be translated by **de** in French (**of, from** etc), the translation of the whole (*preposition + relative pronoun*) will be **dont** in all cases:

  *the people **that** I've talked about* = les personnes **dont** j'ai parlé

## As a conjunction

When used as a conjunction, **that** can almost always be translated by **que** (**qu'** before a vowel or mute h):

*she said **that** she would do it* = elle a dit **qu'**elle le ferait

# the

- In French the definite article, like determiners, agrees with the noun that follows; so **the** is translated as follows:

| | | |
|---|---|---|
| **le** or **l'** + | *masculine singular noun* | **le** chien, **l'**ami |
| **la** or **l'** + | *feminine singular noun* | **la** chaise, **l'**amie |
| **les** + | *masculine plural noun* | **les** hommes, **les** avions |
| **les** + | *feminine plural noun* | **les** femmes, **les** autos |

- When **the** is used after a preposition in English, the two words (*preposition* + **the**) are often translated by one word in French. If the preposition would normally be translated by **de** in French (**of**, **about**, **from** etc), the *preposition* + **the** is translated according to whether the noun is masculine or feminine, singular or plural:

| | | |
|---|---|---|
| **le** or **l'** + | *masculine singular noun* | **du** chien, **de l'**ami |
| **de** + **la** or **l'** + | *feminine singular noun* | **de la** chaise, **de l'**amie |
| **les** + | *masculine plural noun* | **des** hommes, **des** avions |
| **les** + | *feminine plural noun* | **des** femmes, **des** autos |

If the preposition would usually be translated by **à** (**at**, **to** etc) the *preposition* + **the** is translated according to whether the noun is masculine or feminine, singular or plural:

| | | |
|---|---|---|
| **le** or **l'** + | *masculine singular noun* | **au** chien, **à l'**ami |
| **à** + **la** or **l'** + | *feminine singular noun* | **à la** chaise, **à l'**amie |
| **les** + | *masculine plural noun* | **aux** hommes, **aux** avions |
| **les** + | *feminine plural noun* | **aux** femmes, **aux** autos |

- Other than this, there are few problems in translating **the** into French. The following cases are, however, worth remembering as not following exactly the pattern of the English:

| | |
|---|---|
| *the* good, *the* poor, *the* unemployed | = **les** bons, **les** pauvres, **les** chômeurs |
| Charles *the* First, Elizabeth *the* Second | = Charles Ier (Premier), Elizabeth II (Deux) |
| she's *the* actress of the year | = c'est **la plus grande** actrice de l'année |
| *the* Tudors, *the* Batemans, *the* Kennedys | = **les** Tudor, **les** Bateman, **les** Kennedy |
| *the* sporting event of the year | = **le grand** événement sportif de l'année |
| it's *the* film to see | = c'est **le** film à voir |

▶ This dictionary contains usage notes on such topics as **days of the week**, **illnesses**, **the human body**, and **musical instruments**, many of which use **the**; for the index to these notes see ▶ **400** |.

---

**them** *pronoun*
▶ **353** | *See the boxed note on* them *for detailed information and examples.*

**theme park** *noun*
a theme park = un parc de loisirs

**themselves** *pronoun*
- (*when used as a reflexive pronoun*)
  they want to enjoy themselves = ils/elles veulent s'amuser
  they didn't hurt themselves = ils/elles ne se sont pas fait mal
- (*when used for emphasis*)
  they said it themselves = ils l'ont dit eux-mêmes/elles l'ont dit elles-mêmes
  they did it all by themselves = ils l'ont fait tout seuls/elles l'ont fait toutes seules

  ! *Remember that, when talking about mixed groups, the masculine form* eux-mêmes *is used to translate* themselves.

**then** *adverb*
- (*at that point in time*) = alors, à ce moment-là

I was living in Paris then = j'habitais alors Paris
we saw each other a lot then = on se voyait beaucoup à ce moment-là
from then on = à partir de ce moment-là
- (*after, next*) = puis, ensuite
I went for a drink and then had dinner = je suis allé prendre un pot✘ et puis j'ai dîné

**there**
**1** *pronoun*
there is a problem = il y a un problème
there aren't any shops = il n'y a pas de magasins
there was no room = il n'y avait pas de place
there will be a lot of people = il y aura beaucoup de monde
**2** *adverb*
- (*when talking about location*) = là
who's there? = qui est là?
the train wasn't there = le train n'était pas là
go over there = va là-bas
when do we get there? = quand est-ce qu'on arrive?

# them

- When used as a direct object pronoun, referring to people, animals or things, **them** is translated by **les**:

| | |
|---|---|
| *I know them* | = je **les** connais |
| *I don't know them* | = je ne **les** connais pas |
| *do I know them?* | = est-ce que je **les** connais? |

Note that the object pronoun normally comes before the verb in French and that, in tenses like the present perfect and past perfect, the past participle agrees with the direct object pronoun:

| | |
|---|---|
| *he's seen them* | = il **les** a vus |
| | (***them*** *being masculine or of mixed gender*) |
| | = il **les** a vues |
| | (***them*** *being all feminine gender*) |
| *he hasn't seen them* | = il ne **les** a pas vus |
| | = il ne **les** a pas vues |
| *has he seen them?* | = est-ce qu'il **les** a vus? |
| | = est-ce qu'il **les** a vues? |

- In imperatives, the direct object pronoun is translated by **les** and comes after the verb:

| | |
|---|---|
| *catch them!* | = attrape-**les**!* |
| *take them!* | = prenez-**les**!* |

But in negative commands, **les** comes before the verb:

| | |
|---|---|
| *don't take them!* | = ne **les** prenez pas! |
| *don't hit them!* | = ne **les** frappe pas! |

- When used as an indirect object pronoun, **them** is translated by **leur**:

| | |
|---|---|
| *I gave it to them* | = je le **leur** ai donné |
| *I didn't give it to them* | = je ne le **leur** ai pas donné |
| *did I give it to them?* | = est-ce que je le **leur** ai donné? |

- In imperatives, the indirect object pronoun is translated by **leur** and comes after the verb:

| | |
|---|---|
| *write to them!* | = écris-**leur**!* |
| *say it to them!* | = dis-le-**leur**!* |

But in negative commands, **leur** comes before the verb:

*don't show it to them!* = ne le **leur** montre pas!

- After prepositions and the verb to be, the translation is **eux** for masculine or mixed gender and **elles** for feminine gender:

| | |
|---|---|
| *he did it for them* | = il l'a fait **pour eux** |
| | (***them*** *being masculine or of mixed gender*) |
| | = il l'a fait pour **elles** |
| | (***them*** *being all feminine gender*) |
| *it's them* | = ce sont **eux** |
| | ce sont **elles** |

\* Note the hyphen(s).

Note that the entries for **her**, **him**, **me** and **us** are modelled in this note.

---

- (*when drawing attention*)
  **there's** [the sea | my watch | Natalie ...] = voilà [la mer | ma montre | Natalie ...]
  **there they are** = les voilà
  **there you are, there you go** = et voilà

**therefore** *adverb*
= donc, par conséquent

**these**
**1** *determiner*
**these** = ces

**these books aren't mine** = ces livres ne sont pas à moi
**2** *pronoun*
**what are these?** = qu'est-ce que c'est?
**these are your things** = ce sont tes affaires
**these are my friends** = ce sont mes amis
**I prefer** THESE = je préfère ceux-ci/celles-ci
**!** *See the note on* **this** *for further information about the use of* -ci.

**they** *pronoun*
  they = ils/elles
  they'll be there too = ils/elles seront là
    aussi
  there they are! = les voilà!
  they're intelligent girls = ce sont des filles
    intelligentes
  that's how they make yogurt = c'est
    comme ça qu'on fait le yaourt

  ! *Note that* on *is used to translate* they
  *when talking in an impersonal or vague*
  *way about people.*

**thick** *adjective*
  = épais/épaisse

**thief** *noun*
  a thief = un voleur/une voleuse

**thigh** *noun* ▶ 201 |
  the thigh = la cuisse

**thin** *adjective*
  = mince
  to get thin = maigrir

**thing** *noun*
• a thing = une chose, un truc
  I've got things to do = j'ai des choses à
    faire
  that was a stupid thing to do = c'était
    stupide de faire ça
  the best thing would be to call him = le
    mieux serait de l'appeler
  I can't hear a thing = je n'entends rien
• (*belongings*)
  things = les affaires (*feminine*)

**think** *verb*
• (*when talking about opinions*) = penser,
  croire
  what do you think of it? = qu'est-ce que tu
    en penses?
  I think it's unfair = je pense que c'est
    injuste
  'will they come?'—'I don't think so' = 'est-
    ce qu'ils vont venir?'—'je ne crois pas'
  who do you think will win? = qui va
    gagner à ton avis?
• (*to concentrate on an idea*) = réfléchir
  think hard before answering = réfléchis
    bien avant de répondre
• (*to remember*)
  I can't think of his name = je ne me
    rappelle plus son nom
• (*to take into account, to have in mind*)
  to think of someone = penser à quelqu'un
  I thought of you when I saw the dress
    = j'ai pensé à toi quand j'ai vu la robe
  we didn't think of closing the window
    = nous n'avons pas pensé à fermer la
    fenêtre
• (*to have vague plans to*)
  to be thinking of changing jobs
    = envisager de changer de travail
• (*to have an idea about*)
  to think of a solution = trouver une
    solution

**third**
**1** *adjective*
  = troisième
**2** *noun*
• (*in a series*)
  the third = le troisième/la troisième
• (*in dates*) ▶ 222 |
  the third of June = le trois juin
• (*when talking about quantities*) ▶ 317 |
  a third of the population = un tiers de la
    population
**3** *adverb*
  = troisième
  to come third = arriver troisième

**thirsty** *adjective*
  to be thirsty = avoir soif
  I'm very thirsty = j'ai très soif

**thirteen** *number* ▶ 187 |, ▶ 211 |
  thirteen = treize

**thirteenth** *number*
• (*in a series*) = treizième
• (*in dates*) ▶ 222 |
  Friday the thirteenth = vendredi treize

**thirty** *number* ▶ 187 |, ▶ 211 |
  thirty = trente

**this**
**1** *determiner*
  this = ce/cette (! cet + *masculine* + *vowel*
    *or mute h*)
  I like this garden = j'aime bien ce jardin
  do you know this place? = est-ce que tu
    connais cet endroit?
  who is this woman? = qui est cette
    femme?
  I prefer THIS hotel to the others = je préfère
    cet hôtel-ci aux autres

  ! *Note that, since the translations for* this
  *and* that *are the same, the tag* -ci *must be*
  *added to the noun and pronoun if a clear*
  *distinction is to be made.*

**2** *pronoun*
  what's this? = qu'est-ce que c'est?
  who's this? = qui est-ce?
  this is the kitchen = voici la cuisine
  this is my sister = voici ma sœur
  this isn't the right address = ce n'est pas la
    bonne adresse
  how much is THIS? = combien coûte celui-
    ci/celle-ci?

**those**
**1** *determiner*
  those = ces
  those books are yours = ces livres sont à
    toi
**2** *pronoun*
  what are those? = qu'est-ce que c'est?
  those are my letters = ce sont mes lettres
  those are my cousins = ce sont mes
    cousins
  I prefer THOSE = je préfère ceux-là/celles-là
  ▶ 351 | *See the boxed note on* that *for further*
  *information about the use of* -là.

**though** *conjunction*
= bien que
though it's expensive, it's still a good buy
= bien que ce soit cher, ça reste un bon
achat

> **!** Note that the subjunctive is used after
> bien que.

**thought** *noun*
a thought = une pensée

**thousand** *number*
one thousand, a thousand = mille
four thousand pounds = quatre mille
livres
about a thousand people = un millier de
personnes

**thread** *noun*
thread = le fil

**threat** *noun*
a threat = une menace

**threaten** *verb*
= menacer

**three** *number* ▶ 107 , ▶ 211
three = trois
three sisters = trois sœurs
I've got three (of them) = j'en ai trois

**throat** *noun* ▶ 201
the throat = la gorge

**through**

> **!** Often through occurs in combinations
> with verbs, for example: go through, let
> through, read through etc. To find the
> correct translations for this type of verb,
> look up the separate dictionary entries at
> go, let, read etc.

*preposition*
* *(from one side to the other)* = à travers
  to see through the fog = voir à travers le
  brouillard
  to drive through the desert = traverser le
  désert (en voiture)
* *(via, by way of)*
  to go through the town centre = passer par
  le centre-ville
  to look through a window = regarder par
  une fenêtre
* *(past)*
  to go through a red light = brûler un feu
  rouge
  to go through customs = passer la douane
* *(when talking about time)*
  right through the day = toute la journée
  from Friday through to Sunday = de
  vendredi jusqu'à dimanche
  open April through September (*US
  English*) = ouvert d'avril à fin septembre

**throw** *verb*
= lancer
to throw stones at someone = lancer des
pierres à quelqu'un
throw me the ball = lance-moi le ballon
to throw a book on the floor = jeter un
livre par terre

**throw away, throw out** = jeter

**thumb** *noun* ▶ 201
the thumb = le pouce

**thunder** *noun*
thunder = le tonnerre

**thunderstorm** *noun*
a thunderstorm = un orage

**Thursday** *noun* ▶ 222
Thursday = jeudi (*masculine*)

**ticket** *noun*
a ticket (*for a plane, a train, a film, an
event*) = un billet
(*for a bus, the underground, a locker*) = un
ticket

**tickle** *verb*
= chatouiller

**tide** *noun*
the tide = la marée
the tide is out = c'est la marée basse
the tide is coming in = la marée monte

**tidy** *adjective*
(*describing a place, a desk*) = bien
rangé/rangée
(*describing a person*) = ordonné/ordonnée
**tidy up** = ranger

**tie**
**1** *verb*
= attacher
to tie a dog to a tree = attacher un chien à
un arbre
to tie a parcel (up) with string = ficeler un
paquet
**2** *noun*
* (*worn with a shirt*)
  a tie = une cravate
* (*in sport*)
  a tie = un match nul
**tie up** = ligoter

**tiger** *noun*
a tiger = un tigre

**tight** *adjective*
= serré/serrée

**tights** *noun* (*British English*)
tights = un collant (*singular*)

**till¹** ▶ **until**

**till²** *noun*
a till = une caisse

**timber** *noun*
timber = le bois (de construction)

**time** *noun*
* time = le temps
  I don't have time to go there = je n'ai pas
  le temps d'y aller
  we haven't seen them for some time = ça
  fait un moment qu'on ne les a pas vus
  a long time ago = il y a longtemps

T

# Talking about time

▶ For time by the clock, ▶ **211** |; for days of the week, months, and dates, ▶ **222** |.

## How long?

Note the various ways of translating **take** into French:

| | |
|---|---|
| *how long does it take?* | = combien de temps faut-il? |
| *it took me a week* | = il m'a fallu une semaine / cela m'a pris une semaine |
| *it'll take at least a year* | = il faudra au moins un an |
| *it'll only take a minute* | = ça ne prendra qu'une minute |

Use **en** for **in** when expressing the time something took or will take:

*he did it **in** an hour* = il l'a fait **en** une heure

The commonest translation of **for** in the 'how long' sense is **pendant**:

*I worked in a factory **for** a year* = j'ai travaillé en usine **pendant** un an

But use **pour** to translate **for** when the length of time is seen as being still to come:

*we're here **for** a month* = nous sommes là **pour** un mois

And use **depuis** to translate **for** when the action began in the past and is still going on:

| | |
|---|---|
| *she has been here **for** a week* | = elle est ici **depuis** une semaine |
| *I haven't seen her **for** years* | = je ne l'ai pas vue **depuis** des années |

## When?

Use **dans** for **in** when something is seen as happening in the future:

| | |
|---|---|
| *I'll be there **in** an hour* | = j'y serai **dans** une heure |
| ***in** three weeks' time* | = **dans** trois semaines |
| *when did it happen?* | = quand est-ce que c'est arrivé? |
| *a month ago* | = il y a un mois |
| *a week ago yesterday* | = il y a eu huit jours hier |
| *when will you see him?* | = quand est-ce que tu le verras? |
| ***in** a few days* | = **dans** quelques jours |
| *a month from tomorrow* | = **dans** un mois demain |
| *when you see him, tell him to call me* | = quand tu le verras,* dis-lui de m'appeler |

## How often?

| | |
|---|---|
| *how often does it happen?* | = cela arrive tous les combien? |
| *every year* | = tous les ans |
| *five times a day* | = cinq fois par jour |
| *once every three months* | = une fois tous les trois mois |

## How much an hour (etc)?

| | |
|---|---|
| *how much do you get **an** hour?* | = combien gagnez-vous **de** l'heure? |
| *to be paid $20 **an** hour* | = être payé 20 dollars **de** l'heure |
| *to be paid **by the** hour* | = être payé **à** l'heure |
| *how much do you get **a** week?* | = combien gagnez-vous **par** semaine? |
| *$3,000 **a** month* | = 3 000 dollars **par** mois |

\* Note that, when talking about future time, the future tense of the verb is used after **quand**.

---

• (*when talking about a specific hour or period of time*)
the time = l'heure (*feminine*)
what's the time?, what time is it? = quelle heure est-il?
what time does the film start? = à quelle heure commence le film?

to arrive on time = arriver à l'heure
in [five days' | a week's | six months' ...] time = dans [cinq jours | une semaine | six mois ...]
this time last year = il y a exactement un an
by this time next week = d'ici la semaine prochaine
it's time we left = il est temps de partir

- (a moment)
  **a time** – un moment
  **at times** = par moments
  **at the right time** = au bon moment
  **this is no time to argue** = ce n'est pas le
    moment de se disputer
  **any time now** = d'un moment à l'autre
  **for the time being** = pour le moment
- (a period in the past)
  **a time** = une époque
  **they didn't know each other at the time**
    = ils ne se connaissaient pas à l'époque
- (an experience)
  **to have a good time** = bien s'amuser
    (**!** + être)
  **to have a hard time concentrating** = avoir
    du mal à se concentrer
- (an occasion)
  **the first time we met** = la première fois
    que nous nous sommes rencontrés
  **from time to time** = de temps en temps
- (when comparing)
  **three times more expensive** = trois fois
    plus cher
  **ten times quicker** = dix fois plus rapide

**timetable** noun
- (for trains, buses)
  **a timetable** = un horaire
- (in school, at work)
  **a timetable** = un emploi du temps

**tin** noun
- (the metal)
  **tin** = l'étain (masculine)
- (British English) (a can)
  **a tin** = une boîte (de conserve)
  **a tin of beans** = une boîte de haricots

**tin opener** noun (British English)
  **a tin opener** = un ouvre-boîtes

**tiny** adjective
  = tout petit/toute petite

**tip** noun
- (the point, the end)
  **the tip** (of a pen, a stick, a shoe) = la
    pointe
  (of the finger, nose, tongue) = le bout
  **on the tips of one's toes** = sur la pointe
    des pieds
- (given in a hotel, a restaurant)
  **a tip** = un pourboire
- (a piece of advice)
  **a tip** = un conseil

**tire** noun (US English)
  **a tire** = un pneu

**tired** adjective
- (needing rest) = fatigué/fatiguée
  **to get tired** = se fatiguer (**!** + être)
- (needing a change)
  **I'm tired of being a waitress** = j'en ai assez
    d'être serveuse

**tiring** adjective
  = fatigant/fatigante

**tissue** noun
  **a tissue** = un mouchoir en papier

**to** preposition ▶ 211 |
  ▶ 358 | See the boxed note on to. There are
  many adjectives like mean, nice, rude etc
  and verbs like belong, write etc which involve
  the use of to. For translations, look up the
  adjective entries at mean, nice, rude or the
  verb entries at belong, write.

**toast** noun
  **toast** = le pain grillé
  **a piece of toast** = une tranche de pain
    grillé

**toaster** noun
  **a toaster** = un grille-pain

**today** adverb ▶ 356 |
  = aujourd'hui

**toe** noun ▶ 201 |
  **the toe** = l'orteil (masculine)

**toffee** noun
  **toffee** = le caramel

**together** adverb
  = ensemble

**toilet** noun
  **a toilet** = des toilettes (feminine plural)

**toilet paper** noun
  **toilet paper** = le papier hygiénique

**tomato** noun
  **a tomato** = une tomate

**tomorrow** adverb ▶ 356 |
  = demain

**tongue** noun ▶ 201 |
  **the tongue** = la langue

**tonight** adverb
  (this evening) = ce soir
  (during the night) = cette nuit

**too** adverb
- (also) = aussi
  **I'm going too** = j'y vais aussi
- (more than is necessary or desirable)
  = trop
  **it's too** [big | dear | far …] = c'est trop [grand |
    cher | loin …]
  **there were too many people** = il y avait
    trop de monde
  **I ate too much** = j'ai trop mangé

**tool** noun
  **a tool** = un outil

**tooth** noun ▶ 201 |
  **a tooth** = une dent
  **a set of false teeth** = un dentier

**toothache** noun ▶ 266 |
  **to have a toothache** = avoir mal aux dents

**toothbrush** noun
  **a toothbrush** = une brosse à dents

**toothpaste** noun
  **toothpaste** = le dentifrice

**T**

# to

▶ This dictionary contains usage notes on such topics as **The clock**, **Length and weight measurements**, **Games and sports** etc. Many of these use the preposition **to**. For the index to these notes ▶ **400** ].

## As a preposition

● When **to** is used as a preposition with verbs of movement (*go*, *travel* etc), it is often translated by **à** (*à Paris*, *à Londres*), but remember to use **en** with feminine countries (*en France*) and **au** with masculine countries (*au Portugal*).

Remember when using **à** in French that **à** + **le** always becomes **au**:

| | |
|---|---|
| *to the office* | = **au** bureau |

and **à** + **les** always becomes **aux**:

| | |
|---|---|
| *to the shops* | = **aux** magasins |

● When **to** is used as a preposition with verbs such as *speak*, *give*, *say* etc, it is usually translated by **à**:

| | |
|---|---|
| *give the book **to** Jane* | = donne le livre **à** Jane |
| *I'll speak **to** the headmistress* | = je vais parler **à** la directrice |
| *she said it **to** my father* | = elle l'a dit **à** mon père |
| *show it **to** the policeman* | = montre-le **à** l'agent |
| *I pointed it out **to** the stewardess* | = je l'ai signalé **à** l'hôtesse |
| *give the ball **to** the little boy* | = donne le ballon **au***  petit garçon |
| *we gave it **to** the children* | = nous l'avons donné **aux***  enfants |

\* Remember that **à** + **le** = **au** and **à** + **les** = **aux**

● When **to** is used as a preposition with personal pronouns (*me*, *you*, *him*, *her*, *us*, *them*), the two words (*preposition* + *pronoun*) are translated by **me/te/lui/lui/nous/vous/leur**:

| | |
|---|---|
| *she gave it **to** them* | = elle le **leur** a donné |
| *I'll say it **to** her* | = je vais le **lui** dire |
| *will you lend it **to** me?* | = est-ce que tu **me** le prêtes? |

## As part of an infinitive

● When **to** forms the infinitive of a verb taken alone, it needs no translation:

| | |
|---|---|
| *to go* | = aller |
| *to sing* | = chanter |

However, when **to** is used as part of an infinitive giving the meaning **in order to**, it is translated by **pour**:

| | |
|---|---|
| *he's gone into town **to buy** a shirt* | = il est parti en ville **pour acheter** une chemise |
| *I need it **to** do my homework* | = j'en ai besoin **pour faire** mes devoirs |

● **to** is also used as part of an infinitive after certain adjectives: *easy to read* etc. Here **to** is usually translated by **à**:

| | |
|---|---|
| *her writing is easy **to** read* | = son écriture est facile **à** lire |
| *his accent is difficult **to** understand* | = son accent est dur **à** comprendre |

However, when the infinitive has an object, **to** is usually translated by **de**:

| | |
|---|---|
| *it's easy **to** lose one's way* | = il est facile **de** perdre son chemin |
| *it's difficult **to** work at night* | = c'est difficile **de** travailler la nuit |

▶ **to** is also used as part of an infinitive after certain verbs: *she told me **to** wash my hands, I'll help him **to** tidy the room* etc. Here the translation, usually either **à** or **de**, depends on the verb used in French. To find the correct translation, consult the appropriate verb entry: **tell**, **help** etc.

---

## top
**1** noun
* (*the highest part*)
  the top of the hill = le sommet de la colline
  the top of the stairs = le haut de l'escalier

at the top of [the page | the stairs | street ...] = en haut [de la page | de l'escalier | de la rue ...]
* (*a cover, a lid*)
  a top (*on a bottle*) = un bouchon
  (*on a pan*) = un couvercle
  (*on a pen*) = un capuchon

* (*the highest level*)
  **to get to the top** = réussir
  **to be at the top of the class** = être
  premier/première de la classe
  **2** *adjective*
  **the top** [shelf | drawer | button …] = [l'étagère |
  le tiroir | le bouton …] du haut

**top-up card** *noun*
  **a top-up card** = une carte de recharge

**torch** *noun* (*British English*)
  **a torch** = une lampe de poche

**torn** *adjective*
  = déchiré/déchirée

**tortoise** *noun*
  **a tortoise** = une tortue

**total**
  **1** *noun*
  **a total** = un total
  **2** *adjective*
  = total/totale

**touch**
  **1** *verb*
* (*with one's hand*) = toucher
* (*to interfere with*) = toucher à
  **don't touch my things** = ne touche pas à
  mes affaires
  **2** *noun*
  **to** [be | get | stay …] **in touch with someone**
  = [être | se mettre | rester …] en contact avec
  quelqu'un

**tough** *adjective*
* (*not soft, not sensitive*) = coriace
* (*rough*) = dur/dure
  **a tough area** = un quartier dur
* (*difficult*) = difficile
* (*severe*) = sévère

**tour**
  **1** *noun*
* (*by a team, a band, a theatre group*)
  **a tour** = une tournée
  **on tour** = en tournée
* (*by tourists, pupils, visitors*)
  **a tour** = une visite
  **to go on a tour of the castle** = visiter le
  château
  **2** *verb*
  **to tour the United States** = visiter les
  États-Unis

**tourism** *noun*
  tourism = le tourisme

**tourist** *noun*
  **a tourist** = un touriste/une touriste

**tourist office** *noun*
  **a tourist office** (*local*) = un syndicat
  d'initiative

**toward(s)** *preposition*
* (*when talking about place, time*) = vers

**towards the east** = vers l'est
  **towards evening** = vers le soir
* (*when talking about attitudes*) = envers
  **to be friendly towards someone** = se
  montrer cordial envers quelqu'un

**towel** *noun*
  **a towel** = une serviette

**tower** *noun*
  **a tower** = une tour

**tower block** *noun* (*British English*)
  **a tower block** = une tour d'habitation

**town** *noun*
  **a town** = une ville
  **to go into town** = aller en ville

**town hall** *noun*
  **a town hall** = une mairie

**toy** *noun*
  **a toy** = un jouet

**track** *noun*
* (*a path*)
  **a track** = un sentier, un chemin
* (*for sports*)
  **a track** = une piste
* (*the rails*)
  **the track(s)** = la voie ferrée
* (*left by a person, an animal, a car*)
  **tracks** = des traces (*feminine*)

**tracksuit** *noun*
  **a tracksuit** = un survêtement

**trade** *noun*
* **trade** = le commerce
* **a trade** = un métier

**tradition** *noun*
  **a tradition** = une tradition

**traffic** *noun*
  traffic = la circulation

**traffic jam** *noun*
  **a traffic jam** = un embouteillage, un
  bouchon

**traffic lights** *noun*
  traffic lights = les feux (*masculine*)

**train**
  **1** *noun*
  **a train** = un train
  **the train to Paris** = le train à destination
  de Paris
  **2** *verb*
* (*to teach, to prepare*)
  **to train employees** = former des employés
  **to train athletes** = entraîner des athlètes
* (*to learn a job*)
  **to train as a doctor** = suivre une
  formation de médecin
  **she trained as a teacher** = elle a reçu une
  formation d'enseignante
* (*for a sporting event*) = s'entraîner
  (**!** + *être*)

**T**

**trainer** noun (*British English*)
a trainer (*high*) = une basket
(*low*) = un tennis

**training course** noun
a training course = un stage de formation

**tramp** noun
a tramp = un clochard/une clocharde

**translate** verb
= traduire

**translator** noun ▶ 315 |
a translator = un traducteur/une
traductrice

**transport, transportation** (*US
English*) noun
transport = le transport
a means of transport = un moyen de
transport

**trap** noun
a trap = un piège
to set a trap for someone = tendre un
piège à quelqu'un

**trash** noun (*US English*)
trash = les ordures (*feminine plural*)

**trash can** noun (*US English*)
a trash can = une poubelle

**travel** verb
= voyager
to travel abroad = aller à l'étranger
to travel a long way = faire beaucoup de
chemin

**travel agency** noun ▶ 315 |
a travel agency = une agence de voyages

**traveller** (*British English*), **traveler** (*US
English*) noun
a traveller = un voyageur/une voyageuse

**traveller's cheque** (*British English*),
**traveler's check** (*US English*) noun
a traveller's cheque = un chèque-voyage

**tray** noun
a tray = un plateau

**treat** verb
• (*to deal with, to behave with*) = traiter
to treat someone badly = mal se conduire
envers quelqu'un
• (*to pay for*)
to treat someone to a glass of wine
= payer un verre de vin à quelqu'un

**treatment** noun
treatment = le traitement
to receive treatment = être sous
traitement

**tree** noun
a tree = un arbre

**tremble** verb
= trembler

**trendy** adjective
= branché/branchée✖

**trial** noun
a trial = un procès
to go on trial = passer en jugement

**triangle** noun
a triangle = un triangle

**trick**
**1** noun
• (*a joke*)
a trick = un tour, une blague✖
to play a trick on someone = jouer un
tour à quelqu'un
• (*a means of deceiving*)
a trick = une combine
• (*to entertain*)
a trick = un tour
**2** verb
= duper, rouler✖

**trip**
**1** noun
a trip (*abroad*) = un voyage
(*a day out*) = une excursion, une sortie
to be on a business trip = être en voyage
d'affaires
**2** verb
to trip (up) = trébucher
to trip someone (up) = faire trébucher
quelqu'un

**trouble** noun
• (*difficulties*)
trouble = les ennuis (*masculine plural*)
to be in trouble = avoir des ennuis
to get someone into trouble = créer des
ennuis à quelqu'un
to make trouble = faire des histoires✖
• (*an effort*)
to take the trouble to check = se donner la
peine de vérifier
to go to a lot of trouble = se donner
beaucoup de mal

**trousers** noun
trousers = un pantalon (*singular*)

**trout** noun
a trout = une truite

**truck** noun
a truck = un camion

**truck driver** noun ▶ 315 |
a truck driver = un routier

**true** adjective
= vrai/vraie
is it true that he's leaving? = est-ce que
c'est vrai qu'il part?
to come true = se réaliser (**!** + *être*)

**trumpet** noun ▶ 290 |
a trumpet = une trompette

**trunk** *noun*
- (*of a tree*)
  a trunk = un tronc
- (*of an elephant*)
  a trunk = une trompe
- (*US English*) (*in a car*)
  the trunk = le coffre

**trust** *verb*
- (*to believe*) = se fier à (**!** + *être*)
  to trust a friend = se fier à un ami
  I don't trust them = je me méfie d'eux
- (*to rely on*) = faire confiance à
  you can't trust him = on ne peut pas lui
  faire confiance

**truth** *noun*
  the truth = la vérité

**try**
**1** *verb*
- to try = essayer
  to try [to understand | to come | to forget …]
  = essayer [de comprendre | de venir |
  d'oublier …]
  try phoning him = essaie de lui téléphoner
- (*to test*) = essayer
  to try (out) a recipe = essayer une recette
  to try (on) a pair of jeans = essayer un jean
- (*to taste*) = goûter
- (*in court*) = juger
**2** *noun*
  to score a try = marquer un essai

**T-shirt** *noun*
  a T-shirt = un T-shirt

**tube** *noun*
- a tube = un tube
- (*British English*) (*the underground*)
  the tube = le métro

**Tuesday** *noun* ▶ 222 |
  Tuesday = mardi (*masculine*)

**tuna** *noun*
  tuna = le thon

**tunnel** *noun*
  a tunnel = un tunnel

**turkey** *noun*
  a turkey = une dinde

**Turkey** *noun* ▶ 218 |
  Turkey = la Turquie

**turn**
**1** *verb*
- (*to move one's body*) = se retourner
  (**!** + *être*)
  to turn one's face toward(s) the sun
  = tourner le visage vers le soleil
- (*to change direction*) = tourner
  to turn right = tourner à droite
  to turn the corner = tourner au coin de la
  rue
- (*to twist*) = tourner
  to turn the handle = tourner la poignée

- (*to change*)
  to turn the bedroom into an office
  = transformer la chambre en bureau
  to turn someone into a criminal = faire un
  criminel de quelqu'un
- (*to become*)
  to turn into a butterfly = se transformer en
  papillon
  to turn red = rougir
**2** *noun*
- (*a bend*)
  a turn = un tournant, un virage
- (*in games*)
  a turn = un tour
  whose turn is it? = c'est à qui le tour?

**turn around, turn round**
- (*to face the other way*) (*if it's a person*) = se
  retourner (**!** + *être*)
  (*if it's a car*) = faire demi-tour
  to turn the table around = tourner la table
  dans l'autre sens
- (*to go round and round*) = tourner

**turn away** = se détourner (**!** + *être*)
**turn back** = faire demi-tour
**turn down**
- (*to lower*) = baisser
  to turn down the radio = baisser la radio
- (*to reject*) = refuser
  to turn someone down = refuser
  quelqu'un
**turn off**
  to turn the oven off = éteindre le four
  to turn off the light = éteindre la lumière
  to turn the tap off = fermer le robinet
**turn on** = allumer
  to turn on the TV = allumer la télévision
  to turn the tap on = ouvrir le robinet
**turn out**
  to turn out all right (in the end)
  = s'arranger (**!** + *être*)
  to turn out to be easy = se révéler facile
**turn over**
- (*to roll over*) = se retourner (**!** + *être*)
- to turn over the page = tourner la page
**turn up**
- (*to show up*) = arriver
- (*to increase*)
  to turn up the heating = augmenter le
  chauffage
  to turn the music up = mettre la musique
  plus fort

**turtle** *noun*
- a (sea) turtle = une tortue marine
- (*US English*) (*a tortoise*)
  a turtle = une tortue

**TV** *noun*
  a TV = une télévision, une télé**✗**

**twelfth** *number*
- (*in a series*) = douzième
- (*in dates*) ▶ 222 |
  the twelfth of July = le douze juillet

**twelve** *number* ▶ 187 |, ▶ 211 |
  twelve = douze
  twelve pupils = douze élèves
  I've got twelve (of them) = j'en ai douze

**T**

**twenty** *number* ▶ **187 |**, ▶ **211 |**
 twenty = vingt

**twice** *adverb*
 = deux fois
 twice as many people = deux fois plus de
  monde
 twice as much time = deux fois plus de
  temps

**twin**
**1** *noun*
 a twin = un jumeau/une jumelle
**2** *adjective*
 a twin brother = un frère jumeau
 a twin sister = une sœur jumelle

**twist** *verb*
* (*to bend out of shape*) = tordre
* (*to injure*) ▶ **266 |**
 to twist one's ankle = se tordre la cheville

**two** *number* ▶ **187 |**, ▶ **211 |**
 two = deux
 two brothers = deux frères
 I've got two (of them) = j'en ai deux

**type**
**1** *noun*
 a type = un type, un genre
 this type of [person | book | building …] = ce
  genre de [personne | livre | bâtiment …]
 he's not my type = ce n'est pas mon genre
**2** *verb*
 = taper (à la machine)

**typewriter** *noun*
 a typewriter = une machine à écrire

**typical** *adjective*
 = typique

**typist** *noun* ▶ **315 |**
 a typist = un dactylo/une dactylo

**tyre** *noun* (*British English*)
 a tyre = un pneu

# Uu

**ugly** *adjective*
 = laid/laide

**umbrella** *noun*
 an umbrella = un parapluie

**unbelievable** *adjective*
 = incroyable

**uncle** *noun*
 an uncle = un oncle

**uncomfortable** *adjective*
* (*awkward*) = pénible
 to make someone (feel) uncomfortable
  = mettre quelqu'un mal à l'aise

* (*describing shoes, seats*) = inconfortable
 (*describing heat, conditions*) = pénible

**unconscious** *adjective*
 = sans connaissance
 to knock someone unconscious
  = assommer quelqu'un

**under** *preposition*
* under = sous
 to hide under the bed = se cacher sous le
  lit
 I found the newspaper under it = j'ai
  trouvé le journal dessous
* (*less than*)
 to earn under three pounds an hour
  = gagner moins de trois livres de l'heure
 children under five = les enfants de moins
  de cinq ans

**underground** *noun* (*British English*)
 the underground = le métro

**underline** *verb*
 = souligner

**underneath**
**1** *adverb*
 = en dessous
 I want to see what's underneath = je veux
  voir ce qu'il y a dessous
**2** *preposition*
 = au-dessous de, sous
 underneath the building = au-dessous du
  bâtiment

**underpants** *noun*
 underpants = un slip (*singular*)

**understand** *verb*
 = comprendre
 I can't understand what they're saying
  = je ne comprends pas ce qu'ils disent
 to make oneself understood = se faire
  comprendre

**understanding** *adjective*
 = compréhensif/compréhensive

**underwater** *adverb*
 = sous l'eau

**underwear** *noun*
 underwear = les sous-vêtements
  (*masculine plural*)

**undo** *verb*
 = défaire
 to undo a button = défaire un bouton

**undress** *verb*
 = se déshabiller (**!** + *être*)

**uneasy** *adjective*
 = inquiet/inquiète

**unemployed** *adjective*
 to be unemployed = être au chômage, être
  sans emploi

**unemployment** *noun*
 unemployment = le chômage

**unfair** *adjective*
= injuste

**unfortunately** *adverb*
= malheureusement

**unfriendly** *adjective*
(*describing a person*) = peu amical/peu
amicale
(*describing a place*)
= inhospitalier/inhospitalière

**ungrateful** *adjective*
= ingrat/ingrate

**unhappy** *adjective*
(*sad*) = malheureux/malheureuse
(*not satisfied*) = mécontent/mécontente

**unhealthy** *adjective*
(*describing a way of life, food*)
= malsain/malsaine
(*describing a person*) = maladif/maladive
(*describing conditions*) = insalubre

**uniform** *noun*
a uniform = un uniforme

**union** *noun*
a union = un syndicat

**unique** *adjective*
= unique

**United Kingdom** *noun* ▶ 218 |
the United Kingdom = le Royaume-Uni

**United States (of America)** *noun*
▶ 218 |
the United States (of America) = les États-
Unis (d'Amérique)
| ! *Note that* États *is masculine plural.*

**universe** *noun*
a universe = un univers

**university** *noun*
a university = une université

**unkind** *adjective*
to be unkind (*describing a person, an
action*) = ne pas être très gentil/gentille
(*describing a remark*) = être
désobligeant/désobligeante

**unknown** *adjective*
= inconnu/inconnue

**unless** *conjunction*
it won't work unless you plug it in = ça ne
marchera pas si tu ne le branches pas
she can't work unless she finds an au pair
= elle ne peut pas travailler à moins de
trouver une jeune fille au pair
she can't work unless we find an au pair
= elle ne peut pas travailler à moins
qu'on ne lui trouve une jeune fille au
pair
| ! *Note that the subjunctive is used after* à
moins que.

**unlock** *verb*
= ouvrir

**unlucky** *adjective*
= malchanceux/malchanceuse
you were unlucky = tu n'as pas eu de chance

**unpack** *verb*
to unpack a suitcase = défaire une valise
to unpack one's belongings = déballer ses
affaires

**unsuitable** *adjective*
= inapproprié/inappropriée

**untidy** *adjective*
(*in one's habits*)
= désordonné/désordonnée
(*in how one looks*) = peu soigné/peu soignée

**until**
**1** *preposition*
= jusqu'à
I'm staying until Thursday = je reste
jusqu'à jeudi
until now = jusqu'à présent
I'm going to wait until after Christmas = je
vais attendre que Noël soit passé
she won't get an answer until next week
= elle n'aura pas de réponse avant la
semaine prochaine
**2** *conjunction*
I'll wait until I get back home = j'attendrai
d'être rentré
we'll stay until they come = nous
resterons jusqu'à ce qu'ils arrivent
don't look until it's ready = ne regarde pas
avant que ce soit prêt
| ! *Note that the subjunctive is used after*
jusqu'à ce que *and* avant que.

**unusual** *adjective*
(*rare*) = peu commun/peu commune
it's unusual to see so few people = il est
rare de voir si peu de monde
(*different, out of the ordinary*)
= original/originale

**up**
| ! *Often* up *occurs in combinations with
verbs, for example:* blow up, give up, own
up, *etc. To find the correct translations for
this type of verb, look up the separate
dictionary entries at* blow, give, own *etc.*

**1** *preposition*
the cat's up the tree = le chat est dans
l'arbre
to go up the street = remonter la rue
she ran up the stairs = elle a monté
l'escalier en courant
the library is up those stairs = la
bibliothèque se trouve en haut de cet
escalier
**2** *adverb*
up in the sky = dans le ciel
up on (top of) the wardrobe = sur l'armoire
to go up = monter (! + *être*)
to go up to Scotland = aller en Écosse
up there = là-haut
put the picture a bit further up = mets le
tableau un peu plus haut
to climb all the way up = monter jusqu'en
haut

**U**

**3** *adjective*
(*out of bed*)
to be up = être debout
to be up all night = veiller toute la nuit
(*higher in amount, level*)
to be up by 20% = avoir augmenté de 20%
**4 up to**
(*well enough*)
to be up to going out = avoir la force de
sortir
I'm not up to it = je n'en ai pas la force
(*when talking about who is responsible*)
it's up to [me | you | them ...] to decide
= c'est à [moi | toi | eux ...] de décider
(*until*) = jusqu'à
up to now = jusqu'à présent
up to 1996 = jusqu'en 1996

**upset**
**1** *adjective*
to be upset (*annoyed*) = être
contrarié/contrariée
(*distressed*) = être très affecté/affectée
to get upset (*annoyed*) = se fâcher
(**!** + *être*)
(*distressed*) = se mettre dans tous ses états
(**!** + *être*)
**2** *verb*
(*to make someone unhappy*) (*if it's an
event*) = bouleverser
(*if it's a person*) = faire de la peine à
(*to annoy*) = contrarier

**upside down** *adverb*
= à l'envers
you're holding the book upside down = tu
tiens le livre à l'envers

**upstairs** *adverb*
= en haut
to go upstairs = monter (l'escalier)
to bring the cases upstairs = monter les
valises

**urgent** *adjective*
= urgent/urgente

**us** *pronoun*

> **!** us *is always translated by* nous. *Note
> that there is a boxed usage note at* them.
> *The entries* me, him, her *and* us *are
> modelled on this note where you will find
> detailed grammatical information and
> fuller explanations.*

they know us = ils nous connaissent
they don't know us = ils ne nous
connaissent pas
do they know us? = est-ce qu'ils nous
connaissent?
he's seen us = il nous a vus
he hasn't seen us = il ne nous a pas vus
has he seen us? = est-ce qu'il nous a vus?
help us! = aide-nous!
catch us! = attrape-nous!
don't bother us! = ne nous embête pas!
don't hit us! = ne nous frappe pas!

she gave the book to us = elle nous a
donné le livre
she didn't give the book to us = elle ne
nous a pas donné le livre
did she give the book to us? = est-ce
qu'elle nous a donné le livre?
write to us! = écris-nous!
say it to us! = dis-le-nous!
don't show it to us! = ne nous le montre
pas!
he did it for us = il l'a fait pour nous
it's us = c'est nous
stand in front of us = mets-toi devant nous

**USA** *noun* ▶ **218** |
the USA = les USA (*masculine plural*)

**use**
**1** *verb*
(*to make use of*) = se servir de (**!** + *être*)
I use the car to go to work = je me sers de
la voiture pour aller au travail
he uses the room as an office = il se sert
de la pièce comme bureau
what is it used for? = ça sert à quoi?
to use the opportunity to learn French
= profiter de l'occasion pour apprendre
le français
to use a different word = employer un
autre mot
(*to operate on*)
to use petrol = marcher à l'essence
to use water = utiliser de l'eau
(*to go through*) = consommer
it uses a lot of petrol = ça consomme
beaucoup d'essence
(*to take advantage of*)
to use someone = se servir de quelqu'un
**2** *noun*
to make use of a room = utiliser une pièce
to have the use of a car = avoir l'usage
d'une voiture
to lose the use of one's legs = perdre
l'usage de ses jambes
(*when talking about what is useful*)
to be of use to someone = être utile à
quelqu'un, servir à quelqu'un
to be no use = ne servir à rien
the bike is no use any more = le vélo est
hors d'usage
what's the use of complaining? = à quoi
bon se plaindre?
**use up**
to use up all the money = dépenser tout
l'argent
to use up the milk = finir le lait

**used**
**1** *verb*

> **!** *Note that the imperfect tense in French
> is generally used to translate* used to +
> *verb:* she used to live in Toulouse = elle
> habitait Toulouse.

I used to read a lot = je lisais beaucoup
you used not to smoke = tu ne fumais pas
avant
there used to be a castle here = il y avait
un château ici dans le temps

**2** *adjective*
to be used to [children | animals | tourists ...]
= avoir l'habitude des [enfants | animaux | touristes ...]
he's not used to living on his own = il n'a pas l'habitude de vivre seul
to get used to a new job = s'habituer à un nouveau travail

**useful** *adjective*
= utile

**useless** *adjective*
(*not working, having no use*) = inutilisable
(*having no point or purpose*) = inutile
it's useless complaining = il est inutile de se plaindre, ça ne sert à rien de se plaindre
(*describing a person*) = nul/nulle
to be useless at chemistry = être nul/nulle en chimie

**usually** *adverb*
= d'habitude, normalement

# V

**vacant** *adjective*
= libre

**vacation** *noun* (*US English*)
a vacation = des vacances (*feminine plural*)
to take a vacation = prendre des vacances

**vacuum** *verb*
to vacuum a room = passer l'aspirateur dans une pièce

**vacuum cleaner** *noun*
a vacuum cleaner = un aspirateur

**vague** *adjective*
= vague

**vain** *adjective*
= vaniteux/vaniteuse

**valid** *adjective*
(*describing a licence, a passport*) = valide
(*describing a ticket, an offer*) = valable

**valley** *noun*
a valley = une vallée

**valuable** *adjective*
• (*very useful*) = précieux/précieuse
• (*worth a lot of money*)
to be valuable = avoir de la valeur

**van** *noun*
a van (*small*) = une camionnette
(*larger*) = un fourgon

**vandalize** *verb*
= vandaliser

**vanilla** *noun*
vanilla = la vanille

**various** *adjective*
= divers/diverses
there are various ways of saying it = on peut le dire de diverses façons

**vary** *verb*
= varier
to vary from town to town = varier d'une ville à l'autre

**vase** *noun*
a vase = un vase

**VAT** *noun*
VAT = la TVA

**veal** *noun*
veal = le veau

**vegetable** *noun*
a vegetable = un légume

**vegetarian** *noun*
a vegetarian = un végétarien/une végétarienne

**vein** *noun* ▶ 201 |
a vein = une veine

**velvet** *noun*
velvet = le velours

**versus** *preposition*
= contre

**very**
**1** *adverb*
very = très
I don't know him very well = je ne le connais pas très bien
to eat very little = manger très peu
you haven't said very much = tu n'as pas dit grand-chose
we like them very much = on les aime beaucoup
they called me the very next day = ils m'ont appelé dès le lendemain
**2** *adjective*
at the very beginning = au tout début
to sit at the very front = s'asseoir tout devant
to stay to the very end = rester jusqu'au bout
you are the very person I need = tu es exactement la personne qu'il me faut

**vest** *noun*
• (*British English*) (*a piece of underwear*)
a vest = un maillot de corps
• (*US English*) (*a waistcoat*)
a vest = un gilet

**vet** *noun* ▶ 315 |
a vet = un vétérinaire/une vétérinaire

**via** *preposition*
(*on tickets, timetables*) = via
(*in general*) = en passant par
we came via Paris = nous sommes venus en passant par Paris

**V**

**vicious** *adjective*
- (*violent*) = brutal/brutale
- (*nasty, meant to hurt*)
  = malveillant/malveillante

**victory** *noun*
a victory = une victoire
to win a victory = remporter une victoire

**video**
**1** *noun*
- (*a recorded film, programme, event*)
  a video = une cassette vidéo
- ▶ **video cassette**, **video recorder**
**2** *verb*
- (*to record*) = enregistrer
- (*to film*)
  to video a wedding = filmer un mariage
  en vidéo

**video camera** *noun*
a video camera = une caméra vidéo

**video cassette** *noun*
a video cassette = une cassette vidéo

**video game** *noun*
a video game = un jeu vidéo

**video recorder** *noun*
a video recorder = un magnétoscope

**view** *noun*
- a view = une vue
  you're blocking my view = tu me bouches
  la vue
  if you want to get a better view, come
  here = si tu veux mieux voir, viens ici
- (*an opinion, an attitude*)
  a view = un avis, une opinion
  a point of view = un point de vue

**village** *noun*
a village = un village

**vinegar** *noun*
vinegar = le vinaigre

**vineyard** *noun*
a vineyard = un vignoble

**violent** *adjective*
= violent/violente

**violin** *noun* ▶ **290**
a violin = un violon

**Virgo** *noun*
Virgo = Vierge (*feminine*)

**visit**
**1** *verb*
to visit Paris (*to see*) = visiter Paris
(*to stay*) = faire un séjour à Paris
to visit someone (*to call on*) = aller voir
  quelqu'un
(*more formally*) = rendre visite à quelqu'un
(*to stay with* ) = aller passer quelques jours
  chez quelqu'un
**2** *noun*
a visit (*a call*) = une visite

(*a stay*) = un séjour
to pay someone a visit = rendre visite à
  quelqu'un

**visitor** *noun*
- (*a guest*)
  a visitor = un invité/une invitée
  to have visitors = avoir de la visite
- (*a tourist*)
  a visitor = un visiteur/une visiteuse

**vocabulary** *noun*
vocabulary = le vocabulaire

**voice** *noun*
a voice = une voix
to have a good voice = avoir une jolie
  voix
to speak in a low voice = parler à voix
  basse
to sing at the top of one's voice = chanter
  à tue-tête

**volleyball** *noun* ▶ **248**
volleyball = le volley-ball

**vomit** *verb*
= vomir

**vote** *verb*
= voter

# Ww

**wages** *noun*
wages = le salaire (*singular*)

**waist** *noun* ▶ **201**
the waist = la taille

**waistcoat** *noun* (*British English*)
a waistcoat = un gilet

**wait** *verb*
- to wait = attendre
  to wait for someone = attendre quelqu'un
  I'm waiting to use the phone = j'attends de
  pouvoir téléphoner
  to wait for someone to leave = attendre
  que quelqu'un s'en aille
  let's have a beer while we're waiting for
  them = allons prendre une bière en
  attendant qu'ils arrivent

  **!** *Note that the subjunctive is used after*
  attendre que.

  I can't wait to see them = j'ai hâte de les
  voir
- (*in a restaurant*)
  to wait on table, to wait table (*US English*)
  = travailler comme serveur/serveuse
**wait up** = veiller
to wait up for someone = veiller jusqu'au
  retour de quelqu'un

**waiter** noun ▶ 315 |
  a waiter = un serveur

**waiting room** noun
  a waiting room = une salle d'attente

**waitress** noun ▶ 315 |
  a waitress = une serveuse

**wake** verb
  to wake someone = réveiller quelqu'un
**wake up** = se réveiller (! + être)

**Wales** noun ▶ 218 |
  Wales = le pays de Galles

**walk**
**1** verb
  (rather than run) = marcher
  (rather than drive or ride) = aller à pied
  (for pleasure) = se promener (! + être)
  let's walk to the pool = allons à la piscine
    à pied
  to walk down the street = descendre la rue
  to walk the dog = promener le chien
**2** noun
  a walk = une promenade
  to go for a walk = faire une promenade
  it's five minutes' walk from here = c'est a
    cinq minutes à pied d'ici
**walk around** = se promener (! + être)
  to walk around town = se promener en
    ville
  to walk around the lake = faire le tour du
    lac
**walk away** = s'éloigner (! + être)
**walk back** = revenir à pied
  to walk back home = rentrer à pied
**walk by** = passer (! + être)
**walk in** = entrer (! + être)
**walk out** = sortir (! + être)
  to walk out of the room = sortir de la pièce
**walk round** = faire le tour
  to walk round the exhibition = visiter
    l'exposition
**walk up to** = s'approcher de (! + être)

**walkman** noun
  a walkman = un baladeur, un walkman

**wall** noun
  a wall = un mur

**wallet** noun
  a wallet = un portefeuille

**wallpaper** noun
  wallpaper = le papier peint

**walnut** noun
  a walnut = une noix

**wander** verb
  to wander around town = se balader en
    ville
**wander away, wander off** = s'éloigner
(! + être)

**want** verb
• to want = vouloir
  do you want another coffee? = est-ce que
    tu veux un autre café?
  he wants [to go out | to go home | to play ...]
    = il veut [sortir | rentrer | jouer ...]
  she didn't want to stay = elle n'a pas voulu
    rester
  do you want me to come with you? = est-
    ce que tu veux que je vienne avec toi?
  **!** Note that the subjunctive is used after
  vouloir que.

• (to need) = avoir besoin de
  do you want anything in town? = est-ce
    que tu as besoin de quelque chose en
    ville?

**war** noun
  a war = une guerre

**wardrobe** noun
  a wardrobe = une armoire

**warm**
**1** adjective
  = chaud/chaude
  to be warm, to feel warm = avoir chaud
  I'm very warm = j'ai très chaud
  it's nice and warm in the classroom = il
    fait bon dans la salle de classe
  to get warm = se réchauffer (! + être)
  to keep warm = rester au chaud
  to keep a meal warm = tenir un repas au
    chaud
**2** verb
  to warm the plates = chauffer les assiettes
  to warm one's hands = se réchauffer les
    mains
**warm up**
• (to get warm) = se réchauffer (! + être)
• (for a sporting event) = s'échauffer
  (! + être)
• (to make warm) = réchauffer

**warn** verb
  = avertir, prévenir
  to warn someone about the risks = mettre
    quelqu'un en garde contre les risques
  to warn someone to be careful
    = conseiller à quelqu'un de faire
    attention
  I warned him not to take the car = je lui ai
    déconseillé de prendre la voiture

**wash** verb
• (to clean) = laver
  to wash one's clothes = laver ses
    vêtements
  to wash one's face = se laver le visage
• (to get clean) = se laver (! + être)
**wash out**
  to wash out = partir au lavage
  to wash a stain out = faire partir une
    tache au lavage
**wash up**
• (British English) (to do the dishes) = faire la
  vaisselle

**W**

- (*US English*) (*to clean oneself*) = se
  rafraîchir (**!** + *être*)

**washbasin** (*British English*), **wash-
hand basin** *noun*
  a washbasin = un lavabo

**washing** *noun*
  the washing = le linge
  to do the washing = faire la lessive

**washing machine** *noun*
  a washing machine = une machine à laver

**washing-up** *noun* (*British English*)
  the washing-up = la vaisselle
  to do the washing-up = faire la vaisselle

**wasp** *noun*
  a wasp = une guêpe

**waste**
**1** *verb*
  = gaspiller
  to waste energy = gaspiller de l'énergie
  to waste one's time = perdre son temps
**2** *noun*
- it's a waste of money = c'est de l'argent
  gaspillé
  a waste of time = une perte de temps
  it's a waste of time going there = y aller
  est une perte de temps
  to let food go to waste = gaspiller de la
  nourriture
- waste = les déchets (*masculine plural*)

**watch**
**1** *verb*
- (*to look at*) = regarder
  to watch television = regarder la
  télévision
  she watched me making the meal = elle
  m'a regardé préparer le repas
- (*to observe, to follow*) = surveiller
  I feel I'm being watched = j'ai l'impression
  qu'on me surveille
- (*to pay attention to*)
  watch what you're doing = fais attention à
  ce que tu fais
  watch you don't fall = fais attention de ne
  pas tomber
**2** *noun*
  a watch = une montre
**watch out** = faire attention

**water**
**1** *noun*
  water = l'eau (*feminine*)
  drinking water = l'eau potable
  to let in water = prendre l'eau
**2** *verb*
  = arroser

**waterfall** *noun*
  a waterfall = une cascade

**water-skiing** *noun* ▶ 248 |
  water-skiing = le ski nautique

**wave**
**1** *verb*
- (*to signal with one's hand*)
  to wave to someone = saluer quelqu'un
  de la main
  to wave goodbye = faire au revoir de la
  main
- (*to direct*)
  to wave someone on = faire signe à
  quelqu'un d'avancer
- to wave flags = agiter des drapeaux
**2** *noun*
  a wave = une vague

**way**
**1** *noun*
- (*a means, a method*)
  a way = un moyen
  it's a way of earning money = c'est un
  moyen de gagner de l'argent
  it's a good way to make friends = c'est un
  bon moyen de se faire des amis
  he does it the wrong way = il s'y prend
  mal
  that's not the way to do it = ce n'est pas
  comme ça qu'on fait
- (*how one does something*)
  a way = une façon
  I like the way she dresses = j'aime sa
  façon de s'habiller
  I prefer to do it my way = je préfère le faire
  à ma façon
- (*a route, a road*)
  a way = un chemin
  I can't remember the way to the station
  = je ne me souviens plus du chemin
  pour aller à la gare
  we can buy something to eat along the
  way = on peut acheter quelque chose à
  manger en chemin
  on the way back = sur le chemin du
  retour
  I met them on the way back from town = je
  les ai rencontrés en revenant de la ville
  on the way to Paris = en allant à Paris
  where's the way out? = où est la sortie?
  to make one's way to the stairs = se
  diriger vers l'escalier
  to lose one's way = se perdre (**!** + *être*)
- (*a direction*)
  which way are you going? = dans quelle
  direction est-ce que tu vas?
  they went that way = ils sont partis par là
  come this way = venez par ici
- (*someone's route*)
  to be in someone's way = empêcher
  quelqu'un de passer, bloquer le passage
  à quelqu'un
  to be in the way = gêner le passage
  to get out of the way = s'écarter (**!** + *être*)
- (*when talking about distances*)
  it's a long way from here = c'est loin d'ici
  to go all the way to Portugal = aller
  jusqu'au Portugal

- (*what one wants*)
  she always wants her own way = elle ne
  veut en faire qu'à sa tête
  if I had my own way, I'd go alone = si cela
  ne tenait qu'à moi, j'irais tout seul
**2 by the way** = au fait
  what's his name, by the way? = comment
  s'appelle-t-il, au fait?

**we** *pronoun*
  **!** *Note that* we *is generally translated by*
  nous *but that, in informal French,* on *is
  also very common:* we're going to the
  cinema = nous allons au cinéma, on va au
  cinéma.

  we = nous
  we saw her yesterday = nous l'avons vue
  hier, on l'a vue hier
  we didn't agree = nous, nous n'étions pas
  d'accord
  we all make mistakes = tout le monde
  peut se tromper

**weak** *adjective*
- (*not healthy*) = faible
  to have a weak heart = avoir le cœur
  fragile
- (*not good or able*) = faible
  to be weak at languages = être faible en
  langues
- (*easily damaged*) = fragile
- (*having very little power*) = faible
- (*describing tea or coffee*) = léger/légère

**wealthy** *adjective*
  = riche

**wear** *verb*
- (*to be dressed in*) = porter
  to be wearing jeans = porter un jean
  to wear black = s'habiller en noir
- (*to put on*) = mettre
  what will you wear? = qu'est-ce que tu vas
  mettre?
  I've got nothing to wear = je n'ai rien à me
  mettre
**wear out**
  to wear out = s'user (**!** + *être*)
  to wear one's shoes out = user ses
  chaussures
  to wear someone out = épuiser quelqu'un

**weather** *noun*
  the weather = le temps
  what's the weather like? = quel temps
  fait-il?
  the weather is [bad | hot] = il fait [mauvais |
  chaud]
  in [cold | warm | wet ...] weather = quand [il
  fait froid | il fait bon | il pleut ...]

**weather forecast** *noun*
  the weather forecast = les prévisions
  météorologiques, la météo
  **!** *Note that* prévisions *is feminine plural.*

**Web** *noun*
  the Web = le Web

**website** *noun*
  a website = un site web

**wedding** *noun*
  a wedding = un mariage

**Wednesday** *noun* ▶ **222** |
  Wednesday = mercredi (*masculine*)

**week** *noun* ▶ **356** |
  a week = une semaine
  in two weeks' time = dans quinze jours

**weekend** *noun* ▶ **356** |
  a weekend = un week-end

**weigh** *verb* ▶ **285** |
  = peser
  what do you weigh? = combien pèses-tu?
  to weigh oneself = se peser (**!** + *être*)

**weight** *noun* ▶ **285** |
  weight = le poids
  to lose weight = maigrir

**weird** *adjective*
  = bizarre

**welcome**
**1** *verb* ▶ **237** |
  to welcome someone = accueillir
  quelqu'un
**2** *adjective*
- (*when receiving people*)
  to be welcome = être le bienvenu/la
  bienvenue
  welcome to the United States!
  = bienvenue aux États-Unis!
- (*when acknowledging thanks*)
  'thanks'—'you're welcome' = 'merci'—'de
  rien'

**well**
**1** *adverb* ▶ **237** |
- well = bien
  he dresses well = il s'habille bien
  the [exam | interview | class ...] went well
  = [l'examen | l'entretien | le cours ...] s'est bien
  passé
  the work is well paid = le travail est bien
  payé
  she is well able to defend herself = elle est
  tout à fait capable de se défendre
  he's not eating well = il n'a pas d'appétit
- (*other uses*)
  we may as well go home = on ferait aussi
  bien de rentrer
  you may well be right = il se pourrait bien
  que tu aies raison
  **!** *Note that the subjunctive is used after* il
  se pourrait bien que.

**2** *adjective*
  to feel well = se sentir bien
  I hope everyone is well = j'espère que tout
  le monde va bien
  I'm very well = je vais très bien
  to get well = se rétablir (**!** + *être*)
**3 as well** = aussi

**W**

**4 as well as** = ainsi que

**well-known** *adjective*
= célèbre

## Welsh ▶ 275 |
**1** *adjective*
= gallois/galloise
**2** *noun*
• (*the people*)
the Welsh = les Gallois (*masculine plural*)
• (*the language*)
Welsh = le gallois

## west
**1** *noun*
the west = l'ouest (*masculine*)
in the west of France = dans l'ouest de la France
**2** *adverb*
to go west = aller vers l'ouest
to live west of Paris = vivre à l'ouest de Paris
**3** *adjective*
= ouest (**!** *never changes*)
to work in west London = travailler dans l'ouest de Londres

## West Indies *noun* ▶ 218 |
the West Indies = les Antilles (*feminine*)

## wet
**1** *adjective*
• (*damp*) = mouillé/mouillée
your hair is wet = tu as les cheveux mouillés
to get wet = se faire mouiller (**!** + *être*)
she got her feet wet = elle s'est mouillé les pieds
• (*when talking about weather*) = humide
in wet weather = par temps humide
on a wet day = quand il pleut
**2** *verb*
= mouiller

## what
▶ *See the boxed note on* what *for more information and examples.*
**1** *pronoun*
• (*used in questions*)
what's her phone number? = quel est son numéro de téléphone?
what's that box? = qu'est-ce que c'est que cette boîte?
what's this button for? = à quoi sert ce bouton?
what's the French for 'boring'?
= comment dit-on 'boring' en français?
what does he look like? = il est comment?
• (*used as a relative pronoun*)
do what you want = faites ce que vous voulez
what we need is a timetable = ce qu'il nous faut c'est un horaire
**2** *determiner*
do you know what train to take? = est-ce que tu sais quel train il faut prendre?
what a great idea! = quelle bonne idée!

**3** *exclamation*
= quoi!, comment!
**4 what if** = et si
what if I don't get there on time? = et si je n'y suis pas à l'heure?

**whatever** *pronoun*
• (*when anything is possible*)
take whatever you want = prends tout ce que tu veux
whatever you think is useful = tout ce qui vous paraît utile
• (*when it doesn't matter*)
whatever they do, it won't change anything = quoi qu'ils fassent, ça ne changera rien
**!** *Note that the subjunctive is used after* quoi que *(*quoi qu'* before vowel or mute h).*

**wheat** *noun*
wheat = le blé

**wheel** *noun*
a wheel = une roue

**wheelchair** *noun*
a wheelchair = un fauteuil roulant

## when
**1** *adverb*
= quand
when did she leave? = quand est-ce qu'elle est partie?
when is your birthday? = c'est quand ton anniversaire?
I don't know when the film starts = je ne sais pas à quelle heure le film commence
**!** *See the usage note on* The clock ▶ 356 | *for further information on time expressions.*
**2** *conjunction*
= quand
I was asleep when the phone rang = je dormais quand le téléphone a sonné
he didn't like French when he was at school = il n'aimait pas le français quand il était au collège
when I'm 18 I'll have my own car = quand j'aurai 18 ans j'aurai ma propre voiture
**!** *Note that, when talking about future time, the future tense is used after* quand.
**3** *pronoun*
• (*used as a relative pronoun*) = où
in the days when there was no TV = à l'époque où il n'y avait pas de télévision
• (*used in questions*) = quand

## where
**1** *adverb*
= où
where are you going? = où vas-tu?
where do they work? = où est-ce qu'ils travaillent?
do you know where [he is | Tom is | we're going ...]? = est-ce que tu sais où [il est | est Tom | nous allons ...]?
I wonder where he lives = je me demande où il habite
the village where we live = le village où nous habitons

# what

## As a pronoun

### In questions

● When used in questions as an object pronoun, **what** is translated by **qu'est-ce que** (**qu'est-ce qu'** in front of a vowel or mute h):

| | |
|---|---|
| *what is he doing?* | = **qu'est-ce** qu'il fait? |
| *what did you say?* | = **qu'est-ce que** tu as dit? |
| *what are we going to do?* | = **qu'est-ce que** nous allons faire? |

● Alternatively, you can use **que** (**qu'** before a vowel or mute h), but note that, after **que**, the order of subject and verb is reversed and a hyphen is inserted between them if the subject is a pronoun:

| | |
|---|---|
| *what is he doing?* | = **que** fait-il? |
| *what did you say?* | = **qu'**as-tu dit? |
| *what are we going to do?* | = **qu'**allons-nous faire? |

● When used in questions as a subject pronoun, **what** is translated by **qu'est-ce qui**:

| | |
|---|---|
| *what is happening?* | = **qu'est-ce qui** se passe? |
| *what happened?* | = **qu'est-ce qui** s'est passé? |
| *what is going to happen?* | = **qu'est-ce qui** va se passer? |

Again, if you use **que**, the order of subject and verb is reversed, the subject becomes il and a hyphen is inserted between them:

| | |
|---|---|
| *what is happening?* | = **que** se passe-t-il?* |
| *what happened?* | = **que** s'est-il passé? |
| *what is going to happen?* | = **que** va-t-il se passer? |

* In this case, an additional -t- is required for the liaison between the two vowels to be made.

## To introduce a clause

● When used to introduce a clause as the object of the verb, **what** is translated by **ce que** (**ce qu'** before a vowel or mute h):

| | |
|---|---|
| *I don't know what he wants* | = je ne sais pas **ce qu'**il veut |
| *did they have what you wanted?* | = est-ce qu'ils avaient **ce que** tu voulais? |
| *what he said was that he didn't care* | = **ce qu'**il a dit c'est que ça lui était égal |

● When **what** is the subject of the verb, it is translated by **ce qui**:

| | |
|---|---|
| *tell me what happened* | = raconte-moi **ce qui** s'est passé |
| *I want to know what's happening* | = je veux savoir **ce qui** se passe |
| *what matters is that we won* | = **ce qui** compte, c'est que nous avons gagné |

## With prepositions

**What**, when it is used with a preposition in English, is translated by **quoi**. In French, however, the preposition always comes before **quoi**:

| | |
|---|---|
| *what are you thinking about?* | = à **quoi** penses-tu? |
| *I don't know what he is talking about* | = je ne sais pas de **quoi** il parle |

## As a determiner

When **what** is used as a determiner, it is translated by **quel, quelle, quels** or **quelles**, according to whether the noun that follows is masculine or feminine, singular or plural:

| | |
|---|---|
| *what train did you catch?* | = **quel** train as-tu pris? |
| *what time is it?* | = **quelle** heure est-il? |
| *what books do you like?* | = **quels** livres aimes-tu? |
| *what colours do you like?* | = **quelles** couleurs aimes-tu? |

▶ For more examples, see the entry **what**.

**W**

**2** *conjunction*
  that's where she fell = c'est là qu'elle est
  tombée
  I'll leave the key where you can see it = je
  laisserai la clé là où tu peux la voir

**whether** *conjunction*
  = si
  I don't know whether or not to accept = je
  ne sais pas si je dois accepter

**which**
▶ *See the boxed note on* which *for more
information and examples.*
**1** *pronoun*
  the house which I told you about = la
  maison dont je t'ai parlé
**2** *determiner*
  which one of the nurses speaks French?
  = laquelle des infirmières parle
  français?
  ask him which bus leaves first
  = demande-lui quel bus va partir le
  premier

**while** *conjunction*
  = pendant que
  I had a party while my parents were in
  Spain = j'ai fait une fête pendant que
  mes parents étaient en Espagne
  she fell asleep while watching TV = elle
  s'est endormie en regardant la
  télévision

**whisper** *verb*
  = chuchoter

**whistle**
**1** *verb*
  = siffler
**2** *noun*
  a whistle = un sifflet

**white** *adjective* ▶ **213** |
  = blanc/blanche

**who** *pronoun*
• (*used in questions*) = qui
  who told you? = qui (est-ce qui) te l'a dit?
  who did you invite? = qui est-ce que tu as
  invité?
  who did he buy the book for? = pour qui
  a-t-il acheté le livre?
• (*used as a relative pronoun*)
  my friend who lives in Paris = mon ami
  qui habite Paris
  those who can't come by car = ceux/celles
  qui ne peuvent pas venir en voiture
  a friend who I see at work = un ami que je
  vois au travail

**whole**
**1** *noun*
  the whole of [the country | London |
  August ...] = tout [le pays | Londres | le mois
  d'août ...]

**2** *adjective*
  a whole day = toute une journée, une
  journée entière
  three whole weeks = trois semaines
  entières
  I don't want to spend my whole life here
  = je ne veux pas passer toute ma vie ici

**whom** *pronoun*
• (*used in questions*) = qui
  whom did you meet? = qui as-tu
  rencontré?
• (*used as a relative pronoun*)
  the person to whom I spoke on the phone
  = la personne à qui j'ai parlé au téléphone

**whose**
**1** *pronoun*
• (*used in questions*) = à qui
  whose is the dog? = à qui est le chien?
• (*used as a relative pronoun*) = dont
  the boy whose bike was stolen = le
  garçon dont le vélo a été volé
  the woman whose house I'm buying = la
  femme dont j'achète la maison
**2** *determiner*
  whose car is that? = à qui est cette voiture?
  whose pen did you borrow? = à qui as-tu
  emprunté un stylo?

**why**
**1** *adverb*
• (*used in questions*) = pourquoi
  why did you do that? = pourquoi est-ce
  que tu as fait ça?
  why aren't they coming? = pourquoi est-
  ce qu'ils ne viennent pas?
  why not? = pourquoi pas?
• (*when making suggestions*)
  why don't we eat out tonight? = et si on
  allait au restaurant ce soir?
**2** *conjunction*
  = pour ça
  that's why I can't stand him = c'est pour ça
  que je le déteste

**wide** *adjective* ▶ **285** |
• (*in size*) = large
  a wide garden = un jardin large
  the room is ten metres wide = la pièce a
  dix mètres de large
• (*in range*)
  a wide range of games = un très grand
  choix de jeux

**width** *noun* ▶ **285** |
  width = la largeur

**wife** *noun*
  a wife = une femme

**wild** *adjective*
• (*describing animals, birds*) = sauvage
• (*noisy, out of control*) = fou/folle
  to go wild = se déchaîner (**!** + *être*)

**wildlife** *noun*
  wildlife = la faune

# which

## As a pronoun

### In questions

When **which** (meaning *which one* or *which ones*) is used as a pronoun in questions, it is translated by **lequel**, **laquelle**, **lesquels** or **lesquelles**, according to whether the noun it is standing for is masculine or feminine, singular or plural:

| | |
|---|---|
| *there are three peaches,* | = il y a trois pêches, |
| **which** *do you want?* | **laquelle** veux-tu? |

When **which** is followed by a superlative adjective, then the translation is **quel**, **quelle**, **quels** or **quelles**, according to whether the noun it is standing for is masculine or feminine, singular or plural:

| | |
|---|---|
| *(of the apples)* **which** *is the biggest?* | = **quelle** est la plus grosse? |
| *(of the books)* **which** *is the most useful?* | = **quel** est le plus utile? |
| *(of the cars)* **which** *are the fastest?* | = **quelles** sont les plus rapides? |
| *(of the computers)* **which** *are the cheapest?* | = **quels** sont les moins chers? |

### In relative clauses

When used as a pronoun, **which** is translated by **qui** when it is the subject of the verb, and by **que** when it is the object:

| | |
|---|---|
| *the book* **which** *is on the table* | = le livre **qui** est sur la table |
| *the book* **which** *Tina is reading* | = le livre **que** lit Tina |

Note the different word order of subject and verb; this is the case where the subject is a noun but not where the subject is a pronoun.

| | |
|---|---|
| *the book* **which** *I am reading* | = le livre **que** je lis |
| *the book* **which** *he's writing* | = le livre **qu'**il écrit |
| *the film* **which** *we're going to see* | = le film **que** nous allons voir |

Remember that in the present perfect and past perfect tenses, the past participle agrees with the noun **que** is referring back to:

| | |
|---|---|
| *the film* **which** *we saw* | = le film **que** nous avons vu |
| *the car* **which** *they stole* | = la voiture **qu'**ils ont volée |
| *the books* **which** *I gave you* | = les livres **que** je t'ai donnés *(masculine plural)* |
| *the dresses* **which** *she bought yesterday* | = les robes **qu'**elle a achetées hier *(feminine plural)* |

## As a determiner

When **which** is used as a determiner in questions, it is translated by **quel**, **quelle**, **quels** or **quelles** according to whether the noun that follows is masculine or feminine, singular or plural:

| | |
|---|---|
| **which** *car is yours?* | = **quelle** voiture est la vôtre? |
| **which** *dress did she buy?* | = **quelle** robe a-t-elle achetée?* |
| **which** *houses are for sale?* | = **quelles** maisons sont à vendre? |
| **which** *computer doesn't work?* | = **quel** ordinateur ne marche pas? |
| **which** *books did he borrow?* | = **quels** livres a-t-il empruntés?* |

Note that, in the second and third examples, the object precedes the verb or auxiliary verb so that the past participle agrees with it.

\* In this case, an additional **-t-** is required for the liaison between the two vowels to be made.

**W**

---

**will** *verb*

! Note that, when referring to the future, French generally uses the future tense of the verb to translate will + verb: I will sing = je chanterai. When talking about something in the near future, the present tense of aller + verb is also possible: je vais chanter.

• *(when talking about the future)*
she will agree = elle ne sera pas
 d'accord
it will be sunny tomorrow = il va faire beau
 demain
what will we do? = qu'est-ce que nous
 allons faire?

- (*when talking about intentions*)
  **I'll wait for you at the airport** = je
  t'attendrai à l'aéroport
  **we won't stay too long** = nous ne
  resterons pas trop longtemps
- (*in invitations and requests*)
  **will you have some coffee?** = est-ce que
  vous voulez du café?, voulez-vous du
  café?
  **will you ask him for me?** = est-ce que tu
  peux lui demander de ma part?
- (*when making assumptions*)
  **they won't know what's happened** = ils ne
  doivent pas savoir ce qui s'est passé
- (*in short questions and answers*)
  **you'll come again, won't you?** = tu
  reviendras, n'est-ce pas?
  **that will be cheaper, won't it?** = ça sera
  moins cher, non?

**win** *verb*
= gagner

**wind** *noun*
**a wind** = un vent

**window** *noun*
**a window** (*in a house*) = une fenêtre
(*in a shop*) = une vitrine
(*in a car, a bus*) = une vitre

**windsurfing** *noun* ▶ 248 |
**windsurfing** = la planche à voile

**windy** *adjective*
**it's windy** = il fait du vent

**wine** *noun*
**wine** = le vin

**wing** *noun*
**a wing** = une aile

**winter** *noun*
**winter** = l'hiver (*masculine*)
**in winter** = en hiver

**wipe** *verb*
= essuyer
**to wipe one's feet** = s'essuyer les pieds
**to wipe one's nose** = se moucher
(**!** + *être*)

**wireless** *adjective*
= sans fil

**wise** *adjective*
(*describing a person*) = sage
(*describing a decision, a choice*)
= judicieux/judicieuse

**wish**
**1** *noun*
- **a wish** = un souhait
  **to make a wish** = faire un vœu
- (*in greetings*)
  **best wishes** = meilleurs vœux
  (*in a letter*) = amicalement

**2** *verb*
- (*expressing what one would like*)
  **I wish they could come** = si seulement ils
  pouvaient venir
  **she wished she hadn't lied** = elle
  regrettait d'avoir menti
- (*in greetings*) = souhaiter
  **to wish someone a happy birthday**
  = souhaiter un bon anniversaire à
  quelqu'un

**with** *preposition*
- **with** = avec
  **to go away with friends** = partir avec des
  amis
  **I'm living with my parents** = j'habite chez
  mes parents
  **to be pleased with the house** = être
  content/contente de la maison
- (*when describing*)
  **a girl with black hair** = une fille aux
  cheveux noirs
  **the boy with the broken leg** = le garçon à
  la jambe cassée
  **his clothes were covered with mud** = ses
  vêtements étaient couverts de boue
  **he was walking along with his hands in
  his pockets** = il se promenait les mains
  dans les poches
  **she's married with two children** = elle est
  mariée et mère de deux enfants

**without** *preposition*
= sans
**we got in without paying** = on est entré
sans payer

**wolf** *noun*
**a wolf** = un loup

**woman** *noun*
**a woman** = une femme
**a single woman** = une célibataire

**wonder** *verb*
- (*to ask oneself*) = se demander (**!** + *être*)
  **I wonder** [**how** | **why** | **who** ...] = je me
  demande [comment | pourquoi | qui ...]
  **I was wondering when you'd arrive** = je
  me demandais quand tu arriverais
- (*in polite requests*)
  **I wonder if you could help me?**
  = pourriez-vous m'aider?

**wonderful** *adjective*
= merveilleux/merveilleuse

**wood** *noun*
- (*timber*)
  **wood** = le bois
  **made of wood** = en bois
- (*a small forest*)
  **a wood** = un bois

**wool** *noun*
**wool** = la laine

**word** *noun*
**a word** = un mot
**what's the French word for 'break'?**
= comment dit-on 'break' en français?
**in other words** = autrement dit

## work

**1** *verb*
* (*to have or do a job*) = travailler
  to work at home = travailler à domicile
  to work as a doctor = être médecin
* (*to operate properly*) = marcher
  the TV isn't working = la télévision ne
  marche pas, la télévision est en panne
* (*to be successful*) (*if it's an idea, a trick*)
  = marcher
  (*if it's a plan*) = réussir
  (*if it's a medicine, a treatment*) = agir
* (*to use, to operate*) = se servir de (**!** + *être*)
  do you know how to work the computer?
  = est-ce que tu sais te servir de
  l'ordinateur?

**2** *noun*
* work = le travail
  I've got work to do = j'ai du travail
  to be out of work = être au chômage
  the students' work = le travail des élèves
  it's hard work learning French = c'est dur
  d'apprendre le français
* (*for building, for repairs*)
  work(s) = les travaux (*masculine plural*)
  there are road works at the moment = il y
  a des travaux en ce moment
* (*by an artist, a musician*)
  a work = une œuvre

## work out
* (*to find*) = trouver
  to work out the answer = trouver la
  réponse
* (*to understand*) = comprendre
* (*with figures*) = calculer
* (*to go well*) = marcher
* (*to take exercise*) = s'entraîner (**!** + *être*)

## work up
  to get worked up = s'énerver (**!** + *être*)

## worker *noun*
  a worker (*in a factory*) = un ouvrier/une
  ouvrière
  (*in an office, a bank*) = un employé/une
  employée

## world *noun*
  the world = le monde
  all over the world = dans le monde entier
  the biggest city in the world = la plus
  grande ville du monde

## World Cup *noun*
  the World Cup = la Coupe du Monde

## worm *noun*
  a worm = un ver

## worried *adjective*
  = inquiet/inquiète
  to be worried about someone = se faire du
  souci pour quelqu'un

## worry *verb*
* (*to be worried*) = s'inquiéter (**!** + *être*)
  there's nothing to worry about = il n'y a
  pas de quoi s'inquiéter
* (*to make someone worried*) = inquiéter
  it's worrying me = ça m'inquiète

## worse *adjective*
  = pire
  this book is worse than the others = ce
  livre est pire que les autres
  she's worse than me at sports = elle est
  pire que moi en sport
  the weather is going to get worse = le
  temps va empirer
  he's getting worse (*in health*) = il va plus
  mal

## worst

**1** *noun*
  the worst = le pire/la pire
  to be the worst at French = être le plus
  mauvais/la plus mauvaise en français

**2** *adjective*
  = plus mauvais/plus mauvaise
  the worst hotel in town = le plus mauvais
  hôtel de la ville
  the worst film I've ever seen = le plus
  mauvais film que j'aie jamais vu

  > **!** Note that the subjunctive is used after
  > the superlative le plus mauvais… que.

  his worst enemy = son pire ennemi
  the worst thing to do would be to tell him
  = le pire serait de le lui dire

## worth *adjective*
  to be worth £100 = valoir 100 livres
  it's not worth the trouble = ça n'en vaut
  pas la peine

## would *verb*

  > **!** Note that French usually uses verbs in
  > the conditional to translate would + verb:
  > I would buy = j'achèterais.

* (*when talking about hypothetical rather
  than real situations*)
  if I had more money, I would buy a car = si
  j'avais plus d'argent, j'achèterais une
  voiture
  we would have missed the train if we'd
  left later = nous aurions raté le train si
  nous étions partis plus tard
* (*in reported speech*)
  I thought you'd forget to come = je
  pensais que tu oublierais de venir
  we were sure she would like it = nous
  étions sûrs que ça lui plairait
* (*when making an assumption*)
  she'd be 30 now = elle doit avoir 30 ans
  maintenant
  it would have been about midday = il
  devait être à peu près midi
* (*to be prepared to*)
  he wouldn't listen to me = il ne voulait pas
  m'écouter
* (*when talking about one's wishes*)
  I'd like a beer = je voudrais une bière
  we would like to stay another night = nous
  aimerions rester une nuit de plus

**W**

• (*when asking, offering or advising*)
  **would you turn the TV off?** = est-ce que tu
  veux bien éteindre la radio?
  **would you excuse me?** = excusez-moi
  **would you like something to eat?**
  = voulez-vous manger quelque chose?
  **you would do well to check** = tu ferais
  mieux de vérifier

**wrap** *verb*
  = envelopper
  **to wrap (up) a present** = emballer un
  cadeau

**wreck**
**1** *verb*
  (*if it's a person*) = détruire
  (*if it's a fire, a bomb*) = dévaster
**2** *noun*
  **a wreck** = une épave

**wrestling** *noun* ▶ **248** |
  **wrestling** = le catch

**wrist** *noun* ▶ **201** |
  **the wrist** = le poignet

**write** *verb*
  = écrire
  **to write to someone, to write someone**
  (*US English*) = écrire à quelqu'un
  **to write** [an essay | a cheque | a note ...]
  = faire [une rédaction | un chèque | un mot ...]
  **write back** = répondre
  **write down** = noter
  **write out** = écrire

**writing** *noun*
  **writing** = l'écriture (*feminine*)
  **your writing is good** = tu écris bien

**writing pad** *noun*
  **a writing pad** = un bloc de papier à lettres

**wrong** *adjective*
• (*not as it should be*)
  **there's something wrong** = il y a quelque
  chose qui ne va pas
  **what's wrong?** = qu'est-ce qu'il y a?
  **what's wrong with you?** (*if ill, in pain*)
  = qu'est-ce que tu as?
  (*if behaving oddly*) = qu'est-ce qui t'arrive?
• (*not proper or suitable*)
  = mauvais/mauvaise (**!** *before the noun*)
  **I took the wrong key** = j'ai pris la
  mauvaise clé
  **to say the wrong thing** = faire une gaffe
  **to go the wrong way** = se tromper de
  chemin
• (*not correct*)
  **that's wrong** = c'est faux
  **to dial the wrong number** = faire un faux
  numéro, se tromper de numéro
  **it's the wrong answer** = ce n'est pas la
  bonne réponse
  **to be wrong** (*if it's a person*) = avoir tort, se
  tromper (**!** + *être*)

• (*not honest, not good*)
  **it's wrong to steal** = c'est mal de voler
  **she hasn't done anything wrong** = elle n'a
  rien fait de mal
  **there's nothing wrong with trying** = il n'y a
  pas de mal à essayer

**X-ray**
**1** *noun*
  **an X-ray** = une radiographie, une radio
  **to have an X-ray** = se faire radiographier
**2** *verb*
  = radiographier

**yacht** *noun*
  **a yacht** = un yacht

**yard** *noun*
  (*when measuring*) ▶ **285** |
  **a yard** ≈ un yard
  | **!** *Note that a* **yard** = *0.9144 m.*

  (*of a building*)
  **a yard** = une cour
  (*US English*) (*a garden*)
  **a yard** = un jardin

**yawn** *verb*
  = bâiller

**year** *noun*

  | **!** *Note that* **year** *is usually translated by*
  *an in French. However it is sometimes*
  *translated by* **année**, *when there is an*
  *emphasis on the idea of duration.*

  (*when talking about time*) ▶ **356** |
  **a year** = un an
  **last year** = l'an dernier, l'année dernière
  **two years ago** = il y a deux ans
  **to work all year round** = travailler toute
  l'année
  **he's lived there for years** = il y habite
  depuis des années
  **that'll take years!** = ça va prendre une
  éternité!
  (*when talking about age*) ▶ **187** |
  **a year** = un an
  **to be 15 years old, to be 15 years of age**
  = avoir 15 ans
  **a four-year old** = un enfant/une enfant de
  quatre ans

- (*in a school system*)
**first year, year one** ≈ la sixième
**to be in second year, to be in year two** ≈ être en cinquième
**a first year** ≈ un élève/une élève de sixième

## yell
**1** *verb*
= hurler
**to yell at someone** = crier après quelqu'un
**2** *noun*
**a yell** = un hurlement

## yellow *adjective* ▶ 213 |
= jaune
**to go yellow** = jaunir

## yes *adverb*
**yes** = oui
**'are you coming with us?'—'yes I am'**
= 'est-ce que tu viens avec nous?'—'oui'
**'they don't know each other'—'yes they do'** = 'ils ne se connaissent pas'—'(mais) si'
**'didn't he tell you?'—'yes he did'** = 'il ne te l'a pas dit?'—'si'

## yesterday *adverb*
= hier

## yet
**1** *adverb*
= encore
**not yet** = pas encore
**it's not ready yet** = ce n'est pas encore prêt
**have they arrived yet?** = est-ce qu'ils sont arrivés?
**has she met them yet?** = est-ce qu'elle les a déjà rencontrés?
**2** *conjunction*
= pourtant

## yogurt *noun*
**yogurt** = le yaourt

## you *pronoun*
▶ 378 | See the boxed note on **you** for detailed information and examples.

## young
**1** *adjective*
= jeune
**a young lady** = une jeune femme
**young people** = les jeunes (*masculine*)
**she is a year younger than me** = elle a un an de moins que moi
**a younger brother** = un frère cadet
**a younger sister** = une sœur cadette
**to look young** = faire jeune
**2** *noun*
**the young** (*of an animal*) = les petits (*masculine plural*)

## your *determiner*
▶ 379 | See the boxed note on **your** for detailed information and examples. See also the usage note on The human body ▶ 201 |.

## yours *pronoun*
▶ See also the boxed notes on **you** and **your** for more information.
**the red car is yours** (*informal*) = la voiture rouge est à toi
(*polite or to several people*) = la voiture rouge est à vous
**my garden is bigger than yours** (*informal*) = mon jardin est plus grand que le tien
(*polite or to several people*) = mon jardin est plus grand que le vôtre
**her children are older than yours** (*informal*) = ses enfants sont plus âgés que les tiens
(*polite or to several people*) = ses enfants sont plus âgés que les vôtres

**!** *Note that, when comparing objects, people, etc, one of the following translations—le tien, la tienne, les tiens/tiennes, le/la vôtre or les vôtres—will be used. To know which one to use, find out whether the object, person, etc being described is masculine or feminine, singular or plural and whether you are using the polite or the informal form of address.*

## yourself *pronoun*
- (*when used as a reflexive pronoun*)
**you'll enjoy yourself** (*informal*) = tu vas t'amuser
(*polite*) = vous allez vous amuser
**did you hurt yourself?** (*informal*) = est-ce que tu t'es fait mal?
(*polite*) = est-ce que vous vous êtes blessé?
- (*when used for emphasis*)
**you did it yourself** (*informal*) = tu l'as fait toi-même
(*polite*) = vous l'avez fait vous-même

## yourselves *pronoun*
- (*when used as a reflexive pronoun*)
**you'll enjoy yourselves** = vous allez vous amuser
**did you hurt yourselves?** = est-ce que vous vous êtes fait mal?
- (*when used for emphasis*)
**are you going to organize it yourselves?** = est-ce que vous allez l'organiser vous-mêmes?
**you want to be by yourselves** = vous voulez être seuls

## youth *noun*
- (*a young man*)
**a youth** = un jeune
- (*young people*)
**the youth** = les jeunes (*masculine plural*)

## youth club *noun*
**a youth club** = un club de jeunes

## youth hostel *noun*
**a youth hostel** = une auberge de jeunesse

## youth worker *noun*
**a youth worker** = un éducateur/une éducatrice

X
Y

# you

## Used to address people

- In English **you** is used to address everybody, whereas French has two forms: **tu** and **vous**. The usual word to use when you are speaking to anyone you do not know very well is **vous**. This is sometimes called the polite form:

  | | |
  |---|---|
  | *where are* **you** *going?* | = où allez-**vous**? |
  | *I'm thinking of* **you** | = je pense à **vous** |
  | *would* **you** *like some coffee?* | = voulez-**vous** du café? |
  | *can I help* **you**? | = est-ce que je peux **vous** aider? |
  | *what can I do for* **you**? | = qu'est-ce que je peux faire pour **vous**? |

  The more informal pronoun **tu** is used between close friends and family members, within groups of children and young people, by adults when talking to children and always when talking to animals; **tu** is the subject form, the direct and indirect object form is **te** (**t'** before a vowel or mute h) and the form for emphatic use or use after a preposition is **toi**:

  | | |
  |---|---|
  | *where are* **you** *going?* | = où vas-**tu**? |
  | *I'm thinking of* **you** | = je pense à **toi** |
  | *would* **you** *like some coffee?* | = veux-**tu** du café? |
  | *can I help* **you**? | = est-ce que je peux **t'**aider? |
  | *there's a letter for* **you** | = il y a une lettre pour **toi** |

  As a general rule, when talking to a French person use **vous**, wait to see how they address you and follow suit. It is safer to wait for the French person to suggest using **tu**.

  Note that **tu** is only a singular pronoun and **vous** is its plural form.

  Remember that in French the object and indirect object pronouns are always placed before the verb:

  | | |
  |---|---|
  | *she knows* **you** | = elle **vous** connaît |
  | | = elle **te** connaît |
  | *I'll give* **you** *my address* | = je **vous** donnerai mon adresse |
  | | je **te** donnerai mon adresse |

- In tenses like the present perfect and the past perfect, the past participle agrees with the direct object:

  | | |
  |---|---|
  | *I saw* **you** *on Saturday* | |
  | (to one male: polite form) | = je **vous** ai vu samedi |
  | (to one female: polite form) | = je **vous** ai vue samedi |
  | (to one male: informal form) | = je **t'**ai vu samedi |
  | (to one female: informal form) | = je **t'**ai vue samedi |
  | (to two or more people, male or mixed) | = je **vous** ai vus samedi |
  | (to two or more females) | = je **vous** ai vues samedi |

## Used impersonally

When **you** is used impersonally as the more informal form of **one**, it is translated by **on** for the subject form and by **vous** or **te** for the object form, depending on whether the comment is being made amongst friends or in a more formal context:

| | |
|---|---|
| **you** *can do as* **you** *like here* | = **on** peut faire ce qu'**on** veut ici |
| **you** *could easily lose your bag here* | = **on** pourrait facilement perdre son sac ici |
| **you** *never know* | = **on** ne sait jamais |
| *these mushrooms can make* **you** *ill* | = ces champignons peuvent **vous** rendre malade |
| | = ces champignons peuvent **te** rendre malade |

▶ For a guide to the correct verb forms with **vous**, **tu** and **on**, consult the verb in the French-English part of the dictionary and check the number in the box, which will refer you to the French verb tables at the back of the dictionary.

# your

▶ For a full note on the use of the **vous** and **tu** forms in French, see the note on **you ▶ 378 |**.

● In French, determiners agree with the noun that follows:

**your** + *masculine singular noun*
(to one person: polite form or to two or more people)      **votre** chien, **votre** ami
(to one person: informal form)      **ton** chien, **ton** ami

**your** + *feminine singular noun*
(to one person: polite form or to two or more people)      **votre** pomme, **votre** orange
(to one person: informal form)      **ta** pomme, **ton***  orange

\* Note that **ton** is used with a feminine noun beginning with a vowel or mute h.

**your** + *plural noun*
(to one person: polite form or      **vos** chiens, **vos** amis,
to two or more people)      **vos** pommes, **vos** oranges
(to one person: informal form)      **tes** chiens, **tes** amis,
     **tes** pommes, **tes** oranges

When **your** is stressed, **à vous** or **à toi** is added after the noun:

(to one person: polite form) *your* house      = **votre** maison **à vous**
(to two or more people)      = **vos** maisons **à vous**
(to one person: informal form) *your* house      = **ta** maison **à toi**
(to one person: polite form) *your* parents      = **vos** parents **à vous**
(to two or more people)      = **vos** parents **à vous**
(to one person: informal form) *your* parents      = **tes** parents **à toi**

● When used impersonally to mean **one's**, **your** is translated by **son**, **sa** or **ses**, when **you** is translated by **on**:

*you pay your bills at the end of the week*      = on paie **ses** factures à la fin de la semaine
*you get good value for your money*      = on en a pour **son** argent

The translation after an impersonal verb in French is **son**, **sa**, **ses**:

*you have to buy your tickets at the door*      = il faut acheter **ses** billets à l'entrée

Note, however, the following:

*smoking is bad for your health*      = le tabac est mauvais pour **la** santé
*your average student*      = l'étudiant **moyen**

▶ For **your** used with parts of the body, see the usage note on **The human body ▶ 201 |**.

---

**zap** verb
• (to destroy) = détruire
• (British English) (to switch channels)
  to zap from channel to channel = zapper✱
• (to remove from a computer screen)
  = supprimer

**zapper** noun (British English)
  a zapper = une télécommande

**zebra** noun
  a zebra = un zèbre

**zebra crossing** noun (British English)
  a zebra crossing = un passage pour
  piétons

**zero** number
  zero = zéro

**zip** (British English), **zipper** (US English)
noun
  a zip = une fermeture éclair
  to undo a zip = ouvrir une fermeture
  éclair

**zip code** noun (US English)
  a zip code = un code postal

**zodiac** noun
  the zodiac = le zodiaque

**zone** noun
  a zone = une zone

**zoo** noun
  a zoo = un zoo

**Z**

---

# Learning and lifestyle kit

# Glossary of grammatical terms

The list of words and definitions below contains most of the words which you will come across when learning a language and its grammar. Some are used in this dictionary; others you will see in grammars and textbooks.

| | |
|---|---|
| **Abbreviation** | a shortened form of a word or phrase, e.g. (English) exam ▶ examination; (French) imper ▶ imperméable |
| **Accent** | 1. (in writing) a mark associated with a letter, usually showing how the letter is pronounced, e.g. grave accent (è); acute accent (é); circumflex (â)<br>2. (in speech) a person's way of speaking |
| **Adjective** | a word describing a noun, e.g. a *green* shirt = une chemise *verte*; a *small* girl = une *petite* fille |
| **Adverb** | a word that describes or modifies the meaning of a verb, an adjective or another adverb, e.g. he speaks *quickly* = il parle *vite*; fairly big = *assez* grand; very slowly = *très* lentement |
| **Agree, Agreement** | when a word agrees with another, its spelling changes to match the number of that other word, e.g. one child = un enfant; two children = deux enfant**s**; it must also match it for gender, e.g. the **big** dog = **le grand** chien; the **big** house = **la grande** maison |
| **Article** | the definite article 'the'; the indefinite article 'a' or 'an'; the partitive articles 'some', 'any' are all used before a noun (see grammar box on page 352 and also the glossary entry DETERMINER) |
| **Auxiliary, Auxiliary verb** | either of the verbs être or *avoir* which are used to form the perfect, pluperfect, or future perfect tenses, e.g. j'ai mangé = I have eaten; je *suis* revenu = I came back; ils *avaient* vu Bob = they had seen Bob |
| **Base form** | see DICTIONARY FORM |
| **Clause** | a self-contained section of a sentence which contains a subject and a verb |
| **Cognates** | words which resemble each other in more than one language and which historically have the same origin, e.g. republic, république. They do not always retain the same meaning. See FAUX AMI |
| **Colloquial** | refers to a word or an expression used in relaxed, everyday situations. Colloquial language is usually spoken, or used in personal letters or informal writing |
| **Comparative** | the form of the adjective or adverb which allows a comparison to be made, e.g. bigger = *plus* grand; *more* intelligent = *plus* intelligent; cleverer = *plus* malin |
| **Compound noun** | A noun formed from two or more separate words: an airport = un aéroport |

| | |
|---|---|
| **Conditional** | the form of the verb that expresses what might happen IF something else occurred first, e.g. *if* it tasted good, I *would eat* it = *si* c'était bon, je le *mangerais* |
| **Conjunction** | a word used to join clauses together, e.g. *and*, *but*, *because* |
| **Consonant** | a letter representing a sound such as b, c, d, p, t, s, z, etc. Consonants cannot form a complete sound unit or syllable without a vowel. See VOWEL |
| **Construction** | the way the words in a phrase or sentence work together grammatically |
| **Context** | the environment or surroundings within which a word occurs and which affect its meaning. Compare *the* **tank** *fired first* with *he filled the petrol* **tank**. Information about the context of a word helps to pinpoint its exact sense. Knowing the sense and then using the dictionary signposts will guide you to the right translation |
| **Definite Article** | See ARTICLE |
| **Determiner** | a word which is used before a noun to make clear what is being referred to. It describes the function of definite and indefinite articles as well as words like *this*, *my*, and *certain*, e.g. *this* money = *cet* argent; *my* room = *ma* chambre; *certain* people = *certaines* personnes. In French, the determiner will match the gender and the number of the noun it is referring to |
| **Dictionary form** | the form of a word given in the dictionary WORD LIST. For verbs, it is the spelling of the infinitive in English and French; for French nouns, the spelling of the masculine singular form (or the feminine singular form if there is no masculine form); for French adjectives, the spelling of the masculine singular form |
| **Direct object** | the noun or pronoun directly affected by the verb, e.g. she bought *the book* = elle a acheté *le livre*; he carried *it* = il l'a porté; help *me* = aidez-*moi* |
| **Ending** | that part of a noun or an adjective which can be changed to show gender or number and of a verb to show number or tense. The ending doesn't change the basic meaning of the word |
| **Entry** | the information given in a dictionary about the word you have looked up; also the word itself. See HEADWORD |
| **Exclamation** | a sound, word or remark expressing a strong feeling such as anger, fear, or joy, e.g. ouch! = aïe! |
| **Faux ami** | one of a pair of words from two different languages which look alike but which do not have the same meaning, e.g. *sensible* (English) = *having good sense* and *sensible* (French) = *sensitive* |
| **Feminine** | one of the two genders for nouns in French, which is most clearly indicated by the article used with the noun, e.g. *the* girl = *la* fille; *a* table = *une* table. Pronouns and adjectives also carry gender information e.g., *she* eats = *elle* mange; a black dress = une robe noire (because the noun *robe* is feminine) |

| | |
|---|---|
| Gender | marks words in French as being either masculine or feminine (whether they refer to persons *or things*) whereas English does not make the distinction. The gender of a French noun is important because it will affect the form of adjectives which describe it, e.g. a white cow = **une** vache blanc**he**; a white horse = **un** cheval blanc. Gender will also affect the form of pronouns which replace a French noun, e.g. the boy laughed ▶ he laughed = **il** a ri; the beach (feminine) is clean ▶ it is clean = **elle** est propre |
| Headword | the word which is used in the dictionary word list to begin each separate entry. |
| Imperative | a verb form for expressing commands, e.g. *close* the door = *ferme* la porte; *be quiet!* = *taisez-vous!*; *let's go!* = *allons-y!* |
| Imperfect tense | the tense of the verb which refers to a continuous action or state in the past, e.g. I *was singing* = je *chantais*; or to something that used to happen regularly, e.g. he *used to eat* meat = il *mangeait* la viande; I *took* the bus every day = je *prenais* le bus tous les jours |
| Impersonal verb | a verb whose action is not performed by a person or a thing, e.g. *it* is raining = *il* pleut; *it's* going to snow = *il* va neiger |
| Indefinite article | See ARTICLE |
| Indefinite pronoun | a pronoun that does not identify a specific person or object, e.g. *you* never know = *on* ne sait jamais; *one* wonders why = *on* se demande pourquoi; *it's* raining = *il* pleut |
| Indicative | a verb form which is used when indicating or stating a fact, e.g. I don't understand = je ne comprends pas; it was true = c'était vrai. See SUBJUNCTIVE |
| Indirect object | the noun or pronoun indirectly affected by the verb and often following a preposition, e.g. I wrote *to him* = je *lui* ai écrit. The direct object also has an effect on the indirect object, e.g. she gave the book *to the boy* = elle a donné le livre *au garçon*; he tells *us* stories = il *nous* raconte des histoires |
| Infinitive | the basic part or 'name' of a verb before it is altered to indicate tense or number, e.g. to sing = chanter; to drive = conduire. See DICTIONARY FORM |
| Interrogative | a form of wording used to ask questions |
| Intonation | the quality in a human voice which indicates an emotion (surprise, shock) or which shows that a speaker is asking a question, stating a fact or giving an order |
| Inverted commas | punctuation marks used to indicate direct speech, e.g. "come here," she said. They are also referred to as quotation marks. |
| Irregular verb | a verb whose spelling is not predictable or does not follow a regular pattern when it changes to express tense. See REGULAR VERB |

| | |
|---|---|
| **Masculine** | one of the two genders for nouns in French, which is most clearly indicated by the article used with the noun, e.g. *the* boy = *le* garçon; *a* dog = *un* chien. Pronouns and adjectives also carry gender information e.g., *he* eats = *il* mange; a black hat = un chapeau *noir* (because the noun *chapeau* is masculine) |
| **Noun** | a word which names a person, an animal, an object, a feeling or an event, e.g. a student = un étudiant; a dog = un chien; a house = une maison; envy = l'envie; the storm = l'orage |
| **Number** | a form of the word indicating whether it is singular, e.g. a boy = un garçon, or plural, e.g. two boys = deux garçon*s* |
| **Object** | the person, thing or idea affected by or referred to by a verb, e.g. he walked *the dog* = il a promené *le chien*; we crossed *the road* = nous avons traversé *la rue*. See also DIRECT OBJECT, INDIRECT OBJECT |
| **Part of speech** | the grammatical term which describes the function of a word and categorizes it as *noun*, *verb*, *adjective*, *adverb*, etc. All the entries in this dictionary carry information about the part of speech of the word you look up. |
| **Past participle** | the part of the verb used to form compound tenses in combination with an auxiliary verb, e.g. I have *sung* = j'ai *chanté*; we had *stayed* = nous étions *restés*; she's *gone* to bed = elle s'est *couchée* |
| **Past simple** | the tense of the verb which refers to past events which have been completed. In French, it is a verb form which is mostly used in written language |
| **Perfect tense** | the tense of the verb which refers to past events which have been completed, e.g. we *have finished* the work = nous *avons terminé* le travail. She *left* yesterday = elle *est partie* hier. It is also called the *passé composé* in French and is used in spoken language as well as in print |
| **Person** | the 'person' of a verb shows you **who** or **what** is carrying out the action referred to by the verb. There are six persons in the singular: *I, you, he, she, it, one* and three in the plural: *we, you, they* |
| **Phonetics** | the system of sounds of a language. The word can also refer to the symbols used to represent these sounds. The most common system of symbols is the International Phonetic Alphabet |
| **Phrasal verb** | a form of the English verb which combines with a preposition or an adverb to produce a particular meaning, e.g. to *turn up* = *arriver*; to *carry on* working = *continuer* à travailler |
| **Phrase** | **1.** a self-contained section of a sentence which does not contain a full verb<br>**2.** an expression which has a particular meaning which can make it more difficult to translate word for word, e.g. to lay the table = mettre la table; to hang around = traîner |
| **Pluperfect tense** | the tense of the verb referring to (1) past events which precede (2) other events taking place in a more recent past, e.g. he (1) *had sold* the car when (2) he *told me* about it = il (1) *avait vendu* la voiture quand (2) il *m'en a parlé* |

**Plural**

the form of nouns and pronouns which refers to more than one of something, e.g. *boys, we, they*. French ADJECTIVES also have plural forms, e.g. red shoes = des chaussures rouge**s** to agree with the noun they are describing

**Preposition**

a word which stands in front of a noun or pronoun, connecting it to the rest of a sentence, e.g. *between* the chairs = *entre* les chaises; *with* us = *avec* nous; *to* Paris = *à* Paris; *from* Bob = *de* Bob

**Present tense**

the tense of the verb referring to something that is happening now, e.g. I *am watching* television = je *regarde* la télévision; she *understands* = elle *comprend*

**Pronoun**

a word which takes the place of a noun, e.g. is it *your dog*? ▶ is it *yours*?; I sold *the car* ▶ I sold *it*

**Reflexive verb**

a verb whose object is the same as its subject, e.g. he washed *himself* = il s'est lavé; I hurt *myself* = je me suis blessé

**Register**

the style of language used in speech and writing which is suited (and which you can adapt) to the circumstances. These may range from very formal situations to very relaxed or informal contexts

**Regular verb**

a verb which follows a set pattern in its different forms and tenses and can be classified in a fixed group of verbs. In French, there are many verbs ending in, for example, -er (*aimer, chanter, tourner*) which behave regularly. See IRREGULAR VERB

**Sentence**

a set of words usually containing a subject and a verb, which can stand alone and make sense, e.g. she's gone = elle est partie; who is it? = qui est-ce?; (you) leave me alone! = laisse-moi tranquille!

**Singular**

the form of nouns and pronouns which refers to just one of something, e.g. *boy, I, it*. See PLURAL

**Stem**

the part of the verb to which endings which indicate tense, number and gender are added, e.g. the regular verb *chanter* is made up of the stem *chant-* and the ending *-er*. When a verb is regular, the stem doesn't change. When it is irregular, the stem as well as the endings change

**Subject**

the noun or pronoun which causes the action of a verb and can usually be identified by asking **who..?** or **what..?**, e.g. *he* wants to leave = *il* veut partir; *the computer's* broken down = *l'ordinateur* est en panne

**Subjunctive**

a verb form that is used to express a desire, doubt or unlikelihood, e.g. I'm not sure he'll come = je ne suis pas sûr qu'il vienne. It often indicates how the speaker feels about something rather than the fact itself, e.g. I'm happy *that you are back* = je suis content *que tu sois rentré*

**Superlative**

the form of the adjective which makes it 'the most', e.g. *the biggest* = le plus grand; *the smallest* = le plus petit; *the most intelligent* = le plus intelligent

**Syllable**

part of a word which can form a spoken unit built around the VOWEL it contains, e.g. the word **in-tel-li-gent** has four syllables

**Synonym**

a word which has the same (or almost the same) meaning as another, e.g. *enormous* and *gigantic, sure* and *certain*

| | |
|---|---|
| **Tense** | the form of the verb which indicates a particular time frame – past: I *had* = j'*avais*; present: I *have* = j'*ai*; future: I *will have* = j'*aurai* |
| **Verb** | a word which indicates what is being done or which describes a situation, e.g. he *left* the house = il *a quitté* la maison; you *seem* happy = tu *as* l'air heureux; I *am* tired = je *suis* fatigué |
| **Vowel** | a sound which forms the basis of the syllable and which can be spoken by itself, e.g. *a, i, e, o, u*. See CONSONANT, SYLLABLE |
| **Word list** | the list of headwords or vocabulary items which is found in a dictionary |

# A guide to French grammar

This section expands on many of the terms found in the glossary and used in this dictionary to help you to find the information that you need. The numbers in brackets refer to the appropriate exercises in the Dictionary know how section p. 171.

**Adjective** (1, 14) An adjective is used to add extra information to a noun—a *worried* farmer, a *black* cat, a *thick* book. In French: *un fermier* **inquiet**, *un chat* **noir**, *un livre* **épais**. Note that in English, the adjective usually comes before the noun, whereas in French it usually comes after the noun.

Sometimes, of course, the adjective is separated from its noun:

*Your garden is beautiful.*

*Votre jardin est beau.*

**Adverb** (5, 16) An adverb is used to add extra information to a verb, an adjective or another adverb—*to walk* **slowly**, **extremely** *satisfied*, **quite** *often*. In French: *marcher* **lentement**, **extrêmement** *satisfait*, **assez** *souvent*.

**Agreement** There are two kinds of agreement in French which you must be careful about.

The first is the agreement of nouns and adjectives. All nouns in French have a gender, and most can also be either singular or plural. Any adjective which describes a noun must 'agree' with it in both gender (masculine or feminine) and number (singular or plural). In other words, the adjective must also be masculine or feminine, singular or plural: *un garçon* **intelligent**, *une fille* **intelligente**, *deux garçons* **intelligents**, *deux filles* **intelligentes**.

The other kind of agreement is that between a verb and its subject. You must always ensure that the ending of the verb is the one which matches the subject. If the subject is a pronoun, this is fairly straightforward since we usually learn the various forms of a verb together with the appropriate pronoun: *je* **vais**, *tu* **vas**, *il/elle* **va**, *nous* **allons**, *vous* **allez**, *ils/elles* **vont**.

If the subject of the verb is a noun, or a pronoun like *moi*, *toi* etc, you have to be more careful to get the form of the verb right.

*Pierre et son ami vont au cinéma.*
*(Pierre + son ami = ils)*

*La banque ouvre à neuf heures.*
*(la banque = elle)*

*Hélène et moi avons deux enfants.*
*(Hélène + moi = nous)*

*C'est toi qui as acheté ces carottes?*
*(c'est toi qui = tu)*

**Auxiliary verbs** An auxiliary verb is a verb which is combined with another verb in order to form the so-called compound tenses of that verb (the main compound

tenses in French are the perfect, the pluperfect and the future perfect). There are two auxiliary verbs in French, *avoir* and *être*, and each is used with a particular group of verbs.

The auxiliary verb *être* is used first of all to form the compound tenses of all reflexive verbs:

*Vous vous* **êtes** *levé à quelle heure?*
*(What time did you get up?)*

*Je m'étais couché tard.*
*(I had gone to bed late)*

It is also used to form the compound tenses of a small group of verbs. These verbs are:

| | |
|---|---|
| aller | to go |
| arriver | to arrive |
| descendre | to go/come down |
| entrer | to enter |
| monter | to go/come up |
| mourir | to die |
| naître | to be born |
| partir | to leave, to set out |
| passer | to go past, to drop in on |
| rester | to remain, to stay |
| retourner | to return |
| sortir | to go/come out |
| tomber | to fall |
| venir | to come |

*Il est allé au marché.*
*(he went to the market.)*

*je suis descendu.*
*(I went down.)*

The auxiliary verb *avoir* is used to form the compound tenses of all other verbs:

*j'ai fait le ménage.*
*(I've done the housework.)*

*elle a fini son travail.*
*(she has finished her work.)*

*nous avions déjà mangé.*
*(we had already eaten.)*

**Comparative** The comparative, as its name indicates, is the form of the adjective or adverb which enables us to compare two or more nouns or pronouns. In English, this is usually done by putting *more*, *less* or *as* before the appropriate adjective or adverb:

*Anne is* **more** *sensitive (than her sister).*
*Louise is* **less** *tired (than Jacqueline).*
*Léa is* **as** *intelligent (as Louise).*

In French, the equivalent comparatives are *plus*, *moins* and *aussi*:

*Anne est* **plus** *sensible (que sa sœur).*
*Louise est* **moins** *fatiguée (que Jacqueline).*
*Léa est* **aussi** *intelligente (que Louise).*

Note that the French for both *than* and *as* is *que*.

In English, a few adjectives have an irregular comparative form (*good*/**better**, *bad*/**worse**, *little*/**less**, *much* or *many*/**more**) and some shorter English adjectives have a special comparative form ending in *-er* (for example, *bigger*, *smaller*, *happier*, *slower*). In French, there are only three adjectives with a special form: *bon*/**meilleur** (*good*/*better*); *mauvais*/**pire** (*bad*/*worse*); *petit*/**moindre** (*small*/*less*). However, note that *plus petit* is used instead of *moindre* when referring to size: *ma voiture est **plus petite** que la tienne* (*my car is smaller than yours*). The only irregular form which is always used is *meilleur*—don't forget that, like all comparative adjectives, it must agree with its noun: *une **meilleure** chanson* (*a better song*), *de **meilleurs** chanteurs* (*better singers*).

The comparative of adverbs is formed in much the same way:

> Paul walks **more** slowly (than his brother).
> Peter speaks **less** quickly (than Paul).
> Paul goes to Paris **as** often (as Peter).

> Paul marche **plus** lentement (que son frère).
> Peter parle **moins** vite (que Paul).
> Paul va à Paris **aussi** souvent (que Peter).

In both English and French, there are four irregular forms: *beaucoup*/**plus** (*much* or *a lot*/*more*); *bien*/**mieux** (*well*/**better**); *peu*/**moins** (*little*/**less**); *mal*/**pis** or *plus mal* (*badly*/**worse**). However, *pis* is only found in a few fixed expressions and the usual comparative of *mal* is *plus mal*: *je chante **plus mal** que lui* (*I sing worse than he does*).

**Conditional** A conditional sentence is one in which the statement contained in the main clause can only be fulfilled if the condition stated in the subordinate clause is also fulfilled. This condition is usually introduced by *if* in English and by *si* in French.

> If it's fine tomorrow, we'll go to the beach.
> I would be surprised if he came today.

> S'il fait beau demain, nous irons à la plage.
> Je serais surpris s'il venait aujourd'hui.

**Conjunction** (14) A conjunction can be either (i) a word like *and* or *but* which is used to join words or simple sentences together, or (ii) a word like *when*, *although*, *if*, *where*, which is used to form a complex sentence. Look at these examples:

> (i) John **and** Sarah
> Tired **but** happy
> They came down the steps **and** got into the car.

> Sophie **et** Pierre
> Fatigué **mais** heureux
> Ils ont descendu les marches **et** sont montés dans la voiture.

> (ii) **Although** he doesn't like the rain, he agreed to go for a walk.
> He was about to go to bed **when** he heard the noise of an aircraft.

> **Bien qu'**il n'aime pas la pluie, il a accepté de faire une promenade.
> Il était sur le point de se coucher, **quand** il a entendu le bruit d'un avion.

**Determiner** (16) A determiner is used before a noun in order to identify more precisely what is being referred to. Here are some examples of determiners in English: *a* car, *the* car, *my* car, *this* car, *these* cars, *some* cars. Examples of French determiners are: *une* voiture, *la* voiture, *ma* voiture, *cette* voiture, *ces* voitures, *certaines* voitures.

**Exclamation** An exclamation is a word or phrase conveying a reaction such as surprise, shock, disapproval, indignation, amusement etc. In both English and French, it is usually followed by an exclamation mark.

> Well, well!
> What!

> Ça alors!
> Quoi!

**Feminine** (10, 13, 19) ▶ Gender

**Gender** (2, 10, 13, 19) You will see when using the French–English half of this dictionary that some French words are marked (*noun, masculine*) or (*noun, feminine*). Unlike English nouns, every French noun has a gender—it is either masculine or feminine. For example, the French words for *office*, *pen*, *tree*, *roof* are masculine (*un bureau*, *un stylo*, *un arbre*, *un toit*), and the words for *car*, *table*, *house*, *photo* are feminine (*une voiture*, *une table*, *une maison*, *une photo*). When looking up a noun in the dictionary, it is important to note whether the French word is masculine or feminine, because this will determine the form of most adjectives and determiners which go with it—*un grand arbre*, but *une grande maison*.

**Imperative** The imperative is the form of the verb which we use when we want to order someone to do something. In English, there are two imperatives: for example, *leave* and *let's leave*. In French, there are three in order to allow for the *tu* and *vous* forms of the verb: for example, *pars* (*tu* form), *partons*, *partez* (*vous* form).

**Indicative** ▶ Subjunctive

**Infinitive** The infinitive is a form of the verb which has no indication of person or tense. In English, it is often preceded by *to*: *to walk*, *to run*, *to read*, *to receive*. In French, the infinitive ends in *-er*, *-ir*, *-re* or *-oir*: *marcher*, *courir*, *écrire*, *recevoir*. The infinitive is the form you will find at the beginning of verb entries in this and other dictionaries.

**Masculine** (10) ▶ Gender

**Noun** (1, 16, 17) A noun is used to identify a person, an animal, an object, an idea or an emotion—*farmer, cat, book, suggestion, happiness* are all nouns. It can also be the name of an individual, a company or an institution—*Emma, Peter, Robertson's, Parliament* are nouns. Equivalent French nouns are *fermier, chat, livre, suggestion, bonheur, Sophie, Pierre, Boulangerie Fauré, Conseil d'État.*

**Number** (16) As in English, most nouns in French may be singular or plural and change their ending accordingly (usually by adding '-s' in the plural: *a tree, two tree**s***; *un arbre, deux arbre**s***). Unlike English, however, adjectives in French may also be singular or plural and in most cases change their ending in order to agree with the noun they describe: *un grand arbre, deux grand**s** arbre**s**.*

In the French–English half of this dictionary, when a noun has an irregular plural, the plural form is given after the noun. A noun which doesn't change in the plural has the warning (**!** never changes).

**Object** (6) The object of a sentence is the word or group of words which is immediately affected by the action indicated by the verb. So, in the sentence *The dog chewed the bone, dog* is the subject, *chewed* is the verb and ***bone*** is the object. Similarly, in the sentence *Le chien a rongé l'os, chien* is the subject, *a rongé* is the verb and ***os*** is the object.

There may be two kinds of object in a sentence, a direct object and an indirect object. In the examples above, *bone* and *os* are strictly direct objects. However, in the sentence *John gave the dog a bone, John* is the subject, *gave* is the verb, *bone* is the direct object and *dog* is the indirect object. Similarly, in the French sentence *Jean a donné un os au chien, Jean* is the subject, *a donné* is the verb, *os* is the direct object and *chien* is the indirect object. So, in general terms, the indirect object indicates the person or thing which 'benefits' from the action of the verb upon the direct object.

**Phrasal verb** (15) A phrasal verb is a verb combined with a preposition or an adverb and having a particular meaning. For example, *to **run away***, meaning to flee, or *to **see to** something*, meaning to ensure that something is done.

Phrasal verbs don't exist in French and you therefore need to use your dictionary carefully in order to select the correct translation. If you look up *to run away* for example, you will see that phrasal verbs are listed after all the other meanings of the word *run*, and in alphabetical order of the following adverb or preposition.

**Plural** ▶ Number

**Preposition** (11) A preposition is a word, such as *under, beside, across, in*, which is usually followed by a noun: *under the table, beside the road, in the garden; **sous** la table, **au bord de** la route, **dans** le jardin*. Most preposition + noun groups indicate movement

> *he ran **towards the house***
> *il a couru **vers la maison***

position

> *your books are **on the table***
> *vos livres sont **sur la table***

or time

> *I'll be there **at 4 o'clock***
> *je serai là **à six heures**.*

**Pronoun** (3, 14) A pronoun is used instead of a noun in order to avoid repeating it unnecessarily. English pronouns are *I, me, you, he, him, she, her, it, we, us, they, them, mine, yours, his, hers, ours, theirs, this, that, these* and *those*. Equivalent French pronouns are: *je, me, tu, te, il, le, elle, la, nous, vous, ils, les, elles, leur, lui, le mien, la mienne, les miens, les miennes* etc, *ceci, cela, celui, celle, ceux, celles*. All of these are labelled as pronouns in this dictionary. However, some of the English pronouns (but not their French equivalents) can also be used as determiners and you must be careful not to confuse them. Compare these sentences:

> *He lent me **his** book.* (determiner)
> *He lent me **his**.* (pronoun)

> ***These** ideas are important.* (determiner)
> ***These** are important.* (pronoun)

> ***Those** people have just arrived.* (determiner)
> ***Those** have just arrived.* (pronoun)

Now look at the French equivalents:

> *Il m'a prêté **son** livre.* (determiner)
> *Il m'a prêté **le sien**.* (pronoun)

> ***Ces** idées-ci sont importantes.* (determiner)
> ***Celles**-ci sont importantes.* (pronoun)

> ***Ces** gens là viennent d'arriver.* (determiner)
> ***Ceux**-là viennent d'arriver.* (pronoun)

**Reflexive verb** (24) A reflexive verb is one whose action is 'reflected back' upon the subject of the verb. In English, this is indicated by the use of reflexive pronouns such as *myself, yourself, herself, themselves, each other* etc. For example:

> *when he hurts **himself**, he cries.*
> *We speak to **each other** every day.*

In French, this reflexive action is conveyed by the use of the pronouns *me*, *te*, *se*, *nous* or *vous*:

> *Quand il **se** fait mal, il pleure.*
> *Nous **nous** parlons tous les jours.*

Here are the full present tense forms of the reflexive verb *se baigner* (*to go for a swim*):

| | |
|---|---|
| je **me** baigne | nous **nous** baignons |
| tu **te** baignes | vous **vous** baignez |
| il **se** baigne | ils **se** baignent |
| elle **se** baigne | elles **se** baignent |

Remember that many reflexive verbs in French have English equivalents which are not reflexive. Other examples are *se souvenir de* (*to remember*), *se laver* (*to wash*).

### Singular ▶ Number

**Subject** (6) The subject of a sentence is the word or group of words which performs the action indicated by the verb. So, in the sentence *John coughed*, John is the subject of the verb *coughed*. Of course, the verb doesn't necessarily express an action as such. For example, in the sentence *John is tall*, John is the subject of the verb *is*. In the French sentence *Jean a toussé*, Jean is similarly the subject of the verb *a toussé*, and in the sentence *Jean est grand*, Jean is the subject of the verb *est*.

**Subjunctive** The subjunctive is a special form of some tenses of the verb, which in French is mostly used to express doubt and possibility, rather than fact or certainty. It is also used when expressing an emotional reaction to something. This form of the verb is much more widely used in French than in English, where it has almost disappeared, and you will find a fuller explanation and examples on p. 291. Note that the usual form of the various tenses of a verb is known as the indicative because it 'indicates' fact or certainty.

**Superlative** The superlative is the form of the adjective or adverb which is used to express the highest or lowest degree. In English, the adjective or adverb is usually preceded by *most* or *least*, **most** important, **least** important, **most** carefully, **least** carefully. Some adjectives and adverbs (usually of one syllable) have their own form: *best*, *worst*, *biggest*, *smallest*, *fastest*, *slowest* etc. In French, the superlative adjective (which must agree with its noun) is usually formed by putting *le plus*, *la plus*, *les plus*, *le moins*, *la moins* or *les moins* before the adjective: *le livre **le plus** long*, *le livre **le moins** long*, *la question **la plus** importante*, *la question **la moins** importante*, *les avions **les plus** rapides*, *les avions **les moins** rapides*. The superlative adverb is usually preceded by *le plus* or *le moins*: **le plus** *vite*, **le moins** *vite*, **le plus** *soigneusement*, **le moins** *soigneusement*.

Some French adjectives and adverbs have their own form of the superlative, for example:

| | |
|---|---|
| bon/bonne | **le meilleur/la meilleure** |
| mauvais/mauvaise | **le pire/la pire** |
| bien | **le mieux** |
| mal | **le plus mal** |

**Tense** The tense is the particular form of the verb which tells us the approximate time when the action of the verb takes place:

Present tense
> *He **is telephoning** all his friends.*
> *Il téléphone à tous ses amis.*

Future tense
> *He **will telephone** all his friends.*
> *Il téléphonera à tous ses amis.*

The main past and future tenses used in French are:

| | |
|---|---|
| Past tenses | (i) Imperfect |
| | (ii) Present perfect (or Perfect) |
| | (iii) Past perfect (or Pluperfect) |
| Future tenses | (iv) Future (simple) |
| | (v) Future perfect |

For example:

(i) *Il **téléphonait** souvent à tous ses amis.*
(*He often used to telephone all his friends.*)

(ii) *Hier, il **a téléphoné** à tous ses amis.*
(*Yesterday he telephoned all his friends.*)

(iii) *Il **avait** déjà **téléphoné** à tous ses amis.*
(*He had already telephoned all his friends.*)

(iv) *Demain, il **téléphonera** à tous ses amis.*
(*Tomorrow he will telephone all his friends.*)

(v) *Avant 6 heures il **aura téléphoné** à tous ses amis.*
(*By 6 o'clock he will have telephoned all his friends.*)

**Verb** (4, 12, 16) The verb propels the sentence along, telling us what is happening. Look at these examples:

> *Paul **carried** the boxes upstairs to the attic. The storm **did** a lot of damage.*

> *Paul **a monté** les cartons au grenier. La tempête **a fait** beaucoup de dégâts.*

Sometimes, of course, the verb doesn't describe an action, but rather a state of affairs:

> *Paul **has** a back problem.*
> *He **is** often ill.*
> *The damage **appears** less serious than we expected.*

> *Paul **a** un problème de dos.*
> *Il **est** souvent malade.*
> *Les dégâts **semblent** moins importants que prévu.*

## 1 chanter

| Present | |
|---|---|
| je | chante |
| tu | chantes |
| il | chante |
| nous | chantons |
| vous | chantez |
| ils | chantent |

| Future | |
|---|---|
| je | chanterai |
| tu | chanteras |
| il | chantera |
| nous | chanterons |
| vous | chanterez |
| ils | chanteront |

| Imperfect | |
|---|---|
| je | chantais |
| tu | chantais |
| il | chantait |
| nous | chantions |
| vous | chantiez |
| ils | chantaient |

| Perfect | | |
|---|---|---|
| j' | ai | chanté |
| tu | as | chanté |
| il | a | chanté |
| elle | a | chanté |
| nous | avons | chanté |
| vous | avez | chanté |
| ils | ont | chanté |
| elles | ont | chanté |

**Past participle**

chanté/chantée

| Present subjunctive | | |
|---|---|---|
| (que) | je | chante |
| (que) | tu | chantes |
| (qu') | il | chante |
| (que) | nous | chantions |
| (que) | vous | chantiez |
| (qu') | ils | chantent |

| Conditional | |
|---|---|
| je | chanterais |
| tu | chanterais |
| il | chanterait |
| nous | chanterions |
| vous | chanteriez |
| ils | chanteraient |

| Pluperfect | | |
|---|---|---|
| j' | avais | chanté |
| tu | avais | chanté |
| il | avait | chanté |
| elle | avait | chanté |
| nous | avions | chanté |
| vous | aviez | chanté |
| ils | avaient | chanté |
| elles | avaient | chanté |

## 2 oublier

| Present | |
|---|---|
| j' | oublie |
| tu | oublies |
| il | oublie |
| nous | oublions |
| vous | oubliez |
| ils | oublient |

| Future | |
|---|---|
| j' | oublierai |
| tu | oublieras |
| il | oubliera |
| nous | oublierons |
| vous | oublierez |
| ils | oublieront |

| Imperfect | |
|---|---|
| j' | oubliais |
| tu | oubliais |
| il | oubliait |
| nous | oubliions |
| vous | oubliiez |
| ils | oubliaient |

| Perfect | | |
|---|---|---|
| j' | ai | oublié |
| tu | as | oublié |
| il | a | oublié |
| elle | a | oublié |
| nous | avons | oublié |
| vous | avez | oublié |
| ils | ont | oublié |
| elles | ont | oublié |

**Past participle**

oublié/oubliée

| Present subjunctive | | |
|---|---|---|
| (quo) | j' | oublie |
| (que) | tu | oublies |
| (qu') | il | oublie |
| (que) | nous | oubliions |
| (que) | vous | oubliiez |
| (qu') | ils | oublient |

| Conditional | |
|---|---|
| j' | oublierais |
| tu | oublierais |
| il | oublierait |
| nous | oublierions |
| vous | oublieriez |
| ils | oublieraient |

| Pluperfect | | |
|---|---|---|
| j' | avais | oublié |
| tu | avais | oublié |
| il | avait | oublié |
| elle | avait | oublié |
| nous | avions | oublié |
| vous | aviez | oublié |
| ils | avaient | oublié |
| elles | avaient | oublié |

## 3 finir

| Present | | | Perfect | | | Conditional | |
|---|---|---|---|---|---|---|---|
| je | finis | | j' | ai | fini | je | finirais |
| tu | finis | | tu | as | fini | tu | finirais |
| il | finit | | il | a | fini | il | finirait |
| nous | finissons | | elle | a | fini | | |
| vous | finissez | | | | | nous | finirions |
| ils | finissent | | nous | avons | fini | vous | finiriez |
| | | | vous | avez | fini | ils | finiraient |

| Future | | Perfect (cont.) | | | Pluperfect | |
|---|---|---|---|---|---|---|
| je | finirai | ils | ont | fini | j' | avais | fini |
| tu | finiras | elles | ont | fini | tu | avais | fini |
| il | finira | | | | il | avait | fini |

**Future**
je finirai
tu finiras
il finira
nous finirons
vous finirez
ils finiront

**Perfect**
j' ai fini
tu as fini
il a fini
elle a fini

nous avons fini
vous avez fini
ils ont fini
elles ont fini

**Past participle**
fini/finie

**Present subjunctive**
(que) je finisse
(que) tu finisses
(qu') il finisse

(que) nous finissions
(que) vous finissiez
(qu') ils finissent

**Conditional**
je finirais
tu finirais
il finirait

nous finirions
vous finiriez
ils finiraient

**Pluperfect**
j' avais fini
tu avais fini
il avait fini
elle avait fini

nous avions fini
vous aviez fini
ils avaient fini
elles avaient fini

**Imperfect**
je finissais
tu finissais
il finissait
nous finissions
vous finissiez
ils finissaient

---

## 4 offrir

**Present**
j' offre
tu offres
il offre

nous offrons
vous offrez
ils offrent

**Future**
j' offrirai
tu offriras
il offrira

nous offrirons
vous offrirez
ils offriront

**Imperfect**
j' offrais
tu offrais
il offrait

nous offrions
vous offriez
ils offraient

**Perfect**
j' ai offert
tu as offert
il a offert
elle a offert

nous avons offert
vous avez offert
ils ont offert
elles ont offert

**Past participle**
offert/offerte

**Present subjunctive**
(que) j' offre
(que) tu offres
(qu') il offre

(que) nous offrions
(que) vous offriez
(qu') ils offrent

**Conditional**
j' offrirais
tu offrirais
il offrirait

nous offririons
vous offririez
ils offriraient

**Pluperfect**
j' avais offert
tu avais offert
il avait offert
elle avait offert

nous avions offert
vous aviez offert
ils avaient offert
elles avaient offert

## 5 apercevoir

**Present**

| j' | aperçois |
| tu | aperçois |
| il | aperçoit |
| nous | apercevons |
| vous | apercevez |
| ils | aperçoivent |

...........................

**Future**

| j' | apercevrai |
| tu | apercevras |
| il | apercevra |
| nous | apercevrons |
| vous | apercevrez |
| ils | apercevront |

...........................

**Imperfect**

| j' | apercevais |
| tu | apercevais |
| il | apercevait |
| nous | apercevions |
| vous | aperceviez |
| ils | apercevaient |

**Perfect**

| j' | ai | aperçu |
| tu | as | aperçu |
| il | a | aperçu |
| elle | a | aperçu |
| nous | avons | aperçu |
| vous | avez | aperçu |
| ils | ont | aperçu |
| elles | ont | aperçu |

...........................

**Past participle**

aperçu/aperçue

...........................

**Present subjunctive**

| (que) j' | aperçoive |
| (que) tu | aperçoives |
| (qu') il | aperçoive |
| (que) nous | apercevions |
| (que) vous | aperceviez |
| (qu') ils | aperçoivent |

**Conditional**

| j' | apercevrais |
| tu | apercevrais |
| il | apercevrait |
| nous | apercevrions |
| vous | apercevriez |
| ils | apercevraient |

...........................

**Pluperfect**

| j' | avais | aperçu |
| tu | avais | aperçu |
| il | avait | aperçu |
| elle | avait | aperçu |
| nous | avions | aperçu |
| vous | aviez | aperçu |
| ils | avaient | aperçu |
| elles | avaient | aperçu |

## 6 attendre

**Present**

| j' | attends |
| tu | attends |
| il | attend |
| nous | attendons |
| vous | attendez |
| ils | attendent |

...........................

**Future**

| j' | attendrai |
| tu | attendras |
| Il | attendra |
| nous | attendrons |
| vous | attendrez |
| ils | attendront |

...........................

**Imperfect**

| j' | attendais |
| tu | attendais |
| il | attendait |
| nous | attendions |
| vous | attendiez |
| ils | attendaient |

**Perfect**

| j' | ai | attendu |
| tu | as | attendu |
| il | a | attendu |
| elle | a | attendu |
| nous | avons | attendu |
| vous | avez | attendu |
| ils | ont | attendu |
| elles | ont | attendu |

...........................

**Past participle**

attendu/attendue

...........................

**Present subjunctive**

| (que) j' | attende |
| (que) tu | attendes |
| (qu') il | attende |
| (que) nous | attendions |
| (que) vous | attendiez |
| (qu') ils | attendent |

**Conditional**

| j' | attendrais |
| tu | attendrais |
| il | attendrait |
| nous | attendrions |
| vous | attendriez |
| ils | attendraient |

...........................

**Pluperfect**

| j' | avais | attendu |
| tu | avais | attendu |
| il | avait | attendu |
| elle | avait | attendu |
| nous | avions | attendu |
| vous | aviez | attendu |
| ils | avaient | attendu |
| elles | avaient | attendu |

## 7 être

| Present | |
|---|---|
| je | suis |
| tu | es |
| il | est |
| nous | sommes |
| vous | êtes |
| ils | sont |

| Future | |
|---|---|
| je | serai |
| tu | seras |
| il | sera |
| nous | serons |
| vous | serez |
| ils | seront |

| Imperfect | |
|---|---|
| j' | étais |
| tu | étais |
| il | était |
| nous | étions |
| vous | étiez |
| ils | étaient |

| Perfect | | |
|---|---|---|
| j' | ai | été |
| tu | as | été |
| il | a | été |
| elle | a | été |
| nous | avons | été |
| vous | avez | été |
| ils | ont | été |
| elles | ont | été |

**Past participle**

été (invariable)

**Present subjunctive**

| (que) | je | sois |
|---|---|---|
| (que) | tu | sois |
| (qu') | il | soit |
| (que) | nous | soyons |
| (que) | vous | soyez |
| (qu') | ils | soient |

| Conditional | |
|---|---|
| je | serais |
| tu | serais |
| il | serait |
| nous | serions |
| vous | seriez |
| ils | seraient |

**Pluperfect**

| j' | avais | été |
|---|---|---|
| tu | avais | été |
| il | avait | été |
| elle | avait | été |
| nous | avions | été |
| vous | aviez | été |
| ils | avaient | été |
| elles | avaient | été |

## 8 avoir

| Present | |
|---|---|
| j' | ai |
| tu | as |
| il | a |
| nous | avons |
| vous | avez |
| ils | ont |

| Future | |
|---|---|
| j' | aurai |
| tu | auras |
| il | aura |
| nous | aurons |
| vous | aurez |
| ils | auront |

| Imperfect | |
|---|---|
| j' | avais |
| tu | avais |
| il | avait |
| nous | avions |
| vous | aviez |
| ils | avaient |

| Perfect | | |
|---|---|---|
| j' | ai | eu |
| tu | as | eu |
| il | a | eu |
| elle | a | eu |
| nous | avons | eu |
| vous | avez | eu |
| ils | ont | eu |
| elles | ont | eu |

**Past participle**

eu/eue

**Present subjunctive**

| (que) | j' | aie |
|---|---|---|
| (que) | tu | aies |
| (qu') | il | ait |
| (que) | nous | ayons |
| (que) | vous | ayez |
| (qu') | ils | aient |

| Conditional | |
|---|---|
| j' | aurais |
| tu | aurais |
| il | aurait |
| nous | aurions |
| vous | auriez |
| ils | auraient |

**Pluperfect**

| j' | avais | eu |
|---|---|---|
| tu | avais | eu |
| il | avait | eu |
| elle | avait | eu |
| nous | avions | eu |
| vous | aviez | eu |
| ils | avaient | eu |
| elles | avaient | eu |

## 9 aller

| Present | | | Perfect | | | Conditional | | |
|---|---|---|---|---|---|---|---|---|
| je | vais | | je | suis | allé | j' | irais | |
| tu | vas | | tu | es | allé | tu | irais | |
| il | va | | il | est | allé | il | irait | |
| nous | allons | | elle | est | allée | | | |
| vous | allez | | | | | nous | irions | |
| ils | vont | | nous | sommes | allés | vous | iriez | |
| | | | vous | êtes | allés | ils | iraient | |
| **Future** | | | ils | sont | allés | | | |
| j' | irai | | elles | sont | allées | **Pluperfect** | | |
| tu | iras | | | | | j' | étais | allé |
| il | ira | | **Past participle** | | | tu | étais | allé |
| nous | irons | | | allé/allée | | il | était | allé |
| vous | irez | | | | | elle | était | allée |
| ils | iront | | **Present subjunctive** | | | nous | étions | allés |
| | | | (que) | j' | aille | vous | étiez | allés |
| **Imperfect** | | | (que) | tu | ailles | ils | étaient | allés |
| j' | allais | | (qu') | il | aille | elles | étaient | allées |
| tu | allais | | | | | | | |
| il | allait | | (que) | nous | allions | | | |
| | | | (que) | vous | alliez | | | |
| nous | allions | | (qu') | ils | aillent | | | |
| vous | alliez | | | | | | | |
| ils | allaient | | | | | | | |

## 10 faire

| Present | | | Perfect | | | Conditional | | |
|---|---|---|---|---|---|---|---|---|
| je | fais | | j' | ai | fait | je | ferais | |
| tu | fais | | tu | as | fait | tu | ferais | |
| il | fait | | il | a | fait | il | ferait | |
| nous | faisons | | elle | a | fait | | | |
| vous | faites | | | | | nous | ferions | |
| ils | font | | nous | avons | fait | vous | feriez | |
| | | | vous | avez | fait | ils | feraient | |
| **Future** | | | ils | ont | fait | | | |
| je | ferai | | elles | ont | fait | **Pluperfect** | | |
| tu | feras | | | | | j' | avais | fait |
| il | fera | | **Past participle** | | | tu | avais | fait |
| nous | ferons | | | fait/faite | | il | avait | fait |
| vous | ferez | | | | | elle | avait | fait |
| ils | feront | | **Present subjunctive** | | | nous | avions | fait |
| | | | (que) | je | fasse | vous | aviez | fait |
| **Imperfect** | | | (que) | tu | fasses | ils | avaient | fait |
| je | faisais | | (qu') | il | fasse | elles | avaient | fait |
| tu | faisais | | | | | | | |
| il | faisait | | (que) | nous | fassions | | | |
| | | | (que) | vous | fassiez | | | |
| nous | faisions | | (qu') | ils | fassent | | | |
| vous | faisiez | | | | | | | |
| ils | faisaient | | | | | | | |

## 11 créer

| Present | | Perfect | | | Conditional | |
|---|---|---|---|---|---|---|
| je | crée | j' | ai | créé | je | créerais |
| tu | crées | tu | as | créé | tu | créerais |
| il | crée | il | a | créé | il | créerait |
| nous | créons | elle | a | créé | | |
| vous | créez | | | | nous | créerions |
| ils | créent | nous | avons | créé | vous | créeriez |
| | | vous | avez | créé | ils | créeraient |

| Future | | Perfect (cont.) | | |
|---|---|---|---|---|
| je | créerai | ils | ont | créé |
| tu | créeras | elles | ont | créé |
| il | créera | | | |

**Past participle**

créé/créée

**Pluperfect**

| | | | |
|---|---|---|---|
| j' | avais | créé |
| tu | avais | créé |
| il | avait | créé |
| elle | avait | créé |
| nous | avions | créé |
| vous | aviez | créé |
| ils | avaient | créé |
| elles | avaient | créé |

| Future (cont.) | |
|---|---|
| nous | créerons |
| vous | créerez |
| ils | créeront |

**Imperfect**

| je | créais |
|---|---|
| tu | créais |
| il | créait |
| nous | créions |
| vous | créiez |
| ils | créaient |

**Present subjunctive**

| (que) | je | crée |
|---|---|---|
| (que) | tu | crées |
| (qu') | il | crée |
| (que) | nous | créions |
| (que) | vous | créiez |
| (qu') | ils | créent |

## 12 avancer

| Present | | Perfect | | | Conditional | |
|---|---|---|---|---|---|---|
| j' | avance | j' | ai | avancé | j' | avancerais |
| tu | avances | tu | as | avancé | tu | avancerais |
| il | avance | il | a | avancé | il | avancerait |
| nous | avançons | elle | a | avancé | | |
| vous | avancez | | | | nous | avancerions |
| ils | avancent | nous | avons | avancé | vous | avanceriez |
| | | vous | avez | avancé | ils | avanceraient |
| | | ils | ont | avancé | | |
| | | elles | ont | avancé | | |

| Future | |
|---|---|
| j' | avancerai |
| tu | avanceras |
| il | avancera |
| nous | avancerons |
| vous | avancerez |
| ils | avanceront |

**Past participle**

avancé/avancée

**Pluperfect**

| j' | avais | avancé |
|---|---|---|
| tu | avais | avancé |
| il | avait | avancé |
| elle | avait | avancé |
| nous | avions | avancé |
| vous | aviez | avancé |
| ils | avaient | avancé |
| elles | avaient | avancé |

**Imperfect**

| j' | avançais |
|---|---|
| tu | avançais |
| il | avançait |
| nous | avancions |
| vous | avanciez |
| ils | avançaient |

**Present subjunctive**

| (que) | j' | avance |
|---|---|---|
| (que) | tu | avances |
| (qu') | il | avance |
| (que) | nous | avancions |
| (que) | vous | avanciez |
| (qu') | ils | avancent |

## 13 changer

| Present | | Perfect | | | Conditional | |
|---|---|---|---|---|---|---|
| je | change | j' | ai | changé | je | changerais |
| tu | changes | tu | as | changé | tu | changerais |
| il | change | il | a | changé | il | changerait |
| nous | changeons | elle | a | changé | | |
| vous | changez | | | | nous | changerions |
| ils | changent | nous | avons | changé | vous | changeriez |
| | | vous | avez | changé | ils | changeraient |
| **Future** | | ils | ont | changé | | |
| je | changerai | elles | ont | changé | **Pluperfect** | |
| tu | changeras | | | | j' | avais | changé |
| il | changera | **Past participle** | | | tu | avais | changé |
| nous | changerons | | changé/changée | | il | avait | changé |
| vous | changerez | | | | elle | avait | changé |
| ils | changeront | **Present subjunctive** | | | | | |
| | | (que) je | change | | nous | avons | changé |
| **Imperfect** | | (que) tu | changes | | vous | aviez | changé |
| je | changeais | (qu') il | change | | ils | avaient | changé |
| tu | changeais | | | | elles | avaient | changé |
| il | changeait | (que) nous | changions | | | | |
| nous | changions | (que) vous | changiez | | | | |
| vous | changiez | (qu') ils | changent | | | | |
| ils | changeaient | | | | | | |

## 14 espérer

| Present | | Perfect | | | Conditional | |
|---|---|---|---|---|---|---|
| j' | espère | j' | ai | espéré | j' | espérerais |
| tu | espères | tu | as | espéré | tu | espérerais |
| il | espère | il | a | espéré | il | espérerait |
| nous | espérons | elle | a | espéré | | |
| vous | espérez | | | | nous | espérerions |
| ils | espèrent | nous | avons | espéré | vous | espéreriez |
| | | vous | avez | espéré | ils | espéreraient |
| **Future** | | ils | ont | espéré | | |
| j' | espérerai | elles | ont | espéré | **Pluperfect** | |
| tu | espéreras | | | | j' | avais | espéré |
| il | espérera | **Past participle** | | | tu | avais | espéré |
| nous | espérerons | | espéré/espérée | | il | avait | espéré |
| vous | espérerez | | | | elle | avait | espéré |
| ils | espéreront | **Present subjunctive** | | | | | |
| | | (que) j' | espère | | nous | avons | espéré |
| **Imperfect** | | (que) tu | espères | | vous | aviez | espéré |
| j' | espérais | (qu') il | espère | | ils | avaient | espéré |
| tu | espérais | | | | elles | avaient | espéré |
| il | espérait | (que) nous | espérions | | | | |
| nous | espérions | (que) vous | espériez | | | | |
| vous | espériez | (qu') ils | espèrent | | | | |
| ils | espéraient | | | | | | |

## 15 protéger

| Present | | Perfect | | | Conditional | |
|---|---|---|---|---|---|---|
| je | protège | j' | ai | protégé | je | protégerais |
| tu | protèges | tu | as | protégé | tu | protégerais |
| il | protège | il | a | protégé | il | protégerait |
| nous | protégeons | elle | a | protégé | | |
| vous | protégez | | | | nous | protégerions |
| ils | protègent | nous | avons | protégé | vous | protégeriez |
| | | vous | avez | protégé | ils | protégeraient |
| **Future** | | ils | ont | protégé | | |
| je | protégerai | elles | ont | protégé | **Pluperfect** | |
| tu | protégeras | | | | j' | avais | protégé |
| il | protégera | **Past participle** | | | tu | avais | protégé |
| | | | protégé/protégée | | il | avait | protégé |
| nous | protégerons | | | | elle | avait | protégé |
| vous | protégerez | | | | | | |
| ils | protégeront | **Present subjunctive** | | | nous | avions | protégé |
| | | (que) je | protège | | vous | aviez | protégé |
| **Imperfect** | | (que) tu | protèges | | ils | avaient | protégé |
| je | protégeais | (qu') il | protège | | | | |
| tu | protégeais | | | | | | |
| il | protégeait | (que) nous | protégions | | | | |
| nous | protégions | (que) vous | protégiez | | | | |
| vous | protégiez | (qu') ils | protègent | | | | |
| ils | protégeaient | | | | | | |

## 16 mener

| Present | | Perfect | | | Conditional | |
|---|---|---|---|---|---|---|
| je | mène | j' | ai | mené | je | mènerais |
| tu | mènes | tu | as | mené | tu | mènerais |
| il | mène | il | a | mené | il | mènerait |
| nous | menons | elle | a | mené | | |
| vous | menez | | | | nous | mènerions |
| ils | mènent | nous | avons | mené | vous | mèneriez |
| | | vous | avez | mené | ils | mèneraient |
| **Future** | | ils | ont | mené | | |
| je | mènerai | elles | ont | mené | **Pluperfect** | |
| tu | mèneras | | | | j' | avais | mené |
| il | mènera | **Past participle** | | | tu | avais | mené |
| | | | mené/menée | | il | avait | mené |
| nous | mènerons | | | | elle | avait | mené |
| vous | mènerez | | | | | | |
| ils | mèneront | **Present subjunctive** | | | nous | avions | mené |
| | | (que) je | mène | | vous | aviez | mené |
| **Imperfect** | | (que) tu | mènes | | ils | avaient | mené |
| je | menais | (qu') il | mène | | elles | avaient | mené |
| tu | menais | | | | | | |
| il | menait | (que) nous | menions | | | | |
| nous | menions | (que) vous | meniez | | | | |
| vous | meniez | (qu') ils | mènent | | | | |
| ils | menaient | | | | | | |

## 17 peler

| Present | | Perfect | | | Conditional | |
|---|---|---|---|---|---|---|
| je | pèle | j' | ai | pelé | je | pèlerais |
| tu | pèles | tu | as | pelé | tu | pèlerais |
| il | pèle | il | a | pelé | il | pèlerait |
| nous | pelons | elle | a | pelé | nous | pèlerions |
| vous | pelez | | | | vous | pèleriez |
| ils | pèlent | nous | avons | pelé | ils | pèleraient |
| | | vous | avez | pelé | | |
| | | ils | ont | pelé | | |

| Future | | Perfect | | | Pluperfect | | |
|---|---|---|---|---|---|---|---|
| je | pèlerai | elles | ont | pelé | j' | avais | pelé |
| tu | pèleras | | | | tu | avais | pelé |
| il | pèlera | **Past participle** | | | il | avait | pelé |
| nous | pèlerons | | pelé/pelée | | elle | avait | pelé |
| vous | pèlerez | | | | nous | avions | pelé |
| ils | pèleront | **Present subjunctive** | | | vous | aviez | pelé |

| Imperfect | | Present subjunctive | | | Pluperfect | | |
|---|---|---|---|---|---|---|---|
| | | (que) | je | pèle | ils | avaient | pelé |
| je | pelais | (que) | tu | pèles | elles | avaient | pelé |
| tu | pelais | (qu') | il | pèle | | | |
| il | pelait | | | | | | |
| nous | pelions | (que) | nous | pelions | | | |
| vous | peliez | (que) | vous | peliez | | | |
| Ils | pelaient | (qu') | ils | pèlent | | | |

## 18 acheter

| Present | | Perfect | | | Conditional | |
|---|---|---|---|---|---|---|
| j' | achète | j' | ai | acheté | j' | achèterais |
| tu | achètes | tu | as | acheté | tu | achèterais |
| il | achète | il | a | acheté | il | achèterait |
| nous | achetons | elle | a | acheté | nous | achèterions |
| vous | achetez | | | | vous | achèteriez |
| ils | achètent | nous | avons | acheté | ils | achèteraient |
| | | vous | avez | acheté | | |
| | | ils | ont | acheté | | |

| Future | | Perfect | | | Pluperfect | | |
|---|---|---|---|---|---|---|---|
| j' | achèterai | elles | ont | acheté | j' | avais | acheté |
| tu | achèteras | | | | tu | avais | acheté |
| il | achètera | **Past participle** | | | il | avait | acheté |
| nous | achèterons | | acheté/achetée | | elle | avait | acheté |
| vous | achèterez | | | | nous | avions | acheté |
| ils | achèteront | **Present subjunctive** | | | vous | aviez | acheté |

| Imperfect | | Present subjunctive | | | Pluperfect | | |
|---|---|---|---|---|---|---|---|
| j' | achetais | (que) | j' | achète | ils | avaient | acheté |
| tu | achetais | (que) | tu | achètes | elles | avaient | acheté |
| il | achetait | (qu') | il | achète | | | |
| nous | achetions | (que) | nous | achetions | | | |
| vous | achetiez | (que) | vous | achetiez | | | |
| ils | achetaient | (qu') | ils | achètent | | | |

## 19 rappeler

| Present | | | Perfect | | | Conditional | |
|---|---|---|---|---|---|---|---|
| je | rappelle | | j' | ai | rappelé | je | rappellerais |
| tu | rappelles | | tu | as | rappelé | tu | rappellerais |
| il | rappelle | | il | a | rappelé | il | rappellerait |
| nous | rappelons | | elle | a | rappelé | nous | rappellerions |
| vous | rappelez | | | | | vous | rappelleriez |
| ils | rappellent | | nous | avons | rappelé | ils | rappelleraient |
| | | | vous | avez | rappelé | | |
| **Future** | | | ils | ont | rappelé | **Pluperfect** | |
| je | rappellerai | | elles | ont | rappelé | j' | avais | rappelé |
| tu | rappelleras | | | | | tu | avais | rappelé |
| il | rappellera | | **Past participle** | | | il | avait | rappelé |
| nous | rappellerons | | | rappelé/rappelée | | elle | avait | rappelé |
| vous | rappellerez | | | | | nous | avions | rappelé |
| ils | rappelleront | | **Present subjunctive** | | | vous | aviez | rappelé |
| | | | (que) je | rappelle | | ils | avaient | rappelé |
| **Imperfect** | | | (que) tu | rappelles | | elles | avaient | rappelé |
| je | rappelais | | (qu') il | rappelle | | | |
| tu | rappelais | | | | | | |
| il | rappelait | | (que) nous | rappelions | | | |
| nous | rappelions | | (que) vous | rappeliez | | | |
| vous | rappeliez | | (qu') ils | rappellent | | | |
| ils | rappelaient | | | | | | |

## 20 jeter

| Present | | | Perfect | | | Conditional | |
|---|---|---|---|---|---|---|---|
| je | jette | | j' | ai | jeté | je | jetterais |
| tu | jettes | | tu | as | jeté | tu | jetterais |
| il | jette | | il | a | jeté | il | jetterait |
| nous | jetons | | elle | a | jeté | nous | jetterions |
| vous | jetez | | | | | vous | jetteriez |
| ils | jettent | | nous | avons | jeté | ils | jetteraient |
| | | | vous | avez | jeté | | |
| **Future** | | | ils | ont | jeté | **Pluperfect** | |
| je | jetterai | | elles | ont | jeté | j' | avais | jeté |
| tu | jetteras | | | | | tu | avais | jeté |
| il | jettera | | **Past participle** | | | il | avait | jeté |
| nous | jetterons | | | jeté/jetée | | elle | avait | jeté |
| vous | jetterez | | | | | nous | avions | jeté |
| ils | jetteront | | **Present subjunctive** | | | vous | aviez | jeté |
| | | | (que) je | jette | | ils | avaient | jeté |
| **Imperfect** | | | (que) tu | jettes | | elles | avaient | jeté |
| je | jetais | | (qu') il | jette | | | |
| tu | jetais | | | | | | |
| il | jetait | | (que) nous | jetions | | | |
| nous | jetions | | (que) vous | jetiez | | | |
| vous | jetiez | | (qu') ils | jettent | | | |
| ils | jetaient | | | | | | |

## 21 essayer

### Present

| | |
|---|---|
| j' | essaie |
| tu | essaies |
| il | essaie |
| nous | essayons |
| vous | essayez |
| ils | essaient |

### Future

| | |
|---|---|
| j' | essaierai |
| tu | essaieras |
| il | essaiera |
| nous | essaierons |
| vous | essaierez |
| ils | essaieront |

### Imperfect

| | |
|---|---|
| j' | essayais |
| tu | essayais |
| il | essayait |
| nous | essayions |
| vous | essayiez |
| ils | essayaient |

### Perfect

| | | |
|---|---|---|
| j' | ai | essayé |
| tu | as | essayé |
| il | a | essayé |
| elle | a | essayé |
| nous | avons | essayé |
| vous | avez | essayé |
| ils | ont | essayé |
| elles | ont | essayé |

### Past participle

essayé/essayée

### Present subjunctive

| | | |
|---|---|---|
| (que) | j' | essaie |
| (que) | tu | essaies |
| (qu') | il | essaie |
| (que) | nous | essayions |
| (que) | vous | essayiez |
| (qu') | ils | essaient |

### Conditional

| | |
|---|---|
| j' | essaierais |
| tu | essaierais |
| il | essaierait |
| nous | essaierions |
| vous | essaieriez |
| ils | essaieraient |

### Pluperfect

| | | |
|---|---|---|
| j' | avais | essayé |
| tu | avais | essayé |
| Il | avait | essayé |
| elle | avait | essayé |
| nous | avions | essayé |
| vous | aviez | essayé |
| ils | avaient | essayé |
| elles | avaient | essayé |

## 22 appuyer

### Present

| | |
|---|---|
| j' | appuie |
| tu | appuies |
| il | appuie |
| nous | appuyons |
| vous | appuyez |
| ils | appuient |

### Future

| | |
|---|---|
| j' | appuierai |
| tu | appuieras |
| il | appuiera |
| nous | appuierons |
| vous | appuierez |
| ils | appuieront |

### Imperfect

| | |
|---|---|
| j' | appuyais |
| tu | appuyais |
| il | appuyait |
| nous | appuyions |
| vous | appuyiez |
| ils | appuyaient |

### Perfect

| | | |
|---|---|---|
| j' | ai | appuyé |
| tu | as | appuyé |
| il | a | appuyé |
| elle | a | appuyé |
| nous | avons | appuyé |
| vous | avez | appuyé |
| ils | ont | appuyé |
| elles | ont | appuyé |

### Past participle

appuyé/appuyée

### Present subjunctive

| | | |
|---|---|---|
| (que) | j' | appuie |
| (que) | tu | appuies |
| (qu') | il | appuie |
| (que) | nous | appuyions |
| (que) | vous | appuyiez |
| (qu') | ils | appuient |

### Conditional

| | |
|---|---|
| j' | appuierais |
| tu | appuierais |
| Il | appuierait |
| nous | appuierions |
| vous | appuieriez |
| ils | appuieraient |

### Pluperfect

| | | |
|---|---|---|
| j' | avais | appuyé |
| tu | avais | appuyé |
| il | avait | appuyé |
| elle | avait | appuyé |
| nous | avions | appuyé |
| vous | aviez | appuyé |
| ils | avaient | appuyé |
| elles | avaient | appuyé |

## 23 nettoyer

| Present | | Perfect | | | Conditional | |
|---------|---|---------|---|---|-------------|---|
| je | nettoie | j' | ai | nettoyé | je | nettoierais |
| tu | nettoies | tu | as | nettoyé | tu | nettoierais |
| il | nettoie | il | a | nettoyé | il | nettoierait |
| nous | nettoyons | elle | a | nettoyé | nous | nettoierions |
| vous | nettoyez | | | | vous | nettoieriez |
| ils | nettoient | nous | avons | nettoyé | ils | nettoieraient |
| | | vous | avez | nettoyé | | |
| **Future** | | ils | ont | nettoyé | | |
| je | nettoierai | elles | ont | nettoyé | **Pluperfect** | |
| tu | nettoieras | | | | j' | avais nettoyé |
| il | nettoiera | **Past participle** | | | tu | avais nettoyé |
| nous | nettoierons | | nettoyé/nettoyée | | il | avait nettoyé |
| vous | nettoierez | | | | elle | avait nettoyé |
| ils | nettoieront | **Present subjunctive** | | | nous | avions nettoyé |
| | | (que) | je | nettoie | vous | aviez nettoyé |
| **Imperfect** | | (que) | tu | nettoies | ils | avaient nettoyé |
| je | nettoyais | (qu') | il | nettoie | elles | avaient nettoyé |
| tu | nettoyais | | | | | |
| il | nettoyait | (que) | nous | nettoyions | | |
| nous | nettoyions | (que) | vous | nettoyiez | | |
| vous | nettoyiez | (qu') | ils | nettoient | | |
| ils | nettoyaient | | | | | |

## 24 envoyer

| Present | | Perfect | | | Conditional | |
|---------|---|---------|---|---|-------------|---|
| j' | envoie | j' | ai | envoyé | j' | enverrais |
| tu | envoies | tu | as | envoyé | tu | enverrais |
| il | envoie | il | a | envoyé | il | enverrait |
| nous | envoyons | elle | a | envoyé | nous | enverrions |
| vous | envoyez | | | | vous | enverriez |
| ils | envoient | nous | avons | envoyé | ils | enverraient |
| | | vous | avez | envoyé | | |
| **Future** | | ils | ont | envoyé | | |
| j' | enverrai | elles | ont | envoyé | **Pluperfect** | |
| tu | enverras | | | | j' | avais envoyé |
| il | enverra | **Past participle** | | | tu | avais envoyé |
| nous | enverrons | | envoyé/envoyée | | il | avait envoyé |
| vous | enverrez | | | | elle | avait envoyé |
| ils | enverront | **Present subjunctive** | | | nous | avions envoyé |
| | | (que) | j' | envoie | vous | aviez envoyé |
| **Imperfect** | | (que) | tu | envoies | ils | avaient envoyé |
| j' | envoyais | (qu') | il | envoie | elles | avaient envoyé |
| tu | envoyais | | | | | |
| il | envoyait | (que) | nous | envoyions | | |
| nous | envoyions | (que) | vous | envoyiez | | |
| vous | envoyiez | (qu') | ils | envoient | | |
| ils | envoyaient | | | | | |

## 25 mourir

| Present | | | Perfect | | | Conditional | | |
|---|---|---|---|---|---|---|---|---|
| je | mours | | je | suis | mort | je | mourrais | |
| tu | meurs | | tu | es | mort | tu | mourrais | |
| il | meurt | | il | est | mort | il | mourrait | |
| nous | mourons | | elle | est | morte | nous | mourrions | |
| vous | mourez | | | | | vous | mourriez | |
| ils | meurent | | nous | sommes | morts | ils | mourraient | |
| | | | vous | êtes | morts | | | |

**Future**
| | | | ils | sont | morts |
|---|---|---|---|---|---|
| je | mourrai | | elles | sont | mortes |
| tu | mourras | |
| il | mourra | |

**Past participle**

mort/morte

| nous | mourrons |
|---|---|
| vous | mourrez |
| ils | mourront |

**Present subjunctive**

| (que) | je | meure |
|---|---|---|
| (que) | tu | meures |
| (qu') | il | meure |
| (que) | nous | mourions |
| (que) | vous | mouriez |
| (qu') | ils | meurent |

**Pluperfect**

| j' | étais | mort |
|---|---|---|
| tu | étais | mort |
| il | était | mort |
| elle | était | morte |
| nous | étions | morts |
| vous | étiez | morts |
| ils | étaient | morts |
| elles | étaient | mortes |

**Imperfect**

| je | mourais |
|---|---|
| tu | mourais |
| il | mourait |
| nous | mourions |
| vous | mouriez |
| ils | mouraient |

## 26 courir

| Present | | Perfect | | | Conditional | |
|---|---|---|---|---|---|---|
| je | cours | j' | ai | couru | je | courrais |
| tu | cours | tu | as | couru | tu | courrais |
| il | court | il | a | couru | il | courrait |
| nous | courons | elle | a | couru | nous | courrions |
| vous | courez | | | | vous | courriez |
| ils | courent | nous | avons | couru | ils | courraient |
| | | vous | avez | couru | | |

**Future**
| | | ils | ont | couru |
|---|---|---|---|---|
| je | courrai | elles | ont | couru |
| tu | courras | |
| il | courra | |

**Past participle**

couru/courue

| nous | courrons |
|---|---|
| vous | courrez |
| ils | courront |

**Present subjunctive**

| (que) | je | coure |
|---|---|---|
| (que) | tu | coures |
| (qu') | il | coure |
| (que) | nous | courions |
| (que) | vous | couriez |
| (qu') | ils | courent |

**Pluperfect**

| j' | avais | couru |
|---|---|---|
| tu | avais | couru |
| il | avait | couru |
| elle | avait | couru |
| nous | avions | couru |
| vous | aviez | couru |
| ils | avaient | couru |
| elles | avaient | couru |

**Imperfect**

| je | courais |
|---|---|
| tu | courais |
| il | courait |
| nous | courions |
| vous | couriez |
| ils | couraient |

## 27 cueillir

| Present | | |
|---|---|---|
| je | cueille | |
| tu | cueilles | |
| il | cueille | |
| nous | cueillons | |
| vous | cueillez | |
| ils | cueillent | |

| Future | |
|---|---|
| je | cueillerai |
| tu | cueilleras |
| il | cueillera |
| nous | cueillerons |
| vous | cueillerez |
| ils | cueilleront |

| Imperfect | |
|---|---|
| je | cueillais |
| tu | cueillais |
| il | cueillait |
| nous | cueillions |
| vous | cueilliez |
| ils | cueillaient |

| Perfect | | |
|---|---|---|
| j' | ai | cueilli |
| tu | as | cueilli |
| il | a | cueilli |
| elle | a | cueilli |
| nous | avons | cueilli |
| vous | avez | cueilli |
| ils | ont | cueilli |
| elles | ont | cueilli |

**Past participle**

cueilli/cueillie

**Present subjunctive**

| (que) | je | cueille |
|---|---|---|
| (que) | tu | cueilles |
| (qu') | il | cueille |
| (que) | nous | cueillions |
| (que) | vous | cueilliez |
| (qu') | ils | cueillent |

| Conditional | |
|---|---|
| je | cueillerais |
| tu | cueillerais |
| il | cueillerait |
| nous | cueillerions |
| vous | cueilleriez |
| ils | cueilleraient |

| Pluperfect | | |
|---|---|---|
| j' | avais | cueilli |
| tu | avais | cueilli |
| il | avait | cueilli |
| elle | avait | cueilli |
| nous | avions | cueilli |
| vous | aviez | cueilli |
| ils | avaient | cueilli |
| elles | avaient | cueilli |

## 28 faillir

| Perfect | | |
|---|---|---|
| j' | ai | failli |
| tu | as | failli |
| il | a | failli |
| elle | a | failli |
| nous | avons | failli |
| vous | avez | failli |
| ils | ont | failli |
| elles | ont | failli |

**Past participle**

failli

| Pluperfect | | |
|---|---|---|
| j' | avais | failli |
| tu | avais | failli |
| il | avait | failli |
| elle | avait | failli |
| nous | avions | failli |
| vous | aviez | failli |
| ils | avaient | failli |
| elles | avaient | failli |

## 29 fuir

| Present | | Perfect | | | Conditional | |
|---|---|---|---|---|---|---|
| je | fuis | j' | ai | fui | je | fuirais |
| tu | fuis | tu | as | fui | tu | fuirais |
| il | fuit | il | a | fui | il | fuirait |
| nous | fuyons | elle | a | fui | nous | fuirions |
| vous | fuyez | | | | vous | fuiriez |
| ils | fuient | nous | avons | fui | ils | fuiraient |
| | | vous | avez | fui | | |

**Future**

| je | fuirai | ils | ont | fui |
|---|---|---|---|---|
| tu | fuiras | elles | ont | fui |
| il | fuira | | | |

**Past participle**

fui/fuie

**Pluperfect**

| j' | avais | fui |
|---|---|---|
| tu | avais | fui |
| il | avait | fui |
| elle | avait | fui |

| nous | fuirons |
|---|---|
| vous | fuirez |
| ils | fuiront |

**Present subjunctive**

| (que) | je | fuie |
|---|---|---|
| (que) | tu | fuies |
| (qu') | il | fuie |

**Imperfect**

| je | fuyais |
|---|---|
| tu | fuyais |
| il | fuyait |
| nous | fuyions |
| vous | fuyiez |
| ils | fuyaient |

| (que) | nous | fuyions |
|---|---|---|
| (que) | vous | fuyiez |
| (qu') | ils | fuient |

| nous | avions | fui |
|---|---|---|
| vous | aviez | fui |
| ils | avaient | fui |
| elles | avaient | fui |

---

## 30 sortir

| Present | | Perfect | | | Conditional | |
|---|---|---|---|---|---|---|
| je | sors | je | suis | sorti | je | sortirais |
| tu | sors | tu | es | sorti | tu | sortirais |
| il | sort | il | est | sorti | il | sortirait |
| nous | sortons | elle | est | sortie | nous | sortirions |
| vous | sortez | | | | vous | sortiriez |
| ils | sortent | nous | sommes | sortis | ils | sortiraient |
| | | vous | êtes | sortis | | |
| | | ils | sont | sortis | | |

**Future**

| je | sortirai | elles | sont | sorties |
|---|---|---|---|---|
| tu | sortiras | | | |
| il | sortira | | | |

**Past participle**

sorti/sortie

**Pluperfect**

| j' | étais | sorti |
|---|---|---|
| tu | étais | sorti |
| il | était | sorti |
| elle | était | sortie |

| nous | sortirons |
|---|---|
| vous | sortirez |
| ils | sortiront |

**Present subjunctive**

| (que) | je | sorte |
|---|---|---|
| (que) | tu | sortes |
| (qu') | il | sorte |

**Imperfect**

| je | sortais |
|---|---|
| tu | sortais |
| il | sortait |
| nous | sortions |
| vous | sortiez |
| ils | sortaient |

| (que) | nous | sortions |
|---|---|---|
| (que) | vous | sortiez |
| (qu') | ils | sortent |

| nous | étions | sortis |
|---|---|---|
| vous | étiez | sortis |
| ils | étaient | sortis |
| elles | étaient | sorties |

## 31 bouillir

| Present | | Perfect | | | Conditional | |
|---|---|---|---|---|---|---|
| je | bous | j' | ai | bouilli | je | bouillirais |
| tu | bous | tu | as | bouilli | tu | bouillirais |
| il | bout | il | a | bouilli | il | bouillirait |
| nous | bouillons | elle | a | bouilli | | |
| vous | bouillez | | | | nous | bouillirions |
| ils | bouillent | nous | avons | bouilli | vous | bouilliriez |
| | | vous | avez | bouilli | ils | bouilliraient |
| **Future** | | ils | ont | bouilli | | |
| je | bouillirai | elles | ont | bouilli | **Pluperfect** | |
| tu | bouilliras | | | | j' | avais | bouilli |
| il | bouillira | **Past participle** | | | tu | avais | bouilli |
| nous | bouillirons | | bouilli/bouillie | | il | avait | bouilli |
| vous | bouillirez | | | | elle | avait | bouilli |
| ils | bouilliront | **Present subjunctive** | | | nous | avions | bouilli |
| | | (que) | je | bouille | vous | aviez | bouilli |
| **Imperfect** | | (que) | tu | bouilles | ils | avaient | bouilli |
| je | bouillais | (qu') | il | bouille | elles | avaient | bouilli |
| tu | bouillais | | | | | |
| il | bouillait | (que) | nous | bouillions | | |
| nous | bouillions | (que) | vous | bouilliez | | |
| vous | bouilliez | (qu') | ils | bouillent | | |
| ils | bouillaient | | | | | |

## 32 découvrir

| Present | | Perfect | | | Conditional | |
|---|---|---|---|---|---|---|
| je | découvre | j' | ai | découvert | je | découvrirais |
| tu | découvres | tu | as | découvert | tu | découvrirais |
| il | découvre | il | a | découvert | il | découvrirait |
| nous | découvrons | elle | a | découvert | | |
| vous | découvrez | | | | nous | découvririons |
| ils | découvrent | nous | avons | découvert | vous | découvririez |
| | | vous | avez | découvert | ils | découvriraient |
| **Future** | | ils | ont | découvert | | |
| je | découvrirai | elles | ont | découvert | **Pluperfect** | |
| tu | découvriras | | | | j' | avais | découvert |
| il | découvrira | **Past participle** | | | tu | avais | découvert |
| nous | découvrirons | | découvert/ | | il | avait | découvert |
| vous | découvrirez | | découverte | | elle | avait | découvert |
| ils | découvriront | | | | nous | avions | découvert |
| | | **Present subjunctive** | | | vous | aviez | découvert |
| **Imperfect** | | (que) | je | découvre | ils | avaient | découvert |
| je | découvrais | (que) | tu | découvres | elles | avaient | découvert |
| tu | découvrais | (qu') | il | découvre | | |
| il | découvrait | | | | | |
| nous | découvrions | (que) | nous | découvrions | | |
| vous | découvriez | (que) | vous | découvriez | | |
| ils | découvraient | (qu') | ils | découvrent | | |

## 33 pleuvoir

| Present | | | Perfect | | | Conditional | | |
|---|---|---|---|---|---|---|---|---|
| il | pleut | | il | a | plu | il | pleuvrait | |
| ils | pleuvent | | ils | ont | plu | ils | pleuvraient | |

| Future | | | Past participle | | Pluperfect | | |
|---|---|---|---|---|---|---|---|
| il | pleuvra | | plu | | il | avait | plu |
| ils | pleuvront | | | | ils | avaient | plu |

| Imperfect | | Present subjunctive | |
|---|---|---|---|
| il | pleuvait | (qu') il | pleuve |
| ils | pleuvaient | (qu') ils | pleuvent |

## 34 asseoir

| Present | | Perfect | | | Conditional | |
|---|---|---|---|---|---|---|
| j' | assieds | j' | ai | assis | j' | assiérais |
| tu | assieds | tu | as | assis | tu | assiérais |
| il | assied | il | a | assis | il | assiérait |
| nous | asseyons | elle | a | assis | nous | assiérions |
| vous | asseyez | nous | avons | assis | vous | assiériez |
| ils | asseyent | vous | avez | assis | ils | assiéraient |
| | | ils | ont | assis | | |
| Future | | elles | ont | assis | Pluperfect | |
| j' | assiérai | | | | j' | avais assis |
| tu | assiéras | Past participle | | tu | avais assis |
| il | assiéra | | assis/assise | | il | avait assis |
| | | | | | elle | avait assis |
| nous | assiérons | Present subjunctive | | nous | avions assis |
| vous | assiérez | (que) | j' | asseye | vous | aviez assis |
| ils | assiéront | (que) | tu | asseyes | ils | avaient assis |
| | | (qu') | il | asseye | elles | avaient assis |
| Imperfect | | (que) | nous | asseyions | | |
| j' | asseyais | (que) | vous | asseyiez | | |
| tu | asseyais | (qu') | ils | asseyent | | |
| il | asseyait | | | | | |
| nous | asseyions | | | | | |
| vous | asseyiez | | | | | |
| ils | asseyaient | | | | | |

## 35 prévoir

| Present | | Perfect | | | Conditional | |
|---|---|---|---|---|---|---|
| je | prévois | j' | ai | prévu | je | prévoirais |
| tu | prévois | tu | as | prévu | tu | prévoirais |
| il | prévoit | il | a | prévu | il | prévoirait |
| nous | prévoyons | elle | a | prévu | | |
| vous | prévoyez | | | | nous | prévoirions |
| ils | prévoient | nous | avons | prévu | vous | prévoiriez |
| | | vous | avez | prévu | ils | prévoiraient |
| **Future** | | ils | ont | prévu | | |
| je | prévoirai | elles | ont | prévu | **Pluperfect** | |
| tu | prévoiras | | | | j' | avais | prévu |
| il | prévoira | **Past participle** | | | tu | avais | prévu |
| | | prévu/prévue | | | il | avait | prévu |
| nous | prévoirons | | | | elle | avait | prévu |
| vous | prévoirez | | | | | |
| ils | prévoiront | **Present subjunctive** | | | nous | avions | prévu |

| | | | | | vous | aviez | prévu |
|---|---|---|---|---|---|---|---|
| **Imperfect** | | (que) | je | prévoie | ils | avaient | prévu |
| je | prévoyais | (que) | tu | prévoies | elles | avaient | prévu |
| tu | prévoyais | (qu') | il | prévoie | | | |
| il | prévoyait | | | | | | |
| nous | prévoyions | (que) | nous | prévoyions | | | |
| vous | prévoyiez | (que) | vous | prévoyiez | | | |
| ils | prévoyaient | (qu') | ils | prévoient | | | |

## 36 devenir

| Present | | Perfect | | | Conditional | |
|---|---|---|---|---|---|---|
| je | deviens | je | suis | devenu | je | deviendrais |
| tu | deviens | tu | es | devenu | tu | deviendrais |
| il | devient | il | est | devenu | il | deviendrait |
| nous | devenons | elle | est | devenue | | |
| vous | devenez | | | | nous | deviendrions |
| ils | deviennent | nous | sommes | devenus | vous | deviendriez |
| | | vous | êtes | devenus | ils | deviendraient |
| | | ils | sont | devenus | | |
| **Future** | | elles | sont | devenues | **Pluperfect** | |
| je | deviendrai | | | | j' | étais | devenu |
| tu | deviendras | **Past participle** | | | tu | étais | devenu |
| il | deviendra | devenu/devenue | | | il | était | devenu |
| | | | | | elle | était | devenue |
| nous | deviendrons | | | | | |
| vous | deviendrez | **Present subjunctive** | | | nous | étions | devenus |
| ils | deviendront | (que) | je | devienne | vous | étiez | devenus |
| | | (que) | tu | deviennes | ils | étaient | devenus |
| **Imperfect** | | (qu') | il | devienne | elles | étaient | devenues |
| je | devenais | | | | | | |
| tu | devenais | (que) | nous | devenions | | | |
| il | devenait | (que) | vous | deveniez | | | |
| | | (qu') | ils | deviennent | | | |
| nous | devenions | | | | | | |
| vous | deveniez | | | | | | |
| ils | devenaient | | | | | | |

## 37 suivre

**Present**

| | |
|---|---|
| je | suis |
| tu | suis |
| il | suit |
| nous | suivons |
| vous | suivez |
| ils | suivent |

**Future**

| | |
|---|---|
| je | suivrai |
| tu | suivras |
| il | suivra |
| nous | suivrons |
| vous | suivrez |
| ils | suivront |

**Imperfect**

| | |
|---|---|
| je | suivais |
| tu | suivais |
| il | suivait |
| nous | suivions |
| vous | suiviez |
| ils | suivaient |

**Perfect**

| | | |
|---|---|---|
| j' | ai | suivi |
| tu | as | suivi |
| il | a | suivi |
| elle | a | suivi |
| nous | avons | suivi |
| vous | avez | suivi |
| ils | ont | suivi |
| elles | ont | suivi |

**Past participle**

suivi/suivie

**Present subjunctive**

| | | |
|---|---|---|
| (que) | je | suive |
| (que) | tu | suives |
| (qu') | il | suive |
| (que) | nous | suivions |
| (que) | vous | suiviez |
| (qu') | ils | suivent |

**Conditional**

| | |
|---|---|
| je | suivrais |
| tu | suivrais |
| il | suivrait |
| nous | suivrions |
| vous | suivriez |
| ils | suivraient |

**Pluperfect**

| | | |
|---|---|---|
| j' | avais | suivi |
| tu | avais | suivi |
| il | avait | suivi |
| elle | avait | suivi |
| nous | avions | suivi |
| vous | aviez | suivi |
| ils | avaient | suivi |
| elles | avaient | suivi |

## 38 vivre

**Present**

| | |
|---|---|
| je | vis |
| tu | vis |
| il | vit |
| nous | vivons |
| vous | vivez |
| ils | vivent |

**Future**

| | |
|---|---|
| je | vivrai |
| tu | vivras |
| il | vivra |
| nous | vivrons |
| vous | vivrez |
| ils | vivront |

**Imperfect**

| | |
|---|---|
| je | vivais |
| tu | vivais |
| il | vivait |
| nous | vivions |
| vous | viviez |
| ils | vivaient |

**Perfect**

| | | |
|---|---|---|
| j' | ai | vécu |
| tu | as | vécu |
| il | a | vécu |
| elle | a | vécu |
| nous | avons | vécu |
| vous | avez | vécu |
| ils | ont | vécu |
| elles | ont | vécu |

**Past participle**

vécu/vécue

**Present subjunctive**

| | | |
|---|---|---|
| (que) | je | vive |
| (que) | tu | vives |
| (qu') | il | vive |
| (que) | nous | vivions |
| (que) | vous | viviez |
| (qu') | ils | vivent |

**Conditional**

| | |
|---|---|
| je | vivrais |
| tu | vivrais |
| Il | vivrait |
| nous | vivrions |
| vous | vivriez |
| ils | vivraient |

**Pluperfect**

| | | |
|---|---|---|
| j' | avais | vécu |
| tu | avais | vécu |
| il | avait | vécu |
| elle | avait | vécu |
| nous | avions | vécu |
| vous | aviez | vécu |
| ils | avaient | vécu |
| elles | avaient | vécu |

## 39 suffire

| Present | | Perfect | | | Conditional | |
|---|---|---|---|---|---|---|
| je | suffis | j' | ai | suffi | je | suffirais |
| tu | suffis | tu | as | suffi | tu | suffirais |
| il | suffit | il | a | suffi | il | suffirait |
| nous | suffisons | elle | a | suffi | | |
| vous | suffisez | | | | nous | suffirions |
| ils | suffisent | nous | avons | suffi | vous | suffiriez |
| | | vous | avez | suffi | ils | suffiraient |

| Future | | Perfect (cont.) | | |
|---|---|---|---|---|
| | | ils | ont | suffi |
| je | suffirai | elles | ont | suffi |
| tu | suffiras | | | |
| il | suffira | | | |

**Past participle**

suffi

| Future (cont.) | |
|---|---|
| nous | suffirons |
| vous | suffirez |
| ils | suffiront |

**Pluperfect**

| | | |
|---|---|---|
| j' | avais | suffi |
| tu | avais | suffi |
| il | avait | suffi |
| elle | avait | suffi |
| nous | avions | suffi |
| vous | aviez | suffi |
| ils | avaient | suffi |
| elles | avaient | suffi |

| Imperfect | |
|---|---|
| je | suffisais |
| tu | suffisais |
| il | suffisait |
| nous | suffisions |
| vous | suffisiez |
| ils | suffisaient |

**Present subjunctive**

| | | |
|---|---|---|
| (que) | je | suffise |
| (que) | tu | suffises |
| (qu') | il | suffise |
| (que) | nous | suffisions |
| (que) | vous | suffisiez |
| (qu') | ils | suffisent |

## 40 dire

| Present | | Perfect | | | Conditional | |
|---|---|---|---|---|---|---|
| je | dis | j' | ai | dit | je | dirais |
| tu | dis | tu | as | dit | tu | dirais |
| il | dit | il | a | dit | il | dirait |
| nous | disons | elle | a | dit | | |
| vous | dites* | | | | nous | dirions |
| ils | disent | nous | avons | dit | vous | diriez |
| | | vous | avez | dit | ils | diraient |
| | | ils | ont | dit | | |

| Future | | Perfect (cont.) | | |
|---|---|---|---|---|
| je | dirai | elles | ont | dit |
| tu | diras | | | |
| il | dira | | | |

**Past participle**

dit/dite

| Future (cont.) | |
|---|---|
| nous | dirons |
| vous | direz |
| ils | diront |

**Pluperfect**

| | | |
|---|---|---|
| j' | avais | dit |
| tu | avais | dit |
| il | avait | dit |
| elle | avait | dit |
| nous | avions | dit |
| vous | aviez | dit |
| ils | avaient | dit |
| elles | avaient | dit |

| Imperfect | |
|---|---|
| je | disais |
| tu | disais |
| il | disait |
| nous | disions |
| vous | disiez |
| ils | disaient |

**Present subjunctive**

| | | |
|---|---|---|
| (que) | je | dise |
| (que) | tu | dises |
| (qu') | il | dise |
| (que) | nous | disions |
| (que) | vous | disiez |
| (qu') | ils | disent |

* vous interdisez

## 41 lire

| Present | | Perfect | | | Conditional | | |
|---|---|---|---|---|---|---|---|
| je | lis | j' | ai | lu | je | lirais | |
| tu | lis | tu | as | lu | tu | lirais | |
| il | lit | il | a | lu | il | lirait | |
| nous | lisons | elle | a | lu | | | |
| vous | lisez | | | | nous | lirions | |
| ils | lisent | nous | avons | lu | vous | liriez | |
| | | vous | avez | lu | ils | liraient | |
| **Future** | | ils | ont | lu | | | |
| je | lirai | elles | ont | lu | **Pluperfect** | | |
| tu | liras | | | | j' | avais | lu |
| il | lira | **Past participle** | | | tu | avais | lu |
| nous | lirons | | lu/lue | | il | avait | lu |
| vous | lirez | | | | elle | avait | lu |
| ils | liront | **Present subjunctive** | | | nous | avions | lu |
| | | (que) | je | lise | vous | aviez | lu |
| **Imperfect** | | (que) | tu | lises | ils | avaient | lu |
| je | lisais | (qu') | il | lise | elles | avaient | lu |
| tu | lisais | | | | | | |
| il | lisait | (que) | nous | lisions | | | |
| nous | lisions | (que) | vous | lisiez | | | |
| vous | lisiez | (qu') | ils | lisent | | | |
| ils | lisaient | | | | | | |

## 42 écrire

| Present | | Perfect | | | Conditional | | |
|---|---|---|---|---|---|---|---|
| j' | écris | j' | ai | écrit | j' | écrirais | |
| tu | écris | tu | as | écrit | tu | écrirais | |
| il | écrit | il | a | écrit | il | écrirait | |
| nous | écrivons | elle | a | écrit | | | |
| vous | écrivez | | | | nous | écririons | |
| ils | écrivent | nous | avons | écrit | vous | écririez | |
| | | vous | avez | écrit | ils | écriraient | |
| **Future** | | ils | ont | écrit | | | |
| j' | écrirai | elles | ont | écrit | **Pluperfect** | | |
| tu | écriras | | | | j' | avais | écrit |
| il | écrira | **Past participle** | | | tu | avais | écrit |
| nous | écrirons | | écrit/écrite | | il | avait | écrit |
| vous | écrirez | | | | elle | avait | écrit |
| ils | écriront | **Present subjunctive** | | | nous | avions | écrit |
| | | (que) | j' | écrive | vous | aviez | écrit |
| **Imperfect** | | (que) | tu | écrives | ils | avaient | écrit |
| j' | écrivais | (qu') | il | écrive | elles | avaient | écrit |
| tu | écrivais | | | | | | |
| il | écrivait | (que) | nous | écrivions | | | |
| nous | écrivions | (que) | vous | écriviez | | | |
| vous | écriviez | (qu') | ils | écrivent | | | |
| ils | écrivaient | | | | | | |

## 43 rire

| Present | | | Perfect | | | Conditional | | |
|---|---|---|---|---|---|---|---|---|
| je | ris | | j' | ai | ri | je | rirais | |
| tu | ris | | tu | as | ri | tu | rirais | |
| il | rit | | il | a | ri | il | rirait | |
| nous | rions | | elle | a | ri | | | |
| vous | riez | | | | | nous | ririons | |
| ils | rient | | nous | avons | ri | vous | ririez | |
| | | | vous | avez | ri | ils | riraient | |

### Future

| | | | | | | | | |
|---|---|---|---|---|---|---|---|---|
| | | | ils | ont | ri | | | |
| je | rirai | | elles | ont | ri | | | |
| tu | riras | | | | | **Pluperfect** | | |
| il | rira | | **Past participle** | | | j' | avais | ri |
| nous | rirons | | | ri | | tu | avais | ri |
| vous | rirez | | | | | il | avait | ri |
| ils | riront | | | | | elle | avait | ri |

### Imperfect

**Present subjunctive**

| Imperfect | | | Present subjunctive | | | Pluperfect cont. | | |
|---|---|---|---|---|---|---|---|---|
| | | | (que) | je | rie | nous | avions | ri |
| je | riais | | (que) | tu | ries | vous | aviez | ri |
| tu | riais | | (qu') | il | rie | ils | avaient | ri |
| il | riait | | | | | elles | avaient | ri |
| nous | riions | | (que) | nous | riions | | | |
| vous | riiez | | (que) | vous | riiez | | | |
| ils | riaient | | (qu') | ils | rient | | | |

## 44 devoir

| Present | | | Perfect | | | Conditional | | |
|---|---|---|---|---|---|---|---|---|
| je | dois | | j' | ai | dû | je | devrais | |
| tu | dois | | tu | as | dû | tu | devrais | |
| il | doit | | il | a | dû | il | devrait | |
| nous | devons | | elle | a | dû | | | |
| vous | devez | | | | | nous | devrions | |
| ils | doivent | | nous | avons | dû | vous | devriez | |
| | | | vous | avez | dû | ils | devraient | |

### Future

| | | | | | | | | |
|---|---|---|---|---|---|---|---|---|
| | | | ils | ont | dû | | | |
| je | devrai | | elles | ont | dû | | | |
| tu | devras | | | | | **Pluperfect** | | |
| il | devra | | **Past participle** | | | j' | avais | dû |
| nous | devrons | | | dû/due | | tu | avais | dû |
| vous | devrez | | | | | il | avait | dû |
| ils | devront | | | | | elle | avait | dû |

### Imperfect

**Present subjunctive**

| Imperfect | | | Present subjunctive | | | Pluperfect cont. | | |
|---|---|---|---|---|---|---|---|---|
| | | | (que) | je | doive | nous | avions | dû |
| je | devais | | (que) | tu | doives | vous | aviez | dû |
| tu | devais | | (qu') | il | doive | ils | avaient | dû |
| il | devait | | | | | elles | avaient | dû |
| nous | devions | | (que) | nous | devions | | | |
| vous | deviez | | (que) | vous | deviez | | | |
| ils | devaient | | (qu') | ils | doivent | | | |

## 45 valoir

| Present | | Perfect | | | Conditional | |
|---|---|---|---|---|---|---|
| je | vaux | j' | ai | valu | je | vaudrais |
| tu | vaux | tu | as | valu | tu | vaudrais |
| il | vaut | il | a | valu | il | vaudrait |
| nous | valons | elle | a | valu | | |
| vous | valez | | | | nous | vaudrions |
| ils | valent | nous | avons | valu | vous | vaudriez |
| | | vous | avez | valu | ils | vaudraient |
| | | ils | ont | valu | | |
| **Future** | | elles | ont | valu | | |
| je | vaudrai | | | | **Pluperfect** | |
| tu | vaudras | **Past participle** | | | j' | avais | valu |
| il | vaudra | | valu/value | | tu | avais | valu |
| nous | vaudrons | | | | il | avait | valu |
| vous | vaudrez | | | | elle | avait | valu |
| ils | vaudront | **Present subjunctive** | | | | | |
| | | (que) | je | vaille | nous | avions | valu |
| **Imperfect** | | (que) | tu | vailles | vous | aviez | valu |
| je | valais | (qu') | il | vaille | ils | avaient | valu |
| tu | valais | | | | elles | avaient | valu |
| il | valait | (que) | nous | valions | | |
| nous | valions | (que) | vous | valiez | | |
| vous | valiez | (qu') | ils | vaillent | | |
| ils | valaient | | | | | |

## 46 voir

| Present | | Perfect | | | Conditional | |
|---|---|---|---|---|---|---|
| je | vois | j' | ai | vu | je | verrais |
| tu | vois | tu | as | vu | tu | verrais |
| il | voit | il | a | vu | il | verrait |
| nous | voyons | elle | a | vu | | |
| vous | voyez | | | | nous | verrions |
| ils | voient | nous | avons | vu | vous | verriez |
| | | vous | avez | vu | ils | verraient |
| | | ils | ont | vu | | |
| **Future** | | elles | ont | vu | | |
| je | verrai | | | | **Pluperfect** | |
| tu | verras | **Past participle** | | | j' | avais | vu |
| il | verra | | vu/vue | | tu | avais | vu |
| nous | verrons | | | | il | avait | vu |
| vous | verrez | | | | elle | avait | vu |
| ils | verront | **Present subjunctive** | | | | | |
| | | (que) | je | voie | nous | avions | vu |
| **Imperfect** | | (que) | tu | voies | vous | aviez | vu |
| je | voyais | (qu') | il | voie | ils | avaient | vu |
| tu | voyais | | | | elles | avaient | vu |
| il | voyait | (que) | nous | voyions | | |
| nous | voyions | (que) | vous | voyiez | | |
| vous | voyiez | (qu') | ils | voient | | |
| ils | voyaient | | | | | |

## 47 savoir

| Present | |
|---|---|
| je | sais |
| tu | sais |
| il | sait |
| nous | savons |
| vous | savez |
| ils | savent |

| Future | |
|---|---|
| je | saurai |
| tu | sauras |
| il | saura |
| nous | saurons |
| vous | saurez |
| ils | sauront |

| Imperfect | |
|---|---|
| je | savais |
| tu | savais |
| il | savait |
| nous | savions |
| vous | saviez |
| ils | savaient |

| Perfect | | |
|---|---|---|
| j' | ai | su |
| tu | as | su |
| il | a | su |
| elle | a | su |
| nous | avons | su |
| vous | avez | su |
| ils | ont | su |
| elles | ont | su |

**Past participle**

su/sue

**Present subjunctive**

| (que) | je | sache |
|---|---|---|
| (que) | tu | saches |
| (qu') | il | sache |
| (que) | nous | sachions |
| (que) | vous | sachiez |
| (qu') | ils | sachent |

| Conditional | |
|---|---|
| je | saurais |
| tu | saurais |
| il | saurait |
| nous | saurions |
| vous | sauriez |
| ils | sauraient |

| Pluperfect | | |
|---|---|---|
| j' | avais | su |
| tu | avais | su |
| il | avait | su |
| elle | avait | su |
| nous | avions | su |
| vous | aviez | su |
| ils | avaient | su |
| elles | avaient | su |

## 48 vouloir

| Present | |
|---|---|
| je | veux |
| tu | veux |
| il | veut |
| nous | voulons |
| vous | voulez |
| ils | veulent |

| Future | |
|---|---|
| je | voudrai |
| tu | voudras |
| il | voudra |
| nous | voudrons |
| vous | voudrez |
| ils | voudront |

| Imperfect | |
|---|---|
| je | voulais |
| tu | voulais |
| il | voulait |
| nous | voulions |
| vous | vouliez |
| ils | voulaient |

| Perfect | | |
|---|---|---|
| j' | ai | voulu |
| tu | as | voulu |
| il | a | voulu |
| elle | a | voulu |
| nous | avons | voulu |
| vous | avez | voulu |
| ils | ont | voulu |
| elles | ont | voulu |

**Past participle**

voulu/voulue

**Present subjunctive**

| (que) | je | veuille |
|---|---|---|
| (que) | tu | veuilles |
| (qu') | il | veuille |
| (que) | nous | voulions |
| (que) | vous | vouliez |
| (qu') | ils | veuillent |

| Conditional | |
|---|---|
| je | voudrais |
| tu | voudrais |
| il | voudrait |
| nous | voudrions |
| vous | voudriez |
| ils | voudraient |

| Pluperfect | | |
|---|---|---|
| j' | avais | voulu |
| tu | avais | voulu |
| il | avait | voulu |
| elle | avait | voulu |
| nous | avions | voulu |
| vous | aviez | voulu |
| ils | avaient | voulu |
| elles | avaient | voulu |

## 49 pouvoir

| Present | | |
|---|---|---|
| je | peux | |
| tu | peux | |
| il | peut | |
| nous | pouvons | |
| vous | pouvez | |
| ils | peuvent | |

| Future | |
|---|---|
| je | pourrai |
| tu | pourras |
| il | pourra |
| nous | pourrons |
| vous | pourrez |
| ils | pourront |

| Imperfect | |
|---|---|
| je | pouvais |
| tu | pouvais |
| il | pouvait |
| nous | pouvions |
| vous | pouviez |
| ils | pouvaient |

| Perfect | | |
|---|---|---|
| j' | ai | pu |
| tu | as | pu |
| il | a | pu |
| elle | a | pu |
| nous | avons | pu |
| vous | avez | pu |
| ils | ont | pu |
| elles | ont | pu |

**Past participle**

pu

| Present subjunctive | | |
|---|---|---|
| (que) | je | puisse |
| (que) | tu | puisses |
| (qu') | il | puisse |
| (que) | nous | puissions |
| (que) | vous | puissiez |
| (qu') | ils | puissent |

| Conditional | |
|---|---|
| je | pourrais |
| tu | pourrais |
| il | pourrait |
| nous | pourrions |
| vous | pourriez |
| ils | pourraient |

| Pluperfect | | |
|---|---|---|
| j' | avais | pu |
| tu | avais | pu |
| il | avait | pu |
| elle | avait | pu |
| nous | avions | pu |
| vous | aviez | pu |
| ils | avaient | pu |
| elles | avaient | pu |

## 50 falloir

| Present | |
|---|---|
| il | faut |

| Future | |
|---|---|
| il | faudra |

| Imperfect | |
|---|---|
| il | fallait |

| Perfect | | |
|---|---|---|
| il | a | fallu |

**Past participle**

fallu

| Present subjunctive | | |
|---|---|---|
| (qu') | il | faille |

| Conditional | |
|---|---|
| il | faudrait |

| Pluperfect | | |
|---|---|---|
| il | avait | fallu |

## 51 boire

| Present | | | Perfect | | | Conditional | |
|---|---|---|---|---|---|---|---|
| je | bois | | j' | ai | bu | je | boirais |
| tu | bois | | tu | as | bu | tu | boirais |
| il | boit | | il | a | bu | il | boirait |
| nous | buvons | | elle | a | bu | | |
| vous | buvez | | | | | nous | boirions |
| ils | boivent | | nous | avons | bu | vous | boiriez |
| | | | vous | avez | bu | ils | boiraient |

**Future**

| je | boirai |
|---|---|
| tu | boiras |
| il | boira |
| nous | boirons |
| vous | boirez |
| ils | boiront |

**Imperfect**

| je | buvais |
|---|---|
| tu | buvais |
| il | buvait |
| nous | buvions |
| vous | buviez |
| ils | buvaient |

**Perfect** (continued)

| ils | ont | bu |
|---|---|---|
| elles | ont | bu |

**Past participle**

bu/bue

**Present subjunctive**

| (que) | je | boive |
|---|---|---|
| (que) | tu | boives |
| (qu') | il | boive |
| (que) | nous | buvions |
| (que) | vous | buviez |
| (qu') | ils | boivent |

**Pluperfect**

| j' | avais | bu |
|---|---|---|
| tu | avais | bu |
| il | avait | bu |
| elle | avait | bu |
| nous | avions | bu |
| vous | aviez | bu |
| ils | avaient | bu |
| elles | avaient | bu |

## 52 comprendre

**Present**

| je | comprends |
|---|---|
| tu | comprends |
| il | comprend |
| nous | comprenons |
| vous | comprenez |
| ils | comprennent |

**Future**

| je | comprendrai |
|---|---|
| tu | comprendras |
| il | comprendra |
| nous | comprendrons |
| vous | comprendrez |
| ils | comprendront |

**Imperfect**

| je | comprenais |
|---|---|
| tu | comprenais |
| il | comprenait |
| nous | comprenions |
| vous | compreniez |
| ils | comprenaient |

**Perfect**

| j' | ai | compris |
|---|---|---|
| tu | as | compris |
| il | a | compris |
| elle | a | compris |
| nous | avons | compris |
| vous | avez | compris |
| ils | ont | compris |
| elles | ont | compris |

**Past participle**

compris/comprise

**Present subjunctive**

| (que) | je | comprenne |
|---|---|---|
| (que) | tu | comprennes |
| (qu') | il | comprenne |
| (que) | nous | comprenions |
| (que) | vous | compreniez |
| (qu') | ils | comprennent |

**Conditional**

| je | comprendrais |
|---|---|
| tu | comprendrais |
| il | comprendrait |
| nous | comprendrions |
| vous | comprendriez |
| ils | comprendraient |

**Pluperfect**

| j' | avais | compris |
|---|---|---|
| tu | avais | compris |
| il | avait | compris |
| elle | avait | compris |
| nous | avions | compris |
| vous | aviez | compris |
| ils | avaient | compris |
| elles | avaient | compris |

## 53 croire

| Present | | Perfect | | | Conditional | |
|---|---|---|---|---|---|---|
| je | crois | j' | ai | cru | je | croirais |
| tu | crois | tu | as | cru | tu | croirais |
| il | croit | il | a | cru | il | croirait |
| nous | croyons | elle | a | cru | nous | croirions |
| vous | croyez | | | | vous | croiriez |
| ils | croient | nous | avons | cru | ils | croiraient |
| | | vous | avez | cru | | |
| **Future** | | ils | ont | cru | | |
| je | croirai | elles | ont | cru | **Pluperfect** | |
| tu | croiras | | | | j' | avais | cru |
| il | croira | **Past participle** | | | tu | avais | cru |
| nous | croirons | | cru/crue | | il | avait | cru |
| vous | croirez | | | | elle | avait | cru |
| ils | croiront | **Present subjunctive** | | | nous | avons | cru |
| | | (que) | je | croie | vous | aviez | cru |
| **Imperfect** | | (que) | tu | croies | ils | avaient | cru |
| je | croyais | (qu') | il | croie | elles | avaient | cru |
| tu | croyais | | | | | |
| il | croyait | (que) | nous | croyions | | |
| nous | croyions | (que) | vous | croyiez | | |
| vous | croyiez | (qu') | ils | croient | | |
| ils | croyaient | | | | | |

## 54 plaindre

| Present | | Perfect | | | Conditional | |
|---|---|---|---|---|---|---|
| je | plains | j' | ai | plaint | je | plaindrais |
| tu | plains | tu | as | plaint | tu | plaindrais |
| il | plaint | il | a | plaint | il | plaindrait |
| nous | plaignons | elle | a | plaint | nous | plaindrions |
| vous | plaignez | | | | vous | plaindriez |
| ils | plaignent | nous | avons | plaint | ils | plaindraient |
| | | vous | avez | plaint | | |
| **Future** | | ils | ont | plaint | | |
| je | plaindrai | elles | ont | plaint | **Pluperfect** | |
| tu | plaindras | | | | j' | avais | plaint |
| il | plaindra | **Past participle** | | | tu | avais | plaint |
| nous | plaindrons | | plaint/plainte | | il | avait | plaint |
| vous | plaindrez | | | | elle | avait | plaint |
| ils | plaindront | **Present subjunctive** | | | nous | avons | plaint |
| | | (que) | je | plaigne | vous | aviez | plaint |
| **Imperfect** | | (que) | tu | plaignes | ils | avaient | plaint |
| je | plaignais | (qu') | il | plaigne | elles | avaient | plaint |
| tu | plaignais | | | | | |
| il | plaignait | (que) | nous | plaignions | | |
| nous | plaignions | (que) | vous | plaigniez | | |
| vous | plaigniez | (qu') | ils | plaignent | | |
| ils | plaignaient | | | | | |

## 55 éteindre

| Present | | Perfect | | | Conditional | | |
|---|---|---|---|---|---|---|---|
| j' | éteins | j' | ai | éteint | j' | éteindrais | |
| tu | éteins | tu | as | éteint | tu | éteindrais | |
| il | éteint | il | a | éteint | il | éteindrait | |
| nous | éteignons | elle | a | éteint | nous | éteindrions | |
| vous | éteignez | | | | vous | éteindriez | |
| ils | éteignent | nous | avons | éteint | ils | éteindraient | |
| | | vous | avez | éteint | | | |

| Future | | Perfect (cont.) | | |
|---|---|---|---|---|
| j' | éteindrai | ils | ont | éteint |
| tu | éteindras | elles | ont | éteint |
| il | éteindra | | | |

**Past participle**

éteint/éteinte

**Pluperfect**

| Future (cont.) | | Pluperfect | | |
|---|---|---|---|---|
| nous | éteindrons | j' | avais | éteint |
| vous | éteindrez | tu | avais | éteint |
| ils | éteindront | il | avait | éteint |
| | | elle | avait | éteint |

**Present subjunctive**

| Imperfect | | Present subjunctive | | | Pluperfect (cont.) | | |
|---|---|---|---|---|---|---|---|
| j' | éteignais | (que) | j' | éteigne | nous | avions | éteint |
| tu | éteignais | (que) | tu | éteignes | vous | aviez | éteint |
| il | éteignait | (qu') | il | éteigne | ils | avaient | éteint |
| nous | éteignions | (que) | nous | éteignions | elles | avaient | éteint |
| vous | éteigniez | (que) | vous | éteigniez | | | |
| ils | éteignaient | (qu') | ils | éteignent | | | |

## 56 joindre

| Present | | Perfect | | | Conditional | |
|---|---|---|---|---|---|---|
| je | joins | j' | ai | joint | je | joindrais |
| tu | joins | tu | as | joint | tu | joindrais |
| il | joint | il | a | joint | il | joindrait |
| nous | joignons | elle | a | joint | nous | joindrions |
| vous | joignez | | | | vous | joindriez |
| ils | joignent | nous | avons | joint | ils | joindraient |
| | | vous | avez | joint | | |

| Future | | Perfect (cont.) | | |
|---|---|---|---|---|
| je | joindrai | ils | ont | joint |
| tu | joindras | elles | ont | joint |
| il | joindra | | | |

**Past participle**

joint/jointe

**Pluperfect**

| Future (cont.) | | Pluperfect | | |
|---|---|---|---|---|
| nous | joindrons | j' | avais | joint |
| vous | joindrez | tu | avais | joint |
| ils | joindront | il | avait | joint |
| | | elle | avait | joint |

**Present subjunctive**

| Imperfect | | Present subjunctive | | | Pluperfect (cont.) | | |
|---|---|---|---|---|---|---|---|
| je | joignais | (que) | je | joigne | nous | avions | joint |
| tu | joignais | (que) | tu | joignes | vous | aviez | joint |
| il | joignait | (qu') | il | joigne | ils | avaient | joint |
| nous | joignions | (que) | nous | joignions | elles | avaient | joint |
| vous | joigniez | (que) | vous | joigniez | | | |
| ils | joignaient | (qu') | ils | joignent | | | |

## 57 vaincre

| Present | |
|---|---|
| je | vaincs |
| tu | vaincs |
| il | vainc |
| nous | vainquons |
| vous | vainquez |
| ils | vainquont |

| Future | |
|---|---|
| je | vaincrai |
| tu | vaincras |
| il | vaincra |
| nous | vaincrons |
| vous | vaincrez |
| ils | vaincront |

| Imperfect | |
|---|---|
| jo | vainquais |
| tu | vainquais |
| il | vainquait |
| nous | vainquions |
| vous | vainquiez |
| ils | vainquaient |

| Perfect | | |
|---|---|---|
| j' | ai | vaincu |
| tu | as | vaincu |
| il | a | vaincu |
| elle | a | vaincu |
| nous | avons | vaincu |
| vous | avez | vaincu |
| ils | ont | vaincu |
| elles | ont | vaincu |

**Past participle**

vaincu/vaincue

| Present subjunctive | | |
|---|---|---|
| (que) | je | vainque |
| (que) | tu | vainques |
| (qu') | il | vainque |
| (que) | nous | vainquions |
| (que) | vous | vainquiez |
| (qu') | ils | vainquent |

| Conditional | |
|---|---|
| je | vaincrais |
| tu | vaincrais |
| il | vaincrait |
| nous | vaincrions |
| vous | vaincriez |
| ils | vaincraient |

| Pluperfect | | |
|---|---|---|
| j' | avais | vaincu |
| tu | avais | vaincu |
| il | avait | vaincu |
| elle | avait | vaincu |
| nous | avions | vaincu |
| vous | aviez | vaincu |
| ils | avaient | vaincu |
| elles | avaient | vaincu |

## 58 distraire

| Present | |
|---|---|
| je | distrais |
| tu | distrais |
| il | distrait |
| nous | distrayons |
| vous | distrayez |
| ils | distraient |

| Future | |
|---|---|
| je | distrairai |
| tu | distrairas |
| il | distraira |
| nous | distrairons |
| vous | distrairez |
| ils | distrairont |

| Imperfect | |
|---|---|
| je | distrayais |
| tu | distrayais |
| il | distrayait |
| nous | distrayions |
| vous | distrayiez |
| ils | distrayaient |

| Perfect | | |
|---|---|---|
| j' | ai | distrait |
| tu | as | distrait |
| il | a | distrait |
| elle | a | distrait |
| nous | avons | distrait |
| vous | avez | distrait |
| ils | ont | distrait |
| elles | ont | distrait |

**Past participle**

distrait/distraite

| Present subjunctive | | |
|---|---|---|
| (que) | je | distraie |
| (que) | tu | distraies |
| (qu') | il | distraie |
| (que) | nous | distrayions |
| (que) | vous | distrayiez |
| (qu') | ils | distraient |

| Conditional | |
|---|---|
| je | distrairais |
| tu | distrairais |
| il | distrairait |
| nous | distrairions |
| vous | distrairiez |
| ils | distrairaient |

| Pluperfect | | |
|---|---|---|
| j' | avais | distrait |
| tu | avais | distrait |
| il | avait | distrait |
| elle | avait | distrait |
| nous | avions | distrait |
| vous | aviez | distrait |
| ils | avaient | distrait |
| elles | avaient | distrait |

## 59 plaire

| Present | | Perfect | | | Conditional | |
|---|---|---|---|---|---|---|
| je | plais | j' | ai | plu | je | plairais |
| tu | plais | tu | as | plu | tu | plairais |
| il | plaît | il | a | plu | il | plairait |
| nous | plaisons | elle | a | plu | nous | plairions |
| vous | plaisez | | | | vous | plairiez |
| ils | plaisent | nous | avons | plu | ils | plairaient |
| | | vous | avez | plu | | |
| | | ils | ont | plu | | |

| Future | | | Pluperfect | |
|---|---|---|---|---|
| je | plairai | | j' | avais | plu |
| tu | plairas | elles | ont | plu | tu | avais | plu |
| il | plaira | | | il | avait | plu |

**Past participle**
plu/plue

| Imperfect | | | Present subjunctive | | |
|---|---|---|---|---|
| je | plaisais | (que) je | plaise |
| tu | plaisais | (que) tu | plaises |
| il | plaisait | (qu') il | plaise |
| nous | plaisions | (que) nous | plaisions |
| vous | plaisiez | (que) vous | plaisiez |
| ils | plaisaient | (qu') ils | plaisent |

Future
je plairai
tu plairas
il plaira

nous plairons
vous plairez
ils plairont

Imperfect
je plaisais
tu plaisais
il plaisait

nous plaisions
vous plaisiez
ils plaisaient

Perfect
j' ai plu
tu as plu
il a plu
elle a plu

nous avons plu
vous avez plu
ils ont plu
elles ont plu

Past participle
plu/plue

Present subjunctive
(que) je plaise
(que) tu plaises
(qu') il plaise

(que) nous plaisions
(que) vous plaisiez
(qu') ils plaisent

Conditional
je plairais
tu plairais
il plairait

nous plairions
vous plairiez
ils plairaient

Pluperfect
j' avais plu
tu avais plu
il avait plu
elle avait plu

nous avions plu
vous aviez plu
ils avaient plu
elles avaient plu

## 60 mettre

Present
je mets
tu mets
il met

nous mettons
vous mettez
ils mettent

Future
je mettrai
tu mettras
il mettra

nous mettrons
vous mettrez
ils mettront

Imperfect
je mettais
tu mettais
il mettait

nous mettions
vous mettiez
ils mettaient

Perfect
j' ai mis
tu as mis
il a mis
elle a mis

nous avons mis
vous avez mis
ils ont mis
elles ont mis

Past participle
mis/mise

Present subjunctive
(que) je mette
(que) tu mettes
(qu') il mette

(que) nous mettions
(que) vous mettiez
(qu') ils mettent

Conditional
je mettrais
tu mettrais
il mettrait

nous mettrions
vous mettriez
ils mettraient

Pluperfect
j' avais mis
tu avais mis
il avait mis
elle avait mis

nous avions mis
vous aviez mis
ils avaient mis
elles avaient mis

## 61 battre

| Present | | Perfect | | | Conditional | |
|---|---|---|---|---|---|---|
| je | bats | j' | ai | battu | je | battrais |
| tu | bats | tu | as | battu | tu | battrais |
| il | bat | il | a | battu | il | battrait |
| nous | battons | elle | a | battu | nous | battrions |
| vous | battez | | | | vous | battriez |
| ils | battent | nous | avons | battu | ils | battraient |
| | | vous | avez | battu | | |
| **Future** | | ils | ont | battu | | |
| je | battrai | elles | ont | battu | **Pluperfect** | |
| tu | battras | | | | j' | avais | battu |
| il | battra | **Past participle** | | | tu | avais | battu |
| nous | battrons | | battu/battue | | il | avait | battu |
| vous | battrez | | | | elle | avait | battu |
| ils | battront | **Present subjunctive** | | | nous | avons | battu |
| | | (que) | je | batte | vous | aviez | battu |
| **Imperfect** | | (que) | tu | battes | ils | avaient | battu |
| je | battais | (qu') | il | batte | elles | avaient | battu |
| tu | battais | | | | | |
| il | battait | (que) | nous | battions | | |
| nous | battions | (que) | vous | battiez | | |
| vous | battiez | (qu') | ils | battent | | |
| ils | battaient | | | | | |

## 62 traduire

| Present | | Perfect | | | Conditional | |
|---|---|---|---|---|---|---|
| je | traduis | j' | ai | traduit | je | traduirais |
| tu | traduis | tu | as | traduit | tu | traduirais |
| il | traduit | il | a | traduit | il | traduirait |
| nous | traduisons | elle | a | traduit | nous | traduirions |
| vous | traduisez | | | | vous | traduiriez |
| ils | traduisent | nous | avons | traduit | ils | traduiraient |
| | | vous | avez | traduit | | |
| **Future** | | ils | ont | traduit | | |
| je | traduirai | elles | ont | traduit | **Pluperfect** | |
| tu | traduiras | | | | j' | avais | traduit |
| il | traduira | **Past participle** | | | tu | avais | traduit |
| nous | traduirons | | traduit/traduite | | il | avait | traduit |
| vous | traduirez | | | | elle | avait | traduit |
| ils | traduiront | **Present subjunctive** | | | nous | avions | traduit |
| | | (que) | je | traduise | vous | aviez | traduit |
| **Imperfect** | | (que) | tu | traduises | ils | avaient | traduit |
| je | traduisais | (qu') | il | traduise | elles | avaient | traduit |
| tu | traduisais | | | | | |
| il | traduisait | (que) | nous | traduisions | | |
| nous | traduisions | (que) | vous | traduisiez | | |
| vous | traduisiez | (qu') | ils | traduisent | | |
| ils | traduisaient | | | | | |

## 63 connaître

| Present | | |
|---|---|---|
| je | connais | |
| tu | connais | |
| il | connaît | |
| nous | connaissons | |
| vous | connaissez | |
| ils | connaissent | |

| Future | |
|---|---|
| je | connaîtrai |
| tu | connaîtras |
| il | connaîtra |
| nous | connaîtrons |
| vous | connaîtrez |
| ils | connaîtront |

| Imperfect | |
|---|---|
| je | connaissais |
| tu | connaissais |
| il | connaissait |
| nous | connaissions |
| vous | connaissiez |
| ils | connaissaient |

| Perfect | | |
|---|---|---|
| j' | ai | connu |
| tu | as | connu |
| il | a | connu |
| elle | a | connu |
| nous | avons | connu |
| vous | avez | connu |
| ils | ont | connu |
| elles | ont | connu |

**Past participle**

connu/connue

**Present subjunctive**

| (que) | je | connaisse |
|---|---|---|
| (que) | tu | connaisses |
| (qu') | il | connaisse |
| (que) | nous | connaissions |
| (que) | vous | connaissiez |
| (qu') | ils | connaissent |

| Conditional | |
|---|---|
| je | connaîtrais |
| tu | connaîtrais |
| il | connaîtrait |
| nous | connaîtrions |
| vous | connaîtriez |
| ils | connaîtraient |

**Pluperfect**

| j' | avais | connu |
|---|---|---|
| tu | avais | connu |
| il | avait | connu |
| elle | avait | connu |
| nous | avions | connu |
| vous | aviez | connu |
| ils | avaient | connu |
| elles | avaient | connu |

## 64 naître

| Present | | |
|---|---|---|
| je | nais | |
| tu | nais | |
| il | naît | |
| nous | naissons | |
| vous | naissez | |
| ils | naissent | |

| Future | |
|---|---|
| je | naîtrai |
| tu | naîtras |
| il | naîtra |
| nous | naîtrons |
| vous | naîtrez |
| ils | naîtront |

| Imperfect | |
|---|---|
| je | naissais |
| tu | naissais |
| il | naissait |
| nous | naissions |
| vous | naissiez |
| ils | naissaient |

| Perfect | | |
|---|---|---|
| je | suis | né |
| tu | es | né |
| il | est | né |
| elle | est | née |
| nous | sommes | nés |
| vous | êtes | nés |
| ils | sont | nés |
| elles | sont | nées |

**Past participle**

né/née

**Present subjunctive**

| (que) | je | naisse |
|---|---|---|
| (que) | tu | naisses |
| (qu') | il | naisse |
| (que) | nous | naissions |
| (que) | vous | naissiez |
| (qu') | ils | naissent |

| Conditional | |
|---|---|
| je | naîtrais |
| tu | naîtrais |
| il | naîtrait |
| nous | naîtrions |
| vous | naîtriez |
| ils | naîtraient |

**Pluperfect**

| j' | étais | né |
|---|---|---|
| tu | étais | né |
| il | était | né |
| elle | était | née |
| nous | étions | nés |
| vous | étiez | nés |
| ils | étaient | nés |
| elles | étaient | nées |

## 65 résoudre

| Present | | Perfect | | | Conditional | |
|---|---|---|---|---|---|---|
| je | résous | j' | ai | résolu | je | résoudrais |
| tu | résous | tu | as | résolu | tu | résoudrais |
| il | résout | Il | a | résolu | il | résoudrait |
| nous | résolvons | elle | a | résolu | | |
| vous | résolvez | | | | nous | résoudrions |
| ils | résolvent | nous | avons | résolu | vous | résoudriez |
| | | vous | avez | résolu | ils | résoudraient |

**Future**

| | | ils | ont | résolu | | |
|---|---|---|---|---|---|---|
| je | résoudrai | elles | ont | résolu | **Pluperfect** | |
| tu | résoudras | | | | j' | avais | résolu |
| Il | résoudra | **Past participle** | | | tu | avais | résolu |
| nous | résoudrons | | résolu/résolue | | il | avait | résolu |
| vous | résoudrez | | | | elle | avait | résolu |
| ils | résoudront | **Present subjunctive** | | | nous | avons | résolu |

**Imperfect**

| | | (que) | je | résolve | vous | aviez | résolu |
|---|---|---|---|---|---|---|---|
| je | résolvais | (que) | tu | résolves | ils | avaient | résolu |
| tu | résolvais | (qu') | il | résolve | elles | avaient | résolu |
| il | résolvait | | | | | |
| nous | résolvions | (que) | nous | résolvions | | |
| vous | résolviez | (que) | vous | résolviez | | |
| ils | résolvaient | (qu') | ils | résolvent | | |

---

## 66 coudre

| Present | | Perfect | | | Conditional | |
|---|---|---|---|---|---|---|
| je | couds | j' | ai | cousu | je | coudrais |
| tu | couds | tu | as | cousu | tu | coudrais |
| il | coud | il | a | cousu | il | coudrait |
| nous | cousons | elle | a | cousu | | |
| vous | cousez | | | | nous | coudrions |
| ils | cousent | nous | avons | cousu | vous | coudriez |
| | | vous | avez | cousu | ils | coudraient |

**Future**

| | | ils | ont | cousu | | |
|---|---|---|---|---|---|---|
| je | coudrai | elles | ont | cousu | **Pluperfect** | |
| tu | coudras | | | | j' | avais | cousu |
| il | coudra | **Past participle** | | | tu | avais | cousu |
| nous | coudrons | | cousu/cousue | | il | avait | cousu |
| vous | coudrez | | | | elle | avait | cousu |
| ils | coudront | **Present subjunctive** | | | nous | avons | cousu |

**Imperfect**

| | | (que) | je | couse | vous | aviez | cousu |
|---|---|---|---|---|---|---|---|
| je | cousais | (que) | tu | couses | ils | avaient | cousu |
| tu | cousais | (qu') | il | couse | elles | avaient | cousu |
| il | cousait | | | | | |
| nous | cousions | (que) | nous | cousions | | |
| vous | cousiez | (que) | vous | cousiez | | |
| ils | cousaient | (qu') | ils | cousent | | |

# A guide to French pronunciation

While phonetics have not been given for entries in the present dictionary, a simplified, user-friendly table summarizing the main features of French pronunciation and spelling follows.

This table is designed
(a) to help English speakers to bridge the gap between the sound systems of English and French
(b) to connect French sounds to the most frequent written representations of those sounds, illustrating the link by means of examples from basic French vocabulary.

Learners will find in it a useful point of departure for a more advanced study of French phonetics at a later stage. It is not, however, meant to take the place of either a human model—a teacher, for example—or a recording of the same sounds produced by a native speaker.

The table is subdivided into three main categories of phonetic sounds: *vowels*, *semi-vowels*, and *consonants*. The French sounds are presented in order of increasing complexity when compared with the English sound system. In many cases, the sounds are broadly similar, if not actually the same. In others, however, it is only possible in the present format to give an approximation in English terms of the French sound. This is indicated by the symbol ≈. This is particularly true of the French vowels which are nasalized (represented by ɛ̃, ɑ̃, ɔ̃, and œ̃ in the International Phonetic Alphabet) and those which require a marked degree of lip-rounding (represented by ø, œ, y, and ɥ).

A major distinguishing feature of written French is the mute h, as in **homme**, **hôtel**. It functions in the same way as a vowel and spelling or pronunciation adjust accordingly **l'h**omme, **cet h**omme, **les h**ommes [lezɔm]. We have systematically included the mute h in the column dealing with French spelling forms while notes throughout the dictionary text regularly draw users' attention to this important feature.

M. O'N.

## Vowels

| phonetic symbol | sounds like English | written in French as | examples |
|---|---|---|---|
| a | cat, flat | a, à, ha- | acheter, basse, patte, à, voilà, hameau (*note also* femme) |
| ɑ | arm, car | â, as | âgé, gâteau, pâte, bas, las |
| e | hay, tray but *shorter* | -er, -es, -ez, -é, -ée, é-, hé- | aller, des, nez, âgé, année, étage, hélas |
| ɛ | pet, threat | è-, ê-, e-, ai, -ais, ait, -ei-, aï-, -ë-, -et | règle, très, être, bête, elle, cet, aide, faible, français, lait, était, pleine, connaître, Noël, secret |
| i | treat, fleet | i, -ie, -is, î-, hi, y, -ï | il, immeuble, libre, pile, vie, pris, île, hibou, elle y va, type, maïs |
| o | horse, course | au, eau, aux, eaux, o, os, ô, hô- | aussi, gauche, tuyau, beau, château, chevaux, eaux, chose, orage, loto, gros, côte, hôtel (*note also* trop) |
| ɔ | hot, what | o-, ho-, hô- | objet, dommage, randonnée, botte, horaire, hôpital |

## Vowels

| phonetic symbol | sounds like English | written in French as | examples |
|---|---|---|---|
| u | hoot, flute | ou, où, -oû-, -oo-, hou-, -oux | ouvrir, trou, mourir, amour, où, goûter, football, houx, roux (*note also* août) |
| ə | ago, gather (*British English*) | e (*silent at the end of words and may even be left out*) | mère, elle, j'aime, même, premier, grenouille, menu, le, ne, do, petit, fera, chemin, médecin |
| ø | purr, her but shorter | eu, eux | Europe, peu, neveu, bleu, chanteuse, heureux, cheveux, yeux |
| œ | ≈ fun, son | eu, œu-, heu-, œ | peur, déjeuner, meuble, humeur, fauteuil, œuf, sœur, heure, œil |
| y | ee but with rounded lips | u, û, hu | une, utile, rue, vendu, mûr, sûr, humeur, hurler (*note also* eu) |
| ɛ̃ | an/am + nasal twang | in, im, ain, -ein, yn, ym, -en, -aim, hein | intéressant, matin, imbécile, train, copain, plein, peindre, syndical, sympa, italien, rien, faim, hein |
| ɑ̃ | awn/alm + nasal twang | an, -ant, en, em-, -ent, am- | an, chanter, chant, entrer, ennui, empêcher, tempête, souvent, rampe (*note also* temps, paon, banc, sang *and* champ) |
| ɔ̃ | on + nasal twang | on, om, hon- | onze, bon, montrer, jambon, ombre, sombre, tromper, honte |
| œ̃ | fun, son + nasal twang | un, um | un, brun, lundi, parfum |

## Semi-Vowels

| phonetic symbol | sounds like English | written in French as | examples |
|---|---|---|---|
| j | yes, player | -i-, y, -il, -ill- | bien, ciel, tiède, il y a, yaourt, payer, soleil, travail, feuille, fille, billet |
| w | ≈ was | oi, -oî-, ou, -oê-, w- | oiseau, voir, besoin, quoi, oui, jouet, boîte, poêle, K-way |
| ɥ | ≈ we, tweet but with *rounded lips* | -ui-, hui, -uî-, hui- | nuit, lui, aujourd'hui, huit, huître |

## Consonants

| phonetic symbol | sounds like English | written in French as | examples |
|---|---|---|---|
| b | as English | b, -bb- | bain, robe, abbaye |
| d | as English | d, -dd- | devoir, aide, addition |
| f | as English | f, -ff-, ph | fête, neuf, affaires, photo, téléphone |
| k | as English | c, qu-, -q, -cc-, k, -ck-, -ch- | café, sac, quartier, marquer, coq, occupé, kilomètre, kayak, ticket, orchestre |
| l | as English | l, -ll- | lettre, pile, mal, ville, salle |
| m | as English | m, -mm- | mère, madame, femme, sommeil |
| n | as English | n, -nn- | non, animal, panne, donner |
| p | as English | p, -pp-, -bs- | pomme, chapeau, hop, appuyer, observer |
| s | as English | s, -ss-, c, ç-, sc- | son, festival, assiette, poisson, chasse, cette, tracer, cil, garçon, ça, reçu, scène, piscine (note also six, dix) |
| t | as English | t, -tt-, th | tour, auto, patte, thé, bibliothèque |
| v | as English | v, w | venir, lever, grave, wagon, W-C |
| z | as English | -s-, z, -x- | maison, loisirs, brise, zoo, bizarre, dix-huit, sixième |
| g | as English | g, gu-, -gg- | goût, bagarre, gai, guitare, blague, aggressif |
| ʒ | leisure, seizure | j, g-, ge- | j'ai, jeune, déjeuner, plage, geler, gifler, gîte, nageons |
| ʃ | rash, shoe | ch, sh | château, achats, riche, poche, short |
| ɲ | new, onion | gn | ignorer, vignoble, soigner, champignon (note also oignon) |
| ŋ | sing, wrong | -ng | camping, parking |
| ʀ | ≈ a very soft loch sound produced at the back of the throat | r, -rr-, rh- | rouge, partir, arrêter, marre, rhume |

# Numbers

## Cardinal numbers in French

| | | | |
|---|---|---|---|
| 0 | zéro* | 80 | quatre-vingts†§ |
| 1 | un† | 81 | quatre-vingt-un¶ |
| 2 | deux | 82 | quatre-vingt-deux |
| 3 | trois | 90 | quatre-vingt-dix‡ |
| 4 | quatre | 91 | quatre-vingt-onze |
| 5 | cinq | 92 | quatre-vingt-douze |
| 6 | six | 99 | quatre-vingt-dix-neuf |
| 7 | sept | 100 | cent |
| 8 | huit | 101 | cent un† |
| 9 | neuf | 102 | cent deux |
| 10 | dix | 110 | cent dix |
| 11 | onze | 187 | cent quatre vingt-sept |
| 12 | douze | 200 | deux cents |
| 13 | treize | 250 | deux cent◊ cinquante |
| 14 | quatorze | 1 000 | mille |
| 15 | quinze | 1 001 | mille un† |
| 16 | seize | 1 002 | mille deux |
| 17 | dix-sept | 1 020 | mille vingt |
| 18 | dix-huit | 1 200 | mille** deux cents |
| 19 | dix-neuf | 2 000 | deux mille†† |
| 20 | vingt | 10 000 | dix mille |
| 21 | vingt et un | 100 000 | cent mille |
| 22 | vingt-deux | 100 200 | cent deux mille |
| 30 | trente | 1 000 000 | un million‡‡ |
| 40 | quarante | 1 264 932 | un million deux cent |
| 50 | cinquante | | soixante-quatre mille |
| 60 | soixante | | neuf cent trente-deux |
| 70 | soixante dix‡ | 1 000 000 000 | un milliard‡‡ |
| 71 | soixante et onze | 1 000 000 000 000 | un billion‡‡ |

* In English *0* may be called *nought, zero, nil* or even *nothing*; French is always *zéro*: **a nought = un zéro**.

† *one* is *une* in French when it agrees with a feminine noun, so *un crayon* but *une table, des tables, vingt et une tables*, etc.

‡ (70) Also **septante** in Belgium and Switzerland. (80) Also **octante** in Switzerland and Canada, **huitante** in Switzerland. (90) Also **nonante** in Belgium and Switzerland.

§ Note that when *80* is used as a page number it has no *s*: **page eighty = page quatre-vingt**.

¶ **vingt** has no *s* when it is in the middle of a number. The only exception to this rule is when *quatre-vingts* is followed by *millions, milliards* or *billions*, e.g. **quatre-vingts millions, quatre-vingts billions** etc.

◊ **cent** does not take an *s* when it is in the middle of a number. The only exception to this rule is when it is followed by *millions, milliards* or *billions*, e.g. **trois cents millions, six cents billions** etc. It has a normal plural when it modifies other nouns: **200 inhabitants = deux cents habitants**.

Where English would have a comma, French has simply a space. A full stop (period) can be used, e.g. **1.000**. As in English, there is no separation in dates between thousands and hundreds: **in 1995 = en 1995**.

**In dates, the spelling *mil* is preferred to *mille*, i.e. **en 1200 = en mil deux cents**. However, when the year is a round number of thousands, the spelling is always *mille*, so **en l'an mille, en l'an deux mille** etc.

††*mille* is invariable; it never takes an *s*.

‡‡The French words **million, milliard** and **billion** are nouns, and when written out in full they take **de** before another noun, e.g. **a million inhabitants = un million d'habitants**. However, when written in figures, **1,000,000 inhabitants = 1 000 000 habitants**, but is still spoken as *un million d'habitants*. When *million* etc. is part of a complex number, *de* is not used before the nouns, e.g. **6,000,210 people = six millions deux cent dix personnes**.

## Use of *en*

Note the use of *en* in the following examples:

| | |
|---|---|
| *there are six* | = il y **en** a six |
| *I've got a hundred* | = j'**en** ai cent |

**en** must be used when the thing you are talking about is not expressed (the French says literally *there of them are six, I of them have a hundred* etc.). However, **en** is not needed when the object is specified:

| | |
|---|---|
| *there are six apples* | = il y a six pommes |

## Approximate numbers

When you want to say about *…*, remember the French ending *-aine*.

| | |
|---|---|
| *about ten* | = une **dizaine** |
| *about ten books* | = une **dizaine** de livres |
| *about fifteen* | = une **quinzaine** |
| *about fifteen people* | = une **quinzaine** de personnes |

Similarly *une trentaine, une quarantaine, une cinquantaine, une soixantaine* and *une centaine* (and *une douzaine* means a *dozen*). For other numbers, use **environ** (*about*):

| | |
|---|---|
| *about thirty-five* | = **environ** trente-cinq |
| *about four* | = **environ** quatre |
| *thousand pages* | = mille pages |

Note the use of *centaines* and *milliers* to express approximate quantities:

| | |
|---|---|
| *hundreds of books* | = des **centaines** de livres |
| *thousands of books* | = des **milliers** de livres |
| *I've got thousands* | = j'**en** ai des **milliers** |

## Phrases

| | |
|---|---|
| *numbers up to ten* | = les nombres jusqu'à dix |
| *to count up to ten* | = compter jusqu'à dix |
| *almost ten* | = presque dix |
| *less than ten* | = moins de dix |
| *more than ten* | = plus de dix |
| *all ten of them* | = tous les dix |
| *all ten boys* | = les dix garçons |

Note the French word order:

| | |
|---|---|
| *my last ten pounds* | = mes dix dernières livres |
| *the next twelve weeks* | = les douze prochaines semaines |
| *the other two* | = les deux autres |
| *the last four* | = les quatre derniers |

## Calculations in French

| | |
|---|---|
| $10 + 3 = 13$ | dix et trois font *or* égale treize |
| $10 - 3 = 7$ | trois ôté de dix il reste sept *or* dix moins trois égale sept |
| $10 \times 3 = 30$ | dix fois trois égale trente |
| $30 : 3 = 10$ | $(30 \div 3 = 10)$ trente divisé par trois égale dix |

Note how the French division sign differs from the English.

| | |
|---|---|
| $5^2$ | cinq au carré |
| $5^3$ | cinq puissance trois |
| $5^{100}$ | cinq puissance cent |
| $\sqrt{2}$ | racine carrée de deux |
| $\sqrt{25} = 5$ | racine carrée de vingt-cinq égale cinq |
| $B > A$ | B est plus grand que A |
| $A < B$ | A est plus petit que B |

## Decimals in French

Note that French uses a comma where English has a decimal point.

| | say |
|---|---|
| 0,25 | zéro virgule vingt-cinq |
| 0,05 | zéro virgule zéro cinq |
| 0,75 | zéro virgule soixante-quinze |
| 3,45 | trois virgule quarante-cinq |
| 8,195 | huit virgule cent quatre-vingt-quinze |
| 9,1567 | neuf virgule quinze cent soixante-sept or |
| | neuf virgule mille cinq cent soixante-sept |
| 9,3456 | neuf virgule trois mille quatre cent |
| | cinquante-six |

## Percentages in French

| | say |
|---|---|
| 25% | vingt-cinq pour cent |
| 50% | cinquante pour cent |
| 100% | cent pour cent |
| 200% | deux cents pour cent |
| 365% | trois cent soixante cinq pour cent |
| 4,25% | quatre virgule vingt-cinq pour cent |

## Fractions in French

| | say |
|---|---|
| $\frac{1}{2}$ | un demi* |
| $\frac{1}{3}$ | un tiers |
| $\frac{1}{4}$ | un quart |
| $\frac{1}{5}$ | un cinquième |
| $\frac{1}{6}$ | un sixième |
| $\frac{1}{7}$ | un septième |
| $\frac{1}{8}$ | un huitième |
| $\frac{1}{9}$ | un neuvième |
| $\frac{1}{10}$ | un dixième |
| $\frac{1}{11}$ | un onzième |
| $\frac{1}{12}$ | un douzième (etc) |
| $\frac{2}{3}$ | deux tiers† |
| $\frac{2}{5}$ | deux cinquièmes |
| $\frac{2}{10}$ | deux dixièmes (etc) |
| $\frac{3}{4}$ | trois quarts |
| $\frac{3}{5}$ | trois cinquièmes |
| $\frac{3}{10}$ | trois dixièmes (etc) |
| $1\frac{1}{2}$ | un et demi |
| $1\frac{1}{3}$ | un (et) un tiers |
| $1\frac{1}{4}$ | un (et) un quart |
| $1\frac{1}{5}$ | un (et) un cinquième |
| $1\frac{1}{6}$ | un (et) un sixième |
| $1\frac{1}{7}$ | un (et) un septième (etc) |
| $5\frac{2}{3}$ | cinq (et) deux tiers |
| $5\frac{3}{4}$ | cinq (et) trois quarts |
| $5\frac{4}{5}$ | cinq (et) quatre cinquièmes |

45/100ths of = quarante-cinq centièmes de seconde
a second

## Ordinal numbers in French§

| | | |
|---|---|---|
| 1st | 1er‡ | premier (fem. première) |
| 2nd | 2e | second or deuxième |
| 3rd | 3e | troisième |
| 4th | 4e | quatrième |
| 5th | 5e | cinquième |
| 6th | 6e | sixième |
| 7th | 7e | septième |
| 8th | 8e | huitième |
| 9th | 9e | neuvième |
| 10th | 10e | dixième |
| 11th | 11e | onzième |
| 12th | 12e | douzième |
| 13th | 13e | treizième |
| 14th | 14e | quatorzième |
| 15th | 15e | quinzième |
| 16th | 16e | seizième |
| 17th | 17e | dix-septième |
| 18th | 18e | dix-huitième |
| 19th | 19e | dix-neuvième |
| 20th | 20e | vingtième |
| 21st | 21e | vingt et unième |
| 22nd | 22e | vingt-deuxième |
| 23rd | 23e | vingt-troisième |
| 24th | 24e | vingt-quatrième |
| 25th | 25e | vingt-cinquième |
| 30th | 30e | trentième |
| 31st | 31e | trente et unième |
| 40th | 40e | quarantième |
| 50th | 50e | cinquantième |
| 60th | 60e | soixantième |
| 70th | 70e | soixante-dixième¶ |
| 71st | 71e | soixante et onzième |
| 72nd | 72e | soixante-douzième |
| 73rd | 73e | soixante-treizième |
| 74th | 74e | soixante-quartorzième |
| 75th | 75e | soixante-quinzième |
| 79th | 79e | soixante-dix-neuvième |
| 80th | 80e | quatre-vingtième¶ |
| 81st | 81e | quatre-vingt-unième |
| 90th | 90e | quatre-vingt-dixième¶ |
| 91st | 91e | quatre-vingt-onzième |
| 99th | 99e | quatre-vingt-dix-neuvième |
| 100th | 100e | centième |
| 101st | 101e | cent unième |
| 102nd | 102e | cent deuxième |
| 196th | 196e | cent quatre-vingt-seizième |
| 200th | 200e | deux centième |
| 300th | 300e | trois centième |
| 400th | 400e | quatre centième |
| 1,000th | 1 000e | millième |
| 2,000th | 2 000e | deux millième |
| 1,000,000th | 1 000 000e | millionième |

Like English, French makes nouns by adding the definite article:

| | |
|---|---|
| *the first* | = le premier (or la première, or les premiers m pl or les premières f pl) |
| *the second* | = le second (or la seconde etc) |
| *the first three* | = les trois premiers or les trois premières |

Note the French word order in:

| | |
|---|---|
| *the third richest country in the world* | = le troisième pays le plus riche du monde |

* Note that half, when not a fraction, is translated by the noun **moitié** or the adjective **demi**; see the dictionary entry.

† Note the use of **les** and **d'entre** when these fractions are used about a group of people or things: **two-thirds of them = les deux tiers d'entre eux.**

§ All the ordinal numbers in French behave like ordinary adjectives and take normal plural endings where appropriate.

‡ This is the masculine form; the feminine is **1re** and the plural **1ers** (m) or **1res** (f). All the other abbreviations of ordinal numbers are invariable.

¶ (70e) Also **septantième** in Belgium and Switzerland. (80e) Also **huitantième** in Switzerland. (90e) Also **nonantième** in Belgium and Switzerland.

# The French words you must know

**A**
à
accepter
accompagner
acheter
addition l' (f)
adolescent l' (m)
adresse l' (f)
aéroport l' (m)
affreux
âge l' (m)
agent de police l' (m)
agréable
aider
aimer
alcool l' (m)
alimentation l' (f)
aller
allô
alors
ami l' (m); amie l' (f)
amour l' (m)
amusant
an l' (m)
anglais
Angleterre l' (f)
animal l' (m)
année l' (f)
anniversaire l' (m)
août
appareil-photo l' (m)
appeler, s'
apprendre
après
après-midi l' (m/f)
arrêter
arrivée l' (f)
arriver
assez
attendre
attention l' (f)
au revoir
au secours
aujourd'hui
aussi
autobus l' (m)
automne l' (m)
autoroute l' (f)
autre
avant
avec
avion l' (m)
avoir
avril

**B**
bain le
banane la
banlieue la
banque la
bar le
bâtiment le
beau
beaucoup
besoin le
bête
bibliothèque la
bic le
bien
bien sûr

bientôt
bière la
billet le
blanc
bleu
boire
boisson la
boîte la
bon
bon anniversaire
bon appétit
bonjour
bonne année
bonsoir
bouche la
boucherie la
boulangerie la
bouteille la
boutique la
bras le
brosse à dents la
brouillard le
bruit le
brun
bureau le
bureau de renseignements le
bus le

**C**
ça
cadeau le
café le
caisse la
campagne la
camping le
cantine la
car le
carnet le
carrefour le
carte la
carte postale la
casser
célèbre
célibataire
centre le
centre-ville le
cependant
chaise la
chambre la
chance la
changer
chanter
chaque
chat le
château le
chaud
chauffeur le
chaussette la
chaussure la
chemise la
cher
chercher
cheveux les (m)
chez
chic
chien le
chocolat le
choisir
choix le

chose la
cinéma le
circulation la
clé la/clef
cœur le
coiffeur le
coin le
combien
commander
comme
commencer
comment
commissariat le
composer
composter
comprendre
comprimés les (m)
concours le
conducteur le
conduire
confiture la
confortable
connaître
content
continuer
contre
copain le
copine la
corps le
correspondant le
côte la
coucher, se
couleur la
couper
courses les (f)
couteau le
coûter
croire
cuiller/cuillière la
cuisine la

**D**
d'abord
d'accord
d'habitude
dans
date la
de
début le
décembre
décider
défense de
déjà
déjeuner le
délicieux
demain
demander
demi
dentiste le
départ le
(se) dépêcher
depuis
dernier
derrière
descendre
désolé
dessert le
destination la
devant
devoir

difficile
dimanche
dîner le
dire
direction la
discuter
disputer, se
disque compact le
docteur le
donc
donner
dormir
dos le
douche la
droit
droite la
drôle
dur

**E**
eau l' (f)
eau minérale l' (f)
échange l' (m)
écossais
Ecosse l' (f)
écouter
écrire, s'
église l' (f)
embouteillage l' (m)
émission l' (f)
emploi l' (m)
en
en retard
en ville
enchanté
encore
enfant l' (m/f)
enfin
entendre, s'
entre
entrée l' (f)
entrer
environ
envoyer
épicerie l' (f)
équipe l' (f)
escalier l' (m)
espérer
essayer (de)
essence l' (f)
est l' (m)
et
étage l' (m)
été l' (m)
étranger l' (m)
être
étudiant l' (m)
euro l' (m)
exactement
excuser, s'
exemple l' (m); par
extra

**F**
facile
faim la; avoir faim
faire
famille la
fatigué
faux

femme la
fenêtre la
former
février
fille la
film le
fils le
fin la
finir
fleur la
fois la
foot le
fourchette la
frais/fraîche
fraise la
framboise la
français
France la
frère le
frigo le
froid
fromage le
fruit le
fumer

**G**
gagner
gallois
garçon le
gare la
gâteau le
gauche
gens les (m)
gentil
glace la
gorge la
grand
Grande-Bretagne la
grand-mère la
grand-père le
gras
gratuit
grave
grippe la
gris
gros
guichet le

**H**
habiter
haut
heure l' (f)
heureux
hier
histoire l' (f)
hiver l' (m)
homme l' (m)
hôtel l' (m)
hôpital l' (m)
horaire l' (m)
huile l' (f)
hypermarché l' (m)

**I**
ici
idée l' (f)
idiot
île l' (f)
il y a
impoli

important
informations les (f)
instant l' (m)
intelligent
interdit
intéressant
intéresser, s'
irlandais
Irlande l' (f)

**J**
jamais
jambe la
janvier
jardin le
jaune
jeu le
jeudi
jeune
joli
jouer
jour le
journal le
journée la
juillet
juin
jusqu'à
juste

**L**
là
là-bas
lait le
large
laver, se
lent
lettre la
lever, se
libre
lire
lit le
lieu le; avoir lieu
livre le
loin
long
louer
lundi
lunettes les (f)

**M**
madame
mademoiselle
magasin le
mai
main la
maintenant
mais
maison la
mal: avoir mal
malade
malheureusement
manger
marché le
marcher
mardi
mari le
mars
matin le
mauvais
méchant
meilleur
même
menu le
mer la
merci
mercredi

mère la
météo la
métier le
métro le
mettre
midi
mieux
minuit
minute la
miroir le
moche
mode la
moins, au moins
mois le
moment le
monde le
monnaie la
monsieur
montagne la
monter
montre la
montrer
mort
mot le
mur le
musique la

**N**
nager
neige la
nettoyer
Noël
noir
nom le
non
nord le
nourriture la
nouveau
novembre
nuage le
nuit la
numéro le

**O**
octobre
œil l' (m)
œuf l' (m)
oignon l' (m)
oiseau l' (m)
oncle l' (m)
ordinateur l' (m)
oreille l' (f)
ou
où
oublier
ouest l' (m)
oui
ouvert

**P**
pain le
papier le
Pâques
par
parapluie le
parce que
pardon
parfait
parking le
parler
partie la
partir
partout
pas
pas encore
passer, se

passe-temps le
passionnant
pauvre
payer
pays le
Pays de Galles le
péage le
pendant
penser
perdre
père le
permis (de conduire)
le
personne la
petit
petit déjeuner le
petit ami le/petite
amie la
peu
peur la; avoir peur
peut-être
pièce la
pied le; à pied
piscine la
plage la
plan le
plein
pluie la
plus tard
poire la
poisson le
poivre le
police la
pomme la
pomme de terre la
pont le
porc le
porte la
portefeuille le (m)
porte-monnaie le (m)
porter
possible
poste la
poubelle la
poulet le
pour
pourquoi
pousser
pouvoir
premier
prendre
prénom le
préparer
près, tout
presque
prêt
printemps le
privé
prix le
problème le
prochain
professeur le
promenade la
promener, se
propre
public
puis

**Q**
quai le
quand
que
quelqu'un
quelque chose
quelque(s)
quelquefois

question la
qui
quitter
quoi

**R**
raconter
radio la
raison la; avoir raison
ranger
rapide
rappeler
récemment
recevoir
regarder
règle la
rencontrer, se
rentrer
repas le
réserver
rester
retour le
réveiller, se
rez-de-chaussée le
rhume le
riche
rien
rire
rond-point le
rose
rouge
roue la
route la
Route Nationale la
Royaume-Uni le
rue la

**S**
sac le
sac à main le
sage
saison la
salade la
sale
salle la
salon le
salut
samedi
sans
sauf
savoir
savon le
secrétaire le/la
secours le
séjour le
sel le
semaine la
sentir
septembre
serveur le
serviette la
servir
seul
seulement
si
sœur la
soif la; avoir soif
soir le
soirée la
soldes les (m)
soleil le
sortie la
sortir
soudain
sourire
sous

souvent
sport le
station la
stylo le
sud le
super
supermarché le
sur
sympa

**T**
table la
taille la
tante la
tard
tasse la
téléphone (portable)
le
téléphoner
télévision la
température la
temps le
tête la
thé le
timbre le
tirer
toilettes les (f)
tôt
toujours
tous les jours
tout
tout de suite
tout le monde
train le
travail le
travailler
très
triste
trop
trouver, se

**U**
utile

**V**
vacances les (f)
vaisselle la
vendredi
venir
verre le
vert
vêtements les (m)
vie la
vieux
village le
ville la
vin le
violet
visage le
visiter
vite
vivre
voici
voilà
voir, se
voiture la
voyager
vrai
vraiment

**Y**
yeux les (m)

**Z**
zéro

# Phrasefinder

## Contents

| Key phrases | Phrases-clés |
| --- | --- |
| yes, please | oui, s'il vous plaît |
| no, thank you | non merci |
| sorry | désolé/-e |
| excuse me | excusez-moi |
| you're welcome | de rien |
| hello/goodbye | bonjour/au revoir |
| how are you? | comment allez-vous? |
| nice to meet you | enchanté/-e! |

| **Asking questions** | **Poser des questions** |
| --- | --- |
| do you speak English/French? | parlez-vous anglais/français? |
| what's your name? | comment vous appelez-vous? |
| where are you from? | d'où venez-vous? |
| how much is it? | combien ça coûte? |
| how far is it? | c'est loin d'ici? |
| where is...? | où est...? |
| can I have...? | est-ce que je peux avoir...? |
| would you like...? | voulez-vous...? |

| **Statements about yourself** | **Parler de soi** |
| --- | --- |
| my name is... | je m'appelle... |
| I'm English | je suis anglais/-e |
| I'm French | je suis français/-e |
| I don't speak French/English very well | je ne parle pas très bien français/anglais |
| I'm here on holiday | je suis en vacances ici |
| I live near Sheffield | j'habite près de Sheffield |
| I'm a student | je suis étudiant/-e |

| **Emergencies** | **Urgences** |
| --- | --- |
| can you help me? | pouvez-vous m'aider? |
| I'm lost | je me suis perdu/-e |
| I'm ill | je suis malade |
| call an ambulance | appelez une ambulance |
| watch out! | attention! |

# ❶ Going Places

# Se déplacer ❶

| On the road | Par la route |
|---|---|
| where's the nearest petrol station/filling station (US)? | où se trouve la station-service la plus proche? |
| what's the best way to get there? | quel est le meilleur chemin pour y aller? |
| I've got a puncture | j'ai crevé |
| I'd like to hire a bike/car | je voudrais louer un vélo/une voiture |
| I'm looking for somewhere to park | je cherche un endroit pour me garer |
| there's been an accident | il y a eu un accident |
| my car's broken down | ma voiture est en panne |
| the car won't start | la voiture ne démarre pas |

| By rail | Par le train |
|---|---|
| where can I buy a ticket? | où est-ce que je peux acheter un billet? |
| what time is the next train to Paris? | à quelle heure est le prochain train pour Paris? |
| do I have to change? | est-ce qu'il y a un changement? |
| can I take my bike on the train? | est-ce que je peux prendre mon vélo dans le train? |
| which platform for the train to Bath? | de quel quai part le train pour Bath? |
| there's a train to London at 10 o'clock | il y a un train pour Londres à 10 heures |
| a single/return to Nice, please | un aller/aller-retour pour Nice, s'il vous plaît |
| I'd like an all-day ticket | je voudrais un billet valable toute la journée |
| I'd like to reserve a seat | je voudrais réserver une place |

| At the airport | Par avion |
|---|---|
| when's the next flight to Paris/Rome? | quand part le prochain avion pour Paris/Rome? |
| what time do I have to check in? | à quelle heure est-ce que je dois me présenter à l'enregistrement? |
| where do I check in? | où est le comptoir d'enregistrement? |
| I'd like to confirm my flight | je voudrais confirmer mon vol |
| I'd like a window seat | je voudrais une place côté fenêtre |
| I want to change/cancel my reservation | je voudrais modifier/annuler ma réservation |

| Getting there | Trouver son chemin |
|---|---|
| could you tell me the way to the castle? | pourriez-vous m'indiquer la route pour aller au château? |
| how long will it take to get there? | combien de temps est-ce qu'il faut pour y arriver? |
| how far is it from here? | c'est loin d'ici? |
| which bus do I take for the cathedral? | quel bus est-ce que je dois prendre pour aller à la cathédrale? |
| can you tell me where to get off? | pouvez-vous me dire où je dois descendre? |
| how much is the fare to the town centre/center (US)? | quel est le prix d'un billet pour le centre-ville? |
| what time is the last bus? | à quelle heure est le dernier bus? |
| how do I get to the airport? | comment est-ce que je fais pour aller à l'aéroport? |
| where's the nearest underground/subway (US) station? | où est la station de métro la plus proche? |
| can you call me a taxi, please? | pouvez-vous m'appeler un taxi, s'il vous plaît? |
| take the first turning right | prenez la première rue à droite |
| turn left at the traffic lights | prenez à gauche aux feux |
| just past the church | juste après l'église |

# ❷ Keeping in touch

# Rester en contact ❷

### On the phone

where can I buy a phone card?

may I use your phone?

do you have a mobile?

what is the code for Lyons/St Albans?

I want to make a phone call

I'd like to reverse the charges/to call collect (*US*)

the line's engaged/busy (*US*)

there's no answer

hello, this is Danielle

is Alistair there, please?

who's calling?

sorry, wrong number

just a moment, please

would you like to hold?

please tell him/her I called

I'd like to leave a message for him/her

I'll try again later

can he/she ring me back?

my home number is...

my business number is...

my fax number is...

we were cut off

### Au téléphone

où est-ce que je peux acheter une carte de téléphone?

est-ce que je peux utiliser votre téléphone?

avez-vous un portable?

quel est l'indicatif pour Lyon/St Albans?

je veux téléphoner

je voudrais appeler en PCV

la ligne est occupée

ça ne répond pas

allô, c'est Danielle

est-ce qu'Alistair est là, s'il vous plaît?

qui est à l'appareil?

désolé/-e, vous faites erreur

un instant, s'il vous plaît

vous patientez?

pourriez-vous lui dire que j'ai appelé?

j'aimerais lui laisser un message

je réessaierai plus tard

est-ce qu'il/elle peut me rappeler?

mon numéro personnel est le...

mon numéro professionnel est le...

mon numéro de télécopie est le...

on a été coupé

### Writing

what's your address?

here's my business card

where is the nearest post office?

could I have a stamp for France/Italy, please?

I'd like to send a parcel/a telegram

### Écrire

quelle est votre adresse?

voici ma carte de visite

où est le bureau de poste le plus proche?

je voudrais un timbre pour la France/l'Italie, s'il vous plaît

je voudrais envoyer un paquet/un télégramme

### On line

are you on the Internet?

what's your e-mail address?

we could send it by e-mail

I'll e-mail it to you on Thursday

I looked it up on the Internet

the information is on their website

### En ligne

êtes-vous sur Internet?

quelle est votre adresse électronique?

nous pourrions l'envoyer par courrier électronique

je vous l'envoie jeudi par courrier électronique

j'ai vérifié sur Internet

l'information se trouve sur leur site Internet

### Meeting up

what shall we do this evening?

where shall we meet?

I'll see you outside the café at 6 o'clock

see you later

I can't today, I'm busy

### Se retrouver

qu'est-ce qu'on fait ce soir?

où est-ce qu'on se retrouve?

on se retrouve à 6 heures devant le café

à tout à l'heure

je ne peux pas aujourd'hui, je suis occupé/-e

# ❸ Food and Drink

# Boire et manger ❸

---

### Booking a restaurant

can you recommend a good restaurant?

I'd like to reserve a table for four

a reservation for tomorrow evening at eight o'clock

I booked a table for two

### Réserver une table

pouvez-vous me recommander un bon restaurant?

je voudrais réserver une table pour quatre personnes

une réservation pour demain soir à huit heures

j'ai réservé une table pour deux

---

### Ordering

could we see the menu/wine list?

do you have a vegetarian/children's menu?

what would you recommend?

I'd like a white/black coffee
... an expresso,
... a decaffeinated coffee
... a tea/a herbal tea
... a liqueur

could I have the bill, (*Amer*) check?

we'd like to pay separately

### Passer commande

est-ce qu'on pourrait voir la carte/la carte des vins?

est-ce que vous avez un menu végétarien/enfant?

Que (nous) conseillez-vous?

J'aimerais un café/un café noir
... un expresso,
... un café décaféiné
... un thé/une infusion
... un digestif

l'addition, s'il vous plaît

on voudrait payer séparément

---

### You will hear

Désirez-vous un apéritif?

Souhaitez-vous commander?

Désirez-vous une entrée?

Quel plat avez-vous choisi?

Je (vous) conseille le/la...

Souhaitez-vous prendre un dessert?

Désirez-vous un café/un digestif?

Anything else?

Bon appétit!

### On vous dira

Would you like an aperitif?

Are you ready to order?

Would you like a starter?

What will you have for the main course?

I can recommend the ...

Would you like a dessert?

Would you like coffee?/a liqueur?

Désirez-vous autre chose?

Enjoy your meal!

---

### The menu

**starters**

| | |
|---|---|
| hors d'œuvres | hors d'œuvres |
| omelette | omelette |
| soup | soupe |

**fish**

| | |
|---|---|
| bass | perche |
| cod | cabillaud |
| eel | anguille |
| hake | colin |
| herring | hareng |
| monkfish | lotte |
| mullet | mulet |
| mussels | moules |
| oysters | huîtres |
| prawns | crevettes roses |
| salmon | saumon |
| sardines | sardines |
| shrimps | crevettes grises |
| sole | sole |

### La carte/Le menu

**Entrées**

| | |
|---|---|
| hors d'œuvres | hors d'œuvres |
| omelette | omelette |
| soupe | soup |

**Poisson**

| | |
|---|---|
| anguille | eel |
| cabillaud | cod |
| cal(a)mar | squid |
| colin | hake  |
| crevettes grises | shrimp |
| crevettes roses | prawns |
| hareng | herring |
| huîtres | oysters |
| lotte | monkfish |
| moules | mussels |
| mulet | mullet |
| perche | bass |
| sardines | sardines |
| saumon | salmon |

| squid | cal(a)mar | sole | sole |
| trout | truite | thon | tuna |
| tuna | thon | truite | trout |
| turbot | turbot | turbot | turbot |

| **meat** | | **Viande** | |
| beef | bœuf | agneau | lamb |
| chicken | poulet | bifteck | steak |
| duck | canard | bœuf | beef |
| goose | oie | canard | duck |
| guinea fowl | pintade | foie | liver |
| hare | lièvre | lapin | rabbit |
| kidneys | rognons | lièvre | hare |
| lamb | agneau | oie | goose |
| liver | foie | pintade | guinea fowl |
| pork | porc | porc | pork |
| rabbit | lapin | poulet | chicken |
| steak | bifteck | rognons | kidneys |
| veal | veau | sanglier | wild boar |
| wild boar | sanglier | veau | veal |

| **vegetables** | | **Légumes** | |
| artichoke | artichaut | artichauts | artichoke |
| asparagus | asperges | asperges | asparagus |
| aubergine | aubergine | aubergines | aubergine |
| cabbage | chou | carottes | carrot |
| carrot | carrotte | céleri | celery |
| cauliflower | chou-fleur | champignons | mushrooms |
| celery | céleri | chou | cabbage |
| courgettes | courgettes | chou-fleur | cauliflower |
| endives | endives | courgettes | courgettes |
| green beans | haricots verts | endives | endives |
| mushrooms | champignons | épinards | spinach |
| onions | oignons | haricots verts | green beans |
| peas | petits pois | oignons | onions |
| pepper | poivron | petits pois | peas |
| potatoes | pommes de terre | poivrons | peppers |
| spinach | épinards | pommes de terre | potatoes |

| **the way it's cooked** | | **La cuisson** | |
| fried | poêlé | à la vapeur | steamed |
| grilled | grillé | à point | medium rare |
| medium rare | à point | bien cuit | well done |
| pureed | mixé | bleu | very rare |
| rare | saignant | cuit à l'étouffée | stewed |
| roast | rôti | grillé | grilled |
| steamed | à la vapeur | mixé | pureed |
| stewed | cuit à l'étouffée | poêlé | fried |
| very rare | bleu | rôti | roast |
| well done | bien cuit | saignant | rare |

## desserts

| | |
|---|---|
| cheese board | plateau de fromages |
| fruit | fruit |
| ice cream | glace |
| pie | tarte (recouverte de pâte) |
| sorbet | sorbet |
| tart | tarte |

## sundries

| | |
|---|---|
| bread | pain |
| butter | beurre |
| herbs | herbes |
| mayonnaise | mayonnaise |
| mustard | moutarde |
| olive oil | huile d'olive |
| pepper | poivre |
| salt | sel |
| sauce | sauce |
| seasoning | assaisonnement |
| vinegar | vinaigre |

## drinks

| | |
|---|---|
| beer | bière |
| bottle | bouteille |
| carbonated | gazeux |
| half-bottle | demi-bouteille |
| liqueur | digestif |
| mineral water | eau minérale |
| red wine | vin rouge |
| rosé | rosé |
| soft drinks | boissons non alcoolisées |
| still | plat, non gazeux |
| table wine | vin de table |
| white wine | vin blanc |
| wine | vin |

## Fromages et desserts

| | |
|---|---|
| fruit | fruit |
| glace | ice cream |
| plateau de fromages | cheese board |
| sorbet | sorbet |
| tarte | tart |
| tarte (recouverte de pâte) | pie |

## Divers

| | |
|---|---|
| assaisonnement | seasoning |
| beurre | butter |
| herbes | herbs |
| huile d'olive | olive oil |
| mayonnaise | mayonnaise |
| moutarde | mustard |
| pain | bread |
| poivre | pepper |
| sauce | sauce |
| sel | salt |
| vinaigre | vinegar |

## Boissons

| | |
|---|---|
| bière | beer |
| boissons non alcoolisées | soft drinks |
| bouteille | bottle |
| demi-bouteille | half-bottle |
| digestif | liqueur |
| eau minérale | mineral water |
| gazeux | carbonated |
| plat | still |
| rosé | rosé |
| vin | wine |
| vin blanc | white wine |
| vin de table | table wine |
| vin rouge | red wine |

# ❹ Places to stay ☆☆☆                              Où dormir ❶

---

### Camping
can we pitch our tent here?

can we park our caravan here?

what are the facilities like?

how much is it per night?

where do we park the car?

we're looking for a campsite

this is a list of local campsites

we go on a camping holiday every year

### Camper
est-ce qu'on peut planter notre tente ici?

est-ce qu'on peut mettre notre caravane ici?

le camping est-il bien équipé?

c'est combien par nuit?

où est-ce qu'on peut garer la voiture?

on cherche un camping

c'est une liste des campings de la région

nous partons camper chaque année pour les vacances

---

### At the hotel
I'd like a double/single room with bath

we have a reservation in the name of Milne

we'll be staying three nights, from Friday to Sunday

how much does the room cost?

I'd like to see the room, please

what time is breakfast?

bed and breakfast

we'd like to stay another night

please call me at 7:30

are there any messages for me?

### À l'hôtel
je voudrais une chambre double/simple avec bain

nous avons une réservation au nom de Milne

nous resterons trois nuits, de vendredi à dimanche

combien coûte la chambre?

je voudrais voir la chambre, s'il vous plaît

à quelle heure est le petit déjeuner?

chambres d'hôtes

on voudrait rester une nuit de plus

réveillez-moi à 7h30

est-ce qu'il y a des messages pour moi?

---

### Hostels
could you tell me where the youth hostel is?

what time does the hostel close?

I'm staying in a hostel

I know a really good hostel in Dublin

I'd like to go backpacking in Australia

### Auberges de jeunesse
pourriez-vous me dire où se trouve l'auberge de jeunesse?

à quelle heure ferme l'auberge de jeunesse?

je loge à l'auberge de jeunesse

je connais une très bonne auberge de jeunesse à Dublin

j'aimerais bien aller faire de la randonnée en Australie

---

### Rooms to rent
I'm looking for a room with a reasonable rent

I'd like to rent an apartment for a few weeks

where do I find out about rooms to let?

what's the weekly rent?

I'm staying with friends at the moment

I rent an apartment on the outskirts of town

the room's fine – I'll take it

the deposit is one month's rent in advance

### Locations
je cherche une chambre à louer avec un loyer raisonnable

je voudrais louer un appartement pendant quelques semaines

où est-ce que je peux me renseigner sur des chambres à louer?

quel est le montant du loyer pour la semaine?

je loge chez des amis pour le moment

je loue un appartement en banlieue

la chambre est bien – je la prends

l'acompte correspond à un mois de loyer payable d'avance

# ❺ Shopping and money  Achats et argent ❺

### At the bank
I'd like to change some money
I want to change some francs into pounds
do you take Eurocheques?
what's the exchange rate today?
I prefer traveller's cheques/traveler's checks (US) to cash
I'd like to transfer some money from my account
I'll get some money from the cash machine
I usually pay by direct debit

### À la banque
je voudrais changer de l'argent
je veux changer des francs en livres
acceptez-vous les Eurochèques?
quel est le taux de change aujourd'hui?
je préfère les chèques de voyage à l'argent liquide
je voudrais retirer de l'argent sur mon compte
je vais retirer de l'argent au distributeur
d'habitude, je paye par prélèvement automatique

### Finding the right shop
where's the main shopping district?
where's a good place to buy sunglasses?

where can I buy batteries/postcards?
where's the nearest chemist/bookshop?
is there a good food shop around here?
what time do the shops open/close?
where did you get those?
I'm looking for presents for my family
we'll do all our shopping on Saturday

### Trouver le bon magasin
où se trouve le principal quartier commerçant?
quel est le meilleur endroit pour acheter des lunettes de soleil?

où est-ce que je peux acheter des piles/cartes postales?
où est la pharmacie/librairie la plus proche?
est-ce qu'il y a une bonne épicerie près d'ici?
à quelle heure ouvrent/ferment les magasins?
où les avez-vous trouvés?
je cherche des cadeaux pour ma famille
nous ferons toutes nos courses samedi

### Are you being served?
how much does that cost?
can I try it on?
can you keep it for me?
do you have this in another colour/color (US)?

I'm just looking
I'll think about it
I need a bigger/smaller size
I take a size 10/a medium
it doesn't suit me
could you wrap it for me, please?
do you take credit cards?
can I pay by cheque/check (US)?
I'm sorry, I don't have any change
I'd like a receipt, please

### On s'occupe de vous?
combien ça coûte?
est-ce que je peux l'essayer?
pouvez-vous me le/la garder?
est-ce que vous avez ce modèle-ci dans une autre couleur?

je regarde
je vais réfléchir
il me faut une taille au-dessus/au-dessous
je fais du 38/il me faut une taille moyenne
ça ne me va pas
pourriez-vous l'emballer, s'il vous plaît?
est-ce que vous acceptez les cartes de crédit?
est-ce que je peux payer par chèque?
je suis désolé/-e mais je n'ai pas de monnaie
je voudrais un reçu, s'il vous plaît

### Changing things
can I have a refund?
can you mend it for me?
can I speak to the manager?
it doesn't work
I'd like to change it, please
I bought this here yesterday

### Faire un échange
j'aimerais être remboursé/-e
est-ce que vous pouvez me le/la réparer?
je voudrais parler au responsable
ça ne marche pas
je voudrais l'échanger, s'il vous plaît
je l'ai acheté/-e ici hier

# ❻ Sport and leisure                                    Sports et loisirs ❻

---

### Keeping fit

| | |
|---|---|
| where can we play football/squash? | où est-ce qu'on peut jouer au football/squash? |
| where is the sports centre/center (US)? | où se trouve le centre sportif? |
| what's the charge per day? | quel est le prix pour la journée? |
| is there a reduction for children/a student discount? | est-ce qu'il y a des réductions enfants/étudiants? |
| I'm looking for a swimming pool/tennis court | je cherche une piscine/un court de tennis |
| you have to be a member | vous devez être membre |
| I play tennis on Mondays | je joue au tennis le lundi |
| I would like to go fishing/riding | je voudrais aller à la pêche/monter à cheval |
| I want to do aerobics | je veux faire de l'aérobic |
| I love swimming/snowboarding | j'adore nager/faire du snowboard |
| we want to hire skis/rollerblades | nous voulons louer des skis/rollers |

---

### Watching sport

| | |
|---|---|
| is there a football match on Saturday? | est-ce qu'il y a un match de foot samedi? |
| which teams are playing? | quelles sont les équipes qui jouent? |
| where can I get tickets? | où est-ce que je peux acheter des billets? |
| I'd like to see a rugby/football match | je voudrais voir un match de rugby/foot |
| my favourite/favorite (US) team is... | mon équipe préférée est... |
| let's watch the match on TV | regardons le match à la télé |

---

### Going to the cinema/theatre/club

| | |
|---|---|
| what's on? | qu'est-ce qu'il y a au programme? |
| when does the box office open/close? | à quelle heure ouvre/ferme le guichet? |
| what time does the concert/performance start? | à quelle heure commence le concert/ la représentation? |
| when does it finish? | à quelle heure ça finit? |
| are there any seats left for tonight? | est-ce qu'il y a encore des places pour ce soir? |
| how much are the tickets? | combien coûtent les billets? |
| where can I get a programme/program (US)? | où est-ce que je peux me procurer un programme? |
| I want to book tickets for tonight's performance | je veux réserver des places pour la représentation de ce soir |
| I'll book seats in the circle/in the stalls | je vais réserver des places au balcon/à l'orchestre |
| we'd like to go to a club | on voudrait aller en boîte |
| I go clubbing every weekend | je vais en boîte tous les week-ends |

---

### Hobbies

| | |
|---|---|
| do you have any hobbies? | est-ce que vous avez des passe-temps? |
| what do you do at the weekend? | que faites-vous le week-end? |
| I like yoga/listening to music | j'aime le yoga/écouter la musique |
| I spend a lot of time surfing the Net | je passe beaucoup de temps à surfer sur Internet |
| I read a lot | je lis beaucoup |
| I collect comic strips | je collectionne les bandes dessinées |

## ❼ Conversion charts

**Length/Longueur**

| inches/pouces | 0.39 | 3.9 | 7.8 | 11.7 | 15.6 | 19.7 | 39 |
|---|---|---|---|---|---|---|---|
| cm/centimètres | 1 | 10 | 20 | 30 | 40 | 50 | 100 |

**Distance/Distance**

| miles/miles | 0.62 | 6.2 | 12.4 | 18.6 | 24.9 | 31 | 62 |
|---|---|---|---|---|---|---|---|
| km/kilomètres | 1 | 10 | 20 | 30 | 40 | 50 | 100 |

**Weight/Poids**

| pounds/livres | 2.2 | 22 | 44 | 66 | 88 | 110 | 220 |
|---|---|---|---|---|---|---|---|
| kg/kilogrammes | 1 | 10 | 20 | 30 | 40 | 50 | 100 |

**Capacity/Contenance**

| gallons/gallons | 0.22 | 2.2 | 4.4 | 6.6 | 8.8 | 11 | 22 |
|---|---|---|---|---|---|---|---|
| litres/litres | 1 | 10 | 20 | 30 | 40 | 50 | 100 |

**Temperature/Température**

| °C | 0 | 5 | 10 | 15 | 20 | 25 | 30 | 37 | 38 | 40 |
|---|---|---|---|---|---|---|---|---|---|---|
| °F | 32 | 41 | 50 | 59 | 68 | 77 | 86 | 98.4 | 100 | 104 |

**Clothing and shoe sizes/Tailles et pointures**

Women's clothing sizes/Tailles femme

| UK | 8 | 10 | 12 | 14 | 16 | 18 |
|---|---|---|---|---|---|---|
| US | 6 | 8 | 10 | 12 | 14 | 16 |
| Continent | 36 | 38 | 40 | 42 | 44 | 46 |

Men's clothing sizes/Tailles homme

| UK/US | 36 | 38 | 40 | 42 | 44 | 46 |
|---|---|---|---|---|---|---|
| Continent | 46 | 48 | 50 | 52 | 54 | 56 |

Men's and women's shoes/Pointures homme et femme

| UK women | 4 | 5 | 6 | 7 | 7.5 | 8 | | | |
|---|---|---|---|---|---|---|---|---|---|
| UK men | | | | 6 | 7 | 8 | 9 | 10 | 11 |
| US | | 6.5 | 7.5 | 8.5 | 9.5 | 10.5 | 11.5 | 12.5 | 13.5 | 14.5 |
| France | 37 | 38 | 39 | 40 | 41 | 42 | 43 | 44 | 45 |

# ❽ Street signs and information notices

| | |
|---|---|
| accueil | reception |
| appuyer | push |
| arrêt | stop |
| ascenseur | lift |
| billets | tickets |
| caisse  | cash desk |
| chaud | hot |
| dames | ladies |
| défense d'entrer | no entry |
| femmes | women |
| fermé | closed |
| fumeurs | smoking |
| gratuit | free |
| hommes | men |
| interdit | forbidden |
| librairie | bookshop |
| libre | vacant; free |
| à louer | to let |
| messieurs | men |
| ouvert | open |
| péage | toll |
| prière de ne pas... | please do not... |
| rappel | reminder |
| renseignements | enquiries |
| rez-de-chaussée | ground floor |
| sortie | exit |
| sous-sol | basement |
| stationnement | parking |
| tirez | pull |
| toutes directions | through traffic |

# Dates for your diary

## January

| | | | | |
|---|---|---|---|---|
| **1** | 8 | 15 | 22 | 29 |
| 2 | 9 | 16 | 23 | 30 |
| 3 | 10 | 17 | 24 | 31 |
| 4 | 11 | 18 | 25 | |
| 5 | 12 | 19 | 26 | |
| **6** | 13 | 20 | 27 | |
| 7 | 14 | 21 | 28 | |

## February

| | | | | |
|---|---|---|---|---|
| 1 | 8 | 15 | 22 | |
| **2** | 9 | 16 | 23 | |
| 3 | 10 | 17 | 24 | |
| 4 | 11 | 18 | 25 | |
| 5 | 12 | 19 | 26 | |
| 6 | 13 | 20 | 27 | |
| 7 | **14** | 21 | 28 | |

## March

| | | | | |
|---|---|---|---|---|
| 1 | 8 | 15 | 22 | 29 |
| 2 | 9 | 16 | 23 | 30 |
| 3 | 10 | 17 | 24 | 31 |
| 4 | 11 | 18 | 25 | |
| 5 | 12 | 19 | 26 | |
| 6 | 13 | 20 | 27 | |
| 7 | 14 | 21 | 28 | |

## April

| | | | | |
|---|---|---|---|---|
| **1** | 8 | 15 | 22 | 29 |
| 2 | 9 | 16 | 23 | 30 |
| 3 | 10 | 17 | 24 | |
| 4 | 11 | 18 | 25 | |
| 5 | 12 | 19 | 26 | |
| 6 | 13 | 20 | 27 | |
| 7 | 14 | 21 | 28 | |

## May

| | | | | |
|---|---|---|---|---|
| **1** | **8** | 15 | 22 | 29 |
| 2 | 9 | 16 | 23 | 30 |
| 3 | 10 | 17 | 24 | 31 |
| 4 | 11 | 18 | 25 | |
| 5 | 12 | 19 | 26 | |
| 6 | 13 | 20 | 27 | |
| 7 | 14 | 21 | 28 | |

## June

| | | | | |
|---|---|---|---|---|
| 1 | 8 | 15 | 22 | 29 |
| 2 | 9 | 16 | 23 | 30 |
| 3 | 10 | 17 | **24** | |
| 4 | 11 | 18 | 25 | |
| 5 | 12 | 19 | 26 | |
| 6 | 13 | 20 | 27 | |
| 7 | 14 | 21 | 28 | |

## July

| | | | | |
|---|---|---|---|---|
| 1 | 8 | 15 | 22 | 29 |
| 2 | 9 | 16 | 23 | 30 |
| 3 | 10 | 17 | 24 | 31 |
| 4 | 11 | 18 | 25 | |
| 5 | 12 | 19 | 26 | |
| 6 | 13 | 20 | 27 | |
| 7 | **14** | 21 | 28 | |

## August

| | | | | |
|---|---|---|---|---|
| 1 | 8 | **15** | 22 | 29 |
| 2 | 9 | 16 | 23 | 30 |
| 3 | 10 | 17 | 24 | 31 |
| 4 | 11 | 18 | 25 | |
| 5 | 12 | 19 | 26 | |
| 6 | 13 | 20 | 27 | |
| 7 | 14 | 21 | 28 | |

## September

| | | | | |
|---|---|---|---|---|
| 1 | 8 | 15 | 22 | 29 |
| 2 | 9 | 16 | 23 | 30 |
| 3 | 10 | 17 | 24 | |
| 4 | 11 | 18 | 25 | |
| 5 | 12 | 19 | 26 | |
| 6 | 13 | 20 | 27 | |
| 7 | 14 | 21 | 28 | |

## October

| | | | | |
|---|---|---|---|---|
| 1 | 8 | 15 | 22 | 29 |
| 2 | 9 | 16 | 23 | 30 |
| 3 | 10 | 17 | 24 | 31 |
| 4 | 11 | 18 | 25 | |
| 5 | 12 | 19 | 26 | |
| 6 | 13 | 20 | 27 | |
| 7 | 14 | 21 | 28 | |

## November

| | | | | |
|---|---|---|---|---|
| **1** | 8 | 15 | 22 | 29 |
| 2 | 9 | 16 | 23 | 30 |
| 3 | 10 | 17 | 24 | |
| 4 | **11** | 18 | 25 | |
| 5 | 12 | 19 | 26 | |
| 6 | 13 | 20 | 27 | |
| 7 | 14 | 21 | 28 | |

## December

| | | | | |
|---|---|---|---|---|
| 1 | **8** | 15 | 22 | 29 |
| 2 | 9 | 16 | 23 | 30 |
| 3 | 10 | 17 | **24** | **31** |
| 4 | 11 | 18 | **25** | |
| 5 | 12 | 19 | **26** | |
| 6 | 13 | 20 | 27 | |
| 7 | 14 | 21 | 28 | |

**1 January** le jour de l'an (New Year's Day) is a public holiday and a day of family celebration, with a large lunch, traditionally featuring seafood of various kinds.

**6 January** la Fête des Rois (Epiphany or Twelfth Night). Around this time, most families have a *galette des Rois*, a rich pastry cake filled with *frangipane* (almond paste). The cake contains a *fève*, literally a bean, as this is what was originally used. Nowadays the *fève* takes the form of a tiny plastic or ceramic figure. The person who gets the *fève* in their portion puts on the cardboard crown which comes with the cake.

**2 February** la Chandeleur (Candlemas) is celebrated in the church but is not a public holiday. However, it is traditional to eat *crêpes* (pancakes) on this day.

**14 February** la Saint-Valentin (St Valentine's Day). As in many other countries, people celebrate a romantic relationship with gifts of flowers or chocolates.

**1 April** le premier avril (April Fool's Day). The French also take advantage of this occasion to play tricks on one another, calling out *poisson d'avril!* (literally 'April fish').

**1 May** La Fête du Travail (International Labour Day) is a public holiday.

**8 May** le 8 mai or la Fête de la Victoire is a public holiday commemorating Victory in Europe on 8 May 1945.

**24 June** la Saint-Jean (Midsummer's Day). In many areas, bonfires (*les feux de la Saint-Jean*) are lit on Midsummer's Night. People are supposed to jump over these, re-enacting a pagan custom intended to ward off the cold of winter.

**14 July** la Fête Nationale or le 14 juillet is usually called Bastille Day in English and is a public holiday in France. It commemorates the taking of the Bastille prison in Paris and the liberation of its prisoners by the people of Paris in 1789, one of the first events of the Revolution. All over France there are parades on the day of the 14th, and firework displays and *bals* (local dances) either on the night of the 13th or of the 14th.

**15 August** l'Assomption (Feast of the Assumption) is a public holiday. Many people in France are either setting off on holiday around the 15th or else returning home, so this is traditionally a very busy time on the roads.

**1 November** la Toussaint (All Saints' Day) is a public holiday and the day when people remember their dead relatives and friends, although properly speaking it is All Souls' Day the following day that is set aside for this in the church. People take flowers to the cemetery, particularly chrysanthemums, as these are in bloom at this time. Because of this association, it is best to avoid taking chrysanthemums as a gift for someone. Schoolchildren have a two-week holiday around this time.

**11 November** le 11 novembre is a public holiday to commemorate the Armistice of 1918 and a day of remembrance for those who died in the two world wars and in subsequent conflicts. All towns and villages hold parades in which war veterans accompany local officials and a brass band to lay wreaths on the war memorial. In Paris, the President lays a wreath on the tomb of the unknown soldier beneath the *Arc de Triomphe* on the *Champs-Élysées*.

**8 December** la fête de l'Immaculée Conception (Feast of the Immaculate Conception).
In the city of Lyons, this is celebrated as la Fête de la Lumière (Festival of Light) said to commemorate the Virgin's intervention to prevent the plague reaching Lyons in the Middle Ages. People put rows of candles in coloured glass jars on the outsides of their windowsills, so that all the buildings in the centre of the city are illuminated.

**24 December** la veille de Noël (Christmas Eve) is the time when most people exchange presents. Many people go to *la messe de minuit* (midnight mass).

**25 December** Noël (Christmas) is a public holiday and a day of eating and drinking. Lunch will often start with a variety of seafood, oysters being particularly popular. Turkey is often eaten as a main course, sometimes with chestnut stuffing. A variety of cheeses will be followed by *la bûche de Noël*, a rich chocolate cake in the form of a snow-covered log. French people do not usually send Christmas cards, the custom being to send wishes for the coming year to more distant friends and relatives during the month of January.

**26 December** There is no particular name for the day after Christmas Day and it is not a public holiday.

**31 December**  la Saint-Sylvestre (New
Year's Eve). Many people have parties to
celebrate *le réveillon du Nouvel An* (New Year's
Eve Party). Once again, food plays a major
part and, as at Christmas, this is a time to
splash out on luxury foods such as *foie gras*.
There will often be dancing and the New Year
will be welcomed in with champagne.

## Movable feasts and holidays

### Mardi gras
Shrove Tuesday, the last day of carnival before
the beginning of Lent on Ash Wednesday.
Traditionally, *crêpes* (pancakes) are eaten for
supper. In many areas of France, sugared
fritters called *bugnes* in and around Lyons
and *oreillettes* farther south, are eaten between
*la fête des Rois* and *mardi gras*.

### le Vendredi saint
Good Friday is celebrated in the church, but is
not a public holiday.

### Pâques
Easter Sunday, *le dimanche de Pâques*,
is for many people the occasion for a big family
lunch. Easter hunts are organised for children,
with chocolate eggs, rabbits, hens, or fish
traditionally hidden in the family garden.
*Le lundi de Pâques* (Easter Monday) is a public
holiday.

**l'Ascension**, the Thursday forty days after
Easter, is a public holiday in France.

**la Pentecôte** (Whitsun) on the seventh Sunday
after Easter represents for many people the first
long weekend of the summer, as *le lundi de la
Pentecôte* (Whit Monday) is a public holiday.
Many families go to stay with friends
or relatives in the country.

**la Fête des mères** (Mother's Day) is the
Sunday after *Pentecôte*. This is another occasion
for a big family meal, with presents for the
mother. **La fête des pères** (Father's Day) is
celebrated in similar fashion two weeks later.

# Quick reference guide to life and culture

**Académie française** A learned body, founded by Cardinal Richelieu in 1634, whose main role nowadays is to monitor new developments in the French language. It is not always taken entirely seriously by the public at large. Its 40 members are elected for life on the basis of their contribution to scholarship or literature, and are known as '*les Immortels*'.

**Alps, The** A mountain range that runs north to south along the border between France, Switzerland, and Italy. It is 350 km (219 miles) long and 50–60 km (31–37.5 miles) wide. The highest peak in western Europe, Mont Blanc (4,808 m [15,774 ft]) lies in the Alps, straddling the French/Italian border. The Alpine region is home to many popular ski resorts.

**architecture** Since the 1970s, the French state has promoted several major architectural projects, particularly in Paris, including the 1977 Pompidou Centre (also known as Beaubourg), the glass pyramid of the Louvre designed by American architect I. M. Pei and built in 1989, the Grande Arche de la Défense in western Paris, and the Institut du Monde Arabe, designed by Jean Nouvel. In 2004 the Millau viaduct, the tallest in the world, was opened by the French president, Jacques Chirac. Designed by English architect Lord Norman Foster, the 2.5 km (1.6 mile) long, 340 m (1,122 ft) high structure was dubbed 'the bridge in the clouds'.

**bande dessinée** plays a significant cultural role in France. More than a comic book or entertainment for youth, it is a form of popular literature known as the *neuvième art* (the 'ninth art', films being the 'seventh' and TV the 'eighth') and celebrated annually at the *Festival d'Angoulême*. Cartoon characters such as Astérix, Lucky Luke, and Tintin are household names, and older comic books are often collectors' items.

**banlieue** The *banlieue* are the suburbs around main cities, and particularly the poorer residential areas around city centres, which have expanded dramatically in recent decades. The term often has a pejorative connotation, and evokes images of concrete tower blocks ('*grands ensembles*'), urban decay, and crime. The *cités* (deprived estates) are often difficult areas to live in. The government – along with the *banlieusards* (those who live there) – is trying to find ways to rehabilitate the *banlieue*.

**Beur (fem. Beurette)** A term in Verlan derived from the French word *Arabe,* which refers to the French-born children of North African immigrants (primarily Algerian but also Tunisian and Moroccan). The *jeunes Beurs* have been at the heart of anti-racist activity in recent years, but equally at the centre of ethnic tensions in the suburbs (BANLIEUE) of major French cities. Educated within the French school system, many Beurs feel set apart from both French and Arabic culture. Beur artists express this sense of 'in-between-ness' through music, cinema, and literature in works such as *La Haine* (Hate; 1995), a film by Mathieu Kassovitz, which looks at the alienation felt by a Jew, an Arab, and a black African living in a housing project in Paris, and Leïla Houari's *Zeida de nulle part* (Zeida from Nowhere, 1985), a book that explores the hopes and dreams of a young *Maghrébin*. The term is not used so frequently now as it has been in the past. *See also* MAGHRÉBINS.

**Bleus, Les** The French national football team, who wear a blue strip, are known as *Les Bleus*. Supporters shout, '*Allez les Bleus*' ('Come on, Blues !') to urge them on. The team entered footballing legend in 1998 when they won the World Cup at home, beating Brazil in the final. Zinedine Zidane (known as Zizou), who captained the team and scored two goals in their 3–0 victory, achieved iconic status in France. The French rugby union team is also known as *Les Bleus*.

**boules** A type of bowls, also known as *pétanque*, played all over France using metal balls and a jack known as a *cochonnet. Terrains de boules* (playing areas) are set aside for the game in many towns and villages, though one of the beauties of the game is that it can be played virtually anywhere. So a family lunch in the summer will often end in a game of *boules* (*une partie de boules*). There are some regional variations, notably in the size and form of the playing area and the size of the bowls.

**café** Since 1910 the number of traditional cafés or bistros in France has dropped from 510,000 to 57,000, and Paris has even been invaded by branches of Starbucks and McDonalds. In Paris the Café de Flore (which played host to famous French writers and philosophers such as Jean-Paul Sartre and Simone de Beauvoir), Les Deux Magots (a favourite of Pablo Picasso's) and Café de la Gare (opened by Coluche and Depardieu as a theatre) are among many famous cafés with a long history. Parisian waiters often still dress in traditional style, with black waistcoats and long white aprons.

**Cannes film festival** The first Cannes film festival (*Association Française du Festival International du Film*) took place in 1946 at the glamorous Côte d'Azur resort. Now many in the film industry travel from around the world to see and be seen at the May festival, which showcases films 'showing talent deserving encouragement'. The *Palme d'Or* (Golden Palm) is awarded for the best feature film.

**Césars** Prizes awarded annually for achievements in the film industry; the French equivalent of the Oscars.

**champignons** Refers to any mushroom-like fungi, whether edible or not. Hunting for edible mushrooms is a popular leisure activity and many varieties are highly prized. Advice on whether they are edible or not can usually be obtained from a PHARMACIE.

**chanson française** Often referred to as '*chanson à textes*', *la chanson française* is characterized by two main features: the lyrics must be meaningful and the song must be sung in French. The genre was popularized by singers such as Maurice Chevalier and Joséphine Baker during World War II, Edith Piaf and Juliette Gréco in the 1950s and 1960s, and Johnny Hallyday from the 1970s onward. In the 1960s, the lyrics of singer-poets such as Georges Brassens and Jacques Brel reinvigorated the genre; their texts are often studied in schools today. *La chanson française* was taken through the 1980s and beyond by singers such as Patricia Kaas and Alain Souchon, and today MC Solaar, the rap singer, and Corneille (soul) have brought it into the 21st century.

**charcuterie** A shop or supermarket counter selling a wide variety of pork products. As well as cuts of pork, *charcutiers* usually sell chicken both raw and ready-cooked, and various types of raw and cooked ham, pâtés, and a selection of *saucissons*. Most *charcuteries* also offer a variety of salads, savoury pastries, and dishes that can be reheated at home or on the premises. *Charcuteries* offering a catering service usually advertise themselves as *charcutier-traiteur* (*traiteur* means 'caterer'). *La charcuterie* is also used to refer to pork products such as ham and *saucisson*.

**cinéma** Cinema has always been a popular medium in France; it was in Paris in December 1895 that the Lumière brothers first demonstrated their *cinématographe*, showing moving pictures to a paying audience. In the 1920s, French filmmakers such as Louis Delluc and Jean Cocteau experimented with avant-garde cinema, while in the 1930s Jean Renoir produced masterpieces such as *La Grande Illusion*. Marcel Carné's epic tale, *Les Enfants du Paradis*, followed in 1945. In 1959, Jean-Luc Godard's *À Bout de Souffle* established him at the forefront of the *nouvelle vague*, the 'new wave', along with François Truffaut. *Cinéma Beur* (from the slang word meaning second-generation North Africans) arrived in the 1980s with Rachid Bouchareb, and has since coexisted with *cinéma du look*. Visually impressive, with non-naturalistic photography, intense colours, and romantic stories filmed in the studio, the best-known example of the genre is *Le Fabuleux destin d'Amélie Poulain* (2001), which grossed more than $33 million at the box office.

**département** An administrative unit of government in France. Each *département* has a number and this appears as the first two digits in postcodes for addresses within the area, and as the two-digit number at the end of vehicle registration plates.

**DOM-TOM** Acronym for *Département d'outre-mer* and *Territoire d'outre-mer*, the French overseas territories. The DÉPARTEMENTS have the status of a *région*. At present there are four: Guadeloupe, Guyane, Martinique, and Réunion. The *territoires*, which include Nouvelle-Calédonie (New Caledonia) and Tahiti, are constitutionally part of the French republic, and citizens have French nationality.

**énergie nucléaire** Nearly 86 per cent of French electricity is produced by nuclear power; only the United States produces more. There are more nuclear sites in France than in any other European country. Defenders of nuclear power argue that, because of its policy, France creates much less $CO_2$ than most industrialized countries. However, disposal of nuclear waste remains a problem.

**festivals** All year round there are theatre, music, dance, contemporary art, circus, and street festivals, but the majority take place in the summer months between June and September. The most popular are: Vienne for Jazz, La Rochelle for Francofolies (featuring CHANSONS FRANÇAISES), Orange and Aix-en-Provence for opera, Avignon for theatre, Chalon-sur-Saône for street performances, Arles for photography and dance, La Côte-St-André for Berlioz, Lyons for advertising and contemporary art. In Brittany the Festival

Interceltique is becoming more and more popular. *See also* FÊTE DE LA MUSIQUE.

**Fête de la Musique**, created in 1982, is celebrated each year on the summer solstice, 21 June. It is now a major musical event all over France. In Paris amateur and professional musicians alike dust off their instruments and set up in any spare spot, from courtyards to châteaux, parks to doorways. The night echoes to every imaginable style of music as musicians play to large crowds.

**gastronomic** The art or science of good eating is an enduring passion in France. It can be traced through the long history of some Parisian restaurants – *L'Auberge de la Mère Poulard* dates from 1888, Maxim's dates from 1893; through its tradition of great French chefs from Marie-Antoine Carême (1784–1833) to Paul Bocuse (1926– ); through its world-famous culinary academy, *Le Cordon Bleu*, established in 1895; and through the great variety of its regional dishes, from *bouillabaisse* to *pâté de foie gras*. As in the rest of Europe, chefs strive to gain 'chefs' hats' (the mark of excellence from the *Gault Millau Guide*), and stars (the supreme accolade being three) from the *Michelin Guide*.

**GR** or *grandes randonnées* are long-distance footpaths, maintained by the *Fédération française de randonnée pédestre*. *GR* (major hiking routes) are marked by white and red or yellow and red signs; *PR (petites randonnées)* are marked by yellow signs. GR20 is a famous route across Corsica.

**grottes** There are many prehistoric *grottes*, or caves, in France, relics of the cave dwelling peoples who settled in the south of France nearly a million years ago. La grotte Chauvet, in the Ardèche in southeastern France, was discovered by amateur speleologists. It is famous for its more than 300 animal paintings and engravings dating back to the Paleolithic era, between 32,000 and 30,000 years ago. The cave is closed to the public, but a reproduction is being built for visitors at La Mathe. La grotte de Lourdes is a place of pilgrimage; in 1858 a young girl claimed to have seen the Virgin Mary here.

**haute couture** The *Chambre Syndicale de la Couture Parisienne* was founded in 1868 by Charles Worth (1825–95), who was actually born in England but became a highly successful Parisian designer. This association of *haute-couture* ('high-tailoring') houses defined the art of *couture*. Nowadays *haute couture* is a term regulated by the government. Each year the *Chambre Syndicale de la Haute Couture* decides which houses qualify to carry the *haute-couture* label; they have to meet strict criteria in terms of design, production, and presentation of fashion shows. *Haute-couture* clothes are the product of many hours of work, and are therefore extremely expensive. Famous French designers include Christian Dior (1905–57), Yves St Laurent (1936–), and Jean-Paul Gaultier (1952–).

**l'Hexagone** Because of the shape of the map of France, which resembles a six-sided figure, France is often referred to as 'the Hexagon'. *L'Hexagone* refers to mainland France, excluding its islands and other dependencies. *See also* DOM-TOM.

**immigration** Of the 60 million people who live in France, about 4 million (less than 7 per cent) are immigrants (*les immigrés*). Immigration used to be dominated by Europeans (54 per cent of those entering France in 1975 were from Europe), but today most immigrants are Algerians, Moroccans, Tunisians, people from the African colonies, Turks, and Asians (from the former colonies of Vietnam, Laos, and Cambodia). To work in France, incomers have to obtain *une carte de séjour* from the authorities. This is not always easy, particularly for non-EU citizens. People in illegal situations are called '*sans papiers*' (literally, 'without papers'). There are believed to be about 1 million '*sans papiers*' in the country.

**justice** The French Minister of Justice is called *Le Garde des Sceaux (un sceau* is a stamp, or seal). Barristers, or *avocats*, plead at the bar (*le barreau*). Solicitors, known as *notaires*, are very involved in local life, as they deal with property. You may sometimes need to go to see the *notaire*, even when you are just looking for a place to rent.

**laïcité** The concept of *laïcité* has been a fundamental principle in French society since the *Révolution*, which separated religion from the functions of government – though the Church and State were only formally separated in 1905. *Laïcité* literally means secularism, but implies a free expression of religion, although religion is not accorded any special status. The issue has been hotly debated recently in France, after a Muslim girl was expelled from her school for wearing a *hijab*, or veil. In 2004, a law was passed forbidding the wearing of notable religious symbols in a move designed to protect the secular state.

**magasins** Opening and closing times of shops (*les magasins*) vary according to the type of shop and the location. Department stores (*les grands magasins*) are generally open all day from 9 a.m. to 7 p.m. In larger towns, most other shops, with the exception of small food shops, are also open all day. Privately owned food shops such as butchers and fishmongers generally open at 8 a.m. and do not close in the evening until 7 or 7.30 p.m. They usually close, however, between midday and 2 or 3 p.m. In small towns, all the shops, with the exception of bakers, generally close for two or three hours in the middle of the day. In both small and large towns, all types of food shops tend to be open on Sunday mornings until midday. In smaller towns many shops are closed on Mondays.

**Maghrébins** About 1.3 million people of Maghreb origin (from France's ex-colonial territories of Morocco, Algeria, and Tunisia) live and work in France. They came to work in France during the '*trente glorieuses*', the three decades of postwar boom (1945–75). Many worked in car factories. Their children are known as BEURS in Verlan.

**Mai 1968: les événements** Following disputes with university authorities and the police, students all over France went on strike. The government's attempts to suppress dissent using the CRS riot police made the situation much worse; street battles followed, and the students ripped cobbles up from the roads to form barricades. Ten million French workers joined the students in their protest and the country was paralysed for nearly two weeks. In response, President Charles De Gaulle dissolved the Assemblée Nationale and called new elections. The revolutionary fervour of the protesters subsided and de Gaulle was re-elected, though in return he promised major reforms in education.

**mariage** Church weddings are not legally recognized in France, Belgium, or Switzerland (although they are in Quebec), so all couples must be married legally in a civil ceremony, whether or not they want a church wedding (which usually takes place afterwards but can be up to several weeks later). In France, the civil ceremony is a relatively short affair held in the *mairie* (town hall), and conducted by the mayor or his/her deputy. The couple vow to be responsible for the moral instruction and education of their future family, and are presented with a *livret de famille*. If the couple are holding a church ceremony then that is often the 'public' wedding, with the civil marriage usually a private family affair. Guests are often invited to the *vin d'honneur*, which begins the reception, where they can simply

toast the newlyweds with a glass of champagne without staying on for a meal. For those who do stay, celebrations can continue for days, particularly in rural areas. The traditional wedding cake is the *croquembouche*, a magnificent tower of custard-filled profiteroles. The legal age for getting married in France is 18 for men and 15 for women; in Belgium, Switzerland, and Quebec it is 18 for both parties (although it is possible to marry younger with parental consent). Since 2003 same-sex marriage has been legally possible in Belgium. It became legal in Quebec the following year.

**OGM** *Organismes génétiquement modifiés*, or genetically modified foods, cannot be sold in France. The French Ministry of Agriculture is resisting their legalization.

**PACS** *Le pacte civil de solidarité* (contract of civil union), established in November 1999, is designed to safeguard the common interests of partners living together either in mixed or same-sex couples. The PACS does not apply to under-18s, to couples who are blood relatives, or those already in another marriage or relationship. It entails certain obligations on the part of the couple who sign the 'pact', such as a commitment to mutual support and maintenance and shared responsibility for joint expenses. In return, couples are given certain rights, for example over joint property, accommodation, etc.

**partis politiques** In general, French political parties reflect a basic left/right divide. On the left, the main parties are the *Parti Socialiste* (*PS*) and the *Parti Communiste Française* (*PCF*), while the principal party on the right is the new *Union pour un Mouvement Populaire* (UMP), formed by supporters of President Jacques Chirac. There are in addition more extreme groups at both ends of the political spectrum; in the 2002 national election Jean-Marie Le Pen's extreme right *Front National* (*FN*) won about 17 per cent of the popular vote, and was only defeated in the second round by Jacques Chirac's *RPR* (*Rassemblement pour la République*). Beyond the general left/right divide, the ecological movement is represented by *Les Verts* and *Génération Écologie*.

**pharmacie** Pharmacies in France used to sell only medicines and closely related products such as toiletries and some brands of perfume. However, these days they often sell a wider range of goods. Pharmacists generally play an active paramedical role, and people will often consult a pharmacist rather than a doctor in the case of minor ailments, or accidents such as snake bites. Pharmacies are easily spotted by the green cross, lit up when the pharmacy is open. A *pharmacie de garde* (duty chemist) can dispense medicines outside normal opening hours as part of a local rota.

**presse** Also referred to as *le quatrième pouvoir*, the press plays a central role in French cultural life. The best-known and most respected French newspaper is *Le Monde*, which provides in-depth coverage of national and international news. In its new format, it publishes more photographs than in the past. National newspapers reflect the main political trends in public life (*Le Figaro* is associated with the right, while *Libération* is a left-wing publication, and so on). There are also several large-circulation regional newspapers (e.g. *Ouest-France*), as well as specialist publications like *L'Équipe*, the sports daily. France publishes more than 15,000 weekly and monthly magazines. The main French press agency is *l'Agence France Presse* (*AFP*).

**Prix Goncourt** A literary prize awarded every November for a novel published in that year. The event attracts considerable media coverage and speculation.

**religion** Historically and culturally, France is a Catholic country, but the Catholic Church is no longer so influential as it once was. In 1970, 75 per cent of babies were baptized, but by 2000 the figure had dropped to 20 per cent. With 5 million Muslims, more than any other European country, Islam is the second religion in France.

**rentrée** The week at the beginning of September when the new school year starts and around which much of French administrative life revolves. The preceding weeks see intensive advertising of associated merchandise, from books and stationery to clothes and sports equipment. Many stores and supermarkets have a range of special purchases at bargain prices. *La rentrée littéraire* marks the start of the literary year and *la rentrée parlementaire* signals the return of members of parliament after the recess.

**restos du coeur** A charitable organization, *les restos* (*restaurants*) *du coeur* are widely

publicized by virtue of having been set up by a much-loved humourist called Coluche. He died in a motorcycle accident in 1986. *Les restos du coeur* serve meals to the poor and homeless, particularly in winter.

**roller** *Le roller*, or rollerblading, is a very popular sport in France, with an estimated five million practitioners. In Paris on Friday evenings rollerbladers stream through the streets; up to 12,000 people can take part in these impressive displays.

**SMIC** *Salaire Minimum Interprofessionnel de Croissance*: the basic minimum legal wage fixed annually by decree. People earning the SMIC are known as *smicards*. Those under the age of 18 can be paid less than the minimum wage.

**travail** (work) People cannot officially work below the age of 16. In 2000, the working week was reduced to 35 hours (in companies with more than 20 employees), which is now the shortest in Europe. French workers get five weeks' paid holiday per year. Retirement is fixed at the age of 60, but people can take early retirement, known as *'préretraite'*. Those who have children under the age of three can choose to take *un congé parental d'éducation* (parental child-rearing leave). Many French women and men work *à mi-temps* (part-time) or *à temps partiel* (partial time, generally four days a week). One quarter of the workforce is employed by the French state. Unemployment, at nearly 10 per cent, is among the highest in Europe.

**Université** There are 90 universities in France. The State subsidises the French universities but there are also independent establishments, mainly Catholic universities, in Lyons, Paris, Toulouse, Angers, and Lille. The university system now has three levels: *licence* (*baccalauréat* +3), *master* (*Bac* +5), and *doctorat* (*Bac* +8). Some universities have a special reputation for certain subjects (historically the most renowned is the Sorbonne). To enter university students have to have the *baccalauréat*. Fees for the year are minimal, except for private education. The most popular course is humanities, followed by sciences, medicine, and sport.

# Social survival tips

## Talking to and greeting people

**Greetings** To say Hello, use *Bonjour* followed by *monsieur* (to a man), *madame* (to a woman), *mademoiselle* (to a younger woman or an older lady). In the afternoon you can say *Bon après-midi* (Good afternoon), and in the evening *Bonsoir* (Good evening). *Bonne nuit* means good night and is said last thing before going to sleep.

**Tu and vous** You can use *tu* only when you are talking to a good friend, a child, an animal, or, if you are a younger person, someone else your own age who has a similar outlook on life. What you can't do in France is use *tu* to show that you are being friendly, so you shouldn't use *tu* with a bus driver, a receptionist, someone else's parents, etc. In contexts like these the polite form *vous* is used. Similarly, it is best to only use Christian names with friends, and to address everyone else as *monsieur/madame/mademoiselle*. You can use these words without adding a surname.

**Meeting people** French friends and colleagues usually kiss each other on the cheek when they meet. The number of *bises* (kisses) will vary from one area of France to another – anywhere between two and four. When meeting a woman for the first time, a *poignée de main* (handshake) is appropriate. You can switch to the kissing ritual the next time you meet. When two men meet, however, they shake hands as a greeting.

## Going out

**Visiting people** If you are invited to a friend's house, you should take a little gift, for example, a bottle of wine or some chocolates. If you are invited home by your boss or by an older and more traditional person, it's better to take flowers – but remember not to give chrysanthemums as they are a symbol of death.

**Smoking in public** French restaurants always have smoking and non-smoking areas: *zone fumeurs/zone non-fumeurs*. However, it is now forbidden to smoke in the *métro* (underground).

**Tips** Tipping is not compulsory in France, but it's always appreciated in bars, restaurants and taxis. It really depends on how satisfied you are with the service you have received. One euro should be fine for a drink or a taxi, but give more for a meal.

**Hobbies** Some of the most popular French hobbies are: *les dîners entre amis* (dinner with friends); *la pétanque* (boules); *la pêche* (fishing); *la chasse* (hunting); *le ciné* (the cinema); *le théâtre* (the theatre); *les concerts* (concerts). The French like to spend their holidays in France, in their *maison de campagne* (house in the country), *à la mer* (at the seaside) or *à la montagne* (in the mountains).

## Mealtimes

A typical *petit déjeuner* (breakfast) consists of *pain* (bread), *beurre* (butter) and *confiture* (jam), although *les céréales* (cereals) are becoming more popular.

People often have an *apéro* (short for *apéritif*) before a meal, especially at the weekends or on holiday.

Traditionally the midday meal was the big meal of the day, and for people who live in country areas this is still largely the case. Even in big cities many people continue to eat a big meal in the middle of the day, either in a family restaurant near their place of work, or by buying a freshly cooked hot dish from a *charcuterie*. However, people living and working in the larger cities are tending more and more to have a snack lunch and to eat their main meal in the evening. In either case, the main meal virtually always consists of a number of courses, typically a starter such as pâté, *saucisson*, or salad, then meat or fish with a vegetable dish, followed by cheese and dessert. Cheese is virtually always eaten, as one might expect in a country that boasts such a huge variety and number of cheeses, and is always served before the dessert. In town and country alike, Sunday is the day for a big family meal in the middle of the day, and the pâtisseries are usually crowded on Sunday mornings as people queue up to buy a large tart or gâteau for dessert.

Although *le thé* (tea) is becoming more popular in France, coffee or *le café* is still the favourite drink in the morning and after meals. Drink it *noir* (black) or *crème* (with cream).

On special occasions such as birthdays, Christmas, or New Year, you may well start the meal with champagne, or drink some along with dessert, before finishing your meal with *une liqueur* (a liqueur).

## Getting around

**Cars: autoroutes** France has an extensive motorway system, which is largely financed by tolls calculated according to the distance travelled and the vehicle type. Tickets are obtained and tolls paid at *péages* (tollgates). The speed limit for standard vehicles is 130 km/h (approx. 80 mph) and 110 km/h (approx. 70 mph) in wet weather.

**route départementale** These are signalled on French road maps as 'D' followed by a number, and are marked in yellow. They are roads maintained by the *département* and are secondary roads, not intended for fast travel. Many of them have stretches marked in green on maps to highlight areas or views of particular interest.

**route nationale** A *route nationale* forms part of the state-maintained road network, outside the *autoroutes* but providing fast roads for travel between towns and cities. They are signalled by 'N' followed by the road number and are marked in red on French road maps.

**Bison Futé** Symbolized by a little Native American, *Bison Futé* is a creation of the *Centre National d'Information Routière*, the French traffic information service, which reports on travel conditions nationwide, particularly during holiday periods when traffic is heaviest, and recommends alternative routes (*les itinéraires 'bis'*) for travellers keen to avoid traffic jams. The *Bison Futé* traffic tips are broadcast across the full range of media (radio, TV, the national press, the Internet, and Minitel) and appear at regular intervals on the road system itself. Information is updated constantly to reflect actual traffic conditions, enabling motorists to choose the best time to travel. Allied to *Bison Futé* is a colour-coding system to mark the relative intensity of traffic at any time (green, red, yellow, and black), which is a key factor in staggering holiday traffic on the roads.

**Pedestrians** Don't assume that cars will always stop for you at pedestrian crossings, particularly if there is a right filter for traffic coming from behind you. Sometimes the right filter and the pedestrian crossing will both be on green.

**Buses** There are two sorts of *arrêts de bus* (bus stops): the compulsory ones and the ones where you have to flag the bus down.